MW01269053

Language at Large

Language at Large

Essays on Syntax and Semantics

By

Alexandra Y. Aikhenvald and R. M. W. Dixon

Language and Culture Research Centre
James Cook University

BRILL

LEIDEN • BOSTON
2011

This book is printed on acid-free paper.

Library of Congress Cataloging-in-Publication Data

Aikhenval'd, A. IU. (Aleksandra IUr'evna)
  Language at large : essays on syntax and semantics / by Alexandra Y. Aikhenvald and
R. M. W. Dixon.
      p. cm. — (Empirical approaches to linguistic theory; v. 2)
  Includes bibliographical references and index.
  ISBN 978-90-04-20607-6 (alk. paper) 1. Typology (Linguistics) 2. Grammar, Comparative
and general—Syntax. 3. Semantics. I. Dixon, Robert M. W. II. Title. III. Series.

  P204.A45 2011
  415—dc23

                                                                              2011018141

ISSN 2210-6243 (2011)
ISBN 978-90-04-20607-6 (hardback, 2011)
ISBN 978-90-04-20768-4 (e-book, 2011)
ISBN 978-90-04-39281-6 (paperback reprint, 2019)
ISBN 978-90-04-20768-4 (e-book, 2019)

Copyright 2011 by Koninklijke Brill NV, Leiden, The Netherlands.
Koninklijke Brill NV incorporates the imprints Brill, Brill Hes & De Graaf, Brill Nijhoff,
Brill Rodopi, Brill Sense, Hotei Publishing, mentis Verlag, Verlag Ferdinand Schöningh and
Wilhelm Fink Verlag.

CONTENTS

PART B

EXPLAINING LANGUAGE

PART C

ENGLISH GRAMMAR AND LEXICOLOGY

LIST OF TABLES AND FIGURES

PREFACE

Over the past couple of decades, Alexandra Y. Aikhenvald and R. M. W. Dixon have been major players on the world linguistic scene, contributing in a number of areas. The present volume brings together some of the essays they have written—either individually or together— on various themes. Five chapters are published here for the first time. Earlier versions of the remainder have appeared in print but all have been revised for this volume, some very significantly modified and extended. Each essay is self-contained, and can either be read on its own or as part of a themed sequence (for instance, Chapters 8 and 9, and Chapters 2, 3 and 4). There is a little repetition between chapters; this has been retained so that each chapter may be read on its own.

A major field of endeavour has been linguistic typology. Vide Aikhenvald's three volumes: *Classifiers: A typology of noun categorization devices* (2000b), *Evidentiality* (2004) and *Imperatives and commands* (2010a). Plus Dixon's *Ergativity* (1994) and the first two volumes of his *Basic linguistic theory* (2010a, b). The seven chapters in Part A investigate further typological issues.

Chapter 1, 'Versatile cases', explores what happens when cases expand beyond their canonical role of marking the syntactic functions of noun phrases. In many languages, some cases may also be attached to verbs, and may then either take on an aspectual or modal meaning, or mark a type of clause linkage. Chapter 2 presents 'A typology of argument-determined constructions', distinguishing between constructions which transfer an argument (passive, antipassive, causative, applicative), those which focus on an argument, those which manipulate an argument, and those which mark the referential status of an argument ('inverse systems'). A particular grammatical marker may have a central meaning and also secondary functions. Chapter 3 considers 'Causatives which don't cause'. That is, in addition to marking causation, a certain marker may indicate an applicative derivation, or intensity of action, or manipulative effect.

In terms of case marking or clause linking, S (intransitive subject) may be associated with either A (transitive subject) or O (transitive object), giving rise to a nominative-accusative or an absolutive-ergative system. But not all associations between S and A are indications of an 'accusative' system, nor are all associations between S and O to be classified as 'ergative'. Chapter 4 discusses 'Non-ergative associations between S and O'. Then, chapter 5 investigates the ways in which languages show 'Dependencies between grammatical systems'. For example, there may be more tense choices available in positive than in negative clauses, or more genders distinguished in singular than in plural.

In every language, a verb describes an action which relates to a number of participants. Chapter 6 sets out 'The semantic basis for a typology', showing that in some languages the meanings of verbs are oriented towards type of participant (for example, 'eat meat' or 'eat vegetables') whereas in others they relate to type of action ('eat where a good deal of chewing is involved', 'eat by sucking', etc.). For every language, a set of open word classes can be recognised on language-internal criteria (typically: noun, verb and adjective). Languages vary as to the number and types of ways they have for deriving a stem of one class on the basis of a form from another word class. Chapter 7 deals with 'Word-class changing derivations in typological perspective'.

Chapter 8, 'Speech reports: a cross-linguistic perspective', discusses direct speech—as when we hear 'The nurse said to me "Come and see me"'—and indirect speech—'The nurse said to me that I should come and see her'. Monoclausal and multiclausal speech report constructions are discussed, together with their syntactic status and functions. We then venture into a seldom-explored area, constructions which fall between straight direct and straight indirect reports, as when we hear 'The nurse said to me "Come and see her".' Chapter 9 examines 'Semi-direct speech in typological perspective'.

Aikhenvald and Dixon have also been active in providing theoretically-informed documentation of previously undescribed (or scarcely described) languages. Aikhenvald has published on three Arawak languages from north-west Brazil. She worked with the last speaker of Bare (1995), then produced grammars of Warekena (1998) and Tariana (2003). These were followed by her magisterial *The Manambu language from East Sepik, Papua New Guinea* (2008a). Between 1972 and 1991 Dixon published grammars of five Australian languages—Dyirbal, Yidiñ, Warrgamay, Nyawaygi and Mbabaram—plus a full account of the Boumaa dialect of Fijian. From 1991 he undertook immersion fieldwork in Brazil, resulting in his award-winning monograph *The Jarawara language of southern Amazonia* (2004b). The four chapters in Part B are offshoots from this descriptive work.

Speakers of out-of-the-way languages, who 'adopt' a linguist, are typically of high intelligence, but do not have available appropriate terminology which would enable them to explain some tricky point of grammar. Chapter 10, 'Naive linguistic explanation', shows the sorts of 'lateral thinking' which speakers invoke in order to get their point across. The dauntingly complex structure of Tariana involves noun phrases showing double marking for syntactic function—that within a lower clause (or an embedded noun phrase) and that within a higher clause (or an embedding noun phrases). This is explained in Chapter 11, 'Multiple marking of syntactic function and polysynthetic nouns in Tariana'.

Chapter 12, 'Palikur and the typology of classifiers', examines another Arawak language, which is spoken in north-west Brazil and over the border into French Guiana. It has three genders—whose use is motivated by an array of semantic parameters—plus numeral classifiers, two varieties of verbal classifiers, locative classifiers, and possessive classifiers. To round out part B we have Chapter 13, 'Zero and nothing in Jarawara', dealing with a language from the small Arawá family (no connection with Arawak). 'Zero' is a recognised artefact of linguistic analysis (for example to mark singular number in English as opposed to the explicit plural marker, orthographic -s). This chapter follows the great Indian grammarian Pāṇini in showing that 'zero' is not at all the same thing as nothing.

It is natural that a linguist, in between spells of fieldwork in exotic locations, should spend some time analysing their own language. Dixon's *A new approach to English grammar, on semantic principles* (1991) went through half-a-dozen reprints before being expanded (with three chapters added) and revised as *A semantic approach to English grammar* (2005). The first four chapters of Part C extend this work.

Chapter 14, 'Pronouns with transferred reference', begins with the well-known McCawley/Lakoff sentence *I dreamed that I was Brigitte Bardot and that I kissed me*, exploring which pronouns can have their reference transferred and under what circumstances. Following this, Chapter 15 'Comparative constructions in English' works in terms of the general parameters for comparative constructions—as set out in Dixon (2008a)—investigating in some detail how they apply to English. The essential nature of articles, and the grammatical status of *the same*, are dealt with in Chapter 16, 'Features of the noun phase in English', and then Chapter 17 examines the circumstances under which *twice* can or must be used in place of *two times*, and what can be inferred from this concerning constituency.

Dixon has combined interest in the indigenous languages of Australia with that in English, by co-authoring *Australian Aboriginal Words in English: Their origin and meaning*, published as Dixon et al. (1990) with an expanded second edition in 2006. Chapter 18, 'Australian Aboriginal words in dictionaries: A history', sketches the background to this lexicographic endeavour.

<h2 style="text-align:center">Sources</h2>

Chapters 3, 4, 7, 8 and 14 are here published for the first time. We are grateful to the publishers of earlier versions of the remaining chapters to use material from them here.

- 1, 'Versatile Cases', is a revised and enlarged version of a paper from the *Journal of Linguistics* 44: 565–603, 2008; © Cambridge University Press, used with permission.
- 2, 'A typology of Argument-Determined Constructions', is a revised version of a paper published as pp. 71–113 of *Essays on language function and language type*, edited by Joan Bybee, John Haiman and Sandra Thompson, 1997. Used with kind permission of John Benjamins Publishing Company, Amsterdam/Philadelphia (www.benjamins.com).
- 5, 'Dependencies between Grammatical Systems', is a revised version of a paper from *Language* 74: 56–80, 1998.
- 6, 'The Semantic Basis for a Typology', is a truncated and revised version of 'Semantic roles and syntactic functions: the semantic basis for a typology', from the *Proceedings of the 35th Annual Meeting of the Chicago Linguistic Society*, Part 2: *Papers from the Panels*, 323–41, 1999. Parts of this chapter, in very similar form, are in Dixon (2004a: 550–7).
- 9, 'Semi-Direct Speech in Typological Perspective', is a revised version of 'Semi-direct speech: Manambu and beyond', *Language Sciences* 30: 383–422, 2008.
- 10, 'Naive Linguistic Explanation', is a shortened and revised version of a paper from *Language in Society* 21: 83–91, 1992; © Cambridge University Press, used with permission.

- 11, 'Multiple Marking of Syntactic Function and Polysynthetic Nouns in Tariana', is a corrected version of a paper from the *Proceedings of the 35th Regional Meeting of the Chicago Linguistic Society. Part 2: The Panels.* 235–48, 1999.
- 12, 'Palikur and the Typology of Classifiers', is a revised version of a paper from *Anthropological Linguistics*, 40: 429–480, 1998. It is used with permission of the University of Nebraska Press.
- 13, 'Zero and Nothing in Jarawara', is a corrected version of a paper published as pp. 125–37 of *Form and function in language research: Papers in honour of Christian Lehmann*, edited by Johannes Helmbrecht, Yoko Nishina, Yong Min Shin, Stavros Skopeteas and Elisabeth Verhoeven, Berlin, Mouton de Gruyter, 2009.
- 15, 'Comparative Constructions in English', appeared in *Studia Anglica Posnaniensia* 41: 5–27, 2005.
- 16, 'Features of the Noun Phrase in English', is the amalgamation of two papers, 'The articles in English' and 'The grammatical status of *the same*', from *Studia Anglica Posnaniensia* 42: 31–36, 2006 and 45: 3–11, 2009.
- 17, '*Twice* and Constituency', appeared in *Studia Anglica Posnaniensia* 44: 193–202, 2008.
- 18, 'Australian Aboriginal words in Dictionaries—a history', is a revised version of a paper published in the *International Journal of Lexicology* 21: 129–52, 2008.

ABBREVIATIONS

These are abbreviations employed in interlinear glossing of examples; or instance, ERG for ergative and CL for classifier. However, where an example is short, with plenty of room on the line, a full label ERGATIVE or CLASSIFIER is written out. It would be pedantic (and otiose) to insist on always employing ERG and CL when there is no spatial limitation which requires abbreviation. Our aim, through the volume, has been to try to be as reader-friendly as circumstances permit.

1	first person
2	second person
3	third person
A	transitive subject
ABL	ablative
ABS	absolutive
ACC	accusative
ACT.FOC	action focus
AD	location 'ad' (in the vicinity of)
ADDR	addressee
ADESS	adessive
ADJ	adjective, adjectivizer
ADVZ	adverbializer
AG	agentive
AGT	agent
ALL	allative
ANIM	animate
AO	actor orientation
AP	animate plural
APPL	applicative
ART	article
ATT	attributive
AUG	augmentative
AUX	auxiliary
BAS	basic person marking
BAS.NP	basic non-past cross-referencing
BE	bound element

BIV	bivalent
BR	bound root
CAUS	causative
CERT	certain
CL	classifier
CNTR	contrast
COLL	collective
COMIT	comitative
COMPL	completive non-main clause
COMPLZR	complementizer
COND	conditional
CONF	confirmation marker
CONJ	conjugation marker
CONS	consequential
CONT	continuative
CONT.LOC	localization continuative
COP	copula
CS	current speaker
CUST	customary
D	durative marker
DAT	dative
DECL	declarative
DEF	definite
DEM	demonstrative
DENOM	denominal
DEP	dependent
DES	desiderative
DIM	diminutive
DIR	directional
DIR.SP.REP	direct speech report
DIST	distal
DR	bivalent direct
DS	different subject
du	dual
e	eyewitness
E	extended argument of a ditransitive verb
ERG	ergative
excl	exclusive
F, f, fem	feminine

FN	function marker
FOC	focus
FP	far past
FUT	future
GEN	genitive
HAB	habitual
IMM	immediate
IMPF	imperfective
IMPV	imperative
INCH	inchoative
INCL, incl	inclusive
IND.SP.REP	indirect speech report
INDEF	indefinite person
INDIC	indicative
INF	infinitive
INSTR	instrumental
INT	intention
intr	intransitive
IO	indirect object
IP	immediate past
ITER	iterative
ITN	intentional
LK	linker
LOC	locative
LOGOPHOR, log	logophoric
LV	linking vowel
M, m, masc	masculine
MANIP	manipulative
N	noun
n	non-eyewitness
NARR	narrative
NEG	negative
NEUT, n	neuter
nf	non-feminine
NMZR	nominalizer
NOM	nominalization
NOMIN	nominative
NONVIS	non-visual
NP	noun phrase

nsg	non-singular
NT	non-topic
O	transitive object
OBJ	object
obl	oblique
OBLIG	obligative
OPT	optative
OS	Original Speaker
p	person
P	past
PART	participle
PASS	passive
pauc	paucal
PEJ	pejorative
PERF	perfect
PERFV	perfective
PERI	peripheral
PERM	permissive
PL, pl	plural
pl.a	plural absential
POS	positive
POSS	possessive
POSSN	possession
POT	potential
PRES	present
PRET	preterite
PRIV	privative
PRO	free pronoun
PROC	process
PROG	progressive
PROH	prohibitive
PROP	proprietive case
PROPR	proprietive
PROX	proximate
PT	past tense
PURP	purposive
Q	question
QUOT	quotative
REC	reciprocal

REC.P.NONVIS	recent past non-visual
REC.P.VIS	recent past visual
RED	reduplication
REFL	reflexive
REL	relativizer
RELN	relational
REM.P	remote past
REP	reported
RP	reported speech marker
RP	recent past
S	intransitive subject
Sa	subject of active intransitive verb
SEQ	sequential
SF	stem formant
SG, sg	singular
SJ	verb-internal subject agreement suffix, or subject pronoun
So	subject of stative intransitive verb
SS	same subject
SUB	subordinative
SUB.IRR	subjunctive irrealis
SUBJ	subject, subject person marking
SUBST	substitutive case
TAM	tense, aspect, mood and/or modality
TEMP	temporal
TOP	topical
tr	transitive verb
TR	transitivizer; transitive ending
UO	undergoer orientation
V	verb
VBZR	verbalizer
VIS	visual
VOC	vocative

PART A

TOPICS IN LINGUISTIC TYPOLOGY

CHAPTER ONE

VERSATILE CASES

Alexandra Y. Aikhenvald*

Case markers are thought of primarily as nominal morphemes, indicating the function of a noun phrase in a clause. In a few languages of the world case markers also appear on verbal forms. Such 'versatile' cases can express (i) temporal, causal and other relationships between clauses, and (ii) aspectual and modal meanings within a clause. Core cases tend to express aspectual and modal meanings, while oblique cases tend to be used as clause-linkers. For instance, a dative case marks purposive clauses, and a locative case expresses temporal relationships between clauses.

The recurrent semantic differences between case morphemes on noun phrases, as clause-linking devices, and as exponents of clausal categories are rooted in the inherent polyfunctionality of these 'chameleon' morphemes: the specific meaning of any instance is affected by the morphosyntactic context in which it occurs. The conclusions are corroborated by a case study of Manambu, a Papuan language, with extensive use of cases on nouns and on verbs, both as exponents of aspectual and modal meanings, and as clause-linking devices.

1. Case on Verbs?

Case is conventionally defined as a nominal category, whose major function is to mark the role of the noun phrase in a clause (see Blake

* I would like to express my gratitude to those who taught me Manambu, especially Yuamali Ala, Pauline Yuaneng Laki, Gemaj, Jennie Kudapa:kw and numerous others, and to the Brito and Muniz families for teaching me Tariana. Deepest thanks go to Cynthia Allen, Azeb Amha, Ellen Basso, Barry J. Blake, Carol Genetti, Anne-Christie Hellenthal, Luise Hercus, Nerida Jarkey, Brian Joseph, Aet Lees, Frank Lichtenberk, Mark Post, Françoise Rose, Binyam Sisay and Silvia Zaugg-Corelli, for language data, criticisms, comments and suggestions. The late David Watters provided most inspiring comments and information; I owe many of the generalizations to his insights. I am especially grateful to R. M. W. Dixon, for inspiring comments on every page of this chapter. The data on Manambu and on Tariana come from my own fieldwork (and publications based on it). Data on all other languages come from published sources (listed in the references). For the purposes of this chapter, I have consulted over 400 grammars (with special attention to the key areas, mentioned in Appendix 1).

2001: 1; Matthews 1997; and Dixon 2010a: 43). Functions of a noun phrase in a clause can be marked with a bound morpheme, or with an adposition (a preposition or a postposition: see Iggesen 2005: 2, and Blake 2001: 9–12, on 'synthetic' cases expressed with bound morphemes, and 'analytic cases' expressed with adpositions).

In a number of languages of the world, case markers—bound morphemes or adpositions—are not restricted to noun phrases. They also appear on verb roots, or inflected verbal forms. Similarities in meanings between the case markers on nouns and the same forms on verbs are such that it appears counterintuitive to brush them aside as pure coincidence and fortuitous homonymy. Languages for which this phenomenon has been described are listed in Appendix 1 (alongside additional extended uses of case not included in this discussion). This chapter is the first attempt at a cross-linguistic analysis of case morphemes marking categories other than grammatical relations within a clause. 'Verbal' cases can express:

(i)   temporal, causal and other relationships between clauses, and
(ii) aspectual and modal meanings within a clause.

If used as a clause-linking device, a case has a whole clause—rather than just a noun phrase—as its scope. This is comparable to how, in some languages, the same set of conjunctions can be used to coordinate noun phrases and clauses. Cases can mark obligatory (core) arguments or optional obliques (non-core, peripherals, or adjuncts).[1] We will see, throughout the chapter, that core and non-core cases on verbs display somewhat different behaviours. The existence of such 'versatile' cases takes us to a broader issue: a category traditionally associated with one word class can in fact be associated with other classes.

This issue is not entirely new. For instance, tense, aspect and mood are commonly viewed as verbal categories par excellence. Recently,

---

[1] This distinction parallels what Kuryłowicz (1964) called grammatical and semantic case: roughly, grammatical case expresses a purely grammatical relation required by the frame of a particular verb or set of verbs (which can be said to 'govern', or 'require' it—just like the verb 'fear' in Manambu requires dative). Semantic case expresses a semantic relation not obligatorily required by the verb's argument structure, e.g. location (also see Blake 2001: 31–4, on the lack of clear boundaries between these notions). This distinction only partly overlaps with the notions of structural and inherent, or lexical, case, in some formal approaches: see Kiparsky (1998, 2001), and references there. Also see the survey in Iggesen (2005: 1–33).

Nordlinger and Sadler (2004) have demonstrated that these can also be categories of nominals.[2] Another example of a verbal category is evidentiality, that is, the grammaticalized expression of information source (Aikhenvald 2004, and references there). However, in a few languages, a noun phrase within a clause can occur marked with an evidential different from the evidential specification of the clause (marked on its verbal predicate), to signal that the information about this noun phrase was acquired from a different source than that of the verb (see Aikhenvald 2004: 88).

Example (1), from Jarawara, illustrates this. Jarawara has an obligatory firsthand versus non-firsthand distinction in all past tenses, and also a reported evidential. It comes from a story which relates the personal experience of the speaker who had seen the day dawn. This is why the verb is cast in firsthand evidential. The event took place a short time ago: this accounts for the recent past form of the verb 'become dawn' (Dixon 2004a: 193 and p.c.). However, the speaker's source of information about the fact that the place where the day dawned was the mouth of the Banawá river is hearsay (he had not seen the place, but was told what the place was). This is why the oblique noun phrase in (1) is marked for reported evidentiality.[3]

(1) {[[[Banawaa batori]-tee-**mone**] jaa] faja otaa
     Banawá   mouth-CUST-REP.f AT   then 1nsg.excl.S
        ka-waha-**ro**   otaa-ke}
        APPL-become.dawn-REC.P.FIRSTHAND.f   1nsg-DECL.f
     Then the day dawned on us (FIRSTHAND) (lit. we with-dawned) at the
     place REPORTED to be the mouth of the Banawá river

Such differential marking of information source on different clausal constituents is reminiscent of nominal tense marking whereby the time reference of a noun or a noun phrase may be different from that of the clause, as in (2), from Tariana:

(2) [diha panisi-**pena**]   alia-**pidana**
     he   house-NOMINAL.FUTURE   exist-REM.P.REP
     There (reportedly) was his future house

---

[2] For further alternative interpretations, see Tonhauser (2006).
[3] Here and elsewhere phrasal constituents are in square brackets; clauses are in braces.

Tense, aspect, mood, and evidentiality on nominals share their meanings with tense and mood on verbs (even if they are expressed differently: see the discussion in Nordlinger and Sadler 2004). For instance, in Tariana, nominal and verbal future cover future reference, and past covers past (Aikhenvald 2003: 183–7). That is, their meaning does not significantly change depending on whether they occur on a verb, or on a noun.

Some affixes can occur on nouns, and on verbs, with essentially the same meaning. In Classical Sanskrit, the suffix -*tara* was used to form 'the comparative degree of adjectives and rarely... of substantives', 'added (in older language) to adverbs... and (in later language) to verbs' (Monier-Williams 1899: 438). Comparative on adjectives and nouns marks comparison of qualities, e.g. adjective *priyá* 'beloved, dear', comparative *priyátara* 'dearer' (Monier-Williams 1899: 710; Whitney 1891: 175); noun *vīrá* 'man; hero', comparative *vīrátara* 'stronger man; greater hero' (Monier-Williams 1899: 1005: Whitney 1891: 176). Comparative on verbs marks comparison of actions or states, e.g. *vyatháyati* 'to disquiet, agitate' (causative of *vyath* 'tremble, fail'), comparative *vyathayatitarā(m)* 'disturbs more' (Monier-Williams 1899: 1005; Whitney 1891: 176).

In other languages, verbs, just like nouns, may occur with diminutive marking—compare Late Medieval Latin *scribillare* 'scribble, write a bit', a diminutive formation on Latin *scribere* 'write' (containing the same marker as a nominal diminutive, e.g. *asellus* 'young donkey', and many others: Palmer 1954: 236–7). The same morpheme means 'do a bit' with verbs and 'small size; young age' with nouns. This does not mean that we have two different morphemes. Their general meanings remain the same, and the relatively minor semantic difference is a side-effect of the meanings of prototypical verbs, and of nouns. A verb refers to an activity, and a noun to a 'thing'. Along similar lines, in Tariana (Arawak: Aikhenvald 2003: 193–5; 366–7) both diminutive and augmentative enclitics occur with verbs and on nouns. The diminutive with nouns implies a small size or a young age of a referent. With verbs, it marks small extent of action, that is, doing something 'a little bit'. The augmentative on nominals expresses large size of a referent, and on verbs it indicates an intensive action or state (and has an overtone of 'really').[4]

---

[4] Further examples include number marking on nouns and on verbs as different and partly overlapping systems (see Durie 1986; Newman 1990); classifiers and genders in

That is, the meaning of a morpheme used in different morpho-syntactic contexts changes because of the context itself. In line with this, the functions and the meanings of cases on verbal forms, clauses and noun phrases tend to be similar, but not identical. The recurrent semantic correspondences between them can be traced back to the inherent semantic differences between prototypical nouns and verbs, and to the semantic principles behind clause linking. A morpheme is not polysemous (in the sense of having an array of distinct, but related, meanings: Lyons 1977: 561); rather, each has a prototypical, or central meaning specified by the morphosyntactic context.

We start with a typological perspective on verbal case, focussing on the meanings and functions of case morphemes on verbs, as clause-linkers and as markers of clausal categories (§2). A case-study of multiple functions of versatile case morphemes in Manambu, a Papuan language from the Sepik area of New Guinea, is in §3. The last section contains brief conclusions.

2. TYPOLOGICAL PERSPECTIVE ON VERSATILE CASE

2.1. *Where can case morphemes go?*

Case markers can appear on (a) fully or partially inflected verbs; and (b) unmarked verb roots. A case marker with a clausal scope may be able to occur on any constituent in a clause, or on every constituent, or at the margins of a clause. Table 1.1 contains a summary of morpho-syntactic contexts (or loci) of cases, the functions of resulting forms, with example languages.[5] We mentioned in §1 that functions of a noun

---

various morphosyntactic environments (see Aikhenvald 2000b); and different effects of reduplication depending on the word class it applies to (see Beck 2002; Hajek 2004: 355; Lynch, Ross and Crowley 2003: 44). Also see Haude (2006: 239–43) on the applicative suffix used with verbs and with nouns in Movima. The vast majority of languages with such versatile affixes present no difficulty in distinguishing verbs from nouns.

[5] I will not consider adnominal-only 'cases' (that is, cases which only express relationships of a noun phrase within another noun phrase, as opposed to a noun phrase within a clause; adnominal cases include the genitive in Ket, or the 'proprietive' and 'privative' in Australian languages). Some forms mark both the relationship of one noun to another within a noun phrase (adnominal function) and the function of a noun phrase within a clause (clausal, or 'relational', function), as do locational cases in numerous Australian languages and comitative in languages from other areas (see Aikhenvald 2003, on Tariana). These will only be considered as appropriate from the standpoint of their clausal functions.

Table 1.1. Case morphemes on verb roots and on inflected verbs

VERB FORM	FUNCTIONS OF RESULTING FORM	LOCUS	EXAMPLES
I. Inflected verb	Clause-linking device (with fewer categories expressed in subordinate clauses than in main clauses)	on predicate	Tariana (Arawak), Bāgandji, Djambarrpuyngu, Martuthunira (Australian area), Rama (Chibchan), numerous Tibeto-Burman languages, Awtuw (Ram family, Papua New Guinea)
		at clause margins	English, Cantonese (Sinitic), Emerillon (Tupí-Guaraní)
		on any single constituent	Murinhpatha (Australian area)
		on several constituents of non-main clause	Yukulta, Ngarluma and Panyjima (Australian area)
II. Verb root	Aspect and mood in main clause	on predicate	Lepcha (Tibeto-Burman), Kala Lagaw Ya (Australian area)

phrase in a clause can be expressed through bound case morphemes or through adpositions (see Blake 2001). Table 1.1 includes both versatile nominal cases and versatile adpositions (e.g. prepositions in English, and postpositions in Rama). Based on this summary, we can note two tendencies discussed at A and B below.

A. If a case morpheme occurs on an inflected verb, it is most likely to be used as a clause-linking device. In such a use, the 'case-marked' verb is the predicate of a subordinate clause, and thus tends to express fewer

---

I will not consider here non-case-like nominal markers used as clause-linkers (e.g. morphemes like *eng* used as a 'determiner on "given noun phrases"' and a 'subordinating connective' between clauses in Usan (Reesink 1987: 83; 251)).

categories than would be possible in main clauses. For instance, Tariana (Arawak: Aikhenvald 2003: 524) employs two case morphemes on verbs inflected for person. The marker -*se* whose meaning with noun phrases covers location, direction and source means 'as soon as' when used as a clause-linker. The case marker -*ne* 'instrument; reason; location "along"; comitative "together with"' marks clauses with the meaning of 'reason' (Aikhenvald 2003: 530–1; 2006a: 185–6). Example (3), from Tariana (author's fieldnotes), illustrates -*se* on a noun phrase, and with a clausal scope.

(3) {**panisi-se**   **nu-nu-se**}   {nu-wana-de   pi-na}
     house-LOC   1sg-come-LOC/AS.SOON.AS   1sg-call-FUT   2sg-OBJ
     As soon as I come into the house I will call you[6]

In Awtuw, from the Ram family in Papua New Guinea, the object case marker -*re* can occur on the predicate of a complement clause of verbs of speech, perception and cognition. The verb can contain any tense markers, and can have a full set of arguments, core and oblique (Feldman 1986: 160–1).

Alternatively, a case marker with clausal scope may have additional freedom in its position within a clause which a nominal case lacks. For instance, in Murinhpatha (Australian: Walsh 1976: 163; 263–6) the ergative-instrumental inflection—which attaches to nouns—is the same as the affix 'when' which attaches to any constituent (most often to verbs). In Yukulta (Australian: Keen 1983; Dench and Evans 1988: 22–3) a case marker as a clause-linking device occurs on every constituent, except for the subject (similar phenomena have been noted in Ngarluma and Panyjima: Dench and Evans 1988: 23–4; see Dixon 2002: 238–9, for a summary). These facts are relevant for a synchronic description of each language, but hardly so for determining which context of the case marker is diachronically prior.

Other languages provide apparent clues relevant for the path of development of the markers. A case-morpheme with clausal scope can

---

[6] A non-main clause in Tariana cannot express tense or evidentiality. Since the case-marked clause in (3) is a non-main clause, neither tense nor evidentiality are marked. Along similar lines, dative-marked verbs in Bāgandji (Australian: Hercus 1982: 215) can occur with bound pronouns (subjects and objects), but do not mark any other categories (such as tense or mood). Postpositions used as 'subordinating morphemes' in Rama (Chibchan) are suffixed to tenseless verbs (Craig 1991: 469–70). The same holds for case-marked inflected verbs in Djambarrpuyngu (Australian: Wilkinson 1991: 629–53) and Martuthunira (Australian: Dench 1995).

have a different morpho-syntactic status than the same morpheme with a noun phrase. Postpositions in Rama are independent phonological and grammatical words (for instance, they have their own stress, and can be separated from the noun by intervening constituents), while the corresponding subordinators are suffixes. This difference in morpho-syntactic status is relevant for determining the direction of grammaticalization of these morphemes: from a postposition (a free morpheme) to a subordinator (a bound morpheme). A selection of these is shown in (4) (Craig 1991: 470).[7]

(4)   POSTPOSITIONS   SUBORDINATORS
      kama 'goal'   *-kama* 'purpose'
      ka(ng) 'ablative' *-ka* 'time, condition'
      su 'locative'   *-su* 'time, after/upon'

Versatile cases can occupy different positions depending on whether their scope is a noun phrase or a clause. When used adnominally, they may be clitics, or free morphemes (see §1 above, and Blake 2001: 9–12). Once they have clausal scope, they occur on clause margins (similarly to other clause-linkers in a given language). English has a number of such prepositions, as, for instance, *since* which can be used with a noun phrase or with a clause as its scope (see (7a,b)–(8a)).[8]

B. Case morphology on a bare verbal root tends to mark aspectual and modal categories, as in Lepcha (Tibeto-Burman: Plaisier 2006: 120), and also in Kala Lagaw Ya (Kennedy 1984: 162). These morphemes show no differences in their morphosyntactic status, or position in the clause, depending on whether they occur on noun phrases or on verbs. In (5), from Lepcha, the morpheme marking locative case on the noun phrase 'his house' also marks a hortative form of the verb:

(5)   hudo-sá   lí-ká   nóng-ká
      3sg.OBL-GEN house-LOC   go-LOC
      Let's go to his house

We will now turn to a brief survey of case markers as clause linkers, and as markers of clausal categories.

---

[7] Rose (2005) reports a similar situation in Maa (Nilo-Saharan; based on Payne 2004 which was not available to me).
[8] Similar examples are found in Cantonese (Matthews and Yip 1994: 285–99).

2.2. *Cases as markers of clause linking*

2.2.1. *An overview*

Tables 1.2 and 1.3 contain a list of recurrent meaning correspondences between cases with noun phrases, and with clauses, as their scope. Table 1.2 features cases which combine core and non-core (oblique, or peripheral) functions (ergative-instrumental, ergative-ablative, etc.). Table 1.3 features cases with non-core functions (locative, allative, etc.). In each instance, I provide one or two illustrative examples of languages where such a phenomenon has been documented synchronically (the sources are listed in Appendix 2).[9]

2.2.2. *Semantics of cases as clause linkers*

Polysemous cases which combine core and oblique functions appear to be more likely to have a clause as their scope than do purely core cases. The few examples of purely core-cases marking clause linking involve Muskogean languages (e.g. Koasati where the nominative case suffix -*k* is identical to the same-subject switch reference suffix, and the accusative -*n* to the different-subject marker: see Kimball 1991: 225, 391–5, 522–5; parallel phenomena in Chocktaw are in Nicklas 1974: 98, 211; also see Jelinek 1989: 135–7, and Jacobsen 1983: 176). In Yuman languages the erstwhile allative suffix -*m* came to be used as a same-subject marker in clause-linking (Kendall 1975: 4; Langdon 1979: 630). In some Yuman languages it developed into an object case and subsequently acquired the role of a clause complementizer (Jacobsen 1983: 175). The correlation between nominal core objective case and a complementizer was pointed out for Diegueño by Gorbet (1973: 221); also see Gorbet (1976: 121–8; 1979: 261–3) for the putative development of subjective case into a same-subject clause-linking morpheme. Muskogean and Yuman (whose interpretation varies depending on the reconstruction and approach) have not been included in Table 1.2, so as to keep it relatively simple.[10]

---

[9] Further examples can be found in Lichtenberk (1991), and Thurgood and LaPolla (2003). Lichtenberk (1991) also provides a discussion of a comitative adposition developing into a conjunction.

[10] In some instances, it is difficult to decide whether the same form is used to mark a case function on an NP and to link clauses is a matter of pure coincidence or not. For instance, in Dizin, an Omotic language, -*n* marks accusative case (Beachy 2005: 66–7, 114–5); its look-alike is also used as a different subject marker.

Table 1.2. Meanings of cases having core uses, with noun phrases and with clauses

MEANING WITH NOUN PHRASES AS CASE MARKERS	MEANING WITH CLAUSES AS CLAUSE LINKERS	EXAMPLE LANGUAGES
Ergative/ instrumental	because	Bodic (Tibeto-Burman), Limbu (Tibeto-Burman), Tauya (New Guinea area)
	when/while	Bodic (Tibeto-Burman), Murinhpatha (Australian area)
	causal/instrumental; temporal	Djambarrpuyngu (Australian are
Ergative/ablative	'point of origin' and cause of action	Lepcha (Tibeto-Burman)
Accusative, dative, purposive, locative	purposive	Kusunda (isolate, Nepal)
	relative time: simultaneous or sequential to the main clause	Galo (Tibeto-Burman)
	marker of complement clauses of verbs of speech, perception and cognition	Awtuw (Ram family, Papua Ne Guinea)
Dative, goal, purpose	purposive	Bodic (Tibeto-Burman), Djambarrpuyngu (Australian area), Rama (Chibchan), Koore and Yemsa (both Omotic, Afroasiatic)
	purposive; complement clause	Atong (Tibeto-Burman), Garo (Tibeto-Burman)
	purposive (SS)	Manambu (Ndu)
	purposive (DS)	Maale (Omotic, Afroasiatic)
	optative-purposive (DS)	Bāgandji (Australian area)
	contrastive 'though' (together with irrealis) (also see Table 1.3)	Yemsa (Omotic, Afroasiatic)
	locative, relative, destination	Ket (Yenisseic)
Dative-instrumental	causal 'because'	Djambarrpuyngu (Australian area)
Benefactive	causal, conditional	Ket (Yenisseic)

In Lepcha and Bodic languages (Tibeto-Burman), and in Murinhpatha and Djambarrpuyngu (Australian area), the ergative case has an additional, oblique-argument marking function, and is employed to link clauses. In Kusunda, the accusative-purposive case marks direct object, recipient, beneficiary and purpose (in addition to 'dative subject'), and also location; it is also employed as a clause-linking device. Tables 1.2 and 1.3 show that there are few if any semantic differences between core and non-core cases as clause-linking markers. For ease of reference, the two sets of case-markers are presented in separate tables.

Cases and adpositions on noun phrases mark the functions of those noun phrases within the clause (see the overview in Blake 2001). In contrast, the meanings of the same morphemes as clause-linkers are consistent with the major semantic types of clause-linking (see Dixon 2009; and also a partial list in Thompson and Longacre 1985: 177), which include temporal sequence; condition; cause; purpose; possible consequence; location; and manner. Case markers are also used as complementizers (for instance, in Awtuw, from Ram family, they mark complement clauses of verbs of speech, perception and cognition).

Cases with core uses can be used as markers of temporal clause-linking: in Galo, a Tibeto-Burman language, the accusative case *əəm* marks a subordinate clause 'as temporally and/or episodically subordinate to a focal clause, with the relative time relationship as simultaneous or sequential derived from the interaction of supporting and focal clause aspect marking' (Post 2009: 83). So, if the case-marked subordinate clause is cast in perfective, it indicates an action subsequent to that of the main clause. If it takes imperfective (or stative) marking, then the meaning is that of simultaneity. The exact nature of interaction between the categories of the predicate in a non-main clause marked by case morphemes in their clause-linking functions and the resulting semantics of clause-linking is a matter for future investigation. Just a handful of grammar analysts explicitly point out the differences between case markers as clause-linkers depending on aspect, or reality status of the verb (Post 2009, for Galo, and Zaugg-Corelli 2008, for Yemsa).

There appear to be no examples of cases used for expressing addition or disjunction of clauses. Tables 1.2 and 1.3 show that a case may sometimes have a very similar meaning with a noun phrase and with a clause. Other times, there are consistent differences.

Before proceeding to generalizations capturing these differences, we focus on three examples, (a) from English, (b) from Ket, and (c) from Kham.

Table 1.3. Meanings of cases lacking core uses, with noun phrases and with clauses

MEANING WITH NOUN PHRASES AS CASE MARKERS	MEANING WITH CLAUSES AS CLAUSE LINKERS	EXAMPLE LANGUAGES
Locative	if/although, when/while/after	Bodic
	when, while	Kham (Tibeto-Burman), Yamphu (Tibeto-Burman), Eastern Kayah Li (Tibeto-Burman), Manchu (Tungus-Manchurian), Martuthunira (Australian area)
	at the same time as	Galo (Tibeto-Burman)
	clausal complement	Eastern Kayah Li (Tibeto-Burman)
	purposive complement	Lepcha (Tibeto-Burman), Cogtse Gyarong (Tibeto-Burman)
	after, upon	Rama (Chibchan)
	as soon as	Tariana (Arawak), Galo (Tibeto-Burman)
	temporal, cotemporaneous, conditional	Ket (Yenisseic)
	locality; co-reference	Djambarrpuyngu (Australian area)
Ablative	when/while/after, because, condition, when	Bodic (Tibeto-Burman), Atong (Tibeto-Burman)
	causal	Lahu (Tibeto-Burman)
	condition	Rama (Chibchan), Qiang (Tibeto-Burman), Manchu (Tungus-Manchurian)
	after	Alaaba (Cushitic, Afroastiatic)
	after, if, before	Dulong-Rawang (Tibeto-Burman)
	temporal succession, then	Classical Tibetan (Tibeto-Burman)
	since, until	Galo (Tibeto-Burman)
	relative, locative, since (temporal/causal), positive purpose	Ket (Yenisseic) Toqabaqita (Oceanic)
	'precautionary', lest	Kwaio (Oceanic)
	motion from; cessation from; cause; start of temporal span; prior event	Djambarrpuyngu (Australian area)
	comparison 'rather than VERB'	Wolaitta (Omotic, Afroasiatic)

ɔle 1.3 (*cont.*)

EANING WITH ƆUN PHRASES AS ᴀSE MARKERS	MEANING WITH CLAUSES AS CLAUSE LINKERS	EXAMPLE LANGUAGES
ative 'away from'	conditional 'if'	Kham (Tibeto-Burman), Classical Tibetan
	'when'	Classical Tibetan (Tibeto-Burman)
	cause or reason	Yamphu (Tibeto-Burman)
lative	purpose	Bodic (Tibeto-Burman)
	motion towards a situation; the situation in which Object or Indirect Object is engaged	Djambarrpuyngu (Australian area)
lative, purpose	reason, positive purpose	Toqabaqita (Oceanic)
dessive	locative, causal, conditional	Ket (Yenisseic)
tive 'up to'	until	Kham (Tibeto-Burman)
osecutive 'through, along'	temporal cotemporaneous; concurrent background action	Ket (Yenisseic)
olative 'by way/ means of'	reason, 'until'	Toqabaqita (Oceanic)
strumental/ comitative/ perlative	reason; cause	Tariana (Arawak), Classical Tibetan (Tibeto-Burman)
ative, instrumental	purposive, contrastive though (with irrealis) (also see Table 1.2)	Yemsa (Omotic, Afroasiatic)
erlative	concurrent with main clause motion predicate; the situation which is the channel or means for the main clause situation	Djambarrpuyngu (Australian area)
pproximative 'about'	as long as/as much as	Kham (Tibeto-Burman)
milative 'like'	the same way as	Limbu (Tibeto-Burman), Kwoma (Nukuma family, New Guinea)
	when, while, as soon as; if	Yemsa (Omotic, Afroasiatic)
	like, complementizer with verbs of hearing, speech and cogntion	Yemsa (Omotic, Afroasiatic)
	complementizer	Alaaba (Cushitic, Afroasiatic)
ociative 'together'	sequence of events	Yamphu (Tibeto-Burman), Toqabaqita (Oceanic)
omitative	when, after (with realis), until (with irrealis)	Yemsa (Omotic, Afroasiatic)
ausal 'because'	apprehensive 'lest'	Pitta-Pitta (Australian area)

(a) English has a handful of prepositions which can also occur on a clause marking its syntactic relationship with another clause. These are: *after, before, since, until, till,* and *for.* The meaning of most prepositions with a noun phrase and with a clause is the same: compare (6a) and (6b). Brackets indicate the boundaries of the noun phrase and of the clause within the scope of the preposition.

(6) (a) She had a hard time after {the death of her husband}
     (b) She had a hard time after {her husband died}

The preposition *since* is less straightforward: it has a temporal meaning when used with a noun phrase and a temporal or a causal meaning when used with a clause. Both (7a) and (7b) are acceptable. The preposition *since* has a temporal meaning in both examples. In (7a) its scope is a noun phrase; and in (7b) it is a clause.

(7) (a) I've been very lazy since {the end of summer school}
     (b) I've been very lazy since {summer school ended}

However, in its causal meaning *since* can only be used with a clause, as in (8a).

(8) (a) Since {I disliked his manner}, I turned him down

This meaning with a noun phrase argument would not be grammatical:

(8) (b) ?Since my dislike for his manner, I turned him down

Further discussion is in Long (1965); and also Quirk et al. (1985: 659–60). The temporal and the causal meanings are semantically linked—if two events are mentioned together as following each other in time, it may be possible to infer that one is the cause of the other (see Thompson and Longacre 1985: 181ff; Longacre 1985). However, the fact that *since* expresses a causal relationship only when it links clauses alerts us to the fact that the context of use may entail different semantic overtones for what is traditionally considered the same, polysemous, morpheme. Along similar lines, a locational case may have a somewhat different array of meanings with nouns, and with clauses. This takes us to the next example.

(b) Ket (a Yenisseic language: Werner 1997a: 105; 354) has nine clausal cases, six of which can be used for clause-linking.[11] Adessive case means 'at, towards' when used with nouns, as shown in (9) (from Vajda 2004: 27). It can also mark the second argument of verbs denoting thinking (about something) or narrating (about something).

(9) bū   láɣ-ìn-nà-ŋta   òn   sɨkɨŋ
     3masc   Selkup-pl-AP-ADESS   many   years
         du-o-il-daq (surface form: dóldàq)
         3M.SJ-D-PT-live
     He lived among the Selkups (lit. at the Selkups, that is, at their camp)
         for many years

If used with clausal scope, its meaning is causal, locative, or conditional. The causal meaning 'because' is illustrated in (10) (unglossed example from Werner 1997a: 353; glosses from Anderson 2004: 68):

(10) {at   **t-bver-a-vet-diŋta**}   at   sa?j   iñ-d-aq
      I   1-work-PRESENT-SF-ADESS   I   tea   PAST/PERFV-1–give
      Because I work, give me tea

The locational meaning of the adessive case is typical of nominal cases, while causal and conditional meanings are quite typical of clause-linking semantics (see Thompson and Longacre 1985: 177; and especially Dixon 2009).

(c) Kham, from the Tibeto-Burman family, provides a further, spectacular, example of a language in which almost every case marker has a clause-linking function. The case suffixes attach directly to the verb stem. Table 1.4, from Watters (2009: 101–2), summarises these correlations.

---

[11] Absolutive, comitative, and caritive are not employed to link clauses. Cases which 'double' as clause-linkers are dative, benefactive, ablative, adessive, locative, and prosecutive (see Tables 1.2–1.3). Genitive has been excluded from the table, since it only indicates relations within a noun phrase (Werner 1997a: 112); while vocative does not mark grammatical relations and has also been omitted. The related Yugh only employs locative, ablative and benefactive for clause linking (Werner 1997b: 236–7) out of eight cases used with noun phrases (same as Ket, minus adessive).

Table 1.4. Versatile case marking suffixes in nominal and verbal contexts in Kham

Suffix	Case Name	As a Noun Suffix	As a Verb Suffix
-kə	locative	at	when/while
-tə	superessive	on	as soon as
-kin	elative	away from	if
-kin	elative	away from	after (with nominalization)
-kin	comparative	compared to	before, after
-wa	approximative	about	as long as/as much as
-pəi	lative	up to	until
-da	allative	to	provided, first this…
-e	ergative/instrumental	(agency)	because…
-ni	ablative/mediative	from	by means of, through
-e jũ:-ni	benefaction	for the sake of	in order to

Note that the same case marker ('elative', meaning 'away from' when used with nouns) acquires different meanings as a clause linker if attached to a verb which contains a nominalizer, and if attached to a verb which does not. With a nominalized verb, the elative case expresses the meaning of 'after'. If attached to a verbal stem without a nominalizer, the same elative form *-kin* either marks a conditional clause, meaning 'if', or a temporal clause with the meaning of 'before, after'.

As Watters (2009: 101–2) puts it, 'It is not difficult to see the relationship between locative suffixes affixed to nouns and those affixed to verbs—in the former case the suffix specifies location in physical space, and in the latter it specifies location in time. Likewise, an approximation of physical amount (*-wa*) equates to an approximation or duration of time, and distance "up to" a particular location equates to an extension to a point in time. The relationship which holds between a spatial elative ("away from") and a conditional reading is cross-linguistically more rare, but still follows from a reasonable semantic inference—"if" comes from a potential but unrealized state or event. The ergative/instrumental and the ablative/mediative, when affixed to a nominalized verb, names the sub-event in the supporting clause as the "cause" in some larger macro-event, and benefaction marks it as "purpose".'

In a nutshell, a locative marker on a noun phrase is likely to express temporal sequence if used as a clause-linking device. A beneficiary, or a dative marker on a noun is likely to express purpose relationship between two clauses. We turn to this in I and II below.

The meanings of cases on noun phrases are consistent with the semantic functions of noun phrases, as recipients, beneficiaries, instruments, and locations. The meanings of cases as clause-linkers follow the major semantic types in linking clauses: temporal, causal and conditional. These are intertwined: temporal sequence often has overtones of condition and cause. Purposive clause linking may also indicate cause, or consequence, or 'lest' (Dixon 2009). Based on the selection of language-specific correlations between the meanings of a case with a noun phrase and with a clause exemplified in Tables 1.2–1.3, we can suggest a number of semantic correspondences between NP functions and clause-linking devices.

I. Noun-phrase markers with a dative or purposive, or benefactive meaning, tend to have purposive meanings as clause linkers. Table 1.2 shows that this is the case in a number of languages. Dative case marks purposive clauses in languages of the Bodic subgroup of Tibeto-Burman, in Rama (Chibchan), in Djambarrpuyngu, from the Australian area and in Koorete, an Omotic language. In Atong and in Garo, both Tibeto-Burman, dative marking on verbs marks purposive and also some complement clauses. Dative marking on verbs may appear just with same subject clauses, as in Manambu. In contrast, in Maale, from the Omotic subgroup within Afroasiatic, the dative case case shows segmental similarity to the different subject purposive.[12]

Despite its frequency, a dative-on-noun versus purposive-on-verb correspondence is not a steadfast rule: in Ket, the dative case marker is used to mark locative clauses, and even relative clauses (Werner 1997a: 353), alongside 'destination' (Vajda 2004: 25). The dative-instrumental case in Yemsa (Omotic: Zaugg-Corelli 2008: 241–9) has a purposive meaning if attached to realis verbs. With verbs cast in irrealis, its meaning is that of a contrastive 'though'.

---

[12] Dative case -*m* (which always attaches to the absolutive form of the noun) shows segmental similarity to the different subject purposive marker -*óm*. Amha (2001: 186–7) offers evidence in favour of analyzing -*óm* as consisting of two morphemes: the absolutive marker -*ó* and the dative marker -*m*.

II. Noun-phrase markers with locational meanings are likely to develop temporal connotations indicating relative time 'while; as soon as; after, upon, cotemporaneous' and others if they have a clause as their scope. This correlation is akin to a well-documented semantic extension from spatial to temporal notions in the domain of adverbs, and also case markers (Haspelmath 1997; Heine and Kuteva 2002: 40–1; 179–80; 183). This is supported by recent psychological experiments, confirming that 'spatial representations are the source of temporal representations' (Gentner et al. 2002: 557). Martuthunira, an Australian language, offers a further support for this same principle: here, the locative case marker on nouns is employed as a clause-linker with a general temporal meaning which can be interpreted in various ways depending on the context (Dench 2009: 265–79).

The details of meaning overtones for locational cases as clause linking devices vary substantially. A locational meaning of a noun-phrase marker can mirror its meaning with a clause, but within a temporal domain. For example, the perlative case means 'along' in Djambarrpuyngu noun phrases, and 'concurrent with main clause' on clauses containing motion predicates. An additional extension of 'along' with clausal scope is 'the situation which is the channel or means for the main clause situation' (Wilkinson 1991: 641–2). In Kham, lative 'up to' means 'until' when used with a clause (Watters 2002: 317; also see examples in Blake 1999: 307–8, from Australian languages; and especially Genetti 1986, 1991). In Alaaba, a Cushitic language from Ethiopia, the ablative marker suffixed to a finite verb indicates an action completed before that of the main clause has started (Schneider-Blum 2009: 66).

There can be additional extensions. A conditional meaning of a locative case marker as a clause-linker was documented for Ket; this can be viewed as an extension of its temporal meaning (Werner 1997a: 354).[13] Elative and ablative have conditional meanings in a number of languages (Rama, Qiang, Kham and Classical Tibetan). This development can be considered an extension of an erstwhile temporal meaning of a locative morpheme (also see Thompson and Longacre 1985, for links between condition and time in clause-linking). A locational case marker can express purpose. In some Tibeto-Burman languages, a locative marks purpose complement (as

---

[13] The marker for conditional clauses in Sheko, an Omotic language from Ethiopia, could contain a locative marker as its part (Anne-Christie Hellenthal, p.c.).

in Lepcha: Plaisier 2006: 119–20; and Cogtse Gyarong: Nagano 2003: 487). Lichtenberk (1991b: 71–4) provides an explanation of how an ablative postposition came to mark positive purpose in Toqabaqita, and negative consequence, 'lest', in Kwaio. And in Wolaitta, ablative case on an inflected verb marked with future tense has the meaning of 'rather than'. Historically, this may be linked to the use of ablative in comparative constructions, as a marker of the standard of comparison (Azeb Amha, p.c.).[14]

III. Noun-phrase markers with instrumental meaning have a causal or a temporal meaning when used as clause linkers. At least in one of the languages where this development has been attested the instrumental case on a noun can also express cause, as in Tariana (Aikhenvald 2003). We will see, in §3.4.2, that an instrumental case without a causal meaning is used for manner clause-linking.

Other, more 'exotic', non-core cases are relatively straightforward. The similative case 'like' in Kwoma and in Limbu has the same meaning as a clause linker; the sociative marker on nouns expresses sequence of events in Yamphu, and also Toqabaqita. Yemsa has three case forms, each meaning 'like'. Each can be used with a verb, with somewhat different clause-linking meaning. One has the meanings of 'when, while, as soon as', another one means 'if', and the third one means 'like, in a way similar to', and is also used as a complementizer with verbs of hearing, speech and cognition (Zaugg-Corelli 2008: 241–9).[15] Approximative 'about' in Kham develops a more appropriate clause-linking meaning of temporal 'as long as', or quantitative 'as much as' (Watters 2002: 317). The comitative case in Yemsa is used on verbs with the meaning of 'until' (if the verb is cast in irrealis), or 'when, after' if it is realis.

Causal case meaning 'because' has similar overtones of reason, or consequence, when used as a clause-linker. In Pitta-Pitta (Australian area: Blake 1979: 198, 1999: 307, 310), causal case indicates negative consequence (that is, apprehensive 'lest') when employed as a clause

---

[14] As in the following example (the ablative case marker is in bold): *harg-ídí ligaagátt-anaá-**ppe** kaset-ídi naag-étt-iyo-ga* (be.sick-SS:A:CONVERB suffer.badly-FUTURE-ABLATIVE be early-SS:A:CONVERB watch.out/wait-PASS/MIDDLE/NONSUBJECT-IMPERFECTIVE:RELATIVE-NOMINALIZER) 'Rather than suffering from illness (the choice should be that people) take precautions (Azeb Amha, p.c.).

[15] In Alaaba, from the Cushitic branch of Afroasiatic, the similative case marker appears on finite predicates of complement clauses (Schneider-Blum 2009: 70).

linker. In Yidiñ, also from the Australian area (Dixon 1977: 333–5), causal case on nouns, -*m(u),* means 'because'. One suffix, -*m,* also marks what Dixon calls 'causal' clauses. These 'describe something that took place prior to the event described by the main clause (and was in fact finished before the main clause event began)' (p. 334). This alerts us to the fact that many cases may acquire overtones of temporal linkers when used with clauses.[16]

In none of the instances mentioned in Tables 1.2–1.3 does using what looks like a nominal morpheme—a case, or an adposition—on a verb imply an underlying nominalization.[17] In the absence of an overt nominalizing morpheme, saying that a verb has to be nominalized with a zero marker in order to be used with a case, or an adposition, involves pure conjecture. There are no reasons to believe that a verb like *nu-nu-se* 'as soon as I come' in (3) in Tariana is nominalized. If it were, it would have been the only instance of a zero-marked nominalization in the language. The facts of languages such as Kham (see Table 1.4, and comments to it) show that a nominalized verbal form accompanied by a case marker may have a different meaning than a verbal form without an overt nominalizer, with the same case marker attached to it.

In addition, in Tibeto-Burman languages (such as Lepcha: Plaisier 2006), the subject of a nominalization is marked differently from that of a subordinate clause whose predicate takes a case marker as a linking device. English also has a wide variety of nominalizing devices (see Dixon 2005: 322–52); but there are no language internal reasons to consider dependent clauses like the ones in (6b) and (7b) and (8a) as 'nominalized'. Along similar lines, Genetti (1991: 246) argues that

---

[16] Ydiny was not included in Table 1.3 because only one of the allomorphs of the linker is obviously relatable to the case marker. The connection between 'causal' case and 'causal' linking is in all likelihood historical, and not synchronic, as in all examples in Table 1.3. A further example of an historical link between a case marker and marker of a relative clause comes from northern dialects of Dyirbal (Dixon 1972: 354–5), where a nominal genitive suffix -*mi* developed into a marker of relative clause, attaching to a verb carrying the past tense suffix -*ñu* (thus forming a complex morpheme -*ñumi*). This development points towards the functionally unmarked status of verbal past tense form -*ñu.* The issue of a link between genitive markers and exponents of relative clauses goes beyond the scope of this chapter. (Another example is *n* 'of' and -*n* 'marker of verbal relative form known as participle, attested in most Berber languages: Aikhenvald 1987).

[17] Some grammarians tacitly assume this without providing explicit justification (e.g. Hercus 1982: 215).

in Classical Newari, 'the first stage in the development of postpositions to subordinators' was 'the suffixation of nominal postpositions to fully inflected finite' verb forms, 'which lacked overt nominalizing suffixes'.

We conclude that, as expected, the semantics of 'cases' as clause-linkers fits in with the general mould of semantic patterns of clause-linking. A recurrent semantic correspondence is between a spatial meaning of a nominal case and a temporal meaning of a clause linker, confirming that the domains of space and time share conceptual structure (see Boroditsky 2000: 25–6 for experimental results to this effect, and the discussion of the underlying mental representations).

In terms of its historical development, the polysemy of nominal cases and clause-linkers has often been understood as a product of 'grammaticalization' of cases to clause linkers (in the conventional sense of the term, see Meillet 1912; Heine and Kuteva 2002). The facts of Rama (Craig 1991: 471) corroborate this. Postpositions with noun phrase scope in Rama (see (4)) are free morphemes, while the corresponding markers with clausal scope are bound morphemes. This can be interpreted as pointing towards a unilateral grammaticalization path:[18]

(11)   adposition (free morpheme) with a noun phrase scope > adposition
        with clausal scope (developed into a bound morpheme)

The direction of development in (11) is congruent with a general path of semantic change (especially in grammaticalization), whereby more specific meanings, or meanings based on a specific situation, become more general, or 'based on the textual situation' (Genetti 1991: 249).[19]

---

[18] The analysis of correlations between postpositions and related subordinators in Newari (Genetti 1991) points to a development in the same direction (for similar results in a selection of Oceanic languages, see Lichtenberk 1991b: 73–4; also see Blake 1993: 47–9, Dixon 2002: 239, for Australian languages, and Winter 1976: 171–2, Jacobsen 1983: 175–6, Gordon 1980, Miller 2001: 265 and Gorbet 1973; 1976: 110–53, for similar pathways in Yuman languages). Akiba (1977: 616–8) discusses the development of the direct object marker in Old Japanese into a different subject clause-linker. According to Valenzuela (2003: 911–7), Proto-Panoan case markers came to be reanalyzed as sequential markers.

[19] A study of the few prepositions in English whose scope can be either a noun phrase or a clause provides somewhat similar results (also see Traugott 1982, and the historical study in Dill 1986). The *Oxford English Dictionary* (1989) explicitly notes that the prepositional use is primary for *till* and *until* (stating that *till* was originally the preposition governing the demonstrative pronoun *that*, in apposition with the following clause). In at least four instances (*before, till, until* and *for*), the use of the

2.3. *Cases as markers of clausal categories*

Cases as markers of clausal categories of aspect, mood and modalities can historically originate from cases as clause-linkers—see §2.3.1. Cases on noun phrases can also impart aspectual value to the whole clause—see §2.3.2.

2.3.1. *How clause-linking cases come to mark categories of a main clause*

We can recall from Table 1.1 that, when case markers occur on verb roots,[20] they are likely to express clausal categories such as aspect, modality, and mood.

Similar developments occur if case markers attach to deverbal nominalizations used as predicates of dependent clauses. If a dependent clause becomes reinterpreted as a main clause, via ellipsis, the case morphemes are reinterpreted as aspect or modality markers. This path was summarized by Blake (1999, especially Table 3 on p. 304), for Australian languages.[21]

For instance, a dependent apprehensive clause referring to possible negative consequence typically occurs with the main clause expressing a warning, or something to be avoided, as in (12), from Pitta-Pitta (Blake 1999: 307, 310).

(12) Wilakana-ya   kiniyarri [nhan-(nh)a-ka piyawarli-lu
      hide-PRESENT   girl   she-ACC-HERE   dog-ERG
         patya-ka-la]
         bite-[PAST]-LEST
      The girl is hiding lest the dog bite her

---

forms with noun phrase scope predates that with clausal scope. This accords with the direction of change formulated in (11).

[20] All the examples of case morphemes as markers of categories of main clauses identified so far are affixes. Whether the absence of case adpositions in these functions is a coincidence or not remains an open question.

[21] This process—whereby a non-main clause appears on its own with the main clause ellipsed—is known as de-subordination (see Aikhenvald 2004; an alternative, and less felicitous term, is 'insubordination'). This has been described for numerous languages, including Indo-European (such as Italian and English: Vallauri 2004; Stirling 1998). If the construction is no longer elliptical (that is, the ellipsed verb is not recoverable, and does not have to be supplied for the clause to be grammatical), new tense-aspect-mood paradigms emerge (as in Australian languages, e.g. Kayardild: Evans 1995b; Dixon 2002; also see Blake 1993, 1999 and Dixon 2002 for Australian languages in general; or Carib languages: Gildea 1998; Carlin 2004), or a reported evidential paradigm, out of de-subordinated speech report constructions (as in Estonian: Aikhenvald 2004: 281–3 and references there).

The case marker -la—which means 'lest' with clauses—has a causal meaning with noun phrases. It also marks the complement of verbs of fear (Blake 1979: 198), as in (13):[22]

(13)   kiniyari   ṇan-pa-ka   ṭalala   kupakupa-la
       girl   she-NOMIN-HERE   afraid   old.man-CAUSAL
       The girl is frightened of the old man

The main clause may be left out, and then the erstwhile dependent clause comes to be used on its own, with the same 'apprehensive' meaning. (14) is also from Pittta-Pitta (Blake 1999: 310):

(14)   Nhan-(nh)a-ka   piyawarli-lu   patya-ka-la
       she-ACC-HERE   dog-ERG   bite-[PAST]-LEST
       The dog might bite her

In Dixon's (2002: 239) words, 'types of subordinate clauses have been reanalyzed as main clauses, so that what were verbal suffixes marking subordination now take on TAM values'. A typical development involves the aversive case 'for fear of' on a noun phrase to apprehensive modality on a verb in a clause (shown in (13) and (14)), and from dative case on noun phrases to purposive or intentional, or future on clauses (Dixon 2002: 237–9; Blake 1999: 309–10, 1993: 40).

Along similar lines, in Dyirbal -gu (Dixon 1972: 67–77) is used both as dative on nouns and as purposive marker on verbs (of one conjugation). In Kalkatungu (Blake 1999: 315), the dative case marker -ya forms a purposive in combination with past and proprietive markers (the resulting form is: -ny-tya-ya-PAST-PROP-DAT). In this same language, a combination of -ya 'dative' (on nouns) and future -mi forms potential -mi-ya.[23]

Reanalysis of dependent clauses as main clauses does not always go through the intermediary of a nominalization (as in Australian languages). The manifold meanings of -k and -m in Maricopa (Yuman) verbs in independent clauses appear to go back to their uses

---

[22] The difference in spelling for 'girl' in (12) and (13) is due to different orthographic conventions for a flap by Blake (1979) and (1999).
[23] Further examples of case morphemes developing into aspects through the possible intermediary of nominalizations are discussed in Blake (1999: 312) and Dixon (2002: 238).

in dependent clauses (Gordon 1980: 140), but no nominalization is postulated.²⁴

2.3.2. 'Aspectual' cases

A clausal category can be expressed with a case marker on a predicate, or else just by case on a noun phrase, as illustrated in this section. In numerous Balto-Finnic languages, especially Finnish, assigning partitive, or accusative, case to objects of a number of verbs, has aspectual implications.²⁵ Examples (15) and (16) (from Kiparsky 1998) illustrate this semantic effect. The 'irresultative', unbounded, and atelic event in (15) involves having a partitive object. The bear was shot at, but not killed:

(15)   Ammu-i-n   **karhu-a**
       shoot-PAST-1sg   bear-PART
       I shot at the/a bear

In contrast, the resultative and bounded version in (16) involves the object marked with the accusative. (16) 'denotes an accomplishment, "to shoot dead"', while (15) 'denotes an activity' (Kiparsky 1998: 267):²⁶

---

²⁴ In other instances, we cannot decide whether the use of case as a marker of mood or modality results from reinterpretation. We saw in (5) that the locative case marker in Lepcha (Tibeto-Burman: Plaisier 2006: 119–20) doubles as hortative marker 'let's'. In Galo (Tibeto-Burman: Post 2007), dative case on the verb marks optative, or unrealized wish. The origin of these are yet to be ascertained. In Kala Lagaw Ya, a dialect of the Western Torres Strait language (Kennedy 1984: 162), case markers share the same form with tense/aspect morphemes; according to Kennedy, 'the speakers of this language have a single set of abstract categories which can be expounded in both verbal and nominal domains' (cf. Dixon 2002: 239). This requires further investigation.

²⁵ This aspectual overtone has been described in terms of unboundedness versus boundedness of event (e.g. Ikola 1961; Heinämäki 1984), or irresultativity versus resultativity (e.g. Itkonen 1976; Hakulinen and Karlsson 1979: 183; Larsson 1983: 22–3; see a summary by Sands 2000; also see Huumo 2010). Similar aspectual effects of the partitive-accusative case alternation have been described for other Balto-Finnic languages, including Estonian (e.g. Tauli 1980; Tarmo 1981; also see Lees 2004, for a comparison between Finnish and Estonian), Livonian (Tveite 2004), and also Veps (Kettunen 1943). Larsson (1983) offers a general discussion in the light of other Finno-Ugric languages. In Estonian, putting the object in the partitive case imparts the meaning of 'imperfective activity' to the clause, as in *Mees ehitas suvilat* (man build:3sgPAST summer.house:PART.SG) 'The man was building a summer house'. Using a non-partitive object (in Estonian, marked with the genitive case) has overtones of completed action, e.g. *Mees ehitas suvila* (man build:3sg.PAST summer.house:GEN.SG) 'The man built a summer house' (Erelt 2007: 96)).

²⁶ Note that the English translation is somewhat misleading. The alternation of 'shoot somebody' and 'shoot at somebody' in English has similar, but not identical,

(16)   Ammu-i-n   **karhu-n**
        shoot-PAST-1sg   bear-ACC
        I shot the/a bear (it is dead)

Finnish also has intrinsically 'unbounded' verbs (such as 'love', 'touch') which require partitive objects, and intrinsically bounded verbs (such as 'kill', 'find') which require the accusative. The partitive case also denotes objects of indeterminate quantity ('some'), and can be described as a marker of indefiniteness (see Sands 2000; Sands and Campbell 2001).

In addition to this, in Finnish, 'the use of local cases [...] has aspectual implications. The inessive and adessive case imply a continuing activity and so have imperfective aspect, whereas the elative, illative, ablative and allative all imply an end-point of the activity and perfective aspect' (Sands 2000: 277; and a summary in Hakulinen 1961: 333). 'The process as opposed to the result is indicated with the static-location cases (inessive and adessive)' (Sands 2000: 277). If the allative case is used, as in (17), the activity is considered to be a result; this station may be the train's final destination:

(17)   Juna   pysähtyi   **asema-lle**
        train   stop.PAST.3sg station-ALL
        The train stopped at the station (lit. towards the station as its final
           destination)

In (18), the adessive case implies that the station is 'simply a stopping point on the train's journey, and the train continues on'. (Comparable phenomena in Estonian are addressed in Tuldava 1994: 106–7).

(18)   Juna   pysähtyi   **asema-lla**
        train   stop.PAST.3sg station-ADESS
        The train stopped at the station (lit. at the station as a passing point)

In each of these instances, the way in which a noun phrase is marked impacts upon the aspectual value of the clause. The semantic effect of

---

overtones: while 'shoot at somebody' does imply that shooting was not fatal, or the goal has not been attained, 'shooting somebody' simply implies that the O got hit (but did not necessarily die). An in-depth analysis of the partitive-accusative alternation in Finnish for various verb types is in Heinämäki (1984). These overtones are comparable with what Evans (1995: 405–11) exhaustively described as 'modal case' in Kayardild, an Australian language.

case is reminiscent of the absolutive-dative case alternation in Warlpiri: marking the object (O) of a verb like 'shoot' as dative rather
than as absolutive describes 'the situation in which the effect normally
resulting from the action denoted by the verb is, for one reason or
another, aborted or else is subordinated in importance to the action
itself' (Hale 1982: 249). This phenomenon was further characterized
as a 'conative' case alternation which imparts a special 'irresultative'
aspectual value to the whole clause (see Kiparsky 1998: 266, 295–6,
and further references there). This partly confirms the status of aspect
and modality as clausal categories which do not necessarily have to be
marked on the predicate.[27]

Historically speaking, the partitive case in the Balto-Finnic subgroup of Finno-Ugric comes from a locational case with a separative
meaning 'from' (see Laanest 1975; Kiparsky 1998). Correlations of case
marking with aspect are generally considered a later development in
Balto-Finnic. Larjavaara (1991) hypothesizes that the locational 'from'
case developed an aspectual overtone via a 'quantificational' meaning
'some' with a noun phrase. Further historical and comparative evidence indicates that, in Balto-Finnic, 'the partitive's emergence as a
structural case is a precondition for the rise of its aspectual function'
(Kiparsky 1998: 305). That is, the noun phrase-level function of a case
is primary with respect to its other functions, such as marking aspect.
This is comparable to the generalization under (11) above: that a case
or an adposition with a noun phrase scope may develop into a case
or an adposition with a clausal scope and not the other way round.
We now turn to similar phenomena in Manambu, a previously undescribed language from New Guinea.

3. VERSATILE CASE IN MANAMBU

Manambu, from the Ndu family (East Sepik, Papua New Guinea),[28]
offers a particularly rich array of cases employed with noun phrases,

---

[27] In fact, in many languages they are marked with enclitics which may attach to
constituents other than the predicate (see the discussion of Tariana in Aikhenvald
2002b, and further examples of other languages there).

[28] Manambu is spoken by about 2000 people in five villages in Ambunti area of East
Sepik province of Papua New Guinea. Other members of the family are: Ambulas;
Boiken; Iatmul; Yelogu or Kaunga; Gala (or Ngala, or Swakap) (see Aikhenvald
2008a; Jendraschek 2006). Other genetic affiliations are putative. Kwoma/Washkuk
is a neighbouring language spoken by traditional trade-partners of the Manambu. It

and on verb roots. Case morphemes are used as clause-linking devices (cf. §2.2), and as markers of clausal categories (cf. §2.3.1–2).

3.1. *Background information*

Manambu is predominantly suffixing and agglutinating with some fusion, and combines both dependent-marking and head-marking. Nouns and verbs are clearly distinguished in terms of their categories, inflectional possibilities and syntactic behaviour. Nominal categories are gender, number, a system of nine case forms, and a number of derivational processes. Verbal categories include person, number, gender, aspect, mood, modality, direction, and a variety of clause-chaining markers.

Declarative verbs cross-reference two arguments: the subject and any other argument—except copula complement and speech report— which is more topical than the subject. Verbs in different-subject medial clauses cross-reference just the subject. No argument is cross-referenced on verbs marked for modalities such as desiderative and frustrative and a number of aspects. Likewise, predicates in same-subject clauses take no cross-referencing markers.

A verbal root, or an inflected verb, cannot be used as an argument or head a noun phrase. Deverbal action nominalizations are used instead; these are derived from a verbal root via its full reduplication, e.g. *war* 'ascend', *warwar* 'ascension'.

3.2. *Cases on nouns and on verbs in Manambu*

Four of the nine case suffixes in Manambu can occur on verbs. All cases (except for the adnominal comitative) are marked once per noun phrase, almost always on its last word, which is also the head of the noun phrase.[29] When used on verbs, they appear once per clause. Meanings and functions of cases on nouns and verbs are summarized in Table 1.5.

---

shares a number of features with Manambu due to long-standing contact but is not demonstrably related to it. The data presented here are based on original fieldwork.

[29] The case markers which occur only on noun phrases are Ø 'subject case', *-Vb* 'terminative case "until, up to"', two synonymous transportative cases *-Vsa:p* and *-Vsa:y* 'by means of transport', and *-Vwa* 'comitative/perlative'. Every case has a variety of meanings. Only the main meanings are reflected in the glosses (a detailed discussion is in Aikhenvald 2008a). Case-marked forms are in bold type. Case markers attach to a linker *a* or *ə* whose choice depends on the morphological subclass of a noun (Aikhenvald 2008a).

Table 1.5. Meanings and functions of cases in Manambu on nouns and verbs

Case form and label	Meaning on noun	Verb form to which morpheme attaches	Meaning on verb	Function on verb
1. -*Vm* 'objective-locative' (§3.3.1)	Complete involvement of second argument or attained location; definite and referential object	verb root	Completed action or state	Aspect
2. -*Vk* 'dative-purposive' (§3.3.2 and §3.4.1)	Purpose, reason, third argument of ditransitive verb; object of atelic verbs; object of verbs of emotions		(i) Intentional (ii) Purposive same-subject	Modality Clause linking
3. -*Vr* 'allative-instrumental' (§3.4.2)	Direction; instrument		Manner same-subject	Clause linking
4. -*yæy* 'substitutive' (§3.4.3)	Substitution 'instead of something'	verb root if same-subject verb root+ subject marker if different-subject	Substitutive	Clause linking

Cases as markers of aspect and modality are addressed in §3.3. Cases as markers of clause linking are discussed in §3.4.

3.3. *Cases as markers of aspect and modality*

Two cases—the objective-locative and the dative-purposive—can occur on predicates of a main clause, and impart an aspectual or a modal meaning to the whole clause. The resulting verbal forms have the same argument structure as a verb in any other context; they cannot take any cross-referencing. The person reference is either specified with a pronoun, or is recoverable from the context.

3.3.1. *The objective-locative case, and completive aspect*

The objective-locative case -*Vm* on noun phrases marks a second argument if it is completely involved in the action, or if it is completely affected, or if the action is telic. Consider the verb *kwakə-*. It means 'find' if the object is marked with the 'complete involvement case', as in (19), and 'search, look for' if the object is unmarked, as in (20):

(19) {[a   **takwa:m**]   kwakə-ku}
      DEM.DIST:fem.sg   woman:LK:OBJ/LOC   look.for/find-COMPL.SS
      {wiya:r   wula:l}
      house:LK:ALL/INSTR   go.inside:3fem.sgBAS.P
      After having found that woman, she went inside the house

(20) [ñanugw   **amæy**]
      children   mother
      kwakə-ya-bana
      look.for-come-1plSUBJ.NONPAST:3fem.sgBAS.NONPAST
      We keep looking for children's mother

The other major function of the objective-locative case is marking a location which has been reached. An example is at (21). The objective-locative case also conveys an idea of a completed action of reaching the cassowary's breast by climbing. (Cassowary, a flightless bird, is conceptualized as a mythological woman. (21) comes from a myth about a man's head clinging to a cassowary's breast as if he was her baby.)

(21) [a   məd   lə-kə   **muñ-a:m**]
      DEM.DIST:fem.sg   cassowary   she-OBL:fem.sg   breast-LK:OBJ/LOC
      ata   war-də-l
      then   ascend-3masc.sgSUBJ.P-3fem.sgBAS.P
      He (the man's head) went up to the cassowary's breast (reached it and
         stayed on it)

If the destination has not yet been reached, the allative is appropriate, as in (22):

(22) **pətəkaur**   ata   war-də-l
      ladder:ALL/INSTR   then   ascend-3masc.sgSUBJ.P-3fem.sgBAS.P
      Then he went up a ladder (but did not reach the top)

The objective-locative case conflates two functions: it marks a core or an oblique argument, and at the same time contributes an aspectual value of 'completeness' to the whole clause. This is reminiscent of the aspectual overtones of partitive case in Finnish discussed in §2.3.2, and even more so to those of the locative case (see (17) and (18) above).[30]

---

[30] Along similar lines, the locative preposition in Likpe, a Kwa language from Ghana, also has overtones of 'results' of an action (Ameka 2009: 266).

This same case morpheme occurs on verbal roots. There, it indicates completion of an action, or total achievement of a state, e.g. (23):

(23)   wun   [də-kə-m]   **wukəmar-ə-m**
       I   he-LK-OBJ/LOC   forget-LK-OBJ/LOC
       I completely forgot him

The completive meaning of the objective-locative case on a verb is strongly reminiscent of the overtone of 'complete' involvement of an object, or a location, characteristic of the objective-locative used with noun phrases. None of Manambu's relatives has any cognates of the objective-locative case. Consequently, we cannot tell which function of the -*Vm* form is historically prior. This is quite unlike Balto-Finnic languages (see §2.3.2) where—as we know—the primary function of cases with 'aspectual' overtones is marking grammatical relations, while the aspectual overtones represent a later development.

3.3.2. *The dative-purposive case, and intentional modality*
The dative-purposive case -*Vk* with noun phrases expresses intention and purpose, as in the first clause of (24), and the third argument of a ditransitive verb, as in the second clause:

(24)   [**sana:k**   ya-k-na-di]   sa:n
       money:LK:DAT/PURP   come-FUT-ACT.FOC-3PLBAS.NONPAST   money
       dayak   kui-tukwa
       they:DAT   give.to.third.person-PROH
       They will come for money (to get money, with the intention to receive money), don't give them money

The dative-purposive case is also used to mark reason (as in (26), on *agwajapək* 'what for'), the object of verbs of emotions, such as 'like', 'dislike', 'yearn for', 'refuse', and of verbs of fear. It is also used to mark objects of an atelic verb with slightly frustrative overtones.

We can recall, from (19), that the verb *kwakə-* means 'find (telic action)' if its object is marked with the objective-locative case, indicating complete involvement of the second argument. If the object is unmarked, the action is atelic ('look for'), as in (20). If its object is marked with the dative-purposive case, the action is equally atelic with an additional frustrative overtone of 'doing something in vain':

(25) **amæyik** kwakə-dana
mother:LK:DAT/PURP look.for-3plSUBJ.NONPAST:3fem.sgBAS.NONPAST
They are looking for their mother in vain (and not finding her)

The semantic effect of the objective-locative case in (19) as compared to that of the dative-purposive case in (25) is strongly reminiscent of the absolutive/dative case alternation in Warlpiri (see Hale 1982: 249; and §2.3.2 above). The dative-purposive case imparts a modal frustrative value to the whole clause.

The dative-purposive case on a verbal root form marks intentional modality. In (26), it attaches to the verb root *warya-* 'fight':

(26) ñən wun-a-wa **agwa-japək** **warya-k**
you.fem I-LK-COMIT what-thing:LK:DAT fight-DAT/PURP
I am going to fight, why (lit. what for) are you going to fight with me?

The semantic link between the purposive meaning of the dative-purposive on nouns, as in (24), and on verbs, as in (26), is straightforward. The dative-purposive on verb is also used as a clause-linking device—see the next section.

3.4. *Cases as markers of clause linking in Manambu*

Three case forms are used as clause-linking devices. The dative-purposive case occurs on the root of the predicate of a dependent clause marking a same-subject purposive complement. The allative-instrumental case on a verb root produces the predicate of a same-subject manner clause. The substitutive case on a verb root marks a same-subject dependent clause with the substitutive meaning 'instead of doing X, rather than doing X'. If it attaches to a verb inflected just for subject, it marks a different-subject with the same substitutive meaning.

We can recall, from §3.1, that predicates of all same-subject clauses in Manambu are unmarked for subject. Predicates of different-subject clauses do mark subject. The behaviour of case-marked dependent clauses is consistent with this pattern.[31]

---

[31] A different-subject purposive (*-kək* or *-kəkək*, with the choice depending on the number of syllables of the verb stem) may or may not be related to *-k* (see Aikhenvald 2008a: §13.4.3). Of the nine types of Manambu medial clauses, the opposition of same versus different-subject is found only in completive and substitutive clauses; the rest are either same-subject only, or different-subject only (see Aikhenvald 2008a: §18).

3.4.1. *The dative-purposive case, and same-subject purposive clauses*

The intentional, or purposive, meaning of dative-purposive marked predicates echoes the meaning of similarly marked noun phrases. A same-subject purpose complement to a verb of motion is shown in (27):

(27) {wun   {mǝn-a:m   **karda-k}**
        I   you:masc-LK:OBJ/LOC   take:DOWN-PURP.SS
        war-na-dǝwun}
        ascend-ACT.FOC-1masc.sgBAS.NONPAST
        I have come up to take you downwards

A noun marked with a dative-purposive, and a verb marked with the same-subject verb purposive are used in identical contexts. (28) illustrates the dative-purposive marked verb *warya-* 'to fight' expressing purpose of speaking. In (29), a dative-purposive marked noun *di* 'shit' is used.

(28) **warya-k**   wa-na
        fight-PURP.SS   say-ACT.FOC:3fem.sgBAS.NONPAST
        She intends to fight (lit. she said she was going to fight)

(29) **diya:k**   wa-na
        shit:LK:DAT/PURP   say-ACT.FOC:3fem.sgBAS.NONPAST
        She intends to have a shit (lit. she said for shit)

There is no reason to consider a same-subject purposive form, or the intentional, a nominalization. These forms have no nominal properties whatsoever. Neither does the bare root of a verb. The intentional and the same-subject purposive are semantically similar. One may hypothesize that both go back to the dependent purposive, and postulate a subsequent reanalysis of a dependent purposive as a main clause, and of the verb form as intentional modality (along the lines of §2.3.1 above). This analysis is plausible. However, it does not account for the lack of same-subject constraint in intentional modality, and thus remains a mere hypothesis.

Whether an originally nominal case got extended to another, verbal, environment, in Manambu is an open issue. The cognates of the dative-purposive form in Manambu appear on nouns, and also on verbs in related languages. The Maprik dialect of Ambulas (Ndu family, Papua New Guinea: Wilson 1980: 68–75, 119–20) has a 'referential' case *-ke* which marks purpose, goal and theme (of a conversation). The same case-morpheme occurs as a marker of intentional modality in dependent clauses (cf. also Wendel 1993: 88, 102). This suggests that the dative-purposive in Proto-Ndu could have been just as polyfunctional as it is in the present-day languages, and that there is no reason to consider either nominal or verbal context to be diachronically prior.

3.4.2. The allative-instrumental case, and same-subject manner clauses
Unlike the objective-locative and the dative-purposive cases which can mark core arguments, the allative-instrumental case always marks obliques. When used with noun phrases, the allative-instrumental *-Vr* case marks direction, as in (22), and instrument, as in (30):[32]

(30) [am-awa   **nɔbi:r**]   ata   vya-də-di
      bow-LK:COM   arrow:INSTR   then   hit-3masc.sgSUBJ.P-3plBAS.P
      He then hit them with bow and arrow

The allative-instrumental case has an additional meaning of 'along' (e.g. a road). It does not have any comitative overtones; neither is it used to express reason. The allative-instrumental case appears on verbal roots, marking the predicate of same-subject manner clauses, as in (31).

(31) {ñam   **kuyar**}   {**ñanugwa:k**}
      chewed.food   give.to.third.person:INSTR   children:LK:DAT
      kamna:gw   kui-la}
      food   give.to.third.person-3fem.sgSUBJ.P:3fem.sgBAS.P
      She gave food to children by giving (them) chewed food

Tables 1.2–1.3 show that an instrumental case with clauses typically expresses causal or temporal linkage. The unusual meaning of manner linkage of the instrumental case in Manambu may be due to its

---

[32] The syncretism of an allative and an instrumental marking is cross-linguistically infrequent. It is attested in a couple of Australian languages (the same form is used for allative and for instrumental in Patjtjamalh; in Yanyuwa, allative has the same form as ergative, purposive and instrumental: Dixon 2002: 168). In Kwoma/Washkuk (Kooyers 1974: 30), an unrelated neighbour of Manambu, and in a number of other Ndu languages locative and instrumental are expressed with the same morpheme (e.g. Hanga Kundi: Wendel 1993: 105 and Boiken: Freudenburg 1970, 1979). This syncretism is also found in Emerillon (Tupí-Guaraní: Rose 2003) and is rather common in Tibeto-Burman languages, e.g. Atong, where allative and instrumental are expressed with the same morpheme (van Breugel 2014).

lack of causal overtones: this is where it differs from the instrumental case in Tariana (see III at §2.2). An instrumenal case typically acquires a manner extension (Blake 2001). However, Manambu is unusual in that the allative-instrumental case marks manner only when used with verbs as a clause-linking device, rather than expressing other semantic relationships (e.g. reason, as in other languages). A noun expressing manner is unmarked for case. Also note that case markers do not seem to be used for manner linkage in the languages for which descriptions were available (see Table 1.3).

The allative-instrumental case has clear cognates throughout the Ndu family; however, its use with verb roots has not been documented for any language other than Manambu.

3.4.3. *The substitutive case, and substitutive clauses*
The substitutive case with noun phrases means 'instead of'. Just like the allative-instrumental case, it occurs on obliques only, as in (32).

(32) **pilou-a-yæy**   kusu-wapwi   a-tak
      pillow-LK-SUBST   wear-clothes   IMPV-put
      Put clothes (on your bed) instead of a pillow

The substitutive -*yæy* on a verbal root is a same-subject sequencing marker with the meaning 'instead of, rather than':

(33) {awarwa **warya-yæy**}   {aka   kəp
      REC   fight-SUBST:SS   then   just
       lakati-dana}
       sort.out-3plSUBJ.NONPAST:3fem.sgBAS.NONPAST
      Instead of fighting each other, they just sorted it out

If the subjects are different, the substitutive case marker attaches to a partially inflected verb (which, as we can recall, implies cross-referencing just the subject). An example is in (34).

(34) {ñən   **kiya-ñəna-yæy**}   {də-kə-m
       you.fem   die-2fem.sgSUBJ.NONPAST-SUBST   he-OBL-OBJ
        ya-tepul-ke-la-d}
        kill-'hit'-FUT-3fem.sgSUBJ.NONPAST-3masc.sgBAS.NONPAST
      Instead of you dying, she will kill him

The substitutive case has no cognates in other Ndu languages. That is, we have no historical information as to whether its adnominal or its verbal use is diachronically primary.

3.5. *Case on nouns and on verbs in Manambu: a summary*

Manambu demonstrates an unusually rich array of cases used with nouns, and with verbs. In contrast to other verbal predicates of declarative clauses, a 'case-marked' verb never cross-references two arguments. This property is consistent with the categories expressed by 'case-marked' verbs, since in Manambu most modalities, aspects and same-subject clauses take no cross-referencing. Different-subject clauses cross-reference only the subject. None of the case-marked verbal forms has any nominal properties.

We saw above that some languages employ case morphemes as clause-linkers; others use them to express aspectual and modal meanings. Manambu appears to be unique in that it offers both options. Three case markers link clauses—these are dative-purposive, allative-instrumental and substitutive. Two case markers express main clause categories of aspect, and of modality—these are objective-locative and dative-purposive. Case morphemes on verbs in Manambu have a wider array of functions than in any other language described so far which has the versatile case phenomenon.

The meanings of these case morphemes on verbs are transparently related to those of the same case morphemes on nouns. But the detailed correlations are not identical. The objective-locative case has a distinct overtone of complete involvement of the second argument, that is, a completely affected object, as in (19). On an oblique it marks a completely attained location, as in (21). The case on a noun imparts an overtone of telicity to the whole clause. This semantic feature of completeness acquires prominence when the case marker attaches to the predicate: the objective-locative case on verbs marks completive aspect.

The dative-purposive case has 'purpose', the object of intention, or incompletely affected object one is 'seeking' to affect, as components of its meaning (see (24)). This intentional meaning becomes prominent once the marker attaches to a verb root. The result is intentional modality. In addition, the dative-purposive case on a noun may impart a meaning of atelic action (with an overtone of frustrative 'in vain') to the whole clause (see (25)).

One multifunctional morpheme imparts an aspectual meaning of 'completion', and of telicity, to the predicate and to the clause. The other imparts a modal meaning, of intentionality, and an aspectual one, of atelicity. These effects of core cases on verbs are summarized in Scheme 1.

Scheme 1. Semantic overlap in core case markers with noun phrases and with verbs in Manambu.

Object and Location completely affected by or involved in the action } on nouns
Completive aspect } on verbs
Object of purpose and intention } on nouns
Intentional modality } on verbs

The dative-purposive case on verbs also links clauses. So do the allative-instrumental and substitutive cases. Manambu is unusual (see Table 1.3) in that the allative-instrumental case on nouns marks manner clauses rather than having a causal or temporal meaning. As stated above, the allative-instrumental case does not mark manner on nouns. The substitutive case has identical meanings on nouns and on verbs; this is in line with a few other 'exotic' cases mentioned in §2.2, e.g. similative or sociative, which have the same meaning when used on nouns, and as clause-linking devices.

Of the four case forms, the adnominal use of the allative-instrumental can be considered historically older than its verbal use, as predicted by the generalization in (11). For the objective-locative and substitutive cases we cannot tell, due to the absence of cognates. The dative-purposive marker is used both adnominally and with verbs in other languages of the Ndu family. This suggests an old polyfunctionality of the marker -*Vk* with nouns and with verbs.

The Proto-Ndu language may have had other versatile cases. Iatmul, another Ndu language, has an oblique case marker -*(n)kət* which marks recipients, beneficiaries, purpose and intention (and also objects high on the nominal hierarchy: Staalsen 1965). This form is not used with verbs. It is cognate to Manambu -*kər,* a marker of purposive-desiderative modality, e.g. *wun və-kər* (I see-DES) 'I want to see, I intend to see'. The Manambu form is no longer used with nouns. As expected, throughout the history of individual languages, a conventionalized usage of a morpheme in a given environment may result in its reinterpretation.

4. What can we Conclude?

Case morphemes may not be restricted to noun phrases. If they occur on a verb root, or on an inflected verb, they may link clauses or they may express aspects, modalities and moods. The most common semantic correspondences between the same morphemes as markers of the function of a noun phrases and as clause-linking devices are:

I.   Dative or purposive marking on a noun phrase tends to have a purposive meaning as a clause linker.
II. Locational marking on a noun phrase tends to have temporal, or, more rarely, conditional or purposive meaning as a clause linker.
III. Instrumental marking on a noun phrase tends to have a causal, or temporal, or (more rarely) a manner meaning as a clause linker.

The meanings of cases as markers of grammatical functions of a noun phrase, and as clause linkers, are determined by the syntactic environment. In other words, the same set of morphemes marks typical functions of noun phrases, or typical relationships between clauses.

A morpheme may originate as a case with a noun phrase as its scope, and then get extended to be a case with clausal scope, in agreement with the generalization in (11) above. This direction of development is congruent with a general path of semantic change in grammaticalization—more specific meanings become more general.

Alternatively, the case markers may be inherently polyfunctional, being used with noun phrases, and with clauses. Their meanings are then partly conditioned by the syntactic environment. They mark typical semantic functions of noun phrases, such as location, and typical semantic types of clause linking, such as temporal or causal relationships (as outlined by Thompson and Longacre 1985; Dixon 2009). Typically, a locative case marker will occur as exponent of temporal semantics as a clause-linking device (with a wide range of meanings covering; 'when', 'while', 'as soon as' and so on).

The same morphemes can also mark cases, and clausal categories of aspect, modality and mood. This second function may develop out of the first one as the result of reinterpretation of erstwhile dependent clauses as main clauses. Then, case morphemes as exponents of clausal categories can be traced back to their use as clause linkers.

Alternatively, case morphemes on verbs may have aspectual and modal meanings by virtue of their inherent polyfunctionality. A prime example comes from Manambu (also cf. Kennedy 1984: 162, for a similar approach to Kala Lagaw Ya). Since nouns typically have more concrete meanings than verbs, the underlying semantic differences between word classes trigger the meaning differences between the same morphemes on nouns, and on verbs. The inherent polyfunctionality of cases as markers of aspect and modality in Manambu verbs is corroborated by the way in which these cases impart aspectual and modal meaning to a clause even when they occur on a noun phrase (see Scheme 1).

We hypothesize that core cases are likely to impact upon the aspect and modality value of the whole clause. This is corroborated by the evidence from Manambu, and a number of other languages (see Kiparsky 1998). This is also true for cases which can be used both as core and as non-core. In contrast, non-core cases are more likely to 'double' as clause-linkers only.

To conclude: cases which are used on noun phrases and on verbs are 'chameleon' morphemes with fairly generic semantics which acquire more specific meanings appropriate for their morphosyntactic locus (that is, noun phrases or verbs), and scope (that is, noun phrase or clause). This is quite unlike nominal vs. verbal tense and aspect which constitute distinct groups of grammatical categories, each in its own right. To the extent that it has been possible to establish generalisations about the contribution of word class to the specific meanings of these case morphemes, this has implications for word class typology, suggesting a semantic basis underlying the grammar of nouns and verbs as universal word classes.

APPENDIX 1

LANGUAGES WITH CASES ON VERBS, AND THE SOURCES

Case morphemes used with verbs have been noted for the following areas:

- Australian languages (Dixon 1972, 1977, 2002; Hercus 1982; Blake 1987b, 1993, 1999; Dench and Evans 1988; Evans 1995b, Simpson 1988), including Kala Lagaw Ya (Kennedy 1984; Dixon 2002: 239);
- a few languages from Central Siberia, especially Ket and Yugh (Werner 1997a,b; Vajda 2004; Anderson 2004);
- a few languages of the Americas, such as Yuman (Gorbet 1973, 1976, 1979; Gordon 1980: 141; Kendall 1975); Muskogean (Kimball 1991: 225; Nicklas 1974: 98; Jelinek 1989; Jacobsen 1983), Kalapalo (Carib: Ellen Basso, p.c.) and Tariana (Arawak: Aikhenvald 2003);
- a few Oceanic languages (Lichtenberk 1991), and languages from the New Guinea area (Tauya: MacDonald 1988, 1990; Kwoma: Kooyers 1974);
- numerous Omotic languages, from Afroasiatic family, e.g. Maale (Amha 2001), Yemsa (Zaugg-Corelli 2008), Wolaitta (Azeb Amha, p.c.), Sheko (Anne-Christie Hellenthal, p.c.) and Koorete (Binyam Sisay, p.c.);
- Alaaba, a Cushitic language (Schneider-Blum 2009);
- numerous Tibeto-Burman languages (e.g. Genetti 1986, 1991; Watters 2002; Burling 2004; Plaisier 2006; LaPolla 2004, 2006; Post 2007; van Breugel 2014; and papers in Thurgood and LaPolla 2003) and
- the recently discovered isolate Kusunda spoken in Nepal (Watters 2005a, b).

Similarly to bound cases, adpositions may have a whole clause rather than just a noun phrase as their scope (some describe these as adpositions with a subordinating function). This has been described by Long (1965) for English; by Genetti (1986, 1991) for languages from the Bodic subgroup of Tibeto-Burman; and by Craig (1991) for Rama (Chibchan). Rose (2005) offers a partial analysis of this phenomenon in general, adding a few other languages, including Emerillon (from the Tupí-Guaraní group: also see Rose 2003). Other studies include

Ohori (1996) and Akiba (1977). Konow (1909: 9) was perhaps the first scholar ever to notice this phenomenon in a Tibeto-Burman language.

Case markers can also occur on deverbal nominalizations which otherwise have few nominal properties. Such nominalizations—be they action nominalizations, relative forms of verbs, or 'participles', 'infinitives', or 'supines'—already have some non-verbal features (and some may arguably be considered 'defective' nouns or 'defective' adjectives). This has been noted for languages from the Cushitic subgroup of Afroasiatic (Palmer 1957; Hetzron 1969; Hudson 1976; and summary in Dolgopolsky 1991), Turkic and Samoyedic (see an overview in Anderson 2004), Australian (e.g. Dyirbal, Warlpiri, Yidiñ: see Dixon 2002: 237–9), Balto-Finnic and numerous Indo-European languages (see, for instance, Blake 1999: 299–300), and also Japanese (Ohori 1996; Martin 1975: 885). Tibeto-Burman languages where case markers attach to nominalized verbs include Meithei (Chelliah 1997: 172–5), Dumi (van Driem 1993: 271; 245–6), and some instances in Yamphu (Rutgers 1998: 267, 274–5) (also see examples in Moravcsik 1972). An in-depth study of these is a topic for a separate project which is not undertaken here.

Likewise, I exclude the discussion of constructions in which an adposition has to be followed by a subordinator in order to be able to occur with a clause in its scope, as is the case of French *avant* + Noun Phrase 'before, in front' and *avant que* + clause 'before'. Similar examples include preposition + *that* clauses in highly colloquial varieties of American English, e.g. *It's something I loved* **since that** *I was a kid* (Arnold Zwicky, p.c.). Another type of evolving dependent clause structure in some varieties of Modern American English is *wh-* constructions accompanied by an additional subordinator *that*, illustrated in the title of Zwicky (2002), and discussed there. These constructions also lie outside the scope of this discussion. The effects of cases with deverbal nominalizations, and of composite clause-linkers consisting of an adposition and a subordinator, are comparable to those of cases and adpositions with clausal scope; however, they involve different mechanisms (see the discussion in Rose 2005; and Ohori 1996). To limit the scope of the discussion here, I will not consider instances of a case marker on a dependent clause which already contains a marker of syntactic dependency.

APPENDIX 2

SOURCES FOR LANGUAGES CITED IN TABLES 1.2 AND 1.3

Atong (Tibeto-Burman): van Breugel (2006)
Awtuw (Ram family): Feldman (1986: 160–1)
Bāgandji (Australian area): Hercus (1982: 215)
Bodic (Tibeto-Burman): Genetti (1986, 1991)
Classical Tibetan (Tibeto-Burman): DeLancey (2003: 266)
Cogtse Gyarong (Tibeto-Burman): Nagano (2003: 487)
Djambarrpuyngu (Australian area): Wilkinson (1991: 634–6)
Dulong-Rawang (Tibeto-Burman): LaPolla (2006)
Dyirbal (Australian area): Dixon (1972)
Eastern Kayah Li (Tibeto-Burman): Solnit (1997: 213; 249; 259)
Galo (Tibeto-Burman): Post (2008, 2009)
Garo (Tibeto-Burman): Burling (2004: 189; 319)
Ket (Yenisseic): Werner (1997a: 105; 354)
Kham (Tibeto-Burman): Watters (2002: 317, 2009)
Koorete (Omotic, Afroasiatic): Binyam Sisay, p.c.
Kusunda (isolate, Nepal): Watters (2005a: 62–6; 145–50), Watters (2005b)
Kwaio (Oceanic): Keesing (1985); Lichtenberk (1991b: 71)
Kwoma (Nukuma family, New Guinea): Kooyers (1974)
Lahu (Tibeto-Burman): Matisoff (1973: 168; 419)
Lepcha (Tibeto-Burman): Plaisier (2006: 119–23)
Limbu (Tibeto-Burman): van Driem (1987: 230–5)
Maale (Omotic, Afroasiatic): Amha (2001: 58–9, 185–7)
Manambu (Ndu): own fieldwork; Aikhenvald (2008a)
Manchu (Tungus-Manchurian): Holm (2006)
Martuthunira (Australian area): Dench (2009)
Murinhpatha (Australian area): Walsh (1976: 263–4)
Pitta-Pitta (Australian area): Blake (1979: 198, 1999: 307, 310)
Qiang (Tibeto-Burman): LaPolla (2004: 93; 244–5)
Rama (Chibchan): Craig (1991)
Tariana (Arawak): Aikhenvald (2003: 530–1)
Tauya (New Guinea area): MacDonald (1988, 1990b: 236–8)
Toqabaqita (Oceanic): Lichtenberk (1991b: 67)
Yamphu (Tibeto-Burman): Rutgers (1998: 267–8)
Yemsa (Omotic, Afroasiatic): Zaugg-Corelli (2008: 241–9)
Yidiñ (Australian area): Dixon (1977: 333–5)

CHAPTER TWO

A TYPOLOGY OF ARGUMENT-DETERMINED CONSTRUCTIONS

R. M. W. Dixon and Alexandra Y. Aikhenvald*

In this chapter we suggest a typology of syntactic derivations and associated construction types which relate to predicate arguments. Four basic types are distinguished, and a number of subtypes within them. In outline:

(I)   Argument transferring (§1).
      Either removing an argument from the core of a transitive clause (passive, antipassive); or adding an argument to the core of an intransitive or transitive clause (applicative, causative).
(II) Argument focussing (§2).
      Using alternative transitive construction types to focus on different types of argument. These involve no alteration in transitivity, and one construction type cannot usefully be taken as grammatically derived from the others. One example is found in the Philippines subgroup of Austronesian.
(III) Argument manipulating (§3).
      Bringing a non-subject argument into surface subject position, so that it has some, but not all, of the properties of prototypical subjects in that language. (For example, *The Beyer microphone recorded Ravi Shankar well*, in English.)
(IV) Marking the referential status of arguments (§4).
      This covers 'inverse' systems, where different transitive construction types are distinguished depending on the potential-to-control-the-activity of different core arguments, as in Algonquian and some Athabascan languages.

* For their helpful and constructive comments, it is a pleasure to thank Cynthia Allen, Mengistu Amberber, Avery Andrews, Ives Goddard, Nikolaus Himmelmann, Masayuki Onishi, Geoff Pullum, Lucy Seki, Masayoshi Shibatani, Larry Trask and Anna Wierzbicka.

In §5 we compare the grammatical properties of the four types. An appendix surveys some of the terminological confusions which result from using terms, that properly relate to just one type, for describing one or more other types.

All languages distinguish between intransitive and transitive clauses:

- an intransitive clause has a single core argument, in
  S (intransitive subject) function;
- a transitive clause has two core arguments, in
  A (transitive subject) function, and
  O (transitive object) function.

It is probably the case that all languages also have extended transitive (or ditransitive) clauses. These are essentially a sub-type of transitive, involving arguments in A and O functions and one other inherent argument (often marked by dative or locative case, or a corresponding adposition). Some languages also have a type of clause we can call extended intransitive, involving S and one other argument (generally marked in the same way as the third argument in an extended transitive)—see Dixon (1994: 122–4). Many languages also have copula clauses, involving two obligatory arguments (distinct from S, A and O).

Leaving aside copula clauses, we can divide predicate arguments into two main types:

core arguments—S, A and O
peripheral arguments, which can generally occur in both transitive and intransitive clause types; there are two subtypes here:
  - non-local arguments—referring to beneficiary, instrument, etc.
  - local arguments—referring to position at or movement to or from, etc.

In some languages a non-core peripheral argument may be cross-referenced on the verb. It may then be useful to recognise 'dative' as belonging to an 'outer core', with S, A and O constituting the 'inner core'; see, for instance, Morphy (1983: 80f) on Djapu (an Australian language).

1. ARGUMENT TRANSFERRING

By 'argument transferring' we refer to situations where one construction type is formally and functionally basic, and another is derived from it by:

(1) Removing an argument from the (inner) core, and placing it in the periphery (valency reducing)—passive and antipassive (§1.1). Or
(2) Adding an argument to the (inner) core (this will often have had peripheral status in the basic construction) (valency increasing)—applicative (§1.2.1) and causative (§1.2.2).

1.1. *Removing an argument from the core—passive and antipassive*

This type of derivation applies most typically to transitive (including ditransitive) clauses. Since a transitive clause has two core arguments, in A and O functions, there are two possibilities:

(a) The argument in A function is removed from the core and placed in the periphery. The clause now becomes intransitive since there is a single core argument (the original O) which is now in S function. This is a passive construction.
(b) The argument in O function is removed from the core and placed in the periphery. As before, the clause becomes intransitive, since there is a single core argument (the original A) which is now in S function. This is an antipassive construction.

The labels 'passive' and 'antipassive' have been used with a wide range of meanings. Indeed, Siewierska (1984: 255) concluded a survey of the variety of constructions that have been called 'passive' with 'as a group the whole body of so called passives does not have a single property in common'.

To clarify how the terms are used here we propose—following Dixon (1994: 146)—the following criteria for a prototypical passive and a prototypical antipassive. These do accord with the majority of accepted uses of the terms.

PASSIVE DERIVATION
(a) applies to an underlying transitive clause and forms a derived intransitive;

(b) the underlying O becomes S of the passive;
(c) the underlying A argument goes into a peripheral function, being marked by a non-core case, adposition, etc.; this argument can be omitted, although there is always the option of including it;
(d) there is some explicit formal marking of a passive construction (generally, by a verbal affix or by a periphrastic verbal construction).

ANTIPASSIVE DERIVATION
(a) applies to an underlying transitive clause and forms a derived intransitive;
(b) the underlying A becomes S of the antipassive;
(c) the underlying O argument goes into a peripheral function, being marked by a non-core case, adposition, etc.; this argument can be omitted, although there is always the option of including it;
(d) there is some explicit formal marking of an antipassive construction (same basic possibilities as for passive).

If any of conditions (a)–(d) were relaxed, for either construction type, we would find that the labels 'passive' and 'antipassive' could be employed in less than useful ways. For instance, in some languages of the nominative-accusative type an argument in O function can optionally be omitted, e.g. English *We have eaten dinner* and *We have eaten*. This could be termed 'antipassive' (as it is by Heath 1976: 203; see also Postal 1977) if criteria (c) and (d) were ignored. Similarly, languages of the absolutive-ergative type can typically omit specification of an A argument. In Dyirbal we can have *ŋana* (we:A) *dina* (dinner:O) *jaŋa-nyu* (eat-PAST) 'we have eaten dinner' or just *dina jaŋa-nyu*, literally 'eaten dinner' (i.e. 'someone has eaten dinner', 'the dinner has been eaten'). If criteria (c) and (d) were relaxed this could be described as a 'passive'. We simply have, in these instances, a transitive clause in which one core argument need not be accorded surface realisation. This is quite different from an antipassive or passive derivation.

   The argument that is removed from the core (A for a passive, O for an antipassive) is placed in peripheral function and may freely be omitted. In most languages it is omitted in the majority of instances. There are languages with a construction that satisfies (a), (b) and (d) for a passive but always omits the underlying A: this is an 'agentless passive' (a variant on the prototypical passive described above). In similar fashion, a few languages have an antipassive-type construction where the underlying O is obligatorily omitted (but there is marking of a special construction type, criterion (d)). Languages with such a 'patientless antipassive' include Matses (Panoan, Peru; Fleck 2006) and Cavineña (Tacanan, Bolivia; Guillaume 2008: 278–82).

Each of these derivations has a semantic effect. In a passive the original A argument is downgraded in importance and, in consequence, the original O is brought into greater focus. Passive is often used where the O refers to first or second person, or is realised by a definite NP. The situations in which passive is typically used include: to avoid mentioning the A argument; to direct attention onto the O, rather than on the A; to place a topic (which is underlying O) into surface S function; to focus on the result of the activity—see Thompson (1987) and Dixon (1991: 299–305, 2005: 354–9).

An antipassive construction has downgraded the original O, and focusses on the underlying A argument—on the fact that its referent is taking part in an activity which involves a patient (underlying O argument) while paying little or no attention to the identity of the patient.

Both passive and antipassive also typically have syntactic function, to feed a pivot constraint on clause combining. Languages with 'accusative syntax' have an S/A pivot. That is, for certain types of clause combining there must be an argument common to the clauses and it must be in S or A function in each. Passive can be used to place an underlying O argument in surface S function, to meet this constraint. Similarly, in a language with ergative syntax, involving an S/O pivot, antipassive will be required to place an underlying A argument into surface S function, to meet the pivot constraint. (See Dixon 1994: 8–18, 143–81.) Examples of the use of passive and antipassive to feed syntactic pivots are given at the beginning of §2 below.

Mam, from the Mayan family, has one type of antipassive and at least four passives, with similar syntax but different meanings. (Examples from England 1983: 201, 203, 212.) A basic transitive clause is shown at (1) and a general passive, marked by verbal suffix -eet, at (2).

(1) ma   ch-ok   t-b'iyo-'n   [Cheep]ₐ [kab'
    PAST   3plO-DIRECTIONAL 3sgA-hit-DIRECTIONAL José   two
       xjaa]ₒ
       person
    José hit two people

(2) ma   chi   b'iy-eet   [kab'   xjaa]ₛ   ([t-u'n
    PAST   3plS   hit-PASSIVE₁   two   person   3sg-RELN/agent
       Cheep] ₚₑᵣᵢ)
       José
    Two people were hit (by José)

The underlying A argument, 'José', is moved to the periphery and marked with relational noun -u'n; it may be omitted.

(Note that the verbal constituent in Mam includes pronominal elements that show an absolutive-ergative pattern. One form is used for both S and O functions (including 3sg ø and 3pl ch(i)-) and a different form for A (here 3sg is t- and 3pl is ky-)).

The general passive, shown again at (4), can be contrasted with a second variety of passive, marked by -njtz, at (3). This indicates that the referent of the underlying O suffered the action accidentally.

(3) ma   ø-tzeeq'a-njtz   [Cheep]S   ([t-u'n   Kyel] PERI)
     PAST   3sgS-hit-PASSIVE₂   José   3sg-RELN/agent   Miguel
     José was hit accidentally (by Miguel)

(4) ma   ø-tzeeq'a-at   CheepS (t-u'n-Kyel)
              -PASSIVE₁
     José was hit (by Miguel) (on purpose)

Mam also has an antipassive, which focusses on the underlying A and on the activity (e.g. 'They (underlying A, surface S) are winning (antipassive marking)'). Example (5) is a basic transitive clause and (6) is its antipassive correspondent. Note that the underlying O is demoted into the periphery; it is marked with a relational noun or can be omitted.

(5) ma   ø-tzaj   t-tzyu-'n   [Cheep]A   [ch'it]O
     PAST   3sgO-DIR   3sgA-grab-DIR   José   bird
     José grabbed the bird

(6) ma   ø-tzyuu-n   [Cheep]S   ([t-i'j
     PAST   3sgS-grab-ANTIPASSIVE   José   3sg-RELN/patient
        ch'it] PERI)
        bird
     José grabbed (the bird)

As already explained, the prototypical passive and antipassive involve removing one argument from the core of a transitive clause; there were two core arguments and now there is one. In some languages the same derivation, with the same grammatical marking, can be extended also to apply to an intransitive clause. The argument is removed from the core; but there was only one core argument and now none is left. This can be exemplified from Tarahumara, a Uto-Aztecan language from Mexico (data from Langacker 1976: 31, based on Brambila 1953). Example (7) shows the passive of a transitive, marked by verbal suffix

-ru, and (8) the corresponding 'passive' of an intransitive, with the same marking.

(7)   gao   ne   'a-ru
       horse   I   give-PASSIVE
       I was given a horse

(8)   taši   goči-ru
       NOT   sleep-PASSIVE
       One doesn't sleep (lit: not sleeping)

A construction in which the sole argument has been removed from the core of an intransitive clause is the intransitive correspondent of both a passive and an antipassive. Strictly, the erstwhile core argument should optionally be includable, on the periphery. This is reported for a number of Germanic languages, e.g. Dutch in Kirsner (1976). Compare the plain intransitive in (9) with the 'passive' in (10), where original S *de jongens* 'the boys' is now marked by preposition *door* 'by'; it may be included or omitted.

(9)   [de   jongens]$_S$ fluiten
       THE   boys   whistle
       The boys are whistling

(10)   er   wordt   ([door   de   jongens])   gefloten
       THERE BECOMES   BY   THE   boys   whistled
       There is whistling (by the boys)

Constructions like (8) and (10) have been called 'impersonal passive' or 'pseudo-passive' since they show the same marking as regular passives in languages in which they occur. (See Keenan 1985: 272–6; Siewierska 1984: 93–125; Comrie 1976c; and Frajzyngier 1982.) As mentioned already, such a construction could equally be regarded as the intransitive correspondent of an antipassive. However, no example is yet to hand of the transfer of the core argument of an intransitive clause to the periphery, in a language which has an antipassive derivation for transitive clauses, with the two derivations being accorded the same grammatical marking. We predict that such a language may be found.

As with all the construction types discussed in this chapter, there can be variations on the basic theme (see Shibatani, 1985). In English, for instance, a prepositional argument can become passive subject in marked semantic circumstances, e.g. *Charles de Gaulle slept in this bed / This bed was slept in by Charles de Gaulle*, and *Someone has drunk out of this glass* / *This glass has been drunk out of (by someone)*. But note that a prepositional argument can only become passive subject if the clause does *not* include a direct object (from *Someone has drunk whiskey out of this glass* we cannot derive **This glass has been drunk whiskey out of (by someone)*.) See Dixon (1991: 315–20, 2005: 369–74).

There is another kind of valency-reducing derivation which does not fall within the scope of this chapter. The prototypical reflexive involves an underlying transitive clause in which A and O have identical reference. Some languages maintain transitivity and simply place a reflexive pronoun in the O slot. Other languages use a derived intransitive, with the verb marked by a reflexive suffix and the sole core argument, in S function, coding the underlying A = O. The same two grammatical possibilities apply for reciprocals.

We often find a single grammatical marking covering both reflexive and/or reciprocal, and also passive (e.g. *-ru* in Tarahumara) or else antipassive (e.g. Dyirbal, Dixon 1972: 89–93), or both passive and antipassive (e.g. the Australian languages Kuku-Yalanji (Patz 2002: 144–54) and Diyari (Austin 1981a: 151–7); see Dixon (1994: 151–2)).

1.2. *Adding an argument to the core*

In the last section we discussed derivations that extract an argument from the core and place it in the periphery of a clause, from whence it may be omitted. The opposite type of derivation is to add an argument to the core, often one that was already on the periphery.

This applies prototypically to an underlying intransitive clause, deriving a transitive. Just as there are two possibilities for core argument reduction—extracting the A (passive) or the O (antipassive)—so there are two possibilities for argument addition:

(a) Adding an argument that goes into O function in the derived transitive clause, the original S argument taking on A function. This is an applicative construction.
(b) Adding an argument that goes into A function in the derived transitive clause, the original S taking on O function. This is a causative construction.

The grammatical properties and possibilities for applicatives and causatives differ more than do those for passive and antipassive. We discuss them separately.

1.2.1. *Adding an O argument, S becoming A—Applicative*
Just as with passive and antipassive, it is useful to state explicit criteria
for recognising a construction as a prototypical applicative.

APPLICATIVE DERIVATION
(a) applies to an underlying intransitive clause and forms a derived
    transitive;
(b) the argument in underlying S function goes into A function in the
    applicative;
(c) a peripheral argument (which could be explicitly stated in the
    underlying intransitive) is taken into the core, in O function;
(d) there is some explicit formal marking of an applicative construc-
    tion, generally by an affix or some other morphological process
    applying to the verb.

The peripheral argument that is promoted to O may have appeared
with one of a number of cases or adpositional markings in the underlying intransitive clause, depending on the meaning of the verb. This
can be illustrated from the Australian language Yidiñ (see Dixon 1977:
303ff) by a series of example pairs, (a) being an intransitive and (b)
a derived applicative, marked by derivational suffix -*ŋa-* on the verb.
In (11) it is an NP with nominal comitative marking (suffix -*ji* 'with')
that is promoted to O:

(11) (a) wagu:ja$_S$ nyina-ŋ   (waga:l-ji)
           man   sit-PRESENT   wife-COMITATIVE
           The man is sitting (with (his) wife)
      (b) waguja-ŋgu$_A$ wagal$_O$ nyina:-ŋa-l
           man-ERGATIVE   wife   sit-APPLICATIVE-PRESENT
           The man is sitting-with his wife

In (12) the promoted NP was originally in dative case (suffix -*nda*):

(12) (a) wagu:ja$_S$ manga-ŋ   (jaja:-nda)
           man   laugh-PRESENT   child-DATIVE
           The man is laughing (at the child)
      (b) waguja-ŋgu$_A$ jaja$_O$ manga-ŋa-l
           man-ERGATIVE   child   laugh-APPLICATIVE-PRESENT
           The man is laughing-at the child

And in (13) the promoted NP was originally marked with the aversive,
or 'fear', case -*yida*:

(13) (a) wagu:ja$_S$ manŋa-ŋ   (jama-jida)
           man   be frightened-PRESENT   snake-AVERSIVE
           The man is frightened (of the snake)
      (b) waguja-ŋgu$_A$ jama$_O$ manŋa:-ŋa-l
           man-ERGATIVE   snake   be frightened-APPLICATIVE-PRESENT
           The man is frightened-of the snake

In Ainu there is an applicative prefix *e-*. From *mina* 'laugh' is formed *e-mina* 'laugh at', and from *toranne* 'be lazy' we can derive *e-toranne* 'not want to do' (lit. 'be lazy with respect to'). (Tamura 2000: 206–8; Shibatani 1990: 64ff).

There is no fully satisfactory label for this construction type. Sapir (1922: 137) talked of 'comitatives' in Takelma marked by suffix *-(a)g^w-* which has a general meaning 'to do some action (expressed by verb-stem) together with, attended by, having something (expressed by object of verb)'. His examples include (with the comitative allomorph in bold type):

INTRANSITIVE		TRANSITIVE	
wī^i-	'travel'	*wīk'wa-*	'he travels around with it'
lō^ul-	'play'	*lō^ulagwa^ʾn*	'I play with him'
ūyū^ɛs-	'laugh'	*uyu^ɛgwa^ɛn*	'I laugh at him'

(Note that 'with' has different senses in 'run with' and in 'play with'.) Blake (1987: 67) uses the terms 'object creating' and 'advancement'.

We follow current usage and employ the term 'applicative' (which appears to have been taken over from Bantu linguistics—see, for instance, Kisseberth and Abasheikh 1977). Different sub-types of applicative can be named according to the original function of the argument that is taken into the core—comitative, as in (11b), or dative, as in (12b), or aversive, as in (13b), or instrumentive, as in (14b), or benefactive, etc.

The applicative derivation is seldom fully productive, being normally restricted to a limited set of intransitive roots. It is most commonly used with verbs of rest ('sit', 'stand', 'lie', etc.) and of motion ('go', 'run', 'cross', etc.) and with 'laugh (at)', 'cry (over)', 'play (with)' and 'speak (in)'.

Some languages have a verbal affix which just shows applicative sense. But in others a single suffix can have an applicative sense with some verbs and a causative meaning with others, the division being semantically determined. This applies for the suffix *-ŋa-* in Yidiñ, for example. Dixon (2002: 203–6) provides further Australian examples while Dixon (1994: 140) outlines the general semantic principles that are involved.

There can be semantic or syntactic reasons (or both) for using an applicative construction. The speaker may wish to focus on the referent of the promoted O argument. Sentence (12a) basically just states that the man is laughing; it can add, as an extra piece of information what he is laughing at. In contrast, (12b) states that he is laughing-at something, and what he is laughing-at is a child.

Putting an underlying peripheral argument into O function may enable it to be integrated into a discourse sequence. Yidiñ has an S/O pivot for coordination of clauses that share a nominal argument. If one wanted to link 'the child fell down' with 'the man laughed at the child' it would be necessary to employ an applicative construction, with *jaja* 'child' going into O function, in order to coordinate these two clauses and omit the second occurrence of *jaja*.

Some of the languages that show a prototypical applicative (adding an O argument to an intransitive verb) also have a similar derivation applying to transitive verbs (examples are in Blake 1987: 69ff, Comrie 1985). Here we begin with a transitive clause; in the applicative derivation the original A is retained, an erstwhile peripheral argument is promoted into the core to be O, and the original O is pushed out onto the periphery (typically marked by dative or locative case). Sentence (14a) is a plain transitive clause from Dyirbal, with a peripheral NP showing the instrument. In (14b) this has been promoted to O function, with the original O moving to the periphery and now being marked by dative case. (Note that in each clause the core arguments must be stated, but the peripheral arguments—the instrumental NP *garrmay-ju* in (14a) and the dative NP *nuba-gu* in (14b)—may optionally be omitted.)

(14) (a) ŋaja   nuba$_O$ maymba-n   (garrmay-ju)
          1sgA   bark.bag   plaster-PAST   beeswax-INSTRUMENTAL
          I plastered the bark bag (with beeswax) [to seal it and make it watertight]

     (b) ŋaja   garrmay$_O$ maymbal-ma-n
          1sgA   beeswax   plaster-APPLICATIVE-PAST
          (nuba-gu)
          bark bag-DATIVE
          I used the beeswax to plaster (the bark bag)

As before, there can be semantic or syntactic motivation (or both) for using this derived construction. In (14b) the speaker focusses on the fact that they are using beeswax in a plastering operation. And if (14) were to be co-ordinated with a clause that has *garrmay* as pivot (in S or O function) then (14b) would have to be used since it does have *garrmay* in pivot function, e.g. 'bring the beeswax (O) so that I (A) can plaster Ø (O) on the bark bag (dative)' (*garrmay budi ŋaja maymbal-ma-li nuba-gu*).

There are many languages which allow applicative derivation only with an intransitive clause, not directly with transitives. The only way one could express the sense of (14b) in Yidiñ, for instance, would be first to detransitivise the transitive clause (with verb 'plaster') and then apply an applicative derivation to this (see Dixon 1977: 309–11).

1.2.2. *Adding an A argument, S becoming O—Causative*

A causative derivation occurs in the great majority of languages and is much commoner than applicative. Again, it will be useful to provide an explicit set of criteria for the prototypical causative, which relates to an intransitive verb.

CAUSATIVE DERIVATION
(a) applies to an underlying intransitive clause and forms a derived transitive;
(b) the argument in underlying S function goes into O function in the causative;
(c) a new argument is introduced, in A function;
(d) there is some explicit formal marking of the causative construction.

There are differences between these criteria and those put forward for applicative in §1.2.1. In applicative constructions the new O corresponds to a peripheral argument in the underlying intransitive (or transitive) clause. But in many causatives the argument which is now in A function could scarcely have been included in the original intransitive.

Sometimes it could be, as in Jarawara (Arawá family, Brazil—see Dixon 2004b). Consider a man, Yobeto, punching holes in a piece of paper. The result could be described with *babeo* 'paper' in S function to the intransitive verb *-hoti-* 'have holes' and a peripheral NP with *Yobeto* as head and postposition *ehene* 'due to':

(15) babeo~S~   hoti-ke   ([Yobeto
      paper(fem)   have holes-DECLARATIVE(fem)   name(masc)
        ehene])
        due.to(masc)
      The paper has holes (due to Yobeto)

Alternatively, the situation could be described through using the causativised form of *-hoti-, -na-hoti-* 'make holes in', having Yobeto as A and 'paper' as O argument:

(16) Yobeto~A~   babeo~O~   na-hoti-ka
      name(masc)   paper(fem)   CAUSATIVE-have.holes-DECLARATIVE(masc)
      Yobeto made holes in the paper

Intransitive constructions, like (15), with an *ehene* constituent, and transitives like (16), with causative prefix *na-*, are both widely used and are frequently synonymous.

But this is somewhat unusual. In many languages it would not be felicitous to use an intransitive clause, with some sort of 'due to' peripheral constituent, as an alternative to a causative construction. (English is not the ideal language for exemplification since there is no morphological marking of a verbal causative. However, many speakers would consider *burn* to be basically intransitive (e.g. *The cakes burnt*) and say that when used in a transitive construction it has a causative sense (*King Alfred burnt the cakes*). Note the awkwardness of a sentence such as *The cakes burnt due to King Alfred*; this could not be considered an acceptable alternative to *King Alfred burnt the cakes*.)

If a new argument is introduced in A function (the original S becoming O), it appears that the new A will always be a causer. This has such pragmatic/semantic effect that in many languages it can only be stated in a causative construction, as A, and not in a corresponding intransitive in any peripheral function.

Causative is like applicative in that it applies to intransitive verbs in every language in which it is found; only in some languages can it be extended to apply to transitives. In Urubu-Kaapor (Tupí-Guaraní family, Brazil; Kakumasu 1986: 341–2), for example, causatives can only be formed on intransitives. In some languages a causative derivation may potentially apply to any verb but in practice it is used much more with intransitives than with transitives. In Jarawara a few transitive verbs are commonly causativised, e.g. *-fawa-* 'drink', as in

(17b), but for most a construction with *ehene* 'due to' is preferred to a causative.

A transitive clause already has two core arguments, in A and O functions. A causative derivation introduces a new argument in A function (the causer). There are a number of possibilities for what happens to the original A and O. Three of the most common are:

(i)   Original O stays as is, with original A being moved into the periphery. Comrie (1989: 176) shows that the underlying A will go into the first available slot (for this clause) in a hierarchy of grammatical relations, e.g. it will become 'indirect object' if there is not already an indirect object.

(ii) Some languages allow a clause to include two objects—the original O will remain and the original A will now become a second object (Comrie 1989: 178; 1985).

(iii) Original A becomes O within the causative construction, with original O being moved into the periphery. This happens in a scattering of languages including Tolai (Austronesian from New Britian, see Mosel 1984: 155), Warekena (Arawak from Brazil, see Aikhenvald 1998) and Jarawara (Dixon 2004b). Compare the plain transitive from Jarawara in (17a) with the causative in (17b); *inametewe* 'child' is in A function in (17a) and goes into O function in (17b) while *hemejo* 'medicine' was in O function in (17a) and moves into the periphery, from where it can optionally be omitted, in (17b).

(17)   (a)   inametewe$_A$ hemejo$_O$
             child(fem)   medicine(fem)
                fawa-hara-ke
                drink-IMM.PASTeyewitness(fem)-DECL(fem)
             The child drank the medicine
       (b)   inawa$_A$ inamatewe$_O$ na-fawa-re-ka
             shaman(masc)   child(fem)   CAUS-drink-IPe(masc)-DECL(masc)
                ([hemejo jaa]$_{PERIPHERAL}$)
                   medicine
             The shaman made the child drink (the medicine)

A full list of the syntactic possibilities for deriving causative constructions based on transitive verbs, with discussion and exemplifcation, is in Dixon (2000).

There can be a variety of formal mechanisms for marking a causative construction—an affix or other morphological process to a verb, or a periphrastic verb (such as English *make*). And just as a language may have several passives or antipassives with different markings and distinct meanings (but similar or identical syntax) so there may be more than one causative. For instance, in Hindi suffix *-a* indicates direct and *-va* indirect causation (Kachru 1976). In Kamaiurá (Tupí-Guaraní family, Brazil) there are two causative prefixes to intransitive verbs: *-mo-*, indicating that the causer is not involved in the activity, and *-(e)ro-*, indicating that the causer is involved. Compare the intransitive clause in (18a) with its two causatives in (18b) and (18c). (Data from Lucy Seki, personal communication.)

(18)   (a)   ɨar-aₛ   o-pɨta
             canoe-CORE FUNCTION MARKER   3sgS-stop
             The canoe stopped
       (b)   ɨar-a_O   o-mo-mɨta
             canoe-CORE FUNCTION MARKER   3sgA-CAUSATIVE₁–stop
             He stopped the canoe (he was outside it)
       (c)   ɨar-a_O   w-ero-pɨta
             canoe-CORE FUNCTION MARKER   3sgA-CAUSATIVE₂–stop
             He stopped the canoe (he was inside it)

Note that in (18b) the initial consonant of the root, *p*, assimilates to the initial consonant, *m*, of the preceding suffix.

And there are languages which permit a double causative, e.g. Capanahua (Panoan, Peru) has intransitive *mapet* 'ascend', single causative (transitive) *mapet-ma* 'bring (it) up' and double causative (ditransitive) *mapet-ma-ma* 'make/allow (someone) to bring (it) up' (Payne 1990b: 229, quoting data from Eugene Loos).

The grammatical means used to mark a causative construction may have wider functions. This is explored in Chapter 3 'Causatives which don't cause'.

2. ARGUMENT FOCUSSING

One function of passive, of antipassive, of applicative (and occasionally of causative) can be to feed a pivot (grammatical topic) constraint. In English, for instance, we can only omit a repeated argument from the second of two coordinated clauses if this argument is in S or A function (pivot functions for the language) in each clause. For example, in

(19)   John$_A$ saw Mary$_O$ and Ø$_S$ ran away

it is understood that the unstated S argument of *ran away* is identical to the A argument for *saw*, i.e. it is John who ran away.

However, if we wished to coordinate *John came in* and *Mary saw John*, the only way the second occurrence of *John* could be omitted is for the second clause to be passivised. We cannot say **John came in and Mary saw Ø*, only

(20)   John$_S$ came in and Ø$_S$ was seen by Mary

That is, to meet the S/A pivot constraint of English, if one occurrence of a shared argument is in underlying O function it must be placed in surface S function by forming a passive (derived intransitive) construction.

Similarly, in a language with an S/O pivot it is a straightforward matter to coordinate two clauses that share an argument which is in S or O function in each. Thus, in Dyirbal, from

(21)   Jani$_S$ mayi-n
        John   come.in-PAST
        John came in

(22)   Jani$_O$ Mari-ŋgu$_A$ bura-n
        John   Mary-ERGATIVE   see-PAST
        Mary saw John

we can get (note that here coordination is shown by apposition and intonation):

(23)   Jani$_S$ mayi-n   Ø$_O$ Mari-ŋgu$_A$ bura-n
        John   come.in-PAST   Mary-ERGATIVE   see-PAST
        John came in and Mary saw him

However, we cannot simply coordinate (21) and

(24)   Mari$_O$ Jani-ŋgu$_A$ bura-n
        Mary   John-ERGATIVE   see-PAST
        John saw Mary

Although (21) and (24) have an argument in common, *Jani*, it is in S function in (21) and in A function in (24). For coordination to be permitted, (24) must be antipassivised, with underlying A becoming S and O going out onto the periphery, marked by dative case *-gu*. The antipassive construction is marked by derivational suffix *-ŋa-* on the verb:

(25)   Jani$_S$ bural-ŋa-nyu   (Mari-gu)
       John   see-ANTIPASSIVE-PAST   Mary-DATIVE
       John saw (Mary)

Clauses (21) and (25) now share an argument which is in pivot function in each and they may be coordinated, with the second occurrence of *Jani* omitted:

(26)   Jani$_S$ mayi-n   Ø$_S$ bural-ŋa-nyu   Mari-gu
       John   come in-PAST   see-ANTIPASSIVE-PAST   Mary-DATIVE
       John came in and saw Mary

There are many languages which do not operate with a syntactic pivot—that is, they have no syntactic condition on the combining of clauses into complex sentences. The omission of a repeated argument is likely to relate to the meaning of the construction, rather than to the syntactic functions of the argument. In such a language 'John$_A$ hit Mary$_O$ and Ø$_S$ cried' would be likely to be understood as saying that Mary cried (since a person who is hit is likely to be injured, and to cry) whereas 'John$_A$ hit Mary$_O$ and Ø$_S$ laughed' might be understood to say that John laughed (since Mary would be unlikely to do so, in the circumstances). Compare these with English where in both of *John hit Mary and cried* and *John hit Mary and laughed* it is John who is said to be crying (however improbable this might be) and laughing. And Dyirbal, where in corresponding sentences it would be Mary who was laughing and crying.

In the next sub-section we will describe Jarawara, a language which does operate in terms of a pivot, but which does not require intransitivising derivations such as passive and antipassive, which change the syntactic function of predicate arguments. Instead, it has two transitive constructions which maintain the same arguments; one focusses on the A argument and the other on the O. These alternative construction types fulfil the same pivot-feeding function as do passive and antipassive derivations in other languages.

Then, in §2.2, we shall examine a similar series of focussing constructions in Philippines languages. These are grammatically very similar to the alternative construction types in Jarawara but differ in that
they appear not to feed a pivot or discourse topic.

2.1. *Jarawara*

The linking of clauses in Jarawara operates in terms of a pivot. But
there is not a restrictive S/A or S/O pivot. Instead, the language has
two transitive construction types:

(i)   An A-construction (Ac) is used when the pivot argument (an argu-
      ment that is shared with preceding and/or following clause(s)) is
      in A function in this clause.
(ii) An O-construction (Oc) is used when the pivot argument (an
      argument that is shared with preceding and/or following clause(s))
      is in O function in this clause.

An intransitive clause has one core argument, in S function, and
m(asculine)/f(eminine) gender agreement of the verbal mood suffix
(and some other verbal suffixes also) is with the S. This is illustrated in
(15) and in (with square brackets enclosing the predicate constituent):

(27)   Mioto$_S$ [Ø   ki-joma-ke-ka]
       name(m)   3sgS   be in motion-THROUGH.GAP-COMING-DECLARATIVE:m
       Mioto (a man) came in

(28)   Watati$_S$ [Ø   ki-joma-ke-ke]
       name(f)   3sgS   be in motion-THROUGH.GAP-COMING-DECLARATIVE:f
       Watati (a woman) came in

Now consider a transitive clause 'Mioto saw Watati'. This may be
expressed by an A-construction, as in (29a), or by an O-construction,
as in (29b).

(29) (a, Ac)   (Mioto$_A$)   Watati$_O$ [Ø   Ø   awa-ka]
               name(m)   name(f)   3sgO   3sgA   see-DECL:m
     (b, Oc)   (Watati$_O$)   Mioto$_A$ [Ø   Ø   hi-wa   hi-ke]
               name(f)   name(m)   3sgO   3sgA   Oc-see   Oc-DECL:f

If one wanted to say 'Mioto came in and saw Watati', then (27) would
be coordinated with (29a), an A-construction which has *Mioto* as
pivot, giving:

(30) Mioto_S [Ø ki-joma-ke-ka], Ø_A Watati_O [Ø Ø awa-ka]

Note that in an A-construction the mood (and some other verbal suffixes) agree in gender with the A argument—here masculine for *Mioto* (Sentences (16), (17a) and (17b) in §1.2.2 are also A-constructions). The A NP is generally omitted, since it is known from a previous clause in which it was introduced as pivot argument. In an A-construction where both A and O are third person there is no prefix on the verb.

If one wanted to say 'Watati came in and Mioto saw her', then (28) would be linked to the O-construction, (29b), where *Watati* is pivot argument:

(31) Watati_S [Ø ki-joma-ke-ke], Ø_O Mioto_A [Ø Ø hi-wa hi-ke]

In an O-construction, gender agreement is with the O argument—here feminine for *Watati*. The O NP is generally omitted since it is known from a previous clause in which it was introduced as pivot argument. In an O-construction where both A and O are third person there is a prefix *hi-* on the verb (here *hi-* plus *awa* gives *hi-wa*), repeated before the mood suffix.

The transitive clause 'Watati saw Mioto' may also be expressed either by an A-construction, as in (32a) or by an O-construction, as in (32b):

(32) (a, Ac) (Watati_A) Mioto_O [Ø   Ø   awa-ke]
                  name(f)   name(m) 3sgO 3sgA see-DECL:f
         (b, Oc) (Mioto_O)   Watati_A [Ø   Ø   hi-wa   hi-ka]
                  name(m)   name(f) 3sgO 3sgA Oc-see   Oc-DECL:m

Now to say 'Mioto came in and Watati saw him', we coordinate (27) and (32b), in which *Mioto* is pivot, giving:

(33) Mioto_S [Ø ki-joma-ke-ka], Ø_O Watati_A [Ø Ø hi-wa hi-ka]

And to say 'Watati came in and saw Mioto' we combine (28) and (32a), which has *Watati* as pivot:

(34) Watati_S [Ø ki-joma-ke-ke], Ø_A Mioto_O [Ø Ø awa-ke]

Let us now look at the syntactic properties of A-constructions and O-constructions:

(a) Both are fully transitive. Each has two core arguments, in A and O function. When these are realised by NPs, as in (29a/b) and (32a/b), there are ordering preferences but no strict rules. In an A-construction, with explicit A and O NPs, the A precedes the O in 85% of textual examples, and in an O-construction, O precedes A in 73%. (The reverse orders do occur, with no difference in meaning and no possibility of ambiguity; syntactic function is not shown by constituent order in this language.) As already mentioned, the NP in pivot function (A in an A-construction and O in an O-construction) is most often omitted, since it is likely to be coreferential with an argument in preceding clause(s) (and would have been stated at its first occurrence). Note that the verb is always clause-final.

The first constituents of the predicate, immediately preceding the verb, are pronouns in O and A function (3sg is always zero, as in the examples given so far). The important point is that the first slot is always filled by an O pronoun and the second slot by an A pronoun, in both A- and O-constructions. For example:

(35) (a, Ac) [ota-ra$_O$ mee$_A$ haa
                1exc-ACC   3pl   call
                na-ro-ke]
                AUXILIARY-RECENT.PAST:eyewitness:f-DECL:f
                They called out to us (exclusive)
      (b, Oc) [ota-ra$_O$ mee$_A$ haa   na-ro   otaa-ke]
                1exc-ACC   3pl   call   AUX-RPe:f   1exc-DECL:f
                They called out to us (exclusive)

This shows not only that A and O arguments are included in both construction types, but that they are realised in the same way.

(b) As already mentioned, mood (and some other verbal suffixes) agree in gender with the pivot argument—with A in an A-construction and with O in an O-construction. Jarawara has a system of two genders (masculine and feminine) with feminine being the unmarked member. All non-zero pronouns are cross-referenced as feminine (irrespective of the sex of the people they refer to). Thus, feminine agreement is found both in (35a) where the pivot is *mee* 'they' and in (35b) where it is *otaa* 'we exclusive'.

(c) If both A and O are third person, the verb shows a prefix *hi-* in an O-construction (repeated before a mood suffix) but not in an A-construction. There is no *hi-* prefix in any construction if either A or O is first or second person.

(d) If the pivot is a first or second person pronoun it will be repeated (in root form) just before the final mood suffix; the third plural pronoun is not repeated in this position. This property enables us to infer that (35b) is an O-construction—the O pronoun is repeated before mood and so O must be pivot—and that (35a) is an A-construction—there is no repeated pronoun and so O (which is a first person pronoun) cannot be pivot, implying that A must be.

There are other criteria (even more complex) but these will suffice to exemplify the two construction types. What is beyond doubt is that both are fully transitive. It is neither sensible nor feasible to take one as 'active' and suggest that the other is a derived passive or antipassive or whatever. (Although both suggestions have been made—see the Appendix.) Further details, with many textual examples, are in Dixon (2004: 417–45).

A similar system of two transitive construction types is found in other languages of the small Arawá family, e.g. Paumarí—see Chapman and Derbyshire (1991) and Aikhenvald (2009d).

2.2. *Philippines languages*

The fact that the languages of the Philippines subgroup of Austronesian have a number of alternative construction types involving transitive verbs is well known. Much has been written about this, a great deal of it confused or confusing (or both).

Basically, in each clause just one predicate argument is placed in focus (where the term 'focus' is used in a technical sense, indicating that the statement of the clause is orientated towards this argument). This is shown by affix(es) on the verb, indicating the function of the focussed argument, and by a focus marker on the NP which realises the focus argument.

This can be briefly exemplified by quoting from Shibatani (1988b: 86–9) on Cebuano. The set of function (FN) and focus markers on NPs includes:

	CORE FUNCTIONS (S, A, O)	PERIPHERAL FUNCTIONS	FOCUS
common nouns	sa	sa	ang
proper names	ni	kang	si

For the NP which is in focus, the focus marker (*ang* or *si*) replaces the normal function marker (*sa, ni* or *kang*).

A clause with A, O and a peripheral argument can have any of these three in focus (bold type is used to pick out focus, in each sentence):

(36) (a) **ni**-hatag   [**si**   **Juan**]$_A$ [sa libro]$_O$ [sa
A.FOCUS-give FOCUS name FN book FN
bata]$_{RECIPIENT}$
child
Juan gave a/the book to a/the child

(b) **gi**-hatag   [ni Juan]$_A$ [**ang**   **libro**]$_O$ [sa
O.FOCUS-give FN name FOCUS book FN
bata]$_{RECIPIENT}$
child
Juan gave **the book** to a/the child

(c) **gi**-hatag-**an**   [**ang**
RECIPIENT.FOCUS-give-RECIPIENT.FOCUS   FOCUS
bata]$_{RECIPIENT}$ [ni   Juan]$_A$ [sa libro]$_O$
child FN name FN book
Juan gave **the child** a/the book

There are other possibilities (e.g. a locative or instrumental argument can also be in focus) but (36a–c) suffice to indicate the essence of the system.

This is similar to Jarawara in that we have a number of alternative transitive constructions, which differ simply concerning which argument is in focus. Shibatani (1988b), and also De Wolf (1988), reject suggestions that one construction should be called a passive, or another an antipassive, and so on. There are no differences in transitivity between (36a), (36b) and (36c); each involves the same core and the same peripheral arguments. (Shibatani and De Wolf also sensibly reject any characterisation of these constructions in terms of ergativity. The parameter 'accusative/ergative', as it is used for other types of languages, is not easily applicable to the Philippines subgroup.)

Philippines languages are similar to Jarawara (and other Arawá languages) in that they have a number of transitive construction types, in each of which one predicate argument is 'focussed' (a term felicitously employed by Schachter and Otanes 1972: 69). But they differ in the function of this focussing. In Arawá languages it is entirely syntactic, identifying one argument as the pivot, an argument that links this clause to those that precede and/or follow in discourse. In Philippines languages the focussed argument generally has definite reference, as indicated by the translations given for (36a–c) (see Adams and Manaster-Ramer, 1988, for discussion of exceptions). It need not be discourse topic; there is in fact another grammatical device—fronting an NP before the predicate—that marks a topic. But a focussed argument does function as syntactic pivot for relativisation and for the formation of content questions (Shibatani 1991). Focussing in Philippines languages plays a syntactic role but also has pragmatic effect, highlighting the focussed argument, as the centre of attention in that clause.

3. Argument Manipulating

In §1 we discussed derivations that either remove an argument from the core (passive, antipassive) or introduce one (applicative, causative). They necessarily change transitivity and alter the grammatical functions of arguments. In §2 we discussed alternative construction types that have the same transitivity value and identical grammatical relations but just focus on a different argument in each construction. This section will deal with another type of derivation, one which does not affect transitivity but which manipulates predicate arguments at the level of surface structure.

Exemplification will be drawn from Tariana in §3.1 (similar phenomena occur in other North Arawak languages from Brazil) and from English in §3.2.

3.1. *Tariana*

Tariana has both a passive and also what we are calling an argument manipulating derivation. It will be useful first to describe the passive, which shows expected properties, before going on to discuss the more unusual argument manipulating derivation.

The verb in Tariana bears a prefix cross-referencing the person and number of transitive subject (A) or the subject of an active intransitive verb (S_a). Constituent order is fairly free, with a preference for AOV and SV. In a straightforward transitive clause a pronominal NP in non-subject function is marked by suffix -*na*. Any non-subject NP, whether nominal or pronominal, may optionally take topicalising clitic -*nuku*. (Thus, a free pronoun can take both -*na* and -*nuku*.)

The passive derivation, which applies only to transitive verbs, has the following properties:

(a) a passive clause is active intransitive;
(b) the underlying O argument goes into S_a function (and is cross-referenced on the verb);
(c) the underlying A argument is demoted to the periphery and may be optionally omitted; if it is a pronoun it is marked by non-subject suffix -*na* (the demoted A may also take non-subject topicalising clitic -*nuku*);
(d) the verb is marked as passive by prefix *ka*- and suffix -*kana*; it must be followed by an auxiliary which takes the subject prefix.

Compare the active clause in (37a) with its derived passive in (37b).

(37) (a) [hanupe   itʃiri]$_O$ wa-inu-mhade
            many   animal   1plA-kill-FUTURE
            We'll kill many animals
(37) (b) [hanupe   itʃiri]$_S$ ka-inu-kana-mhade   na:
            many   animal   PASS-kill-PASS-FUT   3plS:AUX
              (wa-na)
              1pl-NON-SUBJECT
            Many animals will be killed (by us)

A passive derivation is typically used when the underlying O argument is the new topic for a stretch of discourse.

Now we can examine a quite different type of derivation, of the object manipulating variety. This has the following properties:

(i)   it applies only to transitive and to active intransitive (not to stative intransitive) clauses;
(ii)   a predicate argument NP other than the subject (A or S_a) is placed in subject position in surface structure; it cannot now take either of the non-subject markers -*na* and -*nuku*;
(iii) the verb includes a classifier affix cross-referencing the NP moved into surface subject slot;
(iv)   the original subject (A or S_a) pronominal prefix to the verb is maintained;

(v)   there may be an NP referring to the underlying A or S_a (or else this can be omitted); it must follow the NP promoted into surface subject slot;

(vi)   other argument NPs (besides the original subject, and the NP promoted into surface subject slot) are maintained;

(vii)   the verb bears suffix *-ni* as a marker of this argument manipulating derivation.

Compare the plain transitive clause (38a) with its argument manipulated derivation in (38b):

(38)   (a)   [ha-hipe]$_O$ nu-phu-ka   [pi-na]
                DEM-CLASSIFIER:LAND   1sgA-sell-REC.P.VIS   2sg-NON.SUBJECT
                I sold this land to you

        (b)   [ha-hipe]   nu-phu-ni-hipe-ka
                DEM-CLASSIFIER:LAND   1sgA-sell-ARG.MANIP-CLASSIFIER:LAND-
                [pi-na]   REC.P.VIS
                2sg-NON.SUBJ
                This land, I sold it to you

The points to note here are: (1) the 1sg prefix *nu-* referring to the A argument is retained; (2) the indirect object constituent *pi-na* 'to you' is retained; (3) the underlying O NP is now surface subject, shown by the inclusion of classifer affix *-hipe-* (in this instance identical with the head noun of the NP) in the verb, following the argument manipulating suffix *-ni*—a classifier in the verb always cross-references the subject argument. Thus the NP which is moved to the front of the clause shows all the properties of a subject except pronominal cross-referencing on the verb (which is retained by the underlying subject).

The NP *ha-hipe*, which is moved into surface subject position, is the initial constituent in both (38a) and (38b); however, (39–41) provides examples of NPs which were in each case originally following the verb being moved into initial position.

As has already been stated, any non-subject argument can be promoted into surface subject position. We had an O argument in (38b). Examples (39) and (40) show the promotion of locative NPs, within transitive and intransitive clauses respectively.

(39)   [maka-yawa]   ihñakasi$_O$ na-pe-ni-yawa
        large-CLASSIFIER:HOLE   food   3plA-throw-ARG.MANIP-CL:HOLE
        The hole (here), people throw (leftovers of) food into it

(40) [ha-amaku]   na-ima-ni-amaku
      DEM-hammock 3plS$_a$-sleep-ARG.MANIP-CLASSIFIER
      This hammock, people sleep in it (i.e. this hammock is for sleeping in)

These indicate another detail concerning pronominal prefixes. If there is no explicit reference to the underlying A or S$_a$ (as there is not in (39) and (40)) then the verb takes the 3pl prefix if the unstated agent is implied human.

Example (41) shows the promotion into surface subject position of an instrumental NP:

(41) [ha   sīpi] [itʃiri]$_o$ nu-inu-ni-pi
      DEM   gun   animal   1sg:A-kill-ARG.MANIP-CLASSIFIER:LONG
      This gun, I kill animals with it (i.e. this gun is for me to kill animals
      with)

In examples (38b), (39) and (40) the classifier incorporated into the verb has the same form as a noun or classifier in the manipulated NP (*hipe* 'land' and *amaku* 'hammock' each acts as its own classifier). In (41) *-pi* 'long objects' is the classifier corresponding to *sīpi* 'gun'. (A full discussion of classifiers in Tariana is in Aikhenvald 1994a, 2003: 87–121.)

It will be seen that, unlike in a passive, transitivity is maintained in constructions such as (38b), (39–41). A non-subject argument is placed in subject slot in surface structure but it is still felt to maintain its underlying function (as O or locative or instrumental). The original A or S$_a$ argument is still shown as a pronominal prefix to the verb, even though any realisation as an NP may be omitted.

We mentioned that the clitic *-nuku* can be added (with a topicalising function) to any non-subject NP. It can be used with the demoted A in a passive, but never with an NP referring to underlying A or S$_a$ in an argument manipulated construction.

In a passive construction the new S (underlying O) has all the grammatical properties of the subject (and the original subject has none of them): (i) it can undergo equi-NP deletion; (ii) it can feed a switch-reference (same subject/different subject) constraint. The NPs promoted into surface subject position in (38b), (39–41) have property (i) but not (ii).

In summary, the argument manipulating derivation in Tariana assigns some, but not all, subject properties to a non-subject NP, while still retaining some of the subject properties on the original subject. This derivation is used to mark a constituent which is more topical than the underlying subject, within the section of discourse in which the clause occurs.

(Full information on Tariana grammar will be found in Aikhenvald 2003.)

3.2. *English*

In English (and in a fair number of other European languages, e.g. Russian and Portuguese) a non-subject NP may be moved into surface subject position in semantically specified circumstances, e.g. *These mandarin oranges peel easily.*

The characteristics of this argument manipulating derivation are:

(i)   It is only possible in the presence of one of:
    (a)   One of a small sets of adverbs, e.g. *well, quickly, easily*, as in *This oven cooks well, Those chocolate eggs sold quickly, This jug pours easily.*
    (b)   Negation, e.g. *The thick cream doesn't pour.*
    (c)   A modal, e.g. *The new model of sports car ought to sell.*
    (d)   Emphatic *do*, e.g. *Those romance novels do lend, don't they?*
(ii) Any non-subject NP may potentially be promoted into subject position in surface structure. This can apply to:
    (a)   an O NP, e.g. *Nylon carpet wears well.*
    (b)   an instrumental NP, e.g. *My steel-tipped boots kick (footballs) well.*
    (c)   a locative NP, e.g. *Studio B recorded Oscar Peterson well.*
(iii) Promotion is only possible when the success or lack of success of the activity is due to some quality of the referent of the promoted NP. From *They recorded Oscar Peterson in Studio B* we can get *Studio B recorded Oscar Peterson well*, but from *They recorded Oscar Peterson in Chicago* it is not possible to derive **Chicago recorded Oscar Peterson well*. The acoustic character of Studio B can contribute to the success of the recording activity; the town in which the recording was made does not do so.
(iv) The underlying subject NP is obligatorily omitted from the clause.

There is a clear distinction between promotion to subject and passive in English. Passivisation does not change or add to the semantic relation between object and verb—it merely focusses on the object or on the effect the activity has on it. In *The linoleum was cleaned well* the *well* is taken to refer to the skill of the referent of the transitive subject, even though this is not identified here. Compare this with *The linoleum cleaned well*, where *well* refers to the cleanable quality of the linoleum. Notice also that the underlying A can be included in the passive—*The linoleum was cleaned well by John*—but not in a promotion to subject construction (we cannot say **The linoleum cleaned well by John.*).

There is a further grammatical difference. In English a prepositional NP can become passive subject (if there is no O NP in the clause) but then leaves its preposition behind (e.g. *This glass has been drunk out of (by John)*). When an erstwhile prepositional NP is promoted into subject slot the preposition is lost e.g. from *They recorded Oscar Peterson in Studio B* we can get *Studio B recorded Oscar Peterson well* but not **Studio B recorded Oscar Peterson well in* or **Studio B recorded Oscar Peterson in well*.

A passive based on a transitive clause is always a derived intransitive. In contrast, promotion to subject does not necessarily affect transitivity. Consider (from Dixon 1991: 322ff, 2005: 446ff):

(42) (a) Mary washed the woollens (with Softly) (in the Hoovermatic)

The success of this activity may be due to the subject, Mary; this would be shown by:

(42) (b) Mary washed the woollens well (with Softly) (in the Hoovermatic)

But the garments may be manufactured in such a way that they respond well to washing (to any sort of washing, or to washing with that brand of soap mixture and/or washing in that make of washing machine). To describe this, the NP *the woollens* is moved into surface subject slot, and the adverb *well* is included after the verb:

(42) (c) The woollens washed well (with Softly) (in the Hoovermatic)

Washday success could alternatively be attributed to the type of soap used, and then *Softly* is moved into subject position:

(42) (d) Softly washed the woollens well (in the Hoovermatic)

Or it may be the machine involved which is the critical factor, and to state this *the Hoovermatic* is moved to subject position:

(42)   (e)   The Hoovermatic washed the woollens well (with Softly)

Sentences (42d–e) are similar to corresponding constructions in Tariana, described in §3.1—a non-subject argument is moved into surface subject position, but the transitivity of the clause is maintained. Sentence (42c) plainly belongs to the same paradigm as (42d–e) but it does show a syntactic difference; since it is here the O argument that is moved into surface subject slot, the clause no longer has an object and must be considered intransitive in terms of its surface structure.

Just like Tariana, promotion to subject can also apply within an intransitive clause in English, e.g. *I ran in my new joggers*, and the derived *My new joggers may not look much but they sure run well.*

We mentioned that in Tariana an NP moved into surface subject slot has some, but not all, of the prototypical grammatical properties of a subject—it acts like a subject with respect to equi-NP deletion but not for switch-reference. An NP which is moved into surface subject slot (the first constituent slot in the clause) in English does trigger third person number agreement on the verb, like any normal subject. It also behaves like a subject in coreferential nominal omission, in at least some circumstances, e.g. *We want a carpet which is hard-wearing and cleans easily.* However some (although not all) speakers have an intuition that an argument which is promoted to subject, as in (42c–e), would not show the full possibilities for coreferential omission, parallel to those of a normal subject. This is something that cannot be tested by made-up examples; it requires large-scale investigation of a textual corpus, something that we have not yet attempted to do.

There is one more important difference between the argument manipulating derivation in Tariana (and other North Arawak languages) and that in English (and other European languages). In Tariana argument manipulation has a discourse function, putting a topic argument into surface subject position. In English argument manipulation is used just for semantic effect, together with an adverb, modal, negation, etc., and has little or no discourse role. Note also that in Tariana a non-subject constituent can be moved into surface subject position with any transitive or active intransitive verb, whereas in English there are restrictions on the verbs that enter into this construction type—a full account is in Dixon (1991: 322–35; 2005: 446–58).

In summary, the points in common to argument manipulating derivations in Tariana and in English are:

(i)   A non-subject NP can be placed in surface subject position within a transitive or (active) intransitive clause.
(ii) This NP shows some, but not necessarily all, of the prototypical properties of a subject in that language.
(iii) Arguments other than the original subject, and that which is promoted into surface subject slot, are retained.
(iv) The transitivity of the clause is not necessarily affected.

There are also, of course, grammatical differences. The most notable is that reference to the underlying subject is retained in Tariana but lost in English. And Tariana, but not English, has a verb suffix that acts as formal marker for an argument manipulating derivation.

In Tariana, and also in English, one cannot have both Argument manipulating and Passive applying in the same clause. This is presumably for pragmatic reasons. Once a constituent is moved into surface subject position by an Argument manipulating derivation—for discourse/semantic reasons—it is not plausible to move it out again by applying a Passive derivation.

4. Marking the Referential Status of Arguments—Inverse Systems

The final type of alternative constructions, that are determined by the nature of the predicate arguments, concerns what are called 'inverse systems'. We shall consider two representative examples—one from the Apachean subgroup of Athabascan (exemplified here by Navajo) and the other from Algonquian. (Other examples, some extending the meaning of 'inverse system', are in Givón 1994.)

We are here dealing with two constructions, both transitive and with the same arguments in the same functions, which differ in their specification of which core argument is controller of the activity.

4.1. *Navajo*

Consider the following two sentences (first given in Hale 1973):

(43) (a) łį́į́$_A$ dzaanééz$_O$ yi-ztał
          horse mule   it:it-kick
          The horse kicked the mule (the horse being responsible for what
          happened)
     (b) dzaanééz$_O$ łį́į́$_A$ bi-ztał
          mule   horse   it:it-kick
          The horse kicked the mule (the mule being responsible for what
          happened)

Each transitive clause can potentially occur in either form. In (43a) A precedes O and the verb bears prefix *yi-*; in (43b) O precedes A and the verb shows prefix *bi-*.

Sometimes only the *yi-* construction is possible, e.g. 'The girl (A) drank the water (O)'; sometimes only the *bi-* construction is possible, e.g. 'the snow (A) froze the dog (O)'. Other times each is perfectly acceptable but with different meanings, as in (43a/b).

The underlying principle is that the first position in clause structure (A for a *yi-* and O for a *bi-* construction) must be filled by whichever of A and O has a greater inherent capacity for control of the type of activity referred to by that verb. Basically, if just one of A and O is human, that must be in the first 'controller' position. If just one of A and O is animate, then that must be controller. All this is interpreted in terms of Navajo world-view. For instance, 'horse (A) kicked man (O)' must be a *bi-* construction with the O NP, 'man', in controller position. The Navajo believe that since a man is more intelligent than a horse, if he gets himself kicked by a horse then it must be his fault (if he had used his intelligence and acted in some different way, he could have avoided being kicked).

The actual nature of the activity is only likely to be relevant when two inanimates are involved. We may only use a *yi-* construction (never a *bi-* one) for both 'the rock (A) rolled onto the tree (O)' and 'the tree (A) fell on the rock (O)'. Rocks naturally roll onto trees and trees naturally fall on rocks. A *bi-*construction here would imply that the tree did something (intelligently!) to get the rock to roll onto it, and so on, which is nonsensical.

(This account is based on Hale 1973, Creamer 1974 and Witherspoon 1977, 1980.)

4.2. *Algonquian*

The terms 'direct' and 'inverse' have been used to describe the *yi-* and *bi-* constructions in Navajo. The same terminology is used to describe two kinds of construction in Algonquian languages. But whereas the choice between constructions in Navajo relates simply to which of A and O is seen as controller, in Algonquian direct/inverse marking describes how the referential contrast between A and O agrees with or goes against what would be expected.

The details vary only a little from language to language. Basically, there is a hierarchy:

(44)　(a)　First and second person
　　　(b)　Third person proximate
　　　(c)　Third person obviative

A verb will bear a direct-marking suffix if A is above O on this hierarchy (i.e. if A is first or second person and O third person, or if O is third person proximate and A is third person obviative) and it shows an inverse marking suffix if A is below O. Compare, from Cree (Klaiman 1991: 191–2):

(45)　(a)　ni-wāpam-āw
　　　　　 1sg-see-DIRECT:1sg
　　　　　 I see him/her
　　　(b)　ni-wāpam-ik
　　　　　 1sg-see-INVERSE
　　　　　 He/she sees me

There is a single prefix to the verb, 1sg *ni-*, which is in A function in the direct construction (45a) and in O function in the inverse, (45b). In (45a) suffix *-āw* indicates both direct construction and 1sg subject, while in (45b) *-ik* indicates inverse. That the other core argument here is 3sg is inferred from zero marking; if it were 3pl the suffix *-ak* would follow *-āw* or *-ik*.

There is typically a system of four suffixes, their reconstructed forms for the independent order being: (a) *-a·-* indicating that A is above O on the hierarchy (44); (b) *-ekw-*, inverse marker, used when O is above A on (44), (c) *-eθe(ne)-* used when A is first person and O second person; (d) *-i-* denoting that O is first person and A second person (Goddard 1967: 67; for fuller details see Goddard 1979a, 1979b).

The Algonquian inverse system is related to discourse structure, in a way that the Navajo one appears not to be. There are two varieties of third person marking, generally called 'proximate' and 'obviative', which are of great assistance in referential tracking. In a study of Blackfoot, Pustet (1995) describes how a third person argument which is foregrounded in discourse is likely to be identified as proximate and one which is backgrounded as obviative. That is, the discourse topic will be coded as proximate; if the topic shifts then the new topic will be upgraded from obviative to proximate. (See also LeSourd 1995 on Passamaquoddy, and Klaiman 1991: 196ff.)

We can see that the hierarchy underlying direct/inverse marking in Algonquian languages relates to two parameters: (i) whether A is a speech act participant (first or second person) and O is a non-participant, or vice versa; and (ii) whether A is topic for that part of the discourse and O a non-topic, or vice versa. The relation between speech act participant and non-participant is treated in the same way as that between topic and non-topic. A useful way of interpreting the direct/inverse system is to say that a first or second person participant is more likely to be A and a third person to be O (speech act participants are more likely to be described doing things to other people, rather than the reverse) and a topic is most likely to be A with a non-topic as O (a topic is most likely to be described doing something to a non-topic). In this view, direct marking is used when the relation between argument reference and syntactic function is as expected, and inverse when it is contrary to expectation.

5. COMPARISON

We can now summarise the critical properties which distinguish the four types of argument-determined constructions, described in §§1–4. These are shown in Table 2.1.

(a) *Is there variation in transitivity between associated constructions?*
YES—for (I) Argument transferring derivations. Passive and antipassive have one core argument less than the basic active clause while applicative and causative have one more than the basic clause.
NO—(II) Argument focussing constructions maintain transitivity in both the Jarawara and Philippines subtypes. So also do (IV) Marking the referential status of arguments (inverse systems). With (III) Argument manipulating derivations, transitivity is maintained when a

Table 2.1. Comparison of properties of types (I)–(IV)

		(a) Variation in transitivity?	(b) Functions of arguments changed?	(c) One construction as basic?	(d) Marks control?	(e) Feeds topic/ pivot?
(I)	Argument transferring	YES	YES	YES		
	Passive				NO	(YES)
	Antipassive				YES	(YES)
	Applicative				NO	(YES)
	Causative				YES	(NO)
(II)	Argument focussing	NO	NO	NO	NO	
	Jarawara type					YES
	Philippines type					NO
(III)	Argument manipulating		YES	YES	NO	
	Tariana type	NO				YES
	English type	IN SOME				NO
(IV)	Marking referential role of arguments	NO	NO	NO	YES	
	Navajo type					NO
	Algonquian type					YES

non-O constituent is promoted into surface subject position; this also holds true for O promotion in Tariana, but not in English.

(b) *Are the syntactic functions of predicate arguments changed?*
YES—This obviously happens in (I) Argument transferring, since transitivity is changed. It also applies to (III) Argument manipulating, where a non-subject argument is promoted into subject slot in surface structure and takes on some, but not all, of the grammatical properties of subject.
NO—In both (II) Argument focussing and (IV) Marking the referential status of arguments, the actual grammatical functions of arguments are not affected.

(c) *Can one of the related constructions be taken as syntactically basic and the other(s) as morphosyntactically derived from it?*
YES—(I) Argument transferring—covering Passive, Antipassive, Applicative and Causative—plainly involves a basic clause type (called 'active' for passive and antipassive) and syntactic processes that apply

to it. The basic clause type is unmarked, with there normally being explicit marking (by a verbal affix or auxiliary, etc.) of passive, antipassive, applicative or causative.

Similar remarks apply for (III) Argument manipulating. There is a basic clause type, and in marked circumstances (related to topicality in Tariana and to both the presence of a manner adverb, etc. and the semantic type of the verb in English) a non-subject constituent is moved into surface subject position.

NO—for (II) Argument focussing. There is often one construction that is more frequent in texts, and may be used in discourse-unmarked or pragmatically-unmarked circumstances (this is the A-construction in Jarawara, and the O-focus construction in many Philippines languages) but it is not appropriate to attempt to derive the other construction type(s) from this, because they have the same basic structure and their arguments have the same syntactic functions. There is simply a difference concerning which argument is in discourse/pragmatic focus.

Similar remarks might be taken to apply for (IV), Marking the referential status of arguments. The two constructions in an inverse system show identical transitivity and grammatical functions of their arguments. They differ simply in the reference of A and O arguments. The direct construction may be taken as unmarked from a semantic/pragmatic point of view (in terms of the expected reference of A and of O) and is often formally unmarked at the morphological level, but it may not be unmarked from a syntactic perspective.

(d) *Does one construction type mark the control which a particular argument has over the activity?*
YES—for (IV) Marking the referential status of arguments. This is particularly clear for the Navajo sub-type, where the first position in clause structure must be filled by the argument which has the capacity to be controller (whatever its syntactic status). The Algonquian subtype operates in a slightly different way, marking whether—for the two arguments in core functions—that which would be expected (in terms of its reference) to be controller actually is controller in this instance. NO—for (II) Argument focussing and (III) Argument manipulating, where the alternative construction types pay no attention to the matter of control.

In the case of (I), Argument transferring, we get a YES answer where an A argument is retained in or introduced into the core (antipassive and causative) and a NO elsewhere (passive and applicative). That is, antipassive involves O being moved out of the core and A becoming S; a semantic effect of antipassive is to focus on the underlying A being controller of the activity. Causative involves the introduction into the core of a new argument in A function, the causer, which necessarily exercises control. For passive, A is moved out of the core and with it information about the controller of the activity. With applicative, an O argument is introduced and there need be no idea of control, e.g. (13b) in §1.2.1.

One property that is common to all of (I)–(IV) is that in each construction (each derived construction for (I) and (III)) one particular predicate argument is foregrounded, or brought into focus. Type (II) answered NO to all of questions (a)–(d). Its main characteristic is the fact that in each construction one argument is brought into focus, hence our name 'Argument focussing'.

But there is also focussing in (III) Argument manipulation—on the non-subject argument that is placed in surface subject position. And in (IV), Marking the referential status—the controller is focussed on (being placed in first position in the clause) in Navajo, and whichever of A and O is higher in the hierarchy is focussed on for Algonquian. Similarly for (I), Argument transferring—the argument that is retained in the core (underlying O for passive, underlying A for antipassive) or the argument that is introduced into the core (O for applicative, A for causative) is plainly in focus.

Another property that runs through the types is definiteness. In (II), Argument focussing, the argument in focus is almost always definite, for both the Jarawara and Philippines subtypes. In (III) Argument manipulating, the argument placed in surface subject slot must be definite in Tariana and there is a strong preference for it to be in English. In (I), Argument transferring, there is again a strong preference for the argument which is left in the core (underlying O for passive, underlying A for antipassive) or that which is introduced (O for applicative, A for causative) to be definite. And when (IV), Marking the referential status of arguments, relates to topicality—as in Algonquian languages—there is a clear correlation between being topic and being definite.

There are other properties which do not serve to distinguish the four types of argument-determined constructions but instead establish subtypes within them. For instance:

(e) *Do the different constructions in the type feed a discourse topic or pivot?*

(I).   Argument transferring. In many (but not all) languages in which these derivations occur, one of the functions of passive and of antipassive is to feed a pivot. This is generally also a property of applicative but only very seldom of causative.

(II).   The argument-focussing constructions in Jarawara are entirely oriented towards pivot organisation; those in Philippines languages appear not to be.

(III). The argument-manipulating derivation in Tariana is oriented towards discourse topic; that in English is not.

(IV).   The inverse system in Algonquian languages is oriented towards discourse organisation in that a third person topic is generally marked as proximate and a non-topic as obviative. There is no evidence that inverse marking in Navajo is oriented towards discourse organisation.

6. CONCLUSION

In this chapter we have distinguished between, and briefly described and exemplified, the four types of argument-determined constructions listed on the first page. Their properties are summarised in Table 2.1.

What we have not discussed is the kinds of diachronic change that can apply to the various construction types. It is possible that one type may change into another. Such investigation falls outside our purview here. But it is plain that diachronic shifts will be more readily discernible if the construction types are clearly distinguished—and distinctively named—in the first place.

APPENDIX—TERMINOLOGY

We hope to have made clear the differences between the four types of argument-dependent constructions. Unfortunately, they are often confused because of the terminology used to describe them.

Basic linguistic theory, at any point in time, is the sum of what is understood about human languages. For two thousand years this has been heavily biased towards the familiar languages of Europe and adjacent parts of Asia and Africa.

'Passive' is a familiar concept, in a nominative-accusative language. When linguists first encountered ergative languages they most mis-leadingly described the basic transitive construction as a type of pas-sive. And ergative languages were said not to have any voice contrast. Then it was pointed out by Jacobsen (1985, paper actually written in 1969) that an antipassive derivation in an ergative language is parallel to a passive in an accusative language, and should also be referred to as a 'voice' distinction.

When Bloomfield (1917: 154) worked on Tagalog, he called a clause with A-focus an 'active', and used 'direct passive', 'instrumental pas-sive' and 'local passive' for O-focus, instrument-focus and locative-focus respectively. These construction types do not satisfy the normal criteria for passive, but this was the established label that seemed to Bloomfield to be the least inappropriate to use here. In fact, a new label is needed.

Some of the restricted formal theories that have been developed in recent years place constraints on data interpretation. In early Trans-formational Grammar and in Relational Grammar any set of alterna-tive construction types is taken to involve a derivation. In Relational Grammar the idea of 'advancement' is used for passive, antipassive, argument focussing, argument manipulation, and inverse marking, among other things (e.g. Perlmutter and Postal 1984, Siewierska 1984: 209), Adams de Liclan and Marlett (1991) describe the two transitive clauses in the Arawá language Kulina (very similar to those in Jarawara) in Relational Grammar terms. They call the O-construction 'active' and the A-construction 'antipassive'. Campbell (1985) approaches Jamamadi (another dialect of the same language as Jarawara) from a more traditional stance—she calls the A-construction 'active' and the O-construction 'passive'. Both analyses involve a fundamental lack of understanding of the facts of these languages. We have two transi-tive constructions (with the same A and O arguments) of equivalent syntactic status. Neither can usefully be described as derived from the other. They differ just as to which argument is in focus, as pivot for the section of discourse in which the clause occurs.

While some 'theoreticians' are heavily biased towards derivation, others react against this and shun the idea of syntactic derivation. Each group misses an important distinction. As shown above, the most insightful way of describing both (I), Argument transferring, and (III), Argument manipulating, is to take one construction as basic and the other(s) as derived from it. But the idea of derivation is not applicable for (II), Argument focussing, and scarcely for (IV), Marking the referential status of arguments.

It is clear that we do not have a sufficient stock of generally-accepted terminology in linguistics today. When confronted with a new construction type the tendency is (like Bloomfield) to describe it by a term which properly belongs to a different part of the grammar. Different people extend the meanings of established terms in different ways. The result is that basic typological distinctions are confused.

The label 'middle' is established as the name for a third voice (alongside active and passive) in the grammar of Greek, with the meaning 'doing something for oneself' or 'acting on oneself'. There has been some recent discussion of (III), Argument manipulating, in English (but restricted to the promotion of the O constituent to surface subject position, ignoring the fact that the same possibilities can apply for instrumental and locative constituents). This has been called 'middle', even though its syntactic status and meaning are quite different from the middle in Greek. (For instance Keyser and Roeper, 1984, an article that also follows the misguided practice of recognising 'ergative constructions' in English—see Dixon 1994: 18–22 for a critique of misuse of the term 'ergative'.)

Doris Payne (1994) uses the term inverse in a non-standard way. Tupí-Guaraní languages have one cross-referencing strategy when A is above O on the hierarchy 'first person > second person > third person', and a different strategy when O is above A. She calls the latter 'inverse'. This differs from the normal use of inverse, as described in §4, since in Tupí-Guaraní languages there is never any choice involved, relating to which core argument is controller of the activity (as there may be in Athabascan, Algonquian, and similar cases).

Discussing the inverse construction in Navajo, Hale (1973) described it as generated by 'a syntactic rule which is similar to the passive'. Others have shown less restraint and have simply described inverses as 'passives' (or as 'ergatives'—see references in Klaiman 1991: 186).

The term 'passive' was first used to describe a derivation in which the original A is removed to the periphery and underlying O becomes passive S. But many authors use 'passive' to refer to focus-constructions in Philippine languages (Siewierska 1984: 80–1, mentions those linguists who use 'passive'—including Givón 1979, etc.—and those who prefer 'focus').

Cooreman (1982, 1987) has written on Chamorro, a language that has been provided with an excellent reference grammar by Topping (1973). Chamorro has both what can be described as an agentless passive (marked by verbal prefix *ma-*) and an optional focus system, on the Philippines model. As Topping describes it, this includes Goal Focus, marked by verbal affix *-in-*, and two varieties of Agent Focus, one where the O is indefinite (verbal affix *man-*) and another when O is definite (affix *-um*). Cooreman uses accepted terminology in a non-standard manner, employing the label 'passive' both for the actual agentless passive and also for the Goal Focus construction. She also calls the Actor Focus with indefinite O 'antipassive'. Thus (Cooreman 1982: 368):

(46) CONSTRUCTION TYPE   DEGREE OF TOPICALITY
     antipassive   Agent >> Affected Participant (the
                                   Affected Participant gets
                                   suppressed completely)
     ergative   Agent > Affected Participant
     -UM-construction   Agent = Affected Participant
     -IN-passive   Agent < Affected Participant
     MA-passive   Agent << Affected Participant (the Agent
                                   prototypically gets suppressed)

Note that 'ergative' here refers to a non-focus transitive construction. Cooreman (1987: 76) has a revised diagram, renaming 'ergative' as 'transitive' and omitting mention of the -UM-construction (Agent Focus with definite O):

(47) CONSTRUCTION TYPE   DEGREE OF TOPICALITY
     antipassive   Agent >> Object (where the Object is
                                   prototypically suppressed)
     transitive   Agent > Object
     IN-passive   Agent < Object
     MA-passive   Agent << Object (where the Agent is
                                   prototypically suppressed)

In the introduction to a volume on *Voice and Inversion*, Givón (1994: 8) gives a diagram which he attributes to Cooreman, but which is in fact a substantially modified re-statement:

(48) VOICE   RELATIVE TOPICALITY
      active/direct   AGT >   PAT
      inverse   AGT <   PAT
      passive   AGT << PAT
      antipassive   AGT >> PAT

It appears that Givón has renamed Cooreman's 'IN-passive' (actually a Goal Focus construction) as 'inverse'.

In interpreting these diagrams it is important to bear in mind that 'inverse', 'antipassive' and some uses of 'passive' refer not to Type (IV), Marking the referential status of arguments and Type (I), Argument Transferring, as described above, but to Type (II), Argument focussing. Three of the contributions to Givón (1994) quote either (47) or a combined version of (46) and (47), from Cooreman (p. 116, 122, 235) while another three repeat (48) from Givón, following Givón in attributing it to Cooreman (p. 149, 170, 280). In fact some—but not all—of these contributions do discuss actual inverse systems (comparable to those we exemplified in §4).

In the same volume Thomas Payne (1994) discusses Cebuano, which we mentioned in §2.2; he uses the term 'antipassive' for an A-focus construction, 'passive' for one kind of O-focus and 'inverse' for another kind of O-focus (distinguished in terms of the possibilities of argument omission).

With this sort of cavalier deployment of terminology, across construction types of quite different grammatical statuses, it is difficult to see how any generalisations that are put forward about 'passive', 'inverse' and the like can have interest or validity.

There are, of course, a number of papers by insightful scholars suggesting that such deployment of terms is not useful. We have already mentioned Shibatani (1988b) and De Wolf (1988) who reject suggestions that one kind of Philippines focus construction should be called 'passive' and another type 'antipassive'.

As Shibatani (1988b: 136) states: 'characterizing a particular construction in terms of what is familiar in another language is quite dangerous because the similarity between them may be outweighed by differences.' As Table 2.1 shows, there are similarities between each pair of (I)–(IV), but there are also critical differences.

We suggest that the terms passive, antipassive, inverse, etc., should be used just for the construction types described under these names in this chapter. (And that 'middle' also be restricted to its traditional sense.)

The term 'voice' was originally used to describe an active/passive or (in a language like Greek) an active/middle/passive contrast. Jacobsen (1985) sensibly argued that it should be extended to cover active/antipassive. Others extend the term to refer to quite different construction types. Palmer (1984: 88) employs 'voice' for passive, causative and applicative. Klaiman (1991) uses 'voice' to cover passive and antipassive (but not applicative or causative) and also (II) Argument focussing in Philippine and other languages (called 'information salience voice systems') and (IV) Marking the referential status of arguments (called 'inverse voice systems'). Even Shibatani (1988b) refers to the focus constructions in Philippines-type languages as a type of 'voice'. Presumably Klaiman and Shibatani use 'voice' in these ways simply because there is no other term available. However, it seems to us to be most appropriate to keep 'voice' for the description of valency-reducing derivations (active/passive and active/antipassive) and not also to employ it to describe construction types where transitivity is maintained and where there is no derivation (focus and inverse systems).

The labels we have used here may not be catchy but they are descriptively accurate—Argument transferring (into or out of the core), Argument focussing, Argument Manipulating, and Marking the referential status of arguments. Our aim has been to show that these four types should be distinguished (and that names must not be transferred, willy-nilly between them) if we are to gain a better understanding of how languages work.

It is appropriate to conclude with a plea that grammatical terminology, which in its established use refers to one kind of construction or derivation, should not be redeployed to describe something that, despite some superficial similarities, is in fact fundamentally different in grammatical type. Using a single term to describe distinct grammatical phenomena must tend to obscure the difference between them.

CHAPTER THREE

CAUSATIVES WHICH DO NOT CAUSE: NON-VALENCY-INCREASING EFFECTS OF A VALENCY-INCREASING DERIVATION

Alexandra Y. Aikhenvald*

A causative construction typically involves the introduction of a new argument, a Causer, into a basic clause. The Causer refers to someone, or something, which initiates or controls the activity. A causative is thus primarily a valency-increasing derivation. However, in a number of languages causative is straightforwardly valency-increasing only if applied to intransitive verbs. With transitive verbs, the effect of the same marker may be rather different. We start with two relevant case studies. Causativizers in Manambu, from the Ndu family (Papua New Guinea), express manipulative effort, forceful action, and multiplicity and extent of the object, when applied to transitive verbs. Causativizing markers with transitive verbs in Tariana, from Arawak family (Brazil), have an applicative-like effect with transitive verbs—an additional, erstwhile peripheral, constituent becomes obligatory. The findings of the case-studies are then viewed in cross-linguistic perspective. I discuss other cases where the same morphemes operate as causatives (that is, valency-increasing devices) with transitive, and also with intransitive verbs, and add an extra meaning to the verb, to do with manipulative effort, forceful and intensive action, complete involvement of the object, and/or multiple or large object. These non-causative

* I am indebted to my adopted Manambu family, especially Yuamali Jacklyn Benji Ala, Pauline Agnes Luma Laki, Gemaj, Jenni Kudapa:kw, John Sepaywus and many others, for helping me in my attempts to learn their fascinating language. I am equally grateful to my adopted Tariana relatives—the Britos who speak the Santa Rosa variety, and the Munizes, the speakers of the variety of Periquitos. I am forever in debt to my teachers of Warekena of Xié (especially Humberto Baltar and Pedro Ângelo Tomas), and the late Candelário da Silva, the last speaker of Bare. I am grateful to R. M. W. Dixon for providing invaluable feedback on this and other drafts, and to John Bowden, Eva Csató, Bill Croft, Alan Dench, Nick Enfield, Lars Johanson, Jack Martin, Marc Sicoli and Catherine Travis for comments and suggestions.

meanings of primarily causative morphemes are characteristic only of morphological causatives expressing direct causation with the Causer in control, and can be considered to be their semantic extensions. The Appendix outlines the historical development of polysemous morphological causatives in a number of relevant language families.

1. What this Chapter is About

Causative forms may not always imply causation. What other meanings they may have, and why? This is what this chapter is concerned with.

A causative construction is primarily associated with increasing valency—that is, introducing a new argument, a 'Causer'.[1] In a number

---

[1] In recent years, there has been a considerable amount of typologically and formally oriented literature on the issue of causatives. This chapter is cast within the framework of functionalist typological approach whereby causatives are viewed essentially as mechanisms of introducing an additional argument, a 'Causer', someone or something that initiates or controls the activity (see Comrie 1976a, 1981a, 1989, 2003; Dixon and Aikhenvald 1997, Dixon 2000, and also papers in Comrie and Polinsky 1993). A causative construction can also be described as involving two events (for instance, Frawley 1992: 159 differentiates a 'precipitating event' and a 'result', while Shibatani (1976b) and (2002b) presents causatives as consisting of a 'causing event' and a 'caused event'). In §7, we return to the interpretation of causative construction as involving an 'event fusion' in the light of the polysemy of causative markers discussed in this chapter.

Further seminal work on clause union within relational grammar is also relevant for a multi-event representation of causative constructions (see Aissen and Perlmutter 1983). Causatives viewed as 'fusion' of two events are frequently analysed as semantically complex predicates (this issue was explored within the framework of lexical-functional grammar, e.g. Alsina and Joshi 1991, Alsina 1992, 1996). Along similar lines, Dowty (1972, 1979) offers a bisentential (or biclausal?) representation of causatives (also see Wunderlich 1997: 34, Levin and Rappaport 1995; Härtl 2001 and others). The issue of clausality in causatives is briefly addressed in §2. Further work on complex predication and causativization cast within the Minimalist framework includes Rosen (1989); also see Ackerman and Moore (1999, 2001) on the argument structure of causatives. In a different approach to causative construction, Pylkkänen (2008: 9) argues that causativization involves 'a causative head that introduces a causing event into the semantics of the construction', and that 'external arguments are always introduced by Voice'. Each of these approaches merits attention within a specific formal approach, and it would be a mammoth task to discuss their advantages and disadvantages here. We choose to rely upon a more traditional typology which has withstood the test of time, and which allows us to deal with a broad variety of empirical data, most of them hardly ever discussed in a cross-linguistic perspective. This agrees with a general orientation of this chapter which, in Givón's (1982: v) words, 'leans towards substantive rather than formal linguistics, an interest in language universals of both function and typology, a commitment to a broadly defined data-base'.

of languages, a causative is straightforwardly valency-increasing only if applied to intransitive verbs. With transitive verbs, the effect of the same marker may be rather different. That is, an erstwhille valency-increasing derivation may be polysemous. It may have an additional non-valency-increasing effect, described by some grammarians as 'aspectual', implying increase in intensity of action or force in its performance, and a special manipulative effort required. Or it may imply that the Causer is particularly agentive, or their actions are intentional. This phenomenon has not been accorded the cross-linguistically-based analysis it deserves, within the considerable body of literature on valency-increasing and non-valency-increasing morphology (e.g. Ackerman and Moore 2001; Dixon 2000, and references there).

My aim is to provide a systematic empirically-based investigation of these effects as a component of a semantic complex associated with forceful and direct causation, as a basis for a general inquiry into their nature and motivation. These, in turn, provide support for a view of meaning of morphemes as going beyond one putative central meaning, subsuming the multiple facets of a situation where a morpheme may occur. My further aim is to introduce facts of previously barely known languages, based on my own fieldwork, thus expanding the fact base for future typological and other linguistic research.

I start with a preamble—a brief overview of prototypical causatives within the context of other valency-increasing derivations (§2), and a summary of cross-linguistically relevant semantic features in causatives of different types (§3).

Two relevant case studies are then discussed in some detail. The prefix *kay-* in Manambu, from the Ndu family (Papua New Guinea) causativizes intransitive verbs. When used with transitive verbs, it does not add any participants: instead, it marks manipulative effort, forceful action, or multiplicity and extent of the object (§4). The causative suffix in Tariana, from the Arawak family (Brazil), has a straightforwardly valency-increasing causativizing effect with intransitive and with a handful of transitive verbs. When used with other transitive verbs, the same marker has an applicative-like effect—an erstwhile peripheral constituent becomes an obligatory core argument. And a further causative marker may be added to mark intensive action (§5).

The outcomes of these case-studies both based on my fieldwork are then viewed in cross-linguistic perspective in §6. I discuss other cases where the same morphemes operate as causatives (that is, valency-increasing devices) and also add an extra meaning to the verb, to do with manipulative effort, forceful and intensive action, or complete involvement of the object. These effects are characteristic of morphological causative markers whereby the Causer is acting directly,[2] rather than through an intermediary, and is in control.

The last section offers a tentative explanation for the polysemy and polyfunctionality of causative markers. The Appendix outlines the putative historical development of polysemous morphological causatives in the language families for which this polysemy has been documented.

Causative morphemes can have further meanings (for instance, see Haspelmath 1993a, on the interrelations between morphological causatives and inchoatives, and Saeed 2003: 72, for a general semantic account; also see Dixon 2006a and note 13, for the role of causative markers in transitivity matching). The same morpheme may be used to causativize a verb, and to derive a verb out of a noun or out of an adjective (see Comrie and Thompson 1985, Aikhenvald 2007a; some examples are in Quechua (Cole 1982: 180, 182; Weber 1989); Nyangumarta (Sharp 2002: 203–5); Classical Nahuatl (Comrie and Thompson 1985: 346), Kugu Nganhcara (Smith and Johnson 2000: 412); Rapanui (Du Feu 1996) and Irakw (Mous 1993: 186–8)).

This phenomenon of denominal causatives is reminiscent of other instances whereby affixes occurring on different word classes may have different functions and different meanings. For instance, case morphemes occur on noun phrases to mark grammatical relations, and on verbs and/or clauses as clause-linking devices (see Chapter 1 above). In some languages, verbs, just like nouns, may occur with diminutive marking—compare Late Medieval Latin *scribillare* 'scribble, write a bit', a diminutive formation on Latin *scribere* 'write' (containing the same marker as a nominal diminutive, e.g. *asellus* 'young donkey', and many others: Palmer 1954: 236–7). The same morpheme means 'do a bit' with verbs and 'small size; young age' with nouns.

The general meaning of the diminutive morpheme remains the same, and the semantic difference can be viewed as a side-effect of the meanings of prototypical verbs, and of nouns: a verb refers to an activity, and a noun to a 'thing', or an 'object'. That is, the meaning is conditioned by morphosyntactic context, and has implications for word class typology, suggesting a semantic basis underlying the

---

[2] The terms 'direct' and 'indirect' causation are used with different meanings by other authors, e.g. Dowty (1972, 1979).

grammar of nouns and verbs as major word classes. This issue, and with it the analysis of denominative causatives, is tangential to the present study.

2. Preamble. Causatives and Applicatives

2.1. *Causatives: An introduction*

As described in the previous chapter, a causative construction typically involves the introduction of a new argument, a 'Causer', into a basic intransitive clause. The Causer refers to someone, or something, which initiates or controls the activity. A causative is thus frequently viewed as primarily a valency-increasing derivation which involves introducing a new argument. This transitivity-increasing effect common to all causatives involves:

> *Adding an A (transitive subject) argument, S (intransitive subject) becoming O (object).*

The working definition of a prototypical CAUSATIVE is:

(a) Causative applies to an underlying intransitive clause and forms a derived transitive.
(b) The argument in underlying S function ('the Causee') goes into O function in the causative.[3]
(c) A new argument ('the Causer') is introduced, in A function.
(d) There is some explicit formal marking of the causative construction.

If a language has a causative derivation, it always applies to intransitive verbs. A morphological causative is illustrated in (1) and (2), from Manambu, a Ndu language from the East Sepik area of New Guinea (Aikhenvald 2008a). The relevant markers are in bold type throughout this chapter.

---

[3] The status of a Causee in a causative construction has been a matter for extensive discussion: see Comrie (1976a; 1981a; 1989; 2003). Causee encoding and the issue of double object construction is discussed at length by Ackerman and Moore (1999) (also see references there). Saksena (1982a) demonstrates how different case-marking of a Causee may correlate with different semantic overtones. The issue of the Causee's status and its marking, however important for a general typology of causatives, lies beyond the scope of this chapter.

(1) ba:d   ka:p   wi:-na   —*intransitive*
    egg(s)   by.itself break/split-ACT.FOC+3fem.sgSUBJ.NONPAST
    The egg has broken (by itself)

(2) ñan   ba:d   **kay**-wi:-na-d   —*causativized and thus transitive*
    child(A) egg(o)   CAUS-break/split-ACT.FOC-3masc.sgSUBJ.NONPAST
    A child has broken an egg'[4]

The applicability of a morphological causative may correlate with the verb's semantics. It has been shown that stative intransitive verbs are more prone to forming morphological causatives than, say, motion verbs (see discussion, and further references, in Shibatani 2002b; Dixon 2000; also see Levin and Rappaport 1995; Ackerman and Moore 1999; Alsina 1992, 1996; Alsina and Joshi 1991).[5] In Tariana (Aikhenvald 2000a, 2003), an Arawak language from northwest Amazonia, stative verbs form regular morphological causatives—as seen in (3) and (4). In contrast, many active verbs—including verbs of motion and feeling—do not.

(3) ira-kasi   sakamu-mha   —*intransitive*
    drink-NOMZR(s)   luke.warm-PRES.NONVIS
    The drink is luke-warm

(4) emite   ira-kasi-nuku   di-sakamu-i-ka
    child(A)   drink-NOMZR-TOP.NON.A/s   3sgnfA-luke.warm-CAUS-REC.P.VIS
        —*causativized and thus transitive*
    The child warmed up the drink (partly)

Cross-linguistically, a causative derivation may also apply to transitive verbs. Of these, ingestive verbs—that is, verbs of eating and

---

[4] Data from languages based on my own fieldwork (Manambu, Tariana and Bare) have been collected through original field research, based on large collections of texts of different genres, conversations and participant observation (elicitation was restricted to lexical items). The basics of fieldwork methodology followed are outlined in Aikhenvald (2007b) and Dixon (2007).
[5] There has been a substantial amount of work, by linguists of different theoretical persuasions, on such correlations. This goes beyond the scope of this chapter. In an individual language, the reasons why motion verbs could be less amenable to causativization than verbs of other semantic groups may have to do with language-specific issues. For instance, in Manambu highly polyfunctional motion verbs are restricted in their morphological possibilities, that is, they hardly occur with any suffixes or prefixes (as I showed in Aikhenvald 2008a, 2009a), and are generic in nature. (In other languages, such as Gayo (Eades 2005) causative morphology straightforwardly applies to motion verbs). Limited productivity of morphological causatives in Tariana may be due to increasing impact of contact-induced change under pressure from Tucano (Aikhenvald 2002a).

drinking—are the most likely candidates to allow morphological causativization (see Shibatani 2002b: 6–7; Shibatani and Pardeshi 2002).[6]
And this is indeed the case in Tariana: here, a morphological causative
regularly applies to just a handful of verbs to do with food consump-
tion. The most frequent one of these is 'drink'. (5) shows that this verb
is transitive:

(5)   emite   hinisi-nuku$_O$ du-ira-ka-sita   —transitive
      child(A)   milk-TOP.NON.A/s   3sgnfA-drink-REC.P.VIS-ALREADY
      The child has already drunk the milk

When causativized, with the suffix -ita-, it becomes ditransitive:

(6)   emite-nuku$_{O1}$ hinisi-nuku$_{O2}$ nu-ira-**ita**-de
      child-TOP.NON.A/s   milk-TOP.NON.A/s   1sg-drink-CAUS-FUT.CERT
        —causativized and now ditransitive
      I will make the child drink milk

The newly introduced Causer, 'I', is the transitive subject (A), and the
original A ('the child') is now marked as a topical non-subject, as is the
original O (milk).[7] Comrie (1976a) and Dixon (2000: 47–59) provide
an in-depth discussion of the various options for grammatical roles in
derived transitives—as in (6)—compared with non-derived ones—as
in (5) (also see Ackerman and Moore 1999, 2001 and references there;
and a different perspective in Pylkkänen 2008 and Cuervo 2003). This
issue, however interesting, is tangential to our study here.

A double occurrence of a causative morpheme may have a further
valency-increasing function. The suffix -poj in Movima, an isolate from
Bolivia (Haude 2006: 395), is a marker of direct causation and can be
used on an intransitive verb, or on a transitive verb. Its occurrence on
an intransitive verb is shown in (7):

(7)   ɬok-a-**poj**-a=is   ba:-ra   kis   ko'   —transitive
      fall-DR-CAUS-LV=pl.a   finish-BE.n   ART.pl.a   tree
      They felled all the trees

[6] In Tariana (Aikhenvald 2003) ingestive verbs are transitive. Note that cross-
linguistically, ingestive verbs often display unusual transitivity patterns (see Amberber
2009; Naess 2009).
[7] Tests for grammatical relations in Tariana include pronominal cross-referencing,
case-marking, and passivization (see Chapter 21 of Aikhenvald 2003).

A verb causativized and made transitive with -*poj* can take another causative suffix -*poj*; the result is a causative of a causative, that is, a ditransitive verb with the meaning of 'have someone make something VERB':

(8) loy   iɫ   ɫok-a-**poj-poj**-na   u'ko   n-as   ko'
     ITN   I   fall-DR-CAUS-CAUS-DR   PRO.m   obl-ART.n   tree
     —*ditransitive*
     I'll have him fell the tree[8]

Before turning to the semantics of causatives, we briefly address applicatives, another wide-spread valency-increasing device.

2.2. *Applicatives*

We distinguish two prototypical schemes depending on whether the applicative valency-increasing derivation applies to an intransitive verb or also to a transitive one. This approach to applicatives follows an established tradition: in particular, see Mithun (2001), Peterson (2007), Austin (1997), Dixon and Aikhenvald (2000a). The issue of expressing grammatical relations in applicatives has been discussed, from a formal perspective, by McGinnis (2001) and McGinnis and Gerdts (2004) (these papers also contain critiques of, and references to, other formal approaches to cross-linguistic variation in applicatives).

Scheme 1. Applicative derivation of an intransitive verb.

This involves:

(a) Applicative applies to an underlying intransitive clause and forms a derived transitive.
(b) The argument in underlying S function goes into A function in the applicative.
(c) A peripheral argument (which could be explicitly stated in the underlying intransitive) is taken into the core, in O function.

---

[8] Whether or not a second occurrence of a causative is expected to have the same semantic overtones as the first one is as yet an open question. We will see in (52c) below that the second occurrence of a causative in Godoberi imparts the overtone of particularly forceful causation to the whole construction. This does not appear to be the case in Movima. More investigation is needed (focussed on languages which are still actively spoken, unlike the highly endangered Movima).

Importantly, there is also (d) some explicit formal marking of an applicative construction, generally by an affix or some other morphological process applying to the verb.

This is illustrated by Motuna, a Papuan language from Bougainville (Onishi 2000: 132). An intransitive verb 'get angry' is in (9).

(9)   nii_S [ong-jo   pehkoro]_{Oblique NP} [iirong-ohna-na]_{intr}
      1sg   DEM+M-PURP   boy   get.angry(intr)-1S_a+PRES.PROG-F
      —intransitive
      I am angry for the sake of the boy (that is, the state of "this boy" (who was, for example, unduly mistreated by someone else) is the cause of "my" anger)

In (10), the same verb has an applicative marker. The verb 'get angry with' is now transitive. In Onishi's words, 'the applicative construction indicates that the referent of the new O may potentially be affected by the anger expressed by the referent of A'.

(10) nii_A [ong   pehkoro]_O [iirong-ee-uhna-na]_{tr}   —transitive
      1sg   DEM+M   boy   get.angry(intr)-APPL-3O+1A+PRES.PROG-F
      I am angry with this boy (refers to "my" anger against "this boy", often accompanied by an act of scolding)

The erstwhile oblique ('this boy') has now become an obligatory, core argument (for cross-linguistically-based criteria distinguishing between core arguments and obliques see Dixon and Aikhenvald 2000b).

Scheme 2. Applicative derivation of a transitive verb.

This typically involves valency rearrangement, whereby *a peripheral argument becomes O*:

(a) Applicative applies to an underlying transitive clause and maintains transitivity, but with an argument in a different semantic role filling O function.
(b) The underlying A argument stays as is.
(c) A peripheral argument (which could be explicitly stated in the underlying transitive) is taken into the core, in O function.
(d) The argument which was in O function is moved out of the core into the periphery of the clause (and may be omissible).

(e) There is some explicit formal marking of an applicative construction, generally by an affix or some other morphological process applying to the verb.

We can usefully repeat here examples (14a–b) from §1.2.1 in Chapter 2. Sentence (11), from Dyirbal, illustrates the verb 'plaster' in its transitive use. The oblique, 'beeswax', can be optionally added (and is in parentheses):[9]

(11) ŋaja_A   nuba_O   maymba-n   ([garrmay-ju]_{Optional Peripheral})
    1sg   bark.bag   plaster-PAST   beeswax-INSTR
    —*transitive*
    I plastered the bark bag (with beeswax) [to seal it and make it watertight]

In (12), the verb 'plaster' takes the applicative marker. The verb remains transitive, but the roles of participants—other than the transitive subject ('I')—have changed: 'beeswax' is now the object, and the 'bark bag' is an optional oblique which does not have to be stated.

(12) ŋaja_A   garrmay_O   maymbal-**ma**-n   ([nuba-gu]_{Optional Peripheral})
    1sg   beeswax   plaster-APPL-PAST   bark.bag-DAT
    —*transitive*
    I used the beeswax to plaster (the bark bag) or I plastered the beeswax on the bark bag

Not infrequently, causative and applicative are expressed with the same morphological process, as in a number of Australian languages (Dixon 2002: 202–6; Austin 1997). In Yidiñ (Dixon 1977: 302–19), -*ŋa-l* transitivizes an intransitive verb. This may involve adding an A

---

[9] Applicative derivations are attested in a wide variety of the world's languages; perhaps the most frequently cited examples come from Bantu languages, especially Kinyarwanda, and Romance. One of the objectives of this chapter is to expand the fact base beyond frequently quoted examples; this is one reason why I quote Dyirbal rather than Kinyarwanda. Another reason is the privileged position of Dyirbal and Yidiñ, and a number of other Australian languages, which can boast a comprehensive grammatical description within an areal and genetic context. Applicatives of various types in Salish languages are discussed by Gerdts and Kiyosawa (2005a–b, 2007). Possessive applicatives are hardly mentioned in the existing literature on applicatives. In addition, Australian languages provide a clear instance of causative-applicative polysemy to be discussed shortly.

whereby the transitivized verb becomes a causative, as in (14) (p. 312). The corresponding intransitive is illustrated in (13).

(13) mula:ri$_S$ wanga:jiñu   —*intransitive*
      initiated.man:ABS   get.up+PAST
      The initiated man got up

(14) buriburi:-ŋ$_A$ mula:ri$_O$ wanga:ji-**ŋa**:l   —*transitive*
      old.man-ERG   initiated.man:ABS   get.up-CAUS+PAST
      The old man lifted up the initiated man

Alternatively, this same suffix may transitivize a verb by making an oblique (comitative, locative, dative, instrumental, or 'fear') into an object. The choice depends on the verb's semantics. The intransitive use is shown in (15). The corresponding transitive is in (16) (Dixon 1977: 303):

(15) wagu:ja$_S$ ñina-ŋ   waga:l-ji   —*intransitive*
      man:ABS   sit-PRES   wife-with
      The man is sitting with [his] wife

(16) waguja-ŋgu$_A$ wagal$_O$ ñina:-**ŋa**-l   —*transitivized, now transitive*
      man-ERG   wife:ABS   sit-APPL-PRES
      The man is sitting (with) [his] wife

A conceptual link between applicatives and causatives has been formulated by Lichtenberk (1993: 14): both enable 'the inclusion of the other, complementary, core participant, in a transitive situation'. Also see Shibatani and Pardeshi (2002: 116–22), and especially Peterson (2007: 225) for further instances of causative-applicative syncretism from other parts of the world.

An aside is in order. Causatives are sometimes viewed as complex predicates, involving 'fusion' of two events (e.g. Frawley 1992; Shibatani 1976b), in line with a 'bisentential' approach to causation in Dowty (1972, 1979), Wunderlich (1997: 34) to name but a few. In contrast, applicatives are considered as one basic event (see McGinnis 2001; Gerdts and Kiyosawa 2005a, b), extended by an extra participant (and are thus considered similar to passives where one participant is backgrounded). The existence of the same marking for causatives and for applicatives supports the monopredicative treatment of causatives as of applicatives as valency-increasing devices.

Etymologically, such markers may go back to verbs. For instance, the suffix -*ma*- frequently occurs in Australian languages in both an applicative (illustrated in (12), for Dyirbal) and a causative meaning (as in Margany (53a–b) and other Mayic languages: Dixon 2002: 202–4). This suffix is cognate to the verb meaning 'do, make'; it could have grammaticalized from an erstwhile biclausal construction involving two predicates, one of them *ma* 'do, tell, make'.[10] However, synchronically, forms like the one in (12) are not biclausal.

This takes us to the issue of clausality in causatives. The causatives we have illustrated so far are marked with affixes, and are monoclausal in their realization. Alternatively, causatives can be expressed, monoclausally, with serial verb constructions, complex predicates of other sorts, or multiclausally, by sequences of two clauses (in periphrastic structures). We will see, in the following section, that this surface realization, including differences in their clausal status, has consequences for the semantics of a causative construction. A view that any causative is by definition biclausal since it is regarded as a priori involving two events is the result of projecting patterns of syntactic causatives found in familiar European languages onto languages with bona fide morphological causatives. This essentially outdated approach obscures the underlying principles behind the correlations between the array of marking, and the semantics of causatives, attested cross-linguistically.

3. The Semantics of Causatives

Numerous languages of the world have several causative mechanisms (see the discussion, and references in Dixon 2000). They tend to differ in their meanings, and in their applicability.

3.1. *General parameters*

Relevant parameters in semantic classification of causatives include (Dixon 2000: 62–74):

---

[10] A well attested grammaticalization path involves developing a causative and an applicative out of a component of a serial verb construction, a monoclausal structure consisting of several verbs (see Foley and Olson 1985; Durie 1997 and Aikhenvald 2006a, for further references and a summary of criteria for, and grammaticalization paths in, serial verb constructions). In Alamblak, a Sepik Hill language from Papua New Guinea, the verb *hay* 'give' in serial verb constructions gave rise to both causative and a benefactive applicative (Bruce 1988). Further, similar examples are in Aikhenvald (2006a: 32).

(17) Semantic parameters in causatives
RELATING TO VERB IN TERMS OF ITS SEMANTIC AND SYNTACTIC FEA-
TURES: (1) action/state; (2) transitivity;[11]
RELATING TO THE CAUSEE: (3) control on the part of the Causee or lack
thereof; (4) willingness on the part of the Causee or lack thereof; (5)
affectedness or not of the Causee;
RELATING TO CAUSER AND THE CAUSATION ITSELF: (6) direct or indirect causation; (7) intentional and controlled or accidental and non-
controlled action; (8) naturalness of the activity; (9) involvement of
the Causer in the activity.[12]

A causative in a language may reflect some of these parameters. In the
examples (2) and (6) above, the Causee is fully affected; the causation
is direct; the Causer is acting with intention and effort, and exercising
control.

Semantic parameters within each group interrelate with each other.
For instance, 'direct' causation is often intentional and controlled by
the Causer. However, whether the Causer achieves the result ('causation') intentionally or accidentally may be independent of the parameter 'direct'. A causative marked with a prefix in Kammu (Svantesson
1983: 103–11) is used if the Causer acts intentionally; but the causation
can be interpreted as direct or indirect, since this parameter is not
relevant.

A language may have several markers, each with a different meaning. In Tarascan (Maldonado and Nava L. 2002: 175), -ku- marks a
causative implying lack of 'volitional control' and intention, and -ta-
marks intentional causation. In Mapudungun (Araucanian, spoken
in Chile and Argentina), active verbs and inactive uncontrolled verbs
take different causative suffixes. As shown by Golúscio (2007: 219–20),

---

[11] Transitivity is approached as a syntactic, and not a semantic parameter (in
contrast to Hopper and Thompson 1980). Transitivity is defined in terms of the
number of the verb's arguments.
[12] See Saksena (1980, 1982a, b) for the parameter 'direct' versus 'indirect' causation
as it applies to Hindi causatives (also see Kachru 1976; Masica 1976). For instance,
the 'directness' of causation may correlate with how far the Causer is removed from
the 'caused' action. See Shibatani and Pardeshi (2002: 102–3) for further parameters
within this 'sociative' domain of causation. This issue is addressed in further detail
by Rose and Guillaume (2010). Each of these semantic parameters may acquire
grammatical encoding (as demonstrated in empirically-based cross-linguistic studies
of causatives in Dixon 2000, Comrie 1976a, 1981a) (in some languages, such as
English, a distinction between direct and indirect causation may not be expressed
and is based on pragmatics: see McCawley 1978).

the selection of one of the morphological causatives is governed by features of the Causee as animate, human and individuated and the degree of control over the caused event.

A language may combine a morphological causative with a lexical causative and also analytic, or periphrastic, syntactic causative constructions. Comrie (1981a: 164–7, 1989: 171–4) suggested that the continuum of formal expression of causatives, from analytic/periphrastic to morphological (that is, marked with an affix, reduplication, or another morphological process) to lexical, correlates with their meaning—that is, from less direct to more direct causation, and also from high control to low control on the part of the Causee (also see Haiman 1983: 783–5, 1985: 108–11; and Givón 1990: 556, for similar suggestions concerning the meaning-form correlations in causatives).

Dixon (2000: 74–7) proposes a number of correlations between the various semantic parameters relating to the verb, to the Causer and to the Causee, correlating with 'compactness' of expression. For instance, direct causation tends to be expressed by a more compact mechanism than indirect causation (Parameter 6 in (17))—that is, with morphological rather than with analytic causative if a language has both. Natural and intentional causation tends to be marked in a more compact way than causation involving effort. So, for instance, intentional causation in Kammu (Mon-Khmer) and Chrau (Austronesian) is marked with a morphological causative, accidental causation is expressed with complex predicates in Kammu (Svantesson 1983: 103–11), and with a morphological causative and a periphrastic construction in Chrau (Thomas 1969; Thomas 1971).

Causatives can be arranged on a scale according to the 'compactness' of their expression (what Dixon calls 'compactness scale'). The more compact the expression, the more direct the causation. This is what we would expect following the principles of iconic motivation for expressing grammatical categories (in the spirit of Haiman 1983, 1985). But note that the compactness scale reflects tendencies rather than steadfast rules. These tendencies underlie our expectations for a morphological causative to refer to direct, natural and intentional causation.

Another formal parameter relevant for the semantics of causatives— introduced by Shibatani and Pardeshi (2002: 111–2)—is their productivity: the less productive and more restricted the causative, the likelier it is to express direct—rather than indirect—causation. (Also see

Comrie 1981a: 170; Masica 1976: 58–60; and Nedyalkov and Silnitsky 1973: 7). So, in Tarascan, the lexically restricted causative -ku is only used for direct causation, while the more productive causative -ta can refer to both direct and indirect causation.

This supports the general idea behind the compactness scale. Non-productive, or partially productive, causative markers are somewhat similar to lexical causatives (and often give rise to them, historically). We return to these issues in §4, and then in §7.

The point of the discussion and the examples in this section is to provide a bird's eye view of semantic parameters relevant for causative constructions. These provide a background for further discussion in the following sections.

We will now turn to a series of recurrent polysemous patterns of morphological causatives.

3.2. *Causatives which do not increase valency*

A causative construction involves adding a new participant, a 'Causer'.[13] In other words, a causative implies increasing the number of participants, and affecting the verb's valency (besides imparting other meanings to the constructions: see Saksena 1982a, b, for examples from Hindi). However, in a number of languages, a causative affix is straightforwardly valency-increasing only if applied to intransitive verbs. With transitive verbs, the effect of the same marker may be rather different.

---

[13] The Causer is in the function of a transitive subject (A). That valency-increase by introducing a new subject participant is a syntactically salient feature of causatives is corroborated by causatives' additional syntactic function which has nothing to do with semantics of causation: that of 'feeding' the constraint in same-subject coreference. Causative markers appear on the verbs belonging to different clauses to mark 'transitivity agreement'. This has been documented as a major function of semantically 'bleached' causative morphology in Kalmyk (Say n.d.), and also for Yupik (Mithun 2000), and Galo (Post 2008). In Tariana (Aikhenvald 2006a: 35, 2006b: 186, 195) the causative suffix appears on the second verb in directional serial verb constructions if the first verb is transitive, since matching transitivity is a definitional feature of such constructions. So, *di-ka di-thaka-i* (3sgnf-see 3sgnf-go.across-CAUS) is a directional serial verb construction meaning 'he looked across'. A construction without transitivity matching would have a different meaning, that of sequence of subevents: *di-ka di-thaka* (3sgnf-see 3sgnf-go.across) 'he looked and went across'. Along similar lines, event-argument serial verb constructions in Dyirbal require that the modifying verb should be transitivized if the major verb in the construction is transitive (see Dixon 2006a). This is also an instance of 'causatives that do not cause'; however, causative morphology here does not have any semantic implications.

Such non-valency-increasing uses are restricted to just morphological causatives—see §7.

The non-valency-increasing effects of causative morphology relate to

(i) the A: increase in manipulative effort, intentionality, volitionality and control;
(ii) the ACTION: intensive and/or iterative action;
(iii) the O: complete affectedness of the O, and multiple or large O.

These three groups of meanings are often intertwined. To illustrate them, we start with two case studies, one from New Guinea (§4) and the other from South America (§5). We then turn to further instances of 'causatives that do not cause'—that is, the same morphemes having a causative meaning alongside further meanings of intensive action, increased control and volitionality of A, and more (captured by Harrison 1993: 197–8, in his discussion of this phenomenon in Oceanic languages, under an umbrella term 'act semantic' rather than 'cause semantic'). At no point, however, do I assume that causatives 'give rise' to intensives—it could well be the other way round (see examples in the Appendix).

The exemplification in §6 is fairly exhaustive and representative of the current state of knowledge of the world's languages.

4. CAUSATIVE-MANIPULATIVE DERIVATION IN MANAMBU

I first discuss some general features of Manambu,[14] and then outline the transitivity classes in the language, before turning to the *kay-* derivation with its seemingly different effects with intransitive, and with ambitransitive verbs.

---

[14] Manambu is a member of the Ndu language family, the largest family in the Sepik area in terms of numbers of speakers. The language is spoken by about 2500 people in five villages in East Sepik Province, Ambunti district. A further 200–400 speakers of Manambu live in the cities of Port Moresby, Wewak, Lae, and Madang; a few people live in Kokopo and Mount Hagen. My fieldwork is predominantly based on the Avatip variety (I have also worked with speakers in other villages—Yawabak, Malu, and Apa:n, and to a lesser extent Yambon (Yuanab)). Some issues concerning the causative-manipulative derivation in Manambu are outlined in the author's reference grammar (Aikhenvald 2008a). This section elaborates on these, and explores them further.

4.1. *General features of Manambu*

Manambu is one of the most morphologically complex languages of the Ndu family. In terms of its typological profile, it is nominative-accusative, agglutinating with some fusion, both head- and dependent-marking (with a verb-final tendency), and predominantly suffixing. There are just two prefixes: second person imperative *a-* and *kay-* 'causative, manipulative'—which is the focus of this section.

Nouns and verbs are clearly distinguished in terms of their categories and inflectional possibilities. Nominal categories are gender, number, a system of nine case forms, and a number of derivations. Verbal categories include person, number, gender, aspect, mood, modality, direction, and a variety of clause-chaining patterns. Manambu is synthetic, with a plethora of modalities (desiderative, frustrative, etc.) and aspects, directionals on verbs, and productive verb compounding. There are two classes of adjectives: one closed (which consists of agreeing adjectives 'small', 'big', and 'fine'), and one semi-open (which includes over twenty non-agreeing adjectives, covering colour, physical properties and so on).

Grammatical relations are marked by cases, and also by the cross-referencing of subject and one other argument on the verb. Nouns distinguish nine case forms: (i) a zero-marked subject case (with the same form employed in a number of other functions, including copula complements and second arguments of some extended intransitive verbs); (ii) definite object and locational case *-Vm*; (iii) dative-aversive ('for fear of') *-Vk*; (iv) comitative *-wa*; (v) terminative ('up to a point') *-Vb*; (vi; vii) transportative 'via transport' *-say, -sap*; (viii) allative-instrumental *-Vr*; and (ix) substitutive 'instead' *-yæy*. These latter forms are versatile: they can also occur with verb roots.

4.2. *Transitivity classes*

Manambu has strictly intransitive, transitive and few ditransitive verbs. Strictly intransitive verbs include motion verbs, e.g. *yi-* 'go', *ya-* 'come', *gəp-* 'run', *tabu-* 'escape'; posture verbs, e.g. *kwa-* 'stay', *rə-* 'sit'; and a few others, such as *gra-* 'cry', *warsam-* 'be angry', and *kawi-* 'come ashore'. A few verbs can be used only transitively, e.g. *yi-* 'say, speak' and *kur-* 'do, make, get'. There are few ditransitive verbs, e.g. *kui-* 'give', and derivations based on this.

Over 80% of verbs are S = A ambitransitives. These include ingestive verbs *kə-* 'consume (food, drink, smoke)' and *jə-* 'chew', and verbs

of cognition *wukə-* 'hear, obey, understand' and *laku-* 'know, understand'. The transitive use of the latter is illustrated in (18a). In (18b),
the same verb is used intransitively.

(18a) ma:jₒ   bə   laku-na-wun   —*transitive*
       story   already know-ACT.FOC-1fem.sgSUBJ.NONPAST
       I already know/understand the story

(18b) bə   laku-na-wun   —*intransitive*
       already   know-ACT.FOC-1fem.sgSUBJ.NONPAST
       I already know (I am knowledgeable)

The verb *rali-* 'untie, be untied' is among the few S = O ambitransitives.
Its transitive use is shown in (19a). In (19b) it is used intransitively.

(19a) [wun-a   kwa:r]ₒ   rali-na-wun   —*transitive*
       I-POSS+fem.sg   grass.skirt untie-ACT.FOC-1fem.sgSUBJ.NONPAST
       I untied/have untied my grass skirt

(19b) [wun-a   kwa:r]ₛ   (ka:p)
       I-POSS+fem.sg   grass.skirt (by.itself)
       rali-na   —*intransitive*
       untie-ACT.FOC+3fem.sgSUBJ.NONPAST
       My grass skirt comes/has come untied (by itself)

We now turn to the valency-increasing morphological derivation in
Manambu, and how it applies to intransitive and to transitive verbs.

4.3. *Causative* kay- *with intransitive verbs*

The prefix *kay-* derives a transitive verb from an INTRANSITIVE, as in
(1)–(2) and (20)–(21).

(20) [wun-a   ku-su-wapwi]ₛ   apaw-a   —*intransitive*
      I-POSS+fem.sg   put-UP-clothes   old.fem.sg-3fem.sgCOP
      bəta:y   pərki-na
      already   tear(intransitive)-ACT.FOC+3fem.sgSUBJ.NONPAST
      My clothing (lit. clothing to put on, or wear) is old, it is already torn

(21) [kə   kuprap-ə ñan]ₐ   [wun-a   ku-su-wapwi]ₒ
      this.fem.sg bad-LK   child   I-POSS+fem.sg   put-UP-clothes
      kay-pərki-na   —*causativized transitive*
      CAUS-tear(intransitive)-ACT.FOC+3fem.sgSUBJ.NONPAST
      This naughty girl (fully) tore my clothing

Table 3.1. Causatives of intransitive verbs marked with prefix *kay-*: examples

INTRANSITIVE VERB	KAY-DERIVATION
nawul- 'be stretched; line up'	*kay-nawul-* 'stretch something'
dapu- 'be wrapped'	*kay-dapu-* 'wrap'
napwi- 'be unwrapped'	*kay-napwi-* 'unwrap'
wi:- 'be broken, break'	*kay-wi:-* 'break (e.g. a nut, an egg)' (1)–(2)
pərki- 'be torn' (19)	*kay-pərki-* 'tear something, e.g. a dress or piece of paper' (20)
bətuku- 'become full of air'	*kay-bətuku-* 'pump (something)'

This prefix occurs with about 100 verbs referring to states and processes (the most frequently used ones are listed in Aikhenvald 2008a: 407, and Laki and Aikhenvald forthcoming).[15] That is, the prefix is not fully productive. A few examples are in Table 3.1. It is never used with verbs referring to emotional states (such as 'be angry'), verbs of bodily states and functions, or motion, nor with most copula and posture verbs.[16] The derived transitive verbs containing *kay-* are strictly transitive.

A *kay-* derivation of an intransitive verb can acquire an idiomatic extension. The intransitive verb *blakə-* means 'be turned upside down'. This root is also attested with the causative prefix *kay-*, in *kay-blakə-* 'turn something upside down', as shown in (22a). Or it can be used in a metaphorical sense of 'conquering and fully destroying', as in (22b).

(22a)   [mən-a   val-a:m]ₒ
        you.masc-POSS+fem.sg   canoe-LK+ACC
        a-**kay**-blak
        IMPV-CAUS-be.turned.upside.down
        Turn my canoe upside down!

---

[15] Unlike some Papuan languages (see Pawley 1987, 1993, 2006), Manambu has an extensive verbal lexicon (Laki and Aikhenvald forthcoming list over 1000 monomorphemic verbs).

[16] Verbs of state and of motion do not take either of the two prefixes; so the fact that the causative-manipulative derivation cannot apply to them may be due to a morphological restriction rather than a semantic one. However, this may not be the full story: one consultant suggested that one cannot say 'I made him be angry' in Manambu because anger happens by itself, and one cannot 'force' it upon another person.

b) [kə-də   warya-kə-bana-d-ə   təp-a:m]$_O$
this-masc.sg fight-FUT-1plSUBJ.NONPAST-3masc.sgO.NONPAST-LK village-LK+ACC
  nəbəl **kay**-blakə-kə-bana-d
  today CAUS-overturn-FUT-1plSUBJ.NONPAST-3masc.sgO.NONPAST
Today we will conquer the village which we are going to fight

In terms of the semantic parameters in (17), the morphological causative in Manambu marks direct and intentional causation; the Causer
is in control, and the Causee is fully affected. So, the 'naughty girl' in
(21) tore my clothing fully because she was angry. Similarly, turning a
canoe upside down is an intentional act which involves direct action
(taking the canoe and turning it). And in (22b), 'conquering and fully
destroying' a village implies complete destruction (the Manambu are
well-known for their devastating raids against their neighbours: pic-
turesque accounts of their traditional warfare are in Harrison 1993;
also see a summary in Aikhenvald 2009b).

In other words, the *kay-* derivation is fairly straightforward argu-
ment-adding. As expected for a non-fully productive morphological
causative, it is prone to lexicalization (cf. Shibatani and Pardeshi 2002:
111). When *kay-* occurs with ambitransitive verbs, it has a different
effect.

4.4. *The meanings of* kay- *with ambitransitive and transitive verbs*

The prefix *kay-* can occur on several dozen ambitransitive and transitive verbs, all of them 'affect' verbs. (It never occurs with the few
ditransitive verbs Manambu has.) It does not then increase valency.
Its effects are as follows.

Firstly, it converts an S = A or an S = O ambitransitive verb into a
strictly transitive. That is, the transitivity status of the verb is affected.
However, *kay-* does not make such a verb into a causative: it does not
introduce a new 'Causer'.

Secondly, the semantic effect of *kay-* on ambitransitive verbs relates
to a number of parameters outlined in §3.2:

(i) the A, implying increase in manipulative effort, intentionality,
  volitionality and control;
(ii) the O: multiple or large O;
  or both (i) and (ii).

Table 3.2. Manipulatives of (ambi)transitive verbs marked with prefix *kay-*:
examples

AMBITRANSITIVE VERB	KAY- DERIVATION
lagu- 'pull' (S = A)	*kay-lagu-* 'pull with a special effort'
rapya- 'twist something (e.g. a lid or a top of a bottle); be twisted' (S = O)	*kay-rapya-* 'twist with effort'
puti- 'come off, pass out, faint'; 'take off' (S = O)	*kay-puti-* 'take off' (with effort: e.g. a small child taking shoes off)
TRANSITIVE VERB	KAY- DERIVATION
kraku- 'take (O) outside'	*kay-kraku-* 'take (O) outside applying a physical effort'
gwa- 'pull out, take out or off, e.g. sticky bits of grass or thorns off the body'	*kay-gwa-* refers to the same activity as *gwa-* applied to particularly sticky thorns

The three groups of meanings are illustrated below. For clarity, *kay-* with ambitransitive verbs is glossed as 'MANIP'.

(i) The verb *rali-* 'untie, undo' is an S = O ambitransitive, as shown in (19a) and (19b). In (23), the same verb is used with the prefix *kay-*. The ropes are tangled, and untying them requires special effort:

(23) ya:n   kə-di   ya:p   **a-rali**   **a-kay-rali**
      come+SEQ   DEM.PROX-pl   rope   IMPV-untie   IMPV-MANIP-untie
      Come and untie these ropes; untie them with special effort (since they
          are entangled)

This same verb *kay-rali-* was used to describe the action such as unrolling and disentangling wool which a toddler had messed up—once again, the action involved a lot of effort. Further examples are given in Table 3.2.

(ii) The prefix *kay-* with an ambitransitive or a transitive verb can refer to an action involving a large O, or an O consisting of multiple parts. For instance, the transitive verb *tapu-* means 'carry', e.g. a smallish heap, as in (24a):

(24a) [væs   tukura-ku]
       grass   cover/heap.up-COMPL.SS
         [ata   tapu-kə-tua-di]
         then   carry-FUT-1sgSUBJ.NONPAST-3plO.NONPAST
       Having heaped up (some) grass, I will carry it (in my arms)

The *kay-* derivation *kay-tapu-* refers to carrying heaps of stuff, e.g. a stack of clothes, or grass, in one's arms.

(24b) ñapwi_O   **kay**-tapu-na
       firewood   MANIP-carry-ACT.FOC+3fem.sgSUBJ.NONPAST
       She is carrying (a large amount of) firewood

Along similar lines, the S = O ambitransitive verb *buti-* 'fold (any length of object); be folded' applies to folding a small or a medium-sized object, such as a piece of clothing. In contrast, **kay**-*buti-* means 'fold something carefully, especially a long object, such as a big sheet'.

This meaning is closely linked with the meaning discussed at (i) above, since in this case carrying a large amount of firewood involved a physical effort.

The prefix *kay-* has limited productivity. It cannot be used with ingestive verbs, verbs referring to cognition, or verbs of hitting and killing. But it can occur with the generic verb *məgi-* 'do whatever' (see Aikhenvald 2009a, on other generic verbs in the language). This verb, used as a replacement for a verb a speaker cannot remember, or does not wish to specify, is both S = A and S = O ambitransitive. In (25a) it is used transitively, and in (25b) and (25c) it appears as an intransitive verb. This is the only verb in the language with such properties.

(25a) wun-a:m   məgi-də-d
       I-LK+ACC   do.whatever-3masc.sgSUBJ.PAST-3masc.sgO.PAST
       He did whatever to me (in the context: hit me)

(25b) wulək   məgi-d
       lightning   do.whatever-3masc.sgSUBJ.NONPAST
       Lightning did whatever (in the context: struck)

(25c) lə-kə   mæn atawa   məgi-l
       she-OBL+fem.sg   leg   like.that do.whatever-3fem.sgSUBJ.PAST
         kuprap   ta:l
         bad   become+3fem.sgSUBJ.PAST
       Her leg 'whatevered' like this (in the context: became shrivelled), it
       became bad

The form *kay-məgi-* means 'do whatever with a special effort' and is strictly transitive. This is used as replacement for any verb of affect implying forceful action—such as untying or tying something with effort, or breaking. An example is (26):

(26)   kə-də   təp   a-**kay**-məgi
       this-masc.sg   coconut   IMPV-MANIP-do.whatever
       'Whatever' this coconut! (in the context: break it with force)

Overusing the verb *məgi-* is considered a feature of careless speakers. After I repeated (26), I was instructed by one of my teachers to use a more specific verb instead. In this context, it was a strictly transitive *vya-prapi-* (lit. hit-split) 'hit by splitting' (this is how the coconut was to be broken). Another time the verb *kay-məgi-* (MANIP-do.whatever) was used to refer to breaking stalks of an edible green. Then, its appropriate replacement was judged to be *kay-wuti-* (CAUS-be.broken.in.two). That is, *kay-məgi-* (MANIP-do.whatever) 'do whatever with force' can replace a *kay-* causative or another transitive verb of affect.

That *kay-* can be used on the ubiquitous *məgi-*, highly frequent in everyday conversation, indicates that this morpheme is still active, despite its lack of full productivity. Unlike the *kay-* causative—see (22b)—derivations containing the manipulative *kay-* never develop idiomatic meanings.

4.5. *Other causative techniques in Manambu*

Manambu has a number of other ways of expressing causation. Cause-effect verb compounds, normally consisting of two verbs, may be used to express direct causation. Just like *kay-* causatives, they are not fully productive. The first component is a transitive verb of hitting or stepping on something, and the second component is an intransitive verb expressing the resulting state, e.g. *vya-pərki-* (hit-tear(intransitive)) 'tear by hitting', *væsə-pərki-* (step-tear(intransitive)) 'tear by stepping (on something)'. Cause-effect compounds cannot involve any of the *kay-* derivations. Unlike the *kay-* causatives, they specify the manner in which causation was achieved. Cause-effect compounds can be ambitransitive (unlike the *kay-* formations).[17]

---

[17] Cause-effect compounds form one phonological and grammatical word; their status as bona fide compounds is addressed at length in Aikhenvald (2008a: 344–7), in the context of other verb compounds in the language. These compounds

Cause-effect compounds can develop idiomatic meanings, similarly to *kay-* causatives. For instance, *væsə-blakə-* (step-be.overturned) has an additional meaning of 'exterminate' (for instance, in an attack or in a battle). This is comparable to an extension of a *kay-* derivation *kay-blakə-* (CAUS-be.overturned) to mean 'conquer' (in (22b)).

A further type of causative construction in Manambu is a biclausal structure, a periphrastic causative. This is fully productive, and can be used with verbs of any transitivity value with the meaning of indirect causation. An example is in (27):[18]

(27) [maːj   bla-k-na]
      story   talk-FUT-ACT.FOC+3fem.sgNONPAST
          [kur-na-ñən]
      do-ACT.FOC-2fem.sgSUBJ.NONPAST
      You are acting so that she will talk; you incite her to talk

This example consists of two juxtaposed finite clauses separated by a pause. Just like many Papuan languages of New Guinea, Manambu has extensive clause-chaining, involving non-finite conjoined clauses. These do not participate in causative constructions.

This is quite expected, and fully consistent with the predictions in Dixon (2000) and Shibatani and Pardeshi (2002), that a biclausal periphrastic causative construction is likelier to express indirect than direct causation. Such correlation between meaning and form of a construction agrees with the 'compactness scale' (see §3.1). None of the causative mechanisms other than *kay-* derivations have non-valency increasing meanings.

5. CAUSATIVES AND OTHER VALENCY-INCREASING DERIVATIONS IN TARIANA

We first provide background information on the structure of Tariana[19] and its transitivity classes. Tariana belongs to the Içana-Vaupés

---

are comparable to single-word serial verbs in other languages, such as Alamblak (Aikhenvald 2006a).

[18] A comparison of various causative-marking techniques in Manambu is in Aikhenvald (2008a: 412–16). These are not addressed here because they are not directly relevant to the issue of polysemous causatives.

[19] Tariana is spoken by about 100 people in two villages, Santa Rosa and Periquitos, in the multilingual Vaupés River Basin. The language has undergone massive areal diffusion from the neighbouring East Tucanoan languages. As a result, it is typologically

subgroup of North-Arawak. Its closest relatives are Baniwa of Içana and Piapoco (see §5.4.4 and §6.1.2).

5.1. *Background information*

Tariana is agglutinating with some fusion, and predominantly suffixing, with a few prefixes. It is highly synthetic, with over 21 slots in its verbal structure. As in most Arawak languages, grammatical relations in Tariana are marked with personal prefixes, roughly on an active-stative basis. There is no object marking on the verb. Every verbal root in Tariana is either prefixed or prefixless. Prefixed verbs can be transitive (e.g. *-wapa-ita* 'wait for something'), ditransitive (*-bueta* 'teach'), ambitransitive (A = S_a, e.g. *-ira* 'drink' (3); or O = S_a, e.g. *-thuka* 'break') or active intransitive (S_a, e.g. *-pita* 'bathe'). Most prefixless verbs are stative intransitive S_O (e.g. *kasitana* 'be annoyed'); some are A = S_O ambitransitives (e.g. *harame* 'be scared', *nhesiri* 'like (not food)') or O = S_O ambitransitives (*hui* 'like (food); be tasty'). Ditransitives are few.

Grammatical relations are also marked by cases, on a subject/non-subject basis. This system was calqued from East Tucanoan; but the markers are of Arawak origin (the core case markers go back to reanalyzed locative and oblique markers: see Aikhenvald 2002a).

Examples (5) and (6) illustrate the marking of A with prefixes; the subject of an active intransitive verb (Sa) is also marked with prefixes as in (28):

(28)   nu-a   nu-pita-de   —*intransitive*
       1sgS_a-go   1sgS_a-have.a.bath-FUT.CERT
       I will go and have a bath

No person markers occur on prefixless stative verbs, in agreement with the general split-S profile of Tariana inherited from Proto-Arawak; an example is at (3).

---

different from its Arawak relatives. The differences between Santa Rosa and Periquitos do not impede mutual intelligibility. Aikhenvald (2003) is a reference grammar. Throughout this chapter, 'Tariana' is used as a cover term for both dialects. Dialects are specified only if the forms or functions are different.

5.2. *Increasing valency in Tariana*

Tariana has two suffixes, -*i* and -*i-ta*, which form morphological caus-atives from most intransitive verbs and from five $A = S_a$ ambitransitives. Four of these involve ingestive verbs -*ira* 'drink' (see (6)), -*sita* 'smoke', -*eme* 'sniff snuff' and -*peru* 'lick'. The fifth one is -*ñapa* 'bless (some-one), be capable of blessing (in general)'.

Morphological causatives in Tariana always involve direct causation, as shown in (4), (6) and (29). Other ambitransitive and transitive verbs can be causativized with causative serial verb constructions. Indirect causation is expressed through syntactic causatives (see Aikhenvald 2003 and 2006b for further details of their typological properties).

The semantics and distribution of the two causative markers in Tar-iana are summarized in Table 3.3. Further discussion, and examples, are in §§5.3–4 below. Table 3.3 shows that the two dialects of Tariana share the morphological causatives in their valency-increasing func-tions. They differ in their other extensions: the Tariana of Santa Rosa marks intensity of action and complete involvement of the O, while the Tariana of Periquitos uses the same morphological means to mark multiplicity of O.

Table 3.3. Morphological causatives and their meanings in Tariana

ARKER	INTRANSITIVE VERBS	FIVE $S_a = A$ VERBS	MOST $S_a = A$ VERBS	
(CAUS1)	adding an A argument	—	the verb becomes strictly transitive; a peripheral constituent needs to be stated (30b, 31b, 32b, 33b)	
-*ta* (CAUS1–CAUS2)	• adding an A argument • marking fully affected O and intensive forceful action (37)	adding an A argument (6)	the verb becomes strictly transitive; a peripheral constituent needs to be stated	
			TARIANA OF SANTA ROSA: fully affected O and completed or intensive action (34, 35)	TARIANA OF PERIQUITOS: multiple O (40)

5.3. *Transitivity-increasing suffix* -i

Causatives on intransitive verbs are marked with the suffix *-i*—this is shown in (4) for a stative verb, and in (32) for an active (prefixed) verb. Note that in (29) and in (4) the O is not fully affected.

(29) emite-nuku$_O$ nu-a   nu-pita-**i**-de   —*causativized transitive*
     child.sg-TOP.NON.A/S 1sg-go 1sg-bathe-CAUS1–FUT.CERT
     I will bathe the child (e.g. a little, or just his/her face)[20]

When this morpheme occurs on the majority of ambitransitive verbs, it has a somewhat different meaning, comparable to an applicative (§2.2).

- The verb becomes strictly transitive.
- A peripheral constituent has to be stated, or implied. This is similar to the causative-applicative syncretism discussed in §2 above. Which oblique constituent has to be stated, or implied, depends on the verb, and the conventionalized activities associated with it.

For the ambitransitive verb *-ñha* 'point' (shown in (30a)), it is the 'shaman', as in (30b):

(30a) emite-nuku$_O$ di-ñha-pidana
      child.sg-TOP.NON.A/S 3sgnf-point.at-REM.P.REP
      He pointed at the child

(30b) emite-nuku$_O$ (kañapa-nuku$_{ADDR}$)
      child.sg-TOP.NON.A/S shaman-TOP.NON.A/S
        di-ñha-**i**-pidana
        3sgnf-point.at(tr)-CAUS1-REM.P.REP
      He showed the child to the shaman ('blesser') (briefly; or just one body part affected with disease)

For the ambitransitive verb *-wana* 'call, shout', the oblique to be stated is typically the purpose:

---

[20] For the sake of presentational clarity, examples are given in an underlying form: in modern Tariana *-a-i-* results in *e*. The sequence *a-i* survives in archaic song registers.

(31a) emite-nuku$_O$ nu-wana-de
       child.sg-TOP.NON.A/S   3sgnf-call-FUT.CERT
       I will call the child (just shouting his name)

(31b) emite-nuku$_O$ nu-wana-i-de
       child.sg-TOP.NON.A/S   3sgnf-call(tr)-CAUS1–FUT.CERT
         (di-bueta-karu$_{PURPOSE}$)
         3sgnf-study-PURP
       I will call the child (for some purpose, e.g. to study)

And for the S_a = A ambitransitive verb -*ñapa*, the typical argument is the traditional instrument involved in the activity of 'blessing' by a shaman:

(32a) emite-nuku$_O$ di-ñapa-ka
       child.sg-TOP.NON.A/S   3sgnf-bless(tr)-REC.P.VIS
       He has blessed/has been blessing the child

(32b) emite-nuku$_O$ (tu:me-ne$_{INSTR}$)
       child.sg-TOP.NON.A/S   magic.breath-INSTR
         di-ñapa-i-ka
         3sgnf-bless(tr)-CAUS1–REC.P.VIS
       He blessed the child (or part of his body) with magic breath

If the S = A ambitransitive verb -*wapa* 'wait (for someone), attend to' (33a) is used with the marker -*i*, it typically refers to 'waiting for some-one with gifts' (in the situation of Ritual Offering Feast 'Dabucuri' (Tariana *pudari*)), or 'waiting for a game animal with a weapon, e.g. a rifle', as in (33b):

(33a) dipumi   ka-nu-nuku   wa-wapa-sida
       later   REL-come-TOP.NON.A/S   1pl-wait-YET
       We will be waiting as yet for the one who is coming later

(33b) itʃiri   wa-wapa-i-sida   (sipi-ne)
       game   1pl-wait-CAUS1–YET   rifle-COMIT
       We will as yet be waiting for the game with a rifle

The suffix -*i* has thus a different effect depending on whether it applies to an intransitive, or an ambitransitive verb. In the latter case, it oper-ates as if it were a general applicative. Its semantics depends on the conventionalized situation associated with each verb. So, (31b) does not mean *'call with someone else'. And the form -*wapa-i* in (33b) does not mean *'wait for the purpose of doing something'.

The cultural construal of events in Tariana helps us understand the meanings of each applicative extension of the polysemous -*i*: the appropriate reading of each form is tied to a typical activity of a typical subject and/or a typical conventionalized oblique. So, the applicative of 'bless' (32b) can only be understood as '(shaman) blessing with something'. A reading like 'blessing for some purpose' would not be appropriate (this option has indeed been rejected when I volunteered it), in contrast to the verb 'call' (31b), for which 'purpose' is the appropriate reading of the function of the additional oblique.

Along similar lines, the extension of a causative to an instrumental applicative in Matses (Panoan: Fleck 2002, forthcoming)[21] can only be understood if one has cultural knowledge of Matses hunting practices. As a result, causative-applicatives in Tariana are prone to lexicalization.

The partly unpredictable meaning of applicative-like use of causative markers in Tariana highlights the relevance of cultural conceptualization of events, and the importance of having a knowledge of cultural and traditional background for the language to be investigated. This is reminiscent of how the possibility of putting certain verbs into one serial verb construction depends on whether the whole matches a 'recognizable event-type' (Durie 1997: 322; Jarkey 1991: 169; Aikhenvald 2006a). Thus, in White Hmong, 'dance' and 'listen to music' are normally viewed as distinct events, and thus cannot form one serial verb construction. In contrast, the actions of 'blowing bamboo pipes' and 'dancing' are inseparable; they form one event, and can be combined into a serial verb construction (Jarkey 1991: 169; and Durie 1997: 329). A function of verb serialization is to represent complex events, which are—at least partly—a cultural construct.

This is somewhat similar to how the 'name-worthiness' of an activity provides a reason for nominal and verbal lexical compounds. For instance, in English, compounds like *mountain-climbing* or *berry-picking* are coined as names of recognizable activities. A new compound, for example, *ladder-climbing*, makes one immediately suspect that it must refer to an activity recognized as such in some context

---

[21] The plethora of meanings of the Tariana causative-applicative marker adds another dimension to the observation by Shibatani and Pardeshi (2002: 121) that 'the causative/applicative syncretism is seen when there is a sociative reading associated with the causative construction'.

(see Mithun 1984: 848). In this sense, an applicative, and a serial verb construction, just like compounds, may have a lexical status. Co-conceptualization of culturally associated events thus leads to the creation of idiomatic formations.

Comparable differences in the effect of transitivizing morphology on intransitive, and on transitive verbs, have been noted in other languages. Bare—a North Arawak language from the same family as Tariana—has a suffix -sa which forms causatives of intransitive verbs, e.g. -hetuka 'to be afraid', -hetuka-sa 'frighten', -baraka 'run', -baraka-sa 'make run, hunt', and also of the ingestive verb -dia 'drink' (-dia-sa 'to make drink, make drunk'). When used with a handful of transitive verbs, the effect of -sa is applicative-like. For instance, the verb -d'ekada means 'do or make something', and -d'ekada-sa means 'do something to somebody; make something for somebody'. How productive this was remains an open question: my grammar was based on work with the last fluent speaker of the language (Aikhenvald 1995).

In Panyjima (Dench 1991: 190–1), the 'placement' suffix -thu- 'modifies the sense of the root such that the verb action generally has a specific locational endpoint and is clearly controlled'. This suffix 'operates as a causative' on intransitive verb stems, e.g. panti-thu-L (sit(intr)-PLACE-CONJ) 'set, sit (someone) down (tr)', karipa-thu-L (go. up(intr)-PLACE-CONJ) 'lift up (tr)'. On transitive stems 'there is not the same increase in valency', e.g. thaa-thu-L (send(tr)-PLACE-CONJ) 'pour (into) (tr)', ngarna-thu-L (eat(tr)-PLACE-CONJ) 'bite into (tr)'. From these examples, it appears that transitive verbs marked with -thu- require an obligatory location.[22]

5.4. The valency-increasing marker -i-ta

The suffix -i-ta consists of the causative -i and an additional morpheme -ta glossed here as 'second causative' (CAUS2). This is used as a straightforward causative on the five ambitransitive verbs mentioned at the beginning of §4: see (6) and (37). Verbs -ira 'drink', -eme 'sniff snuff', -sita 'smoke' and -peru 'lick' can never occur with just -i to form a causative; the verb -ñapa 'bless' behaves somewhat differently (see below). These uses are shared by the two dialects of Tariana. We

---

[22] However, examples are too few to judge; the behaviour of a cognate morpheme in Martuthunira (Dench 1995: 161) is suggestive but inconclusive (Alan Dench, p.c.).

now turn to the meanings of the marker *-i-ta* with other verbs, first in the Tariana of Santa Rosa (§5.4.1–2), and then in the Tariana of Periquitos (§5.4.3).

5.4.1. *The marker* -i-ta *with the majority of ambitransitive and transitive verbs in the Tariana of Santa Rosa*
With the majority of ambitransitive and transitive verbs, adding the suffix *-ta* to a verb already marked with *-i* relates to:

(ii) the O/CAUSEE: complete affectedness of O/Causee which tends to be topical or definite;
(iii) the ACTION OF CAUSATION: completed and/or intensive action.

We can recall that a morphological causative with *-i* of the intransitive verb 'wash', implies that the O, 'child', is not fully affected, as in (29). In (34), the same verb was used with the accompanying *-ta* and it implies that the action was intensive and the O completely involved:

(34) [emite-nuku]$_O$ nu-a   nu-pita-**i-ta**-de
      child.sg-TOP.NON.A/S   1sg-go   1sg-bathe-CAUS1–CAUS2–FUT.CERT
      I will bathe the child (all over and a lot)

Along similar lines, *-wapa-i* in (33b) does not carry any implications as to whether the O was affected or whether the action was intensive or not. In contrast, the verb *-wapa-i-ta* in (35) implies that I am waiting for all my relatives. The intensity of the process of waiting is underscored by *kiaku* 'strongly, patiently':

(35) kiaku   nu-wapa-**i-ta**-naka   nu-kesi-nipe-nuku
      strongly   1sg-wait-CAUS1–CAUS2–PRES.VIS   1sg-friend-PL-TOP.NON.A/S
      pumeni-peri-ne
      sweet-COLL-INSTR
      I am patiently waiting for my relatives with drinks and sweet things
      (as an offering)

The ambitransitive verb *-ñapa* 'bless', illustrated in (32a), is unique in Tariana. When it occurs with the suffix *-i*, the meaning of the resulting derivation is applicative-like, similar to most other ambitransitive verbs—see (32b). When an additional *-ta* is added, the resulting form may refer to intensive action performed fully with the O also being fully affected:

(36) emite-nuku$_\text{O}$ (tu:me-ne$_\text{INSTR}$)
     child.sg-TOP.NON.A/S   magic.breath-INSTR
       di-ñapa-**i-ta**-ka
       3sgnf-bless(tr)-CAUS1–CAUS2–REC.P.VIS
     He fully blessed the child with magic breath (fully performing the
       procedure of blessing)

We can recall that *-ñapa* was mentioned in §5.2 as one of the five
ambitransitive verbs which derive a morphological causative. This
causative can only be derived with *-i-ta* (never with *-i*: see Table 3.3).
So, *-ñapa-i-ta* can have a causative reading:

(37) emite-nuku$_\text{O1}$ ka-ñapa-nuku$_\text{O2}$ (tu:me-ne$_\text{INSTR}$)
     child.sg-TOP.NON.A/S   REL-bless-TOP.NON.A/S   magic.breath-INSTR
       di-ñapa-**i-ta**-ka
       3sgnf-bless(tr)-CAUS1–CAUS2–REC.P.VIS
     He made the shaman (lit. 'blesser') bless the child

The arguments marked with the topical non-subject case (used for any
non-subject constituent, including objects), 'child' and 'shaman', differ
in one syntactic property: only the 'original' object, 'child', can be passivized upon (see, e.g., Aikhenvald 2003: 258–60). The two readings—
'make someone bless the child' and 'fully bless the child'—can only be
distinguished by context.

5.4.2. *Repetition of the marker* -i-ta *in the Tariana of Santa Rosa*
The suffix *-i-ta* can be repeated, and then it expresses the intensity of
causation. The only examples of this are with causativized prefixless
(stative) verbs. The verb *pusa* 'be wet' is intransitive. It can be causativized with either *-i* or *-i-ta*, with a difference in meaning. This is shown
in (38a–b).

(38a) iya   nu-na   di-pusa-**i**-ka
      rain   1sg-OBJ   3sgnf-be.wet-CAUS1–REC.P.VIS
      The rain made me (partly) wet

(38b) iya   nu-na   di-pusa-**i-ta**-ka
      rain   1sg-OBJ   3sgnf-be.wet-CAUS1–CAUS2–REC.P.VIS
      The rain made me (fully) wet

If the marker *-i-ta* is repeated, the implication is that the O was made
wet through and through (further examples are in Aikhenvald 2003:
273–4):

(39)   iya-yāna   piaça-pu-nuku
       rain-PEJ   piaçaba-CL:BUNDLE-TOP.NON.A/S
          di-pusa-**i-ta-i-ta**-na
          3sgnf-be.wet-CAUS1–CAUS2–CAUS1–CAUS2–REM.P.VIS
          The naughty rain made my bundle of piaçaba leaves well and truly wet
          through indeed

That is, repeating the 'double causative' does not result in two separate
events of causation. This is quite unlike Movima (see (7)–(8)) where a
double causative has a straightforward meaning, of two events of causation. In Tariana, the 'double causative' indicates increased intensity,
and—at least in this case—also complete involvement of the object.
Tariana does not have any verbal reduplication; and no grammatical
morpheme other than the causative can be reduplicated.[23]

   This repetition of the causative markers is a well-established feature of the language. It is consistently used by most competent older
speakers, while younger speakers tend to ignore and even fail to rec-
ognize them. This repetition is reminiscent of Warekena of Xié (see
(45) below).

5.4.3. *The marker* -i-ta *with the majority of ambitransitive and transitive verbs in the Tariana of Periquitos*

The meanings of intensive action and complete involvement of the
O are a feature of the marker -*i-ta* in the Tariana of Santa Rosa. In
the Periquitos variety, adding -*ta* to causative-applicative form marked
with -*i* indicates multiple O. That is, the meaning of (35) is 'I am waiting for my many relatives'. Since -*ta* on the verb implies a plural O,
(34) is ungrammatical. The grammatical version in the Periquitos
variety is (40). Note an additional difference in meaning: -*ta* does not
impart the overtone of intensive action:

(40)   emipeni-nuku   nu-a   nu-pita-**i-ta**-de
       child.pl-TOP.NON.A/S   1sg-go   1sg-bathe-CAUS1–CAUS2–FUT.CERT
       I will bathe the children

---

[23] There is no reason to surmise that reduplication was a more general pattern in
an earlier stage of the language (as suggested by an anonymous referee), since there
are no traces of reduplication elsewhere in the grammar, nor in the closely related
languages Baniwa of Içana/Kurripako, Piapoco and Guarequena.

Speakers of the Periquitos variety do not use the forms with the repeated *-i-ta* (as in (39)). This may well be due to the grammatically innovative character of the Periquitos Tariana (this issue, tangential to our present discussion, was discussed in Aikhenvald 2003: 620–6).

5.4.4. *Is* -ta *a causative marker?*

There is no doubt that *-i* is a bona fide morphological causative with intransitive verbs, marking valency increase with transitive verbs. Below, I offer further arguments to justify glossing *-ta-* as a causative marker.

Firstly, *-ta* forms part of the suffix *-i-ta* which is the only causativizing morpheme used with the five ambitransitive verbs (§5.2). Secondly, this formative appears in a fair number of transitive verbs which may or may not have been historically derived, e.g. *-nawaita* 'separate, pull apart' (possibly related to *-nawa* 'go by, pass by'), *-adaita* 'prevent'. Thirdly, *-ta* and *-i-ta* are in free variation in a few examples where they are used as verbalizers, e.g. *di-rawa* 'his provision', *di-rawa-i-ta, di-rawa-ta* 'he provides (someone) with provisions or food)'. This alternation is quite unusual in the context of Tariana phonology (Aikhenvald 2003), since this is the only instance in the language when a vowel sequence *a-i* is in free variation with *i* (there is a tendency towards free variation of the sequence *ai*, a diphthong *ay*, and a single vowel *e*, e.g. *kai* 'be painful', *kay* 'like this' can be both pronounced as [ke] in a rapid register).

And finally, the marker *-ta* is a reflex of Proto-North-Arawak **-ta* 'causativizer; marker of valency increase' (Aikhenvald 1998: 380; 2001). In some North Arawak languages—e.g. Yucuna (Schauer and Schauer 2000: 521; 2005: 307) and Guarequena (González Ñáñez 1997: 135)—*-ta* is used only to causativize intransitive verbs. In Achagua (Wilson 1992: 94) the reflex of Proto-North-Arawak **-ta, -da* 'causative', is used with both intransitive and transitive verbs, e.g. *wáa* 'sit down', *wáa-ida* 'put; make sit down', *wéni* 'buy', *wéni-da* 'sell, make buy'. In Warekena of Xié, this same morpheme *-ta* is used with intransitive verbs, and with just two ambitransitive verbs, *-kurua* 'drink' (causative *-kurua-ta* 'make drink') and *-gura* 'peel' (causative *-gura-ta* 'make peel'). Further discussion of Warekena is in §6.1.2 below (especially (44) and (45)).

The causative *-sa* in Bare (a regular reflex of Proto-Arawak **-ta*) has different meanings with transitive and with intransitive verbs—see the end of §5.3. There is thus ample historical evidence that *-ta* was an older causative form; however, synchronically in Tariana it does not have a straightforwardly causative function.

The form *-i-ta* as a marker of causative in Tariana is shared with its closest relatives, Baniwa of Içana (Taylor 1990; my own data) and Piapoco (Klumpp 1990)—see §6.1.2.[24]

We now turn to a cross-linguistically-based appraisal of non-valency-increasing overtones of causative morphology.

6. NON-VALENCY INCREASING CAUSATIVES: A CROSS-LINGUISTIC PERSPECTIVE

The non-valency-increasing semantic effects of causative morphology relate to three groups of semantic parameters listed in §3.2. We now discuss the examples relevant to each group of these parameters one by one. Languages where non-valency-increasing meanings of causative morphology are restricted to transitive and ambitransitive verbs are considered in §6.1. In §6.2 we turn to languages where there are no such restrictions.

6.1. *Non-valency-increasing morphological causatives with transitive and ambitransitive verbs*

In terms of their semantics, morphological causatives with a non-valency-increasing effect can relate to the properties of the subject (A)—see §6.1.1. Or they can relate to the properties of the action—see §6.1.2; or to both—see §6.1.3. They can also reflect the features of the object (O)—see §6.1.4.[25]

6.1.1. *Relating to the A*
Causative markers can relate to (i) the A, involving increase in *manipulative effort, intentionality, volitionality* and *control*, as illustrated for Manambu in §4. In Manambu, the marker used to derive causatives of intransitive verbs marks increase in the manipulative effort on behalf of the A when used with transitive verbs.

---

[24] The causative marker *-i* appears to go back to Proto-North-Arawak (see Aikhenvald 2001).

[25] The issue of morphological causative with ditransitive verbs is only addressed here inasmuch as it is mentioned in individual grammars (see §6.1.4, for Gayo, based on Eades 2005).

A similar pattern has been described for Hunzib (Northeast Caucasian: van den Berg 1995: 107–8). The suffix -*k'(V)* derives a morphological causative of intransitive and of transitive verbs:

(41a) abu-l~A~   si~O~   b-iƛe-r
      father-ERG   bear.CL.4   CL.4–kill-PRET
      Father killed the bear

(41b) maduhan-li-l~A~   abu-g   si~O~   b-iƛ'e-**k'**-er
      neighbour-OBL-ERG   father-ADESS   bear.CL.4   CL.4–kill-CAUS-PRET
      The neighbour made father kill the bear

When the suffix -*k'(V)*- occurs twice on an intransitive verb, the effect is 'double causative', as shown in (42a–c).

(42a) habur~S~   k'arƛe-r
      wheel.CL.3   turn-PRET
      The wheel turned

(42b) ož-di-l~A~   habur~O~   k'arƛe-**k'**-er
      boy-OBL-ERG   wheel.CL.3   turn-CAUS-PRET
      The boy turned the wheel

(42c) abu-l~A~   ož-di-g   habur~O~   k'arƛe-**k'e-k'**-er
      father-ERG   boy-OBL-ADESS   wheel.CL.3   turn-CAUS-CAUS-PRET
      Father made the boy turn the wheel

When the second causative marking appears on an erstwhile transitive verb—such as the verb 'kill', in (41), the result is not a double causative. The double occurrence of the causative suffix implies 'forceful' causation, but does not add any extra participants—see (43):

(43) maduhan-li-l~A~   abu-g   si~O~
      neighbour-OBL-ERG   father-ADESS   bear.CL.4
          b-iƛ'e-**k'e-k'**-er
      CL.4–kill-CAUS-CAUS-PRET
      The neighbour forced father to kill the bear

The second causative marker in Turkish has a similar semantic overtone of 'forceful causation', as noted by Zimmer (1976: 411–2): 'Another possible interpretation of a morphological double causative is as a single act of causation, with emphasis on its forcefulness' (also has been confirmed by Lars Johanson and Birsel Karakoç, p.c.). This phenomenon is described by Göksel and Kerslake (2005: 147–8) as follows: 'If the root verb is transitive (e.g. *kes-* 'cut'), an additional causative suffix is often used simply as a means of emphasizing causation, but it may also imply the addition of another intermediary. In most cases, a transitive stem with two causative suffixes is identical in meaning to its single causative counterpart'.[26]

Adding a causative marker to a transitive stem may imply intentional action, as in Tarascan (Maldonado and Nava L. 2002: 175), Tsez (Comrie 2000: 365, 368) and Finnish (Kittilä 2009: 80).

6.1.2. *Relating to the action*

A causative morpheme can express intensive action. Prefix *va-* in Leti, an Austronesian language from Southwest Maluku, derives causatives from intransitive verbs referring to states or processes, e.g. *n-tèrsa* (3sg-be.firm) 's/he/it is firm', *n-va-tèrsa* (3sg-CAUS-be.firm) 's/he/it makes (something) firm'. When used with transitive dynamic verbs, the prefix does not affect the verb's valency. Instead, it derives a verb with an 'iterative-intensive' meaning, e.g. *n-teti* (3sg-chop) 's/he/it chops (something)', *n-va-teti* (3sg-CAUS/INTENSIVE/ITERATIVE-chop) 's/he/it minces (something)' (van Engelenhoven 2004: 146–7).

The intensifying function of a causative marker in Tariana was shown in examples (34), (35) and (39). This pattern is found in a number of related languages. In Warekena of Xié (North Arawak, Brazil: Aikhenvald 1998: 366–74), the causative *-ta* derives causatives from all intransitive verbs and two transitive verbs (see §5.4.4). (44) shows the intransitive verb *kune* 'be afraid' and its causative version, *kune-ta* 'scare, make afraid'.

(44)   kune-na   ema-hã   i-kune-**ta**-paɾu
        be.afraid-I(S$_o$) 3sgnfS$_a$+shout-PAUSAL.FORM   3sgnf-fear-CAUS-PURP
        ñamari$_O$
        people
        I am afraid, (he: the evil spirit) shouts to scare people

The causative marker can be used twice, to express the extent of intensive action:

(45)   i-kune-**ta-ta**-mia   ñamari$_O$
        3sgnf-fear-CAUS-CAUS-PERFV   people
        He has already scared people very much

---

[26] No clear example of 'emphasizing causation' has been given by either author.

Baniwa of Içana, Tariana's closest relative, has a suffix -*ita*, cognate with Tariana -*i-ta* but, in contrast to Tariana, not analyzable synchronically. Its causative meaning is restricted to intransitive verbs, e.g. -*dia* 'return (intr)', -*dia-ita* 'return (something)'. When used with transitive verbs, -*ita* has an intensive or prolonged meaning, e.g. *nu-wapa* 'I am waiting', *nu-wapa-ita* 'I am waiting intensively or for a long time' (Taylor 1990: 48; my own data).

Piapoco, a North Arawak language from the same subgroup as Tariana and Baniwa of Içana, also has a causative suffix -*ída* (cognate to Baniwa -*ita* and also not analyzable synchronically). When used with intransitive verbs, this suffix produces morphological causatives, as in (46a–b) (Klumpp 1990: 88–90):

(46a)   i-chàca-ca-wa
        3sg-extinguish-POS-INTRANSITIVIZER
        It went out (a fire dies)

(46b)   i-chàca-(i)**da**-ca   lámpara$_O$
        3sg-extinguish-CAUS-POS   lamp
        He extinguished the lamp

With transitive verbs, this suffix has 'the function of intensifying the action', as in (47):

(47)   wa-chùulia-ca   *versus*   wa-chùulia-(i)**da**-ca
       1pl-command-POS   1pl-command-CAUS-POS
       We command   We strictly command

(48a) features a simple transitive verb 'wrap'. In (48b) and (48c) this same verb appears with the causativizer -*ída*. As was explained by a Piapoco speaker, in (48a) 'the boy was simply covered up with a blanket, probably just one time and on one particular night'.

(48a)   nu-épua-ca   nu-ìri-wa$_O$ táiyápi   bàwina
        1sg-wrap-POS   1sg-son-REFL   at.night   early
        I wrapped my son (in a blanket) last night

In contrast, (48b) describes 'a regular practice of heavily bundling up the child against habitual cold, as in Bogotá'.

(48b)   nu-épùa-(i)**da**-ca   nu-ìri-wa$_O$ ca-salíni-íri   i-ícha
        1sg-wrap-CAUS-POS   1sg-son-REFL   ATT-chill-masc   3sg-away.from
        I (regularly) bundled up my son against the cold

And in (48c), the causative suffix 'indicates the extra effort it takes to fold stiff, green banana leaves around crumbly, ground corn mash and tie up the bundle carefully so nothing leaks out during boiling':

(48c)   nu-épùa-(i)da-ca   síipina$_o$
        1sg-wrap-CAUS-POS   corn.tamales
        I wrapped corn tamales (in banana leaves before boiling)

In summary, the causative suffix with transitive verbs in Piapoco indicates intensive action, with a tinge of regularity and manipulative effort on behalf of the Causer. Other examples given by Klumpp (1990: 89) include a transitive verb *nu-émia-ca* (1sg-hear-POS) 'I hear' versus *nu-émìa-(i)da-ca* (1sg-hear-CAUS-POS) 'I listen carefully', invoking the idea of perceiver's controlled action. This is reminiscent of the group of meanings discussed under §6.1.3.

6.1.3. *Relating to the A and to the action*

Not uncommonly, causative markers in their non-valency-increasing uses combine reference to the manipulative effort and control on behalf of the A with reference to intensity or repetition of actions.

The multifunctional prefix *va'a-* in Boumaa Fijian (Dixon 1988: 50; 188–9; ms) forms causatives from intransitive verbs (which have a corresponding S = A ambitransitive verb) supplied with a transitive ending, e.g. *vuli* 'study (intr)', *vuli-ca* 'study (tr)', ***va'a-vuli-ca*** 'teach'.

When the prefix ***va'a-*** applies to transitive verbs and ambitransitive verbs, it may have an additional—a non-strictly-causative—meaning. It then 'implies special volition or effort on the part of the agent—one may "hear" a noise involuntarily, but "listening" involves intent', e.g. *rogo* 'be heard' (intr), *rogo-ca* 'hear (tr)', ***va'a-rogo-ca*** 'listen to' (Dixon 1988: 51).

Other examples include: *rai-ca* 'see', ***va'a-rai-ca*** 'watch, inspect, look after'; *sogo-ta-* 'close (e.g. a door) (tr)', ***va'a-sogo-ta*** 'try hard to close (e.g. a door that may not fit too well into the door frame)', *muri-a* 'follow (e.g. follow a person you can see)', ***va'a-muri-a*** 'follow, where there is some difficulty involved'. This same connotation of volition or 'effort on the part of the agent' is also present in the causative marked by ***va'a-***, e.g. ***va'a-vuli-ca*** 'teach', literally, 'exert an effort to make (someone) learn' (Dixon 1988: 51; ms).

Besides its meaning of a special effort on the part of the A (see §6.1.1), the prefix *va'a-* with S = A ambitransitives may also mean 'do many times' (iii), as in *taro-ga* 'ask', ***va'a-taro-ga*** 'ask many times (either ask many people or repeatedly ask the same question of one person)'. Some verbs are polysemous—combining both meanings, as in *cega-a* 'turn upwards (tr)', ***va'a**-cega-a* 'turn upwards assiduously'; 'keep turning up and down (e.g. many mats if looking for something)'.

Meanings, of 'deliberateness or intensity or frequency', are also characteristic of the prefix *faka-* in Tongan (a close relative of Fijian) whose primary role is to form causatives from intransitive verbs (see Churchward 1953: 31–2).

Harrison (1982: 197–8) mentions similar meanings of the causative *ka-* in Gilbertese (also Oceanic), and of *vaka-* in Bau Fijian (the standard language of the Fiji Islands). The transitivizer *-akina* in Gilbertese also has overtones of 'the additional dimension of increased actor involvement', in some instances suggesting 'purposeful intentional action towards a salient object' (Harrison 1982: 209).

The causative prefix *ka-* in Ponapean, a Micronesian language, is productively used with intransitive verbs, e.g. *ketiket* 'to be numb', ***ka**-ketiket-ih* (CAUS-be.numb-TRANSITIVIZER) 'to cause to be numb' (Rehg 1981: 215–19). In the honorific speech register of Ponapean, causativized verbs are used without implying causation, as indicators of the high status of the addressee. As Fischer (1969: 419–20) puts it, in Ponapean 'there are honorific forms of some verbs which appear analogous to forms of other verbs which are causative [...], e.g. the verb *itek* "to ask"', which has both a pseudo-causative honorific form *ke-idek* "to ask"'.[27] Using the causative prefix in the 'exaltive' honorific speech register is indicative of what Keating (1998: 87) refers to as 'implications about high-status persons being perceived as direct instigators of actions'. Once again, a causative marker indicates increased agency of the subject (the A).[28]

Along similar lines, the causative suffix *-(n)en* in Gayo, an Austronesian language of Sumatra (Eades 2005: 186–91) has a straightforward causative effect if applied to an intransitive verb root. With a transitive verb root, the same suffix may specify 'an increase in volition or intensity of the action specified'. In (49a) a simple transitive verb 'kick' is used. In (49b), this verb is marked with the causative, but there is no

---

[27] Causative markers are used honorifically in Japanese (Fischer 1969: 419), and in Nahuatl (Pittmann 1948).
[28] In some cases, the meanings of the causative derivation in Ponapean are hardly predictable. For instance, the noun *mehel* 'truth' combined with the causative *ka-* is used 'to describe an officially sanctioned final outcome, as in the final heat of a race' (Peterson 1993: 350).

additional participant—instead, the action of kicking is more intensive and, according to Eades, involves stronger volition.[29] That the kicking resulted in splitting shows the intensity of the action.

(49a)　I-tipak=è　　　　　　aku
　　　　UO-kick-3.NOM.SUBJ　I
　　　　He kicked me

(49b)　I-tipak-**ni**　　akang　asu,　mu-belah　ulu=é
　　　　UP-kick-CAUS　deer　dog　AO-split　head-3POSS
　　　　The deer kicked the dog, splitting its head

The causative marker in Atong, a Tibeto-Burman language of the Bodo-Kosh subgroup spoken in north-east India (van Breugel 2014), applies to intransitive verbs, as in (50a):

(50a)　may$_O$　tuŋ-**et**-ni-ma
　　　　rice　hot-CAUS-FUT-Q
　　　　Shall [I] make the rice hot?

This same causative marker on a transitive verb does not increase the number of arguments. Similarly to Manambu, Hunzib, and Boumaa Fijian, it indicates the A's volition, intention, and special effort. The transitive verb *cay-* 'see (tr)' is illustrated in (50b). In (50c), *cay-et* (see-CAUS) means 'look (attentively into the hole, inspecting it)' and not *'make see':

(50b)　[aŋ-mi　jora-aw]$_O$　　　　cay-na　　　　　　man?-ni-ma
　　　　1sg-GEN　love.match-ACC　see/look.at-PURP　be.able-FUT-Q
　　　　Will (you) be able to see my match in love?

(50c)　ətəkəy　cay-**et**-wa-ci=e　　　　　　　　　　phalthaŋ=aw$_O$
　　　　like.that　look-CAUS-FACTIVE-LOC-NONTOPIC　self=ACC
　　　　nuk=ok
　　　　see=PERFV
　　　　[Then he saw a deep hole with water at the bottom.] When [he] looked like that he saw himself

---

[29] Eades (2005: 190) notes that the suffix *(n)en* has somewhat different overtones with different verbs. For instance, with verb 'hear' it 'signals that the act is intentional on the part of the actor, i.e. the hearer', the meaning of the suffixed form being 'listen to'—which is similar to the effect of *va'a-* in Boumaa Fijian. See §6.1.4, for further overtones of the Gayo *-(n)en*, with the ditransitive verb 'give'.

The same suffix can express iterative action. As a result, transitive verbs accompanied with the suffix -*et* can be polysemous, and their meanings have to be disambiguated by context, e.g. *say*- 'write', *say-et* 'write with effort; write many times'.[30]

In Godoberi (Northeast Caucasian: Kibrik 1996b: 128–9) causatives can be formed on verbs of any transitivity value. Causatives of some strictly transitive verbs may not involve addition of an extra argument; 'rather, the original agent gets reinterpreted as a Causer, and the action gets intensified'. Consider the following pairs:

(51a) mak'i-di$_A$ ɫeni$_O$ čibi   —–volition of A
child-ERG   water   splash.PAST
The child splashed the water (perhaps involuntarily)

(51b) mak'i-di$_A$ ɫeni$_O$ čib-**ali**   —+volition of A
child-ERG   water   splash-CAUS.PAST
The child splashed the water (purposefully and repeatedly)

(52a) wač-u-di$_A$ ʕali-qi$_O$ q$_o$ard-i   maɫi   —+volition of Causee
brother-OBL-ERG   Ali-AD   write-INF   teach.PAST
The brother taught Ali how to write (Ali studied voluntarily)

(52b) wač-u-di$_A$ ʕali-qi$_O$ q$_o$ard-i   maɫ-**ali**   —–volition of Causee
brother-OBL-ERG   Ali-AD   write-INF   teach-CAUS.PAST
The brother taught Ali how to write (overcoming his resistance)

The causative form in (52b) can alternatively be used with the meaning of direct forceful causation; the resulting verb is then ditransitive. An example is (52c):

(52c) im-u-di$_A$ wač-u-č'u$_O$ ʕali-qi$_O$ q$_o$ard-i
father-OBL-ERG   brother-OBL-CONT.LOC   Ali-AD   write-INF
maɫ-**ali**
teach-CAUS.PAST
Father forced brother to teach Ali how to write

---

[30] A similar phenomenon appears to exist in the closely related Garo (Burling 2004: 143–4). Along similar lines, in Lachixio Zapotec the same morpheme, 'marker of activity/causation', derives causatives from intransitive verbs; when applied to transitive verbs, it indicates that the A is more active and is acting in a more purposeful manner (Mark Sicoli, p.c. 2008).

This is reminiscent of the polysemy of the Santa Rosa Tariana -*ñapa-i-ta* 'bless fully with something' in (36) and 'make someone bless someone' in (37).

6.1.4. *Relating to the O*

A morphological causative may involve marking complete affectedness of the O, and multiple or large O. In (40), from the Tariana variety of Periquitos, the erstwhile second causative marker -*ta* had just the function of indicating a multiple O. Similar examples come from Margany, and Creek.

The suffix -*ma*- in Margany, an Australian language, derives a causative, or an applicative from an intransitive verb, similarly to Yidiñ exemplified above (see Breen 1981: 319–20; and Dixon 2002: 202–4, on a pan-Australian perspective). This is shown in (53a–b).

(53a)   inda_A   gala**ma**:ṇi
        2sg   fear+CAUS+RECENT.PAST
        You frightened him

(53b)   wanduṇa_O   inda_A   ṇaṇḍi**ma**:ṇi
        who+ABS   2sg   talk+APPL+REC.P
        Who was that man you were talking to before?

Adding a causative-applicative suffix -*ma* to a transitive verb does not change the verb's valency: it marks a plural object. In (54a), 'it signifies that the verb acts on (or affects) a number of objects':

(54a)   bari   ṇaya   iḍa**man**
        stone 1sg   put.down+PL+PRES
        I am piling up rocks

In (54b), 'it signifies that the verb causes the object to become more than one object':

(54b)   ṇat^yungu   bamaṇgu   yuḍi   babi**maṇi**
        1sgGEN+ERG   brother+ERG   meat   cut+PL+PRES
        My brother is butchering some meat

A similar phenomenon has been observed in Creek (Muskogean: Martin 2000: 394–6; 1991). The marker of direct causative -*ic* in Creek is polysemous with the plural marker for objects and intransitive subjects (see §6.2 in chapter 4 below concerning how, if there is a verbal suffix indicating plurality of core arguments, this is likely to refer to S/O arguments). The direct causative is not fully productive, and is 'most commonly applied to nonagentive states or inchoatives'. It is in bold type in the following examples (in agreement with Martin 2000: 394): *fikhonn-itá* 'to stop', *fikhonneyc-itá* 'to stop (something)'; *kiil-íta* 'to die (of one)', *iliᴄ-itá* 'to kill (of one)'; *noł-íta* 'to be cooked', *nołeyc-ta* 'to cook something'; *kiłł-itá* 'to know', *kiłłeyc-itá* 'to inform'.

This same suffix marks multiple S (intransitive subject), as in *tamk-itá* 'to fly (of one)', *tamiᴄ-itá* 'to fly (of three or more)', or a multiple O, as in *halat-itá* 'to hold (one)', *halatheyc-itá* 'to hold (two or more)'. The plural use of *-ic-* appears to take priority over the direct causative use.

The same form is used as a causative marker and as an exponent of verbal plural in other Muskogean languages, e.g. Koasati (Kimball 1991: 329; 341) (also see Broadwell 1990; and William Davies 1981, 1986, for Chickasaw). Both are reconstructed for the proto-language by Martin and Munro (2005: 302; 311) (also see the Appendix).

We can recall, from §6.1.3, that the morpheme *-(n)en* in Gayo (Eades 2005: 190–1) has a straightforwardly causative meaning with intransitive verbs; with transitive verbs it marks intensity and increased volition on the part of the A. When used with a ditransitive verb 'give', '*-(n)en* signals that the act of giving involves increased volition, often involving multiple undergoers, i.e. meaning "give out"'.

A further link between plurality of a non-subject and causative has been documented in languages with the so called 'distributive causative'. The distributive causative in Yukaghir (Maslova 2003: 220–1) 'signifies that the causative action is applied to multiple entities […], or to multiple locations within one entity […], or otherwise just multiple times', e.g. *ǯel-ge-j* 'break (once, at one place)' (itr), *ǯel-ge-de-j* 'break' (tr), *ǯel'-ge-t-* 'break (several things, at a number of places, in a number of pieces; tr)'. This causative applies to a closed set of intransitive verbs.

In Aleut (Golovko 1993: 386; also Dixon 2000: 73), a distributive causative suffix *-dgu* indicates that a set of Causees is involved (then the O has to take plural marking). The Causees are distributed in space, e.g. 'the woman is making the hides dry'. In both Yukaghir and Aleut distributive causatives are valency-increasing markers. Their meanings to do with multiplicity of objects or locations are additional to their primary use as direct causatives. This is rather different from languages such as Margany or Creek where the causative and the non-singular object readings of the same morpheme are mutually exclusive.

We saw in §5.4.1 that the function of the 'double causative' marker *-i-ta* with the majority of ambitransitive and transitive verbs in the Tariana of Santa Rosa relates to complete affectedness of the O/Causee and to the intensity of the action of causation. Along similar lines, the manipulative *kay-* in Manambu (see §4.4 and especially example (24b)) combines the meanings relating to the A (implying increase in manipulative effort, intentionality, volitionality and control), and the O (reference to complete affectedness of the O, and multiple or large O). This is understandable—handling a large object requires a special manipulative effort on the part of the agent, as in (24).

These polysemous patterns, just like those described in §6.1.3, point in one direction: that the meanings of non-valency-increasing causatives outlined in §3.2 are closely interrelated. There is no reason to assume that multifunctionality of causative markers as indicators of forcefulness or volition on the part of the Causer, or greater affectedness of the object should a priori point towards the direction of semantic change, from causative to intensive: it may just as well be the opposite, or neither. We return to this in §7.

6.2. *Non-valency-increasing morphological causatives with verbs of any transitivity value*

In all the example languages discussed so far, the non-valency-increasing effects of morphological causatives are apparent only with transitive verbs. That is, polysemous readings—like in the Tariana of Santa Rosa (36) and (37), and Godoberi (52b–c)—are only characteristic of transitive verbs.

We now turn to languages where non-valency-increasing effects of morphological causatives are not restricted to any particular transitivity class. In the vast majority of such cases described in the linguistic literature, the polysemous causative has overtones of intensive and/or iterative action (parameter (ii) in §3.2), and manipulative effort on the part of the A ((i) in §3.2).

In Taba (South Halmahera, Austronesian: Bowden 2001: 198; 202), the prefix *ha-* is used to derive transitive verbs with a causative meaning from verbs of any transitivity value. The meaning is that of direct causation, as in (55a–b), and e.g. *sung* 'enter (intr)', *ha-sung* 'make go in':

(55a) Paramalam$_S$ n=mot
       lamp   3sg=die
       The lamp has gone out (lit. the lamp has died)

(55b) I$_A$ n=**ha**-mot   paramalam$_O$
       3sg   3sg=CAUS-die   lamp
       He turned the lamp off (lit. he made the lamp die)

The same prefix also derives forms with intensive meanings, as in (56b). An intransitive verb 'stay awake all night' is shown in (56a):

(56a) tit$_S$ t=wonga   maliling   ya
       1pl.incl   1pl.incl=stay.awake.all.night   night   up
       We stayed awake all last night ('night' is a temporal constituent, not
       an O)

(56b) tit$_S$ t=**ha**-wonga   maliling   ya
       1pl.incl   1pl.incl=CAUS-stay.awake.all.night   night   up
       We stayed awake all last night ('night' is a temporal constituent, not
       an O)

In Bowden's (2001: 202) words, 'both of these sentences could be used to describe the same event, but' (56b) 'emphasizes the intensity of the staying awake: it may be used to brag about how much fun was had at a big party for instance. Intensive causative marking also has an extended meaning whereby increased duration can be indicated'.
    Another example of *ha-* is on an ambitransitive verb:

(57) manusia   maleo   l=surat   John   n=**ha**-surat   tarus
      people   other   3pl=write   John   3sg=CAUS-write   all.the.time
      Other people write, John writes (on and on) all the time

The verb *surat* 'write' can be used transitively or intransitively (as an A = S ambitransitive). John Bowden (p.c.) confirms that (57) exemplifies an intransitive usage of *ha-*, and states that 'it could equally be used transitively if you were referring to, say, someone writing a lengthy book' (5 February 2007), adding that 'intensive meanings of *ha-* are more commonly found on transitive verbs'.
    The exact meaning may depend on the verb's semantics. The prefix *p-* in Mangap-Mbula, an Oceanic language from New Guinea, turns

intransitive verbs into causatives, e.g. *-bayou* 'be hot', *-**pa**-bayou* 'heat up (something)' (Bugenhagen 1995: 174–5). It is said to have the same function with verbs encoding non-volitional actions and little change of state of the O. When used with transitive verbs considered by Bugenhagen to have 'high transitivity', the prefix indicates 'an increased amount of effort or struggle on the part of the Agent':

(58a) aŋ-kaaga   kataama
      1sg-open   door
      I open the door

(58b) aŋ-**pa**-kaaga   kataama
      1sg-CAUS-open   door
      I managed to get the door open

The Taba prefix *ha-* and the Mangap-Mbula *p-* are etymologically related to Fijian *va'a-*: the former is a reflex of Proto-Austronesian **pa-* and the latter of Proto-Oceanic **pa[ka]-* (see Evans 2003: 252–66; also see Wolff 1973: 81, for Proto-Austronesian causative **pa-*). We return to this in the Appendix.

Along similar lines, in Chichewa (Bantu, Malawi: Hopper and Thompson 1980: 264; based on Anonymous 1969: 78–9), 'the causative morpheme is interpreted as a signal of intensity'.[31] The intransitive verb is illustrated in (59a), and its causative and intensive versions are shown in (59b) and (59c) respectively.

(59a) Mwana'yu$_S$ w-a-dy-a   —*intransitive*
      child.this   he-TENSE-eat-INDIC
      The child has eaten

(59b) Mai$_A$ a-ku-dy-**ETS**-a   mwana$_O$
      woman   she-TENSE-eat-CAUS-INDIC   child
      —*causativized transitive*
      The woman is feeding the child

(59c) Mwana'yu$_S$ w-a-dy-**ETS**-a   —*intensive intransitive*
      child.this   he-TENSE-eat-CAUS-INDIC
      The child has eaten too much

[31] Anonymous (1969: 79) describes this as follows '*-tsa* suffix sometimes conveys a notion of intensity in the action, or superlative "much", "too much", according to the context and intonation'.

Similar pairs are in (60a) and (60b):

(60a) Gwir-a-ni   chingwe$_O$!   —*transitive*
      hold-IMPV-2pl   string!
      Hold the string!

(60b) Gwir-**ITS**-a-ni   chingwe$_O$!   —*intensive transitive*
      hold-CAUS-IMPV-2pl   string
      Hold the string firmly!

The same technique is used to mark a causative and an intensive in a number of more familiar languages. In Arabic and Hebrew, the verb stem which involves gemination of the second root consonant expresses causative and/or intensive meaning, e.g. Arabic *fariha* 'be glad', *farraha* 'make glad'; *kasara* 'break', *kassara* 'break in (small) pieces' (Premper 1987: 89–90; Hopper and Thompson 1980: 264, and discussion in Masica 1976: 96). The polysemy of the stem with 'doubled second radical' as causative and intensive in Semitic languages was summarized by Moscati (1969: 124) (also see Grande 1972: 210–11; Diakonoff 1989: 104; also see Tsarfaty 2007, forthcoming, for this phenomenon in Modern Israeli Hebrew). It appears to be a Proto-Semitic feature. Whether or not this can be reconstructed for Proto-Afro-asiatic remains a question for further investigation. The directions in historical development of polysemous patterns in causatives are addressed in the Appendix.

7. Causatives which do not Cause: An Appraisal

By its definition, a causative adds a core participant to a verb. If a language has more than one causative technique, a morphological causative is expected to mark direct, volitional and intentional causation. In addition to that, morphological causatives may have other, 'valency-preserving', meanings, which have little to do with changing valency. We have identified three groups of meanings, all intrinsically related:

(i)   reference to the A: increase in manipulative effort, intentionality, volitionality and control;
(ii) reference to the ACTION: intensive and/or iterative action;[32]

---

[32] The examples from Arabic, some of the Boumaa Fijian examples, and a few other (less certain) ones were mentioned by Kulikov (1999) as instances of what he called

(iii) reference to the O: complete affectedness of the O, and multiple
       or large O.

In a number of languages, non-valency-increasing meanings of causative morphemes are restricted to transitive and ambitransitive verbs.
This is consistent with the generally accepted thesis that if a language
has a causative, it will primarily apply to intransitive verbs (see Shibatani 2002b: 6; Dixon 2000). In other languages, causative morphemes
have non-valency-increasing overtones with verbs of any transitivity
class.

In languages such as Manambu, causatives have a valency-increasing
effect only with intransitive verbs. In languages like Tariana, or Godoberi, causatives straightforwardly increase the valency of intransitive
verbs. With transitive verbs, they may or may not do so. This results
in polysemous patterns illustrated in (36–7), from Tariana of Santa
Rosa, and (52b–c), from Godoberi. These usually have to be resolved
by context, and ultimately rely on inference.

Table 3.4 summarizes the semantic parameters shared by morphological causatives in their valency-changing and valency-preserving
functions. Table 3.5 provides an overview of non-valency-increasing
meanings of causative markers (with the example languages). Morphological causatives appear to express reference to A (parameter (i))
and to O (parameter (iii)) only in those languages where non-valency-
increasing effects are restricted to transitive and ambitransitive verbs.
Reference to the action (parameter (ii)) in terms of its intensity, iteration

---

'split causativity': what he called 'aspectual' effect of causative morphology. However,
the non-valency-increasing effects of causative morphology go beyond aspectual
overtones. The term 'split' is quite inappropriate. As will be seen further on in this
section, non-valency-increasing effects of causative morphology represent a semantic
extension of these morphemes. This is very different from the conventional use of the
term 'split', as in 'split ergativity' or a 'split' gender system. A 'split' system involves
different subsystems operating in different contexts. That this is not typically the case
with causatives is corroborated by (a) numerous examples of polysemous forms, such
as Godoberi (52b, c) and Tariana (36–7); and (b) by the existence of non-aspectual
overtones of these morphemes, as discussed above.

Some of the semantic effects of causative markers have been briefly discussed by
Kittilä (2009: 79–81), under the umbrella term 'agentivization', without distinguishing
the semantics of A, of O and of the action. He mentions 'intensification' as one
meaning of causative morphology (using one example each from Tariana, Hunzib,
Taba and Chichewa), without mentioning further overtones of causative morphemes
in these languages.

and manipulative effort involved is shared by all the languages where morphological causatives have non-valency-increasing meanings.

Table 3.4 shows that morphological causatives in their valency-increasing and non-valency-increasing—that is, valency-preserving—meanings (columns 1 and 2) have numerous features in common. This involves intentional and volitional action on the part of the Causer, effort involved in the Causer's actions, and the involvement of the Causee.

We saw in §§4–5 above that only morphological causatives which express direct causation with a volitional and intentional Causer have overtones relating to parameters (i)–(iii). This follows from the

le 3.4. Semantic parameters shared by morphological causative markers in their valency-increasing and valency-preserving functions

ORPHOLOGICAL USATIVES VALENCY-CREASING DEVICES	MEANINGS AS NON-VALENCY-INCREASING DEVICES	EXAMPLE LANGUAGES	
		non-valency-increasing effects with transitive and ambitransitive verbs only	non-valency-increasing effects with any verbs
user acts tentionally and litionally	(i) reference to A: increase in manipulative effort, intentionality, volitionality and control	Manambu, Tariana, Boumaa Fijian, Tongan, Gilbertese, Atong, Gayo	
	(ii) reference to the ACTION: manipulative effort	Manambu, Tariana, Piapoco, Godoberi	Mangap-Mbula
user's action volves effort	(ii) reference to the ACTION: intensive and/or iterative action	Warekena, Baniwa, Piapoco, Tariana, Leti, Boumaa Fijian, Tongan, Gilbertese, Atong	Taba, Chichewa, Arabic, Hebrew
	(iii) reference to the O: multiple or large O	Manambu, Tariana of Periquitos, Margany, Creek	
usee completely volved	(iii) reference to the O: complete affectedness of the O	Tariana	

Table 3.5. Non-valency-increasing meanings of causative markers: summary
of examples

SEMANTIC PARAMETER	EXAMPLES DISCUSSED	
	with (ambi)transitive verbs only	with verbs of any transitivity value
(i) reference to A: increase in *manipulative effort, intentionality, volitionality* and *control*	Manambu, Tariana, Boumaa Fijian, Tongan, Gilbertese, Atong. Gayo	Mangap-Mbula
(ii) reference to the ACTION: *manipulative effort, intensive* and/or *iterative* action	Manambu, Tariana, Piapoco, Godoberi, Warekena, Baniwa, Piapoco, Tariana, Leti, Boumaa Fijian, Tongan, Gilbertese, Atong	Taba, Chichewa, Arabic, Hebrew
(iii) reference to the O: *complete affectedness of the O*, and *multiple* or *large O*	Manambu, Tariana of Santa Rosa, Tariana of Periquitos, Margany, Creek	

(i)   reference to the A: increase in manipulative effort, intentionality, volitionality and
      control;
(ii) reference to the ACTION: intensive and/or iterative action;
(iii) reference to the O: complete affectedness of the O, and multiple or large O

semantics of direct causation, which typically involves manipulative force. The intensity (and repetition) of action can be conceived of as its semantic corollary.

These shared features suggest the combination of semantic features for morphological causatives which have non-causative meanings of intensity, volition and control shown in Figure 3.1. This figure does not represent a grammaticalization cline; nor does it reflect a historical development of causative, or of intensive, markers.

Morphological causatives in their valency-changing and valency-preserving functions have yet another feature in common. A prototypical morphological causative makes an intransitive verb into a transitive one, and a transitive verb into a ditransitive. In other words, it increases the transitivity of the verb.

A morphological causative in its function other than introducing an agent affects the parameters typically associated with transitivity

---

tional and Intentional Causer (A) ~ marking of volitionality and intention of A (as 'Causer') (i)

Causer who has the capacity of directly affecting the action, or of direct causation marker ~ of
intensive action involving manipulative effort (ii); marker of repetitive action (ii)

lly affected O and/or complete involvement of Causee ~ marker of completely involved O or
multiple and/or large O (iii)

Figure 3.1. Semantic features of causative markers with non-valency-increasing uses

increase in at least two further ways. As we saw in §§4–5, it makes an
ambitransitive verb into an obligatory transitive one. This effect may
be called 'transitivity-fixing'. And, by adding the semantic features
(i)–(iii), it makes the verb more prototypically transitive: a prototypically transitive verb (or, in Hopper and Thompson's 1980 terminology, 'highly transitive verb') involves volitional A high in potency, and
highly affected O: see further parameters in Dixon (2010b: 115–42).

This functional similarity between the valency-increasing and non-
valency-increasing functions of morphological causatives underlies the
semantic patterns featured in Figure 3.1 and Table 3.4. The semantics
of the markers we have discussed here can be presented in terms of a
complex of meanings directly related to each other. The exact meaning
of each morpheme is not restricted to an abstract 'central' component
(be it an intensive, or a causative): the general constellation of meaning features subsumes numerous aspects of the situation in which the
form can be used. Each of the features may be considered salient and
then provides motivation for an extension, from a historical perspective. 'Causatives that don't cause' and 'intensifiers that do not inten-
sify' reflect different sides of the same coin: this is captured by the
notion of heterosemy (Lichtenberk 1991a; Persson 1988) where two or
more meanings or functions are borne by reflexes of a common source
element. This is different from the classical understanding of polysemy
as the association of distinct (albeit related) meanings within one and
the same lexeme, or morpheme (Lichtenberk 1991a; Lyons 1977: 561).
What we are dealing with here is one meaning complex, with some
features more prominent than others.[33]

---

[33] A similar approach could be taken to analyze other semantically rich markers—
for instance, diminutives which may have endearing or pejorative overtones, or
augmentatives (see Bauer 1983, 1996, on English diminutives; Aikhenvald 2000b, for

Why do morphological causatives rather than causatives of any other types have non-causative meanings to do with intensity of action, control and volition of the Causer and the involvement of the Causee? The answer lies in the nature of meaning-mechanism correlations between values of semantic parameters relevant to causatives and types of mechanisms (morphological, periphrastic, or lexical). According to Dixon's (2000: 74–7) scale of compactness, direct causation is associated with more compact (that is, morphological) rather than less compact (periphrastic) expression. Interestingly, in a number of languages discussed here—including Manambu and Tariana—the 'causatives that do not "cause"' are not fully productive. (This is not to say that they are lexical forms learned individually; they are just not formed on any verb in the language.) The lack of productivity partly correlates with directness of causation: according to Shibatani and Pardeshi (2002: 113), non-productive causatives tend to express direct rather than indirect causation.

The meanings of 'causatives that do not cause' can be viewed as corollaries of their primary meanings as exponents of direct causation, volitionality and intention of the Causer (A), associated manipulative effort and hense intensity of action (which may be also extended to repetitive action).[34]

In a number of the languages discussed in this chapter, the historical development of relevant markers indicates a directionality from valency-increasing to non-valency-increasing meanings. However, this pathway is far from universal: in other cases, a development in the opposite direction could be postulated. A number of languages— including Indo-European, Semitic, Austronesian and also Zapotec (see note 30)—provide inconclusive evidence. The relevant literature, and examples are addressed in the Appendix.

A final remark is in order. We can recall that a causative may have an applicative-like effect. Do applicatives ever develop overtones to do with involvement of A, or intensity of action, or involvement and number of O? There is no information about this in the literature; for now, this question remains open.

---

the overtones of value associated with diminution and augmentation in noun class and classifier systems).

[34] See, for instance, Heine and Kuteva (2002), for a recurrent connection between repetitive and intensive action. Note that the causative-repetitive polysemy cannot be utilized as an argument in favour of two-event interpretation of a causative, because repetition of the same event marked by the same means as the causative always has overtones of a single intensive action.

APPENDIX

CAUSATIVES THAT DO NOT CAUSE: EVIDENCE FOR HISTORICAL DEVELOPMENT

We now address the issue of historical directionality in the development of the polysemous extensions of morphological causatives as exponents of manipulative effort, intensive action and also multiple O. In a number of cases, the original causative has developed a variety of non-valency-increasing meanings. These cases are discussed below.

I. Evidence from the Arawak Language Family

The data from Arawak languages show that the original Proto-Arawak morphological causative *-ta* (Aikhenvald 1999; 2002a: 306) acquired overtones of manipulative effort, complete involvement of O and intensive action as a secondary development. This is a feature of North Arawak, particularly the Içana-Vaupés subgroup (including Tariana, Piapoco and Baniwa of Içana). The Tariana variety of Periquitos has developed an additional meaning to do with multiple Causee.

An additional lesson to be learnt from Tariana is the potential historical development of a causative marker. The Proto-North-Arawak causative *-ta* survives in causative and applicative functions in Bare (see §5.3, §5.4.4). In Warekena, it is used as a causative, but can be repeated to express intensive action (meaning (ii)). In the Tariana of Santa Rosa, the same marker follows a different path—combining (i) and (ii).

II. Evidence from the Austronesian Language Family

Evidence from the Austronesian domain points towards the same direction, albeit less conclusively. Taba *ha-*, Boumaa Fijian *va'a-*, Bau Fijian *vaka*, Tongan *faka-*, and Mangap-Mbula *p-* come from Proto-Austronesian causative **pa(ka)-* (Bowden, Pawley: p.c.; cf. Evans 2003: 254–66, 305; Lynch, Ross and Crowley 2002: 83).

The Proto-Austronesian causative **pa-* was reconstructed by Wolff (1973: 81).[35] In his discussion of the Proto-Oceanic **paka-*, Harrison

---

[35] According to Evans (2003: 266), Proto-Oceanic had two causative prefixes **pa-* and **paka-*, both inherited from Proto-Austronesian; the distinction between the

(1982: 197–8) suggests that its polysemy as a causative and as a marker of what he calls 'act semantic' go back to Proto-Oceanic.[36]

Since most scholars agree that the meaning of the relevant morpheme(s) in Proto-Austronesian was causative, the semantic path from causative to the combination of non-valency-increasing meanings (i) and (ii) appears to be the consensus opinion.

Along similar lines, Chichewa -ets/-its (see examples (59–60)) possibly comes from the Proto-Bantu causative extension *-ci or *-ti (Williamson and Blench 2000: 39). The same morpheme -či marks causative and the verbal plural, or distributive, in Muskogean languages (Martin and Munro 2005: 302; 311). According to Jack Martin (p.c.), the two are related (they share at least one morphological feature: both trigger the deletion of the middle voice marker). The causative function appears to be older.

All these instances provide historical support for the idea of extension of a prototypical morphological causative to cover manipulative effort on the part of the A, intensive and iterative action, and multiple objects. That is, Figure 3.1 appears to reflect a historical reality as reconstructed for Arawak, Austronesian, and perhaps also Bantu and Muskogean.

However, the relevant markers may have been polysemous in the proto-language. The evidence from Semitic and from Indo-European is inconclusive.

III. Evidence from the Semitic Branch of the Afro-Asiatic Family

The evidence in favour of causative being the original meaning of polysemous causative-intensive forms is not fully conclusive. According to Moscati (1969: 124), the stem with doubled second radical 'which is attested over the whole Semitic area, seems to have a primarily

---

two is believed to have been no longer productive in Proto-Oceanic. This justifies the notation of the Proto-Oceanic causative as *pa[ka]-. See Evans (2003 and references there) for further discussion. See Blust (2003: 451–61) for a reconstruction of a variety of Proto-Austronesian causative markers.

[36] According to Harrison (1982: 196), '"act semantic" increases the actorhood of the Causer argument, indicated that that (sic) it is a more conscious, active, volitional participant'.

"factitive" significance, i.e. as a causative in relation to a state or condition…to this meaning-aspect must be added the denominative one and the intensive aspect'. Diakonoff (1989: 104) is non-committal, stating that reduplicated forms 'usually denote an action as either intensive, or iterative, factitive, declarative, or causative'.

IV. EVIDENCE FROM INDO-EUROPEAN LANGUAGES

Transitivizing, or causativizing, markers have intensifying meanings in some Indo-European languages. Matras (2002: 42) mentions 'an older marker of causativity' found in the transitivizer or intensifier affix -ar- in Romani ('possibly from Old Indo-Aryan/Middle Indo-Aryan kar 'do'). In the Slavic-Hungarian contact zone in Central Europe, the common Romani transitivizer -ker- (Matras 2002: 124–5) survives 'in an iterative function, modelled on the system of Slavic aspect' (detailed examples and argumentation is in Hübschmannová and Bubeník 1997: 140–1). The Common Romani causative suffix -av- is the reflex of a reanalyzed Old Indo-Aryan causative suffix -aya- (see Hübschmannová and Bubeník 1997: 135; according to Kuryłowicz 1964: 89, this suffix was originally iterative and became causative as a result of a later development). This also survives as an iterative marker in Northern varieties of Eastern Slovak Romani; the two erstwhile causative suffixes are often 'strung together which intensifies the iterative meaning', e.g. čiv-el > čiv-av-el/čiv-ker-el > čiv-av-ker-el 'throw' > 'be throwing all the time (frequently)' (see Hübschmannová and Bubeník 1997: 141).

A historical link between causativity and iterativity is no news in Indo-European comparative linguistics. A well-known example is the Proto-Indo-European verbal suffix *-sk reflexes of which are used to mark duratives and iteratives (in present and in preterite) in Hittite, and causative in Tocharian and Armenian. Szemerényi (1996: 273) comments on the traces of an iterative or durative meaning of this morpheme in Tocharian B, pointing out that 'it is therefore probable that all later shades of meaning have arisen from a basic iterative-durative sense' (p. 273, and further references there; also Szemerényi 1970: 253).

Other authors effectively acknowledge that this and other markers could have been polysemous as causative-iterative in the proto-language (e.g. Watkins 1998: 58–9; and also Meillet 1964: 211–13; Kuryłowicz 1964: 86, 107–8; Klein 1984: 135; Ivanov and Gamkrelidze

1984: 178; and Hübschmannová and Bubeník 1997: 141). Thus, for instance, Watkins (1998: 58) discusses the 'CAUSATIVE-ITERATIVE formation with *o-* grade root and suffix **-éje/o-*' which is 'well attested throughout the family'. The difficulty of reconstructing the exact function of each suffix in the proto-language is addressed by Ivanov and Gamkrelidze (1984: 347). This suggests reconstructing a polysemous morpheme at the level of the proto-language.

Along similar lines, the etymology of the Manambu *kay-* 'causative (intransitive verbs); manipulative (ambitransitive and transitive verbs)' is inconclusive. Iatmul, from the same family as Manambu, lost the productive prefix *kay-*. The formative *ka-* survives only in one ambitransitive verb *kabuluk* 'turn over; capsize' (cognate to Manambu *kay-blakə-*). That is, a limited morphological causative in Manambu has survived as part of a fully lexicalized 'lexical' causative in Iatmul. The prefix *kay-* does not appear to have cognates in other languages of the Ndu family, except for Ambulas. The non-productive causative *ke-* in Ambulas (Wilson 1980: 61–2) occurs as a causativizer on two intransitive verbs and on one transitive verb (where its semantic effects are unclear). More study is needed before we can trace the development of this morpheme.

CHAPTER FOUR

NON-ERGATIVE ASSOCIATIONS BETWEEN S AND O

Alexandra Y. Aikhenvald and R. M. W. Dixon

1. Introduction

The message of this chapter is that terms 'ergative' and 'accusative' are appropriately used to describe ways of marking the functions of core arguments in a clause, and syntactic constraints on shared arguments in clause linking. In this usage the terms have a coherent conceptual value. However, there has recently arisen a tendency to extend the use of 'ergative' to cover *any* association between intransitive subject (S) and transitive object (O) functions; and similarly to use 'accusative' for any association of S with transitive subject (A). Our point is that these further types of association are quite different from the established meanings of 'ergative' and 'accusative' and that to extend the terms beyond their established conceptual domains can be both unhelpful and confusing.

In §§2–4 there is recapitulation of the main features of ergative and accusative systems for marking core syntactic relations and for clause linking; this is a necessary preliminary to what follows. After a mention of universal associations between S and A other than those in accusative systems, in §5, there is then, in §6, discussion of six ways in which S and O may be grouped together, quite apart from their linking in ergative systems. §7 puts forward a tentative explanation for the S/O associations described in §6. Then, further ways in which S and A, or S and O, may be linked are discussed in §8. Finally, §9 integrates the findings, emphasising that the varied recurrent associations between S and O found throughout the grammars of very many languages should not all be labelled 'ergative' (and those between S and A should not all be labelled 'accusative'). The labels are best restricted to describing systems of core argument marking and of constraints on shared argument function in clause linking.

The chapter aims at a summary statement of the varied types of association between S and O (and between S and A). It does not attempt an exhaustive account of each association (to have done this would have resulted in a book-length study). Many previous publications have alluded to some of the things discussed here. We have made no attempt to refer to all of these. To have done so would have resulted in a long and unwieldy catalogue, whereas we aimed to be pithy and to-the-point.

A fair number of the illustrative examples here come from the authors' own field work—Aikhenvald's on Warekena (1998) and Tariana (2003), both from Brazil, and on Manambu (2008a), from Papua New Guinea; and Dixon's on Dyirbal (1972) from Australia, on Fijian (1988), from Oceania, and on Jarawara (2004b), from Brazil. These can be referred to for in-depth statements of the associations highlighted below.

2. CORE SYNTACTIC RELATIONS

In every language, each clause has an internal structure, consisting of a predicate (which typically relates to a verb) and a number of arguments—some of which must be either stated or understood from the context (these are 'core arguments'), and others which are optional (these are 'peripheral arguments', sometimes called 'adjuncts').

As mentioned in earlier chapters, there are two main clause structures across the languages of the world, one 'intransitive', with one core argument ('intransitive subject'), and the other 'transitive', with two core arguments ('transitive subject' and 'transitive object').[1] As in other chapters, it is useful to employ the following standard abbreviatory letters:

S for intransitive subject
A for transitive subject
O for transitive object

---

[1] There are further subtypes of both major clause structures. A few languages have an 'extended intransitive' clause type, with core argument S (marked and functioning in the same way as S in a plain intransitive) plus a second core argument that can be called E ('extension to core'). A rather larger number of languages have an 'extended transitive' (alternatively called 'ditransitive') clause type which involves three core arguments: A, O and E. It is noteworthy that E in extended intransitive and E in extended transitive clause types have very similar properties. (See Dixon 1994: 120–4; Dixon and Aikhenvald 2000b: 2–4.) These do not impinge on the discussion of A, S and O in the present chapter.

Note that no special significance attaches to the use of letters S, A and O. These are simply convenient abbreviations for the longer labels, in the same way that 'USA' is a convenient abbreviation for 'United States of America'.

Transitivity is a syntactic (not a semantic) matter, as are subject and object. In this spirit, the letters A, S and O should only be used to refer to syntactic functions. 'O' was the obvious choice as abbreviation for 'object'.[2] Different abbreviations were needed for 'intransitive subject' and 'transitive subject'. On a fairly arbitrary basis, 'S' was selected for the former and 'A' for the latter (alternatives would have been I and T, or S and T, or I and S).

One point which cannot be stressed too strongly is that 'A' does *not* stand for 'agent' or 'actor', which are semantic labels; it stands for 'transitive subject', a syntactic function. Each type of verbs has its characteristic semantic roles (Dixon 1994: 7–8). There are a number of disparate semantic roles—each associated with a distinct verb type—which are mapped onto the syntactic relation A. These include the Agent for a verb of Affect (such as 'hit' or 'cut'), the Donor for a verb of Giving, the Speaker for a verb of Speaking, the Perceiver for a verb of Attention (such as 'see', 'hear'); see Dixon (1994: 7–8, 1991, 2005). Some of these could be described as 'Actor' or 'Agent'; but they could not all be. For instance, 'John' could not be called 'Actor' or 'Agent' in *John*$_{A:PERCEIVER}$ *saw* [*the burglar*]$_{O:IMPRESSION}$ *as he ran by.*

In exactly the same way, 'O' stands for the syntactic function of 'transitive object', *not* for 'patient' or any other semantic notion. A number of diverse semantic roles are typically mapped onto transitive object (O) function. In some languages a verb of Giving has the Gift as O, in others the Recipient is O, and in a further set of languages there are two construction types, covering both possibilities. This can be exemplified from English:

(1)   John$_{A:DONOR}$ gave [a signed copy of his new book]$_{O:GIFT}$ to Mary
(2)   John$_{A:DONOR}$ gave [the janitor]$_{O:RECIPIENT}$ [some old clothes]

---

[2] The abbreviations A, S and O were first used in Dixon's (1968) PhD thesis and first appeared in print in the published revision of this (1972). Note that Dixon (1972: xii) does gloss 'A' as 'subject (or agent) of a transitive verb'. The inclusion of 'agent' here was ill-thought and something which Dixon now regrets.

One could scarcely label both *a signed copy of his new book* in (1) and *the janitor* in (2) as 'patient'. Nor would this label be appropriate for *the burglar* in *John*_{A:PERCEIVER} *saw* [*the burglar*]_{O:IMPRESSION} *as he ran by*.

3. WAYS OF MARKING CORE ARGUMENTS—ACCUSATIVE AND ERGATIVE SYSTEMS

There is generally some grammatical mechanism for showing which of the two core arguments in a transitive clause is in A and which is in O function. That is, A and O need to be marked differently. S is a different syntactic function from A and O, and one might expect S to be marked in a third way. This is seldom encountered. Since A and O occur in a different clause type from S, a grammar can operate economically and either (i) mark A in the same way as S, or (ii) mark O in the same way as S.

Grammatical tradition grew out of study of the classical Indo-European languages Sanskrit, Greek and Latin. Here we find:

(i) One case, called 'nominative' used to mark S and A functions, and a further case, called 'accusative', used to mark O function.

Within the past hundred years, descriptions have been provided for languages with a different kind of marking pattern:

(ii) One case is used just for A function. Following Dirr (1912), this has been called 'ergative'. A second case marks both S and O functions. This was originally called 'nominative', a label which could be confusing in view of the established use of 'nominative' for the case which marks S and A function in a system of type (i). From the mid-1970s, the label 'absolutive' (taken over from Eskimoist terminology) has been preferred.

A language of type (i) is said to have a 'nominative-accusative' case system, or 'accusative' for short. One of type (ii) is said to have an 'absolutive-ergative' system, or 'ergative' for short. Languages with case marking of these types are said to be 'morphologically accusative' and 'morphologically ergative' respectively.

There are other grammatical mechanisms for indicating the syntactic functions of core arguments. Some languages have bound pronouns, which typically attach to the verb. One language may have a series of bound pronouns with a single form for S and A and another for O, while another language has one series for S and O and a distinct series for A. Labels 'accusative' and 'ergative' were extended to apply to such systems of bound pronouns.

Or syntactic function can be shown by the order in which NPs realising core arguments occur in relation to the predicate (or verb, V). English shows orders AVO and SV. Both A and S occur before the V, and O after it. This has been called an 'accusative' pattern of constituent ordering. The combination of OVA and VS would also be called 'accusative'. If A is on a different side of V from S and O, we get 'ergative' constituent order—AVO and VS, as in the Mayan language Huastec (Edmonson 1988), or OVA and SV, as in the Western Nilotic language Päri (Andersen 1988).

'Ergative' and 'accusative' labels are not so easily assigned where all three core arguments are on the same side of the verb. For instance, in a language with SV and OAV, one could maintain that S and O are treated in the same way since both occur initially, or that S and A are treated in the same way since both occur immediately before V. It can be seen that no clear classification—in terms of 'accusative' and 'ergative' types—is possible here. Similarly for SV and AOV, VS and VAO, VS and VOA. However, the placement of peripheral constituents can be a critical factor. The ordering of core constituents in Sanuma (from the Yanomami dialect continuum, in northern Brazil and southern Venezuela) is SV and AOV. But the placement of peripheral constituents (which can be shown as X) is critical—XSV and AXOV (Borgman 1990). There is here an ergative pattern of constituent ordering, with S and O coming between peripheral constituents and V.

Labels 'morphological accusativity' and 'morphological ergativity' are appropriate when only case inflections are involved. Less so when other mechanisms for marking the functions of core arguments are included—such as constituent order, which is a syntactic matter. We should best refer to 'accusative' and 'ergative' systems for *core argument marking*.

Many languages combine the two basic types of core argument marking in one of several ways. Pronouns may have accusative while nouns have ergative inflection. There may be an ergative system in clauses which are marked by past tense or perfect aspect, and accusative elsewhere. In a number of languages, some intransitive verbs mark

S like A (this is called Sa) while others mark S like O (So), producing a 'split-S' system. A variant on this is where there is a further subclass of intransitive verbs which may mark S either like A or like O, with a difference in meaning—a 'fluid-S' system. There is a full account of these and other types of 'split systems' in Dixon (1994: 70–110).

4. INTER-CLAUSAL OR SYNTACTIC ACCUSATIVE AND ERGATIVE PATTERNS

The idea of 'accusative' and 'ergative' alignment originated from morphological marking, being then extended to any marking of core arguments. It was further extended to the syntactic level, dealing with the constraints on the building up of complex sentences in terms of the treatment of core arguments. If two clauses—in a coordinate or subordinate relationship—require for a certain purpose a common argument which is in S or A function in each, the language may be said to have 'accusative syntax'. This applies to English. If in this language two clauses which are coordinated have an argument in common, it can be omitted from the second clause *only* if it is in S or A function—called the 'pivot' function—in each clause. In the following four coordinations, *John* is in S or A function in each and can either be replaced by a pronoun or omitted from the second clause (shown here by placing the pronoun in parentheses). The common arguments are in bold type.

John$_S$ laughed and (**he**$_S$) sat down   **John**$_A$ saw Mary$_O$ and (**he**$_A$) patted Fido$_O$

John$_S$ laughed and (**he**$_A$) patted Fido$_O$ **John**$_A$ patted Fido$_O$ and (**he**$_S$) sat down

However, when the common argument is not in a pivot function (S or A) in each clause, it cannot be omitted from the second clause. There are no parentheses around the pronouns in:

John$_S$ laughed and Mary$_A$ heard **him**$_O$ **John**$_A$ patted Fido$_O$ and Mary$_A$ watched **him**$_O$

Mary$_A$ saw John$_O$ and **he**$_S$ sat down   Mary$_A$ saw **John**$_O$ and **he**$_A$ patted Fido$_O$

Mary$_A$ saw John$_O$ and Fido$_A$ bit **him**$_O$

(One could omit the pronoun from three of these sentences but the meaning would then be changed. For example, *Mary saw John and sat down* implies that it was Mary, and not John, who sat down.)

Some languages combine S or O as pivot functions. For instance, Warekena (an Arawak language from north-west Brazil)[3] has a relative clause construction in which the common argument must be in S or O function in the relative clause and in S or O (or locative or instrumental, but not A) function in the main clause, as in:

(3) enu-waba   ʃia   weruami$_S$ [wa-weya-ri
     sky-LOC   3sgmS:live   1pl:father   1plA-want-RELATIVISER
        weda]$_{RELATIVE.CLAUSE}$
        1plA:see
     Our father, who we want to see, lives in the sky

Here 'our father', the common argument, is in S function for the main clause and in O function for the relative clause.

'Terminative clauses' in Warekena also operate with an S/O pivot, as in:

(4) wahã   yaranawi$_A$ peta   kavayu$_O$ ate   parahã
     THEN   white.man   3sgmA:hit   horse   until   3sgmS:run
     Then the white man hit the horse until he (the horse) ran off

No S argument is stated for the second clause in (4) but—in terms of the S/O pivot—it is understood to be identical with the O argument of the first clause. That is, it is the horse that runs off, not the man. (Discussion and further examples of these two construction types in Warekena will be found in Aikhenvald 1998: 273–8, 283–6.)

The Australian language Dyirbal has a strong S/O pivot. For instance, two clauses may only be coordinated if they share an argument which is in S or O function in each. If one of the arguments is in A function, then the antipassive syntactic derivation must be applied. This places the erstwhile A argument into S (a pivot function) and converts the original O into a peripheral argument (marked by dative case), which can either be included or omitted (as exemplified in (25)).

Since this chapter is not about ergativity—but about ways in which S and O arguments pattern together *other than* core-argument-marking (or morphological) and inter-clausal (or syntactic) ergativity—it would be otiose to here include extensive details of the workings of an S/O pivot in a syntactically ergative language. There is detailed discussion

---

[3] In terms of the marking of core arguments, Warekena has a split-S system.

and exemplification concerning Dyirbal and other languages in Dixon
(1994: 8–18, 143–81).

It should be noted that most, but not all, languages can be characterised as accusative or ergative in terms of the marking of core arguments. The classification is not available for languages with no case
marking or bound pronouns and with fixed constituent order which
have core arguments all on the same side of the predicate (with no critical evidence from the positioning of peripheral NPs, such as occurs in
Sanuma). And there are some languages which lack any grammatical
means for recognising core arguments (no cases, no bound pronouns,
and free constituent order), but instead rely on the pragmatics of the
discourse situation for this. These also fall outside the classification.

Quite a number of languages have an 'accusative' S/A pivot and a
few have an 'ergative' S/O pivot. Some even employ the two types of
pivot for different kinds of complex sentence construction. But many
languages have no pivot at all, and so cannot be classified as either
'accusative' or 'ergative' at the syntactic level. That is, they have no
syntactic constraints on the functions of shared arguments between
clauses but operate on an entirely semantic principle.

It has been necessary to outline how S and A are grouped together
for core-argument marking (or morphological) accusativity and also
for inter-clausal (or syntactic) accusativity. And how S and O are
grouped together for the corresponding varieties of ergativity. Quite
apart from this, there are a number of recurrent cross-linguistic associations between S and A, summarised in the next section. We then
turn to the main focus of this chapter, recurrent associations between
S and O, a topic which has thus far been discussed in the literature
only a little.

5. ASSOCIATIONS BETWEEN S AND A
(APART FROM ACCUSATIVE MARKING)

Syntactic functions S and A can be grouped together—in accordance
with tradition—as 'subject'. There are a number of recurrent grammatical properties which link S and A in every sort of language (whether
of accusative or ergative profile in terms of the parameters presented
in the last two sections). These are discussed in Dixon (1994: 131–42)
and can be summarised here:

(a) In an imperative construction the most common—often, the only—referent for S (in an intransitive) or A (in a transitive imperative) is second person. Moreover, many languages allow the S or A argument of an imperative not to be explicitly stated when it is second person (or, when it is second person singular).

(b) When a concept such as 'can', 'try' or 'begin' is realised by a lexical verb, it is likely to have the same subject (S or A) as the verb to which it is linked. For example, in English, *John tried to run, and Mary began writing*. A further example of this concerns Serial Verb Constructions; see, for example, Aikhenvald (2006a).

(c) A reflexive construction involves two underlying arguments which have the same reference. In a common variety of reflexive construction, one argument is fully stated (we can call this the 'controller') while the second argument is realised as a reflexive pronoun. If one of the two arguments has subject (A or S) function, then this will always be the controller with the other argument shown by a reflexive pronoun. For example *John$_A$ cut himself$_O$* and *Mary$_S$ looked at herself in the mirror* in English

These associations between S and A apply equally to languages with accusative or ergative marking of core syntactic functions. See Dixon (1994: 174), Du Bois (1987: 839–43) and further references therein. (They relate to the fact that the topic around which a discourse is organised is in the great majority of instances human, and generally the controller of an activity, and thus in A or S function.) It is not appropriate to describe them as 'accusative' features.

6. ASSOCIATIONS BETWEEN S AND O
(APART FROM ERGATIVE MARKING)

There are a number of pervasive links between S and O which recur in all types of languages, irrespective of their profiles—accusative, ergative, mixed or neither—in terms of core argument marking and inter-clausal linking. They should not be regarded as some further instance of ergativity (although this has sometimes been said). Keenan (1984/1987) and Dixon (1994: 55) mention some of the links for which a fuller account is given below. Note that all the associations discussed in §§6.1–5 have fairly widespread occurrence.

6.1. *Suppletive verb forms referring to number specification of an argument*

Many languages have suppletive forms for a small number of the most common verbs, the choice of form depending on whether a core argument has singular or plural reference.

This can be illustrated from Jarawará (Arawá family, Brazil), a language with an entirely accusative system for core argument marking. First, a pair of intransitive clauses:

(5) awa$_S$ sona-ke
     tree(fem)   fall(singular.S)-DECLARATIVE(fem)
     A tree fell over

(6) awa$_S$ foro-ke
     tree(fem)   fall(non.singular.S)-DECLARATIVE(fem)
     Several trees fell over

The verb 'fall' has form *sona* when the S argument has singular and *foro* when it has non-singular reference. We can now illustrate with transitive clauses:

(7) fana$_A$ mato$_O$ ibana-ke
     woman(fem)   pequiá.fruit(masc)   roast(singular.O)-DECLARATIVE(fem)
     A woman roasted a pequiá fruit

(8) fana$_A$ mato$_O$
     woman(fem)   pequiá.fruit(masc)
        joka-ke
        roast(non.singular.O)-DECLARATIVE(fem)
     A woman roasted several pequiá fruit

Verb 'roast' has form *ibana* when the O argument has singular and *joka* when it has non-singular reference. (Note that the declarative ending on the verb shows feminine agreement in (5–8); it agrees with the S argument of an intransitive clause and with the A of this variety of transitive construction.)

Jarawara has about twenty verbs with suppletive forms. Some are transitive, and all are like 'roast' in that which form is chosen depends on the number reference of the O argument; these verbs include 'take out', 'pierce', 'kill', 'throw', 'hold in the hand' and 'tie onto hook (e.g. hammock)'. There are a number of intransitive verbs (including 'fall' and 'be big/much') which have suppletive forms depending on whether the S argument is singular or non-singular. And a further set of verbs has three suppletive forms, depending on whether the S argument has singular, dual or plural reference; these are posture verbs relating to sitting, standing and lying plus 'be hanging' and 'be inside'. (Full details are in Dixon 2004b: 543–6.)

The critical point is that the choice of suppletive verb forms depends on the number reference of the S argument (in an intransitive clause) or of the O argument (in a transitive clause). It *never* relates to the A argument. This association between S and O, just described for Jarawara, is found to apply *in every language*—from across the world—which has number-determined suppletive verb forms.

For instance, nine verbs with suppletive forms are reported for Comanche (Uto-Aztecan; Charney 1993: 114–5), including:

singular S	plural S		singular O	plural O	
iHpii	iHkoi	'sleep'	yaa	himi	'hold, carry'
hapi	kwapi	'lie down'	kweʔya	kweyuʔi	'remove'
ika	weekwi	'go inside'	yikwi	nikwi	'tell'

It will be seen that there are some similarities between the forms, but these appear to be ad hoc for each pair.

There can be different kinds of number specification. For instance, Meryam Mir (a Papuan language, spoken on the eastern islands of Torres Strait, between Australia and New Guinea; Piper 1989: 81–5) has more than twenty verbs with one form for when the S or O argument has singular or dual reference, and a different form where it has paucal ('a few') or plural ('many')' reference. They include:

	sg/dual O	pauc/pl O		sg/dual S	pauc/pl S	
(i)	ep	ays	'carry'	baw	barot	'enter'
	batawered	dikri	'throw'			
(ii)	epaytered	epayt	'pour'	ekwey	eko	'stand up'
	dími	dim	'close'	éydi	éyd	'lie down'
	ísmer	is	'pull out'	éwsmer	ews	'come out'

It will be seen that the pairs under (i) are suppletive, while for those under (ii) the paucal/plural form is a truncation of the singular/dual one (for 'stand up', *ekwey* is reduced to *ekw* with the final *w* being reinterpreted as *o*, giving *eko*).

Durie (1986) provides a wide-ranging discussion, identifying S and O as the relevant arguments for number marking of suppletive verbs across several dozen languages.[4] Durie suggests there must be many further examples beyond those that he collected. Among these many other languages are Northern Paiute (Uto-Aztecan, Thornes 2003), Cupeño (Uto-Aztecan, Hill 2005) and Thompson (Salish, Thompson and Thompson 1992) from North America; Sawu, an Austronesian language from Indonesia (Walker 1982); Koiari, a Papuan language from New Guinea (Dutton 1996); and Sumerian (Thomsen 1984).

There are some languages which appear to have suppletive verbs that are all intransitive and relate to the number of the S argument; for example, Karo, spoken in Brazil, from the Tupí family (Gabas 1999). And there are some whose suppletive verbs are all transitive and relate to the number of the O argument; for example, Amele, a Papuan language from New Guinea (Roberts 1987), and Emmi, from the Australian linguistic area (Ford 1998). (Further discussion and examples of suppletive verbs according to number of S or O argument are in Dixon 2012: 62–5.)

6.2. *Verbal affixes, and adverbs, referring to quantification or number specification of an argument*

When there is an affix to the verb which specifies the number reference of a core argument, it typically relates to an S argument in an intransitive and an O argument in a transitive clause. Manambu (Ndu family, Papuan area; Aikhenvald 2008a: 260) has an accusative profile in terms of both core argument marking and clause linking. There is verbal suffix -*tu*-, 'all', which refers to the S or O argument, as in:

(9)   [a-də   ñan]$_A$ takwagw$_O$ ata
       THAT-masc:SG   young.person:SG   woman:PL   THEN
       vya-tu-d
       kill-ALL(O)-3masc.sgA
       That young man then killed all the women

(10)   [a-di   takwagw]$_S$ ata   gəpə-tu-di
       THAT-PL   woman:PL   THEN   run.away-ALL(S)-3plS
       All those women then ran away

---

[4] There is further discussion and examples in Mithun (1999a: 84–6) and Corbett (2000: 252–3). Veselinova (2003, 2005) presents a very partial account, incorporating only a few of Durie's insights—for instance, she does not mention the S/O association—and only a few of his example languages.

Warekena—which, as mentioned before, shows a split-S system for marking core arguments—has a quantifier adverb *ʃupe* 'many' which refers to the S argument in an intransitive and the O argument in a transitive clause:

(11) ʃupe   ñamari$_S$ ni-wayata
     many   people   3pl:S-speak
     Many people spoke

(12) ʃupe   ñamari$_O$ neda
     many   people   3plA:see
     They saw many people

Note that *ʃupe* in (12) can only relate to the O argument; that is, it could *not* mean *'many of them saw people'.

Dyirbal, which is split ergative/accusative in terms of core argument marking but has an exclusively S/O (that is, ergative) syntactic pivot, has verbal suffix *-ja-* (Dixon 1972: 249) which can indicate 'many S' in an intransitive or 'many O' in a transitive clause:

(13) [balan   yibi]$_S$ banin-ja-ñu
     THERE:ABSOLUTIVE:FEMININE   woman   come-MANY(S)-PAST
     Many women came

(14) yara-ŋgu$_A$ jiyil$_O$ gundal-ja-ñu
     man-ERGATIVE   starling   put.in-MANY(O)-PAST
     The man was putting many starlings (into his bag)

Alternatively, suffix *-ja-* can indicate that an action is repeated (often being performed not with respect to some known goal but blindly, everywhere, in the hope of encountering a goal), as in:

(15) [bayi   yara]$_S$ ŋandan-ja-ñu
     THERE:ABSOLUTIVE:MASCULINE   man   call-REPEATED-PAST
     The man called out in all directions (not knowing if there was anyone there to hear him)

A number of Chadic languages—which share an accusative system for marking core arguments—have a morphological process applying to verbs that shows rather similar semantic effect to that in Dyirbal. It can indicate either an action performed many times, or many referents of the S or O argument. Newman (1990: 53–87, and see further references therein) employs the term 'pluractional' and summarises its occurrence in Bura, Lele, Margi, Pero and other Chadic languages.

All the examples we have gathered of number-determined suppletive verb forms (discussed in §6.1) appear to relate to S and O arguments. The great majority of number suffixes on verbs also relate to S and O. There are, however, other possibilities here. Just a few languages show a number affix which appears to relate to S in an intransitive and to A in a transitive clause; these include Tagalog (Schachter and Otanes 1972: 334–6) and Amuesha, an Arawak language from Peru (Duff-Tripp 1997: 98–9).[5]

6.3. *Derived nouns based on a verb and a core argument*

Many languages derive nouns by compounding a verb with a core argument—this is always in underlying S or O function. A small selection of examples from English is:

	noun in O function plus verb	noun in S function plus verb
(a)	punchball	hovercraft
	pickpocket	driftwood
(b)	toothpick	sunset
	haircut	snowdrift

Note that in examples (a) the underlying verb comes first in the compound whereas in (b) it comes last.

In Jarawara (which, like English, has an entirely accusative profile), nominalisations typically involve the reduplicated form of a verb plus an NP in S or O function. For example:

nominalisation	from	intransitive verb	and	NP	
ee-tati-fo.fore		fore		ee	tati
'pillow (lit. place where we lay our heads)'		'lie on raised surface'		'our'	'head'

nominalisation	from	transitive verb	and	NP
jama-jo-jowi		jowi		jama
'broom'		'sweep'		'thing'

---

[5] There are languages with a number suffix which only occurs with intransitive verbs and then relates to the S argument. In some languages a number suffix on transitive verbs can relate to either A or O, so that its reference may be ambiguous—for example, Piro, an Arawak language from Peru (Matteson 1965: 94) and varieties of Quechua (Adelaar 2004: 221–2; Weber 1989: 143–4).

Note that *ee tati*, 'our head', is in underlying S relation to *fore*, 'lie on raised surface', while *jama*, 'thing' is in underlying O relation to *jowi*, 'sweep'. (Further examples are in Dixon 2004b: 534–5.)

Similar derivations are found in Movima, an isolate from Bolivia (Haude 2006: 200–1). For example *am-me* 'vehicle (such as bus, taxi, boat)' is, literally, 'enter-person' while *pul-pul-ta* 'litter' is, literally, 'swept.away-stuff' (with the verb *pul-* 'sweep' being reduplicated in this derivation). Hixkaryana, a Carib language from Brazil, exhibits a similar pattern (Derbyshire 1985: 222). Both Movima and Hixkaryana have a mixed accusative/ergative profile. Urarina, an isolate from Peru, is entirely accusative and forms nominal derivations on an S/O basis (Olawsky 2006: 321–2).

6.4. *Nominal incorporation*

If nominal incorporation relates to a core function, this is almost always S or O (and not A). There is a considerable literature on this, including Mithun (1984), Keenan (1987: 173–4), Fortescue (1992) and de Reuse (1994). For example, in the Australian language Rembarrnga (McKay 1975: 290–1), the incorporated adjective *kartpurr* 'wounded' refers to the S argument in the intransitive clause of (16) and to the O argument in the transitive clause of (17):

(16)   ø-kartpurr-mañ
        3sgS-wounded-go:PAST
        The wounded [buffalo] went off

(17)   yarr-kartpurr-perte?-miñ   nənta-ma$_O$
        3sgO:1plA-wounded-carry-PAST   THAT-man
        We carried that wounded man

(Further examples from Australian languages are in Dixon 2002: 423–9.)

6.5. *Verbal classifiers*

Verbal classifiers are morphemes which occur on the verb and characterise a core argument in terms of its shape, form, consistency and other semantic properties (often to the exclusion of animacy and humanness). See the discussion and exemplification in Aikhenvald (2000b: 149–61). Verbal classifiers typically categorise S and O (hardly ever A).

In Mundurukú (Tupí family, Brazil; Gonçalves 1987: 42–3), a language of predominantly accusative character, we find (superscript numbers here indicate tones):

(18)   a²ko³-ba⁴ₛ   i³-ba²-dom³
       banana-CL:LONG.RIGID   3sg:POSS-CL:LONG.RIGID(S)-stay:FUT
       [ko⁴be³   be³]
       canoe   LOC
       A banana will remain in the canoe

(19)   be³kit²kit²ₐ   a²ko³-ba⁴ₒ
       child   banana-CL:LONG.RIGID
       o'³-su²-ba²-do³bu²xik³
       3sg-POSS-CL:LONG.RIGID(O)-find:PAST
       A child found a banana

The classifier -ba- 'long rigid object' is added to the noun 'banana' and to the verb, where it refers to the S argument in (18) and to the O in (19). The noun which shows the same classifier as the verb in a transitive clause is presumably identified as being in O function.

6.6. Demonstratives with limited syntactic function

In most languages, a demonstrative with deictic (or pointing) effect can occur as any core argument. But there are languages with constraints on the functions in which a demonstrative may occur. In all the instances we are aware of, demonstratives are restricted to S and O functions.

In Manambu, which (as already mentioned) has an accusative system for core argument marking, there is a type of demonstrative which refers to a previously established topic that has not been mentioned for some time and is now being 'reactivated'. A reactivated topic demonstrative may only be used in S function, as in (20), or in O function, as in (21).

Sentence (20) was said to a child who was running around at a local market, in order to remind her of the existence of two relatives (who she ought to be following):

(20)   abraₛ   yi-na-bər
       THAT:REACTIVATED:dual   go-ACTION.FOCUS-3duS
       Those two are going! (I am reminding you of them; or else you will
       be left behind)

In (21), the bundle of sago has been established as a topic in a previous stretch of the discourse and is now being brought back into attention.

(21)   na:gw$_O$ ada$_O$
       sago(masc)   THAT:REACTIVATED:sg:masc
         ka-war-la-d
         carry-go.up-3sg.femA-3sg.mascO
       She has carried up that (previously mentioned) sago

Note that the reactivated topic demonstrative has different forms for singular, dual and plural and, if singular, for feminine and masculine.

A reactivated topic demonstrative cannot be used in A function. How this is handled in Manambu is for an intransitive clause to be used to reintroduce the topic, and this is followed by a transitive clause in which the reactivated topic is in A function, now referred to just by a bound pronoun. For example:

(22)   ñan$_S$ ada$_S$ tad;
       young.person   THAT:REACTIVATED:sg:masc   be:3sg.masc
         takwagw$_O$ vya-də-di
         woman:PLURAL   hit-3sg.mascA-3plO
       That (previously mentioned) young man was there; he hit the women

Note that the reactivated topic demonstrative is in apposition to the O NP in (21) and to the S NP in (22). (Detailed analysis is in Aikhenvald 2008a: 219–22.)

Dyirbal is another language in which demonstratives may only appear in S function, as in (23), or in O function, as in (24):

(23)   [giyi   yara]$_S$ bungi-n
         THIS:MASCULINE   man   lie.down-PAST
       This man lay down

(24)   [giyi   yara]$_O$ ŋaja$_A$ bura-n
         THIS:MASCULINE   man   1sg   see-PAST
       I saw this man

This language has a different technique from that in Manambu for dealing with the situation when a person referred to by a demonstrative would be in A function. The antipassive derivation applies. This puts an underlying A argument into S function, with the erstwhile O now being marked with dative case, as in:

(25)   [giyi   yara]ₛ   bural-ŋa-ñu   ŋaygun-gu
         THIS:MASCULINE   man   see-ANTIPASSIVE-PAST   1sg-DATIVE
         This man saw me

As mentioned before, Dyirbal is mixed ergative/accusative in terms of the marking of core arguments and operates with an exclusively S/O pivot for clause linking. The antipassive derivation 'feeds' this, converting an argument which is underlying A (a non-pivot function) into derived S (a pivot function). The restriction of demonstratives to S or O function thus accords with this language's syntactic profile.

The point we are making is that if there is a functional constraint on demonstratives it is always to S and O functions, whether the language has an accusative profile (such as Manambu) or a largely ergative one (such as Dyirbal). As a further example, Daguman (2004: 207) reports that for Northern Subanen (an Austronesian language from the Philippines) 'in verbal clauses, demonstrative heads occur just in S and O core functions'. This language is of mixed accusative and ergative character.

7. Why S and O?

There are two reasons for the recurrent associations between S and O (quite distinct from ergative marking) as set out in §§6.1–6. The first relates to the fact that there is often a close semantic correlation between a transitive verb and its O argument (rather than there being one between a transitive verb and its A argument), and also between an intransitive verb and its S argument.

We do find some limitations on the kind of referent for the A argument of a given type of verbs, but these are invariably rather general. Only a being with eyes can *see*, only someone who has a brain can *think*, only living organisms (animals and plants) and certain kinds of machine can *eat*, and so on. In contrast, limitations on the referent of the O argument for a given type of verbs tend to be much more specific. The O argument of a verb of singing can only refer to a song (or, say, an opera, which is a composite of songs). The O of *polish* is generally a piece of furniture, for *knit* the O is likely to be a garment, for *knead* it is likely to be dough, for *impeach* a person in high authority and for *survey*, in one of its senses, some geographical entity. (Further examples are in Keenan 1987: 172.)

It naturally follows that a noun in O function, if it is one of a limited set of typical O arguments, may be incorporated into a transitive verb, but not one in A function. In Fijian, a transitive verb may incorporate a noun in O function—the verb loses its transitive suffix, the noun loses the article it would have had when functioning as an O NP, and the verb-plus-noun combination functions as an intransitive verb. Consider the simple transitive clause:

(26) e_A laga-ta   [a   sere]$_O$
      3sg   sing-TRANSITIVE   ARTICLE   song
      He/she is singing a song

Object incorporated yields:

(27) e_S laga-sere
      3sg   sing-song
      He/she is singing songs

When the noun *sere* is head of an O NP, as in (26), it refers to a distinct entity: 'sing a song'. When it is incorporated into the verb, as in (27), *laga-sere* has a generic meaning, 'singing songs' (literally 'song-singing').

In Fijian, object incorporation is fully productive for just a few verbs. 'Eat', 'drink, suck' and 'board (a vehicle)' can incorporate any kind of object. Other transitive verbs may incorporate only a limited set of nouns. Thus, *laga* 'sing' may only incorporate a noun referring to a song, such as *sere* in (27). *Sara* 'watch' may incorporate 'film' or 'sports' or 'place'. *Waawaa* 'wait for' may incorporate a noun such as 'bus'. (Further examples are in Dixon 1988: 226–9.)

For some intransitive verbs the possible S arguments are fairly restricted. In English, *drip* is used of taps, holes in the ceiling, blood from a wound, and not much more. For *growl*, the S is likely to be a dog or bear, or someone who makes similar noise, or thunder, a stomach or some kinds of musical instrument. Only horses, or people behaving like horses, are found to *gallop*. And so on.

In summary, there is often a close association between the semantics of a transitive verb and its O argument, and between the semantics of an intransitive verb and its S argument. It is this that underlies the association of S and O in number-marking for suppletive forms of verbs (§6.1), in verbal affixes and adverbs which provide quantification or number specification (§6.2), in nouns derived by compounding (§6.3), in nominal incorporation (§6.4) and in verbal classifiers (§6.5). (Note that incorporated nouns often develop historically into verbal classifiers, which also operate on an S/O basis—see Aikhenvald 2000b: 355.)

As noted before, each of these kinds of recurrent association between S and O is found in languages with every type of profile—whether accusative, or ergative, or a mixture of these, or neither of them. None of the S/O associations discussed in §§6.1–6 should be described as 'ergative' (a term which relates to grammar); the motivation for these further associations between S and O lies in the domains of semantics and pragmatics.

Nor should that in §6.6, relating to demonstratives only occurring in S or O functions in some languages. This is also found in languages with both ergative and accusative profiles. There is a rather different explanation for it from that just offered for §§6.1–5, relating to the seminal finding by Du Bois (1987: 805) that 'arguments comprising new information appear preferentially in the S or O roles, but not in the A role.' A demonstrative with deictic effect, which draws attention to something in the context of speech, is likely to be introducing a new entity into the discourse. We return to this point in §9, after briefly discussing other types of S/A and S/O grouping, in §8.

8. OTHER S/O AND S/A GROUPINGS

There are some parts of a grammar where we may get an association of S with A in some instances and of S with O in others. These mixed groupings are found in all types of languages—of accusative and of ergative profile—and should not themselves be labelled as 'accusative' or as 'ergative'.

(a) Nominalisations

Many languages have an agentive nominalisation which applies to verbs, deriving a noun which relates to the underlying A argument of a transitive and S argument of an intransitive verb. For example, the suffix *-er* in English as in *runner, speaker* (underlying S) and *employer, admirer* (underlying A). The fact that a nominalising process operates on an S/A basis should not be taken as an 'accusative' feature—of English or of any other language.

There may also be nominalisations which relate to underlying O or S arguments. One example is *-ee* in English. Originally, all nouns derived by this suffix related to the underlying O argument of the verb; they include *employee, nominee, lessee, grantee*. The nominalisation process was then extended to describe an underlying S, such as *escapee, retiree*, and *attendee* (Dixon 2005: 343). The fact that this derivational process operates productively on an S/O basis should not be taken as an 'ergative' property.

A further example of a nominalisation process which operates on an S/O basis comes from the Carib language Apalai (Koehn and Koehn 1986: 92). Suffix *-senano*, added to a verb, derives a noun indicating 'brand new object'. This relates to the S argument of an intransitive verb, as in (28), or to the O argument of a transitive verb, as in (29):

(28)   enuru-senano
         born-NOMINALISER
         new-born one

(29)   iyri-senano
         make-NOMINALISER
         freshly-made object

In essence, each nominalising process in each language is likely to have its own syntactic orientation, which may be S/A or S/O (or it may have some other syntactic character).

(b) *Ambitransitive verbs*

In some languages all verbs are either strictly intransitive, occurring exclusively in an intransitive clause, or else strictly transitive, occurring exclusively in a transitive clause. But many languages have ambitransitive (or 'labile') verbs, which may occur in either clause type. There are two varieties of ambitransitives, according to whether the S of an intransitive clause relates to the A or to the O of a transitive clause involving the same verb. For example, in English we find:

S = A type of ambitransitive
 eat, as in *John$_S$ has eaten* and *John$_A$ has eaten lunch$_O$*
 knit, as in *Mary$_S$ is knitting* and *Mary$_A$ is knitting socks$_O$*
S = O type of ambitransitive
 spill, as in *[The water]$_S$ spilled* and *John$_A$ spilled [the water]$_O$*
 melt, as in *[The ice block]$_S$ melted* and *Mary$_A$ melted [the ice block]$_O$*

In a language with accusative profile it is generally the case that an S or A argument must be stated (or understood from context) whereas an O argument can be omitted, at least with some verbs. There may be a temptation to put forward the idea that S = A ambitransitives are basically transitive verbs which can omit the O NP. (Although this is often not possible, for instance if S and A are marked differently on bound pronouns, or in some other way.)

In similar fashion, a language with ergative profile generally requires an S or O argument to be stated (or understood) but the A argument may be omitted. This opens a possibility for treating S = O ambitransitives as basically transitive verbs from which the A NP can be omitted. (Again, there may be other properties of core functions which preclude such a treatment.)

Some linguists have suggested that ambitransitives of type S = O are an 'ergative' feature; presumably, those of type S = A would then be an 'accusative' feature. The approaches suggested in the last two paragraphs could mean that a language of accusative profile would only have ambitransitives of type S = O, while one with an ergative profile would be restricted to ambitransitives of type S = A. If ambitransitives were labelled as 'accusative' and 'ergative', this would mean that a language with an accusative system for marking core arguments would have ergative ambitransitives, and vice versa. If no other counter-argument could be adduced, this would surely demonstrate the unproductive nature of such approaches.

In fact, careful grammatical analysis shows that both types of ambitransitive verb can be recognised for all kinds of language—whether with an accusative or an ergative profile or any mix of these. (That is, the analyses mentioned in the last paragraph are in error.)

Just looking at languages which the authors know well, in Fijian (Dixon 1988: 204), most verbs can be ambitransitive, about 53% being of type S = A with the remainder S = O. Jarawara (Dixon 2004b: 82) has just a couple of dozen S = A ambitransitives but several hundred of type S = O, while for Tariana (Arawak family, Brazil; Aikhenvald 2003:

66–7) these figures are roughly reversed. (All three languages have an accusative profile in terms of core argument marking.)

Just as it is not appropriate to refer to an S/A nominaliser (such as -er in English) as 'accusative' and an S/O one (such as -ee) as 'ergative', so it is quite inappropriate to refer to S = A ambitransitives as 'accusative' and the S = O variety as 'ergative'. This has been done a fair number of times. Most notoriously, formal grammarians of the 'generativist' school have not only dubbed a sentence pair such as *John opened the window* and *The window opened* as 'ergative' but have misunderstood traditional terminology to the extent of using 'ergative' as a label for S and O arguments, rather than for A. (See Dixon 1994: 26 and further references therein.)[6]

9. Conclusion

We now point to three critical features of languages (A1–A3) which link together S and A, or S and O, but do not directly relate to 'accusativity' or 'ergativity'. These features provide the motivation for why many languages show either an accusative or an ergative profile (or a mixture of the two) in terms of marking core arguments and/or clause linking (B1–2).

A1. *New information typically introduced in S or O function*

At the end of §7, we alluded to Du Bois' (1987) important finding that when some new information is introduced into a discourse it is predominantly in S or O function for first mention. Further work since 1987 has confirmed this insight, which applies to languages of both accusative and ergative profile (see, among others, Genetti and Crain 2003).

Demonstratives with deictic (pointing) effect are typically used to introduce a new participant and it is in view of point A1 that, if demonstratives are limited in their syntactic role, they will be restricted to S and O functions. Languages have different ways of dealing with

---

[6] The terms 'unergative' and 'unaccusative' have been used for S = A and S = O ambitransitives, respectively. These labels have also been employed in several other ways such as to engender a considerable degress of confuson; they are best avoided. See the discussion in Dixon (2010b: 155–6, 158).

the situation when some participant would be in A function for its first appearance in a discourse. We saw in §6.6 that Manambu will introduce the new participant in S function within an existential clause (effectively saying 'here this is'), following it with a transitive clause with the already-introduced new participant in A function. In contrast, Dyirbal uses an antipassive version of the clause for which the new participant is underlying A, so that it is put into derived S function.

A2. *The topic running through a stretch of discourse is most likely to be in A or S function in each clause*

This was also pointed out by Du Bois (1987). The criterion for recognising an argument to be in A function is that it should have the potentiality for initiating or controlling the action or state being referred to by its transitive verb. And if there is an initiator/controller for the action or state referred to by an intransitive verb, it must be in S function. Thus, A and S link together as 'controllers' and as a consequence they predominantly—but by no means exclusively—function as topic.

A topic will be stated at the beginning of the stretch of discourse to which it applies, and is not likely to be restated in each following clause. Because of this, there are likely to be more explicit statements of NPs in O function than of those in A function. This was shown by Du Bois (1987: 822) to apply for Sacapultec Maya—which has an ergative system for core argument marking—and it also holds for Jarawara—which has an exclusively accusative system. Sample counts for transitive clauses in Jarawara show that for stated NPs there are almost five times as many in O as in A function.

The linking of S and A as 'potential controller' explains the fact that—in languages with both accusative and ergative profiles—A and S are treated in the same way in imperatives, in reflexives, and with respect to 'can', 'try' and 'begin', as outlined in §5.

A3. *There may be a close semantic association between a verb and its O or S argument*

As pointed out in §7, the meaning of a transitive verb may be closely tied to the meanings of possible referents of its O argument, and similarly for the meaning of an intransitive verb and the possible referents of the S argument. This explains the five types of links between S and O described in §§6.1–5—number marking by suppletive verbs, quantification or number shown by adverb or verbal affix, derived nouns, nominal incorporation, and verbal classifiers. (This is a quite different kind of association between S and O from that in A1.)

Note that A2 is not to be described as an 'accusative' feature, just as A1 and A3 are not to be described as 'ergative'. These features apply to all types of language, irrespective of their accusative or ergative orientation.

We can now move on to types of linguistic organisation which *are* to be labelled 'accusative' and 'ergative'.

B1. *Systems for marking core arguments*

It is rare for a language to have different marking for all of A, O and S. Since S occurs in a different clause type, it can be marked in the same way as A, or in the same way as O. Which to select?

If S and A are marked in the same way, this will reflect their association as typical topic functions, point A2. If S and O are treated in the same way, this will reflect their joint role in being the favourite functions for introducing new information, point A1. (And also, a much more minor matter, the semantic association that a verb may have with O or with S, point A3.)

As Du Bois (1987: 850) wisely muses, an accusative system of core argument marking will reflect point A2, and an ergative one point A1. Many languages have an exclusively accusative system. A largish minority of languages have an ergative system—in whole or in part—for marking core arguments.

B2. *Inter-clausal linking*

Some languages have a grammatical mechanism for telling which core argument is in topic role for that clause. Such a grammatical topic is called a 'pivot'. Many languages lack a pivot. If successive clauses in discourse share a common argument, and statement of this is omitted from the second clause, then—as explained in §4—its identity will be inferred on pragmatic grounds. A fair number of languages have an S/A ('accusative') pivot, naturally reflecting point A2, the association of A and S as typical topic functions. A much smaller number have an S/O ('ergative') pivot, reflecting point A1, the shared role of S and O in introducing new information.

It is noteworthy that many languages with an ergative system of core argument marking, under B1, employ an S/A pivot. Those languages with an S/O pivot (said to have 'ergative syntax') are all at least partly ergative with respect to core argument marking, and all have an antipassive derivation for putting an argument in underlying A (non-pivot) function into derived S (pivot) function, as demonstrated by (25) in §6.6. (See the discussion in Dixon 1994: 143–82.)

The features mentioned in §8 were:
C1. *Nominalisation.* Some nominalisation processes relate to A and S, others to O and S.
C2. *Ambitransitive verbs.* Most languages which include ambitransitive verbs have both S = A and S = O varieties.

Many languages show S/O and S/A features, of both C1 ad C2 types, irrespective of whether they have an accusative or ergative profile.

The crux of this chapter is that labels 'ergative' and 'accusative' are best restricted to description of features B1 and B2. Points A1, A2, A3, and also C1 and C2 cover a variety of associations between S and A, and between S and O, that have nothing to do with ergativity and accusativity in the generally accepted use of these terms.

The fact that some languages are accusative and others ergative in terms of core argument marking and clause-linking (B1 and B2) relates to the general properties of human languages given under A1 and A2 (and, to a lesser extent, A3). An accusative system reflects point A2, that a topic is most likely to be in S or A function, while an ergative system reflects point A1, that new information is typically introduced in S or O function.

C1 and C2 are quite different—simply ways in which S and A, or S and O, pattern in the same manner in parts of grammar; they apply equally for accusative and for ergative languages.

It appears that about one-quarter of known languages have an ergative system for core argument marking (B1), and some of these are also ergative in respect of constraints on clause-linking (see Dixon 1994: 2–5.) This is the primary and well-established usage of the label 'ergative'.

Almost every language has some part of its grammar in which S and O are treated in the same way—those topics discussed in §6 and §8, and doubtless many more besides. To label number-marking suppletive verbs, or nominal incorporation, or ambitransitives of type S = O, and so on—in sum, any association of S and O—as 'ergative' would be to assign ergative properties to virtually every language. Following this path would confuse the basic meaning and value of the term—in terms of B1 and B2—and would obscure its descriptive and explanatory power.

This chapter serves as a call for more care in the use of terms like 'ergative' and 'accusative' (and 'absolutive' and 'nominative').

CHAPTER FIVE

DEPENDENCIES BETWEEN GRAMMATICAL SYSTEMS

Alexandra Y. Aikhenvald and R. M. W. Dixon

1. INTRODUCTION

In this chapter we consider eight grammatical systems—Polarity, Tense, Aspect, Evidentiality, Person, Reference classification, Number and Case—and examine their co-occurrence within grammars. In many instances there is no dependency between systems. For instance, a language may have a two-term number system, singular and plural, and a three-term case system, nominative, accusative and dative, with all combinations of these choices being attested (nominative singular, accusative singular, dative singular, nominative plural, accusative plural, dative plural). In another language we may find a distinction between three cases in singular number, but only a two-way contrast in plural number—a nominative plural (corresponding in function to nominative singular) and a single accusative-dative plural (functionally corresponding to both accusative singular and dative singular). We can then say that there is a *dependency* between the Number and Case systems in this language, specifically that *Case depends on Number* since the Case choices that are available depend on the choice that is made from the Number system.

We have gathered all the examples we could find of dependencies between the eight systems and examined the direction of dependencies. For some pairs of systems there is a one-way dependency; for instance, if there is a dependency between Polarity (positive versus negative) and Case it is always Case that depends on Polarity, never the other way around. For other pairs the dependency can operate in one direction in one language and in the reverse direction in another; for instance, we have examples of Case depending on Number, and also Number depending on Case (but never in the same language, only in distinct languages). Putting together the full set of dependencies, from our data, reveals a hierarchy of dependencies between the systems. This helps to explain the way in which human language is intrinsically organised.

We have not restricted ourselves to a particular selection of languages. Rather, we have looked for dependencies between systems in all the languages on which we (or the colleagues we consulted) have available data, more than five hundred in all.[1] We give, in this chapter, examples of all the dependencies that we have found.[2] Our methodology was basically inductive (see §6).

§2 presents the eight systems that we consider, and then §3 briefly mentions formal and functional markedness within systems. §4 begins by explaining the idea of dependency, as we use the term, before getting down to the main business of the chapter, statement of the dependencies we have found. §5 gives a hierarchy that summarises the dependencies and then §6 suggests a rationale that underlies the hierarchy. §7 is a brief conclusion, with suggestions for further work. The appendix extends the discussion to also include the system of Definiteness.[3]

2. SYSTEMS CONSIDERED

All languages have a number of grammatical systems—closed sets of choices one of which must be selected for a construction of a certain type. Some systems are found in all languages (e.g. Polarity, Person) while others occur in many but not all languages (e.g. Tense, Case).

---

[1] Dependencies of the type investigated here are typically found in agglutinative and especially in fusional languages. They are rarer in isolating languages. The fact that we quote few examples from isolating languages should not be taken as an indication that we have ignored this typological class; on the contrary, we have assiduously searched the grammars of isolating languages.

[2] We give an example of every type of dependency found. We do not, of course, mention every example of each type; for some dependencies we found scores of examples but have just quoted a couple of typical ones here.

[3] This chapter is concerned with paradigmatic dependencies between grammatical systems. A related question concerns the syntagmatic co-occurrence of different grammatical systems, either as portmanteau morphemes, or as separate but contiguous morphemes. In some instances this can be entirely fortuitous and does not imply a semantic connection between the systems involved, e.g. the surface realisation through one portmanteau verb suffix in Latin of person and number of subject, tense, voice and mood. In other instances syntagmatic connection does indicate a semantic link between systems, e.g. in most languages pronouns combine person and number in one form (which is not analysable into separate person and number morphemes); this correlates with the fact that non-singular number is interpreted differently in different persons. We plan, in a later study, to examine the varied semantic bases of syntagmatic co-occurrences of grammatical systems.

We will here consider eight types of grammatical system: (I) Polarity, which is a property of a complete clause; (II) Tense, Aspect and Evidentiality, which are generally taken to be properties of a predicate; (III) Person, Reference classification and Number, which are properties of a predicate argument; and (IV) Case, marking the syntactic function of a predicate argument.

(I) *Relating to a clause*

(a) *Polarity.* All languages make a choice between positive and negative main clauses. (In many, but not all, languages there are also mechanisms for negating NPs, adverbs, quantifiers, pronouns, conjunctions, lexemes, etc.)

(II) *Relating to a predicate*

It is probably the case that every language has some grammatical marking for the non-spatial setting of an action or state.[4] (We take this to relate to the predicate, but an alternative position is to consider it a feature of the clause as a whole).[5] There are a number of possibilities, those most often encountered being:

(b) *Tense.* A closed system of choices referring to the time of an action or state in relation to a temporal focus—generally 'now', the moment of speaking; sometimes 'today' (and sometimes a combination of these focuses). Tense systems can involve two choices (most often past/non-past, sometimes future/non-future) or three (past, present and future) or more (see, for instance, Foley 1991: 235f on the system of eight tenses in Yimas, East Sepik family, Papuan region).

(c) *Aspect.* We here use this term in a fairly narrow sense to refer to the temporal composition, or the completion, of an event (see Comrie

---

[4] We use 'non-spatial setting' to cover grammatical marking for Reality, Modality, Evidence, Extent, Boundedness, Composition, Aspect and Tense—see Dixon (2010a: 152–5; 2012: 1–44). Useful recent publications on some of these parameters include Chung and Timberlake (1985), Palmer (1986) and Bybee, Perkins and Pagliuca (1994).

[5] While there is no disputing that Polarity is a property of the clause, opinions vary as to whether Tense, Aspect and Evidentiality should be taken as relating to the clause as a whole or to the head of the clause, its predicate. Foley and Van Valin (1984: 208–9) and Van Valin (1993: 8) regard Aspect as a category of the nucleus (i.e. predicate) but Tense and Evidentials as properties of the clause (see also Lyons 1966: 224). Note, however, that many languages combine information about Tense and Aspect into one grammatical system.

1976b). There is frequently a two-term system of perfective (the event is regarded as a whole, without regard for its temporal composition) and imperfective (focussing on the temporal composition of the event). (The term 'aspect' is often used with a wider sense to refer to any type of Aktionsart, e.g. do repeatedly, begin to do, do quickly; we do not include this type of grammatical specification in the present discussion.)

(d) *Evidentiality.* Languages from many parts of the world require specification of the evidence underlying any statement—whether the narrator actually saw what is being described, or inferred it, or was told about it, etc. Evidentiality systems can consist of just two terms (generally eyewitness and non-eyewitness) or of more than two. A classic treatment is Barnes (1984) who describes the five-term system in Tuyuca (Tucanoan family, Colombia): visual evidence; non-visual evidence; apparent evidence; second-hand evidence; assumed. (See also Aikhenvald 2004 and the chapters in Aikhenvald and Dixon 2003.)

(III) *Relating to a predicate argument*

(e) *Person.* Every language has a Person system, making a distinction between first person (referring to speaker) and second person (referring to addressee). Many languages also include in the system third person (referring to someone other than speaker and addressee); in some languages there is no third person pronoun per se, and the system of deictics must be used for third person reference (e.g. Yidiñ, see Dixon 1977).

(f) *Reference classification.* We group together here a number of different types of mechanism which all relate to the categorization of nominals (see Aikhenvald 2000b for an inclusive study of these mechanisms).

(i) Almost every language involves a grammatical contrast between *human/non-human* or between *animate/inanimate.* This is sometimes marked only in an indirect way, e.g. there may just be a distinction between human and non-human interrogatives, 'who' and 'what' (as in Uralic languages such as Finnish—Collinder 1965: 138, 141),[6] or

---

[6] Ewe is one of the few languages that lacks a human/non-human or animate/inanimate distinction in its grammar, even in interrogative words. There is a question marker *ka* that can co-occur with any noun, e.g. *nú* ('thing') *ka* 'which thing, i.e. what', *ame* ('person') *ka* 'which person, i.e. who', *afi* ('place') *ka* 'which place, i.e. where',

a plural marker may be restricted to use with animate nouns (as in Athapaskan languages such as Slave, see Rice 1989: 247). In Jarawara (Arawá family) from Brazil, only animates may be referred to by the third person plural pronoun *mee* (Dixon 2004b: 74–8). In Comanche dual and plural marking is obligatory for human nouns, optional for animates and seldom used for inanimates (Charney 1993).

(ii) Many languages have a *gender* system (masculine/feminine, or masculine/feminine/neuter) or a larger system of *noun classes*, placing every noun in one of a closed system of classes (with no necessary distinction between masculine and feminine), as in Bantu languages.[7] We here employ a narrow sense of 'gender' and 'noun class', requiring that there should be agreement in gender/noun class between a noun and some other word(s) in the clause.[8] (The terms gender and noun classes are often used interchangeably in the literature—see Corbett 1991; it is, however, necessary to distinguish them since some languages show both gender and noun classes.)[9]

(iii) There can be a set of *classifiers*. Most (but, generally, not all) nouns are each associated with a certain classifier which should accompany it in certain syntactic environments, and describes its physical structure or form or use or animacy. Some classifier sets have just a few members (e.g. five in Bengali—Barz and Diller 1989: 167–8) while others may be very large, and cannot be exhaustively listed (over 200 have been reported for Burmese, in Burling 1965, and over 400 for Tzeltal, in Berlin 1968).

Mechanisms (i), (ii) and (iii) are alternative ways of classifying nouns according to the nature of their referent. It is probably the case that a classifier set always includes a contrast human/non-human or animate/inanimate, as in (i). A gender/noun class system almost always includes (i), and even if it does not there will be a distinction of type

---

awu ('garment') *ka* 'which garment' (Ameka 1991, and personal communication). It is thus at the lexical—not at the grammatical—level that a distinction is made between human/non-human and animate/inanimate.

[7] We are only concerned with gender marking of a predicate argument, not of differences of speech-style determined by the sex of the speaker.

[8] This excludes semantically-based gender shown just on third person pronouns (which is not an agreement category), as in English.

[9] For instance, Paumarí (Arawá family, southern Amazonia) has (i) a system of two genders, feminine and masculine, marked on third person singular pronouns, demonstratives, adjectives and some verbal suffixes; and (ii) a system of two shape-based noun classes, marked by presence or absence of a verbal prefix. See Aikhenvald (1994a: 415–7, 2000b: 70–5) and Chapman and Derbyshire (1991).

(i) elsewhere in the grammar. Languages are known in which a gen-der/noun class system and a set of classifiers co-occur (e.g. Achagua, Arawak family, from Colombia—Wilson 1992: 63; and Malto, Dravidian family—Mahapatra 1979).

(g) *Number*. Every grammar includes a Number system—describing how many individuals are referred to by a predicate argument—although size and applicability vary. We can have just two numbers (singular/plural) or three (singular/dual/plural) or four (singular/dual/paucal/plural, or sometimes singular/dual/trial/plural). Most languages have a Number system applying—obligatorily or optionally—to nouns, to adjectives and/or to verbs (cross-referencing number for an argument of the verb).[10] There is almost always a Number system applying to pronouns, although it has a different semantic effect for third person (being here similar to number on a noun) and to first and second person.[11]

(IV) *Marking the function of a predicate argument*

(h) *Case*. Many languages have some overt marker on an NP indicating its syntactic function in the clause.[12] Case marking can be by inflection (which can go onto every word in an NP, or onto just one word, or onto several words) or by clitics or particles. Case generally marks core syntactic functions—intransitive subject (S), transitive subject (A) and transitive object (O)—and also other non-local functions (e.g. dative, instrumental) and local specification (locative, allative,

---

[10] We are here restricting 'Number' to a description of the referents of a predicate argument. That is, we specifically exclude—as something semantically quite different—iterative- or frequentative-type marking on a verb (e.g. 'do once', 'do many times'). See Dressler (1968), Greenberg (1991) and references therein.

[11] The familiar second person plural is 'addressee and one or more others, not including speaker' whereas first person plural is typically 'speaker and one or more others, which can include the addressee'. Many languages make a distinction between first person plural exclusive (specifically excluding the addressee) and what is called first person plural inclusive (better: 'first-plus-second person').

Sanuma (Yanomami family) has four pronouns, referring to: (a) speaker (first singular); (b) addressee (second singular); (c) speaker and at least one other person, not the addressee (first plural exclusive); (d) addressee and at least one other person, which can include the speaker (combining second plural and first plural inclusive, from more familiar systems). Here 'first-plus-second person' is grouped with second person, whereas in most other languages it is grouped with first person (Borgman 1990: 149).

[12] Blake (2001) is both an up-to-date discussion of this topic and also a guide to the earlier literature.

ablative). Some languages have limited case marking, e.g. just for local specification.

Of the eight types of grammatical system listed here, (e) Person and (b) Tense are shifters, whose reference varies according to the identity of speaker, addressee, and time of event. (Deictics, such as 'this' and 'that', are a further variety of shifter, whose reference relates to the location of the event.)

This is an exploratory venture, examining just a selection of the types of grammatical systems that recur across the languages of the world. We are not here considering systems of mood (interrogative, imperative, etc.) and modality[13] or types of possessive marking; these undoubtedly do interrelate with the types of system discussed here. We have investigated systems of Definiteness, which differ from (a)–(h) in that they relate primarily to the organisation of discourse; there is discussion of Definiteness (and deixis) in the Appendix.

We are also excluding, from the present discussion, categories such as transitivity, voice, causative, applicative, and reflexive/reciprocal; these relate to clause types, syntactic derivation, and argument coreferentiality, which are rather different matters from (I)–(IV). In fact a number of grammatical systems do have varying sets of choices in different clause types. Another point of relevance is the different possibilities for various grammatical systems in main clauses and in types of subordinate clause (for instance, there are often fewer Tense, Aspect, or Evidentiality choices in subordinate clauses). Systematic study of these topics is a matter for future research.

3. MARKEDNESS

The idea of markedness applies to some—but by no means all—of the grammatical systems in a language. There is a fundamental distinction between two kinds of markedness—formal and functional. A formally unmarked term will be the only one in its system to have zero realisation (or a zero allomorph).

---

[13] Mood and modality were not included in this first attempt to examine the dependencies between grammatical systems for a number of reasons. A major factor is that the terms 'mood' and 'modality' are used with a wide range of meanings so that it is hard to find two linguists who would agree on the scope of the terms. A study (even a preliminary one) of the dependencies between mood and other types of system would really require a study to itself, first defining the terms. But see the remarks on mood in §5 below.

Functional markedness relates to the situation of use—the marked term(s) may be used each in a restricted, specifiable situation, with the unmarked term being used in all other circumstances. In Portuguese, for instance, a masculine/feminine choice is made when the sex of the referent is known and unambiguous. But when it is unknown, or when there is a mix of referents, of both sexes, then the functionally unmarked term, masculine, is used, e.g. *o filho* 'the son', *a filha* 'the daughter' and *os filhos* 'the children'. (There are further examples, from Australian languages, in Sands 1995: 264–5).[14]

It should be noted that formal and functional markedness do not necessarily coincide—a term from a system that is functionally unmarked need not be formally unmarked, and vice versa (see Dixon 1994: 56).

We are here concerned with situations in which the choices available in one grammatical system vary, depending on the choice made in another system. This often relates to functional markedness but need not necessarily do so. Some gender systems, for example, show no formal or functional markedness, but can still be open to neutralisation[15] (say, in plural number). There may be no way to relate the gender-neutral plural form of a noun to any of the gender-specific singular ones, either formally or functionally.

However, if a system does show functional markedness it is generally the case that (i) when the number of choices in the system is reduced, in a particular context, the unmarked term will always be retained, and will have its semantic scope extended; and (ii) if the choices in system X depend on that made in system Y, we will always expect more choices in X to be associated with the unmarked than with the marked terms from Y.

For three of the systems listed in §2 we can make general remarks about markedness:

---

[14] Greenberg (1966) and Croft (1990: 64–94) have extensive and useful discussions of markedness but do not distinguish between formal and functional varieties. They make further distinctions that are not relevant to our discussion in this chapter. Modern work on markedness is based on the pioneering ideas of Trubetzkoy (for instance 1962: 146ff) and Jakobson (for instance, the papers reprinted in Jakobson 1984).

[15] The term 'neutralisation' (first used in phonology) is used here as a grammatical term, in preference to the synonymous 'syncretism' (Trask 1993: 181). See also the papers in Plank (1991).

POLARITY. In every language positive is—functionally and almost always also formally—the unmarked and negative the marked term.[16]

NUMBER. Singular is almost always functionally (and often also formally) unmarked. A rare exception is Kiowa (Kiowa-Tanoan family) where there is a three-term number system and a number of noun classes. For one class singular/dual is unmarked and plural is shown by suffix -gɔ; for another dual/plural is unmarked and singular shown by -gɔ; for a third class dual is unmarked with singular/plural being shown by -gɔ (Watkins 1984: 79).[17]

PERSON. If one term in a full pronominal system is formally unmarked it appears always to be third person; in a system of bound pronouns, 3sg is often zero. As noted earlier the pronoun system in some languages involves just first and second person (reference to third person then involving deictics); if either term is unmarked in such a system it will generally be first person. For instance, the Australian language Warnman has replaced its (first and second person) pronoun paradigm, basing new free forms on a root *parra-* with suffixes added to show Number and Person; just *parra* is used (with no suffix) for 1sg (O'Grady, Voegelin and Voegelin 1966: 136). The paradigm is:

---

[16] In Old Tamil positive clauses required a choice from the tense system—past, present or future; there was no tense marking is negative clauses. Negation was overtly marked (by the suffix -*aa*-) only for third person neuter subject. For first and second person, and third person masculine and feminine, negation was simply shown by the absence of a tense suffix (which were always non-zero). We here have a situation where negation is functionally marked but, in a sense, formally unmarked. (Data from Lehmann 1993: 68–9.)

[17] In some languages there is a small set of nouns (referring to things that typically occur in groups) whose bare stem has a collective meaning (that, is the formally unmarked term in the number system has a type of plural reference), and there are explicit affixes for singular and for non-collective plural reference (see Tiersma 1982 and Croft 1990: 66).

Another unusual—but rather different—type of number system is found in languages spoken in north-west Amazonia (from the Guahibo, Tucanoan and North Arawak families). Here inanimate nouns have a formally and functionally unmarked form which is used when number is not specified and also has a collective sense; explicit singular or plural reference is achieved by the addition of a classifier (in derivational function) to the specific noun. Thus in Tariana (North Arawak) we have *deri* 'banana/bananas (number not in focus); bananas (collective)'. Adding the 'long curved' classifier -*pi* we get *deri-pi* '(one) banana'; to this can be added the plural suffix -*pe*, giving *deri-pi-pe* 'bananas (individuated plural)'.

(1)

	singular	dual	plural
1st person	parra	parra-kutjarra	parra-warnta
2nd person	parra-ŋku	parra-ŋku-kutjarra	parra-ŋku-warnta

For the other systems there is often no unmarked term or if there is one it varies from language to language. In Tense, that term which includes reference to present time is most often formally unmarked but there are exceptions, e.g. past is unmarked in the Tibeto-Burman language Ao (Gurubasave Gowda 1975: 49–50) and remote past is unmarked in Manambu (see under (b) Tense in §4.1). Concerning Aspect, there is often no markedness in the system and when there is there seems to be no cross-language consistency as to which term is unmarked (see Comrie 1976b: 111–22). Similar remarks apply to Evidentiality.

In Case, that term which covers S function is generally the unmarked one—this is nominative in a nominative/accusative and absolutive in an absolutive/ergative system. But there are some languages where accusative is formally unmarked—see Dixon (1994: 63–7).

Turning to Reference classification, we find that in two-term gender systems masculine is most often functionally unmarked; but there are a sprinkling of exceptions, with unmarked feminine, e.g. Jarawara (Dixon 1995; 2004b: 286–7) and Seneca (Chafe 1967: 13–6); see also Alpher (1987).[18]

4. Dependencies

In many instances, grammatical systems are independent of each other. One may get a Polarity system, a Tense system and a Case system with no dependency between them. But in other instances we do find dependencies. The number of Tense choices available may depend on Polarity; the number of Case choices available may vary with Tense. (In the extreme instance, a Tense system may only apply in positive polarity, or a Case system only in one tense.)

We shall now look at the interrelations between our eight types of grammatical system. If the choices in system Y depend on that made

---

[18] Systems of noun classes and classifiers often have one 'residue' term, covering anything not included under the positive specification of the other terms; this can sometimes be used when one does not wish to make a specification from the system.

from system X, in some language(s), but never vice versa, we shall say that there is a dependency relation between X and Y, i.e. X > Y. For instance, if there are fewer case distinctions in plural than in singular number, we shall say that the number of choices available in the Case system depends on the choice that is made in the Number system, i.e. Number > Case.[19]

Note that a dependency relation may apply just in one part of the grammar of a language and not necessarily in other sections of the grammar. For instance, a Person distinction may be neutralised for plural number in bound pronominal affixes, attached to the verb, but be retained in free-form pronouns (this happens in a number of north Australian languages such as Kunwinjku—see Carroll 1976).

For some pairs of categories, X and Y, we find that if there is a dependency between them this always applies in one direction, e.g. X > Y. For other categories the dependency may be one way in some languages (X > Y) but the opposite way in others (Y > X). In the latter case we say that, cross-linguistically, there is a mutual dependency between X and Y.[20]

We shall show that a hierarchy of dependencies can be established, connecting the eight types of system.

4.1. *Polarity*

Polarity—the choice between positive and negative—is found to come at the beginning of the dependency hierarchy. Most other types of grammatical system can depend on Polarity; Polarity never depends on anything else.

The type of dependency is simple. Since positive is always the unmarked term, another type of grammatical system, if it depends on Polarity, will have more choices available in the positive than in the negative.

---

[19] Note that we are simply examining synchronic dependencies within a grammar. The present study does not venture into the question of diachronic development or the matter of cause and effect.

[20] We have not yet unearthed any example of a dependency X > Y in one part of the grammar of a language and the opposite dependency, Y > X, in another part of the grammar of the same language. Such a situation is not impossible, but would surely be transitory. It might evolve as the result of phonological changes and would be likely to be eliminated by grammatical changes of an analogical nature.

PERSON; REFERENCE CLASSIFICATION; and NUMBER. Some languages which have bound pronominal forms (attached to the verb)—expressing two or three of these categories—lose or neutralise them in the negative. Thus, all Person and Number contrasts are lost from this position in Estonian (here there is no gender system). Consider the verb 'to be'. In positive polarity, it inflects for three persons and for number in first and second persons. However, in negative clauses there is a single form covering all persons and numbers:

(2)   POSITIVE   NEGATIVE
    1sg olen   1pl oleme   ⎫
    2sg oled   2pl olete   ⎬   ei ole
          ⎵⎵⎵⎵⎵⎵⎵⎵⎵⎵⎵⎵   ⎭
              3 on

In Manambu (Ndu family, Papuan area; Aikhenvald 2008a: 298–303), and Tariana (Arawak family; Aikhenvald 2003: 400–8), all specifications of Person, Number and Gender, within the verb, are neutralised in the negative. In Ainu just the positive existential verb has distinct forms which signal the number of the subject (singular or plural) while the negative existential verb has a single form (Refsing 1986: 152). In Bengali all Person/Number distinctions of the subject argument are neutralised in the negative existential verb (Basu 1955: 9).

CASE. In Estonian (as in other Balto-Finnic languages), the direct object NP of some verbs can—in positive clauses—be marked by either objective[21] or partitive case, with a meaning difference. The difference indicates (i) totality versus partiality of the involvement of the object, i.e. 'all' versus 'some'; and/or (ii) definite/indefinite categorisation of the object; and/or (iii) perfective versus imperfective aspect.

(3)   jõi-n   vee   ära
      drink.PAST-1sg   water.OBJECTIVE.SG   away
      I drank (up) all the water

---

[21] We here use 'objective' for the marking of a 'total' object (note that there is a tradition in Estonian grammar to refer to 'total' and 'partial' objects). A 'partial' object is always marked by partitive case. 'Objective' is either genitive or nominative case, the choice being conditioned by number and by construction type—nominative for the 'total' object of an imperative or impersonal clause, or if it is plural; and genitive otherwise. (There is also a contrast between 'total' and 'partial' subject, which we do not consider here.)

(4) jõi-n   vett
     drink.PAST-1sg   water.PARTITIVE.SG
     I was drinking some water

However, in the negative only partitive can be used:[22]

(5) mina   ei   joonud
     1sg.NOM   NEGATIVE   drink.PAST PARTICIPLE
       vett   (ära)
       water.PARTITIVE:SG   (away)[23]
     I didn't drink (up) the water; OR I wasn't drinking any water

That is, the case system includes a contrast between 'total' and 'partial' marking for direct object, in the positive, but this is neutralised in the negative.[24]

TENSE. Many languages have a larger set of tense distinctions in the positive than in the negative.[25] In Amharic, for example, there are distinct inflections for past and perfect in positive clauses (Leslau 1995: 292–303 and Mengistu Amberber, personal communication).

(6) säbärä   'he broke'

(7) säbroal   'he has broken'

---

[22] In positive clauses the verb takes a suffix marking person and number of subject. This is not included in a negative clause and here a free form pronoun (which could optionally be added to (3) and (4)) is required.

[23] Examples (3–5) were provided by Aet Lees.

[24] Some languages present a more complicated situation. In Russian most positive transitive verbs can mark the object with either accusative or genitive case (genitive here having a partitive sense), but a few may only use accusative (and other sets of verbs have other possibilities) while almost all negative verbs allow either accusative or genitive. There are complex meaning alternations. For instance, proper nouns and common nouns with animate and/or definite reference tend to take accusative case, while common nouns with inanimate and/or indefinite reference tend to take genitive case (see Timberlake 1986 for a detailed discussion). Since it is difficult to formulate general rules, we do not consider it appropriate to resort to this data in the present discussion of dependencies.

[25] Hagège (1982: 85), in one of the few studies of cross-linguistic dependencies, states that in 42% of languages there is neutralisation or reorganisation of tense in the negative (the sample of languages employed is not specified). He also comments on dependencies between negation and mood, case, and subordinate clause types.

but this distinction is neutralised in the negative:

(8)   al-səbbərə-mm   'he did not break' or 'he has not broken'

(Note that negation is here marked by combination of prefix *al-* and suffix *-mm*.) Many Niger-Congo languages also show this dependency, e.g. in the Kolokuma dialect of Ịjọ simple past and present are distinguished in positive but not in negative (Williamson 1963: 74–5). In Amele (Gum family, Papuan region) the distinction between today's past, yesterday's past and remote past is neutralised in the negative, as is that between future and relative future (Roberts 1987: 110, 223–6). Kayardild, an Australian language, also shows fewer distinctions in its TAM system in negative than in positive polarity (Evans 1995b: 255).

ASPECT. In the Nilo-Saharan language Kresh, positive clauses distinguish perfective, perfect and imperfective aspects; in the negative a single marking covers all three aspects—Brown (1994: 165–6). In Pero, from the Chadic branch of Afroasiatic, the distinction between completive and non-completive aspect is neutralised in negative clauses—Frajzyngier (1989: 98).

EVIDENTIALITY. In Maricopa, from the Yuman family (Gordon 1986: 85), the evidential system consists of 'witnessed visually', 'witnessed through another sense' and 'reported'. Evidentiality and Polarity are notionally distinct and potentially applicable in either order. In fact, the eyewitness evidential may be specified after negation (note that negation involves discontinuous marking *waly-. . . -ma*), as in:

(9)   waly-marsh-ma-'-yuu
       NEGATIVE-win.DUAL-NEGATIVE-1sg-EYEWITNESS
       I saw them not win (i.e. lose)

Applied in the reverse order—eyewitness evidential plus negation—we would get 'I didn't see them win'. This order of morphological processes is not acceptable in Maricopa; one has instead to use a biclausal construction involving the independent verb 'see', as in:

(10)   marsh-m   waly-'-yuu-ma-k
       win-DUAL.DIFFERENT SUBJECT   NEGATIVE-1sg-see-NEGATIVE-ASPECT
       I didn't see them win

(Note that the eyewitness evidentiality suffix is homonymous with the lexical verb 'see', and has undoubtedly developed from it.)

Thus Evidentiality itself cannot be negated in Maricopa—an evidentiality specification cannot be made within the scope of the negative marker.[26]

We would predict that languages will be found where there are some evidentiality choices in negative clauses but not so many as in positive ones; that is, certain Evidentiality contrasts may be neutralised in the negative, just as certain Tense and Aspect choices are, in some languages.

4.2. *Person, Reference classification and Number*

As shown in the last section, all of Person, Reference classification and Number can be dependent on Polarity. When we examine the interrelations between these three types of system we find a mutual dependency between each pair.

PERSON > NUMBER. [The choices available in the Number system depend on the choice that is made in the Person system.] In some languages a number distinction is made in certain person(s) but is absent from other(s). English is an example of this—we find a singular/plural contrast in first person (*I* versus *we*) and in third (*he/she/it* versus *they*) but in second person *you* has both singular and plural reference.

Foley (1986: 70–1) describes neutralisations of this type among Papuan languages. In Kuman a singular/plural distinction is made only for first not for second or third person free pronouns while in Asmat it is made in first and second person but not in third.

(11)

	Kuman			Asmat	
	SG	PL		SG	PL
1	na	no	1	no	na
2	ene		2	o	ca
3	ye		3	a	

---

[26] In Yimas (Lower Sepik family, Papuan region) the positive copula has two forms with evidentiality values 'seen' and 'unseen'; this quasi-evidential contrast is neutralised in the negative (Foley 1991: 112–3, 225–7, 262–3).

NUMBER > PERSON. [The choices available in the Person system depend on the choice that is made in the Number system.] Here there are fewer person distinctions made in one or more non-singular numbers than in the singular. This is a typical feature of Papuan languages from the highlands of New Guinea (Foley 1986: 71–2). In Kalam, for example, there is a single form covering second and third person in the dual, but separate forms in singular and plural; whereas in Wiru second and third person fall together in both dual and plural. In Dogon, from the Niger-Congo family, first and second person bound pronouns fall together in the plural (Plungian 1995: 30).

We pointed out, in §3, that singular is almost always the (formally and functionally) unmarked term in a number system. Neutralisations in another grammatical system almost always take place in one or more non-singular numbers, never in the singular. We also said that if any term in a full system of bound pronouns is formally unmarked it will be third person singular (or first person singular in a system restricted to first and second persons). We did not attempt any general comments concerning functional markedness in Person systems.

NUMBER > REFERENCE CLASSIFICATION. [The choices available in the Reference classification system depend on the choice that is made in the Number system.] In some languages a gender distinction is made in singular pronouns (for all persons) but not in the plural, e.g. Manambu (Ndu family, Papuan region). In Amharic a gender distinction is made for second and third person in the singular, but not in the plural (Leslau 1995: 46ff). Many languages show a gender distinction in third person singular but not in third non-singular (or in first or second persons). Examples include German, Russian and other Indo-European languages. Heine (1982) gives examples from a number of African languages where several noun class distinctions are neutralised in the plural, e.g. in Mba, from the Ubangi branch of Niger-Congo, there are seven noun class markers in the singular but only three in the plural.

This dependency relates to Greenberg's (1963: 95) 'Universal 37. A language never has more gender categories in non-singular numbers than in the singular'. There is, however, a well-attested set of exceptions to this generalisation. In one group of Austronesian languages, there is an animate/inanimate distinction in pronouns only in plural number, e.g. Biak (where the distinction occurs in plural, not in singular, dual or trial—Steinhauer 1986). For additional counter-examples, see Plank and Schellinger (1997).

REFERENCE CLASSIFICATION > NUMBER. [The choices available in the Number system depend on the choice that is made in the Reference classification system.] In a number of Australian languages number distinctions are made only in some noun classes—those with human referents. Thus in Ngandi (Heath 1978: 35) we find seven noun classes. Those with non-human referents have the same prefix marker for all numbers (*rni-, rna-, a-, gu-* and *ma-* respectively). Masculine and feminine classes have prefixes *rni-* and *rna-* in the singular; there is a prefix *bari-* covering masculine dual, and *ba-* which is used for masculine and feminine plural, feminine dual and mixed masculine/feminine dual.

Other examples of this dependency were given under (f–i) in §2.

PERSON > REFERENCE CLASSIFICATION. [The choices available in the Reference classification system depend on the choice that is made in the Person system.] One typically finds gender or noun class specification made just in third person. First and second person are uniquely specified and their sex is presumably known, so gender specification here would be communicatively redundant. However, just a few languages do also show gender in second (but not in first) person, e.g. Hebrew and other Semitic languages; or—more rarely—in first (but not second) person, as in possessive pronouns in Kalaw Kawaw Ya, the West Torres Strait language (Ford and Ober 1991: 138) where a male possessor will use *ngaw* and a female will use *nguzu* for 'my'.

REFERENCE CLASSIFICATION > PERSON. [The choices available in the Person system depend on the choice that is made in the Reference classification system.] We have an example where Person depends on a combination of Reference classification and Number (but we do not yet have an example of Person depending on Reference classification alone). Future tense forms of the verb in Hebrew have distinct second and third person forms for both masculine and feminine genders in the singular; in the plural we find: second person masculine, third person masculine and a single form covering both second and third person feminine. That is, the contrast between second and third persons is neutralised in feminine gender and plural number. The future paradigm of *katav* 'to write' is:

(12)

	SINGULAR	PLURAL
1st	extov	nixtov
2nd masculine	tixtov	nixnəvu
3rd masculine	yixtov	yixtəvu
2nd feminine	tixtəvi	tixtovna
3rd feminine	tixtov	tixtovna

4.3. *Case*

We now consider the interrelation of Person, Reference classification and Number with Case. There are one-way dependencies Person > Case and Reference Classification > Case:

PERSON > CASE. [The choices available in the Case system depend on the choice that is made in the Person system.] In a number of Australian languages, first and second person singular pronouns distinguish case forms for each of S, A and O while 3sg has one form for S and O and another for A, e.g. Warrgamay (Dixon 1981: 40). In Dhalandji, also from Australia, S and A fall together for 1sg but are distinguished in all other pronouns (Austin 1981b: 216).

REFERENCE CLASSIFICATION > CASE. [The choices available in the Case system depend on the choice that is made in the Reference classification system.] We often get more case distinctions for nouns with human or animate than for those with non-human/inanimate reference. In Yessan-Mayo, from the Papuan region, dative case marker *-ni* can also be used to mark O function just with animate nouns (Foley 1986: 101). In Spanish a noun in O function is marked with the preposition *a* only if it has definite human reference. In both Dyirbal, from the Australian region (Dixon 1972: 43), and Dogon, from the Niger-Congo region (Plungian 1995: 12), there is an accusative marker, used for O function only with proper names of people and some nouns with human reference such as kin terms 'mother' and 'father'.

In Latin (and some other Indo-European languages), case distinctions relate to gender in connection with declensional classes (Aronoff 1992). All nouns belonging to masculine and feminine declensions (whether their reference is human, animate or inanimate) distinguish nominative and accusative cases, but this distinction is neutralised for all nouns belonging to neuter gender.

Looking now at Number we find dependencies in each direction with Case:

NUMBER > CASE. [The choices available in the Case system depend on the choice that is made in the Number system.] There are many examples of a larger case system in singular (the unmarked term from the number system) than in non-singular. We can again quote Latin, where nouns of all but the second declension have distinct dative and ablative forms in the singular, but a single form covering both functions in the plural. In all Indo-European languages that show a dual, there are fewer case distinctions in dual than in singular or plural, e.g. Sanskrit where nominative, accusative and vocative fall together in the dual, as do instrumental, dative and ablative, and also genitive and locative.

In many Australian languages, singular pronouns show distinct forms for each of S, A and O while dual and plural pronouns have a single form covering S and A, e.g. the Girramay dialect of Dyirbal (Dixon 1972: 50). In Kalaw Lagaw Ya, from West Torres Strait, there are two case systems for singular and dual nouns—common nouns have an ergative case for A and an absolutive one covering S and O, while proper nouns have an accusative case for O function and nominative covering S and A. But in plural number there is no case marking at all (that is, case suffixes cannot co-occur with the plural suffix). See Comrie (1981b).

CASE > NUMBER. [The choices available in the Number system depend on the choice that is made in the Case system.] In Chukchi there is a number distinction for all common nouns just in absolutive case, not in oblique (Skorik 1961 and Michael Dunn, personal communication). A similar situation is found in Erzya and Moksha Mordvin (Uralic) where the number distinction is neutralised in oblique cases just for nouns with indefinite reference (Feoktistov 1975: 289–93, 1966: 180, 204). For definite nouns in Kurdish number is distinguished for oblique cases, not for nominative (Bakaev 1966: 263).

4.4. *The hierarchy thus far*

We can summarise the dependencies discussed in terms of the hierarchy in (13).

(13)

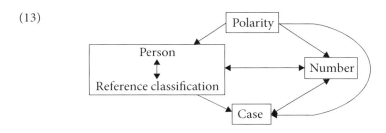

Diagram (13) states that any of the other grammatical systems may be dependent on Polarity—with more distinctions in positive than in negative—but that Polarity does not itself depend on anything else.

There is a mutual dependency between (e) Person and (f) Reference classification, between both of these and (g) Number, and between (g) Number and (h) Case. Other dependencies are unidirectional.

4.5. *Tense, Aspect and Evidentiality*

We can now turn our attention to the three types of grammatical system listed under (II) Relating to a predicate, in §2. In §4.1 we gave examples of all of Tense, Aspect and Evidentiality depending on Polarity. When we examine interrelations between these systems we find that—just as with Person, Reference classification and Number—there appears to be a mutual dependency between each pair.

TENSE > ASPECT. [The choices available in the Aspect system depend on the choice that is made in the Tense system.] When a language has Tense and Aspect as separate grammatical systems, we may get fewer aspectual distinctions in one tense than in others. Comrie (1976b: 71ff) reports that in many Indo-European languages, a distinction between perfective and imperfective aspect is only made in past tense. Further examples are discussed in Dahl (1985).

In Yimas (Papuan region) the Tense system has 'today' as focus; here a distinction between perfective and imperfective aspect is only

made in present tense ('completed during today' versus 'ongoing')—
Foley (1991: 241ff).[27]

ASPECT > TENSE. [The choices available in the Tense system depend
on the choice that is made in the Aspect system.] Most descriptions
of Russian state that three tenses—past, present and future—are distinguished in imperfective aspect, but only two—past and future—in
perfective. This reflects the historical development where the original
non-past imperfective became present (with no aspectual distinction),
the original non-past perfective became future perfective and a new
periphrastic form developed for future imperfective.

In the dependencies noted in §§4.1–4.3 there is typically neutralisation with the neutralised form, X, covering both X value and Y value.
Here there is simply a gap in the paradigm: there is no present perfective. As noted, it is usually said that in Russian Tense depends on
Aspect (there is no present tense in perfective aspect); an alternative
way of describing this situation would be with Tense determining
Aspect—one could say that an aspectual distinction is made in past
and future but is neutralised in present tense.[28]

TENSE > EVIDENTIALITY. [The choices available in the Evidentiality system depend on the choice that is made in the Tense system.]
Some languages may have Tense and Evidentiality as independent
systems, with the full set of evidentiality choices made in each tense
(e.g. Quechua—Weber 1986, 1989) but this is rather rare. In Jarawara,
for instance, there is a two-term evidentiality system (eyewitness/

---

[27] The verbal inflectional system in Yimas has nine terms: (1) irrealis (used of events
that are timeless, or in the legendary past, or in the indefinite future); (2) remote past
(more than about five days); (3) far past (two to about five days); (4) near past (yesterday); (5) near future (tomorrow); (6) remote future (after tomorrow); (7) present
perfective (completed during today, which is taken to extend from sunset to sunset);
(8) present imperfective (ongoing at the moment of speaking); (9) present habitual
(recurs, and could happen today). Terms (1)–(6) refer to past and future time outside
today (with no additional reference to aspect), while terms (7)–(9) provide aspectual
specification within the tense choice 'today'.

[28] Note that in the other examples given in this section the direction of the dependency is unequivocal. In Yimas, for instance, the only way of stating the dependency
is that an aspectual distinction is only made in present tense; and in Jarawara there is
no alternative to saying that the evidentiality system only applies in past tense.

non-eyewitness) which applies just in past tenses (Dixon 1995: 271, 2004b: 203–7).

As already mentioned, Tuyuca (Barnes 1984) has five evidentiality choices—visual evidence; non-visual evidence; apparent evidence; second-hand evidence; and assumed—in past tense. In present tense there are just four choices (not 'second-hand evidence') while no evidentiality specification can be made in future tense.

EVIDENTIALITY > {TENSE and ASPECT}. [The choices available in a combined Tense/Aspect system depend on the choice that is made in the Evidentiality system.] In Tariana, a Tense/Aspect specification can only be made in eyewitness evidentiality (the unmarked term from the system). In Estonian there is a four term system, combining Tense and Aspect, in clauses showing non-reported evidentiality: present/ future, imperfect (also called simple past), perfect and pluperfect.

In clauses with reported evidentiality there are just two choices available: present/future, and a neutralisation of imperfect, perfect and pluperfect. Bulgarian also has a grammatical system combining Tense and Evidentiality; this has nine choices available in non-reported but just five in reported evidentiality—present and imperfect fall together, as do perfect and past perfect, etc. (Scatton 1984: 330–1; see also Jakobson 1971 and Friedman 1986.)

We have no example of a dependency Aspect > Evidentiality [the choices available in the Evidentiality system depending on the choice that is made in the Aspect system], but predict that one may be found as more languages with evidentiality systems are described. This is the only gap in our illustration that there can be dependencies in either direction between any pair of Tense, Aspect and Evidentiality.

4.6. Tense, Aspect, Evidentiality and other systems

In §4.4 we established a hierarchy, beginning with Polarity, then having Person and Reference classification in one block, with Number in another, followed by Case. In the last section we dealt with a second hierarchy, again beginning with Polarity, followed by Tense, Aspect and Evidentiality in a block (where each system within a block shows mutual dependency with the others).

As the first step in relating together the two hierarchies, we can examine the links between Tense, Aspect and Evidentiality, on the one hand, and Person, Reference classification and Number, on the other. The dependencies here are fairly complex, involving a combination of two or more systems on one (or both) sides.

{TENSE and ASPECT} > PERSON. [The choices available in the Person system depend on the choices that are made in the Tense and Aspect systems.] Verbs in Veps (Balto-Finnic) distinguish three persons and two numbers in present and simple past tenses; however, in past perfect only number is distinguished, all three persons falling together (Laanest 1975: 91). In Old English verbal forms, 1sg and 3sg were distinguished in present tense but fell together in the past. For instance, the verb 'see' declined as (Quirk and Wrenn 1957: 46–7):

(14)

	PRESENT	PAST
2sg	syhst	sáwe
1sg	sēō	seah
3sg	syhō	seah
1/2/3pl	sēōð	sāwon

EVIDENTIALITY > {PERSON and NUMBER}. [The choices available in the Person and Number systems depend on the choice that is made in the Evidentiality system.] In Estonian, verbs in a clause with non-reported evidentiality distinguish Person and Number of subject. However, in a reported clause, no persons or numbers are distinguished on the verb, the two systems being neutralised.

{TENSE, REFERENCE CLASSIFICATION and NUMBER} > PERSON. [The choices available in the Person system depend on the choices that are made in the Tense, Reference classification and Number systems.] This was given in §4.2—in Hebrew, second and third person fall together in feminine gender, just in future tense and plural number.

TENSE (AND NUMBER) > {PERSON and REFERENCE CLASSIFICATION}. [The choices available in the Person and Reference classification systems depend on the choices that are made in the Tense and Number systems.] In Russian the verb in non-past tenses inflects for person and number of subject but not gender; in past tense the verb marks singular and plural and, within singular, masculine, feminine and neuter gender, but not Person. We thus find the Person system applying only in non-past and gender only in past singular. The paradigm of *dela-t'* 'do' includes:

(15)

	PRESENT				PAST	
1sg	delaju	1pl	delaem	masculine sg	delal	
2sg	delaeš	2pl	delaete	feminine sg	delala	} plural delali
3sg	delaet	3pl	delajut	neuter sg	delalo	

In Modern Hebrew (where there are just two genders) we find that in present tense the verb is inflected for gender and number (the gender distinction is made in both singular and plural). In other tenses the verb inflects for number and person, with gender being specified just for second and third person. That is, person is only distinguished in non-present, and gender is restricted to second and third person in non-present (it is marked for all types of subject in the present).[29]

{TENSE, ASPECT and NUMBER} > PERSON. [The choices available in the Person system depend on the choices that are made in the Tense, Aspect and Number systems.] In Livonian, a Balto-Finnic language, second and third person plural are distinguished in the present but fall together in all other tenses/aspects (imperfect, perfect, pluperfect) (Laanest 1975: 98 and T. R. Viitso, personal communication).

{TENSE and EVIDENTIALITY} > PERSON. [The choices available in the Person system depend on the choices that are made in the Tense and Evidentiality systems.] In Udmurt (from the Permic subgroup of Uralic), verbs show neutralisation of second and third persons (in both singular and plural) in past tense, non-eyewitness evidentiality and positive polarity. And note that all persons are neutralised in negative polarity. (Tepljashina and Lytkin 1976: 179).

{POLARITY, TENSE and EVIDENTIALITY} > {PERSON and NUMBER}. [The choices available in the Person and Number systems depend on the choices that are made in the Polarity, Tense, and Evidentiality systems.] In Udmurt all three persons and both numbers are neutralised in past non-eyewitness, within a negative clause.

---

[29] In these instances there are diachronic reasons for the split in grammatical marking. The past in Russian and the present in Hebrew have both developed out of deverbal adjectives (or participles), and inflect in a manner typical of nominals. For most of the examples of dependencies given here we lack information about their historical development. The diachronic dimension of dependencies is a question for future study.

Komi, a closely related language, maintains distinct forms for all persons and numbers in past non-eyewitness for positive polarity, but has one form covering second and third person in the plural in a negative clause. Here we get person neutralisation depending on a combination of Tense, Evidentiality and Polarity (Tepljashina and Lytkin 1976: 179).

TENSE > CASE. [The choices available in the Case system depend on the choice that is made in the Tense system.] Roth (1897: 7ff) reported the following case marking system for the Australian language Pitta-Pitta:

(16)

	NON-FUTURE	FUTURE
intransitive subject (S)	ø	-ngu
transitive subject (A)	-lu	-ngu
transitive object (O)	-nha	-ku
indirect object	-ku	-ku

Blake (1979: 193) reports that his informants would alternate -*ku* and -*nha* for O function in a future clause (these were the last speakers, and this variation concerning O marking in a future clause may well have been a feature of a language death situation). In both Roth's and Blake's descriptions, there are fewer case distinctions in future (two case forms for Roth and three for Blake) compared with non-future (four distinct case markers).

A similar situation is found in another Australian language, Yukulta, but here the two types of case choice are conditioned by a combination of Tense, Aspect and Person—see Keen (1983) and Dixon (1994: 105–6).[30]

---

[30] In Yukulta there are two construction types: (a) with the NP in A function marked by ergative case and that in O function by absolutive; (b) with A marked by absolutive and O by dative. Roughly, (a) is used for statements of past fact and future intention, and (b) in all other circumstances. (Construction (b) must also be used, whatever the tense/polarity choice of the clause if (i) A is third person and O is first or second person, or (ii) A is second person and O is non-singular first person.)

ASPECT > CASE. [The choices available in the Case system depend on the choice that is made in the Aspect system.] Hindi has distinct schemes for case marking of core syntactic relations according to Aspect—there is an ergative (for A function)/absolutive (S and O functions) system just in perfective.

Many other languages have two case systems, conditioned by Aspect or Tense; we always find an ergative system in past tense, or perfective aspect, and an accusative system in non-past or in imperfective—see discussion and references in Dixon (1994: 97–101).

No dependency is known between Evidentiality and Case. Evidentiality is closely linked to Tense and Aspect (as markers of non-spatial setting). Since there are dependencies Tense > Evidentiality and Aspect > Evidentiality, we would predict a direction of dependency: Evidentiality > Case.

5. The Overall Hierarchy

The dependencies that have been described can be summarised as an integrated diagram in (17).

(17)

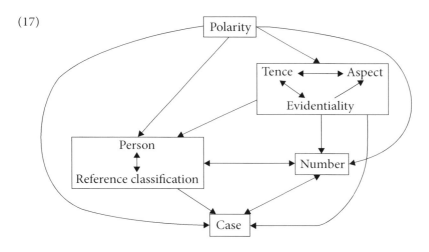

Diagram (17) combines the individual dependencies between Person and Reference classification with other types of grammatical system, and also those between Tense, Aspect and Evidentiality and other systems.

Stating the hierarchy more simply, without arrows, we get (with I, II, III and IV relating to the grouping of systems, in §2).

(18) DEPENDENCY HIERARCHY BETWEEN GRAMMATICAL SYSTEMS:

1.   Polarity (I)
2.   Tense; Aspect; Evidentiality (II)
3.   ⎰ Person; Reference classification (gender, etc.) (III)
4.   ⎱ Number (III) ⎱
5.   Case (IV)   ⎰

This basically indicates that a grammatical system may be dependent on any system above it in the hierarchy (but not vice versa). That is, the lower system may have a different set of choices available according to which term is chosen from the higher system. The braces indicate mutual dependencies (i) between Person and Reference classification, and Number; and (ii) between Number and Case.

6. RATIONALE BEHIND THE HIERARCHY

We began this study by simply looking to see what kinds of dependencies there were between various types of grammatical systems, without any notion that a hierarchy of dependency might arise. It was only as our examples accumulated that the idea of a hierarchy inductively emerged.

It will be noted that these grammatical systems occur on the hierarchy in a principled order. This is, in fact, the order in which the systems were presented, in §2. First comes Polarity, which relates unequivocally to the clause as a whole—(I) in §2. This is followed by Tense, Aspect and Evidentiality, three types of system that relate to the predicate (or, alternatively, to the clause as a whole)—(II) in §2. Then come the types of system which provide semantic specification of a predicate argument, Person, Reference classification, and Number—(III) in §2. At the bottom of the hierarchy comes Case, which is not itself concerned with semantic specification, but provides surface marking of the syntactic function of a predicate argument—(IV) in §2.

The dependencies between these systems relate to dependencies in grammatical organisation. We take the clause to be the basic unit of grammar. A clause must include a predicate as its head, and a number of arguments, which are the dependents of the predicate. The number and nature of the arguments depends on the choice of predicate. Some verbs are intransitive and require one core argument, others are transitive and require two, while a few are ditransitive and require three. Some verbs (e.g. 'think') must have a human or higher animate subject, others (e.g. 'drink') require a certain kind of object.

Polarity—the contrast between positive and negative—is unequivocally associated with the unit clause, in every language. Every language makes a distinction between positive and negative main clauses (at the very least). It is thus to be expected that Polarity should be at the top of the hierarchy—any of the other types of system discussed here may depend on Polarity, but Polarity may not depend on any of them.[31] We suggest that it is a priori implausible for the possibility of negating a clause to depend on the choice made from a system such as Tense or Gender or Number (i.e. that some language would be able to negate a clause only in present tense, or just if the subject was of masculine gender or plural number).

We have not—in this preliminary foray into the topic of dependencies between grammatical systems—looked at systems of Mood. The basic Mood system (consisting of just indicative, interrogative and imperative) is also associated with the clause. We would make a prediction—that the choice from a basic Mood system would never depend on any of the eight types of system discussed here. That is, possibilities of mood specification would not depend on the choice made from an Aspect or Number or Case system.[32] Nor should there be any dependency, in either direction, between Polarity and Mood.[33]

---

[31] At the end of §1 we noted that there may be correlations of a different type between grammatical systems and clause types. The situation here is quite different and the applicability of a Polarity system can depend on the choice of clause type. In Jarawara, for instance, negation may be marked in a main clause, a relative clause or a nominalised clause, but not in a complement clause. In Jarawara one cannot say 'I saw you not working (when you were supposed to be working)', only 'I didn't see you working'.

[32] Many other systems will of course depend on mood. Imperative, in particular, typically implies restricted choices in Tense, Aspect, Evidentiality and Person (in some— but by no means all—languages, the subject of an imperative must be second person).

[33] We can conceive of a language in which there is no polarity choice for polar questions, so that there is no such thing as a polar question in the negative (one could not ask 'Hasn't she gone?', only 'Has she gone?'). However, we suggest that no human language would have this restriction.

The dependencies between systems follow the dependencies just outlined between the kinds of constituents they are associated with. A predicate argument depends on the predicate, which is the head of the clause. As the hierarchy shows, systems associated with the predicate argument (Person, Reference classification and Number) depend on the systems associated with the predicate (Tense, Aspect and Evidentiality) and on that associated with the clause as a whole (Polarity). And systems associated with the predicate of the clause (Tense, Aspect and Evidentiality) depend on that associated with the entire clause (Polarity).

It is significant that the three types of system associated with the predicate (Tense, Aspect and Evidentiality) are all on the same level in the hierarchy. Save that we have as yet no example of Aspect > Evidentiality, there are dependencies in each direction between these (for instance, we find Tense > Evidentiality in one language and Evidentiality > Tense in another). This is consistent with them all being associated with the same grammatical unit, the predicate.

In the same way, each pair of Person, Reference classification and Number show dependencies in each direction (in different languages). This is also consistent with the fact that they are all associated with the same grammatical unit, the predicate argument.

Case is a different type of system from the others in that it marks the function of a predicate argument in the clause. It is natural that Case should come at the bottom of the hierarchy since it is a surface marking of the function of the predicate argument, which is dependent on the predicate, which is head of the clause. If there should be any dependency between Case and another system, we would expect Case to be dependent on the other system.

This expectation is generally borne out. There is, however, one exception. In some languages Case depends on Number (as we would predict) but there are also clear examples (given in §4.3) of languages in which Number depends on Case. This appears to occur only in limited and specifiable circumstances—a number distinction may be neutralised in oblique cases (Chukchi) or for indefinite nouns (Kurdish) or both (Erzya and Moksha Mordvin). What is unusual is that in Kurdish

---

Note that there are some languages that have questions of the type 'V-not-V' (e.g. 'Is he at home or not at home?'). However, to the best of our knowledge all such languages do also have straightforward positive ('Is he at home?) and negative ('Is he not at home?) questions, e.g. Mandarin Chinese.

a number distinction is made only for definite nouns in oblique cases, not in the nominative. The types of dependencies between Number and Case, and their conditioning environments, is a fascinating topic for further study.

Most of the dependencies we have described are well-attested; for some there are only one or two examples available at present. Note that we do not suggest that no counter-example will ever be found for the surest unidirectional dependencies—simply that these will be rare, and will represent an unstable and transitory stage in language change.

There are a number of typological parameters in terms of which the grammars of languages vary. These parameters are not independent of each other; there are certain typical combinations. Some of these were investigated in Greenberg's (1963) classic study of language universals. Another is that a system of switch-reference marking is only found in languages with an accusative syntax. (Further examples are in §9.1 of Dixon 1997.) The kinds of dependencies between grammatical systems, reported in this chapter, provide another example of the preferred grammatical organisation of human languages. The net result of these typical combinations of features is that certain typological profiles are very common across the languages of the world, and other profiles are quite uncommon (often being transitional phases, as a language shifts from one common profile to another).

Each language is the product of its history. Phonological changes (and some kinds of grammatical change) may produce a kind of grammatical organisation that does not exactly accord with any of the common typological profiles.[34] There may then be further changes, grammatically-motivated,[35] which will assist the grammar to accord more closely with universal preferences, such as the kinds of dependencies outlined above. The hierarchy put forward in this chapter should assist in predicting possible directions of change.

---

[34] The Kurdish example, in which number is only distinguished in oblique cases, is an instance of this.

[35] Diachronic changes in Rushan (from the Pamir subgroup of Iranian) have produced a system in which A (transitive subject) and O (transitive object) are marked in the same way, differently from S (intransitive subject), in past tense. This arrangement is highly unusual and unstable (besides being clearly communicatively inefficient). In fact, two kinds of change are in progress for younger speakers: (a) a tendency to use the same kind of case marking in past as in present, where A and O are marked differently; and (b) a tendency to us the preposition *az* 'from' before an O NP, in both tenses. (See Dixon 1994: 202–3 and further references there.)

A topic for future study is how mechanisms of grammatical change are susceptible to and motivated by the hierarchy of system dependencies established here.

7. Conclusion

By gathering examples of dependencies between grammatical relations across a variety of languages, we have been able to show that there is a hierarchy of dependencies, set out in (17). And, in §6, we discussed the grammatical and semantic rationale behind the hierarchy.

This hierarchy is put forward as a preliminary hypothesis, a first attempt to describe and explain the ways in which some grammatical systems interrelate. We are only familiar with the grammatical organisation of a fraction of the world's languages. We welcome further information—more examples of the dependencies described here, and examples of those for which we do not yet have attestation (Aspect and Evidentiality, Evidentiality and Case).

This kind of investigation could be extended to consideration of other grammatical systems, and of construction types, etc. Indeed, it should be possible to predict the kinds of dependencies that should or should not be encountered (as we did for Mood, in §6), and then verify these predictions by examining data from a wide selection of languages.[36]

Appendix—Definiteness

Definiteness is a quite different type of system from those just discussed. The data we have on it is less extensive than that for other systems. For this reason, our preliminary results concerning dependencies between Definiteness and the other systems discussed here are presented separately.

All languages have some mechanism for indicating Definiteness. However, a grammatical system 'definite/indefinite' is probably only found in a minority of the world's languages. Definiteness is essentially

---

[36] Languages of the fusional type show phonological integration of grammatical morphemes and, hand-in-hand with this, have a tendency towards integration of grammatical systems. That is, the highest proportion of dependencies between grammatical systems are found in fusional languages. But, as the examples in this chapter show, there are also a number of dependencies in agglutinative and isolating languages.

a discourse category, relating to whether the predicate argument in question is fully specified by the referential information included in the NP (e.g. *the man who lives next door*—when there is only one man who does so—or *the King of Spain*) or whether it refers anaphorically to a participant already introduced in the discourse (e.g. *A snake came into our house. My brother screamed but then my father killed <u>the snake</u>* (sc. the one which had come into our house)).

Every language has deictic terms (always 'this', almost always also 'that', etc.) used for pointing to something in the context of speech and often—although not always—also with anaphoric function. These are semantically similar to markers of Definiteness (the definite member of a definiteness system often developed from a deictic).

We have searched for dependencies between a system of Definiteness and the eight types of system discussed in this chapter. We find no dependency, in either direction, between system of type (II)—Tense, Aspect and Evidentiality—and Definiteness.

There can be a dependency: POLARITY > DEFINITENESS [the choices available in the Definiteness system depend on the choice that is made in the Polarity system]. First consider English, where clausal negation and definiteness are independent parameters, e.g. one can say, in the positive:

(19)   I saw some books   [indefinite]
(20)   I saw the books   [definite]

and in the negative:

(21)   I didn't see any books   [indefinite]
(22)   I didn't see the books   [definite]

In French there is an indefinite/definite contrast in the positive:

(23)   J'ai vu des livres   [indefinite]
(24)   J'ai vu les livres   [definite]

But this distinction is neutralised in the negative. Both (21) and (22) would be translated by:

(25)   Je n'ai vu pas de livres   [indefinite/definite]

We also get definiteness neutralised in some languages when an NP (not a clause) is negated. In Portuguese, for instance, one can say, in the positive, *um cachorro* 'a dog', with the masculine indefinite article, or *o cachorro* 'the dog', with the masculine definite article. There is a negative adjective, with masculine form *nenhum*, which replaces articles; thus *nenhum cachorro* can mean either 'not a dog' or 'not the dog'.

With Case we find dependencies in each direction:

CASE > DEFINITENESS. [The choices available in the Definiteness system depend on the choice that is made in the Case system]. In Modern Eastern Armenian a distinction between definite and indefinite is made in the nominative-accusative and genitive-dative cases, but not in ablative, instrumental or locative (here the interpretation can be definite or indefinite) (Bernard Comrie, personal communication.) In Basque nouns are marked for case and definiteness with just definite (not indefinite) being further specified for number. However, there are two cases—partitive and prolative—which cannot be specified for definiteness (Saltarelli 1988: 300).

DEFINITENESS > CASE. [The choices available in the Case system depend on the choice that is made in the Definiteness system]. In some languages a particular case inflection is used only on definite, never on indefinite, nouns. This can apply for ergative—as in languages from the Circassian subgroup of North-west Caucasian—or to accusative—as in Aari, from the Omotic family (Hayward 1990: 442), and in Hebrew and Amharic, from the Semitic family. (See Dixon 1994: 91; Kirtchuk 1993; Mallinson and Blake 1981: 62; and Leslau 1995: 181.)

Similarly with Number, there are dependencies in each direction:

NUMBER > DEFINITENESS. [The choices available in the Definiteness system depend on the choice that is made in the Number system]. In Sinhala, a definite/indefinite contrast is made only in singular number (Matzel 1987: 66–7); and the same restriction applies in Kabardian (Kumakhov and Vamling 1995: 92).

DEFINITENESS > NUMBER. [The choices available in the Number system depend on the choice that is made in the Definiteness system]. In Gimira (Omotic family) plural marking is rarely used on a noun unless it is definite (Breeze 1990: 11). And in Kurdish only indefinite (not definite) nouns distinguish singular from plural (Bakaev 1966: 263–4). See also the examples from Erzya, Moksha-Mordvin and Kurdish, given at the end of §4.3.

We have no clear examples of a dependency between Reference classification and Definiteness.[37] With respect to Person, we can remark that first and second person singular pronouns (in their central meanings) are uniquely specified and necessarily definite; a definite/indefinite contrast can only apply in the third person.
    Definiteness is different in nature from the eight types of grammatical system discussed in the body of this chapter, since it is basically a discourse category, relating to how a predicate argument functions in speech. However, the information available suggests that it can be placed in the hierarchy already established, as in (26).

(26)

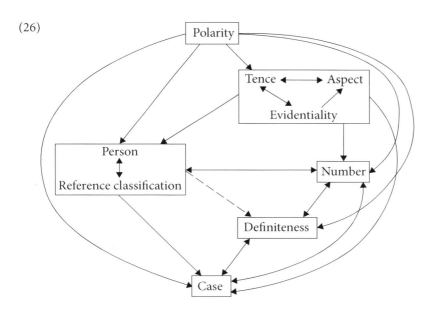

---

[37] Corbett (1991: 124–5) describes how in Swedish an adjective will only inflect for gender in an indefinite NP, not in a definite one. However, this appears to be a matter of agreement, not of basic choice from a grammatical system. The gender of the head noun will always be marked within the NP, on the article; it is just that, if the article is indefinite, gender is marked a second time, on the adjective.

SOURCES AND ACKNOWLEDGEMENTS

We have not thought it necessary to provide literature citations for references to well-known languages for which there are many grammars available—Estonian, French, German, Hebrew, Hindi, Latin, Mandarin Chinese, Portuguese, Russian, Sanskrit, Spanish and Swahili. But we have included citations for information quoted from lesser-known languages. (Care has been taken only to use information from sources that we consider to be reliable.) We have, of course, made use of information from languages on which we have done field work ourselves, including Tariana, Manambu and Estonian (Aikhenvald) and Jarawara, Dyirbal and Warrgamay (Dixon).

For critical comments on an earlier draft of this chapter, we owe a considerable debt to Mengistu Amberber, Felix Ameka, Wallace Chafe, Adam Chapman, Greville Corbett, Desmond Derbyshire, Mark Donohue, Matthew Dryer, Michael Dunn, Nicholas Evans, Zygmunt Frajzyngier, Joseph Greenberg, Martin Haspelmath, Bernd Heine, George Hewitt, Nikolaus Himmelmann, Leonid Kulikov, Aet Lees, Ilse Lehiste, Winfred Lehmann, Frank Lichtenberk, Tony Liddicoat, Edith Moravcsik, Ulrike Mosel, Nicole Nau, Masayuki Onishi, Vladimir Plungian, Alan Rumsey, Tim Shopen, George Silnitsky, Tiit-Rein Viitso, Anna Wierzbicka and especially Bernard Comrie.

CHAPTER SIX

THE SEMANTIC BASIS FOR A TYPOLOGY

R. M. W. Dixon*

1. Syntactic Functions and Semantic Roles

Syntax and semantics are distinct but interrelated components of a language. It is important to distinguish between:

- SYNTACTIC FUNCTIONS. These are the functions of arguments (which may be expressed by NPs and/or bound pronouns). An intransitive clause has one core argument, in S (intransitive subject) function, and a transitive clause has two, in A (transitive subject) and O (transitive object) functions. There is almost always a subtype of transitive—extended transitive (or ditransitive), with three obligatory arguments—A, O and E, for 'extension to core' (this is typically marked by dative case).
- SEMANTIC ROLES. Verbs divide into a number of semantic types, each being associated with a set of semantic roles. Illustrating for English (fuller details are in Dixon 1991, 2005):
  - One set of verbs of MOTION (including *go* and *wiggle*) typically has just one semantic role, the Moving (thing).
  - Verbs of the ATTENTION type (such as *see* and *hear*) typically have two semantic roles, Perceiver and Impression.
  - Verbs of the THINKING type (such as *believe* and *suppose*) typically have two roles, Cogitator and Thought.

* My major debt is to Okomobi, Soki, Mioto, Kamo, Botenawaa, Kakai, Wero and all the other Jarawara people of the village of Casa Nova, for their friendship and skilled instruction. I am grateful to Alan Vogel, who invited me to share his field location and assisted with the grammar of Jarawara (Dixon 2004b). And also to Alexandra Y. Aikhenvald, Timothy Jowan Curnow and Suzanne Kite, who provided most useful comments on a draft of the chapter.

In many languages, each semantic role corresponds to (that is, is mapped onto) a consistent syntactic function. In English, the Moving role is associated with S, Perceiver and Cogitator roles with A, and Impression and Thought roles with O.

2. CORRESPONDENCES BETWEEN FUNCTIONS AND ROLES

In some language a certain semantic roles is always mapped onto the same syntactic function. In others there is a degree of fluidity.

The most extreme fluidity I have encountered is found in Jarawara, spoken in the dense jungle of southern Amazonia. This can be illustrated for two verbs.[1] (Note that all the examples given here are taken from texts.) Consider *tisa -na-*, a transitive verb which describes using an arrow (or slingshot) to hit something; it is most frequently used for shooting fish in the water. The A argument will be the hunter, but the O argument can be any of the other semantic roles involved in the activity. It is most frequently the animal or fish that is shot at:

(1) aba$_O$ mee   otaa   tisa   na   otaa-ke
     fish(m)   3nsgO   1exclA   shoot   AUXILIARY   1excl-DECL:f
     We shot lots of fish

(Note that Jarawara has two genders, feminine (f) and masculine (m). Feminine is the unmarked gender. For instance, all pronouns are cross-referenced as feminine, irrespective of the sex of their referent. Thus in (1) the declarative suffix has f form *-ke* (m would be *-ka*), agreeing with the 1st person non-singular exclusive pronoun, *otaa*, in A function.)

Alternatively, the arrow that is used in the action can be placed in O function:[2]

---

[1] Note that there are two classes of verb in Jarawara: inflecting (e.g. *-tafa-* 'eat') and non-inflecting (e.g. *hoo -na-* 'snore'). Verbal prefixes and suffixes are added directly to an inflecting verb but to an auxiliary (generally *-na-*) which follows a non-inflecting verb. The auxiliary *-na-* is omitted with certain prefix and suffix combinations; this happens in (5) and (22).
[2] Jarawara has three past tenses: immediate past (IP), recent past (RP) and far past (FP). Each must be accompanied by an evidentiality marker: eyewitness (e) or non-eyewitness (n).

(2) faja   wati$_O$ mee   tisa   ne-mete-mone-ke   fahi
     THEN   arrow(m)   3nsgA   shoot   AUX-FPnf-REP:f-DECL:f   THERE
     They are then said to have shot off arrows there

And we also have an example where the O argument is 'water':

(3) faha$_O$ ee   tisa   ne-ne
     water(f)   1inclA   shoot   AUXILIARY-IRREALIS:f
     We could shoot into the water (to try to catch fish)

The verb *ori -na-* is generally used to describe paddling a canoe. It is
an ambitransitive of type S = A. An intransitive example is:

(4) faja   Motobi$_S$ ori   na-re-ka   fahi
     THEN   name(m)   paddle   AUXILIARY-IPem-DECL:m   THERE
     Then Motobi paddled there

Or the verb can be used transitively. Again, there is variation in which
semantic role is mapped onto O syntactic function. It can be the boat
that is paddled:

(5) kanawaa$_O$ ori   o-ne   o-ke
     canoe(f)   paddle   1sgA-CONTINUOUS   1sg-DECL:f
     I am paddling the canoe

Or it can be the river or lake that is paddled on:[3]

(6) faha$_O$ otaa   ori   na
     water(f)   1exclA   paddle   AUXILIARY:f
     We paddled in the water

Dyirbal is a language of quite different type, where—with few exceptions—each semantic role can be associated with only one syntactic function. Comparing with *tisa -na-* in Jarawara, a Dyirbal verb

---

[3] When the applicative derivation (marked by prefix *ka-*) is applied to *ori -na-*, the
O argument can be the paddle, or the goods or passengers in the canoe. The applicative of *ori -na-* can also be used to describe 'mixing together (e.g. bananas and fish
broth) with a spoon'. As noted under (III) in §3, this relates to the nature-of-action
characterisation of *ori -na-* as 'moving a piece of wood though some liquid'.

such as *jurrga-* 'spear something that can be seen, holding on to the spear'.[4] For this verb, the thing that the spear is aimed at must be in O function:

(7) ŋaja$_A$ [bayi   jabu]$_O$ jurrga-nyu
     1sg:NOM   DET:ABS:m   fish(m):ABS   spear-PAST
     [baŋgul   jirrga-ŋgu]   yuramu-ga
     DET:INSTR:m   multi.prong.spear(m)-INSTR   river-LOC
     I speared the fish with a multi-prong spear in the river

There is an applicative derivation (marked by suffix *-ma-* to the verb) which puts an instrument argument into O function and marks the original O (here, the thing aimed at) with dative case (see Dixon 1972: 95–6). But the underived verb, as in (7), can *only* have the thing aimed at in O function, the Instrument role marked with instrumental case, and the Locus role marked with locative case.

English falls between these two extremes, showing a modicum of variation in role/function correspondences for simple transitive verbs. A familiar example from English (which tends to be quoted so often partly because examples like this are relatively rare in English, as compared with Jarawara) is (adapted from Anderson 1971):

(8) John$_A$ loaded the hay$_O$ (onto wagons)

(9) John$_A$ loaded the wagons$_O$ (with hay)

In (8) the (thing that becomes) Resting role is in O function whereas in (9) the Locus role is in O function. These sentences do of course have different meanings: (8) implies that all the hay has been put on wagons, whereas (9) implies that all the wagons have been filled with hay. This correlates with specification of definiteness, and properties of the O function: a role in O function is more likely than one in peripheral function to be definite, and to refer to something specifically affected by the activity.

Verbs of giving are an interesting topic for study. There are here three semantic roles: Donor, Gift and Recipient. In some languages

---

[4] We should remark that the Jarawara do not employ spears and generally kill fish with bow and arrow. The bow and arrow is unknown in Australia and the Dyirbal generally kill fish with a spear.

the Gift must be placed in O function, in others the Recipient must be O. English shows variation here, with both alternatives being possible: one can say either *I gave some money to John* (where the Gift, *some money*, is in O function) or *I gave John some money* (where the Recipient, *John*, is the O). (See Dixon 2010b: 134–7 for fuller discussion of verbs of giving.)

There is a *continuum of role/function correspondences*:

(10) (a)   (b)   (c)
      fixed   some fluidity   great fluidity
      correspondences   (for a few verbs)   (for many verbs)
      as in Dyirbal   as in English   as in Jarawara

It is likely that there is a correlation between place on the continuum in (10) and transitivity profile:

- Some language show fixed transitivity—each verb is either strictly transitive or strictly intransitive. Dyirbal if of this type. Preliminary investigation suggests that there may be a correlation between fixed role-function correspondences in (a) and strict transitivity.
- Other languages have fluid transitivity. That is, many verbs can be used in either a transitive or an intransitive constriction. There are ambitransitives of type S = O and others of type S = A. (See §8 in Chapter 4.) Jarawara demonstrates this profile, and it is likely that a language with fluid transitory will also have fluid function-role correspondence (c) in (10).

English lies between these extremes; there is a limited number of ambitransitive verbs (see Dixon 2005: 305–11). This fits in with its middle position in the continuum at (10).

3. A SEMANTIC TYPOLOGY

Language is about meaning, the communication of meaning. Everything in the grammar of a language must have—or must once have had—a broad semantic basis. It can be shown that the typological continuum of role/function correspondences in (10) is a consequence of a certain semantic orientation within a language.

(11) A SEMANTIC TYPOLOGY OF VERBS
A prototypical verb describes an action that involves a number of par-
ticipants. Languages differ as to whether:
(A) verbs are taken to describe a kind of action with respect to the
    (articulation of) types of participants that are involved; or
(B) verbs are taken to describe a kind of action per se.

We can refer to (A) as the 'nature-of-argument' type and to (B) as
the 'nature-of action' type. These types can be illustrated with verbs of
eating in Dyirbal, a language of type (A) and in Jarawara, a language
of type (B).

The Girramay dialect of Dyirbal has three rather specific verbs of
eating, depending on the nature of the foodstuff that is being consumed (the foodstuff is the O argument):

(12)   rubima-   eat fish
       burnyja-   eat meat
       nanba-   eat vegetables

Jarawara also has a number of transitive verbs of eating, but these
describe the nature of the action, not the type of object involved.
We find:

(13)   -kaba-   eat where a lot of chewing is involved (this would be used
                    of meat, fish, sweet corn, yams, manioc, biscuits, etc.)
       jome -na-   eat where little or no chewing is needed, e.g. eating an
                    orange or banana (also used for swallowing a pill)
       komo -na-   eating which involves spitting out seeds (e.g. jifo, the fruit
                    of the murity palm, *Mauritia vinifera*)
       bako -na-   eating by sucking (e.g. water melon, cashew fruit, sugar
                    cane)

For some foods there is a choice of verbs available, e.g. eating a pine-
apple could be described by *jome -na-* or by *bako -na-*.

Characterisations (A) and (B) are not polar alternatives but rather
the ends of a continuum.[5] Dyirbal is close to one extreme and Jarawara at the other; English lies somewhere between them. The differ-

---

[5] I It may well be that a given language will be of type (B)—with correspondingly
wide role/relation correspondences—just for verbs of certain semantic types, and of
type (A) for other semantic types of verbs. This is a matter for further study.

ence between English and Jarawara may be illustrated with verbs of speaking.

VERBS OF SPEAKING involve three basic semantic roles—the Speaker, the Addressee, and the Message (what is talked about). Many verbs of speaking in English have a fixed correspondence between semantic role and syntactic function. Compare *report* and *inform* in

(14)   I reported the accident to the police

(15)   I informed the police of the accident

For *report* the Message must be O, with the Addressee being in peripheral function (marked here by *to*), whereas for *inform* the Addressee is O with the Message being in peripheral function (marked by preposition *of* or *about*). The alternative role/function assignment is not allowed; that is *I reported the police of the accident* and *I informed the accident to the police* are unacceptable. In other words, each of these verbs is restricted to a specific configuration of participants—type (A) in (11).

  In Jarawara we have *-hijara-*, a verb of S = A type. It can be used intransitively with the meaning 'talk, speak', as in

(16)   o-hijara-mati-be
       1sgS-talk-SHORT.TIME-IMMEDIATE:f
       I'll talk now for a bit [the opening of a story]

or transitively, generally with the Addressee as O, e.g.

(17)   ijo$_O$ mee   o-hijara-hara   o-ke
       Indian   3nsgO   1sgA-talk.to-IPe:f   1sg-DECLARATIVE:f
       I talked to the Indians

It is possible to have the Message in O function:

(18)   [Jesowi   mee   ati]$_O$ otaa   hijara-bone   otaa-ke
       name(m)   AUG   word   1exclA   talk.about-INT:f   1excl-DECL:f
       We'll talk about the words of Jesus and his companions

Note that in Jarawara the first slots of the predicate carry obligatory pronominal reference to O and A/S arguments (with 3sg always

zero). There can be NPs in core functions (S, or A and/or O, in either
order) before the predicate; these receive no marking. Non-core NPs
(e.g. indirect object, instrument, temporals, locationals) take the all-
purpose peripheral postposition *jaa* and come at the beginning or end
of the clause, as in (30–32). Thus, any NPs not marked by a postposition, and positioned before the verb, must be in S, A or O function. In
(17) the A argument is coded by 1sg prefix *o-*, so *ijo* must be the other
core argument, in O function. Similarly in other examples.

The verb *-kamina-* is of S = O type. It is generally used transitively,
with the Message in O function, meaning 'narrate, tell a story about',
e.g. (note that there is here vowel assimilation, *-kamina* becoming
-komina after prefix *o-*.):

(19) okobi$_O$ o-komina-mati-be
      1sgPOSS:father(m)   1sgA-tell.about-SHORT.TIME-IMMEDIATE:f
      I'll tell a story about my father [another story opening]

However, the Addressee can be in O function, as in 'I'll tell a story to
the tape-recorder's microphone', or

(20) era   kamina-tee   ama-ka
      1inclO   tell.stories-HABITUAL   EXTENT-DECLARATIVE:m
      He would tell us stories

This verb has also been heard used intransitively, with an S = O sense:

(21) [jama   [kamina-ba]$_{RELATIVE.CLAUSE}$]$_S$ wata-ma-ka-re
      thing(f)   be.told.about-FUTURE:f   exist-BACK-DECL-NEGATIVE:f
      There's no more to be told (lit. things which are to be told don't exist)

When working on Jarawara I thought at first that *-hijara-* required the
Addressee as O and *-kamina-* the Message as O (like *inform* and *report*
respectively in English). These are in fact the most frequent role/func-
tion assignments; but a larger corpus revealed that both role/function
correspondences are possible for each verb.

   The underlying difference here is not in the configuration of arguments involved, but in the type of action; *-hijara-* refers to a casual
act of speaking, whereas *-kamina-* refers to something more deliberate, a story-telling. With *-kamina-* the focus is likely to be on what is
being talked about (so that the Message is most frequently O), and

with -*hijara*- the focus is more likely to be on who is being addressed than on what is being said (so the Addressee is most frequently O). These most frequent role/function correspondences follow from the meanings of the verbs—the type of speaking that is being described— rather than being a defining characteristic of the verbs.

Note also the different syntactic orientations of these two verbs: -*hijara*- is an ambitransitive of type S = A while -*kamina*- is of type S = O. These verbs are most frequently used in transitive clauses, but each can also be used intransitively. With -*kamina*- it is the O argument which becomes S; this is the argument that typically codes the Message role. With -*hijara*- it is the A argument which becomes S; this codes the Speaker role. All of this relates to the meanings of the verbs: -*hijara*- basically focuses on the act of speaking whereas -*kamina*- describes a deliberate act of story-telling, with focus on the story.

We now give further examples, from Jarawara, of how verbs tend to refer to a type of action, paying relatively little regard to the type of participant involved. As a consequence, there is considerable freedom concerning what semantic role is mapped onto a given syntactic function.

(I) There are three verbs which describe the expelling of material from the body: *soo -na-* 'pee', *mii -na-* 'shit' and *saa -na-* 'vomit'. Each is of type S = A. They can be used intransitively, to describe the activity, e.g.

(22) mii   o-mati-be
      shit   1sgS-SHORT.TIME-IMMEDIATE:f
      I'll just have a shit (lit. I'll now shit for a short time)

They can also be used transitively, either with what is expelled from the body as O argument:

(23) inamatewe$_A$ ama$_O$ mii   na-ka
      child   blood(f)   shit   AUXILIARY-DECLARATIVE:m
      The boy child shat blood

or with what it is expelled onto as O:

(24) inamatewe$_A$ [mesa   mese]$_O$ mii   na-ka
      child   table(f)   top.of   shit   AUXILIARY-DECL:m
      The boy child shat on top of the table

The verb *mii -na-* simply describes a type of activity: expelling something through the anus. The O argument can be whatever semantic role (other than that which is mapped onto A function) is focussed on in that instance of use—either what comes out or what it comes out onto.

Similarly, the S = O ambitransitive verb *sika -na-* 'pour' can have either 'what is poured' or 'what it is poured onto' as O argument.

(II) The basic meaning of the verb *rara -na-* is 'push with the foot'. It is used nowadays to describe working an old-fashioned sewing machine by pushing the treadle with one's foot:

(25) Hinabori$_A$ makina$_O$ rara   ni-ne-ke
      name(f)   machine(f)   press with foot   AUX-CONT-DECL:f
      Hinabori is sewing with the machine (lit. pressing the machine with
         her foot)

Here *makina* '(sewing) machine' is the O argument. But the O argument could equally well refer to whatever is being sewn, e.g. *makari* 'clothing' in:

(26) Hinabori$_A$ makari$_O$ rara   ni-ne-ke
      name(f)   clothing(f)   press.with.foot   AUX-CONT-DECL:f
      Hinabori is sewing a garment

It will be seen that *rara -na-* describes a type of action, that's all; either of the objects involved in the action—the machine itself, or the garment that is sewn using the machine—can be in O function.

(III) We now return to the verbs exemplified in (1–5). *Tisa -na-* simply describes a type of action, shooting an arrow with a bow or setting in motion a projectile with a slingshot (this is never done randomly, only to hit some target). It may bring into focus, in O function, any role other than that in A function—the target (the fish) as in (1), the arrow as in (2), or the water that the fish is in, as in (3).

Ori -na- simply describes the action of moving a piece of wood (or anything similar) through some liquid. It is generally used to describe paddling a canoe and then the role in O function can be the canoe, as in (4), or the river or lake that is paddled on, as in (5); again, any role other than that in A function can be the O argument. This verb can also be used to describe using a spoon to mix something into a liquid (see note 3).

(IV) *fata -na-*. This can be used as an intransitive verb meaning '(a flower) opens out into blossom', 'explode (e.g. a fruit when placed in the fire)' or '(the inside of a peach palm fruit) opens out (displaying its seeds)'. It can also be used transitively with the meaning 'push away with force'; e.g. if attacked by a jaguar one would push it off with maximum aggression. The transitive sense was used in one text to describe a woman pushing a man from on top of her, with force, after he had failed to satisfy her sexually.

My consultants stated that there is a single verb involved (rather than homonyms, in which Jarawara is particularly rich), presumably of type S = O. The meaning of *fata -na-* as is thus '(make) move suddenly, with distinctive effect (to a different place, or into a different state)'. As seen, it can relate to a variety of types of participant.

(V) It is hard to imagine any place with more biting insects than Jarawara territory. The transitive verb *taro -na-* is used to describe waving one's hand back and forth in front of one's face to clear away the insects. The same verb is also used to described kicking a football (the national game of Brazil was one of the first cultural importations into this region). It appears that *taro -na-* simply characterises a type of activity—the action of making something move as quickly as possible away from one. The 'something' can be a horde of insects or a football.

(VI) The verb *wete -na-* is of S = O type. Used intransitively it refers to a person returning to a place. Used transitively it is used to describe wrapping string round and round an object, preparatory to tying it. The string is moved away from the speaker, then back towards them, then away, then back, and so on. This verb simply describes a type of motion, something which has gone away then coming back. The S/O argument can be a person or a piece of string.

(VII) For some time I thought that there were in Jarawara three distinct verbs with the form *-wasi(ha)-*:

- (a) An intransitive verb *-wasi(ha)-* 'be caught', typically used of fish, with the causative prefix *-na-* we get *-na-wasi(ha)-* 'catch (e.g. fish)'. These uses are illustrated in (27) and (28).

(27) awita$_S$ wasi-bote   ne-mari   ama-ka
   piau(m)   be.caught-SOON   AUXILIARY-FPem   EXTENT-DECL:m
   The piau (fish) soon got caught (i.e. it took the bait)

(28) awita$_O$ mee   ee   na-wasi-haba   ee-ke
   piau(m) 3nsgO 1inclA CAUSATIVE-be.caught-FUTURE 1incl-DECL:f
   We'll catch piau (fish)

- (b) An S = O ambitransitive verb -*wasi(ha)*- 'find'. Here the S/O argument can be a path, a river, a game animal, some footprints, a person, etc., while the A argument may be a hunter or his dogs.[6] For example:

(29) kobaja$_O$ jomee$_A$ mee   mee   wasiha
   wild pig (m)   dog(m)   3nsgO   3nsgA   find
   The [hunting] dogs found the wild pigs

- (c) A transitive verb -*wasi(ha)*- 'cook, prepare (food)'. Note that there are specific verbs for different modes of cooking—roasting, toasting, boiling, etc. In contrast to these, -*wasi(ha)*- is a general verb which can apply to any kind of cooking. And whereas the specific cooking verbs can have as O argument the name of whatever foodstuff is being prepared, the O for -*wasi(ha)*- can only be the generic free noun *yamata* 'food' or the generic possessed noun (which must take a pronominal prefix), e.g. *o-tefe* 'my food'.

Speakers of Jarawara consistently affirm that (a–c) are all one verb. There is a single meaning involved. This appears to be something like 'be in/get into a desired state'. Sense (c) refers to bringing food into a state where it can be eaten. Sense (b) is used for meeting up with something that is sought, such as a game animal or a friend (and it is extended to also cover an unexpected meeting). Sense (a) is intransitive and is used to describe fish, or some other animal, being caught. There is a causative derivation from sense (a) to describe a causer (A) making the fish (O) be caught.

It is relevant to ask why a hunter meeting up with some game animal is described using the transitive sense of -*wasi(ha)*- while a fisherman catching fish is described using the causativisation of the intransitive

---

[6] In the Jarawara world view one does not 'catch a bad cold'. Instead the bad cold (noun *ito*, in A function) finds (verb -*wasi(ha)*-) a person (O function).

sense, i.e. *-na-wasi(ha)-*. The answer appears to be that these are different kinds of activity. A fisherman sees fish swimming around in the river, puts some bait on his line and knows that he is certain to catch enough for the evening meal; the fish are, effectively, there to be caught. But a hunter may track through the forest for hours without coming across the tracks of a tapir, a deer or a wild pig, and even then he is by no means certain to catch it. The transitive sense of *-wasi(ha)-* is considered appropriate to describe a hunter encountering his prey.

(VIII) The S = O ambitransitive verb *behe -na-* means 'turn the opposite way from normal orientation'. It can be used to describe a plate or a book placed face down, a shirt that is inside out, or a canoe that is overturned. Here we can get different roles in A function. In one story a canoe simply overturned together with the people in it; the canoe is the A argument of *behe -na-* and the people the O argument. In another story a legendary hero turned into an alligator and placed himself under a canoe containing his brothers and tipped it over; here the alligator is the A argument of *behe -na-*, with the people in the canoe again being the O argument.

(IX) The examples thus far have all involved ambitransitive or transitive verbs. We will now look at a number of intransitives. Firstly, *moo -ka-na-* 'be full'. The S argument here can be the container that is full, or the thing that fills it. Thus:

(30) faha_S   moo   ka-na-hara-ke   waha (wije   jaa)
     water(f) be.full INSIDE-AUX-IPef-DECL:f NOW   (container PERI)
     The water was now full (in the container)

(31) wije_S   moo   ka-na-hara-ke   waha (faha   jaa)
     container(f) be.full INSIDE-AUX-IPef-DECL:f NOW   (water   PERI)
     The container was now full (with water)

Note that the role which is not coded as S argument can optionally be included as a peripheral argument, marked by the postposition *jaa*— the container in (33) and the contents (here, water) in (34).

(X) The intransitive verb *bete -na-* means 'break, snap off'. If a pig is tied up and tugs at the rope so that it snaps then *bete -na-* can be used to describe this. The interesting feature is that the S argument can either be the rope, or the pig.

(XI) Now consider the intransitive verb *bere -na-* which has the meaning 'be across something'. It can describe the positioning of the cross-piece (on which the people sit) in a canoe, or a road meeting another road and continuing on the far side of it, or a flood lying across the land, or a log lying across a stream (as a bridge), e.g.

(32)   awa_S   bere   ni-ne-ke
       wood(f)   be.across   AUXILIARY-CONTINUOUS-DECLARATIVE:f
       [faha   tori   neme   jaa]
        water(f)   inside:f   above   PERIPHERAL
       A log is lying across a stream (lit. in the space above the inside part
       of the water)

The fluidity of role/function correspondence is demonstrated by (33), where the S argument refers to a person walking on a log that is across a muddy patch:

(33)   bere   o-na-ma-bone
       be across   1sgS-AUXILIARY-BACK-INTENTION:f
       I intended to walk back (on a log) across (the mud)

The next sentence from this text also features *bere -na-* (plus the dual prefix *ka-*), but in a quite different sense. The narrator has slipped off the log and fallen astride it, one leg in the mud on either side:

(34)   o-wisi_S   bere   ka-n-isa
       1sgposs-lower leg   be across   DUAL-AUXILIARY-DOWN:f
       My two legs were astride (the log) down (on either side of it)

This demonstrates that *bere -na-* simply indicates a position—something across something else. The verb holds no expectations whatsoever as to what reference its core (and peripheral) arguments should have.

(XII) The last verb to be discussed here is the intransitive *-wana-* 'be in contact with'. This can describe a wide range of situations—a mosquito sitting on someone's arm, an ant on a leaf, a fruit skin adhering to someone's foot, a microphone clipped to a person's chest, a vine growing around a tree, thatching placed on a house, people on a trail, boards joined together in carpentry, two pieces of paper stuck together with glue, a hoe stuck in a hole, boats linked by a tow-rope, and people holding hands in a dance. The causative form of this verb, with prefix *na*-, is used to describe a shaman putting someone's soul back in their body (after rescuing it from evil spirits who had taken it away). All that this verb describes is contact—between anything and anything; the identity of the participants is irrelevant.

The conclusion we can draw from these examples is that a language of the nature-of-action type, (B), places relatively little restriction on what role goes into which syntactic function. The role/function correspondences are then determined by discourse considerations. There is seldom any chance of ambiguity. For instance, the O argument for *tisa -na-* 'shoot arrow' is *aba* 'fish' in (1), *wati* 'arrow' in (2) and *faha* 'water' in (3). A listener will know, from their knowledge of the world, that *aba* is the Target, *wati* is the Instrument and *faha* is the Locus of the activity. At the opposite end of the semantic continuum in (11), a language of the nature-of argument type, (A), is likely to require that each core function relate to a constant semantic role.

Thus, the semantic typology of verbs in (11) underlies the typology of role/function correspondences in (10), with (B) of (11) relating to (c) of (10) and (A) of (16) to (a) of (10).

We can now briefly return to the parameters of transitivity, which it was suggested might correlate with that of role/function correspondences. It does seem that a nature-of-argument language is likely to pay attention to both the *number* and *nature* of arguments of a verb. In terms of number, this would imply strict transitivity; in terms of nature it would imply—as just discussed—strict role/function correspondences. Contrariwise, a nature-of-action language is likely to be little concerned with the number or nature of arguments that a verb has. In terms of number this implies a rather fluid transitivity, with many ambitransitive verbs. In terms of nature it implies fairly fluid role/function correspondences.

That is, we can relate together the role/function correspondence parameter, in (10), with the parameter of transitivity. But they are not related directly. Rather, each is connected—in a different way—with the semantic typology of verbs whose extremes are nature-of-argument and nature-of-action types, in (11).

4. Envoi

The lesson to be learnt from this brief study is that meaning is the central element of language and must be the basis for any worthwhile linguistic explanation. Grammatical typology should be founded on the study of interlinguistic meaning, and a meaning-based explanation should be sought for any correlations between different parts of a grammar.

This chapter has been necessarily exploratory. It has not been possible to extend the number of languages investigated beyond those that I am familiar with, simply because grammars and dictionaries of languages seldom pay much attention to role/function correspondences (indeed, few of them really deal with the matter of ambitransitive verbs). My hope is that this initial window into these matters will encourage others to study them in languages that they know well and to provide further examples of types of correspondences. One does, of course, require hypotheses as the basis for any scientific study; but then useful linguistic generalisations are only possible *on an inductive basis*, from study of how an hypothesis can be interpreted for a wide range of languages.

CHAPTER SEVEN

WORD-CLASS-CHANGING DERIVATIONS IN TYPOLOGICAL PERSPECTIVE

Alexandra Y. Aikhenvald

1. What this Chapter is About

The backbone of every grammar is recognising major word classes, and providing grammatical criteria for these. Word classes can be open or closed. Open word classes are amenable to accepting new members either through loans, or due to word-class-changing derivations. In a language like English, nouns, adjectives, adverbs and verbs can be derived from each other. Onomatopoeia and interjections may be considered open to new members, but never by derivation.

Languages vary in their possibilities for extending open classes through derivation. In Setswana (Bantu), verbs can also be derived from ideophones and adverbs. In Yidiñ (Australian area: Dixon 1977: 364ff), just about any non-verbal stem can be verbalised. But in Djabugay (Patz 1991: 291), verbalisation is said to apply just to adjectives. Other languages have no ways of deriving verbs from any other word class—these include Babungo (Bantu: Schaub 1985), Supyire (Gur: Carlson 1994), Tauya (Papuan area: MacDonald 1990b), and numerous Tibeto-Burman languages. In contrast, Kobon (Papuan area: Davies 1981) has no derived nouns; however, verbs can be derived from adjectives, and adjectives derived from nouns and verbs.

No nominalizations have been attested in a few Australian languages—these include Watjarri (Douglas 1981), Yidiñ (Dixon 1977), and Panyjima (Dench 1991). Maale, an Omotic language from Southwest Ethiopia, has only one word-class-changing derivation: from adjectives to nouns (Amha 2001: 74–5).

The purpose of this chapter is to investigate the principal types of derivations which change word classes. We consider their semantic and syntactic properties, patterns of polysemy, and distribution across the world.

We will not focus on derivations which do not change word class. So, for instance, we will not discuss the ways in which an intransitive verb can be made transitive, or a noun can be derived from another noun. Not infrequently, however, a marker of a word-class-changing derivation has an additional meaning. For instance, a verbalizer which applies to nouns and adjectives may double as a causative marker on verbs. Some derived forms can develop additional uses—markers of nominalizations can be employed as evidentiality strategies, and even develop into independent word classes. Derived members of a word class may display signs of 'mixed parentage'—for instance, a deverbal noun may well keep some verbal features not found in non-derived members of the same broad class of nouns. These features of derived forms will be discussed throughout §§3–7.

And then comes the question 'why' some languages have only nominalizations, and others mostly verbalizations? Are there any language properties which correlate with the presence, or with the absence, of word-class-changing derivations? This is the topic of §8.

Before going any further, we recapitulate the major criteria used in defining word classes. These criteria can then be applied to potentially problematic derived forms.

2. Delineating Word Classes

A statement of word classes is an integral part of any grammar. For each word class, we need to know if it is open or closed (and if it is closed, approximately how many members it has). The most important criteria involve morphological structure, grammatical categories and syntactic functions. As an additional, 'optional extra', members of different word classes may display different patterns in terms of their phonological possibilities. There is typically a semantic core to each word class but this cannot be used as a criterion for their identification.

2.1. *How to establish word classes*

The essential criteria for distinguishing between word classes include:

(i) Morphological structure and categories, that is, obligatory inflections or optional derivations that apply for each word class, and
(ii) Syntactic functions of the representatives of the class.

2.1.1. *Morphological criteria*

Typical morphological categories of nouns include case (marking grammatical function of a noun phrase in a clause), inherent number, inherent gender, classifiers, possession marking, as well as degree (diminutive, augmentative). Typical categories associated with a verb are person, number, and gender of core arguments, tense, aspect, modality, mood, evidentiality, and valency-changing derivations. Typical categories of adjectives are comparison, agreement gender (determined by the noun), and agreement number (see Dixon 2004a).

This is not an exhaustive list. There may also be nominal tense (usually independent of tense on verbs), and verbal classifiers (which may be completely independent from classifiers with nouns).

The marking of categories on nouns and verbs can overlap. For instance, throughout the Arawak language family, the same set of prefixes marks possessor on nouns and the A/S$_a$ on verbs. In Carib, Tupí and Jê languages the same set of affixes marks possessor on nouns and S$_o$/O on verbs. In many familiar Indo-European languages, inherent gender on nouns can be expressed in the same way as the agreement gender on adjectives, e.g. Portuguese *menino* (boy:inherent.masc.sg) *bonito* (handsome:agreement.masc.sg) 'handsome boy'.

And there can be polyfunctional morphemes used with more than one word class. In Classical Sanskrit, the suffix -*tara* was used to form 'the comparative degree of adjectives and rarely...of substantives', 'added (in older language) to adverbs...and (in later language) to verbs' (Monier-Williams 1899: 438). Comparative on adjectives marks comparison of qualities, and comparative on verbs marks comparison of actions or states.

In Tariana (Arawak: Aikhenvald 2003: 193–5, 366–7) degree markers—diminutive and augmentative—occur on verbs, on nouns and on adjectives. The diminutive with nouns implies a small size or young age of a referent. With verbs, it marks small extent of action, that is, doing something 'a little bit', and with adjectives it expresses small degree of a property. The augmentative on nominals expresses large size of a referent, on adjectives it indicates the degree of quality (e.g. 'very big'), while on verbs it marks an intensive action or state (and also has an additional overtone of 'really').[1] The differences in meanings are conditioned by the semantic core of each word class.

---

[1] Cf. also diminutive markers on verbs and nouns, in Late Medieval Latin. Further examples include number marking on nouns and on verbs as different and partly overlapping systems (see Durie 1986; Newman 1990); classifiers and genders in various morphosyntactic environments (see Aikhenvald 2000b); and different effects of reduplication depending on the word class it applies to (see Dixon 2004a: 17, 25; Beck 2002; Hajek 2004: 355; Lynch, Ross and Crowley 2003: 44). Also see Haude

The comparative in Sanskrit is primarily an adjectival category, extended to verbs and adverbs. In contrast, 'degree' in Tariana is a category equally characteristic of nouns, of adjectives and of verbs. Such versatile categories cannot be used as primary criteria for word classes. Their existence is concomitant to the word-class divisions.

2.1.2. *Syntactic criteria*

Syntactic criteria reflect the relationships between word class and functional slot. It is important to distinguish between function in clause structure and word class.

The crucial functions are:

WITHIN A CLAUSE:

- obligatory predicate;
- obligatory core arguments A, S, O and E (extended argument, for instance, of a ditransitive verb), and also copula subject;
- copula complement;
- peripheral arguments.

WITHIN A PHRASE:

- head of a noun phrase (including possessor and possessee in a noun phrase);
- head of predicate;
- modifier of a noun phrase;
- modifier of a verb.

Individual languages offer numerous options. In some languages—e.g. Latin and Dyirbal—verbs are always heads of (transitive or intransitive) predicates, while arguments and obliques can only be nouns, and adjectives are copula complements and modifiers in a noun phrase. At the other extreme are Nootka and other languages from the Wakashan, and also Salishan, families, where predicates and core arguments can be nouns or verbs.

(2006: 239–43) on the applicative suffix used with verbs and with nouns in Movima. Further examples from Kwaza are in van der Voort (2000: 454–66). Note that the vast majority of languages with such versatile affixes present no difficulty in distinguishing verbs from nouns.

This is how Schachter (1985: 12) puts it: 'Since the characteristic function of nouns is as arguments and that of verbs is as predicates, a functional distinction between nouns and verbs becomes difficult to establish to the extent that nouns occur as predicates and verbs as arguments without any distinctive marking'.

A similar problem appears to exist in Tagalog. However, Schachter and Otanes (1972: 59–85) showed that the morphological differences between nominals, adjectivals, verbals and adverbials in Tagalog are sufficient for distinguishing between the word classes. In particular, only verbs can be inflected for aspect.

For English, a statement can be made that all verbs can function as predicates and some also as arguments and obliques (e.g. *walk, dance, smile*); all nouns can function as arguments and some can also function as predicates (e.g. *mother, stone, table*). We return to this in §2.1.4.

In Tariana, a North Arawak language from northwestern Amazonia, verbs, nouns, adjectives and adverbs can head an intransitive predicate. Only verbs can head a transitive predicate. Nouns and adjectives, but not verbs or adverbs, can be heads of NPs. Only adjectives are typical modifiers in NPs, and only adverbs modify verbs. This is in addition to morphological differences between the four word classes. In Boumaa Fijian (Dixon 1988: 238), verbs, adjectives and nouns can head an intransitive predicate, but only verbs can head a transitive one. All three can head an NP (though this is a primary function only for nouns), and only adjectives can be consistently used as modifiers in noun phrases. So much for those who might claim that Boumaa Fijian does not distinguish word classes.

Representatives of different word classes can take different subsets of morphology depending on their function. For instance, in Turkish, nouns and adjectives as predicate heads take agreement suffixes, but cannot take the nominal plural marker (Underhill 1976: 40).

The option of having a noun or an adjective as predicate head should not be confused with zero-derivation, from a non-verb to a verb. For instance, in Tariana any noun can head a predicate. Then, it takes only a subset of verbal categories—for instance, it cannot occur with the imperative mood. But it has all other grammatical properties of a noun.

If a noun cannot be used to head a predicate in a language, an obvious way out is to make it into a verb. And if a verb cannot be used as an argument or an oblique, it needs to be 'nominalized'. As we will see below, more often than not, derived forms have fewer properties of the classes they are adopted into than other, non-derived members.

2.1.3. Concomitant features

Word classes also differ in terms of their discourse functions, and semantic core. Nouns can be said to designate objects (including humans and other animates, places, things, etc.); verbs designate activities, processes and states, adjectives denote qualities, attributes and states, while adverbs denote manner, time, location and further attributes of actions or properties.

Such semantic features are intuitively obvious. But in practice they are difficult to apply as steadfast criteria. 'States' can be denoted by verbs, such as 'be poor', and by adjectives, such as 'poor'. Verbs denote activities, but so do deverbal nouns. This is why semantics is concomitant, rather than criterial, to distinguishing word classes.[2]

Nevertheless, a comment on semantic content of each word class remains essential—for instance, specifying if the verb class in language X includes stative verbs which correspond to adjectives in other languages (that is, express concepts to do with qualities and attributes). An implication of this may be that X has only a small closed adjective class. Or the noun class may only include nouns with concrete reference—in some languages there are no abstract nouns (e.g. sincerity, beauty, truth, height). In a number of highly synthetic languages of North America and Northern Australia some kinship terms are subtypes of verb, and not of noun.

This alerts us to the fact that major word classes are not homogenous: they are composed of subclasses defined in terms of grammatical and also semantic properties.

---

[2] In some languages different word classes have different segmental phonological possibilities; in other languages different word classes have different root structure. For example, in most Arawak languages polysyllabic roots are always nominal. In the Bantu language Setswana, the majority of verbs end in -a, and nouns never start with a vowel. In Lango (Western Nilotic, Uganda) nouns have lexical tones; their roots can be longer than one syllable, and verb roots are one syllable long, and their tone is determined by aspect-mood marking. In Hua (East Central Highlands family, Eastern New Guinea Highlands stock) verb stems always end in a vowel; nouns have no constraints (but some sublasses of nouns—proper nouns and most kin terms—end in a glottal stop). These facts are important facts but, once again, not necessarily criterial.

2.1.4. *Major word classes, and their subdivisions*
Subclasses of nouns, verbs, adjectives, and also adverbs are defined in terms of grammatical properties (in conjunction with semantic groupings). Subclasses of nouns often include body parts (which may be obligatorily inalienably possessed), kinship tems, place names, and personal names. Subclasses of verbs relate to the argument structure (e.g. transitive, intransitive, S = O and S = A ambitransitives), and grammatically motivated semantic groups (weather verbs, stative verbs, active verbs, etc.). Dixon (2004a) and individual chapters in Dixon and Aikhenvald (2004) show how grammatical subgroups of adjectives are motivated by their semantics. Size adjectives often behave differently from value adjectives, and so on. Within a broad class of adverbs, one often distinguishes manner, locationals, and time groupings.

How does this relate to our main topic? More often than not, forms derived from another word class would constitute a separate subdivision with limited grammatical properties. We will see throughout this chapter that these limitations can go along various lines. Derived nouns may have fewer grammatical categories than normal nouns. For instance, in Tariana deverbal action nominalizations cannot be pluralised. So-called infinitives in Finnish and Estonian take a reduced number of cases. And they may have fewer syntactic possibilities than other nouns—in Tariana nominalizations do not occur in A or S functions.

Or they may have more possibilities. For instance, in Latin, participles—traditionally considered adjectives derived from verbs—distinguish present, past and future. Alternatively, their categories may be different from those of declarative verbs: in Turkish (Lewis 1967: 254; Comrie and Thompson 1985: 362) the action nominals have relative tense and not absolute tense.

Derived verbs are often restricted in their meanings. In Irakw (South-Cushitic), verbs derived from adjectives are either inchoative, e.g. 'black'—'become black', or causative 'black'—'make black' (Mous 1993: 186–8). Their syntactic possibilities are determined by the transitivity class they are assigned to. Denominal verbs in North-East Ambae are derived only from words for clothing, and mean 'to dress in this type of clothing' (Hyslop 2001: 356).

What is a 'derivation', and how do we distinguish between polyfunctional (sometimes called 'precategorial') roots, and zero-derivation or conversions? This takes us to the next section.

2.2. *Derivations, zero-derivations, 'pre-categorial' roots, and 'referring expressions'*

Derivation is traditionally defined as involving creation of a new word in the lexicon. This is what word-class-changing derivations are good for.[3]

The means for deriving a member of one word class from another include affixation, internal segmental change ('apophony'), reduplication, prosodic modification, subtraction, repetition, and also compounding (and a variety of other, often marginal, means of combining more than one stem, as in blends of the type *choco-holic*: see Algeo 1977: 49–55; Aikhenvald 2007a).

The major challenges to the idea of word-class-changing derivations, and perhaps even major word classes themselves, come from two quarters: polyfunctional roots, and verbs as 'referring expressions'.

2.2.1. *Polyfunctional forms: pre-categorial roots, zero-derivations, and conversions*

What if the same form can be used as a 'verb' and as a 'noun', in terms of both their syntactic and morphological properties? English offers numerous examples (see Bauer and Huddleston 2002: 1640–3; Dixon 2005: 57–8). Pairs like *spy* (verb)—*spy* (a person who spies), *sleep* (verb)—*sleep* (action noun), *knife* (noun)—*knife* (verb: use a knife to attack someone), and *mother* (noun)—*mother* (verb: behave as a mother) can be considered instances of zero-derivation.[4]

Can we say which function is primary? The answer is yes. The vast majority of polyfunctional roots in English can be identified by speakers either as primarily verbal, and secondarily nominal, or the other way round. *Stand, call, drink* and *spill* are primarily verbs, and the nominal usage of *stand* (as in a stadium), *call* (as in *phone-call*), *drink* (as in *have a drink*) and *spill* (as in *have a spill*) is clearly secondary. The reverse applies to *mother, father* and *knife* which are primarily nouns. And note that typically only generic nouns tend to develop a

---

[3] Various sets of prototypical properties of inflection versus derivation have been suggested (see references and summary in Aikhenvald 2000b: 30 and 2007). The notions of inflection and derivation are of limited applicability to highly synthetic languages where most grammatical markers are optional.

[4] Another, practically equivalent, way of looking at zero-derivations is considering them 'conversions' ('changing a word's syntactic category without any concomitant change of form': Bauer and Huddleston 2002: 1640–3).

verb-like usage—for instance, a primary noun *stone* can be used as a verb, as in *to stone*, but more specific nouns, such as *pebble, rock, granite* are not used this way. Only the general noun *flower* has a verbal usage (as in *the tree is flowering*), but specific names for flowers do not (*to lily, *to tulip, *to daisy). (See Dixon 2005: 57–8). The meaning correspondences are idiosyncratic, even for nouns from the same semantic field: *to mother* means 'behave as a mother to', and *to father* means 'to be the progenitor of'. Other kinship terms are hardly ever used this way, unless as a joke. And nouns used as verbs develop numerous idiosyncrasies. The verb *to table* is one example: in British English it means 'bring forward for discussion or consideration at a meeting', and in American English it means the opposite: 'postpone consideration (of a matter)' (*Oxford English Dictionary*). (Also see Clark and Clark 1979.)

Polyfunctionality of forms, and roots, is pervasive in numerous Austronesian languages (especially Philippine and Oceanic languages), and in Wakashan and Salish languages from the Pacific Northwest. In the Lolovoli dialect of North-East Ambae (Hyslop 2001: 91–2), in Taba (Bowden 2001: 113–4), and in Tukang Besi (Donohue 1999: 86–90) there is a number of roots which can act as verbs and as nouns, depending on morphological markers and syntactic environment. In each of these cases, a special argument needs to be made as to whether the roots are really polyfunctional, or whether some can be considered primarily nominal, and some primarily verbal. An exemplary analysis is in Hyslop (2001: 91).

Some scholars consider such roots 'pre-categorial'—that is, neither nominal nor verbal. Their exact status as nouns or as verbs would then depend on the type of morphology one attaches to them, and the syntactic slot they occur in.

Having polyfunctional roots does not rule out having word-class-changing derivations. Tukang Besi has a number of nominalizers and two verbalizers (each of limited use). North-East Ambae has a number of nominalizing devices, and employs reduplication to derive an intransitive verb from some nouns, and verbal modifiers (= adverbs) from verbs. Taba (Bowden 2001: 395–6) also has a nominalizing derivation. That is, verbs and nouns are distinct grammatical classes.

2.2.2. *Lexicalised 'referring expressions'*
In a few highly synthetic languages of North America and northern Australia, a fully inflected verb can be used as a core argument or an

oblique. In Bininj Gun-Wok (Australian: Evans 2003: 123), *ka-lobme-n* (3-run-NONPAST) is a verb meaning '(s)he runs'. This same form can also be used as an argument or an oblique meaning 'good runner'. *Ga-bo-man.ga-n* (3-liquid-fall-NONPAST) is a verb meaning 'water falls'. And in its nominal usage it means 'waterfall'. The semantics of these is sometimes compositional and straightforward, and other times not. The resultant form can be considered a noun for all syntactic purposes, and is the result of lexicalization of an inflected verb. Further examples of inflected verbs which 'serve as descriptive labels for objects' and 'can function syntactically as nominals, cooccurring with determiners and serving as arguments of clauses' come from Iroquoian languages (Mithun 1999a: 58; 1999b). The existence of such lexicalizations does not imply that there is no distinction between nouns and verbs.

Similar lexicalizations are found in well known Indo-European languages, e.g. English *Johnny-come-lately, wanna-be, (an) also-ran, forget-me-not*, or a *what-I-don't-know-won't-hurt-me* attitude (Toman 1992: 286), Portuguese *tomara-que-cáia* (may-it-fall) 'a type of camisole without shoulder straps', *bem-te-vi* (well-you-I-saw) 'tyrant-flycatcher bird', German *Stell-dich-ein* (stand-you:ACC-in) 'rendez-vous' (Motsch 1994: 5022). These are just curious rareties, which do not seriously impinge upon the composition of word classes.

We now turn to word-class-changing derivations, and their properties.

3. WORD-CLASS-CHANGING DERIVATIONS

We distinguish the following basic types of word-class-changing derivations:

(i)   Verbalizations: derivations whose end-product has properties of a verb—see §4.
(ii) Nominalizations: derivations whose end-product has properties of a noun. Deverbal nominalizations present somewhat different problems, and often have different properties, than nouns derived from other word classes. See §5.
(iii) Adjectivizations: derivations whose end-product has properties of an adjective—§6.
(iv) Adverbializations: derivations whose end-product has properties of an adverb—§7.

For each derivation we will consider:

- word class it can be derived from (for instance, a verb can be derived from a noun, from an adjective, an adverb, and more);
- semantic types associated with each;
- polysemous patterns for markers of word-class-changing derivations.

Cross-linguistically, nominalizations and verbalizations appear to be more frequent than adjectivizing and adverbializing derivations. Languages tend to have more varied devices for deriving nouns and verbs than for deriving adjectives or adverbs. One obvious reason is the absence of adjectives or adverbs as an open class in quite a number of languages. And languages where adjectives are used to modify verbs tend not to have adverbs derived from other word classes.

How do derived nouns, verbs, adjectives, and adverbs compare to underived members of the same word class, in terms of their morphological, syntactic and perhaps also semantic features? This is a major question which we will address separately in each of §§4–7.

There may be further, language-specific, problems. A word-class-changing derivation can be productive, or restricted to just a few items. Individual word-class-changing derivations may apply more than once. English *tru-th-ful-ness* is a noun derived from an adjective which, in its turn, is derived from a noun itself derived from an adjective. (Also see Newman 2000: 725, on 'double derivations' in Hausa).

Direction of derivation—whether from a noun to a verb, or a verb to a noun—may be problematic. In English *rain* can be thought of as primarily a verb, or primarily a noun. Languages with numerous productive word-class-changing derivations may allow back formations, e.g. English *sculpt* from *sculptor* or *baby-sit* from *baby-sitter*. The choice of a derivational device may depend on a combination of semantic, morphological and sometimes also phonological factors (see Dixon 2014).

A further problem concerns potential lexicalization, and semantic idiosyncrasies, in word-class-changing derivations of most types. For instance, in Hixkaryana intransitive verbs can be derived from a few obligatorily possessed nouns with a broad meaning of 'have a N or a property of N', however, the exact meaning is hard to predict, e.g. *-amusu-* 'weight of', *-amus-na-* 'be heavy'; *-onu-* 'eye of', *-on-ta-* 'be awake', *-eherkotu-* 'flower of', *-eherkotuh-ta* 'be in flower' (Derbyshire

1985: 221–2). I hypothesize that fully productive derivations tend to lexicalize less than those which are restricted to just some semantic, or other, types. These issues appear to be too language-specific to warrant a typological perspective.

Word-class-changing derivational devices include affixes (suffixes, prefixes, infixes and circumfixes), morphological processes such as apophony, reduplication, prosodic modification, and subtraction, and compounding.

4. Derived Verbs, and their Properties

Verbs can be derived from nouns, from adjectives and—less frequently—from other word classes. We first discuss the semantic types of verbs derived from nouns (§4.1), adjectives (§4.2), and adverbs and other word classes (§4.3) and the polysemous patterns for each derivation. We then consider the properties of derived verbs, and the origins of verbalizing morphology.

4.1. *Verbs derived from nouns*

4.1.1. *Semantic types*
Commonly attested semantic types of verbs derived from nouns are as follows:

I. Inchoative 'become N', 'acquire a property of a N', e.g. Hausa *Mùsùlmī* 'muslim', *Mùsùluntà* 'become a Muslim' (Newman 2000); Movima *jo'me:* 'bird', *jo'me:-ni* 'turn into a bird (intransitive)' (Haude 2006: 493); numerous Australian languages (Dixon 2002: 75), e.g. Dyirbal *baryan* 'youth', *baryan-bi-* 'become a youth' (Dixon 1972: 86); Nyangumarta *karukaru* 'nausea', *karukaru-jarri* (nausea-INCH) 'become nauseated' (Sharp 2002: 19).

Inchoative derivations can derive inherently progressive verbs, as in Yagua (Payne and Payne 1990: 411) *rimityu* 'old person', *rimityu-y* 'be getting old'.

A further subtype of 'become' derivations is 'achieve N', e.g. English *econom-ize* (that is, achieve economy), *monopol-ize*, German *Hunger* 'hunger', *ver-hungern* 'starve to death, die of hunger'.

II. PROPRIETIVE 'have N; have a property of N': e.g. Urarina *lana* 'husband', *lana-oka* 'she has a husband' (Olawsky 2006); Indonesian *anak* 'child', *ber-anak* 'have children' (Sneddon 1996); Ainu *tum* 'strength', *tum-asnu* 'be strong' (Tamura 2000: 218–9); Cupeño -*ash* 'pet', *ash-lyu* 'have a dog', *pa-l* 'water', *pa-lu* 'be watery' (Hill 2005: 279); Tamambo *bwero* 'ear', *bwero-bwero* 'be deaf', *bange* 'stomach', *bange-bange* 'be pregnant' (Jauncey 1997).

A semantically comparable derivation from a noun referring to a body part or emotional state can mean 'feel emotion' or 'have something wrong with a body part'. In Panyjima verbalizations can be formed on any nominal, and there is a special psycho-inchoative derivation from nominals referring to body parts or psychological states, e.g. *putha* 'head', *putha-nguli-* 'have a headache' (Dench 1991: 188–92).

III. EXISTENTIAL 'be N', e.g. Bare *yahane* 'day', *yahane-ka* 'be day, daytime'; Hausa *jāhìlī* 'ignorant person', *jàhiltā̀* 'be unaware of or ignorant about' (Newman 2000: 723); Nyangumarta *karli* 'moon', *karli-karri-* 'be moon; be new moon' (Sharp 2002); Jarawara *tone* 'bone', *tone.tone -na-* 'be skin and bones' (Dixon 2004b: 536).

IV. CAUSATIVE, covering the following:

(a) 'produce or manufacture N', e.g. Indonesian *telur* 'egg', *ber-telur* 'lay an egg'; Movima *juve* 'dugout canoe', *juve-ni-ti* 'construct a dugout' (Haude 2006: 486);

(b) 'provide with N', e.g. German *Waffe* 'arms', *be-waffnen* 'arm, provide with arms'; Tariana -*ipitana* 'name', -*ipitaneta* 'bestow a name on O';

(c) 'transform, make into N', e.g. Hausa *kurmā* 'deaf person', *kurùntā* 'deafen, make deaf' (Newman 2000: 723); Matses *shubu* 'house', *shubu-wa* 'make a house' (Fleck forthcoming: 364); numerous Australian languages, e.g. Dyirbal *waru* 'bend', *waru-mal-* 'to make bendy' (Dixon 1972: 85–6), Nyangumarta *yirti-ji-* (stick-AFFECT) 'point'; *yini-ma-* (name-CAUS) 'name (someone)' (Sharp 2002: 78); Hungarian *park* 'park', *park-osít* 'create parks' (Kenesei et al. 1998: 358); Chukchi *ra* 'house', -*ta-ra-ŋ-* 'make a house' (Dunn 1999: 270); Khalkha Mongolian *alta* 'gold', *alta-la-* 'turn to gold' (Poppe 1951: 46) (also German *Gold* 'gold', *ver-golden* 'paint gold, turn into gold'; English *victim-ize, crystal-ize*).

(d) 'make N come about', e.g. English *glori-fy* 'make have glory' (Dixon 2014).

V. Manipulative, covering:

(a) 'apply/use N', e.g. Indonesian *topi* 'hat', *ber-topi* 'wear a hat'; Lolo-voli dialect of North-East Ambae *malo* 'loincloth', *malo-malo* 'be dressed in loincloth' (Hyslop 2001: 356); Hixkaryana derivation meaning 'make X for, making an effort', e.g. *-yho-* 'plantation of', *-yho-to-* 'make a plantation for (making an effort)' (Derbyshire 1985: 221–3); Boumaa Fijian *wai.ni.mate* 'medicine, fly spray' (lit. liquid of illness/death), *va'a-wai.ni.mate* 'use fly spray on' (Dixon 1988: 182–4);

(b) instrumental 'use N as instrument', e.g. German *Gift* 'poison', *vergiften* 'poison', *Heirat* 'marriage, wedding', *er-heiraten* 'obtain something through marriage' (Comrie and Thompson 1985: 347); Chukchi *yatya* 'adze', *-yatya-tko-* 'work with an adze' (Dunn 1999: 269);

(c) 'apply or give N to the object', e.g. Indonesian *andatangan* 'signature', *men-andatanhan-i* 'sign, apply signature' (Sneddon 1996); Hixkaryana *woku-* 'a drink', *-wok-ha-* 'give a drink to' (Derbyshire 1985: 221–3);

(d) activity which uses the noun, e.g. Tamambo *boe* 'boar', *boe-hi* 'make a special payment to someone (often a pig)' (Jauncey 1997: 11); typical activity and a process involving the noun, e.g. Panyjima *wilka-pi-L* (gap-PROC-CONJ) 'move through gap in hill' (Dench 1991: 190); Khalkha Mongolian *dū* 'song', *dū-la-* 'sing' (Poppe 1951: 46);

(e) 'get N', e.g. Sm'algyax *hoon* 'salmon, fish', *si-hoon* 'get fish' (Stebbins 2001); Khalkha Mongolian *šuwū* 'bird', *šuwū-la* 'hunt birds' (Poppe 1951: 46).

VI. Depriving of N (or 'cause not to have N'), e.g. English *de-caffeinate; dis-arm,* German *Waffe* 'arms', *ent-waffnen* 'disarm'; Panyjima *kulu-pi-l* (louse-PROC) 'delouse, remove head lice' (Dench 1991: 190); Hixkaryana *-kamsuku-ru-* 'blood of', *-kamsuh-ka-* 'make bleed' (Derbyshire 1985: 221–3).

VII. Delocutive 'call N', 'say N', e.g. Bininj Gun-Wok *gogok* 'older brother', *gogok-me* 'call (O) older brother' (Evans 2003: 343); Indonesian *bapak* 'father', *ber-bapak* 'to use "father" when addressing someone'; Jacaltec *-mi'* 'mother', *-mi'layi* 'mention mother' (Day 1973: 47–9).

VIII. SIMILARITY:

(a) 'behave/work as N', e.g. Hungarian *szónok* 'orator', *szónok-oskodik* 'work as an orator', *atya* 'father', *atyá-skodik* 'behave like a father' (Kenesei et al. 1998: 358); English *burglar-ize, bowdler-ize* (e.g. a salacious literary work, in the way Dr. Thomas Bowdler expurgated Shakespeare 'for family reading') (Dixon 2014);

(b) 'be/seem like N', e.g. Sm'algyax *mełiitk* 'bile', *xs-mełiitk* 'be greenish' (Stebbins 2001); Jarawara *fanawi* 'woman', *fa.fanawi-* 'be like a woman';

(c) 'treat O as if O were N', e.g. English *lion-ize* (a celebrity) 'treat as special and unusual (as a lion is among animals) (Dixon forthcoming-a);

(d) '(make) take on the character of N', e.g. English *cit-ify, lad-ify.*

IX. TEMPORAL, LOCATIVE, DIRECTIONAL:

(a) 'be located in N', e.g. Movima *beń'i* grassland', *beń'i-m-maj* 'be located in grassland' (Haude 2006: 492); Evenki *d'u* 'house, tent', *d'u-ta-* 'live in a tent' (Nedjalkov 1997: 301); Panyjima *mangka-thu-L* (straw-PLACE-CONJ) 'put a drinking straw into' (Dench 1991: 190);

(b) 'put O in a location N', e.g. Indonesian *makam* 'grave', *me-makam-kan* 'cause something to be put in a grave'; English *hospitalize (a patient)*; Huallaga Quechua *uma* 'head', *uma-kaku-* 'put (O) on one's head' (Weber 1989: 30–2);

(c) 'put N in a location O', e.g. *bitumen-ize (a road)*;

(d) 'move in the direction of N', e.g. Movima *chaṁmo:* 'bush', *chaṁmo:-na* 'go into the forest' (Haude 2006: 493);

(e) 'spend time of N', e.g. Russian *zima* 'winter', *zimovatj'* 'spend winter'; Estonian *suvi* 'summer', *suvetama* 'spend summer'.

X. INGESTIVE 'consume N', e.g. Chukchi *caj* 'tea', *-caj-o-* 'drink tea' (Dunn 1999: 269); Evenki *-ty* 'consume': *ulle* 'meat', *ulle-ty-* 'eat meat' (Nedjalkov 1997: 301).

XI. RECIPROCAL 'be/do N to each other', e.g. Indonesian *tetangga* 'neighbours', *ber-tetangga* 'be neighbours with each other'; Evenki *turen* 'word, speech, language', *turet-met-* 'talk with each other, swear at each other' (Nedjalkov 1997: 301).

Derived verbs may have further, even more specific meanings. Evenki has denominal verbal derivational suffixes meaning 'hunt', e.g. *mo:ty* 'elk', *moty-ma:-* 'hunt elk, go and gather', e.g. *dikte* 'berries', *dikte-le:-* 'go and gather berries', 'gather and bring', e.g. *dikte-le-* 'gather and bring berries', and also 'smell', 'play' and 'test' (Nedjalkov 1997: 301). Imbabura Quechua has a desiderative denominal derivation, as in *yaku* 'water', *yaku-naya-* 'want water' (Cole 1982: 180). And Ainu has a special derivation *-asap* 'be poor at N', e.g. *mon* 'work', *mon-asap* 'be slow in one's work' (Tamura 2000: 219).

Languages with numerous specific verbalizers tend to have one generic affix with a meaning of 'perform an action involving N', as do Evenki and Nyangumarta. Some languages—such as Chukchi—have no such generic markers. I hypothesize that languages have temporal, locative, directional, ingestive, reciprocal and further, even more specific, denominal verbs if they have at least one of the semantic types I–VIII. In other words, types I–VIII are 'core'—this correlates with their relative frequency across the world.

4.1.2. *Polysemous patterns*
Which meanings are likely to be expressed with one morpheme? A particularly recurrent pattern of polysemy involves using the same morpheme to derive verbs with CAUSATIVE (IV) and MANIPULATIVE (V) meanings, as in Cavineña (Guillaume 2008: 129) *-diji* 'path', *diji-ne-* 'provide O with path', *situ* 'friend', *situ-ne-* 'make O one's friend', *espiki* 'wall', *espiki-ne* 'provide O with a wall'; and Khalkha Mongolian (Poppe 1951: 146). The motivation behind this polysemy is intuitively clear: causation can be viewed as a type of manipulation.

There are other possibilities. The Indonesian prefix *ber-* has PROPRIETIVE, CAUSATIVE, MANIPULATIVE, DELOCUTIVE and RECIPROCAL meanings.

The verbalizer *-ti* in Cavineña combines INCHOATIVE (*makei* 'enemy', *ka-makei-ti-* 'become enemy', *chipiru* 'money, *ka-chipiru-ti-* 'get rich' (acquire money)), PROPRIETIVE (*-tsa* 'flower', *ka-tsa-ti-* 'blossom, have flowers', and CAUSATIVE (*jucha* 'sin', *ka-jucha-ti-* 'commit a sin') meanings (Guillaume 2008: 127–9).

In Movima, the form *kape-lo:-ti'* (coffee-BR.LIQUID-VBZR) can mean either 'make coffee' (CAUSATIVE) or 'drink coffee' (INGESTIVE).

The verbalizer *-ta* in Hausa combines INCHOATIVE, CAUSATIVE and MANIPULATIVE meanings (Newman 2000: 723).

English *-ize* has a wide variety of meanings which include CAUSATIVE (*victim-ize*), LOCATIVE (b) and (c) (*hospital-ize, bitumen-ize*), MANIPU-LATIVE 'provide N to/for O' (*summar-ize*), INCHOATIVE (*econom-ize*), SIMILARITY 'behave/act like N' (*burglar-ize*) and a few additional ones such as 'represent N of/for O' (*symbolize*), 'subject O to N' (*pressur-ize*), and 'follow the pursuit of N' (*theor-ize*).

The polysemous verbalizer *-z* in Hungarian covers PROPRIETIVE (*ülés* 'session', *ülés-ezik* 'have a session'), CAUSATIVE (*keret* 'frame', *keret-ez* 'to frame', *fal* 'wall', *fal-az* 'build a wall'), MANIPULATIVE (*autó* 'car', *autó-zik* 'drive a car', *rádió* 'radio(set)', *rádió-zik* 'listen to the radio'), DEPRIVING (*csont* 'bone', *csont-oz* 'take bones out of'), and DELOCU-TIVE (*bácsi* 'uncle', *bácsi-z* 'call X uncle'). The general semantic core of such polysemous derivations is 'typical activity to do with N' (Kenesei et al. 1998: 357).

In each case, polysemies involve at least one 'core' meaning (types I–VIII in §4.1.1). Another major feature of verbs derived from nouns is that their semantics is often determined by that of the noun—see §4.4.1.

4.2. *Verbs derived from adjectives*

4.2.1. *Semantic types, and polysemous patterns*
Commonly attested semantic types of verbs derived from adjectives are listed below (we use the same headings as in §4.1.1 wherever appropriate):

I. INCHOATIVE 'become ADJ', as in Bare *kunaba* 'thin', *-kunaba-d'a* 'to lose weight'; Hungarian *kemény* 'hard', *kemény-edik* 'become hard'; Russian *krasnyj* 'red', *krasnetj'* 'become red'; Djabugay *wigi* 'thin', *wigi-mayi-y* 'become thin' (Patz 1991: 294);

   Ia. 'become more ADJ', e.g. Russian *mjagkij* 'soft', *mjaknutj* 'become soft; become softer'; English *fatten, soften*.

II. EXISTENTIAL 'be ADJ', e.g. Boumaa Fijian *rewa* 'high', *va'a-rewa-* 'be raised (of a flag)'; *tautauvata* 'same, level', *va'a-tautauvata-* 'be level with (e.g. in a race)' (Dixon 1988: 184); Dagbani *tul-li* 'hot', *tul-a* 'be hot' (Olawsky 2001: 18).

III. Causative 'make ADJ', e.g. Hungarian *szép* 'beautiful', *szépi-ít* 'beautify', *kemény* 'hard', *kemény-ít* 'make hard'; Russian *belyj* 'white', *belitj'* 'make white, bleach'; English *American-ize, regular-ize*.

IV. Consider or Acknowledge as ADJ, e.g. Basque *on* 'good', *on-etsi* 'consider good' (Saltarelli 1988: 259–60); Ilocano *dakes* 'bad', *tagi-daksan* 'consider bad' (Rubino 1998a: 14); Khalkha Mongolian *saiŋ* 'good', *saiša-* 'acknowledge as good' (Poppe 1951: 47); Turkish *garip* 'strange', *garip-se* 'consider something strange' (Kornfilt 1997: 455–6).

V. Exposure to ADJ, e.g. Tagalog *angháng* 'piquant', *ma-anghang-an* 'be affected by the spice' (Rubino 1998b: 17).

VI. Similarity 'behave as if ADJ', e.g. Hungarian *kemény* 'hard', *kemény-kedik* 'behave as if he/she was tough' (Kenesei et al. 1998: 362, 358).

Types I–IV are cross-linguistically more frequent than V–VI. Languages with types V–VI also have types I–IV. A deadjectival verb may combine EXISTENTIAL and INCHOATIVE meanings, e.g. Russian *beletj* 'be white', and 'become white' (especially in the perfective aspect, and in formations with prefixes, e.g. *po-beletj* 'become white'). Further possibilities for polysemous patterns remain to be disclosed.

4.2.2. *Denominal and deadjectival verbs: comparison, and overlap*
A striking feature of deadjectival verbs is how poor they are in terms of semantic types expressed, compared with the wealth of meaning of verbs derived from nouns. I have found no deadjectival verbs of PRO-PRIETIVE, MANIPULATIVE, DELOCUTIVE, DEPRIVING, INSTRUMENTAL, TEMPORAL, LOCATIONAL, DIRECTIONAL, INGESTIVE or RECIPROCAL types. Evenki is a typical example of such semantic asymmetry: this language is exceptionally rich in semantic types of denominal verbs, while all deadjectival verbs fall into just two types: INCHOATIVE and CAUSATIVE (Nedjalkov 1997: 303). These are the most typical deadjectival verbs. And it comes as no real surprise that in some languages the same set of affixes is used to derive INCHOATIVE and CAUSATIVE verbs from both nouns and adjectives, as in Jacaltec. Nouns in Jacaltec occur with a few additional verbalizing markers—such as delocutive and manipulative—which are not applied to adjectives.

The INCHOATIVE, EXISTENTIAL, CAUSATIVE and SIMILARITY types are shared by verbs derived from nouns and from adjectives. These are indeed among the four core semantic types for both denominal and deadjectival verbs.

The subtype Ia ('become more ADJ') has not been attested with denominal verbs and presumably is linked to the inherently gradable nature of some adjectives.

The relative poverty of deadjectival verbs appears to be independent of the status of adjectives—that is, whether they share grammatical features with nouns or with verbs. Numerous languages seem not to derive verbs from adjectives at all.

Yet other languages have polyfunctional deadjectival and denominal verbalizations. This is a feature of languages where adjectives share properties with nouns. CAUSATIVE and INCHOATIVE derivations from nouns and adjectives in Jacaltec (Day 1973) were mentioned above. In Australian languages (Dixon 2002: 75–6) INCHOATIVE and CAUSATIVE verbalizing derivations tend to apply equally to nouns and to adjectives (see, for instance, Haviland 1979: 118–20 on Guugu Yimidhirr). In Panyjima (Dench 1991: 188–92) verbalizations can be formed on any nominals, e.g. inchoative 'become', and causative 'make'. Meanings vary depending on the nominal: with an entity, the verb describes the controlled creation of that entity by typically agentive A, e.g. *karla* 'fire', *karla-ma-L* 'light a fire'. With nouns referring to noises emanating from the body, the result is an intransitive verb, as in *ngayiny* 'breath', *ngayiny-ma-L* 'breathe'.[5]

Hungarian has a deadjectival derivational suffix with the meaning of SIMILARITY 'behave as if ADJ/in an ADJ way'. The same suffix derives verbs from nouns, meaning 'behave/work as if N', e.g. *kemény* 'hard', *kemény-kedik* 'behave as if he/she was tough'; *hős* 'hero', *hős-ködik* 'behave like a hero, brag' (Kenesei et al. 1998: 362, 358).

There may be further options. The verbalizer *-ya:* in Huallaga Quechua has INCHOATIVE meaning with nouns, adjectives, and a few closed word classes, e.g. *runa* 'man', *runa-ya:-* 'become a man', *hatun* 'big', *hatun-ya:-* 'become big', *ima* 'what?', *ima-ya:-* 'become what' and DELOCUTIVE meaning with onomatopoeia, e.g. *hachin* 'the sound of a

---

[5] Djabugay (Patz 1991: 294) appears to be an exception: only adjectives can form inchoative verbs. This may be a feature of language obsolescence.

donkey braying', *hachin-ya:-* 'bray' (Weber 1989: 30–1). This takes us
to verbs derived from other word classes.

4.3. *Verbs derived from adverbs, and other word classes*

In a language where verbs can be derived from adverbs, and closed
classes, they can also be derived from nouns and adjectives. In terms
of their semantic types, such derived verbs offer fewer options than
verbs derived from nouns, and from adjectives.

The most recurrent types are INCHOATIVE and CAUSATIVE, as in
Khalkha Mongolian *xemxe* '(adverb) piece-like, in pieces', *xemxere-*
'become broken into pieces', *xemxel-* 'break (something) in pieces'
(Poppe 1951: 47) (see examples from Yidiñ in Dixon 1977: 364–8;
and Evenki in Nedjalkov 1997: 304). INCHOATIVE and CAUSATIVE
verbs can also be derived from some members of closed classes, e.g.
numbers, as in Finnish *kahdentaa* 'duplicate' (from *kaksi* 'two'), *moni-
staa* 'multiply' (from *moni* 'many') and Estonian *ühinema* 'be united',
ühendama 'unite' (from *üks*, genitive stem *ühe* 'one'). Verbs derived
from time adverbs may have a TEMPORAL meaning, e.g. Evenki *d'uga*
'in summer', *d'uga-d'an-* 'spend summer' (Nedjalkov 1997: 304).

DELOCUTIVE verbs (meaning 'say X': Benveniste 1971b) can be
derived from personal pronouns: this is the case in many European
languages, e.g. Estonian *sina-ta-ma* (2sg-DENOM-INF) vs *teie-ta-ma*
(2pl-DENOM-INF), German *du-zen* (2sg-VBZR) vs *sie-zen* (2pl-VBZR),
French *tutoyer* vs *vouvoyer*, Spanish *tutear* vs *vosear*, Russian *tykatj*
vs *vykatj*, which all mean 'say thou' and 'say you (pl) as a mark of
respect', respectively.

They can also be derived from onomatopoeia and interjections.
In Dyirbal (Australian: Dixon 2002: 208; 1979), the delocutive suffix
-(m)ba-y derives intransitive verbs, e.g. *yabu-yabu-ba-y* 'call yabu yabu
(a call of terror)'. In Yankunytjatajara (Goddard 1983: 219–23), the
delocutive verbalizer *-(n)ma-* derives intransitive verbs from nouns
referring to sounds or animal noises, e.g. *muun-ma-* 'say "moo" (of a
cow)', and transitive verbs from interjections and kinship terms, e.g.
mama-nma- 'address someone as mama' (further references in Dixon
2002: 208–9). The verbalizer *-da* in Turkish has a similar meaning with
onomatopoeia, e.g. *horul* 'sound of snoring', *horul-da* 'snore' (Kornfilt
1997: 456; see further similar examples from Khalkha Mongolian in
Poppe 1951: 48).

Only occasionally can verbs be derived from other word classes with
other meanings. In Setswana (Tsonope 1997: 17) verbs derived from

ideophones and expressives have the meaning of 'a quick instantaneous action' implied by the ideophone, e.g. *phapha* 'sound of flap; being awoken suddenly', *phapha-ma* 'flap, awake suddenly', *nwê* 'sound of sinking', *nwê-la* 'sink'. Along somewhat similar lines, Ainu has verbs derived from onomatopoeic expressions with the meaning of 'action associated with the sound denoted by the onomatopoeia', e.g. *top* 'a sound of spitting out', *top-se* 'spit out'. This is also used for delocutive verbs, e.g. *e* 'yes', *e-se* 'say "yes"'. A number of further suffixes occur with onomatopoeia, deriving verbs with the meaning of 'continuous action', e.g. *sasun* 'rustling sound', *sasun-itara* 'keep on rustling'; or 'become ONOM suddenly and temporarily', e.g. *noy* 'falling down', *noy-kosanpa* 'suddenly fall down' (Tamura 2000: 216–18).

A polyfunctional verbalizer can allow one to derive verbs from several word classes. In Rapanui (Du Feu 1996), the prefix *haka-* derives verbs from nouns (broad meaning of make/produce N, e.g. *reka* 'amusement', *haka-reka* 'amuse'), and also from adjectives, numerals and adverbs (*ra'e* 'first', *haka-ra'e* 'put first'). In Taba, the prefix *ha-* can derive an intransitive verb 'from almost anything' (Bowden 2001: 201). In Boumaa Fijian, the polyfunctional verbalizer *va'a-* derives manipulative verbs from nouns (see (a) at V in §4.1.1), existential verbs from adjectives (see II in §4.2.1), and delocutive verbs when applied to greetings and interjections, e.g. *bula* 'hello', *va'a-bula* 'say "bula" (hello)', *io* 'yes', *va'a-io* 'say "yes"' (Dixon 1988: 182). Polyfunctionality of *va'a* goes way beyond just this: it can also derive adverbs, and even nouns (Dixon 1988: 182–4).[6]

4.4. *Derived verbs and their features*

Derived verbs can be transitive or intransitive. In some languages verbalizations are assigned to one particular transitivity class. For instance, in Tariana most are transitive, and in Matses (Fleck forthcoming) all are transitive. In other languages, such as English, and most languages from the Australian area, derived verbs can belong to any class in terms of transitivity. But they hardly ever form a special subclass of verbs in any of their grammatical features. This is quite unlike nominalizations: we will see, in §5, that these often constitute a special subclass within the class of nouns, in terms of their morphological and syntactic properties.

---

[6] The forms *haka-*, *ha-* and *va'a-* are cognates.

4.4.1. *What determines the choice of a verbalizer?*

For each language, the type of verbalization is likely to be determined by the semantic type, and also etymology and sometimes phonology of the source (noun, adjective, or other). Dixon (2014) shows how the principles for deriving verbs in English reflect an interplay of etymology, semantics and segmental and suprasegmental phonological factors. Unveiling these principles for each language is an important analytic task for every grammarian.

A. Semantics (including a typical activity to do with the 'source')—be it a noun, an adjective, or another word class—is what often determines the choice of the verbalizer, and the meaning of the resulting derivation. In English, *-ify* means 'make the state come about', e.g. *glory* versus *glorify* 'make have glory', and is used with fairly abstract terms.

The suffix *-ate* attaches to concrete nouns and means 'apply, put', e.g. *hyphen-ate, oxygen-ate*. The meaning of the denominal derivation is dictated by what can be conceivably done to a referent: one inserts hyphens, but oxygenating implies treating something with oxygen or dissolving oxygen in it.

This principle helps determine the limits of derivations: for instance, in Movima, a highly productive MANIPULATIVE verbalizer *-ti'* 'produce N; make N' cannot occur with nouns whose referents cannot be modified or produced, e.g. 'sky'.

There is often semantic matching of a noun and a verbalizing affix. The INSTRUMENTAL marker *-tko* in Chukchi is only used with nouns referring to tools, while the INGESTIVE *-o-* can only be used with nouns whose referents can be eaten. Desiderative denominal verbs in Imbabura Quechua can be derived only from nouns compatible with conventional bodily desires ('thirst', 'hunger', 'sex').

There are many more examples of how the use, and the semantics, of a derived verb are dictated by the 'source'. The MANIPULATIVE *-ma* derivation in Cupeño applies only to body parts, e.g. *-yu* 'head, hair', *yu-ma* 'wear a hat', *-naq* 'ear', *naq-ma* 'hear' (Hill 2005: 281). And in Urarina, the PROPRIETIVE verbalizing derivation *-oka* meaning 'have N' applies only to long-term possession of body parts, kinship terms and important items (such as machete, money, clothing, house, canoe).

The DELOCUTIVE verbalizer *-me/hme* in Bininj Gun-Wok (Evans 2003: 343) is restricted to kinship nouns (used as address terms). In the Lolovoli dialect of North-East Ambae denominal MANIPULATIVE verbs ('use as N') are derived only from words for clothing, and mean 'to dress in this type of clothing' (Hyslop 2001: 356). INCHOATIVE verbs with progressive overtones in Yagua are formed only on a small subset of animate nouns (*rimityu* 'old person', *rimityu-y* 'be getting old') (Payne and Payne 1990: 411).

Both the transitivity value and the semantics of a derived verb can be determined by the noun referent. In Panyjima the meaning of the causative 'make' as a verbalizer varies depending on the nominal: with an entity, the verb describes the controlled creation of that entity by typically agentive A, e.g. *karla* 'fire', *karla-ma-L* 'light a fire'. With nouns referring to noises emanating from the body, the result is an intransitive verb, as in *ngayiny* 'breath', *ngayiny-ma-L* 'breathe' (Dench 1991: 188–92).

Restrictions on deriving verbs from adjectives often depend on their semantic types. In English, the suffix *-en* derives CAUSATIVE verbs only from adjectives of the DIMENSION and PHYSICAL PROPERTY semantic types, e.g. *deep-en, light-en*, from one adjective of the SPEED type (*quick-en*) and three from colour type (*blacken, widen, redden*) (Dixon 1982: 21–4). It cannot derive verbs from adjectives referring to HUMAN PROPENSITY. (This is in addition to phonological motivation: see Dixon 1982: 21–4.) Only VALUE adjectives can be verbalised in Tariana and in Manambu. In Egyptial Colloquial Arabic, CAUSATIVE verbs can be derived only from some adjectives of COLOUR, PHYSICAL PROPERTY and DIMENSION (Gary and Gamal-Eldin 1982: 117), e.g. *jizarraʔ* 'make blue', *ʔazraʔ* 'blue'.

B. Etymology of the source may determine the choice of a verbalizer. There may be special verbalizations applying just to loans. Noun/verb pairs involving a stress difference in English are all of Romance origin (e.g. noun /ˈinsʌlt/, verb /inˈsʌlt/). The verbalizer *-ate* typically applies to loans from Greek, Latin and French (Marchand 1969; Dixon 2014). In Swahili, verbs are derived predominantly from nouns of Arabic origin (Ikoro 1996).

4.4.2. *Recurrent semantic types*

Derived verbs vary in terms of the wealth of their semantics. Deadjectival verbs offer fewer semantic options than verbs derived from nouns. Even fewer types are available for verbs derived from other word classes.

The recurrent semantic types of derived verbs are INCHOATIVE and CAUSATIVE. These can be formed from any word class. DELOCUTIVE verbs also also recurrent, but somewhat more restricted: they can be derived from nouns, onomatopoeia, and even pronouns, but not from adjectives or adverbs. I hypothesize that if a language has any verbalizing derivations at all, these will, in all likelihood, belong to one of these three classes.[7]

Just one of these semantic types, the causative, correlates with other, non-word-class-changing uses of verbalizers—see the next section.

4.4.3. *Non-word-class-changing uses of verbalizers*

Verbalizers can be polysemous: besides their word-class-changing use they can have a number of other meanings.

Most frequently, a word-class-changing verbalizer with a CAUSATIVE meaning 'make N/ADJ' doubles as a VALENCY-CHANGING marker on verbs, transforming intransitive verbs into transitive, as in Imbabura Quechua *ali* 'good', *ali-chi-* 'make O good', *wañu-* 'die', *wañu-chi-* 'kill' (Cole 1982: 180, 182). (Further examples can be found in Tariana; Warekena of Xié; Bare (Arawak); Huallaga Quechua (Weber 1989); Nyangumarta *-ji-* 'affective' (Sharp 2002: 203–5); Movima bivalent voice marker 'make into something similar to N' (Haude 2006: 494); Boumaa Fijian (Dixon 1988: 181); Classical Nahuatl (Comrie and Thompson 1985: 346); Kugu Nganhcara (Smith and Johnson 2000: 412); Rapanui (Du Feu 1996)).

A verbalizer may have a causative meaning with some verbs, and intensive meaning with others. The ubiquitous prefix *va'a-* in Boumaa Fijian (Dixon 1988: 185–9) derives causatives from intransitive verbs, as in *'oto* 'lie', *va'a-'oto-ra* 'put'. When applied to a few transitive verbs, it adds the nuance of 'do intensively, with special effort', as in *rai-ca* 'see', *va'a-rai-ca* 'watch, inspect'. The verbalizing prefix *ha-* in Taba derives transitive verbs from intransitives, e.g. *mot* 'die', *ha-mot* 'kill', and also marks intensive activity (with verbs of any transitivity), e.g. *surat* 'write', *ha-surat-* 'write a lot' (Bowden 2001: 198–202).

Or a verbalizer can double as an applicative-like valency-increasing device. The 'locative' verbalizer in Panyjima derives transitive verbs to do with putting referents into a location, e.g. *yapan* 'hot stone', *yapan-tu-* 'put hot cooking stones into O'. This same marker also adds

---

[7] This statement reflects a tendency, and not a universal rule. The only denominal verbalization in Urarina is of PROPRIETIVE type.

a locational endpoint to a verb, making an intransitive verb transitive, e.g., *panti-* 'sit (intr)', *panti-thu-* 'set, sit down' (Dench 1991: 190).

A verbalizer can double as a VALENCY-DECREASING DEVICE. For instance, a verbalizer *-ti* with INCHOATIVE meaning in Cavineña marks verbal reflexives.[8] And in Irakw, the marker *-t* derives intransitive EXISTENTIAL verbs from nouns, e.g. *xure* 'doubt', *xuruut* 'be in doubt', *muuná* 'heart', *munuut* 'be in a bad mood'. In addition, it has an intransitivizing reflexive and an anticausative effect with verbs, e.g. *tuuʔ* 'to uproot', *tuʔut* 'to pull oneself out', *gweer* 'to open', *gweeriit* 'to be open' (Mous 1993: 174; 190).

A polyfunctional verbalizer may not affect the valency of the verb it applies to. The MANIPULATIVE verbalizer denoting 'typical activity and process using N' in Panyjima (Dench 1991: 189–90) has iterative meanings with verbs, e.g. *kulu* 'louse', *kulu-pi* 'delouse', *paka-* (break into pieces: tr), *paka-pi* 'break into pieces'. This is reminiscent of the polysemy of *va'a-* in Boumaa Fijian.

A modal desiderative verbalizer in Imbabura Quechua is used as a DESIDERATIVE marker on verbs, e.g. *yaku* 'water', *yaku-naya-* 'want water', *miku-* 'eat', *miku-naya-* 'want to eat' (Cole 1981: 180–1; also see Weber 1989: 33, 170–1).

There may be further options. In Movima (Haude 2006: 495), a PROPRIETIVE verbalizer 'have N/ADJ' doubles as instrumental marker on nouns (it also appears as a bound element on intransitive verbs). The PROPRIETIVE *ka-* in Tariana and its PRIVATIVE counterpart *ma-* derive a few verbs from obligatorily possessed nouns, e.g. *nu-sa-do* (1sg-spouse-feminine) 'my wife', *ka-sa-do* (PROPR-spouse-feminine) 'marry (of a man)', *ma-sa-do* 'not marry'. These same markers also impart proprietive and privative meanings respectively to some adjectives, e.g. *ka-sawite* (PROPR-horn:ADJ.ANIM) 'horny (e.g. deer)' and *ma-sawite* (PRIV-horn:ADJ.ANIM) 'without horns (e.g. deer)', and stative verbs, e.g. *ka-weni* (PROPR-be.pricey) and *ma-weni* (PRIV-be. pricey) 'be cheap'. This pattern is widespread in many Arawak languages (Aikhenvald 2001; 2003: 410–1).

---

[8] A marker of INCHOATIVE denominal verbs hardly ever marks inchoative ('begin') on verbs. I am yet to find an example of a DELOCUTIVE verbalizer which comes from a speech verb. (In Bare, some denominal inchoative verbs are S = O ambitransitives, which may give a false impression of inchoative-causative polysemy, e.g. *waye* 'merry', *waye-d'a* 'be merry; make O merry'.)

An additional function of verbalizing morphology can be INTE-
GRATING LOANS. Kugu Nganhcara (Smith and Johnson 2000: 414)
and Guugu Yimidhir (Haviland 1979: 120–1) have special transitive
verbalizers employed for this purpose; a similar function of Hungarian
suffix -(iz)ál is discussed by Kenesei et al. (1998: 358). The verbalizer
-wa in Matses forms transitive borrowed verbs.

4.4.4. The origins of verbalizers, and alternatives to derived verbs

Where do verbalizers come from? Take Proto-Arawak. Here, the
proprietive-attributive prefix ka- and its negative counterpart ma- are
reconstructible for the protolanguage. It may have been a causative
marker as well. This is an instance of old inherent polysemy which
goes back to the protolanguage.

But this is far from being the only option. Verbalizers come from
lexical sources, and from reanalysis and reinterpretation of complex
constructions.

Denominal verbs in Australian languages 'undoubtedly originated
in coverb-plus-simple-verb-constructions. The coverb slot could have
been filled by one of a number of nominal forms; the simple verb
was then reanalysed as a derivational suffix and the pattern genera-
lised to apply to all (semantically appropriate) adjectives and nouns'
(Dixon 2002: 75). The recurrent causative verbalizer -ma is 'undoubtedly related to one of the two widely occurring simple verbs ma-l 'do,
make, tell' and ma(:)-nj/n 'hold, take, get' (76). Along similar lines, the
verbalizing -wa in Matses appears to have originated from a free transitive verb meaning 'make'. In Bininj Gun-Wok, the causative verbalizer -wo- appears to result from grammaticalization of the verb 'give',
and the inchoative -da/-rra comes from an independent root meaning
'stand, reach a standstill' (Evans 2003: 327, 343).

This takes us to the next issue. Quite a few languages have more
nominalizing than verbalizing derivations. In just some languages
from the Australian linguistic area the situation is the reverse. Not
infrequently, verbalizations are less productive than nominalizations.
For instance, the two verbalizations in Cavineña apply to just sixteen
and seventeen nouns respectively, while nominalizations and adjectivizations are fully productive.

Why is this so? If a noun can head a predicate, this reduces a functional need for a verbalization. Another possible answer to this question may have to do with the existence of syntactic constructions which
may be used in lieu of verbalizations. Many languages have 'light' verb
structures where a noun occupies a complement slot and the whole

construction acts like an inflected verb. Such constructions are found throughout the world—see, for instance, Haig (2001) on Kurdish and other languages. Consider Manambu: *du taːd* (man become:3masc. sgSUBJECT) is the only way of saying 'he became a man'. A complex construction is used as a 'verbalization' stategy. And the data from the Australian languages above (based on Dixon 2002: 75) show that at least some synchronic verbalizations go back to analytic structures of this kind.

5. DERIVED NOUNS, AND THEIR PROPERTIES

The vast majority of languages have some means of deriving nouns from verbs, and/or other word classes. Semantic types of nouns derived from verbs, adjectives, adverbs and other classes are discussed in §5.1–2.

Derived nouns may share all, or just some, nominal properties with nouns of other types. They may differ from underived nouns in that they also have categories associated with verbs—including tense, aspect and modality. This is discussed in §5.3.

Word-class-changing derivations are a means of producing grammatical words belonging to a word class different from that of the source. A derived nominalization is expected to have properties of a noun. Suppose a language has a deverbal form that occurs in a syntactic slot which is typically associated with a noun. Does this form automatically qualify as 'a nominalization'? A short answer is 'no'. Further discussion is in §5.4.

Nominalizers may also function as non-word-class-changing markers. Nominalizations may undergo reanalysis and give rise to new word classes. This, and the origin of nominalizing morphemes, is discussed in §5.5–7.

5.1. *Nouns derived from verbs*

5.1.1. *Semantic types*
Nouns derived from verbs fall into three semantic types.

(A) They describe an activity, state or property of the verb.
(B) They represent a core argument of a verb: A, S, or O. The presence of S/O and S/A based nominalizations in a language has nothing to do with its being accusative or ergative. See Chapter 4 above.

(C) They represent an oblique: instrument, location, destination, manner, reason or time.

The major semantic subtypes of each of these are listed below.

A. ACTIVITY, STATE OR PROPERTY NOMINALIZATIONS

A1. ACTIVITY or PROCESS NOMINALIZATION, e.g. English *shouting* (as in *Your shouting woke me up*) (Dixon 2005: 322); Urarina *ate-su-naa* (fish-kill-NMZR) 'fishing', *amiane-naa* (work-NMZR) 'working'; Apalaí *j-oepy-ry* (1sg-come-NMZR) 'my coming';

A2. UNIT OF ACTIVITY NOMINALIZATION, e.g. English *shout* (as in *Her loud shout woke him up*) (Dixon 2005: 322);

A3. COLLECTIVE or MUTUAL ACTION NOMINALIZATION, e.g. Tagalog *hábul* 'chase', *habul-án* 'rumble, many people chasing one another' (Rubino 1998b: 15), Motuna *onoh* 'decide', *non-ono* 'decision (by many)', *taapu-* 'help', *taa-taapu* 'helping (each other)' (Onishi 1994: 122–5);

A4. STATE NOMINALIZATION, e.g. English *hatred* (Dixon 2005: 322);

A5. PROPERTY NOMINALIZATION, e.g. English *resemblance* (Dixon 2005: 322), Turkana *-ro* 'be bad', *a-ro-n-i-sɨ* 'badness' (Dimmendaal 1983: 270).

B. NOMINALIZATIONS REPRESENTING CORE ARGUMENTS

B1. A/S 'AGENTIVE' NOMINALIZATION, e.g. English *employ-er, kill-er, organiz-er*; Movima *pul-a-cho:-pa* (sweep-BIV.DIRECT-BOUND.ROOT-AG) 'sweeping person; the sweeper' (Haude 2006: 475–6); Huallaga Quechua *pishta(ku)-* 'slaughter', *pishtakuw* 'slaughterer' (Weber 1989: 53); Dyirbal *ɖanay* 'stand', *ɖanaymuŋa* '(someone who habitually stands (a lot)' (Dixon 1972: 81).

'Agentive' nominalizations can develop overtones of 'habitual activity', or 'habitual actor', as in Dyirbal, Jamul Tiipay (Miller 2001: 116) and Movima. Wardaman has a special word-class-changing A/S oriented derivation with the meaning of 'be liable or prone to do/be X' (usually with negative connotations), e.g. *gajigaji* 'walk', *gajigaji-werreng* 'liable to walk around', *mambang* 'chase', *mambang-berreng* 'liable to chase after' (Merlan 1994: 274–5). It has a negative counterpart 'unable to do/be V'. Huallaga Quechua has an agentive nominalization with the meaning of 'one who does excessively', e.g. *a:ya-* 'yawn, have the mouth open', *a:yara:chi* 'one who stands around with his mouth open' (Weber 1989: 53) (cf. the Dyirbal example above).

An 'agentive' nominalization can have a potential meaning, e.g. Makushi *iwí-ton* (kill-NMZR) 'potential killer, capable of killing' (said of a poisonous snake) (Abbott 1991: 95).

'Agentive' nominalizations can distinguish male and female referents, as does Lahu nominalization with an additional meaning of 'expert in V; someone in charge of V-ing', e.g. *mɔ̀ chî ̱ šē-phâ* (things-wash-male expert) 'laundryman', *yâ pɔ pî šē-ma* (child-born-benefactive-female expert) 'midwife' (Matisoff 1973: 457).

B2. S/O BASED NOMINALIZATION, e.g. English *employee, nominee, escapee, attendee*; Urarina *baha-j* (ask-S/O.NOM) 'what I asked for', *lauhu-i* (sit-S/O.NOM) 'the one sitting' (Olawsky 2006: 271–2); Apalaí *-senano* 'result of recently performed action' (Koehn and Koehn 1986: 90–2).

B3. O-BASED 'OBJECT' NOMINALIZATION, e.g. English *convert, payment*; Apalaí *y-ny-mero-ry* (1-NMZR-write-NMZR) 'the thing I am writing'.

There can be further variations. Apalaí distinguishes two agentive nominalizations: one for A, e.g. *o-pipoh-ne* (2–beat-NMZR) 'the one who hits you', and the other one for S, e.g. *wa-kety* (dance-NMZR) 'one who dances' (Koehn and Koehn 1986).

B4. RESULT NOMINALIZATIONS are semantically similar to object nominalizations, e.g. English *arrangement* (as in *flower arrangement*); Urarina *baune-naa* (apply magic-NMZR) 'magic' (Olawsky 2007: 273); Khalkha Mongolian (Poppe 1951: 34) *bitši-* 'write', *bitšig* 'writing, letter'.

C. NOMINALIZATIONS REPRESENTING OBLIQUES

C1. NOMINALIZATION DESCRIBING AN INSTRUMENT OR MATERIAL USED IN THE ACTIVITY, e.g. English *mower, swimmers* (Dixon 2005: 323); Movima *iwani-wamba:-ni* (speak-INSTR:BOUND.ROOT.round-PROCESS) 'telephone' (Haude 2006: 480); Yukaghir *čahat-ī* (paint-INSTR.NOM) 'paint (what one paints with)' (Maslova 2003: 130).

An instrumental nominalization can have a PURPOSIVE meaning, as in Eastern Kayah Li *dé thã ʔi-dɛ kū* (water INSTR.NOM-dip.up(water) hole) 'water hole' (lit. hole with the purpose of dipping up water) (Solnit 1997: 35).

C2. LOCATION NOMINALIZATION, e.g. English *entry*; Yukaghir *modi-be* (reside-LOC.NMZR) 'place of residence' (Maslova 2003: 130); Amharic *manor* 'reside', *manorya* 'residence' (Amberber 1996: 9).

A location nominalization in Cavineña refers to a place where an event can be performed occasionally, e.g. *ani-* 'sit', *e-ani-kware* 'place to stay temporarily' (Guillaume 2008: 437–9).

C3. DESTINATION OF LOCATION NOMINALIZATION, e.g. Urarina *eno-ala-naha* (cook-PURP.LOC) 'place (as a destination) for cooking food' (Olawsky 2006: 646).

C4. MANNER NOMINALIZATION, e.g. Supyire *jyiile* 'cross (a river)', *jyiile-ŋka-* 'manner of crossing' (Carlson 1994: 108–116); Amharic *sbr* 'break', *assababar* 'manner of breaking' (Amberber 1996: 9); Turkish *ye-* 'eat', *ye-yiš* 'way of eating' (Lewis 1967: 172–3).

C5. REASON NOMINALIZATION, as in Sundanese *dataŋ* 'arrive', *paŋ-dataŋ* 'reason for arriving' (Robins 1959: 357).

C6. TIME NOMINALIZATION, e.g. Supyire *kaan-* 'give', *tèè-kaan-* 'time to give, pay' (Carlson 1994: 108–16); Amharic *maššä* 'become evening', *mˈššˈt* 'evening' (Amberber 1996: 9).

There can be further, rarer types. Apalaí has a nominalization with the meaning of 'payment for the action', e.g. *upo kurika-tamity* (clothes wash-NMZR.PAYMENT) 'payment for washing clothes' (Koehn and Koehn 1986: 90). There is another nominalization meaning 'companion in the action': Apalaí *eroh-tozo* (work-NMZR) 'his work partner' (Koehn and Koehn 1986: 93).

Nominalization types which have not been encountered include recipient or gift, topic (of conversation), and source. Destination (C3) appears to be very rare.

So far we have only mentioned positive nominalizations. Negative nominalizations also exist, but there are typically fewer negative than positive ones—which is hardly surprising given that fewer categories tend to be expressed under negation (see Chapter 5 above). Negative nominalizations are either of type (A) or of type (B), never (C).

Apalaí has eleven nominalizations, only one of which—S/A nominalization—is inherently negative: *nyh-pyny* (sleep-NEG.NMZR) 'one who does not sleep', *kana an-anȳ-pyny* (fish 3O-lift-NEG.NMZR) 'one who does not fish' (Koehn and Koehn 1986: 89–90). The only privative nominalization in Supyire (Carlson 1994: 108–16) negates the action, e.g. *jàcyí* 'consider important', *jàcyí-m̀bàà-* 'lack of considering something important'.

5.1.2. *Polysemous patterns*

Deverbal nominalizers are often polysemous. English *-ing* (Dixon 2005: 340) covers the following meanings: A1. ACTIVITY or PROCESS, e.g. *running*; A2. UNIT OF ACTIVITY, e.g. *happening*; A4. STATE, e.g. *liking*; B4 OBJECT often overlapping with A1, e.g. *building*; B5 RESULT often overlapping with A2, e.g. *building, wrapping*. English *-(a/i)tion* (Dixon 2005: 341) has all of these meanings (except for A1 ACTIVITY): A2 in *installation*, A4 in *admiration*, B4 e.g. *assumption*, B5 as in *information*, and also marks A3 PROPERTY, as in *distinction*. These nominalizers span A (nominalizations to do with activity, process and state), and B (core arguments).[9]

A nominalizer can span A, B and C, as does English *-ment* (Dixon 2005: 341–2). It expresses:

A2. UNIT OF ACTIVITY, e.g. *arrangement, commencement*;
A3. PROPERTY, e.g. *measurement*;
A4. STATE, e.g. *enjoyment, bewilderment*;
B4. OBJECT, e.g. *payment*;
B5. RESULT, e.g. *arrangement* (also see A2); and
C2. LOCATION, e.g. *settlement, enbarkment*.

One nominalizer may cover A and C semantic types, e.g. MANNER, REASON and ACTION in Ilocano *agsangit* 'cry', *panagsangit* 'act of crying; reason for crying; manner of crying' (Rubino 1998a: 12).

---

[9] A full account of deverbal nominalisation in English is in Dixon (2005: 317–52). Polysemy of A and B is cross-linguistically common. One other example of a polysemous ACTION/RESULT nominalization comes from Urarina: *ajtōō-hwā* (say-NMZR) 'process of saying, what was said', *baune-naa* (apply.magic-NMZR) 'magic' (Olawsky 2006: 273).

B and C types often overlap. Such CORE-OBLIQUE polysemous patterns involve:

- 'AGENT' (A/S)-INSTRUMENT, as in Yukaghir *čekč-il'* (be.skillful-NMZR) 'foreman' (lit. the one who is skillful), *šer-il'* (cover-NMZR) 'covering' (the one used for cover)' (Maslova 2003: 134); Yankunytjatjara (Goddard 1983: 151–2) *inka-* 'sing', *inka-payi* 'singer', *atul-* 'chop, pound', *atul-payi* 'chopper, i.e. axe or axeman'; Indonesian *mencetak* 'print', *pencetak* 'printer' (person or instrument) (Sneddon 1996).
- AGENT-INSTRUMENT-LOCATION, e.g. English *singer, mower, printer, feeder* (e.g. someone who feeds kangaroos and the place where they feed).
- S/O-INSTRUMENT, e.g. Desano *kóā-bu-ri-ru* (throw.away-POT-NMZR-CL:SPHERICAL) 'clothes to be thrown away', *sĩrĩ-ri-yũ* (die-NMZR-CL:PLANT) 'a dying (banana plant)', *wi-ri-ru* (fly-NMZR-CL:SPHERICAL) 'airplane (instrument for flying)' (Miller 1999: 143–4).
- AGENT-LOCATION, e.g. Movima where *-pa* nominalization derives AGENTIVE nominalizations from intransitive, and locative nominalization from transitive verbs, e.g. *pul-a-cho:-pa* (sweep-BIV.DIRECT-BOUND.ROOT-AG) 'sweeping person; the sweeper', *dewaj-na:-pa-'ne* (see-BIV.DIRECT-AG-fem) 'place where (I) see her' (Haude 2006: 475–7).
- OBJECT, S/A, INSTRUMENT and LOCATION, e.g. Supyire *jo* 'swallow', *ya-jo-ŋɔ* 'bait', *si* 'give birth', *ya-sé-gé* 'child', *filili* 'crawl', *ya-fili-ge* 'creeping thing', *bàhàrà* 'play', *ya-baha-ga* 'toy' (Carlson 1994: 108–116).
- LOCATION and RESULT, e.g. Tamambo (Jauncey 1997: 10) *ate* 'sit', *ate-i* 'chair, place to sit'; *rongovosai* 'know (something)', *rongovosai* 'knowledge'.

A nominalizer of type C can cover several meanings, for instance:

- INSTRUMENT and LOCATION, as in Turkana (Dimmendaal 1983: 283–4), e.g. *-pɪ* 'sweep', *a-pɪ-ɛṭ* 'broom', *-ŋɔl* 'slaughter', *a-ŋɔl- ɛṭ* 'slaughter place'.
- TIME and LOCATION, e.g. Ainu (Tamura 2000: 222) *mokor* 'sleep', *mokor-usi* 'place/time where/when people sleep'; Desano (Miller 1999: 144) *bõẽʔbẽ-di-ro-ge* (work-PAST-NMZR-LOC) '(place) where (we) worked', *boyo-ro* (be.light-NMZR) 'at dawn', and also prefix *ha'li-* in Sm'algyax (Stebbins 2001: 14).

Some combinations have not been attested—no language seems to have one nominalizer just for TIME and S/A, or for REASON and S/O. Alternatively, there can be one multi-task non-subject nominalization. In Jamul Tiipay (Miller 2001: 123), one single 'oblique' nominalization refers to a typical argument or oblique of a verb: OBJECT/RESULT, e.g. *nyii* 'put around the waist', *a'nyii* 'belt', *cheyaw* 'sing', *sha'yaw* 'song'; INSTRUMENT, e.g. *shuukwil* 'sew', *sha'kwiil* 'that which is used for sewing'; LOCATION, e.g. *allymar* 'to burn', *llya'maar* 'fireplace'.

To what extent does the verb's semantics determine the choice of the meaning for a polysemous nominalizer? A full answer to this question requires further study.

5.2. *Nouns derived from adjectives, adverbs, and other word classes*

Nouns can be derived from adjectives, with the following meanings.

I. PROPERTY, OR STATE ASSOCIATED WITH THE PROPERTY. Abstract nouns derived from adjectives typically refer to a PROPERTY, e.g. English *white, white-ness, delicate, delicac-y*; Maale, an Omotic language from Southwest Ethiopia *dalgi* 'wide', *dalg-um-ó* 'width' (Amha 2001: 74–5); Setswana *sesane* 'narrow', *bo-sesane* 'narrowness' (Tsonope 1997: 15); Somali *cád* 'white', *caddáan* 'whiteness' (Tosco 1999: 27) and many others.

A noun derived from an ADJECTIVE can denote a state associated with the property word, as *hard-ship* 'having to undergo circumstances that are hard' (Dixon 2014).

As a variation on this semantic type, Japanese has a suffix *-mi* 'flavour, savour, tinge' which derives nouns from adjectives, e.g. *atarashi-i* 'new', *atarashi-mi* 'modern touch', *omosorio-i* 'interesting', *omosiro-mi* 'interest, fun' (Nerida Jarkey, p.c.).

II. PERSON CHARACTERISED BY A PROPERTY, e.g. Indonesian *besar* 'big', *pembesar* 'important person' (Sneddon 1996); Lango *mwòl* 'soft, humble', *à-mwóló* 'humble person' (Noonan 1992: 75), Akan *kétewa* 'little', *a-kétewa* 'a little person' (Christaller 1875: 47); Setswana *golo* 'old', *mo-golo* 'an elderly person' (Tsonope 1997).

In Awa Pit, a deadjectival noun always has an animate referent, and can be either unmarked for number, e.g. *tlapa* 'old', *tlapa-mika* 'the old one [elder brother]', or have a collective plural meaning, e.g. *kutnya* 'three', *kutnya-tuz* 'the three [people]' (Curnow 1997: 88–90, 284–6).

Nouns derived from adverbs usually belong to just one type: they have an abstract meaning, e.g. Setswana *ruri* 'indeed', *bo-ruri* 'being true to something', *pila* 'fine' (adverb), *bo-pila* 'fineness', *gaufi* 'near, nearby', *bo-gaufi* 'nearness'.

Very few languages have a special derivation of nouns from adverbs, let alone from minor word classes.

Instead, there may be a general nominalizer deriving nouns from verbs, adjectives, and adverbs. The Hixkaryana action nominalizer *-no* derives action nouns (AI) from verbs, e.g. *omok* 'come', *omok-no* 'coming'. It derives nouns with the meaning of 'person characterised by a property' from some adjectives, e.g. *karyhe* 'strong (adjective/adverb)', *karyhe-no* 'one who is strong', and abstract nouns from others, e.g. *kawo* 'long (adjective/adverb)', *-kawo-no-* 'length of' (Derbyshire 1985: 234–5). This same suffix can derive nouns from postpositional phrases, e.g. *nĭmno yawo* (house in) 'in the house', *nĭmno yawo-no* 'the one in the house'. A similar phenomenon has been observed in Yagua (Payne and Payne 1990: 360, 449–50). In Hua (Haiman 1980: 295–9) nouns can be derived from various classes with a nominalizer *-'a*. The meanings of the derived nouns are not always predictable, e.g. *hauva* 'new', *hauva-na* '(too) early, early days', *hava'* 'bad', *hava-'a* 'nothing'; *aiga'* 'this, same', *aiga'-'a* 'which one'. This same form has a number of other, non-word-class-changing functions: for instance it derives abstract nouns from other nouns.

In a handful of languages, nouns with human referents can also be derived from members of closed classes, e.g. Setswana *kae* 'where?', *mo-kae* 'a person of which culture/ethnicity?', and from ideophones, e.g. *se-thuuthuu* 'motorcycle' is derived from *thuu* 'imitation of the sound a motorcycle makes'.

We hypothesize that only a language with deverbal and deadjectival nouns will have nouns derived from other word classes.

Nouns can be derived from word classes other than verbs and adjectives in a 'roundabout' way. In English, a noun cannot be derived from an adverb, or from a member of a closed class. But one can derive an adjective from, say, a connective, and then derive a noun from this adjective. An example is *iffiness*. How cross-linguistically frequent such multiple derivations are remains an open question.

Semantic types of nouns derived from word classes other than verbs are few, compared with the wealth of meanings of deverbal nouns. This is comparable to how denominal verbs have many more meanings than verbs derived from adjectives and other word classes (see

§4.1–3). This is to do with the fact that nouns and verbs are most likely to be open to derivational processes.

Nouns derived from word classes other than verbs tend to have all the nominal morphological and syntactic properties. This is not always the case with deverbal nouns. How do they compare—in terms of their properties—to underived nouns?

5.3. *Deverbal nouns, and their features*

Some deverbal nouns have all the morphological and syntactic properties of a noun—these include English action/result nominalization *arrival* or object nominalization *building*. Others do not have all such properties—see §5.3.1. On the other hand, deverbal nouns may differ from nouns of other types in that they have some verbal categories—see §5.3.2. A criterial feature of nominalizations is how the arguments are marked—see §5.3.3.

Why are some nominalizations more 'verb-like' than others? Nominalizations used as strategies for clausal arguments tend to express more verb-like categories than those which do not. But not all clausal arguments are nominalizations. We return to this in §5.4.

Activity and process nominalizations (A1), and state and property nominalizations (A4 and A5) tend to have fewer nominal features than underived nouns. Unit-activity (A2) and core-, and oblique-oriented nominalizations (B and C) appear to be always more nominal. We hypothesize that if a language has any nominalizations, it will have core nominalizations rather than any of the other types.

5.3.1. *Nominal properties of deverbal nouns*
Deverbal nouns may not have the full set of morphological and syntactic features of an underived noun. Deverbal nouns may show restrictions in the following:

(i) NUMBER AND QUANTIFICATION. Deverbal nominalizations referring to activity may not be able to be pluralised (or quantified). In Tariana nominalizations cannot be pluralised, and always require singular agreement on the verb. In English a unit of activity-nominalization, such as *shout,* is likelier to be pluralised than an activity one, e.g. *singing,* or *painting.*[10]

---

[10] Note however that restrictions on expression of number in nominalizations may be determined by the rules of number marking in the language. In Apalaí only agent

This is linked to a restriction on QUANTIFICATION: for instance, in Lahu (Matisoff 1973: 446) nominalizations do not appear in quantifying noun phrases (they cannot be quantified).

(ii) GENDER AND CLASSIFIER CHOICE. In Tariana action nominalizations require just one classifier in constructions with numerals and adjectives whose general meaning is 'collective'. An action nominalization cannot occur with a demonstrative classifier, or a possessive classifier. In Tucano and Desano, nominalizations have three gender forms but do not take any classifiers.

(iii) CASE MARKING AND FUNCTIONS. Within a NOUN PHRASE, a deverbal nominalization may not be able to have the syntactic function of possessor or possessed, as is the case in Manambu. The Turkish deverbal noun formed with the suffix -mek does not have adnominal genitive case (Lewis 1967: 167–9) and cannot be the possessor.

In some languages a nominalization can be part of an adpositional phrase, as in Lahu: here ve-nominalizations (Matisoff 1973: 446) can be 'followed' by noun particles pa-tɔ 'because of' and thàʔ 'accusative'; and this constitutes the proof of their nominal nature. In others, nominalizations do not occur with all the adpositions nouns can occur with.

Within a clause, a nominalization often has fewer functions and occurs in fewer case forms than a noun. In Estonian, the so-called -ma infinitive, traditionally called 'action noun' (tegevus-nimi) has only four cases (out of over twelve).

This highlights the limitations on SYNTACTIC FUNCTIONS of activity and process nominalizations. It is simplistic to state that 'a nominalization can occur wherever a noun phrase is called for' (Comrie and Thompson 1985: 393). In a number of languages nominalizations cannot occur in A function at all, as in Tariana.

Nominalizations are expected to be able to occur with definite articles. And if they are modified, we expect them to be modified just like any other noun, with an adjective, as in English his beautiful singing. In each instance, we need to check what morphological and syntactic features of underived nouns nominalizations have.

(S/A) nominalizations can be pluralised, following the principle that only human referents can be pluralised (Koehn and Koehn 1986: 90–2).

5.3.2. *Verbal properties of deverbal nouns*

Deverbal nouns may allow the expression of clausal categories traditionally associated with the predicate, and typically marked on the verb. These are:

(i) RELATIVE TENSE. Apalaí (Koehn and Koehn 1986: 90–2) distinguishes recent past versus non-past in agentive and object nominalization: *-senano* 'nominalization for result of recently performed action (S/O based)', e.g. *enuru-senano* (be.born-NMZR) 'newborn', *-semy* 'product of action either future or present', e.g. *etapa-semy* 'one who is to be killed'.

There tend to be fewer tense distinctions in nominalizations than in main clause predicates: for instance, Turkish (Lewis 1967: 254) distinguishes non-future versus future activity nouns, rather than past versus non-past as in main clauses. Desano (Miller 1999: 140–1) distinguishes just present, past and future in nominalizations, while main clauses also distinguish remote and recent past and three types of future (depending on degree of certainty). Tucano distinguishes present, past and future in nominalizations, and present, recent and remote past and two futures in main clause predicates (Ramirez 1997: 278–9). In contrast, Matses distinguishes three degrees of past in nominalizations, and in main clauses (Fleck forthcoming).

The meanings of relative tense in nominalizations are reminiscent of 'propositional' nominal tense. This is when nominal arguments and obliques are inflected for tense whose reference depends on that of the main clause perdicate (Nordlinger and Sadler 2004).

(ii) ASPECT. In Desano a nominalization can occur with any aspect marker, e.g. *wai ba-bĩrĩ-di-ro* (fish eat-HAB-PAST-NMZR:TEMP.LOC. CONCEPT) 'place where they always ate fish' (Miller 1999: 141). Deverbal nominalizations in Polish have the same distinction between perfective versus imperfective aspect as do predicates of the main clause (see Comrie and Thompson 1985: 363). The verbal activity noun 'reading' derived from the imperfective verb *czytać* 'read' refers to the process itself, as in *czytanie tej ksążki* 'reading (imperfective) of this book'. In contrast, the verbal activity noun derived from perfective verb *przeczytać* 'read, have read' refers to the completed act of reading, as in *przeczytanie tej ksążki* 'accomplished reading (perfective) of this book'.

Alternatively, nominalizations can be derived from a verb marked for aspect, without actual aspectual pairs. In Yukaghir, the locative nominalizer -bE- can attach to verbal stems marked only for imperfective aspect (never for perfective), e.g. *madā-nu-be* (sit-IMPF-LOC.NOM) 'seat', or for iterative, e.g. *čoh-uj-be* (cross.river-ITER-LOC.NOM) 'place where a river is crossed' (Maslova 2003: 130–1).

(iii) VALENCY CHANGING. Deverbal nominalizations can be derived from verbal forms which contain valency-changing affixes. In Jarawara a derived deverbal noun can include applicative marker *ka-*. And in Tariana a noun can be derived from causative-marked stem, e.g. *dhe* 'he enters', *dheta* 'he makes (something) enter', *dheta-nipe* 'the action of him making something enter'. In Yagua (Payne and Payne 1990: 354–5) action nominalizations can contain markers of valency-increasing and valency-decreasing derivations.[11]

(iv) MODALITY. In Desano, a nominalization can occur with a marker of any modality, e.g. *buʔe-dia-biri-di-rā* (study-DESID-NEG-PAST-ANIM. pl) 'the ones who didn't want to study' (Miller 1999: 141). In Meithei, a nominalization can take potential or neccessitative modality (Chelliah 1997: 156). In Cupeño (Hill 2005: 310–1) one deverbal derivation contains the irrealis marker *-pi-* and has 'a slight orientation towards near future'; in the examples given it appears as a modifier or head of predicate, e.g. *maayis-i wel-in-pi-ch-i* (corn-O grow-IN-SUB.IRR-NMZR-O) '(they will eat) the corn that will be grown'.

Alternatively, aspectual and modal meanings in nominalizations can be expressed with special markers. In Kayardild (Evans 1995b: 464–5), 'proprietive' nominalization which involves attaching the suffix *-kuru* to a nominalized verb may have potential meaning, e.g. *dara-n-kuru dangka-a* (break-NMZR-PROPR person-NMZR) 'man who has to do the circumcising'. The consequential nominalization indicates prior action, as in *dara-n-ngarrba dangka-a* (break-NMZR-CONS person-NMZR) 'man who has circumcised (someone) before'.

---

[11] Also see examples of deverbal nominalizations of synthetic passive in Turkish in Comrie and Thompson (1985: 364–5). Only some of the nominalizations in Finnish form 'impersonal' (Sands 2000: 292–6). Languages with analytic valency-changing constructions usually do not have such distinctions in nominalizations. So, Tariana, Estonian and English tend not to have passive nominalizations.

(v) EVIDENTIALITY. Meithei (Chelliah 1997: 156) distinguishes evidentiality in action nominalizations. Just as with tense, fewer distinctions may be made in nominalizations than in main clauses. In Matses, two evidentiality distinctions are made in nominalizations, and three in main clauses (Fleck 2006; forthcoming).

Of the verbal-like categories expressed in nominalizations, some are plainly more frequent than others. Having evidentiality and modality distinctions in nominalizations is not as common as having relative tense. (Many languages with rich systems of evidentials in main clauses make no evidential distinctions in nominalizations—these include Quechua, Tucano, Desano and Tariana.)

No languages have been found where mood—declarative, interrogative, and imperative—distinctions can be made in nominalizations. The explanation for this may be that mood is a main clause category. (The ways in which nominalizations are questioned can be criterial for their nominal status: see the discussion of Meithei in Chelliah 1997: 138–9).

How are nominalizations negated? If negation is exclusively a clausal category, and a constituent cannot be negated, neither can a nominalization. This is the case in Dyirbal, Hausa, Jarawara, Tariana, Warekena and Manambu.

In a language where a constituent can be negated, so usually can a nominalization. English nominalizations are negated just like any noun, with *non-*, e.g. *non-arrival*. Or they can be negated just like verbs, as in Kwaza and Movima, e.g. Kwaza (van der Voort 2000: 246–9) *kui-ˈhe-(c)wa-ki* (drink-NEG-INDEF.SUBJ-DECL) 'he did not drink'; *kui-ˈhe-cwa-hy*) (drink-NEG-INDEF.SUBJ-NMZR) 'that (stuff) which he didn't drink'. Alternatively, there can be special negative, or privative, nominalizations (see end of §5.1.1).[12]

In a nutshell, activity and process nominalizations are likely to have fewer nominal properties than other derived, and underived, nouns. Activity and process nominalizations may have to be always derived.

---

[12] As we saw at the end of §5.1.1, there tend to be fewer of these than of non-negative nominalizations. Matses (Fleck 2006: 233) distinguishes five non-negative and three negative nominalizations. This agrees with the general principle that fewer distinctions tend to be made in negative than in positive constructions. In Finnish, some nominalizations ('infinitives') cannot be negated at all.

The major issue in the properties of nominalizations is the way in which the core arguments of an erstwhile verb are marked.

5.3.3. *Argument marking, and deverbal nouns*
Core arguments (A, S and O) of the verb can be expressed in a nominalization in the same way as the arguments of the predicate of the main clause. In Tamil, the subject is unmarked, and the object can take the suffix *-ai* if definite and/or animate (see Comrie and Thompson 1985: 373; Lehmann 1993):

(1) Nīṅkaḷ   it-ai   cey-t-irkaḷ
     you   this-OBJ   do-PAST-2pl
     You did this

A nominalized verb takes the subject and the object in exactly the same form:

(2) Nīṅkaḷ   it-ai   cey-tal   tarmam
     you   this-OBJ   do-VERBAL.NOUN   right.conduct
     Your doing this is right

Alternatively, a nominalized verb occurs with its arguments in what looks like a possessive construction: A, S, and O are expressed as 'possessors'. In English, *John arrived* can be nominalized as *John's arrival*— a noun phrase similar in its structure to *John's cat*. *John* is marked with the prenominal *'s* genitive. *The enemy destroyed the city* is nominalized as *the enemy's destruction of the city*. The marking of arguments of the verb *destroy* is parallel to the structure of a noun phrase.

There can be variations on this. The A/S can be marked as a 'possessor', and the O expressed just like in a main clause. This can be exemplified from Turkish: (3) is a noun phrase with a possessor marked with genitive case, and (4) is an intransitive clause. This clause can be nominalized as (5).

(3) Hasan-ın   kapı-sı   Hasan's door
     Hasan-GEN   door-his

(4) Hasan   gel-di   Hasan came
     Hasan   come-3sgPAST

(5) Hasan-ın   gel-me-sı   Hasan's coming
     Hasan-GEN   come-VERBAL.NOUN-his

A transitive clause is at (6); and it can be nominalized as (7). The O, 'letter', appears in the direct object case.

(6) Hasan   mektub-u   yaz-dı   Hasan wrote a letter
     Hasan   letter-OBJ write-3sgPAST

(7) Hasan-ın   mektub-u   yaz-ma-sı   Hasan's writing a letter
     Hasan-GEN letter-OBJ write-VERBAL.NOUN-his

A nominalized verb can mark its O argument in a way distinct from main clause verb, and its A/S in the same way as does the main clause verb. This is illustrated with the following, from Tariana:

(8) ne:ri   i-hwida   deer's head
    deer   INDEF-head

(9) ne:ri   di-eku-ka   Deer ran
    deer   3sgnf-run-RECENT.PAST.VISUAL

(10) ne:ri   di-eku-nipe   deer's running
     deer   3sgnf-run-NMZR

(11) tʃiari   ne:ri-nuku   di-inu-ka   Man killed the deer
     man   deer-OBJ   3sgnf-kill-RECENT.PAST.VISUAL

(12) tʃiari   ne:ri   di-inu-nipe   man's killing of the deer
     man   deer   3sgnf-kill-NMZR

That is, the A argument of a nominalization in (12) is cross-referenced in exactly the same way as the A argument of an inflected verb (as in (11)), but differently from a possessor (in (8)). However, the O of a nominalization cannot be marked with the object case, unlike the O of a clause (as in (11)).

The syntax of action nominals can deviate from that of nouns and of corresponding inflected verbs. In German and Russian, emotion verbs 'love' and 'hate' take accusative objects. When nominalized, the erstwhile objects are marked in an idiosyncratic way, with prepositions. Objects and subjects of nominalizations of other verbs are typically marked with genitive, similarly to English.

It is as if some nominalizations are simple nouns, while others have more clausal properties. How do we draw the line?

5.4. *The limits of nominalizations*

5.4.1. *Are all clausal arguments nominalizations?*

Certain verbs—including verbs of perception ('see', 'hear'), cognitive processes ('know'), wanting and others—can take a clause, rather than a noun phrase, as a core argument. This is called a complement clause (Dixon 2006b provides relevant parameters for defining complement clauses). The predicate of a complement clause can be inflected just like the main clause predicate, as in English *that*-clauses in (13a). The O argument of the verb *hear* can be a clause, or a noun phrase, as in (13b).

(13a)   I heard {that Brazil beat Argentina}$_O$

(13b)   I heard [the result]$_O$

Or the predicate may occur in a form specific for a complement clause construction. Consider English (14a), where *-ing* form of the verb is in the O slot. Once again, the O argument of the verb *hear* can be a noun phrase, as shown in (14b):

(14a)   I heard {Brazil beating Argentina}$_O$

(14b)   I heard [the game]$_O$

The complement clause occupies the slot reserved for a noun phrase. Hence a tendency for some linguists to call such clauses 'clausal nominalizations'. Some even go as far as distinguishing 'non-finite clausal nominalizations'—equivalent of English (14a)—and 'finite clausal nominalizations'—equivalent of English (13a) (e.g. Foley 1991). Hardly any scholar of English would call a *that*-clause in (13a) a 'syntactic noun'. But many do call the *-ing* form in (14a) a nominalized clause.[13]

But what is nominal about the constituents in braces in (13a) and (14a) except for the syntactic slot they occupy? The answer is, not much.

---

[13] An alternative is a verbal noun, or a 'gerund'. I concur with Wilkins who said in 1668 (quoted from OED) that 'gerunds and supines are unnecessary inflections of Verbs'. Terms like gerund, gerundive and supine are fine within the context of traditional Latin grammar. But they need to be applied with care—if at all—to other languages.

A complement clause—as any other clause—is expected to have the internal constituent structure of a clause. A complement clause functions as a core argument (S, A, O) of a higher clause (see Dixon 2006b: 5–6, 15–7).

The marker -*ing* in English is polysemous: it can mark the predicate of a complement clause, as in (14a) and (15a). Or it can form a deverbal noun, as in (15b) (or also mark progressive). Consider the following pair of examples.

(15a)   {John's playing the national anthem}$_{\text{clausal A}}$ pleased Mary$_{\text{O}}$

(15b)   [John's playing of the national anthem]$_{\text{NP A}}$ pleased Mary$_{\text{O}}$

In (15a) the complement clause has the internal structure of a clause:

(i)   it has an A NP (marked with possessive *'s*, characteristic for this variety of a complement clause in English);
(ii) it has an O NP marked like any other O NP of a clause in the language.

In contrast, the -*ing* form in (15b) is a noun because:

(i)   the underlying O is marked by *of*, making this a type of possessive noun phrase;
(ii) in (15b) *John's* is a modifier of the head noun *playing* and can be replaced by another modifier, such as an article, an adjective, a quantifier or a demonstrative.

In addition to this, the predicate of the complement clause in (15a) can only be modified by an adverb, which follows the O, just like it would in a main clause, e.g. *John's playing the national anthem poorly* pleased Mary. In contrast, the head of the NP in (15b) has to be modified by an adjective, like any common noun would. And the adjective has to precede the noun, as it always does: *John's poor playing of the national anthem annoyed Mary.*

And the predicate of the complement clause in (15a) can express tense, e.g. *{John's **having played** the national anthem at the funeral yesterday}$_{\text{clausal A}}$ pleased Mary$_{\text{O}}$*. Needless to say, the -*ing* form in (15b) cannot.

This is because the -*ing* form in (15a) is a verb. And the -*ing* form in (15b) is a noun. As a noun it is slightly deficient: it cannot easily form a plural, as a noun is expected to. But this may be due to a semantic restriction: verbal nouns in *-ing* which have a concrete semantics of unit-nominalizations, e.g. *happening*, or object-nominalizations, e.g. *building*, can be pluralized. So can some activity nominalizations, e.g. *drowning* (*there have not been many drownings of babies this summer*), and *misunderstanding*.

In addition, the *-ing* form in (15a) would be negated as a verb (*John's not singing the national anthem*), and the *-ing* form in (15b) would be negated as a noun, with a prefix *non-*, as in *non-entity, non-arrival*, and *John's non-singing of the national anthem*. It can also be passivised: *its being sung in church*. That this 'passive *-ing* form' is not a form of (15b) is corroborated by how it is negated (*not being sung,* **non-being sung*) and by the fact that it cannot occur with the definite article.

Note however that the *-ing* verb in (15a) does not have all the 'trappings' of a main clause verb. It cannot take the same tense distinctions as a declarative main clause. Just like other complement clauses in English whose predicates are marked with *-ing, from -ing* and *to*, the auxiliary *have* has to be employed. This auxiliary indicates perfect aspect in main clauses, and in *that* and *wh-* complement clauses. Here it conflates the meanings of perfect aspect, past tense, and perfect plus past tense. That is, fewer tense-aspect distinctions are expressed in these dependent clauses than in declarative clauses (see further discussion in Dixon 2005: 50).

That the verb in a main clause expresses more categories than the verb in a dependent clause is the case in many languages from across the world.[14] But this does not mean that a dependent clause is a 'noun' and its predicate is 'nominalised'.

English provides a clear example of how one can distinguish between a verbal *-ing* form marking the predicate of a complement clause, and a bona fide deverbal noun. The criteria are summarised in Table 7.1.

---

[14] This statement is reminiscent of the concept of 'finiteness'. A finite verb can be used in a main declarative clause, and a non-finite verb appears in all other clauses. Traditionally, in Indo-European languages, finite verbs are expected to be inflected for person, number (and gender), and tense. Verbal forms which do not express all of these categories and are used in complement clauses or dependent clauses are called 'less finite', or 'non-finite'. In the Latin tradition, these include infinitives, gerunds, gerundives, and supines. The notion of 'finiteness' is highly tradition-specific and difficult to define. It is better avoided altogether.

Table 7.1. Distinguishing polysemous -*ing* forms in English

ITERIA	VERB IN COMPLEMENT CLAUSE	SIMILARITY TO VERBS	DEVERBAL NOUN	SIMILARITY TO NOUNS
Expressing A	Possessive *'s*	–	Possessive *'s*	+
Expressing O	postposed, unmarked	+	like nouns (marked with *of*)	+
Modification	with postposed adverb	+	with preposed adjective	+
The A can be replaced with a modifier	no	+	yes	+
Tense can be expressed	yes	+	no	+
Overt nominal number marking	no	+	some	+
Negation	*not*	+	*non-*	+

Terms such as 'syntactic noun', 'clausal nominalizations' and 'nominalized clauses' are better avoided, if we want to achieve clarity. But for each 'suspect' form one needs to provide a set of criteria why it should be an instance of a nominalization as a word-class-changing derivation, and not an essentially verbal form characteristic of a given clause type. We now provide an illustration of a potentially problematic instance.

5.4.2. *Derived deverbal nouns, or clause types?*
Distinguishing nouns and clause types which share properties with noun phrases is crucial for drawing the limits of the notion of 'nominalization'.

Boumaa Fijian (Dixon 1988: 268) has two broad types of complement clauses: relator-introduced clauses (roughly like English *that* clauses, in (13a)) and 'clausal NPs' (roughly like the English -*ing* complement in (14a)). Clausal NPs are similar to simple NPs: they contain a common article, and the A/S is coded as possessor. See (16):

(16) au aa   rogo-ca {a   o-dra   qaaqaa [a   cauravou yai]}$_O$
     1sg PAST hear-TR ART CL.POSS-3pl win   ART youth   this
     I heard these youths' winning

A clausal NP can be introduced with a preposition. Such an NP can even function as possessor or possessed in associative construction NP *ni* NP, meaning 'NP associated/of NP'.

Why is this NP better analysed as a special clause type, and not as a noun? Firstly, arguments and obliques other than the S/A are marked in exactly the same way as in a declarative main clause. An example is at (17) (Dixon 1988: 132; p.c.):

(17) au   rogo-ca [a   o-na   laga-ta   [a   same]$_O$
     1sgA   hear-TR ART CL.POSS-3sg sing-TR   ART psalm
     [o   Maritina]$_A$ i   na   lotu]
     ART.NAME Maritina   in ART church
     I heard {Maritina$_A$ singing a psalm$_O$ in church}$_O$

A clausal NP can also include a peripheral NP marked with preposition *i*. And all of the various constituents of the predicate can occur in a clausal NP—these include past tense *aa* and future *na*, and the verbal modifier *mai* 'here'. See (18) (also see Dixon 1988: 333):

(18) au   tadra-a   {a   o-mu   aa/na   la'o   mai}$_O$
     1sgA dream-TR ART CL.POSS-2sg PAST/FUT come HERE
     I dreamt that you had/would come

If a verb takes nominal morphology, this does not automatically make it into a noun. In many languages, cases can have a clausal scope. Case markers can attach to inflected verbs, or to verb roots. In (19), from Tariana, the instrumental case *-ne* marks a reason clause:

(19) {heku   nuha hñaka-si-nuku **mheta-kade-ne**}   mhaisiki
     yesterday I   eat-NMZR-OBJ   NEG:bring-NEG-REASON hunger
     pi-ñami-nihka
     2sg-die-RECENT.PAST.INFERRED
     Since I did not bring you food yesterday, you (inferred) are dying of hunger

There is nothing nominal about the form in bold type: it is negated like a verb, and takes a case-marked object; there is also an oblique. This is similar to how in English, and many other languages, a preposition can be used to link clauses, e.g. *She had a hard time after {the death of her husband}* and *She had a hard time after {her husband died}.* The clause *after her husband died* is not a noun. See further discussion of clause-linking functions of cases and adpositions in Chapter 1 above and Genetti (1986, 1991).

That is, if a clause, or a word, has some noun-like syntactic functions, this is not enough to declare it a noun. And if a form takes some nominal morphology, it does not mean that it should be declared 'nominalized'. We need to look at all the properties—syntactic and morphological—of a given form before we make a decision.

Verbal forms and deverbal derivations can be plotted on a continuum from those which have all the trappings of a main clause declarative verb to those that are fully nominal.[15] For instance, English allows for a tripartite division:[16]

Full set of verbal properties	Verbal: Tense/aspect; modification	No verbal properties
No nominal properties	Marking subject as possessor	Full set of nominal properties
main clause declarative verb	*-ing* complement clause	*-ing* deverbal noun *-ment* deverbal noun, etc.

Word-class membership is defined on synchronic, and not on etymological, grounds. Historically speaking, some of the so-called 'infinitive' verb forms which appear in complement clauses and purpose clauses go back to a case-marked verbal noun. For instance, the Udmurt 'infinitive' *-ny* and the Hungarian *-ni* go back to a deverbal action noun plus a lative (directional) case ending (see Haspelmath 1989: 292, and references there). The infinitives in Latin, Ancient Greek, Old

---

[15] And see Kornfilt (1997: 450), on Turkish deverbal nouns and 'elements...which, while nominal, aren't full nouns', 'referred to as "action nominal", "factive nominal" and "infinitival"'. They display a range of nominal properties: all can be suffixed with case morphemes, their subjects are marked with genitive case, and the agreement suffixes—if any—are taken from the nominal, not verbal, paradigm. All of them can be passivised, can take complements (including accusative-marked direct objects), and can be modified by adverbs.

The forms differ as to (a) whether they can be affixed with plural; (b) whether they can co-occur with nominal determiners such as demonstratives, and if they can be coordinated with the nominal comitative conjunction *-(y)lA* (Kornfilt 1997: 450–1).

[16] This continuum is only partly reminiscent of Lehmann's (1988: 200) 'continuum of desentialization': his assumption that only an inflected verb can constitute a 'sentence', or be a proper head of predicate, holds only for those languages where nouns cannot head a predicate.

Indo-Iranian, Slavic, and Hittite go back to verbal nouns in the dative, accusative, or locative cases (also see Jeffers 1975: Gippert 1978). Synchronically, these forms are not nouns. They tend to have the argument structure of verbs. For instance, in Ancient Greek the infinitive suffixes have lost connection with the nominal case paradigm. The infinitive distinguishes voices and tenses/aspects (there is a future and a perfect infinitive). This verb form characteristic of complement and purpose clauses is considered part of a verb's paradigm.

5.5. *What can nominalizations be good for?*

Nominalizations—deverbal derivations with mostly nominal morphological and syntactic features—can be 'versatile' (Noonan 1997).

If a language lacks a special grammatical construction for complementation, it will still have a grammatical mechanism for stating 'what a proposition is which is seen, heard, believed, known, liked, etc.,' (Dixon 2006a: 1). Such mechanisms are called 'complementation strategies'. They involve coopting an already existing structure in a language, to occur where a complement clause would be expected. These strategies include, among others, nominalizations (see examples and discussion in Dixon 2006a: 36–8). Nominalizations as complementation strategies have been described for Matses, Akkadian, Tariana, Goemai, and also Kham (Watters 2002: 331–41), and North-East Ambae (Hyslop 2001: 392).

A prime example comes from Carib languages, e.g. Apalaí (Koehn and Koehn 1986: 89–95). Nominalizations have the argument structure and the categories of typical nouns. The S and O of a nominalized verb are marked as possessor noun phrase, or possessive prefix on the verb, e.g. *j-oepy-ry* (1sgPOSS-come-NMZR) 'my coming'; *j-etapa-ry* 'my being killed'.

The A of a nominalized verb can be expressed with an oblique noun phrase, or prefix attached to the postposition *a* 'to, by', e.g. *karau apoi-topo-Ṽpyry y-a* (bird catch-NMZR-PAST 1sgPOSS-by) 'my having caught the bird'.

Nominalizations can be used as heads of predicates, as in (20), as S and as O, and as complementation strategies, as in (21):

(20) a-yto-ry   ropa   moro   isawã   pona
      3-go-NMZR   again   that   sand   to
      He is going to the beach (again)

(21) {{t-ōxi-ry   ekaro-ry} se   to-exi-ry-ke}
3REFL-daughter-POSSN give-NMZR want 3REFL-be-NMZR-REASON
Because he wanted to give (lit. giving) his own daughter (in marriage)

Multifunctional nominalizations are a prominent feature of many
other languages, among them Tupí-Guaraní (see Seki 2000), and especially Tibeto-Burman languages. Chantyal employs nominalizations as
complementation strategies, in purpose clauses, in relative clauses, as
modifiers, and predicate heads—this is why a paper on these is appropriately called 'Versatile nominalizations' by Noonan (1997).

Multifunctional nominalizations are likely to undergo reanalysis
and develop into special verbal paradigms—see below.

5.6. *Multifunctional nominalizers*

Nominalizers can have a variety of additional uses and functions.

They can be used to mark NON-WORD-CLASS-CHANGING DERIVA-
TIONS. Action nominalizers can derive nouns denoting a property or
an object associated with another noun, e.g. English *bedding* 'things
which go on a bed, e.g. sheets and blankets'. Agent nominalizers in
Lahu (Matisoff 1973: 457) can derive nouns from verbs, e.g. *mô chî
šē-phâ* (things wash male.expert) 'laundryman', *yâ pɔ pî šē-ma* (child
born benefactive female.expert). When used with nouns, they refer
to 'the owner of' or 'master of a trade', e.g. *yɛ̀=šē-phâ* (house-male
expert) 'owner of the house', *yɛ̀=šē-ma* (house-female expert) 'lady of
the house', *nâʔ-chî=šē-phâ* (medicine-male expert) 'doctor'.

In many languages with CLASSIFIERS and NOUN-CLASS MARKERS
used in multiple environments, these are employed as markers of
object, result and A/S nominalizations. In Yagua (Payne and Payne
1990: 354–6), all classifiers can occur on verbal, adjectival or adverbial
roots to form nouns. So, the animate singular classifier forms an agent
noun with a specific referent, as in *dapuuy-nù* (hunt-CLASS.ANIM:SG)
'the one who is hunting or hunting person'. The neuter classifier can
be used to derive an agent noun with a more generic, habitual meaning, e.g. *dapuuy-ra* (hunt-CL:NEUT) 'the hunter, or professional hunter
qualified in the action of hunting'. Similar functions of classifiers have
been described for Movima (Haude 2006: 477–8), Tucano, Desano,
and Tariana, and Bantu languages (Mufwene 1980; Aikhenvald 2000b:
84, 220–2).

Nominalizations can undergo partial REANALYSIS, and be used in independent clauses. Nominalizations are often used as EVIDENTIAL-ITY STRATEGIES, as in Meithei where a nominalization marked with *-jat* expresses the inferred evidential meaning (Chelliah 1997: 295–6; see further examples in Aikhenvald 2004: 117–20). They can be used in lieu of commands, as in Korean, where formal and official commands involve nominalised clauses.

Or they can be a source for NEW TENSE AND ASPECT PARADIGMS. In numerous Carib languages nominalizations as predicate heads have been reanalysed as tense and aspect forms. In Trio (Carlin 2004: 293) an activity nominalization marked with *-se* is now used as a habitual past. Further examples are in Derbyshire (1999: 39–40) and Gildea (1998: 119–51). Nominalizations as copula complements are reanaly-sed as one simplex predicate with a unitary tense and aspect value. This is similar to how a periphrastic construction consisting of a deverbal adjective, or participle, accompanied by a copula verb, can develop into one predicate (Bhat n/d: 14, on Old Kannada; also Dia-konoff 1988).

Erstwhile nominalizations can undergo reanalysis of another sort: they can develop into verbal forms predominantly used in non-main clauses. For instance, the deverbal noun in the locative case has taken on an independent life as an 'infinitive' marked with *-t'* or *-ti* for most Slavic languages. This form does not have any nominal properties, and has been completely integrated into the verbal paradigm. Many verbal categories can be expressed in it. It is considered 'non-finite' since it does not have person and number agreement and tense. The origin of such 'defective' verbal forms—known under a plethora of terms including infinitive, gerund, and supine—is often non-verbal. But to lump them together as 'nominalizations' obscures the actual relation-ships between word classes in a language.

5.7. *The origins of nominalizers*

In terms of their origins, nominalizers can come from other word-class-changing devices. The subject nominalizer in Jamul Tiipay (Miller 2001: 119–20) comes from a marker of relative clause forms of verbs. Along similar lines, the nominalizer *-wa* in Chantyal may have devel-oped from a number of nominalizing suffixes (including the agent-patient nominalizer and the action nominalizer) (Noonan 1997).

Or they can come from full nouns. The marker of temporal nominal-ization in Supyire (Carlson 1994: 108–16) *kaan-* 'give', *tèè-kaan-* 'time to give, pay' goes back to the noun *tèrè* 'time, moment'. In Meithei (Chelliah 1997: 155), two nominalizers come from nouns: -*pót* 'type of action, state or result' comes from *pót* 'thing'. Numerous further examples are found in Tibeto-Burman languages (including Lahu: Matisoff 1973).

This implies that word-class-changing affixal derivations develop from compounds. This is an additional reason why compounds should not be excluded from a general study of word-class-changing devices.

6. Derived Adjectives, and their Properties

Adjectives can be derived from verbs and from nouns, and, rarely, from adverbs and other word classes. By and large, derived adjectives appear to span the same semantic types and have the same properties as underived adjectives.

6.1. *Adjectives derived from verbs*

Adjectives derived from verbs relate to (a) the activity or its result, or to (b) a property of a core argument, usually A/S or O.

The major semantic subtypes of each of these are listed below.

a. Property associated with activity or with its result.

a1. Property associated with the action, e.g. Hungarian *visz-ket* 'itch', *visket-ős* 'itchy' (Kenesei et al. 1998: 367); Turkish (Kornfilt 1997: 458) *ak* 'flow', *ak-ıcı* 'fluent, fluid' (this derivation is said to have an overtone of regularity); Tamambo (Jauncey 1997: 11) *mana* 'laugh', *manamana* 'friendly', *sale* 'float', *salesale* 'light (in weight)'.

a2. Property associated with the result of an action, e.g. Amharic (Amberber 1996: 10) *saffa* 'become wide', *saffi* 'wide'; Turkish (Kornfilt 1997: 458) *dol* 'get full', *dol-u* 'full'; Awa Pit (Curnow 1997: 11) *ii* 'die', *iita* 'dead'; Lango *ɲàkkò* 'to grind coarsely', *à-ɲák-á* 'coarse'.

b. Property of a core argument.

b1. Potential property of the A/S or of the O argument, as in English *forget-ful, turn-able, attract-ive* (A/S), *forfeit-able* (O); Hungarian *olvas* 'read', *olvas-ható* 'readable' (Kenesei et al. 1998: 366); or to the object (*forget-able*); Basque (Saltarelli 1988: 260) *farre* 'laugh', *farre-garri* 'laughable', *jan* 'eat', *jan-garri* 'edible'. In English, the suffix *-able* also has a potential meaning, e.g. *walk-able, breath-able*, as in *breathable tissues*.

This type also covers 'purposive' adjectives, e.g. Awa Pit (Curnow 1997: 11) *ku* 'eat, drink', *(chicha) ku-m* '(chicha) for drinking', adjectives with the meaning of 'having facility/propensity for action', as in Basque (Saltarelli 1988: 260) *irrista-tu* 'slip', *irrista-kor* 'slippery', 'prescriptive adjectives', as in Hungarian *kinyit* 'open', *kinyit-andó* '(something) to be opened' (Kenesei et al. 1998: 367), and 'desiderative' adjectives, as in Quechua (Cole 1982).

b2. ACTUAL PROPERTY OF THE A/S ARGUMENT OF THE VERB, e.g. Jacaltec *tz'unu* 'plant something', *tz'un-bil wu* (plant-ADJ by.me) 'planted by me', *tx'ixwi* 'be ashamed', *tx'ixwi-naj* 'ashamed' (Day 1973: 48); Amele *bebes* 'terrify', *bebes-ec* 'terrifying' (Roberts 1987: 325–6); Babungo *léy* 'clear, clean', *lēy* 'clear, clean' (Schaub 1985: 245); Indonesian *menangis* 'cry', *penangis* 'cry-baby' (adjective) (Sneddon 1996: 48).[17]

b3. PROPERTY OF THE O ARGUMENT OF THE VERB, e.g. Amele *ab* '(be) separate', *ab-ec* 'separate', *cagas* 'forgive', *cagac-ec* 'forgiven' (Roberts 1987: 325–6).

Adjectives of any type may have a special 'privative' counterpart, e.g. Hungarian *olvas-hatatlan* 'unreadable', or simply negative, e.g. *olvas-atlan* 'unread'.

Deverbal adjectives exemplified above have all the properties characteristic of underived adjectives. Derived adjectives of type (a) tend to belong to the semantic type of PHYSICAL PROPERTY (Dixon 2004a), while those of type (b) cover HUMAN PROPENSITY and PHYSICAL PROPERTY. In some languages—for instance, Warekena of Xié (Aikhenvald 1998: 304–8)—all adjectives are derived from verbs; these cover all the semantic types of adjectives. Unlike nominalizations, deverbal adjectives do not appear to treat S/O together.

Participles, or 'deverbal modifiers', deserve a special mention. In numerous languages, such modifiers can be regularly derived from

---

[17] A meaning of such 'property' can be rather broad: for instance, in Tagalog, the prefix *naka-* derives adjectives from verbs whose meanings encompass manner, bodily positions and 'wearing', e.g. *upó* 'sit', *nakaupó* 'seated', *baróng* 'kind of shirt', *nakabaróng* 'wearing a barong' (Rubino 1998b: 17).

verbs, and thus can be considered part of the verbal paradigm. These 'participles' tend to have verbal categories which include ASPECT, RELATIVE TENSE, MODALITY, and VALENCY-CHANGING. Their argument structure and marking is the same as that of verbs. Participles can be A/S oriented ('active' participles), S/O oriented ('passive' participles), or have no orientation. 'Resultative' participles are always S/O oriented, e.g. English *a fallen leaf, a recently recorded song*. In terms of expressing tense and aspect, A/S and S/O oriented participles may display assymmetry, as is the case in Latin (see further examples and discussion of participles in Haspelmath 1994):

	A/S oriented, active participle	S/O oriented passive participle
present	*scrib-ens* 'writing'	—
past	—	*scriptus* 'written'
future	*scrip-turus* 'going to write, about to write'	*scrib-endus* 'to be written'

'Participles' may, however, differ from adjectives in their grammatical properties (contrary to the assumption that they 'behave like adjectives with respect to morphology and external syntax': Haspelmath 1994: 152). For instance, in Hungarian participles have no comparative forms, and cannot be used with intensifiers or head a predicate (Kenesei et al. 1998: 366). In Latin, participles have nominal tense, and adjectives do not. In Tariana, A/S participles agree in gender and number with the A/S, just like adjectives do. However, the number marking is different from that on nouns and that on adjectives. Participles distinguish nominal tense (rather than verbal tense and evidentiality). The marking of arguments is the same as with verbs, and so is negation. In all such instances, it would be a simplification to lump them together with 'deverbal adjectives'. They are best considered a special category of verbs whose major function is marking the predicate of a relative clause.

Deverbal modifiers ('participles') can give rise to complex predicates. S/O oriented participles play a role in developing passive constructions, e.g. *the book was written by a famous author*. Periphrastic constructions consisting of a past participle of the main verb followed by the future forms of the verb *a:gu* 'to become' in Old Kannada gave rise to simple forms with future subjunctive meanings in non-coastal dialects of Kannada (Bhat n/d). This is similar to how nominalizations undergo reinterpretation and give rise to new verbal paradigms (§5.6–7).

6.2. *Adjectives derived from nouns*

Adjectives derived from nouns cover the following semantic types:

(I) MATERIAL: 'made of N', as in English *wood-en*, Evenki *altan* 'gold', *alta-ma* 'golden' (Nedjalkov 1997: 305).

(II) SIMILARITY: 'be like N; behave like N', as in English *mann-ish*; Turkish *masa* 'table', *masa-msɪ* 'table-like' (Kornfilt 1997: 457); Hungarian *könyv* 'book', *könyv-szerű* 'like a book'; Kobon *imgup rö* (snake. species like) 'like an imgup (snake species)' (Davies 1981: 211–12); Japanese (Onishi 1996b) *otoko* 'man', *otoko-rasii* 'manly'.

(III) PROPERTY: 'BE CHARACTERISED BY', as in English *passionate, beauti-ful,* Jacaltec *pojoj* 'dust', *pojoj-taj* 'dusty' (Day 1973: 49); Amharic *mïdir* 'earth', *mïdrawi* 'earthly' (Amberber 1996: 11); Turkish *bilim* 'science', *bilim-sel* 'scientific' (Kornfilt 1997: 457); Ponapean *ilok* 'wave', *ilokin* 'wavy' (Rehg 1981); Tagalog *gútom* 'hunger', *gutóm* 'hungry', *bigát* 'weight', *mabigát* 'heavy' (Rubino 1998b: 17); Evenki *kungakan* 'child', *kungaka-dy* 'childish' (Nedjalkov 1997: 305–6); cf. 'propensity for object', as in Basque *negar* 'tear', *negar-ti* 'tearful' (Saltarelli 1988: 260).

(IV) PROPRIETIVE: 'having N', e.g. English *hair-y*; Hungarian *kazetta* 'cassette', *kazettá-s* 'having cassettes' (Kenesei et al. 1998: 362–3); Evenki *dyl* 'head', *dyli-migda* 'with a big head' (Nedjalkov 1997: 305); 'pertaining to N', e.g. Hungarian *Budapest* 'Budapest', *budapest-i* 'from Budapest' (Kenesei et al. 1998: 362–3); Egyptian Colloquial Arabic *ʕamiid* 'dean', *ʕamiid-i* 'pertaining to the dean' (Gary and Gamal-Eldin 1982: 117).

The opposite of proprietive is privative, as English *joy-less*; Hungarian *könyv* 'book', *könyv-telen* 'bookless'; Bengali *sim(a)* 'boundary'; *ɔ-sim* 'boundless' (Onishi 1997).

There may be further distinctions: English has two privative markers which derive adjectives from nouns. One, *-less*, as in *parent-less*, refers to the lack of N as something one would expect and hope to have. The other one, *-free*, as in *dust-free (environment)* and *parent-free (evening)*, conveys the idea that the absence of N is somehow welcome or desirable.

(V) QUANTIFICATION, e.g. Hungarian *marok* 'hand', *marok-nyi* 'handful of' (Kenesei et al. 1998: 365); Motuna (Onishi 1994: 152–3) *-no(h)i* 'as big as', e.g. *irihwa-noh-ni* (finger-as.big.as-DIM) 'as big as this finger'; Bengali (Onishi 1997) *jɔl(o)-moy* 'full of water', *jɔl* 'water'.

There may be a special derivation relating to TIME, e.g. Evenki (Nedjalkov 1997: 305) *b'ega* 'month', *b'ega-pty* 'monthly', or to location, e.g. Evenki (Nedjalkov 1997: 305) *do:* 'interior', *do:-gu/do:-vu* 'inner'.

An adjectivizing derivation can be polysemous. Meanings of (ii) and (iii) are combined by *-s* adjectives in Hungarian (Kenesei et al. 1998: 362–3), e.g. *szerence* 'luck', *scerencsé-s* 'lucky', *ezüst* 'silver', *ezüst-ös* 'silvery'.

Adjectives in Hungarian can be formed on noun phrases, e.g. *rövid függöny* 'short curtain', *rövid függöny-ös* 'with short curtains'; *nagyon rövid haj-ú* (very short hair-ADJ) '(someone) with very short hair'. The same applies to Tariana.

6.3. *Adjectives derived from other word classes, multifunctional derivations, and the origins of derivational markers*

The same suffix can be used to derive adjectives from nouns, and from verbs, with similar meanings. Examples from English include *-less, -able, -ful, -y* and more (see Dixon 2014). In Colloquial Welsh (King 1993: 86–9), the suffix *-ol* derives adjectives from verbs, e.g. *cefnogi* 'support', *cefnogol* 'supportive', and from nouns, e.g. *trosedd* 'crime', *troseddol* 'criminal'. The meaning is roughly 'having property of'. The suffix *-gar* derives adjectives with habitual meaning from verbs, e.g. *ennill* 'gain', *enillgar* 'lucrative', and from nouns, e.g. *dialedd* 'vengeance', *dialeddgar* 'vengeful'.

Adjectives may be occasionally derived from other word classes, e.g. from prepositions, as in Egyptian Colloquial Arabic (Abbul-Fetouh 1969: 109) *fo:ʔ* 'on/up', *fo:ʔami* 'upper'. In Evenki (Nedjalkov 1997: 306) adjectives can be derived from adverbs, with a general meaning 'relating to', e.g. adverb *tyma:tne* 'in the morning', adjective *tymar* 'pertaining to the morning', adverb *amaski* 'backwards', adjective *amaski-pty* 'former, backward'.

Adjectivizing derivations from nouns may involve noun class markers, as in Tariana *panisi* 'house', *panisite* (house:NOUN.CLASS.ANIMATE) 'the one of the house (its owner or the one living in it)'.

Adjectivizers can come from lexical nouns, e.g. the suffix-*szerű* in Hungarian *könyv-szerű* 'like a book' comes from *szer* 'tool' (Kenesei

et al. 1998: 365). This is reminiscent of how compounding can be used
as a means of deriving adjectives, with somewhat non-compositional
meanings, e.g. Tamambo (Jauncey 1997: 11) *mata-suri* (eye-follow)
'jealous', *batu-dira* (head-strong) 'naughty'. Compounds may function
as modifiers, in which case they can be treated as derived adjectives,
e.g. Irakw *ii'a-tleer* (ear-long) 'widely known', *gur-boo'* (stomach-black)
'discontent' (Mous 1993: 208).

An adjectivizing morpheme can be limited to loans, e.g. suffixes *-i,
-wi-, -iah* in Indonesian can derive adjectives only from nouns of Sanskrit or Arabic origin, e.g. *alam* 'nature, the world', *alami* 'natural'
(Sneddon 1996).

In terms of their semantic types, adjectives derived from nouns
show somewhat more diversity than adjectives derived from verbs. We
saw above that they cover HUMAN PROPENSITY, PHYSICAL PROPERTY,
SIMILARITY, QUALIFICATION and QUANTIFICATION. This correlation
appears independent of whether the language has noun-like or verb-
like adjectives.

7. DERIVED ADVERBS, AND THEIR PROPERTIES

7.1. *Recurrent semantic types*

Derived adverbs are less widespread than derived adjectives, nouns or
verbs. Adverbs can be derived from each of these word classes. A typical meaning of a derived adverb is 'manner', as in Basque (Saltarelli
1988: 260–1) where manner adverbs can be derived from nouns and
from verbs, e.g. *harri* 'a stone', *harri-ka* 'by stoning', *jo* 'to hit', *jo-ka*
'by hitting'; and Evenki (Nedjalkov 1997: 306–7) *ajav-* 'the love', *ajav-
ne* 'lovingly', *helinche-* 'to hurry/hasten', *helinche-ne* 'in a hurry'.

In some languages, manner adverbs can be derived just from
nouns, e.g. Egyptian Colloquial Arabic (Gary and Gamal-Eldin 1982:
117) *surʕa* 'speed', *bi-surʕa* 'speedily' and Jacaltec *ewan* 'dark', *ewan-
taj* 'secretly' (where the same suffix is also used to derive adjectives
from nouns: Day 1973: 49). The ubiquitous prefix *va'a-* in Boumaa
Fijian (Dixon 1988: 109–11, 183–4; 2004a: 21) can derive adverbs from
adjectives and from some nouns, but not from verbs, e.g. adjective
levu 'big', *va'a-levu* 'greatly', *Viti* 'Fiji', *va'a-Viti* 'Fijian way', *tuuraga*
'chief', *va'a-tuuraga* 'chiefly'. In Goemai (Hellwig 2011), the prefix *N-*
can derive an adverb from any verb. A derived adverb can refer to time
of the action or state implied by the verb, as in (22).

(22) Goe=tarap   s'onkwa   m-b'arak
      2sg.masc.S=snap(PL)   maize   ADVZ-wet
      Break the maize freshly (i.e. while it is wet)

Or a derived adverb can occur together with the verb 'to emphasize the state of affairs':

(23) Tù   bí   hók   n-tú
      kill(SG)   thing   DEF   ADVZ-kill(SG)
      Kill the thing killing

Adverbs derived from adjectives typically refer to manner in which the property is realised, e.g. Colloquial Welsh *cyflym* 'quick', *yn gyflym* 'quickly' (King 1993: 238) and Basque (Saltarelli 1988: 261) *eder* 'handsome', *ederki* 'well'. In English, many adjectives form an adverb by adding *-ly*, meaning 'do it in that way'; for example, *clever-ly*. (There is discussion of which adjectives from which semantic types form which type of adverb, in English, in Dixon 2005: 381–5.) Just occasionally, a deadjectival adverb may have a slightly idiosyncratic meaning, e.g. Indonesian (Sneddon 1996) 'as ADJ as possible', e.g. *baik* 'good', *se-baik-baik-nya* 'as good as possible'.

Adverbs derived from nouns in English have a broadly directional meaning, e.g. *home-wards* 'towards home', *clock-wise* 'circular motion in the same direction that the hands of a clock move', and *side-ways* 'with the side of an object facing forwards instead of, as would be expected, the front facing forwards' (also see Dixon 2010a: 149–50).

Adverbs derived from numbers may cover the meaning of 'quantification', e.g. Boumaa Fijian (Dixon 1988: 110), e.g. *vitu* 'seven', *va'a-vitu* 'seven times', and also English *ten-fold* as in *It increased tenfold*, meaning that it became ten times as big as before.

Adjectives may be able to modify verbs, as is the case in Tariana, in Japanese (Dixon 2004a: 21), and in most Carib languages. Then, a language is not expected to have a special class of adverbs derived from adjectives.

7.2. *The limits of adverbializations*

Just like many other word-class-changing derivational markers, adverbializers can be grammaticalised from independent nouns: a prime example is English *-ways* as in *side-ways*. Or they can arise through reintrepretation of other categories.

Cross-linguistically, the reinterpretation of case-marked nouns or combinations of nouns with prepositions as manner adverbs is rather common, e.g. Evenki *amar* 'back/rear', *amar-duk* (rear-ABL) 'from the rear', *amar-du* (rear-DAT) 'behind' (Nedjalkov 1997: 306–7), English *besides, underneath*; Russian *tolkom* (sense/reason:INSTR.SG) 'properly', *putëm* (road:INSTR.SG) 'in the right way'; and many others (also see Kornfilt 1997: 462, on Turkish). Whether or not such case-marked forms are to be treated as members of the class of adverbs depends on how they compare to non-derived members of the same word class.

Predicates of adverbial dependent clauses can be reinterpreted and reanalysed as verbal modifiers. This is the case in Manambu, Iatmul (Staalsen 1965), Urarina, and Ket (Vajda 2004: 41). So, in Manambu the form *səbən-ən* (return-SEQ) literally translates as 'by manner of returning, on coming back'. It can be used as a verbal modifier meaning 'back'. The two usages can be distinguished: the verb in a dependent clause can have its own arguments and obliques and can be negated, and the verbal modifier cannot.

The dependent clause verb *səbən-ən* in its negative and positive form is illustrated in (24). The relevant forms are in bold type.

(24) [lə   wiya:r   **səbən-ən**]   [ñanugwa:k   kamna:gw
      she   house:LK:ALL   return-SEQ   children:LK:DAT   food
        kui-k-la]   **səbən-ma:r-ən**]   kui   ma:
        give.to.third.p-FUT-3fem.sgSUBJ return-NEG.DEP-SEQ give.NEG   NEG
        On returning to the house (or: by returning to the house) she will give
          children food, on not returning (or: by not returning) she won't give
          (it to them)

The same form *səbənən* reanalysed as an adverb is given in (25). It cannot be negated, since negation is a clausal category in Manambu, and an individual constituent cannot be negated.

(25) kamna:gw   **səbənən**   kui-k-la
      food   back   give.to.third.p-FUT-3fem.sgSUBJ
      She will give food back (to them)

And this takes us to a more general question. If a special verbal form is used as a predicate of a dependent clause which, in its turn, has the syntactic functions of an oblique within the sentence as a whole, is this form a deverbal adverb?[18]

This question is similar to that concerning special verbal forms used in complement clauses (see (14a) and (15a)). We saw in §5.4.1 above that such forms do not have to be nominalizations, inasmuch as they may not have the morphological and syntactic properties of nouns. The same holds for the predicates of subordinate clauses.

The predicate of the Manambu clause in (24) has syntactic and morphological properties of an uninflected verb; but not of an adverb. Along similar lines, the predicate of a 'participial' clause in Dolakhā Newar (Genetti 2005: 35, 40) is not inflected for the 'full range of verb morphology'; 'its status with respect to the surrounding text is determined by the morphology on the final verb.' 'Participial clauses' form a clause chain, and are 'neither a nominal argument, a nominal modifier, nor a complement of the following verb or clause'; the semantic relation between the non-main and the main clause is determined by the context.[19]

Dependent clauses expressing 'concomitant action' and a variety of other meanings are pervasive in Tibeto-Burman (see further examples in Genetti 2005, 2007; Rutgers 1998), Dravidian (e.g. Krishnamurti and Behnam 1998), and Papuan languages. They cannot be considered on a par with lexical derived adverbs—just like a 'that' complement clause in English (13a) is not a noun. The predicates of these clauses can be reanalysed as adverbs—this is what we saw for Manambu (24–5 above). To what extent this reanalysis is a common phenomenon is an open question.

---

[18] In some recent literature (Haspelmath 1994, 1995) a term 'converb' has been introduced to cover special verbal forms restricted to manner, temporal and other subordinate clauses. To what extent the notion of 'converb' is cross-linguistically valid in terms of meanings and categories expressed is still an open question.

[19] An example of a dependent 'participial' clause in Dolakhā Newar is:

(26) [kāsi   oŋ-an   jal-ai   ju-en]
     Kāsi   go-PARTICIPLE   burn-BORROWED.VERB   be-PARTICIPLE
          citrāŋga   bicitrāŋga   sit-a
          Citrāŋga   Bicitrāŋga   die-3sg.PAST
     Going to Kāsi and burning (committing self-immolation), Citrāŋga and Bicitrāŋga died

8. Summing Up

We have surveyed the four major types of word-class-changing derivations—verbalizations, nominalizations, adjectivizations, and adverbializations. The relevant parameters involve:

- what word classes they can be derived from,
- typical semantics of derived forms,
- properties of derived forms as compared to the underived ones;
- possible polysemy of derivational markers, and
- potential pathways of reinterpretation and reanalysis of derived forms.

8.1. *Verbalizations*

A language is more likely to have verbs derived from nouns than from other word classes. Derived verbs are typically full-fledged verbs in terms of all properties. Denominal verbs have many more semantic types than verbs derived from adjectives and other word classes. Verbalizers can double as non-word-class-changing derivational devices. The most frequent polysemy involves verbalizers and causative markers.

Quite a few languages have no verbs derived from other word classes. These languages typically allow for nouns and other word classes to occupy the predicate slot (which reduces the functional need for a verbalizing derivation). A language with no verbalizations is likely to have a syntactic construction consisting of a non-verbal element and a support verb ('light' verb, or a copula verb). This can be viewed as a 'verbalization' strategy—and is another way in which a language can avoid verbalization.

8.2. *Nominalizations*

Nouns can be derived from any word class. Deverbal nouns are the most frequent type, and they are the richest in terms of their semantics. Deverbal nouns can refer to:

(A) activity, state, or property of the verb;
(B) core arguments A, S, O; or
(C) oblique arguments (time, location, reason, manner; hardly ever destination).

There do not seem to be any special derivations relating to E as a core argument. Individual derivational markers can be polysemous between these three categories.

Deverbal nouns tend to be a special subclass of nouns, while nouns derived from other word classes have all the properties of underived nouns. Deverbal nouns—especially those referring to activity—may have a reduced set of nominal properties. They may not have the full set of number and gender and classifier choices, and they may not be able to appear in the full set of nominal syntactic functions and take all the nominal cases, or definiteness markers. They may also have some verbal features—these include relative tense, aspect, valency-changing, and just occasionally, modality and evidentiality. They never distinguish mood.

The way arguments of deverbal nouns are marked varies: in some languages arguments are marked similarly to the way they are marked for inflected verbs, while in others they are marked as they would be in a possessive construction. And in others, the marking combines features of both, or deviates from both. That is, some nominalizations are fully nominal in terms of argument marking, and some are less so.

A clausal argument should not be automatically equated with a nominalization. In §5.4.1, we discussed English -*ing* forms and concluded (Table 7.1) that one should distinguish between the -*ing* verb in a complement clause (as in *John's singing the national anthem in church*) and a bona-fide nominalization (as in *the singing of the national anthem in church*). For each 'suspect' form one needs a set of criteria showing why this is a nominalization—that is, a noun—or not.

In languages with few, or hardly any nominalizing derivations, relative clauses can be used in lieu of these. For instance, Manambu has no agentive nominalizations. The only way of saying 'teacher' in Manambu is using a relative clause, 'man who teaches', or 'woman who teaches'. The head can be omitted, and a headless relative clause is another valid alternative to what would be a derivational device in another language.

Nominalizations themselves can be quite versatile: they may be used in lieu of complement or other clause types. And they can be reanalysed as main clause and non-main clause predicates, giving rise to new paradigms.

There are often more nominalizing than verbalizing derivations. It appears that some languages are predominantly verbalizing and others are predominantly nominalizing. This requires further investigation.

8.3. *Adjectivizations*

Adjectives derived from verbs can relate to:

(a) the activity or its result, or
(b) a property of the core argument, A, S, or O.

Deverbal adjectives never relate to an oblique argument. In this sense, they are more restricted than deverbal nouns. Type (a) adjectives tend to belong to the semantic type of physical property, and those of type (b) tend cover human propensity and physical property. Adjectives derived from nouns belong to a wider variety of semantic types (material, similarity, proprietive, and quantification). However, it appears to be the case that by and large derived adjectives are restricted in terms of their semantic types. They may be grammatically restricted, too—this requires further investigation.

Modifiers derived from verbs (traditionally called 'participles') are only sometimes fully-fledged members of the adjective class. Depending on their syntactic and morphological features, they may have to be considered forms of verbs restricted to a clause type, typically, a complement or a relative clause. A language may have no derived adjectives, but instead employ an array of relative clauses, and also nouns as modifiers.

8.4. *Adverbializations*

Derived adverbs are less frequent cross-linguistically than other derived word classes. By-and-large, they are limited to manner and quantification. Derived adverbs are marginal members of the adverb class: there are typically few of them, and they may be semantically limited. Adverbs may arise from reanalysis of case-marked nouns, or combinations of noun with adposition. Or they may come from reanalysis of dependent verb forms. This does not imply that dependent clauses with a special form of the predicate have to be treated as 'syntactic adverbs', or 'converbs'.

If adjectives can be used as modifiers to a verb, a language may not have any adverbializing derivation.

8.5. *Predicting word-class-changing derivations*

We can suggest further tentative GENERALIZATIONS to do with what kinds of word-class-changing derivations we may expect:

I.   It appears that if word-class-changing derivations can be applied to a closed class, they can also be applied to open classes.
II. Analytic alternatives to verbalizations incolve complex verbs. Headless relative clauses can be considered alternatives to nominalizations. A syntactic alternative to adjectivization is a relative clause.
III. Languages where adjectives can modify verbs are expected to have fewer adverbializing derivations (if any at all).
IV. Derived members of all classes, except verbs, tend to be grammatically and semantically somewhat 'impoverished' compared to the underived members which are more central. So, activity nominalizations can be 'incomplete' nouns. But verbalizations are never 'incomplete' verbs. (Note that nominalizations can apply to only some verbs or adjectives; and verbalizations can apply only to some nouns, or adjectives.)
V.   It appears that languages with dependent marking favour nominalizing derivations.

Further hypotheses are:

- If a language has an adjectivizing derivation, and adjectives share grammatical properties with verbs, we hypothesize that it will also have a verbalizing derivation.
- If a language has an adjectivizing derivation, and adjectives share grammatical properties with nouns, we hypothesize that it will also have a nominalizing derivation.
- If a language has just one verbalization, this tends to be causative and/or inchoative.
- If a language has a nominalization, this tends to be an agentive (A/S) nominalization, one of the most nominal of all types.

It also appears that a full array of derivational devices, including affixation, internal segmental change ('apophony'), reduplication, prosodic modification, subtraction, repetition, and also compounding (see §2.2), is available only to nouns, while members of other word classes are usually derived via affixation or compounding.

While there are languages where all adjectives and all adverbs are derived, there appear to be no languages where all verbs, or all nouns, are derived from other classes.

It is plainly the case that some languages have more word-class-changing derivations than others. Why so?

We hypothesize that languages with more freedom of the occurrence of word classes in various functional slots in a clause will have fewer word-class-changing derivations than languages with less freedom. Word-class-changing derivations in such languages as Manambu, Tariana or Boumaa Fijian are 'impoverished' compared with German, English, and other familiar Indo-European languages. But Manambu, Tariana and Boumaa Fijian offer a wider variety of options for members of different word classes to occur in various functional slots in a clause.

A language with a closed class of verbs will not be likely to have derived verbs. Yet another reason for not having word-class-changing devices may lie in the nature of distinctions between word classes. In Manambu, the phonological differences between verbal and non-verbal roots create a potential impediment for easily changing classes.

9. QUESTIONS AND SUGGESTIONS FOR FIELDWORKERS

What follows is a brief list of suggestions and questions for fieldworkers analyzing word-class-changing derivations in a language of their expertise. They need not be dealt with in this order. The relevant section of the chapter is mentioned after each point.

A. Word classes—see §2

- Provide a statement of word classes, in terms of their morphological, syntactic and other properties. (For instance, if the language has phonological differences between nouns and verbs, this needs to be stated). For each word class, delineate the relevant subclasses (this may prove to be important for establishing semantic principles for the choice of a word-class-changing derivational marker).
- State what types of words can function as head of a transitive predicate (transitive verbs, anything else?) and as head of an intransitive predicate (intransitive verbs, anything else?); which word classes can be used as arguments within a clause (without overt marking of derivation), and as modifiers within a noun phrase and within a clause. State members of which word class can be possessors, and which can be 'possessed' within a noun phrase.

If needed, provide a very brief statement of relevant clause types, inasmuch as this is required for discussing the syntactic function of each of the word classes.

For each word class, provide information on whether it is open or closed. For a closed class, say approximately how many members it has.

B. Word-class-changing derivations—see the brief overview in §3.

Does the language have any of:

(i)   Verbalizations: derivations whose end-product has properties of a verb—see §4.
(ii) Nominalizations: derivations whose end-product has properties of a noun. Deverbal nominalizations present somewhat different problems, and often have different properties from those of nouns derived from other word classes. See §5.
(iii) Adjectivizations: derivations whose end-product has properties of an adjective—§6.
(iv) Adverbializations: derivations whose end-product has properties of an adverb—§7.

For each word-class-changing derivation, please discuss:

- the word class it can be derived from (for instance, a verb can be derived from a noun, from an adjective, an adverb, or any other word class; if relevant, explain how the derivation applies to a multiword constituent);
- the semantic types and patterns associated with each (following the types suggested in §§4–7, and perhaps going beyond these);
- polysemous patterns for markers of each word-class-changing derivation. Do any of the word-class-changing derivations also have a non-word-class-changing function?

For each derivation, please mention:

- its productivity;
- its lexicalization patterns, if any;
- other potential problems, such as the direction of derivation.

Word-class-changing derivational devices include affixes (suffixes, prefixes, infixes and circumfixes), morphological processes such as apophony, reduplication, prosodic modification, and subtraction, and especially compounding.

C. Derived verbs—§4

Can verbs be derived from nouns, adjectives, adverbs, and closed classes?

C-1 Semantic types (inchoative, causative, other?)—see §4.1.1; §4.2.1 and §4.3.
     If verbs can be derived from nouns, and from members of other word classes, is it true that denominal verbs cover more semantic types than other derived verbs (see §4.2.2 and §4.3)?
C-2 Features of derived verbs: what factors determine the choice of a verbalizer (such as, for instance, the grammatical class of a noun if a verb is derived from a noun; or the semantic group the noun belongs to)? (§4.4.1)
C-3 Polysemous patterns of derivational markers, and their further functions: do any of the verbalizers have non-word-class-changing functions (such as causative)? (§4.4.3)
C-4 Do you have any idea about the origin of verbalizers? (§4.4.4).
C-5 Further potential problems.

For instance, if the language does not have verbalizing derivations, are there any alternative structures—for instance, 'support verb' constructions, or the option of employing a noun or an adjective as head of predicate? (§4.4.4)

D. Derived nouns—§5

Can nouns be derived from verbs, adjectives, adverbs, and closed classes? We need to address the following issues:

D-1 If nouns can be derived from verbs, please specify their semantic types (relating to (A) action, to (B) core arguments, or to (C) oblique arguments) (§5.1.1).

D-2 For each nominalization, please address the polysemous patterns of derivational markers (for instance, nominalizations relating to core arguments can be polysemous with nominalizations relating to action) (§5.1.2).

D-3 What are the features of derived nouns: how do they compare to underived nouns in terms of their morphological properties and syntactic functions? Do they have all the nominal properties (§5.3.1) and any of the verbal properties (§5.3.2)? How are the arguments of nominalizations marked (§5.3.3)?

D-4 Do nominalizations have any additional syntactic functions (for instance, can they be employed as complementation strategies, or as relativization strategies, or as part of complex predicates)? Have any of the nominalizers been reanalyzed? (§5.4–5.6)?

If the language has special forms of verbs restricted to complement clauses or relative clauses, a case should be made for whether these forms are nominalizations or not (looking at the relevant properties of word classes established for the language in §2, 'Word classes'; also see §5.4).

If nominalizations can be derived from a serial verb construction or from a complex predicate, how is this achieved?

D-5 If nouns can be derived from word classes other than verbs (e.g. adjectives, adverbs, or any other), please specify their semantic types and any other relevant features (§5.2). Are there any multifunctional nominalizers? (§5.6).

If possible, address the issue of the factors which condition the choice of a nominalizer (semantic or other).

D-6 Do you have any idea concerning the origin of any of the nominalizers? (§5.7).

E. Derived adjectives

Can adjectives be derived from verbs, nouns, adverbs, and closed classes? We need to address the following issues:

E-1 Semantic types of adjectives derived from verbs (§6.1)
E-2 Semantic types of adjectives derived from nouns (§6.2)

E-3   Semantic types of adjectives derived from other word classes (§6.3)

E-4   Polysemous patterns of derivational markers, and their further functions (§6.3)

E-5   How do derived adjectives compare to underived adjectives? (§6.3)

E-6   Do you have any idea concerning the origin of any of the adjectivizers? (§6.3)

If the language has special forms of verbs restricted to relative clauses (these forms are sometimes called 'participles'), a case should be made for whether these forms are derived adjectives or not (looking at the relevant properties of word classes established for the language in §2, 'Word classes'; also see §6.3).

F. Derived adverbs

Can nouns be derived from verbs, adjectives, adverbs, and closed classes? We need to address the following issues:

F-1   Semantic types of adverbs derived from verbs, nouns, adjectives and other word classes (§7.1)

F-2   Polysemous patterns of derivational markers, and their further functions (§7.2)

F-3   How do derived adverbs compare to underived adverbs? (§7.2)

F-4   Do you have any idea concerning the origin of any of the adverbializers? (§7.2)

If the language has special forms of verbs restricted to dependent clauses (these forms are sometimes called 'converbs'), a case should be made for whether these forms are adverbializations or not (looking at the relevant properties of word classes established for the language in §2 'Word classes', and §7.2).

G. General issues

§§8.1–4 contain a summary of general features of word-class-changing derivations. A number of hypotheses predicting types of word-class-changing derivations were formulated in §8.5. We recapitulate them here, for ease of reference. Do any of these make sense, for the language of your expertise?

I   It appears that if word-class-changing derivations can be applied to a closed class, they can also be applied to open classes.
II Complex predicates can be considered analytic alternatives to verbalizations, while relative clauses (especially those which can be used without an overt 'head') can be considered analytic alternatives for nominalizations.
III Languages where adjectives can modify verbs are expected to have fewer adverbializing derivations (if any at all).
IV Derived members of all classes, except verbs, tend to be grammatically and semantically somewhat 'impoverished' compared to the underived members which are more central. So, activity nominalizations can be 'incomplete' nouns. But verbalizations are never 'incomplete' verbs.
V   It appears that languages with dependent marking favour nominalizing derivations.

Further hypotheses are:

- If a language has an adjectivizing derivation, and adjectives share grammatical properties with verbs, we hypothesize that it will also have a verbalizing derivation.
- If a language has an adjectivizing derivation, and adjectives share grammatical properties with nouns, we hypothesize that it will also have a nominalizing derivation.
- If a language has just one verbalization, this tends to be causative and/or inchoative.
- If a language has a nominalization, this tends to be an agentive (A/S) nominalization, one of the most nominal of all types.

While there are languages where all adjectives and all adverbs are derived, there appear to be no languages where all verbs, or all nouns, are derived from other classes. BUT in some languages certain subclasses of nouns can consist only of derived items; these typically include abstract concepts, activity and unit of activity (A-type at §5.1.1).

CHAPTER EIGHT

SPEECH REPORTS: A CROSS-LINGUISTIC PERSPECTIVE

Alexandra Y. Aikhenvald

1. Speech Report Constructions: An Overview

A speech report situation involves at least two speakers—the 'author' of the original speech, and the 'reporter'. A speech report construction contains: (i) the speech report content, (ii) the reporting marker, or 'quote framer', and (iii) a linker between these. In a direct speech construction, the speech report content corresponds exactly (or more or less so), to what the original author of the speech report content had said. In the English sentence (1)

(1) He said: 'I needed more money yesterday'

the direct speech report—marked with quotes in the written language—is postposed to the reporting verb 'say'. There is no overt link between the two.

Alternatively, the report may be made without 'using his or her exact words' (Trask 1993: 140), as 'indirect speech'. Then the author's speech is 'adapted' to the 'perspective' of the reporter. In (2),

(2) He said (that) he had needed more money the previous day

the person who made the pronouncement was someone other than the author. Hence, the original 'I' is changed to 'he'. And since the pronouncement was prior to the report, *needed* is 'back-shifted' to the 'past perfect', or past with respect to the past, *had needed*. The time adverb *yesterday* is changed to *the previous day*. The optional complementiser *that* is a marker of syntactic link between the reporting clause and the speech report content.

A reporting marker is often a verb of speech, or an expression 'be like' or 'do like', or a combination of both. An intonation break, or a complementiser, typically mark the link between the reporting marker and the speech report. Speech report constructions may consist of more than one clause—as in (1) and (2); see §2. Or they can be monoclausal—see §3.

A 'verbatim' report and 'indirect' speech differ in a variety of ways: in the marking of person, tense, intonation patterns, and many more. 'Verbatim' quotation option also opens up a potential for mimetic, or 'theatrical effect' (Wierzbicka 1974): one can try and reproduce or imitate the intonation, expression and so on of what had been originally said. A quote can be of more than one clause; or it can consist of just one word, or one morpheme, or not contain any speech as such—just a gesture (Partee 1973). In multiclausal speech reports, the reporting clause is a full clause.

Monoclausal speech reports can be of three kinds:

- (a) construction with a reported or a quotative evidential (see an overview in Aikhenvald 2004: 68–85, and Aikhenvald 2008b);
- (b) construction with double person marking (as in Kwaza: van der Voort 2000: 291–6);
- (c) free indirect discourse (see Quirk et al. 1985; Landeweerd and Vet 1996, for French).

Monoclausal speech reports often originate from reanalysis of multiclausal reports (see Aikhenvald 2004: 68–85, 2008b, and Travis 2006). A major difference between monoclausal speech reports with reported and with quotative evidentials lies in the possibility of an overt statement of the author of the report. A purely reported evidential does not allow for the author of the speech report to be specified. This is in contrast to a quotative evidentials where the source of speech report is to be present. The distinction between direct and indirect speech reports does not apply to monoclausal speech reports. We turn to their further properties in §3.

A list of points to be addressed in an analysis of speech reports in any language is given in §8.

2. MULTICLAUSAL SPEECH REPORT CONSTRUCTIONS

Direct and indirect speech are the most straightforward and cross-linguistically frequent speech reports. We first discuss the formal differences between the two (§2.1), and show that neither is uniform cross-linguistically. Some categories but not others are shifted to the perspective of the external 'reporter': we are then faced with a construction which has come to be called 'semi-direct' speech—this is the topic of Chapter 9. There may be more than one 'intermediate' construction—see §2.2. Distinguishing between several multiclausal speech reports may not be straightforward—several constructions in a language may form a continuum (§2.3). Or a language may have just one multiclausal speech report structure (§2.4).

Within a multiclausal construction, a reporting marker can be a verb of speech, an expression 'be like' or 'do like' (see Romaine and Lange 1998), or a combination of both. An intonation break, a pause, or a complementizer, typically mark the link between the reporting marker and the speech report.

Most languages of the world distinguish two multiclausal speech report constructions: direct and indirect speech. Direct speech (also called quote clause; or quote content) lacks the adjustment of personal, temporal and spatial deixis to the Original Speaker's perspective. It is expected to have all, or most, properties of a main clause. An indirect speech report is typically a kind of embedded complement clause.

Direct speech aims at close, if not fully verbatim, reproduction, of what has been said; direct discourse may involve 'show', not just speech (Wierzbicka 1974: 272; and also see Partee 1973). This is the basis for functional differences between direct and indirect speech. A quote can be of more than one clause; or it can consist of just one word, or one morpheme, or not contain any speech as such—just a gesture (Partee 1973).[1]

2.1. *Distinguishing direct and indirect speech*

Most languages of the world distinguish two multiclausal speech report constructions: direct and indirect speech. A direct speech (also called quote clause, or quote content) lacks the adjustment of personal, temporal and spatial deixis to the narrator's perspective. It is expected to have all, or most, properties of a main clause. An indirect speech report is typically a kind of embedded complement clause.

Direct speech closely reproduces what has been said; 'direct discourse is "show" as well as speech, indirect discourse is speech only'

---

[1] Li (1986: 30–1) and Partee (1973) argue against an earlier transformationalist claim that all indirect speech should be derived from direct speech. Further discussion on how to differentiate between direct and indirect speech reports can be found in Coulmas (1986a), Güldemann (2001), and Güldemann and von Roncador (2002).

(Wierzbicka 1974: 272; and also see Partee 1973). This is the basis for functional differences between direct and indirect speech: see §6.

Major points of difference between direct and indirect speech reports are as follows.

(i) SHIFT IN PERSONAL DEIXIS, to fit in with the perspective of the Original Speaker is a major defining property of indirect speech report constructions (see §1.1 of Chapter 9). An indirect speech report construction may require a simple person shift in pronouns—as when the original *I* of the direct speech in *John$_i$ said 'I$_i$ saw Fred yesterday'* has been shifted to *he* in indirect speech *John$_i$ said that he$_i$ saw Fred yesterday*. A language can employ logophoric (see §3.5 of Chapter 9), reflexive or emphatic pronouns for marking co-reference between the subject of the reporting clause and the subject of the indirect speech report (Culy 1994a: 1055; Carlson 1994: 444–5 on Supyire).[2]

Person shift is the most prominent feature for distinguishing direct and indirect speech. It is the only way of telling direct and indirect speech apart in Hatam (Papuan area: Reesink 1999: 105), Abun (Berry and Berry 1999: 177), Nigerian Pidgin (Faraclas 1996: 6) and Babungo (Schaub 1985: 1). All other features can be considered concomitant to it.

(ii) SHIFT IN SPATIAL AND IN TEMPORAL DEIXIS. Indirect speech report constructions may also involve change in SPATIAL DEIXIS. In Lango (Noonan 1992: 227), the direct speech report in (3) employs a proximal locative 'here'. If the statement is framed as indirect speech, the deictic changes: what was 'here' for the author of the speech report, is 'there' for the Current Speaker in (4).

Lango
(3) òkòbò   nî   [àkétò   pàlà   kân]
     3sg+say+PERF   COMPL   1sg+put+PERF   knife   here
     He said, 'I put the knife here'

(4) òkòbò   nî   [èkétò   pàlà   kỳnỳ]
     3sg+say+PERF   COMPL   3sg+put+PERF   knife   there
     He said that he put the knife there

---

[2] See further references and discussion in Güldemann (2003); Dimmendaal (2001).

In English, an indirect speech report requires changing a time adverb—as in (1) and (2)—and also spatial and other deictics, to fit in with the perspective of the Current Speaker. 'Here' and 'this' in direct speech (5) become 'there' and 'that' in an indirect speech report, and 'come' becomes 'go' (6a,b), due to a switch in the 'deictic orientation' from that of the Original Speaker ('John' in (5)), to that of the Current Speaker (Li 1986; Wiesemann 1990). The Current Speaker's perspective may be different from that in the speech report content, as in (6a,b). (6a) and (6b) are alternatives (see further discussion in Leech and Svartvik 1975: 149–50).

(5)   John told Paul, 'Come here and take care of this mess'

(6a)   John told Paul to go there and take care of that mess

(6b)   John told Paul that he should go there and take care of that mess

In English—but not in Lango and many more languages—what was past in a direct quote changes to 'past in the past' in indirect speech as shown in (4). Such rules of TENSE SHIFT, also known as back-shifting, are prominent in many European languages. (Dixon 2005: 223–5 gives an instructive outline of the rules of back-shifting in English. An overview of back-shift in other European languages is in Janssen and van der Wurff 1996b; also see Sakita 2002 on how these rules apply in spoken English, and Sulkala and Karjalainen 1992: 2, on Finnish.)

   Indirect speech can be marked with a special verb form: this is how conditional (Konjunktiv) is used in German and jussive in Estonian (ten Cate 1996: 202; Erelt 2002). Or the meaning of tenses may be different in indirect speech reports, and in direct speech reports and main clauses. In Finnish, the present tense in indirect speech may indicate that the action is continuous. In Rumanian (Mallinson 1986: 3), the use of conditional in indirect speech implies no responsibility for the truth of the report ('say that V-indicative' means 'say that V' and 'say that V-conditional' means 'allege that V'); no such connotations are found elsewhere in the language.

(iii) SPECIAL MARKING OF REPORTED COMMANDS. The occurrence of IMPERATIVE is likely to be restricted to direct speech and main clauses in general, and an alternative construction used in indirect speech: (5) and (6a, b) show how a *to*-infinitive and a *that* + *should* construction in indirect speech replace an imperative in direct speech (also see McGregor 1994: 73). In Hdi (Frajzyngier 2002: 451) a simple verb form in the indirect speech report corresponds to the imperative in the direct speech report; and in Finnish conditional is used in reported commands. In Taba (Western Austronesian: Bowden 2001: 390–1), the equivalent of an imperative in direct speech reports is a resultative form of the verb. It is not uncommon to employ a different construction type for an indirect speech report of a statement and of a command, as is the case in English, and in Gulf Arabic (here a complementizer marks an indirect speech report unless it is a reported command—then it is omitted: Holes 1990: 2).

(iv) Reported questions ('indirect questions') may take special complementizers when they occur in indirect speech reports (such as *whether* or *if* in English and their equivalents in Taba). There may be differences in constituent orders—a question in a main clause and in a direct speech report in English requires the inversion of subject and verb, while no such inversion is required if a question occurs in indirect speech. No tag questions occur in indirect speech in English (Quirk et al. 1985: 1032).

(v) Overt marker of syntactic link between the reporting expression and the speech report may be required for indirect speech, but not for direct speech. In (2a,b), from English, the optional COMPLEMENTIZER *that* differentiates statements in indirect speech from direct speech. All types of complement clause in English can mark indirect speech, in line with the fact that, cross-linguistically, indirect speech reports are often a subtype of complement clause (Dixon 2005). In Manambu (see Table 3), a speech introducer may occur with direct speech reports, but not with indirect ones.

A complementizer may be used with both direct and indirect speech reports in Lango (see (3) and (4) above), Nkore-Kiga (Bantu: Taylor 1985: 5), Lele (Frajzyngier 2001: 374) and Koromfe (Rennison 1997). Or neither can include a complementizer of any sort, as in Gooniyandi and Taba (McGregor 1994; Bowden 2001: 390–1). In Ndyuka, a complementizer is equally optional with both (Huttar and Huttar 1994: 1–3).

If both direct and indirect speech reports occur with a complementizer, the difference between the two may lie in its frequency. In Supyire a complementizer is rarer with direct speech than with indirect speech (Carlson 1994: 447), while in Tikar (Jackson 1987: 100) it is the other way round. And in Ainu (Bugaeva 2008; Tamura 2000) different complementizers are used with direct, and with indirect speech reports. This takes us to our next point:

(vi) PRESENCE AND TYPE OF REPORTING VERB OR MARKER often differentiate direct and indirect speech reports. A direct speech report—but not indirect speech—may occur without a framing clause of speech, as in Modern Hebrew (Zuckermann 2006), Gooniyandi, Tuvaluan (Besnier 2000: 3), Paumarí (Chapman and Derbyshire 1991: 242–3) and Urubu-Kaapor (Kakumasu 1986: 338). In Maori, many more verbs of speech introduce indirect reports than direct reports (Bauer 1993: 1). In Ainu, it is the opposite (Bugaeva 2008). In many cases if a verb can occur with a direct speech report it can occur with an indirect one. There are exceptions—in colloquial English *go* and *(be) like* only occur with direct speech reports (see Buchstaller 2005, 2006 on their functions, and attitudes to them in modern British and American Englishes). Modern Hebrew employs the verb 'do' as a marker of direct speech reports (Zuckermann 2006: 475). Verbs which do not normally refer to speech acts often introduce direct speech reports (but are not employed for indirect speech); examples include Vinitiri (Oceanic, Austronesian: Van Der Mark 2007) *lari* 'be like', Aguaruna (Jivaroan: Overall 2008) *wahát* 'stop; call' and Dyirbal (Australian: Dixon 1972, p.c.) *yalama-y/l* 'do like this'; also see Golato (2000) on *so* 'so' as a speech report introducer in colloquial German.

(vii) POSITION OF THE SPEECH REPORT IN THE SENTENCE differentiates direct and indirect speech reports in Evenki (Nedjalkov 1997: 1–3) where indirect speech reports follow the reporting verb while direct speech reports may follow or precede it. Direct speech in Awtuw (Feldman 1986: 160–1, 169) follows a speech verb preceded by an adverb meaning 'thus', and indirect speech reports can occur clause-medially. And in Turkish (Kornfilt 1997: 3) indirect speech reports may occur anywhere in the sentence, while direct speech reports may occur only to the immediate left of the report verb 'say'. In Gooniyandi the reporting marker may precede or follow a direct speech report, and always precedes an indirect speech report.

This is directly linked to:

(viii) SPECIFIC CONSTITUENT ORDER WITHIN THE SENTENCE WITH SPEECH REPORT. In Russian (a language with relatively free constituent order), if a direct speech complement precedes the reporting verb, the subject obligatorily follows the verb (see Clarke 2005, and further references there; and Malinson 1986: 1–2, for a similar tendency in Rumanian). The direct speech report in English can be placed before or after the reporting clause—as shown in (7). The reporting clause may interrupt the speech report. This is characteristic of the written language (but not so much of the spoken language).

(7)   'Please,' John said, 'don't do this'
       'Please,' said John, 'don't do this'
       John said, 'Please, don't do this'
       'Please, don't do this,' said John
       'Please, don't do this,' John said
       Said John, 'Please, don't do this'

The subject in a direct speech report is often placed after the reporting verb—unless it is a personal pronoun:

(8)   ⎰ John exclaimed
       'I need more money,'   ⎨ exclaimed John
                                 ⎱ he exclaimed
                                   *exclaimed he (Leech and Svartvik 1975: 117)

The starred option would have been fine if the verb of speech were *say*: *'I need more money,' said he.*

(ix) SPECIAL INTONATION CONTOUR for direct speech report—different from that of an independent clause and an indirect report—has been described for Maltese (Borg and Azzopardi-Alexander 1997: 1–3) and Cairene Egyptian Colloquial Arabic (Gary and Gamal-Eldin 1982: 3).[3] A sentence containing a direct speech report in Modern Greek has an intonational break before the start of the direct speech itself, unlike other sentence types including indirect speech (Joseph and Philippaki-Warburton 1987: 3).

(x) VOCATIVES AND EXCLAMATIONS occur only in direct speech reports, and not in indirect speech in most languages.[4] This is in line

---

[3] Similar examples are Nunggubuyu (Heath 1984: 559), Tuvaluan (Besnier 2000: 5), Ndyuka (Huttar and Huttar 1994: 7) and Maybrat (Dol 1999: 222–3).
[4] Further similar examples include Korean, Finnish, Nunggubuyu and Tuvaluan (Sohn 1994: 13; Sulkala and Karjalainen 1992: 1; Heath 1984: 559; Besnier 2000: 5).

with 'mimetic', or 'theatrical' character of direct speech reports pointed out by Clark and Gerrig (1990), and by Wierzbicka (1974).

FURTHER MARKERS OF DIRECT SPEECH REPORTS include the use of quotative or reported evidentials. An evidential particle in Tamil occurs only with direct speech reports (Asher 1985: 1–3). In Japanese both direct and indirect speech reports can contain one of several quotative particles; according to Hinds (1986: 4–5), only in indirect speech may a quotative particle be replaced by a qualifying phrase, meaning 'something like' or 'like'. In many languages the direct—but not the indirect—speech report may be discontinuous: this applies to English, Modern Hebrew (Zuckermann 2006), Gooniyandi and Ungarinjin (McGregor 1994: 74; Rumsey 1982: 164).[5] This property is far from universal: Colloquial Russian (Clarke 2005: 380) allows both direct and indirect speech reports to be discontinuous.

There may be further, language specific, differences between direct and indirect speech. In Korean, honorific forms are typical of independent clauses and direct speech reports; in indirect speech they are replaced with neutral forms (Sohn 1994: 11). In Hungarian (Kiefer 1986), if the verb 'say' takes the headless proximal demonstrative *ez* as its object, it can only be followed by a direct speech report. In contrast, the distal demonstrative in the same function requires an indirect speech report introduced by the complementizer *hogy* 'that, how'. Direct speech reports in Awtuw cannot take case-marking—unlike indirect speech reports (Feldman 1986). And we saw in §2.2.2 that indirect speech reports in Manambu are never introduced with a cataphoric *ata* 'thus', while direct speech reports always are.

We saw in (iii) and (iv) above that speech act distinctions (commands, and questions) appear in direct speech reports just as in any other main clause. In contrast, when used in indirect speech reports, both commands and questions are often replaced with other clause types. We saw in §2.2.2 that in some languages reported commands are the only instance of indirect speech.

---

[5] If a direct speech report can be discontinuous, can it be placed between any constituents, or between parts of one phrasal constituent? This requires further study.

And last, but not least: an indirect speech report is typically a full clause, while a direct speech report may be less than a clause, or may consist of several sentences.[6]

So far, we have identified a number of properties which should allow us to unambiguously distinguish between the two varieties of speech reports.

This distinction is irrelevant for those languages which have just one multiclausal speech report construction—a direct speech report. This is the case in numerous Australian languages, e.g. Dyirbal, Ngalakan (Merlan 1983: 151–2) and Mangarayi (Merlan 1982: 1–4), and also many Amazonian languages (e.g. Urubu-Kaapor (Tupí-Guaraní: Kakumasu 1986), Matses (Panoan: Fleck forthcoming), in Chamling (Tibeto-Burman) and Nepali (Indic) (Ebert 1986). Then the direct speech report accompanies the verb of speech which can precede or follow it, depending on the language. A direct speech report can be accompanied by the quotative evidential in Kombai (de Vries 1990) and a number of Uto-Aztecan languages (Munro 1978).

And in some languages indirect speech reports are employed only for certain clause types (reported commands), while direct speech reports are predominant in others. This is the case in Manambu—see §2.2 of Chapter 9.

2.2. *Further kinds of multiclausal speech report constructions*

Navajo and other Athabaskan languages distinguish between (i) direct quotation whereby speech is quoted verbatim; (ii) direct discourse whereby some deictic markers—e.g. time—can be shifted, and (iii) indirect discourse, with the shift of all the relevant deictic markers (see Schauber 1979: 19–29; Saxton 1998). Different reporting verbs occur in each case. Consider Dogrib. This language distinguishes four speech report constructions, each with its own grammatical properties (Saxton 1998). Just like other Athabaskan languages, Dogrib distinguishes indirect speech reports, direct speech reports and direct quotations.

---

[6] Direct and indirect speech reports can also differ in terms of their syntactic status. Indirect speech reports are usually a type of complement clause, while direct speech reports may share similarities with complement clauses (see, for instance, Genetti 2006), but may have a special syntactic status (further discussion is in Aikhenvald 2015).

Verbs which take speech report complements include those of speech, causation and desire (see §5).

An indirect speech report in (13) contains an optional complementiser, absent in all other types of speech report. The pronominal reference is shifted to the point of view of the Current speaker, that is 'I':

Dogrib
(9)   Nàèdì k'èèzhǫ [semǫ   k'arehta   (gha)]   ʔasìlà
       doctor   1sg.mother 1sg.IMPERF.check   COMPL 1sg.3.PERF.cause
       The doctor had me check on my mother

In contrast, pronouns in a direct speech report are understood from the perspective of the person who reports the speech 'complement' (the doctor in (10)). Since the complementiser in indirect speech report is optional a direct speech report can also receive an indirect speech interpretation:

(10)   Nàèdì k'èèzhǫ [semǫ   k'arehta   ha]   niwǫ
        doctor   1sg.mother 1sg.IMPERF.check   FUT   3.IMPERF.want
        The doctor_i wants me to check on his_i (own) mother—direct speech
           interpretation
        or
        The doctor had me check on my mother—indirect speech interpretation, complementiser omitted

Direct quotations are distinguished from direct speech complements in that they do not allow indirect discourse interpretation. (11) cannot be interpreted as 'John asked where my/his friend is'.

(11)   John   [Saàgịal   aedì]   ndi
        John   1sg.friend   where?   3.IMPERF.say
        John asked, 'Where is my friend?'
        *John asked where my/his friend is

These three constructions discussed may also occur as main clauses. The fourth speech report construction—called 'direct discourse control complements' by Saxton (1998)—cannot. It can only occur as a complement of just one verb, the 'direct discourse-taking' verb *ts'eniwǫ* 'think, want'. This 'direct-discourse control complement' is characterized by the use of first person optative verb inflection and reflexive pronoun to signal coreferentiality between the subject of the main clause and that of the complement:

(12)   [Kwik'ìi   ?edekwi   ghàwehtįh]   niwǫ
       gun   REFL.grandchild   1sg.OPT.give   3.IMPERF.want
       He wants to give the gun to his grandchild (lit. He wants: I may give
       gun to own grandchild).

If used in a main clause the reflexive possessive *?ede-* in Dogrib
requires a third person antecedent. That is, constructions like (12) are
somewhat similar to 'semi-direct' speech in languages like Akɔɔse: the
verb in the speech report inflects as if it were in a direct speech report,
but the reflexive is 'adjusted' to the third person of the narrator as
if it were indirect speech (Saxton 1998: 208; and see also Chapter 9
below).

   While in Dogrib all 'direct-discourse' verbs can also optionally select
indirect discourse complements, the converse is not true (Saxton 1998:
206). Only a subset of direct discourse verbs can occur with direct
quotations—which are a limited set of constructions such as interrogative clauses and cannot be embedded. Only one verb takes 'direct
discourse control' complement (as in (12)).

2.3. *A continuum approach to multiclausal speech report constructions*

The grammatical distinction between quotations and direct speech
reports in Athabascan languages alerts us to further complications in
distinguishing direct and indirect speech.

   Direct speech reports often vary as to how 'faithful' to the original they are. Let's take a couple of naturally occurring examples (with
names changed). On a Saturday, John said: 'I will go to Sorrento on
Friday'. On this same Saturday, his girlfriend repeated what he'd said,
quoting him verbatim:

(13)   John said, 'I will go to Sorrento on Friday'

When Thursday came, she repeated what John had said as (14), read-
justing the time word to her perspective:

(14)   John said, 'I will go to Sorrento tomorrow'

This is not exactly what John had said—his words have been slightly
rephrased to agree with the Current Speaker's time perspective. Yet

this is still a direct speech report: there is no person shift, and no back-shifting of tense.

An even clearer differentiation between quotations and direct speech reports has been described for Athabaskan languages. We can recall from §2.2 that different speech-reporting verbs are used depending on whether the speech report is (i) direct quotation whereby speech is quoted verbatim; (ii) direct discourse whereby some deictic markers— e.g. time—can be shifted, or (iii) indirect discourse, with the shift of all the relevant deictic markers (see Schauber 1979: 19–29, for Navajo; Saxton 1998, for Dogrib).

   And more often than not, a direct quote is a distilled version of what the person has actually said—hesitation marks or false starts (and sometimes grammatical errors) may be omitted or adjusted (also see Clark and Gerrig 1990).

   We can safely assert that in English, the direct speech report in (13) will be 'less direct' than in (14)—simply because the time word's reference has been shifted as one would expect in indirect speech, while other categories have not. To account for such intermediate cases, we suggest that the difference between speech reports, from verbatim quote to indirect speech, be considered as a continuum—shown in Figure 8.1.

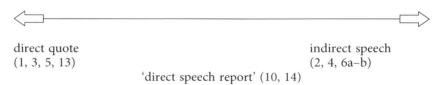

direct quote   indirect speech
(1, 3, 5, 13)   (2, 4, 6a–b)
                 'direct speech report' (10, 14)

Figure 8.1. Speech reports as a continuum

For each language, different 'cut-off' points have to be plotted separately on such a continuum, depending on how many grammatical features of indirect speech allow 'exceptions' (as in (14))—that is, whether the shift of a deictic category is strictly obligatory, or less so (see Saxton 1998 and Schauber 1979, on further grammatical differences between quotes and direct speech reports in Athabaskan languages).

   Even with the continuum approach, 'direct speech' is not always easy to distinguish from 'indirect speech'. English has a variety of grammatical features distinguishing the two, including the rules of 'sequence of tenses', and shift of person and other deictic categories, all exemplified above. Nevertheless, the distinction between direct and indirect speech can get 'blurred'—see the discussion by Huddleston (2002b: 1029). Compare direct speech in *Tell Richard: 'Fred's my best friend'* with indirect speech in *Tell Richard that Fred's my best friend* (Quirk et al. 1985: 1023). If *that* is omitted, the resulting sentence *Tell Richard Fred's my best friend* becomes ambiguous. In the written text, both direct and indirect speech interpretations are possible (the quotation marks make it clear). In the spoken language, the intonation may help, but only partly. In an isolating language, like Thai, with extensive ellipsis difficulties in distinguishing direct and indirect speech may be even greater. Since there is no grammatical marking of person (and personal pronouns are frequently omitted), even 'person shift' is hard to rely upon as an ultimate criterion. Instances where no criterion is strictly applicable fall into a general category of speech reports of indeterminate type whose exact interpretation depends on the context.

2.4. *Languages with one multiclausal speech report construction*

Languages with one multiclausal speech report construction may employ a direct speech report as their only strategy. This is the case in numerous Australian languages, e.g. Dyirbal, Ngalakan (Merlan 1983: 151–2) and Mangarayi (Merlan 1982: 1–4), and also in Chamling (Tibeto-Burman) and Nepali (Indic) (Ebert 1986) and Urubu-Kaapor. Then the direct speech report accompanies the verb of speech which can precede or follow it, depending on the language. A direct speech report is accompanied by the quotative evidential in Kombai (de Vries 1990) and a number of Uto-Aztecan languages (Munro 1978).

Rules for the deletion of the report marker (often a verb) vary from language to language. In Luiseño (Uto-Aztecan, Munro 1978: 155) it can be deleted if its subject is the same as the subject of the quoted sentence. The reporting verb may be omitted and is then recoverable from the context in Udihe (Nikolaeva and Tolskaya 2001: 669–70) and Urubu-Kaapor (Kakumasu 1986: 367):

Urubu-Kaapor
(15) [a-ho   ta   kỹ]   aja   pandu [ere-jywyr   ym   ta
      1sg-go   FUT   FUT.DEP.PURP   thus   3p+say 2sg-return   NEG   FUT
      nde   ke   mámy]   aja   ihẽ   i-pe
      you   FOC   perhaps   thus   I   3p-to
      'I'm going', thus he said; 'Perhaps you won't return', thus I (said) to
      him

3. Monoclausal Speech Report Constructions

Monoclausal speech reports can be of three kinds: (a) construction
with a reported or a quotative evidential; (b) construction with double
person marking; and (c) free indirect discourse.

(a) Reported and quotative evidentials as speech report
markers are by far the most frequent monoclausal speech report strategies. About half of the world's languages have a special morpheme
whose main meaning is to indicate that the speaker's information is
that of verbal report, as is the case with *-lda* in Lezgian:

Lezgian
(16) Baku.d-a   irid   itim   gülle.di-z   aq̂ud-na-lda
      Baku-INESSIVE   seven   man   bullet-DAT   take.out-AORIST-REP
      They say that in Baku seven men were shot

A language may have a special synthetic verbal form to convey the fact
that the information is reported:

Estonian
(17) Ta   on   aus   mees
      he   is   honest   man
      He is an honest man

(18) Ta   olevat   aus   mees
      he   be.REP.PRES   honest   man
      He is said to be an honest man

Reported evidentials vary in their semantic complexity: in Estonian,
their connotation is that of lack of reliability of information ('he is said
to be honest, but I don't vouch for it'). Reported evidentials in Kham
(19), and in Quechua do not have such connotations. (A survey of the
semantics of reported evidentials is in Aikhenvald 2004: 167–85.)

Kham
(19) ba-zya   di
      go-CONT   REP
      He is going (it is said)

Reported is typically the only evidential used in commands; the meaning is that of reported command (see Aikhenvald 2004): 'eat-reported' means 'eat because you were told to'.

Evidentials can differentiate several kinds of speech reports. Comanche and a few other North American Indian languages have separate reported and quotative evidentials. A narrative past particle *kɨ* in Comanche (Uto-Aztecan: Charney 1993: 188–91) shows that information is reported (but does not specify who by). The quotative particle *me* occurs if there is a direct quotation:

Comanche
(20) hãã   me-se   sutɨ   patsi
      yes   QUOT-CNTR   that.one   older.sister
      The older sister said, 'yes'

The reported and the quotative evidentials can even appear together, if a quotation happens to occur in a text told in narrative past.

(21) sutɨ-se   'yes'   me-kɨ
      that.one-CNTR   yes   QUOT-NARRATIVE.PAST
      He (Coyote) said 'yes', it is said

In Tariana and Quechua, the reported evidential never indicates who the author of the speech report is (Floyd 1999: 130–1); neither can it occur with direct speech. The same evidential may combine the meanings of a reported and a quotative, as in Jinghpaw (Tibeto-Burman: Saxena 1988: 377) and in Copala Trique (Otomangean: Hollenbach 1992: 241)

Quoting the exact words of the person is the only way of reporting their speech in Semelai (Kruspe 2004: 402). This is done with a quotative marker, *kʰləŋ* (a particle likely to derive from an erstwhile verb of speech, but which has lost its verbal properties: it cannot be negated, derived, take arguments or aspectual modifiers). The 'author' of the quote can be stated explicitly (as in 22), or omitted if understood from the context (23).

Semelai (Aslian)
(22) 'kˣ   smaʔ   haʔ   hɔ̃nʔ?'   kʰləŋ   puyˣŋ
      2f   person   at   where?   QUOT   shaman
      'You (are) a person from where?' (asked) the shaman

(23) ˈbeh,   daʔ   ŋ=khˈʔˈ   kʰləŋ
      no   NEG   1fA=know   QUOT
      'No, I do not know', (he) (replied)

The quotative marker can appear at a clause or a phrase boundary, or even occur several times within a clause (it cannot break up a constituent, and is a significant syntactic test for constituency).

Few languages with quotative evidential lack any other speech report strategy (as does Semelai). Most have at least a direct speech report (or quotation)—as do Matses and Hixkaryana. The 'division of labour' of various speech reports will be discussed in §6.

(b) CONSTRUCTION WITH DOUBLE PERSON MARKING has been described for Kwaza, an isolate from Brazil (van der Voort 2000: 291–6). Person and mood markers corresponding to the person of the reporter and the mood of 'reporting' are encliticised to the 'report'. In (24), I am reporting what I had said myself.

(24) kukuiˈhỹ-da-ˈki-da-ki
      be.ill-1sg-DECL-1sg-DECL
      I said that I am ill (lit. ill-I-I)

In (25) the persons of the 'reporter' and of the original speaker are different:

(25) MagaˈriDa   kukuiˈhỹ-da-ˈki-tsˈ
      Margarida   be.ill-2sg-DECL-DECL.3p.NARR
      Margarida says you are ill[7]

(c) FREE INDIRECT SPEECH comes about if the reporting clause introducing indirect speech is omitted and left implicit 'except when retained as a parenthetical clause' (Quirk et al. 1985: 1032). It is used extensively to 'report speech or (particularly in fiction) the stream of thought'; and 'the potentialities of the direct-speech sentence structure are retained (for example, direct questions and exclamations, vocative, tag questions, and interjections). 'It is therefore only the back-shift of

---

[7] If the narrator is third person and the mood of narrative is declarative, the final -ki is replaced with -tsɛ. Third person cross-referencing marker is ø. A somewhat similar structure is found in Amele (Roberts 1987: 14–16), and (36).

the verb, together with equivalent shifts in personal pronouns, demonstratives, and time and place references, that signals the fact that the
words are being reported, rather than being in direct speech.' The itali-
cised verbs below are backshifted to the past tense:

> So that *was* their plan, *was* it? He well *knew* their tricks, and *would show*
> them a thing or two before he *was* finished. Thank goodness he *had been*
> alerted, and that there *were* still a few honest people in the world!'(Quirk
> et al. 1985: 1032).

Free indirect speech coexists with other, multiclausal, speech reports,
and is by no means restricted to familiar Indo-European languages,
where it is a widely used stylistic device (e.g. Romanian: Malinson
1986: 3). Nikolaeva and Tolskaya (2001: 669) describe such structures
for Udihe, a Tungusic language.

'Free indirect speech' in English is often recognisable by the presence of 'backshifting'. Or it can be identified by the type of past tense
forms used (see Landeweerd and Vet 1996: 158–9, on this phenomenon in French; and Matthews 1997: 136). A reported speech complement in German can appear on its own as a 'de-subordinated' main
clause. The conditional form of the verb marks the sentence in square
brackets below as something that had been claimed by Miks (Feuillet
1996: 80).

(26) Miks bestritt   natürlich alles.   [Von dem
      Miks disputed   of.course everything.   Of   ART.DEF.masc.sg+DAT
      Bock **wiss-e**   er   nichts.]
      goat know-COND.PRES   he   nothing.
      Miks disputed everything, of course. [(According to him), he **knew**
      nothing about the goat.]

Such conditional has stylistic overtones: it marks reported speech in
journalistic discourse 'mainly to distinguish reported speech from
utterances by the reporter' (Starke 1985: 165; ten Cate 1996: 202), creating a 'distancing' effect: the author does not vouch for the veracity
of the statement.

Free indirect speech is obviously derivative of a biclausal indirect
speech report, and presupposes its existence in the language. It plainly
results from ellipsis of the reporting verb. So does free direct speech,
often employed as a stylistic device in fiction.[8]

---

[8] Consider the following example of free direct speech *A fly kept buzzing around,*
occasionally trying to settle on me. I brushed it off. **Keep calm! Wait until it feels safe.**

Forms typical of free indirect speech can develop into a reported evidential; that is, a monoclausal speech report structure which is not an obvious result of ellipsis. In (26), the verb form alone indicates that the information is part of a verbal report. Once this becomes the main context for the verbal form, a reported evidential evolves. This scenario has been reconstructed for present reported evidentials in Standard Estonian, and also Livonian, Latvian and Lithuanian (Aikhenvald 2004: 281–3; Wälchli 2000: 194–5).

Reported and quotative evidentials often derive from a grammaticalised verb 'say', as in Semelai. Grammaticalisation is a gradual process. In some varieties of South American Spanish and Portuguese, the verb 'say' (Spanish *decir*, Portuguese *dizer*) plus the complementiser *que* appear fused into a particle *dizque* which is on its way towards grammaticalisation into a reported and general non-firsthand evidential (see Kany 1944; Travis 2006 and Aikhenvald 2002a; 2004: 140–2). In Kambera (Western Austronesian: Klamer 2002) the root *wà* 'say' in report constructions can still be analysed as a verbal root. But its grammatical properties are somewhat unusual: it has limited morphological possibilities and discourse functions, and is prosodically deficient compared to any other verb. This suggests that 'say' is midway towards becoming fully grammaticalized as a marker of monoclausal speech report construction.

The unusual monoclausal speech report construction with double person marking in Kwaza—as in (30)—could also have originated from ellipsis of the verb of saying. Kwaza also has a biclausal paratactic speech report construction involving verbs of saying: what translates as 'she said (to me) that I am ill' would literally translate as ''you are ill', she talked to me, notifying'. These could be underlying structures for the 'double person' speech reports (van der Voort 2000: 293).

Alternatively, a reported evidential may come from a noun ('noise' in Xamatauteri, a Yanomami language: Ramirez 1994: 170), or a noun or an adverbial expression meaning 'rumour, fame' or 'news; reportedly', as in Basque: Jacobsen 1986: 7, and Jarawara: Dixon 2003: 186). In such cases, there is no evidence that a monoclausal speech report has once been biclausal (Aikhenvald 2004: 284–5; 2011).

There! Got it. *On my hand was a disgusting flattened fly, oozing blood. I wiped my hand on the grass.* **Now I can relax** (Quirk et al. 1985: 1033).

4. Syntactic Status of Speech Reports

The role of direct and of indirect speech report in multiclausal constructions depends on the transitivity of the reporting verb.[9] A reporting verb may be intransitive, as in Godié (Kru), and Urarina, or Samoan and Yup'ik Eskimo (here, the lack of ergative case marking on the subject of 'say' indicates that it is intransitive: Munro 1982: 304–5). All, or some, reporting verbs can be transitive, as in Ku Waru and Boumaa Fijian. Semantically, reporting verbs score rather low on the transitivity hierarchy (Munro 1982: 316). In Dolakha Newari, the reporting verb is ditransitive (Genetti 2006).

The cross-linguistic properties of DIRECT SPEECH REPORT have been a 'bone of contention' for some time. Traditional grammars used to take it for granted that reporting verbs—such as *say* in English—take a speech complement as their object (cf. Rosenbaum 1967, and criticism in Munro 1982). In contrast, Partee (1973) argued that 'quoted sentence is not syntactically or semantically a part of the sentence which contains it'. Direct speech reports are treated as special clause types in Lower Grand Valley Dani (Bromley 1981: 272), Telefol (Healey 1964) and Wai Wai (Hawkins 1998: 26). Table 8.1 exemplifies their syntactic possibilities.

Table 8.1. Syntactic possibilities for direct speech report

SYNTACTIC FUNCTION	EXAMPLE LANGUAGES
A. Complement clause or other constituent in O function	Jarawara, Dolakha Newari, Ku Waru, Bunuba, Urubu-Kaapor, Tikar, Koromfe, Ndyuka, Dogrib, Navajo
B. Construction with some similarities to a complement clause but not identical to it	English, Russian
C. An oblique, or non-core, construction different from any clausal constituents	Cahuilla, Pima, Manambu, Mohave

---

[9] In the available literature, there is hardly any conclusive information concerning the syntactic status of 'semi-direct' speech complement.

A. Direct speech report as a complement clause or other constituent in O function. This has been described for Jarawara, where the direct speech report occurs with the ambitransitive verb *ati -na-* 'say; ask; order' as a reporting marker (Dixon 2004b: 394). In Ku Waru, a language with semantic marking of A and S, the subject of the transitive reporting verb *nyi-* frequently takes the agentive marking when it occurs with a direct speech report. This justifies considering direct speech on a par with other objects (Merlan and Rumsey 1991: 342; 2001). A similar argument applies to Bunuba (Rumsey 1994).

In Dolakha Newari the reporting verb is ditransitive and takes two objects: the addressee, and the speech report content. Direct speech report has all the properties of a complement clause in O function, including flexibility in constituent order, the ergative case on the A of the reporting verb, and the lack of intonation break between the reporting verb and the speech report. Unlike other complement clauses, a direct speech report may consist of less than a clause (e.g. an interjection). For this reason, Genetti (2006) suggests calling them 'complement constituents' (rather than just 'complement clauses').

B. Direct speech report has some similarities to a complement clause. Traditional analyses of English assumed that the direct speech report occurs in what looks like the direct object function.[10] Indeed, it can be questioned with *what* just like any NP object. It can also occur in what Quirk et al. (1985: 1022) call pseudo-cleft construction: *What Dorothy said was 'My mother's on the phone'*. And yet it differs from a complement clause in O function in a number of significant ways.

And yet, unlike any other clause or other constituent, a direct speech report can be discontinuous (also see McGregor 1994, on Gooniyandi). Again, unlike any other clausal constituent, a direct speech report may require verb-subject inversion, unless the subject is a pronoun: see (8). In addition, this inversion is grammatical only if the direct speech report occurs sentence-initially or sentence-medially. If it occurs sentence finally, the verb-subject in the reporting clause results in an ungrammatical construction, as in (27b).

---

[10] Most reporting verbs, including *say* in English, are transitive; *say* appears to be A=S ambitransitive—it can take an NP object, but there are a few contexts where a pronominal object is impossible, as in *You don't say!* or *Who says?* (Munro 1982: 305).

(27a)   McDougall replied 'On the contrary, Mary doesn't resemble Jane'

(27b)   *Replied McDougall, 'On the contrary, Mary doesn't resemble Jane'

(27c)   'On the contrary', replied McDougall, 'Mary doesn't resemble Jane'

(27d)   'On the contrary', McDougall replied, 'Mary doesn't resemble Jane'

(27e)   'On the contrary, Mary doesn't resemble Jane', replied McDougall

(27f)   'On the contrary, Mary doesn't resemble Jane', McDougall replied

A direct speech complement can contain more, or less, than one clause. Unlike both *that* complement clauses and NP objects, it cannot be target of passive (Munro 1982: 307–8). A direct speech complement can be in apposition to an NP, as in *Dorothy used the following words: 'My mother's on the phone'.*[11]

Direct speech reports in Russian are basically similar to English, except that they can be targets of passive. There may be further differences between direct speech reports and NP objects. Direct speech reports can be questioned differently from NPs and complement clauses in O function. In most Yuman languages (Munro 1982: 314–15) the NP object of the transitive 'say' verb is questioned with an interrogative pronoun, and the direct speech complement can only be questioned with an indefinite/interrogative prefix on the verb 'say'. This suggests that a direct speech report ought to be considered a special type of core constituent; see more on this below.

C. DIRECT SPEECH REPORT MAY BE AN OBLIQUE, OR NON-CORE, CONSTRUCTION DIFFERENT FROM ANY CLAUSAL CONSTITUENT. This is the case if the reporting verb is intransitive. Colloquial English has a variety of direct speech reports introduced by intransitive verbs *go* and *be like* (not used for indirect speech reports). The syntactic role of a direct speech report in a structure like *And he goes, 'Yeah, right!'*, is even more contentious than with the verb *say*; but hardly anyone would claim that it is an object complement clause.

In Cahuilla (Munro 1982), Wardaman (Merlan 1994: 205; examples 484 and 486) and Manambu, the reporting verb is transitive. The addressee—rather than the direct speech report—has the object properties (such as being cross-referenced on the verb).

---

[11] Quirk et al. (1985: 1023) recognise a 'gradient from direct speech that is clearly independent to direct speech that is clearly integrated into the clause structure', in English.

A direct speech report can behave similarly to an oblique (e.g. Mojave: Munro 1982: 308–9); or be unlike any as a non-constituent, as in Pima (Munro 1982: 310–11). In Tariana, an NP object is questioned with a pronoun 'what', and a direct speech complement—with the pronoun 'how', which is also used to question oblique constituents. But unlike an NP or a clausal constituent, a direct speech report cannot take any case marking, or be target of passive. If it is an oblique, it is a class on its own. If there are no language-internal reasons to treat a direct speech report as a clausal constituent, it may be considered paratactically juxtaposed to the clause containing the reporting verb, as in Kambera (Klamer 2002), Dyirbal, Maale (Amha 2001: 1999), and Lavukaleve (Terrill 2003: 229–30).

Direct speech reports tend to have a special syntactic status in a variety of further ways:

(1) A direct speech report construction does not have to be coextensive with a clause, or a sentence. It can be a stretch of discourse, 'a meaningless string of sounds' (Munro 1978: 153), or a combination of speech with mimicking—and often derogatory—intonation and facial and other gestures. A direct speech report often displays idiosyncratic syntactic properties: for instance, it can be discontinous.

(2) The expectation that a direct speech report is like a matrix clause perfectly capable of occurring on its own—unlike an indirect speech report which is a subordinate clause—is not quite borne out by the facts. A direct speech report cannot always be considered equal to an independent main clause: it often has its own intonational and syntactic characteristics (as we saw in §2.1, especially (ii) and (ix)). Furthermore, a direct speech report can contain a complementiser (and thus technically speaking marked as embedded: cf. de Roeck 1994: 338–9), as in Tikar, Lango and Ocotepec Mixtec (Alexander 1988: 292). Or a direct speech report can contain marking not found in any other clause type, e.g. an obligatory reported evidential in biclausal speech report constructions in Udihe (Nikolaeva and Tolskaya 2001: 663–4; 668) and Kiowa (Watkins 1984: 84–5).[12]

---

[12] Similar examples come from Nganasan (Samoyedic), Latunde (Nambiquara), Tamil (see Asher 1985: 1–3), Malayalam (Asher and Kumari 1997: 3), Marathi (Pandharipande 1997: 1), Cora (Casad 1984: 397), Kobon (Davies 1981: 1–3) and Kombai (de Vries 1990).

(3) A direct speech report can be obligatory in a clause with a report-ing verb, as in Ambae, Maybrat and Lower Grand Valley Dani, and Western Tarahumara (Burgess 1984: 125–6). In Mixtec languages the direct speech report is obligatory in a construction involving the verb 'say' preceding and following the direct speech report (see Johnson 1988: 136–7 on Jamiltepec Mixtec; Alexander 1988: 290–2; on Ocotepec Mixtec, Shields 1988: 435, on Silacayoapan Mixtec, Hills 1990 243–4 on Ayutla Mixtec, and Small 1990: 441–2 on Coatzopan Mixtec).

(4) Finally, a sentence containing a direct speech report can differ from other sentence types in properties such as constituent order. In Ku Waru, Bunuba and Manambu the reporting verb follows the direct speech report, in agreement with the general verb final tendency of these languages. In Udihe it can only precede it—and this goes against the predominantly verb-final character of this language. In English— a language with a strict constituent order—direct speech reports are unusual in their ordering flexibility with respect to the reporting verb. Even the argument structure of the reporting verb in a sentence con-taining a direct speech report may differ from its argument structure in other sentence types. In Udihe the addressee of the imperative as part of direct speech report is marked as direct object of the reporting verb (Nikolaeva and Tolskaya 2001: 670–1).[13]

In summary: cross-linguistically, there is enough evidence to suggest that direct speech reports are special construction types. In each case, language-internal criteria need to be sought so as to establish the sta-tus of direct speech reports as core or non-core components and with respect to their similarities with complement clauses in a language.

INDIRECT SPEECH REPORTS are cross-linguistically much more uni-form. Unlike direct speech reports, they are almost always coextensive with a clause and are typically a subtype of complement clause used with other verbs which take clausal arguments—as in English (Dixon 2006b), Russian (Barentsen 1996), Akkadian (Deutscher 2000; 2006), and Paumarí (Chapman and Derbyshire 1991: 240). Both direct and

---

[13] Just occasionally does a language have different strategies for monoclausal and multiclausal direct speech reports. Kolyma Yukaghir distinguishes short quotations (equalling one finite clause) which occur preposed to the ambitransitive verb *mon-* 'say' (Maslova 2003: 500–1). Long quotations—which constitute a piece of discourse—can follow any verb of speech (Maslova 2003: 501); these can be interrupted by converbs of *mon-*.

indirect speech reports are treated as subtypes of complement clause
in Dogrib and Navajo (Saxton 1998), and also in Tikar (Jackson 1987),
Koromfe (Rennison 1997), and Ndyuka (Huttar and Huttar 1994: 1).
Or an indirect speech report can constitute a separate type of complement clause. Indirect speech reports in Jarawara are unlike any other
complement clause in that they include a tense-modal suffix (Dixon
2004b; 2006c).

How indirect speech reports fit into the overall system of complement clauses in a language requires further study. All seven complement clause types in English are used in indirect speech reports. Not
so in Tariana: a different type of clause, used in lieu of complement
clause, occurs in indirect speech reports. In languages without complement clauses as a special type, another clause type is 'coopted' as a
functional equivalent of indirect speech. In Lavukaleve (Terrill 2003:
440–1), a purposive clause or a subordinate anterior clause can be
used as functional equivalents of indirect speech clause: 'their chief
told them to go' is literally 'Upon their chief telling them, they went'.
A different clause type—nominalized clause (Terrill 2003: 423–4)—is
used in lieu of complement clause in other languages (e.g. with verbs
of wanting).

5. REPORTING VERBS AND 'QUOTE FRAMERS'

Reporting markers vary. A reporting marker can be a verb, or an
adverbial expression 'thus, like this', as in Sanskrit *iti* 'thus' (the accusative form of *idam* 'this, that'). A reporting marker can be the same
as a similarity marker; a prime example of this is *be like* in colloquial
English: *And I'm like, 'Gimme a break, will you!'*. Similar examples
from Finnish, German and Swedish are given by Heine and Kuteva
(2002: 274). In English, *word(s)* can introduce a speech report, as in
English *Dorothy used the following words: 'My mother's on the phone'*.
In Tariana, the word for 'speech' is used similarly to *words* in English,
while Manambu employs the word for 'language'. Non-verbal (that
is, nominal, adverbial and the like) reporting markers are typically an
alternative to reporting verbs in multiclausal speech reports.

A reporting marker may precede or follow the speech report (or
even be placed inside it). It can occur more than once with one speech
report. In numerous Tibeto-Burman languages, a quote is followed by
a participial form of the verb 'say' directly preceding an inflected form
of the same verb (Genetti 2006):

Dolakha Newari
(28) [chi   do-ō]   haŋ-an   hat-cu
       2sg   PROH-go   say-PART   say-3sgPAST
       She said: 'Don't you go' (lit. Don't you go, she saying said)

This pattern is considered an areal feature throughout South Asia (see Noonan 2001; Saxena 1988). It is also attested in a few Papuan languages (and even in some varieties of the Creole Tok Pisin).

Or speech report can be both preceded and followed by the speech verb: a combination of 'quotation introducer' and 'quotation closer' is a feature of numerous Mixtecan languages:

Jamiltepec Mixtec (Johnson 1988: 136)
(29) kātyí   ra   [kwāhán]   kātyí   ra
       CONT:say   he   IMPERATIVE:go   CONT:say   he
       He says, 'Go!', he says

A 'quote framer' may be even more elaborate. In Amele (Roberts 1987: 12–16), a speech verb immediately precedes the quote, and a copy of the suffixation of the speech verbs follows it. The suffixes are in bold type:

Amele
(30) Mala   uqa   cudumac   ma-**don**
       chicken   3sg   wallaby   say-3sg-3sg-REM.P
         'Se   qai-ni [...]'   **don**
         Hey   friend-1sg.POSS   3sg-3sg-REM.P
       The chicken said to the wallaby: 'Hey, my friend [...]'

Quote framers are not used with indirect speech in any of these languages. The choice of a reporting marker is what often differentiates direct and indirect speech reports. The options are:

(I) A subset of indirect-speech reporting verbs can frame direct speech in Lower Grand Valley Dani (Bromley 1981: 272), Macushi (Abbott 1991: 28–9, 62), Paumarí, Maori, Abkhaz (Hewitt 1979: 5–8) and Korean (Sohn 1994: 13). In Chadic languages, such as Lele, verbs of speech and cognition occur with indirect speech, but only verbs of speech occur with direct speech reports (Frajzyngier 2001: 374–6). In Kolyma Yukaghir, only a few verbs of speech allow a monoclausal quotation; all of them allow multisentence quotations and indirect speech complements.

(II) The sets of direct and indirect speech report framing verbs are fully, or largely, identical in Gooniyandi, Amele, Basque, Evenki, or Russian.

(III) Different verbs occur with indirect and direct speech reports, as in Athabaskan languages.[14] In Urarina the verb 'say' can only take a direct speech report, while other verbs of speech occur with indirect speech complement clauses (Olawsky 2006).

Even if the same set of verbs is used for both direct and indirect speech, their behaviour may be different. In Supyire three verbs of speech and some verbs of cognition take direct speech reports (Carlson 1994: 448–9); speech reports with verbs of cognition can only be in the indicative form, while those of verbs of speech can be either indicative or subjunctive. The reporting verb can be omitted with direct, but not with indirect speech report in Amele, Boumaa Fijian and Udihe (Nikolaeva and Tolskaya 2001: 660–70). In Lower Grand Valley Dani, the reporting verb is never omitted with direct speech. It is omitted with indirect speech only if the construction refers to 'speaker's inner reactions', that is, thought and suppositions, rather than actual speech (Bromley 1981).

In English the sets of verbs occurring with direct and with indirect speech largely overlap; grammars list forty or so verbs which are most frequently used with direct speech. Two direct speech report verbs, *go, be like* and others used in colloquial English, never occur with indirect speech.

So far, I have found no language where more verbs would be able to occur with direct speech than with indirect speech. If direct and indirect speech are distinguished at all, the set of indirect-speech-taking verbs tends to be more extensive. This may have to do with the syntactic nature of indirect speech complement clause: it is tends to also occur with complement-clause taking verbs other than verbs of speech.

---

[14] These sets overlap in different ways in different languages—sets may be mutually exclusive, as they appear to be in Slave; or largely overlapping, as in Dogrib (Rice 1989: 988–9; Saxton 1998). Only some direct discourse complement taking verbs occur with direct quotations. In Dogrib, a fourth type of speech report, similar to semi-direct speech (see (16)), can only occur with one verb.

Verbs and expressions marking speech reports can be of various kinds:

(a) They may include only the general verb 'say' (as in Bunuba, Ku Waru, Manambu, and Jamiltepec Mixtec). Or a verb of speech or cognition has to form a serial verb construction with the generic 'say' to be able to occur with a direct speech report, as in Maybrat (Dol 1999: 227–30), Lolovoli dialect of North-East Ambae (Hyslop 2001: 289–91), Erromangan (Crowley 1998: 254–7) and Tariana.

(b) They may include numerous verbs of speech, as in Coatzospan Mixtec, Lower Grand Valley Dani and Tucano (Ramirez 1997: 370).

(c) They may also include verbs of cognition and thought, as in Ayutla Mixtec, Ocotepec Mixtec, as well as of perception, as in Nigerian Pidgin (Faraclas 1997: 6–7); verbs of speech and communication in general, verbs of opinion, assertion, decision and verbs referreing to emotions, cognition and certainty, as in Kashmiri (Wali and Koul 1997: 4–5). In Tuvaluan (Besnier 2000: 2), any verb which refers to an emotion and presupposes verbal exchange (such as 'be angry') can occur with a speech report.

The semantic types of verbs which can occur with speech reports are reminiscent of the patterns of polysemy of the reporting marker attested cross-linguistically. As Munro (1982: 316) put it, 'the meaning of "say" must [...] go beyond the idea of simply communicating facts by uttering words, and must probably include at some level a recognition of the general human reaction to speech as a characteristic indicator of personality and intention'.

Verbs of 'saying', especially those capable of taking a direct speech report, are typically employed in expressions of thought, emotions and intention. In Dolakha Newari, a direct quote construction which consists of a direct speech report followed by the participial form of 'say' is used to express hope, thought or fear. To say 'He was afraid the dog would bite' one says (Genetti 2006):

(31) ām   [khicā=n   ŋyā-eu]   haŋ-an   gyāt-a
     3sg   dog=ERG   bite-3sgFUT   say-PART   fear-3sgPAST
     He was afraid the dog would bite him (Lit. Saying 'the dog will bite',
     he feared)

This construction, and its whole array of meanings, is an areal property shared by numerous South Asian languages (Noonan 2001; Saxena 1988): a direct speech construction expresses reason and cause, purpose and intention. For instance, a sentence like 'Because the cow wanted to get into the field, it made me hurry' literally translates into Chantyal as 'The cow will go in the field, having said, it made me hurry'.

Direct speech reports express thinking, desire, intention and cognition in Maybrat (Dol 1999: 228–30), and also purpose in Tauya (MacDonald 1990b), in Korowai (van Enk and de Vries 1997: 104–5), in Kombai (see de Vries 1990), and in a number of Western Austronesian languages (Klamer 2000). Besides these meanings, Aguaruna (Larsen 1984: 86–114) uses the direct speech report construction to express reason and warnings. In Urubu-Kaapor, direct speech construction is used to express desire. Thought and motives are represented as quoted speech in languages of Marind and Awyu families (Drabbe 1955, 1957, 1959), in Telefol, and in Manambu. In Erromangan (Crowley 1998: 255–8) the same type of direct speech report construction occurs with verbs of speech and mental processes (including fear). In Tariana, 'think' translates as 'say in one's heart' or as 'say think'.

There can be further meaning extensions. In Erromangan (Crowley 1998: 257), a speech report construction appears in a resultative construction to introduce a direct result of the event described in the preceding clause: 'so that he would go ashore' literally translates as 'saying he will go ashore'. And in Awtuw (Feldman 1986: 169–70), an indirect speech report construction is used in comparative constructions—'he makes noise like a pig eating' is literally 'he makes such noise, you would say a pig is eating'.

A direct speech report construction introduces onomatopoeia in many Papuan and South Asian languages, and in Urarina. In Yuman languages 'say' constructions involve onomatopoeia and numerous descriptive expressions reflecting characteristic configurations, or noises objects make (Langdon 1977).

A monoclausal speech report construction can express a similar range of meanings. The quotative marker in Semelai is used to report thought and also to frame expressives, interjections, exclamations and onomatopoeic noises: $p^hur\ khl\partial\eta$ (noise.of.jumping.down QUOT) is the way of saying 'there was a noise p^hur (of the hero) jumping down' (Kruspe 2004: 403). In Kwaza, a speech report construction is used for internal speech and thought. The quotative construction gave rise to purposive, intentional and desiderative constructions (van der Voort 2000: 295–6).

Reported and quotative evidentials develop overtones of unreliable information, and action over which the speaker has no control—as in Jamul Tiipay, or Estonian. In Kwaza the quotative construction also has overtones of doubt. The uninflected form of 'say' in Erromangan has become a hesitation marker (Crowley 1998: 263).

In Australian languages, one verb often means 'do' and 'say'. Ngalakan *yini-* means 'say' and 'do thus' (it may even be accompanied by a gesture if it indexes something present in the speech situation) (Merlan 1983: 152). The basic meaning of *ma* in Ungarinjin is 'do'. This verb also occurs with direct speech report, and can then be translated as 'say'. But given that for the Ungarinjin, 'speech is a form of action, perhaps its most salient form', 'do' is arguably still the verb's core meaning (Rumsey 1982: 158–63; 1990). A somewhat different construction with the same verb is used for intention and causation. This same root is also used for internal speech, that is, thought, in Bunuba. In Tuvaluan, the verb used in direct speech reports has a general meaning 'do' and also appears in desiderative, causative and purposive constructions (Besnier 2000: 657). And in the Lolovoli dialect of North-East Ambae, a direct speech report construction is used for imitating another person's action (Hyslop 2001: 299).

These recurrent patterns of polysemy for speech report constructions are summarised in Figure 8.2 (also see Aikhenvald 2009c, on the role of polysemous speech reports in clause linking).

resultative
↑
deliberate action
↑
intention; purpose
↑
wish
↑
dubious information; hesitation < SPEECH REPORT CONSTRUCTION > comparison or
similarity, reason and causation
↓
reported thought
↓
cognition and perception

Figure 8.2. Polysemous patterns in speech report constructions

Each of these meanings can become the main meaning, and serve as basis for patterns of grammaticalisation of the 'say' verb into desiderative, intention and purpose marker, as well as a marker of resultative and comparative constructions, and of doubt. In Obolo (Aaron 1996/7) the reporting verb 'say' became a future marker. In Yimas (Foley 1991: 291) and Manambu the verb 'say' has become a causative marker.

Alternatively, in multiclausal constructions, 'say' often becomes a complementiser (Deutscher 2000: 67–91 followed various stages of this development through the history of Akkadian). Or a 'say' verb can undergo depletion and become a marker of a monoclausal reported construction—that is, a reported or a quotative evidential.[15] These processes belong to one grammaticalisation path as follows:

> SPEECH REPORT MARKER → marker of syntactic link between two clauses → once speech report stands on its own, SPEECH REPORT MARKER becomes a reported/quotative marker

A reporting verb can grammaticalize in different ways in one language. In Lezgian the verb 'say' has undergone such polygrammaticalization: it has given rise to a reported evidential (see (16)), and to a marker of similarity (Haspelmath 1993b: 247).

An additional issue concerns the ways in which direct speech reports may provide bases for lexical derivations. Well-known expressions like *memento* and *habeas corpus* go back to Latin direct speech constructions, with a literal meaning '(you) remember!' and 'you must have the body', respectively. And consider expressions like English *forget-me-not* or a *what-I-don't-know-won't-hurt-me attitude* (Toman 1992: 286), or French *un je-ne-sais-quoi* 'something; lit. I don't know what', (slang) *je-m'en-foutard* 'someone who doesn't care, lit. I-don't-care-er', *je-m'en-foutisme* 'I don't care-type attitude', Brazilian Portuguese *não-me-esqueças* 'forget-me-not', *não-me-toques* (lit. touch me not) 'a type of thorny plant' (with a derivative *não-me-toquense* to refer to a part of this plant), and even German *Stell-dich-ein* (stand-you:ACC-in) 'rendez-vous' (Motsch 1994: 5022) which keep the surface make-up

---

[15] Factors that influence grammaticalisation of a speech report marker as a marker of syntactic link or an evidential have to do with (i) syllabic length and prosodic status (that is, cliticization), and (ii) position in the sentence (see Klamer 2000, on the interaction of these factors in the different grammaticalisation paths of speech reports in Buru and Tukang Besi). These require a separate study.

of a direct speech construction, and yet are compounds. How pervasive such derivations are in non-Indo-European languages is an open question.

6. Functions of Speech Reports

Why quote? In Kate Burridge's words (2001), 'it's comforting to see that there are others around with the same thoughts as our own, and at the same time a quote lends credence to these thoughts. What's more, we are usually giving them a far more brilliant, more catchy manner of expression than we could manage alone—and perhaps too we convey an impression of being well read'. No one could phrase it better than this—so why not quote? And, as we all know, quoting the right thing at the right time, may show that you are a member of an in-group.[16] A right quotation from the right source can help you achieve the needed effect. Burridge tells us (2001: 190) that 'a quote from the Bible in communities like the horse-and-buggy Amish and mennonite groups in North America [...] can resolve a conflict in a non-threatening way'. Jean, the main character of Noel Shute's *A Town Like Alice*, managed to get the recalcitrant headman of a village in Malaya to let her have a well built for women by artfully quoting the Koran. Quotations are often a mark of solidarity (Brown and Levinson 1987: 122). But quoting something wrong, or wrongly, may spoil your reputation forever: the last advice of a dying professor to his devoted pupils was 'Verify your quotations' (as reported by Churchill 1951: 616).

Quotations and direct discourse in general are not just speech. Quotations are 'demonstrations', and they often convey not just the words, but the intonation, the look, the gestures and so on. 'The internal structure of quotation is really the structure of what is being depicted, and that can range from the raging of a person to the racket of a machine'—another nice quotation, this time from Clark and Gerrig (1990: 772). Preference for quotations can have its roots in cultural conventions. Extensive use of direct speech in Kombai, a West Papuan language with no other speech report constructions, correlates with a tendency to be highly explicit and specific in depicting events (de

---

[16] Note that quotes can be implicit; If I say 'All this man wants is to dream an impossible dream', I have a song from *The man of LaMancha* in mind. But am I really quoting?

Vries 1990: 301–2). In Ungarinyin, as in many other Australian languages, speech is tantamount to action, and direct speech reports are a way to enact what had happened, drawing upon the full 'dramatic possibilities not only of "wording", but of intonation, gesture, and the full range of expressive dimensions' (Rumsey 1990: 354–5).

There is another side to direct quotes—in Burridge's words again (2001: 190), 'quotes can offer protection too, a kind of verbal escape hatch for those moments when you might want to distance yourself, when you don't want to take full responsibility for your words, particularly if those words might cause offence'. And indeed, in many languages quotations are used just for this purpose. In Arizona Tewa, I can say '"I am sick"-reported, he says'—and that would imply that I do not vouch for the veracity of the information. If I want to sound neutral, I would use an indirect speech construction—'He said that he was sick' (Kroskrity 1993: 146; Aikhenvald 2004: 139). Not so in Tariana—a direct speech report is a neutral strategy. Only when talking about one's own experience does a direct speech complement sound odd—and then an indirect speech report expressed through one of the complementation strategies is appropriate.

And, as Wiesemann (1990: 75) pointed out, conventions vary, across cultures and languages, as to whether rephrasing what someone else had said is appropriate or not. In Tuvaluan (Besnier 1992: 173) 'another person's speech must be represented as the faithful rendition of the original utterance'. Same applies to Tariana. Not so in Manambu, and in many Indo-European languages, including English (see discussion by Clark and Gerrig 1990: 795–6) where even quotations do not have to be verbatim, and are often rephrased.

If a language has more than one speech report construction, why choose one over the other? We have seen that a reported evidential and a direct quote can have unwanted epistemic overtones, as in Arizona Tewa. Or one may want to be more specific: a direct speech report allows one to explicitly state who the author of the information is, while a reported evidential simply indicates that the information comes from some verbal report, as in Menomini (Bloomfield 1962: 444; 506–7). Similarly, a reported evidential in Kham (Watters 2002: 316–17) marks the information as reported; and also occurs as a stylistic 'token' of folktales and narratives as a genre. Using a direct speech report allows the speaker to express further subtle distinctions—for instance, internal cognitive processes like thinking, and to state the 'authorship'.

Discourse organization provides another reason. Contrary to Haiman's (1985: 228) sweeping statement that 'the perception that indirect quotations represent backgrounded material is totally unsupported', direct speech in Cerma (Gur) discourse represents foregrounded information, while indirect speech is a way of backgrounding it (Lowe and Hurlimann 2002); somewhat similar examples are in Tikar (Jackson 1987: 107–8), and Adioukrou (Hill 1995: 103–5). In Babungo a shift from direct to indirect speech leads to a climax in the story (Schaub 1985: 5–6).

Quotes are a feature of a rhetorical speech style in Chantyal (Noonan 2001). Perhaps, the more colloquial the register in English, the higher the ratio of direct to indirect speech reports (suggestion by R.M.W. Dixon). In Aguaruna narratives, important information is often presented in the form of quoting what some other participant said about the event (Larson 1984: 60–84). Descriptive passages in Mangarayi narratives tend to be summed up with a direct speech report (Merlan 1982: 3–4). Just like reported evidentials, reported speech can be a token of traditional stories, as in Kunama (Nilo-Saharan) and Bedauye (Cushitic) (Güldemann 2001: 330).

Using direct speech makes the text more polyphonous and the description more vivid—it is a powerful stylistic device. In English if novelists 'wish to engross readers in the characters' world, that might demand direct quotation' (Clark and Gerrig 1990: 794).

In summary, different speech report strategies are hardly ever fully synonymous. Each has its own connotations, and discourse or stylistic functions (Aikhenvald 2004: 140).

7. FURTHER ISSUES

Direct and indirect speech reports can be viewed as extremes on a continuum, ranging from a verbatim rendering of what someone else said, to its reinterpretation according to the perspective of the reporter. Some languages have an array of multiclausal speech report constructions, while others have one monoclausal type. The choice of one of the many speech report constructions is often conditioned by stylistic preferences; or may be coloured by attitude to information. Whether any of this correlates with any non-linguistic parameters—such as attitudes to information and the requirement to be always specific—is an open question.

It appears that, like many other categories, speech report constructions are easily diffused. Logophoricity is an areal, rather than a genetic, property spread across unrelated African languages (demonstrated by Güldemann 2001, 2002, 2003 and 2008; see Frajzyngier 1985 on Chadic languages). The emergence of indirect speech reports in Maale is the result of an influence from Amharic; traditional Maale has only direct speech report constructions (Amha 2001: 199–200). In Evenki, clauses with indirect speech reports had to be nominalised; under Russian influence, Evenki allows the use of verbal indicative forms in indirect speech (Nedjalkov 1997: 1–3). Yet exactly what patterns of speech report marking are more diffusible than others remains to be investigated. Their diffusion is often a corollary of the diffusion of some other category—such as evidentials in the Vaupés area (Aikhenvald 2002a, 2004).

8. POINTS TO BE ADDRESSED WHEN INVESTIGATING SPEECH REPORTS IN A LANGUAGE

The following are among the main questions to be addressed when analyzing speech reports in a language. These will be of use to fieldworkers, working on previously undescribed or poorly described languages, and also to those scholars who are working on better-known languages.

A. What are the constructions employed for reporting speech? How many multiclausal and/or monoclausal speech report constructions does the language have?

If the language has a distinction between indirect and direct speech reports, what are their distinguishing features in terms of:

(i)   shift in person deixis (with particular attention to co-reference and disambiguation of third person referents);
(ii)   shift in spatial and temporal deixis (and in tense on verbs);
(iii) changes in mood and modality;
(iv)   report of commands (also known as indirect commands);
(v)   report of questions (also known as indirect questions);
(vi)   presence or absence of a complementizer.

Additional distinctions may include: intonational differences; different use of interjections and exclamations; differences in constituent order; differences in behaviour of demonstratives, and perhaps more.

Can a direct speech report be discontinuous? If so, are there any rules or tendencies as to how it is placed with respect to other constituents? Can it intervene between parts of a constituent? Can a direct speech report be longer or shorter than a clause?

Are there any instances of semi-direct speech (Type I, Original-Speaker-oriented, or Type II, Current-speaker-oriented)? How do semi-direct speech reports compare to speech reports of other kinds (direct and indirect)? Are semi-direct speech reports obligatory or optional?

What kind of monoclausal speech report construction does the language have (if any); frequent possibilities include an evidential, or free indirect speech.

B. Syntactic role of speech report content

B–1 Provide a statement of transitivity of reporting verb(s) and speech report constructions.

B–2 If the language has indirect speech, is it similar to a complement clause, or is it a separate clause type? If the language does not have complement clauses as a special type, is another clause type, or complementation strategy, co-opted as a functional equivalent of indirect speech?

What is the syntactic status of direct speech? Can a speech report be questioned, or referred to with an anaphoric pronoun? What is the position of a reporting verb or a quote framer within the sentence?

B-3 Are reporting verbs or quote framers obligatory? Which verbs or other, non-verbal, expressions, can be used as quote framers? How do they differ from each other? Can they differentiate direct and indirect speech constructions?

C. Polysemous patterns for reporting verb and quote framers
Are speech report constructions used for the expression of reported thought, intention and/or purpose, wish, cognition and perception, dubious information, comparative or causative marker? Are speech report constructions obligatorily employed for introducing onomatopoeia?

D. Grammaticalization effects
Can you say anything about the grammaticalization patterns of
the reporting verb and of quote framer(s) and/or the speech report
construction?

E. Functional, stylistic and discourse implications of speech report
constructions
If a language has a choice between several speech report constructions,
what are the conditioning factors for the preferential choice of one
over the other? For instance, are there any differences in degree of
commitment to the veracity of the statement, or correlations with the
person of the narrator, or information structure? Are direct or indirect
speech reports, or any other speech report construction, a feature of
any particular style (e.g. historical narrative)?

F. Effects of langage contact
Have any of the speech report constructions in the language been
influenced by a neighbouring language, or have arisen as the result of
areal diffusion and language contact?

CHAPTER NINE

SEMI-DIRECT SPEECH IN TYPOLOGICAL PERSPECTIVE

Alexandra Y. Aikhenvald[*]

Every language has some way of reporting what someone else has said. To express what Jakobson (1990: 130) called 'speech within speech', the speaker can use their own words, recasting the original text as their own, within an 'indirect' speech construction. Or the other person may be quoted 'directly', just as they said it, or more or less so. One major difference between direct and indirect speech lies in the way person specification within the speech report is cast. In direct speech, person reference is expressed exactly as it was in the original speech report. In indirect speech, the person reference is shifted to the perspective of the speaker. There is a third option—a 'middle ground' situation known as 'semi-direct' speech—with incomplete person shift. Semi-direct speech often involves coreferentiality between the current speaker—rather than the author of the speech report—and a participant within the speech report. In Manambu, a Ndu language spoken in the New Guinea area, semi-direct speech differs from both direct and indirect speech in a few interesting ways. Further examples of semi-direct speech and its various guises come from a number of African languages, other languages from New Guinea area, and Colloquial English. The existence of a semi-direct speech construction brings an additional dimension to the typology of speech reports: the necessity of including the perspective of current speaker in the overall picture.

[*] I am grateful to those speakers of British and Australian English who allowed me to quote their informal speech (Simon Tully, Rowena Dixon, Sam Trustrum and Simon Trustrum), and to the members of my adopted family in the village of Avatip (East Sepik, Papua New Guinea) who taught me their native Manambu, especially Jacklyn Yuamali Benji Ala and Pauline Yuaneng Luma Laki. I am grateful to R. M. W. Dixon, Anna Bugaeva, Carol Genetti, Tida Syuntarô, Michael Daniel and the anonymous referees, for comments and suggestions.

1. THE PROBLEM: SPEECH REPORTS WITH INCOMPLETE PERSON SHIFT

1.1. *Direct and indirect speech reports*

Every language has some way of reporting what someone has said. To express what Jakobson (1990: 130) called 'speech within speech', the speaker can use their own words, recasting the original text as their own, within an 'indirect' speech construction. Or the other person can be quoted 'directly', just as they said it, or more or less so. In some languages, such 'direct' speech is the only type of speech report. Others have an array of structures on a continuum between 'direct' quotation and 'indirect' speech. One major difference between direct and indirect speech lies in the person of participants within the speech report.

In a direct speech construction, the speech report content corresponds exactly (or more or less so), to what the 'Original Speaker', that is, the author of the speech report content, had said. Consider the English sentences (1a) and (1b):

(1a)   John$_i$ said: 'I$_i$ saw Fred yesterday'

(1b)   John$_i$ said: 'He$_j$ saw Fred yesterday'

In both examples, the direct speech report—marked with quotes in the written language—is postposed to the reporting verb 'say'. There is no overt link between the two. In (1a), the personal pronoun 'I' is co-referential with the Original Speaker, 'John', and is used within the speech report. In (1b), the personal pronoun 'he' is not coreferential with the Original Speaker. The subject of the speech report is someone other than John.

Alternatively, the report may be made without using his or her exact words, cast as 'indirect speech'. Then the person reference within a speech report is adapted to the perspective of the Current Speaker. In (2a), the original 'I' (used by John in (1a)) is changed to 'he':

(2a)   John$_i$ said (that) he$_i$ had seen Fred the previous day

And in (2b) 'he' used by John in (1b) is preserved.

(2b)   John$_i$ said (that) he$_j$ had seen Fred the previous day

English has no grammatical means of distinguishing different third person referents here. In contrast, languages with logophoric systems do—we return to these in §3.5.

Indirect speech reports in English differ from direct speech in a number of other features. Since the speech report content of (1a) and (1b) was prior to the report by John, *saw* in both (2a) and (2b) is 'back-shifted' to the 'past perfect', or past with respect to the past, *had seen*. The time adverb *yesterday* is changed to *the previous day*. The optional complementizer *that* is a marker of syntactic link between the reporting clause and the speech report content. Chapter 8 contains a survey of features which serve to differentiate speech reports across languages. A list of points to be addressed in an analysis of speech reports in any language is given in §8 of Chapter 8.

In this chapter we focus on SHIFT IN PERSONAL DEIXIS, which is a major property distinguishing direct and indirect speech reports. Suffice it to say that in many languages it is indeed the only way of telling direct and indirect speech apart—examples include Hatam (Papuan area: Reesink 1999: 105), Abun (Berry and Berry 1999: 177), Nigerian Pidgin (Faraclas 1996: 6) and Babungo (Schaub 1985. p. 1).[1] But is such person shift always straightforward? This takes us to the next section.

1.2. *Person shift, and coreferentiality in speech reports*

A speech report may involve:

- the Current Speaker (CS)—that is, the person who produces the speech report;
- the Original Speaker (OS), e.g. John in (1a,b) and (2a,b);
- and the participants within the speech report itself—the subject 'I' in (1a), 'he' in (1b)–(2a,b), and the object 'Fred' in (1a,b) and (2a,b). There can be further participants—such as the addressee, and a variety of obliques.

---

[1] Cross-linguistic statements within this chapter are based on a comprehensive typological account of speech reports presented in the position paper for the Local Workshop on Direct and Indirect speech at the Research Centre for Linguistic Typology in 2004. The data for this chapter was collected over 12 years of fieldwork, mostly with speakers of the Avatip variety. The corpus consists of over 1500 pages of transcribed texts, notes and conversations, from over fifty speakers.

When a direct speech report is recast as indirect speech, and if the Original Speaker is coreferential with a Speech Act Participant within the report (that is, first person 'I' or second person 'you'), a non-third person shifts to third person—compare (1a) and (2a). If there is no coreferentiality, there is no person shift—compare (1b) and (2b).

A selection of options for coreferentiality between the Original Speaker (OS) and the participants within the speech report is given in Table 9.1. For the sake of simplicity, at this stage, I have not included either the option for a second person for the Original Speaker, or any ungrammatical options with the lack of shift in indirect speech reports (e.g. *John_i said that Paul had seen me_i).

This table contains a set of grammatical options. Further options would be ungrammatical in standard English. These involve person shift within a direct speech report. So, a sentence *John_i said: 'He_i

Table 9.1. Coreferentiality of the Original Speaker and the participants within speech reports

CS	OS	PARTICIPANTS WITHIN SPEECH REPORT		EXAMPLES	SPEECH REPORT
		A/S ('SUBJECT')	O ('OBJECT')		
me	John	Fred	Paul	John said: 'Fred saw Paul'	Direct
				John said (that) Fred had seen Paul	Indirect
me	John	John	Paul	John_i said: 'I_i saw Paul'	Direct
				John_i said (that) he_i had seen Paul'	Indirect
me	John	Fred	John	John_i said: 'Fred saw me_i'	Direct
				John_i said (that) Fred had seen him_i	Indirect
me	John	John	John	John_i said: 'I_i saw myself_i'	Direct
				John_i said (that) he_i had seen himself_i	Indirect

saw Paul' where 'he' refers to John would be nonsensical. A sentence *John$_i$ said: 'Fred saw him$_i$,' where 'him' refers to John would also be impossible, if He saw Paul and Fred saw him are direct speech reports. These examples could be grammatical only if seen as a variation on an indirect speech report with that omitted, John$_i$ said he$_i$ saw Paul with no tense back-shift. We will see below, however, that such 'strange' speech reports—'semi-direct speech'—are a legitimate option in some languages.

The Current Speaker (CS) may be coreferential with the Original Speaker, and/or with a participant within a speech report situation. A selection of relevant options is given in Table 9.2.

Here again, a number of further options would be ungrammatical in standard English. These involve person shift within direct speech reports which cast the Current Speaker (here 'me') as if the Current Speaker were also the Original Speaker when she is not, as in *John$_i$ said: 'I$_{CurrentSpeaker}$ saw Fred'. This may be acceptable as an indirect speech report with that omitted and no tense back-shift, but not as a direct speech report.

If I am simultaneously the Current Speaker and the subject of a statement within the speech report, the option *John$_i$ said 'She$_{CurrentSpeaker}$ saw him$_i$' would also be ungrammatical, as would be *John$_i$ said 'I$_{CurrentSpeaker}$ saw me$_i$' (the grammatical option in both cases would be John said 'She saw me'). Another ungrammatical option would involve preserving the first person reference for the Current Speaker as object within a direct speech report, as in *John$_i$ said 'I$_i$ saw me$_{CurrentSpeaker}$'.

A further ungrammatical option involves casting the Current Speaker as if she were not the Original Speaker when in fact she was, as in *I$_{CurrentSpeaker=OriginalSpeaker}$ said 'She $_{CurrentSpeaker=OriginalSpeaker}$ saw Fred'. It is equally impossible to say *I$_{CurrentSpeaker}$ said 'Fred saw her$_{CurrentSpeaker}$'.[2]

These ungrammatical starred examples can be viewed as weird instances of direct speech with unexpected person shift. The starred examples discussed after Table 9.1 contain what looks like 'illegitimate' shift of person of the Original Speaker. Those discussed after Table 9.2 contain peculiar shifts of person of the Current Speaker. The value of

---

[2] Other ungrammatical examples which involve lack of shift in indirect speech reports, such as *John$_i$ said that he$_i$ had seen her$_{CS}$ are not included, for the sake of simplicity.

ALEXANDRA Y. AIKHENVALD

Table 9.2. Coreferentiality of the Current Speaker, the Original Speaker and the participants in speech reports (the Current Speaker is feminine)

CS	OS	PARTICIPANTS WITHIN SPEECH REPORT		EXAMPLES	SPEECH REPORT
		A/S ('SUBJECT')	O ('OBJECT')		
me	me	John	Fred	I$_{CS}$ said: 'John saw Fred' I said (that) John had seen Fred	Direct Indirect
me	John	me	Fred	John said 'She$_{CS}$ saw Fred' John said (that) I had seen Fred	Direct Indirect
me	John	me	John	John$_i$ said 'She$_{CS}$ saw me$_i$' John$_i$ said (that) I had seen him$_i$	Direct Indirect
me	John	John	me	John$_i$ said 'I$_i$ saw her$_{CS}$' John$_i$ said (that) he$_i$ had seen me$_{CS}$	Direct Indirect
me	me	me	Fred	I$_{CS}$ said 'I$_{CS}$ saw Fred' I$_{CS}$ said (that) I$_{CS}$ had seen Fred	Direct Indirect
me	me	Fred	me	I$_{CS}$ said 'Fred saw me$_{CS}$' I$_{CS}$ said (that) Fred had seen me$_{CS}$	Direct Indirect
me	me	me	me	I$_{CS}$ said: 'I$_{CS}$ saw myself$_{CS}$' I$_{CS}$ said (that) I$_{CS}$ had seen myself$_{CS}$	Direct Indirect

other persons remains the same as it was produced by the Original Speaker.

Speech report constructions with such 'incomplete' person shift, also known as 'semi-direct' speech, are in fact a legitimate option in a number of languages, many of them spoken in the Highlands of New Guinea. In some, semi-direct speech is obligatory.[3]

---

[3] Whether any language has indirect speech reports similar to *John$_i$ said that he$_i$ had seen her$_{CS}$* is an open question. In addition, if one reports speech by someone

In summary, such semi-direct speech reports can be:

Type I. Original-Speaker-Oriented which correspond to the options
discussed after Table 9.1;

Type II. Current-Speaker-oriented, which correspond to the options
discussed after Table 9.2.

We start with a brief outline of speech reports in Manambu, a Ndu
language from the Papuan area, which has both options for semi-
direct speech (§2). In §3 we consider further examples of semi-direct
speech documented in the literature, and the conditions under which
it is used. There, we also discuss the possibility of semi-direct speech
constructions in English. The last section (§4) contains brief conclusions.

2. Speech Report Constructions in Manambu

2.1. *Background*

Manambu belongs to the Ndu family, and is spoken by about 2000
people in five villages in the Ambunti region of the East Sepik Province of Papua New Guinea. It is a highly synthetic, predominantly
suffixing and agglutinating language, with a strong tendency towards
verb-final constituent order. Its morphological structure is quite complex (Aikhenvald 2008a). Manambu has contrastive word stress, and
no tones.

Nouns distinguish two genders, three numbers and nine case forms.
Verbs have an array of grammatical categories, including several
modalities, aspects and tenses fused with person, number and gender
marking; a complex system of negation; and clause-chaining. Only
declarative verbs are fully inflected: they can cross-reference two participants (the subject and another topical argument or oblique) and
take a full array of aspect markers. Desideratives and same-subject
purposives do not take any person inflection. The different subject
purposive cross-references just the subject.

The imperative has its own paradigm of subject marking. Importantly, there is one verb form for second person singular, dual and

---

else—as in, for instance, *Paul said: 'John said: 'I saw Fred yesterday'*—both Paul and
John will be 'original speakers'. For the sake of simplicity, we restrict most of our
discussion to the situation with one original speaker.

plural imperative. The exact reference is distinguished by using free personal pronouns: *a-wuk* (IMPV.2pers-listen) may mean 'you (singular)
listen!' or 'you (dual) listen!', or 'you (plural) listen'. To disambiguate these, one can say *mən a-wuk* (you.masc IMPV.2pers-listen) 'you
(masculine) listen!', *ñan a-wuk* (you.fem IMPV.2pers-listen) 'you (feminine) listen!', *bər a-wuk* (you.du IMPV.2pers-listen) 'you two listen!',
gur a-wuk (you.pl IMPV.2pers-listen) 'you many listen!'

Direct speech reports in Manambu are highly frequent, and semantically versatile. Any speech act—statement, question or command—
can be cast as a direct speech report. In contrast, indirect speech
reports are restricted to reported commands, and are less semantically
versatile. In §2.2, we address the differences between direct and indirect speech reports. 'Semi-direct' speech with incomplete person shift
along the lines of §1.2 is considered in §2.3.

2.2. *Distinguishing direct and indirect speech reports*

Speech reports in Manambu are multiclausal. They are by far the most
frequent clause type in Manambu discourse of all genres. An over-
whelming majority of speech reports are direct speech. These aim at
reproducing what has been said without any shift in personal, temporal
or spatial deixis. Direct speech reports are often quotations. And, more
often than not, they convey not just the words, but the intonation, the
look, the gestures, the particular tone of voice and so on—depending
on the 'theatrical effect' the speaker wants to produce. A direct speech
report can be separated from the reporting clause by a short pause.

Direct speech reports in Manambu cover statements, reported commands and reported questions. Indirect speech reports exclusively
cover reported commands. The distinguishing properties of direct and
indirect speech reports are listed in Table 9.3. Most of these properties
are mentioned in Chapter 8 as potentially criterial for distinguishing
direct and indirect speech reports cross-linguistically. The numbers of
examples from Manambu which illustrate the points in the Table are
given in brackets.

2.2.1. *Direct speech reports, and their properties in Manambu*
As expected, a direct speech report does not display any shift in
personal, temporal or spatial deixis to fit in with the perspective of
the reporter. This is illustrated in (3). Here, the locative *kəlam* 'here'
reflects the location of the female addressee's 'staying'. (We can recall,
from §2.1, that the second person imperative does not distinguish

Table 9.3. Direct and indirect speech reports in Manambu: a comparison

PROPERTIES OF SPEECH REPORT	DIRECT SPEECH REPORTS	INDIRECT SPEECH REPORTS
1. Shift in personal, temporal or spatial deixis	none (3), (5), (6), (7)	yes (14), (15), (16)
2. Co-extensive with a clause	not necessarily (3), (5)	yes (14), (15), (16)
3. Speech report introducer *ata* 'then, thus'	yes (3), (4), (5), (6), (8)	no
4. A pause between reporting verb and the speech report	optional (3)	no
5. Vocatives and exclamations	yes (4)	no
6. Discontinuous speech report	possible (5)	no
7. Speech report can precede or follow the reporting clause	yes (3)–(5)	always precedes (14), (15), (16)
8. Types of speech act reported	statement (4)–(5), question (9), command (3)	only command (14), (15), (16)
9. Can be conventionalized	yes (8)	no
10. Speech report implies a speech event	not necessarily (10)–(13)	always
11. Different forms of verb in speech reports mark involvement of the Original Speaker in performing activity	no	possible (15), (16)

gender and number of the addressee: this is why the second person
imperative form *adakw* is used.) A direct speech report is typically
introduced with the demonstrative adverb *ata* 'then, thus' within the
reporting clause with the verb *wa-* 'say, speak'. There is an optional
pause between the speech report and the reporting verb. (Here and
throughout the chapter, clauses are in square brackets. Speech reports
are in italics.)

(3) [*ñən*   *kəta*   *kələm*   *adakw*]   [PAUSE]
     you.fem.sg   now   here   stay:IMPV.2pers   PAUSE
     [ata   wa-bər   ləkə-k]
     then   say-3duSUBJ.P   she-LK-DAT
     'You stay here now,' thus they said to her

A direct speech report can be co-extensive with a clause, or a sentence.
It may contain part of a clause, for instance, just a vocative, as in (4).
Or it may consist of several sentences and be discontinuous, as in (5).
Such discontinuity only occurs on clause boundaries.

(4) [gra-n]   [ata   wa-na]
     cry-SEQ   then   say-ACT.FOC+3fem.sgSUBJ.NP
     [*wun-a-də*   *mam-eee*]
     I-LK-masc.sg   older.sibling-VOC
     She said crying: 'Oh my older brother!'

(5) [*də-kə-k*   *və*   *ma:*]   [*wun*   *warya-u*]
     he-OBL-DAT   see:NEG   NEG   I   fight-1sgPERM
     [ata   wa-də-di]
     then   say-3masc.sgSUBJ.P-3plOBJ.P
     [*də-kə-wa*   *kəta*   *warəa-k*
     he-OBL-COMIT   now   fight-PURP.SS
     yi-na-dəwun-ək]
     go-ACT.FOC-1masc.sgSUBJ.P-CONF
     'She is not to see him, let me fight,' thus he said to them, 'I am going
     to fight with him now'

Speech reports can precede or follow the framing clause containing
the speech verb, with a slight preference for the former. (In the corpus
about 70% of direct speech reports precede the framing clause.)

Direct speech covers all speech acts. A statement was illustrated in
(5), while (6) features a command. Direct speech reports are preferred
in reported commands if the Original Speaker chooses to preserve the
exact wording of the command.

If a command is part of a larger speech report which contains a justification for the command, a direct speech report is a preferred strategy. The reported command in (6) was accompanied by an explanation in (7): the older brother felt he ought to be killed by the enemy before they killed his younger sibling:

(6) [kə   təpa:m   wun-a:k   a-vi]
     this   village+LK+LOC   I-LK+DAT   IMPV-hit/kill
       [ata   wa:d]
       then   say+3masc.sgBAS.P
     'Kill me in this village,' thus he said

(7) [wun   kiya-u   ta:y]   [wun   ma:m]
     I   die-PERM   first   I   older.sibling
     Let me die first, I am the older brother

A conventional greeting which has the form of a command is always cast as a direct speech report:

(8) [yara   ma:y]   [ata   wa:l]
     well   go   then   say+3fem.sgSUBJ.P
     'Good-bye (lit. you go well),' she said

A question within a direct speech report is illustrated in (9).

(9) [[ñə   kas]   wa-ku]   [bassa:d]
     sun   how.much say-COMPL:SS   ask+3masc.sgSUBJ.P
     He asked what time it is (lit. He asked saying 'What time is it?')

This example illustrates an additional point: the verb *wa-* 'say, speak' is the only speech verb which consistently introduces speech reports.[4] Other verbs referring to speech acts (e.g. 'ask' in (9), and 'cry' in (4)) can only occur with a speech report if they are preceded by a

---

[4] Manambu has three verbs of speech—*bla-* (allomorph *bəl-*) 'say/tell (something)', *yi-* 'say X, speak (a language)', and *wa-* 'say, tell'. Of these, only the verb *wa-* occurs with speech reports of any kind. This is in contrast to those languages where the choice of reporting verb may differentiate speech reports (see Chapter 8). The verb *yi-* occurs with just a few interjections as speech reports, as in *ay yi-da-d* (INTERJECTION say-3plSUBJ.NP-3masc.sgBAS.NP) 'they shouted' (lit. they said ay), and with a noun phrase object, e.g. *yarək yi-da-d* (news say-3plSUBJ.NP-3masc.sgBAS.NP) 'they told the news'. The verb *bla-* can take a limited number of noun phrase objects, including *kudi* 'language', *ma:j* 'talk', *yanu* 'witchcraft' (e.g. *ñaura kudi bla-* (Iatmul language speak-) 'to speak Iatmul language').

dependent medial clause containing the verb *wa-* which, in its turn, introduces the speech report, as in (9). In such cases the direct speech report introducer *ata* 'then, thus' can be omitted: it is indeed omitted in (9), but not in (4).

Direct speech reports in Manambu are extremely versatile: besides reporting an actual speech event, they are employed to express internal speech and thought, desire and intention of third person, warning, reason and purpose. In these cases, *ata* is often omitted.

Example (10) is cast as a direct speech report. It did not involve any actual speech act. As I was coming downstairs with a loaded camera (without saying anything, but with a clear intention to take pictures, as requested prior to that), my adopted sister said to make sure the girls were ready for me to take their picture.

(10) [*kayik*   *kurək*]   [wa-na]
      picture/image   do/get+PURP.SS   say-ACT.FOC+3fem.sgSUBJ.NP
      She wants or intends to take pictures (lit. She says '(I) am intending
         to take pictures')

One day a duckling was brought inside the house. The cat did not dare touch him, but its desires were clear from the way it looked at the bird. (11)—a comment on this—could not have referred to an actual speech act: cats do not talk.

(11) [pusi   væn   tə-na-d]
      cat   see+SEQ   keep-ACT.FOC-3masc.sgSUBJ.NP
         [*papər*   *kə-kə-tua*]
         later   eat-FUT-1sgSUBJ.NP+3fem.sgO.NP
         [wa-na-d]
         say-ACT.FOC-3masc.sgSUBJ.NP
      The cat keeps looking (at the duckling), he wants to eat her later (lit.
         He says 'I will eat her later')

Direct speech reports are the only way of expressing someone's intention—Manambu has no other way of expressing the notion of 'intending', or 'wanting'. They can also express reason, as in (12):

(12) [[*asayik*]   wa-ku]   gra-na
       father+DAT   say-COMPL:SS   cry-ACT.FOC+3fem.sgSUBJ.NP
      She is crying because of her father (lit. Having said 'because of father'
         she is crying)

This was said about a baby who was crying because her father had gone off to a meeting, leaving her. The baby could not talk, so there was no actual speech act involved. Similarly, in (13), a speech report is a way of expressing the end result of counting: this was a question to a mother about the age of her toddler:

(13) [*nabi*   *kas*]   wa-na-d
      year   how.many   say-ACT.FOC-3masc.sgSUBJ.NP
      How old is he? (lit. How many years does he say?)

Internal speech and thought are also cast as direct speech reports, using the same verb *wa-* 'say' whose meaning can be viewed as far more general than simply reporting a speech act.

Such versatility is hardly unusual. Multifunctional speech reports are a feature Manambu shares with a number of other Papuan and Austronesian languages. Direct speech reports express thinking, desire, intention and cognition in Maybrat (Dol 1999: 228–30), and also purpose in Tauya (MacDonald 1990a), in Korowai (van Enk and de Vries 1997: 104–5), in Kombai (see de Vries 1990), and also in a number of Western Austronesian languages (Klamer 2000). Lower Grand Valley Dani also employs direct speech reports to express the speaker's intention (Bromley 1981: 245). Thought and motives are represented as quoted speech in languages of the Marind and Awyu families (Drabbe 1955, 1957, 1959).[5]

2.2.2. *Indirect speech reports, and their features in Manambu*
In contrast to direct speech reports which are not limited to any speech act, indirect speech reports cover just reported commands. An

---

[5] These do not exhaust potential polysemies of reporting verbs. In Australian languages, one verb often means 'do' and 'say'. Ngalakan *yini-* means 'say' and 'do thus' (it may even be accompanied by a gesture if it indexes something present in the speech situation) (Merlan 1983: 152). The basic meaning of *ma* in Ungarinjin is 'do'. This verb also occurs with direct speech reports, and can then be translated as 'say'. But given that for the Ungarinjin, 'speech is a form of action, perhaps its most salient form', 'do' is arguably still the verb's core meaning (Rumsey 1982: 158–63, 1990). A somewhat different construction with the same verb is used for intention and causation. This same root is also used for internal speech, that is, thought, in Bunuba. In Tuvaluan, the verb used in direct speech reports has a general meaning 'do' and also appears in desiderative, causative and purposive constructions (Besnier 2000: 657). And in the Lolovoli dialect of North-East Ambae, a direct speech report construction is used for imitating another person's action (Hyslop, 2001: 299).

alternative to (6) is (14). Then, the exact words of the actual command
are not preserved. The predicate in reported commands appears in the
different subject purposive, if the Original Speaker is not involved in
performing the activity. The person shift in the verb 'hit/kill' and in the
spatial deictic are indicative of an indirect speech report.

(14) [a   təpa:m   də-kə-k   vya-mən-kək]
      that   village+LK+LOC   he-OBL-DAT   hit/kill-2masc.sg-PURP.DS
      [wa:d]
         say+3masc.sgSUBJ.P
      He told (you) to kill him in that village

Indirect speech reports cannot contain the speech report introducer
ata 'then, thus'. A speech report is always preposed to the reporting
verb *wa-* and there is no pause. Unlike direct speech reports, an indirect speech report cannot be discontinuous, consist of more than one
clause, or be shorter than a clause. If the subject of the speech report
is different from the Original Speaker, different subject purposive is
used, as in (15). The Original Speaker is not going to join the subject
of the speech report in 'eating sago'.

(15) [na:gw   kə-lə-kəkək]   [wa-tua-l]
       sago   consume-3fem.sg-PURP.DS   say-1sgSUBJ.P-3fem.sgBAS.P
      I told her to eat sago

But if the original speaker is involved in performing the required
activity, the same subject purposive is used within the indirect speech
report, as in (16):

(16) [na:gw   kəka:k]   [wa:d]
       sago   eat+RED+PURP.SS   say+3masc.sgBAS.P
      He told (them) to eat sago (he was eating with them)

This is somewhat similar to the phenomenon of logophoricity (see
§3.5).

   In contrast to direct speech reports which have a number of semantic extensions, indirect speech reports in Manambu always imply an
actual speech event. There are no conventionalized uses of indirect
speech reports (see (8) above, for a conventionalized direct speech
report).

In terms of their syntactic status, neither the direct speech nor the indirect speech report is an object of the verb *wa-* 'say, speak' since they cannot be cross-referenced on the verb as a direct object or an oblique (such as, for instance, location or manner) would. The verb *wa-* can be used either transitively or intransitively; when used transitively, the addressee can be cross-referenced—this is illustrated in (5) ('he-said-to-them'). Speech reports are best considered a special type of obligatory grammatical relation different from any other (see Mittwoch 1985; Partee 1973; Munro 1978, 1982, and Chapter 8 above, on the special syntactic status of speech reports).

2.3. *Semi-direct speech reports in Manambu*

Direct and indirect speech reports are very common in Manambu. Semi-direct speech constructions are less frequent, but nevertheless are a recurrent and acceptable pattern. Of the total of direct speech reports in the corpus, semi-direct speech reports account for about 10%. All involve free personal pronouns.

2.3.1. *Formal properties of semi-direct speech*
While in indirect speech reports the person reference 'shifts' to the perspective of the Current Speaker, there is no such shift in direct speech reports. In semi-direct speech, the reference for some participants is shifted, while for others it is not.

Example (18) illustrates such an 'intermediate' speech report in Manambu. Before the two brothers had left the house, they said (17) to their sister. This is cast as a direct speech report within the narrative. The imperative, 'you-stay', is in bold type.

(17) [*ñən*   *ata*   *wiya:m*   **adakw**   *an*   *ma:*
      you.fem.sg   then   house+LOC   stay:IMPV.2pers   1du   again
      kami:k   *yi-tək*]   [wa-ku]   [*ata*   *yi-bər*]
      fish+DAT   go-1duIMPV   say-COMPL:SS   then   go-3duBAS.P
      'You stay at home, let us two go fishing again,' having said (this) the
      two went off

We can recall, from §2.1 above that second person imperative in Manambu does not distinguish number or gender of the addressee. The second person free pronoun *ñən* 'you feminine' appears here: it is now fully clear that the girl is the addressee.

Later in this story, a stranger approaches the girl and makes an attempt to kidnap her. She tells him that she will stay at home after what her brothers have told her to do. This is how she reports her brothers' speech:

(18) [wun   wiya:m   **adakw**]   [wa-bər-kəkəb]
      I:IND.SP.REP house+LOC stay:IMPV.2pers:DIR.SP.REP say-3du-AS.SOON.AS
      [wiya:m   kwa-kə-na-wun-ək   wun]
      house+LOC   stay-FUT-ACT.FOC-1fem.sgBAS.NP-CONF   I
      Since the two told me to stay (lit. I you-stay) in the house I will stay
      in the house

Example (18) contains reported speech within reported speech. This example, like further instances below, comes from a story told by a narrator. However, the narrator's identity as a 'Current Speaker' is of no relevance to person shift. The Original Speaker (i.e. the girl) in (18) is the 'second level' reporter, which can be considered a 'surrogate' Current Speaker.

The speech report in (18) is an example of Type I semi-direct speech. The speech report contains a token of direct speech report: the second person imperative form of the verb. This is exactly what the brothers had said to the girl, in (17) in the direct speech report (hence the note DIR.SP.REP in the gloss). On the other hand, the speech report in (18) contains one feature of indirect speech: the free pronoun has been shifted to first person 'I', to fit in with the perspective of the 'surrogate' Current Speaker, that is, the girl (hence the note IND.SP.REP in the gloss). The token of indirect speech is coreferential with the Original Speakers—the two brothers.

The differences and similarities between a direct speech report in (17) and a semi-direct report in (18) are summarised in Scheme 1.

Scheme 1. Differences between direct and semi-direct speech reports
in Manambu (17–18)

DIFFERENT FROM DIRECT SPEECH REPORT: change of pronoun ñən 'you' to
                                        wun 'I'
SAME AS DIRECT SPEECH REPORT: imperative verb form adakw

Semi-direct speech reports found in the corpus do not always contain commands. They can be declarative statements. A mother (who has recently died but keeps an eye on her orphaned children) tells her son that the things belonging to him and his sister are here:

(19) [bər-a-di   ja:p   kədiya   taka-tua-di]
      you.du-LK-pl   thing   this.pl.here put-1sgSUBJ.P-3PLBAS.P
      [ata   wa:l]
      then   say+3fem.sgBAS.P
      She said thus: 'The things belonging to you two I put here'

The son then reports to his sister what the mother had said:

(20) [an-a-di   ja:p   kədiya
      we.two-LK-pl:IND.SP.REP   thing   this.pl.here
       taka-tua-di]   [ata   wa:l]
      put-1sgSUBJ.P-3plBAS.P:DIR.SP.REP   then   say+3fem.sgBAS.P
      She₍ᵢ₎ said thus: 'The things belonging to us two I₍ᵢ₎ put here'

Just as in (18), the person shift within the speech report is incomplete.
The first person singular cross-referencing on the verb is exactly the
same as in the original speech, in (19), and thus can be considered a
token of direct speech (DIR.SP.REP in the gloss). The possessive pronoun ('belonging to us two') is 'adjusted' to the Original Speaker's
(that is, the son's) perspective, and can thus be considered a token of
an indirect speech report (IND.SP.REP in the gloss). The spatial deixis
has not been 'shifted'—the form 'here' is the same in both (19) (what
the mother had said) and in (20) (her speech reported by her son).
This is another example of semi-direct speech of Type I: the person
reference of the subject of the speech report has been partially adjusted
to the perspective of the Original Speaker (the boy).
    A speech report with incomplete person shift may contain an unin-
flected verb—a desiderative form with no person cross-referencing, in
(21). A man says to two sisters, in an attempt to frighten them:

(21) [wun   kə-kə-tua-digur-ək]   [wun   kəta
      I   eat-FUT-1sgSUBJ.NP-2plBAS.NP-CONF   I   now
       bra:m   kə-kər]
      you.two+LK+OBJ   eat-DES
      I will eat you up, I want to eat you two

The younger sister is scared, and says (22) to her older sister, recasting
the man's speech as follows:

(22) [lə-kə   mamək   ata
      she-LK+fem.sg   elder.sibling+LK+DAT   then
         wa-lə-l]
         say-3fem.sgSUBJ.P-3fem.sgBAS.P
         [a-də   du   [pause]] [wun   kəta
          DEM.DIST-masc.sg man [pause]]   I:DIR.SP.REP   now
          an-a:m   kə-kər]   [ata   wa-na-d]]
          1du-LK+OBJ:IND.SP.REP   eat-DES   thus say-ACT.FOC-3masc.sgBAS.NP
      She said to her elder sister thus: 'That manᵢ: "Iᵢ want to eat us now' "(heᵢ)
      said'

The girl did not quote the man's speech exactly—she partly recast it,
transforming it into a semi-direct speech report. The subject reference
('I') is not adjusted to her, that is, the 'Original Speaker's' perspective.
This is a token of direct speech report, and is exactly the same as in the
man's original speech in (21). So is the temporal deictic, kəta 'now'. In
contrast, the object referent ('us two') is adjusted to the perspective of
the girl as the Original Speaker, and is a token of indirect speech. This
is another example of semi-direct speech report of Type I.

Examples (17)–(22) come from traditional stories, told by a story-
teller. As mentioned above, for each of (18), (20) and (22), one can
postulate two sets of 'Original Speakers', if the story-teller is to be
considered a Current Speaker. For instance, in (18) brothers are the
'primary' Original Speakers whose speech appears in (17), and the girl
who is reporting their speech can be treated as a 'secondary' Original Speaker. The secondary Original Speaker can be considered, for
all effects, a 'surrogate' Current Speaker, since the perspective of the
story-teller appears to be irrelevant for person shifts. The reference
within the speech report is shifted to that of this Current Speaker—
the girl in (18), 'us two' in (20), and in (22).

Similar constructions are used in spontaneous conversations where
there is no speech report within a speech report. A mother told her
child to listen to the care-taker:

(23) [sa!   mən   lə-kə-k   a-wuk]
      hey!   you.masc   she-OBL-DAT   IMPV.2pers-listen
      Hey! You listen to her!

Later on, the care-taker grumbled at the child, reminding the child of
what the mother had said, and using the same imperative intonation
and the same interjection sa 'Hey!' as the one in (23):

(24) [*sa!* *mən*   *wun-aːk*   *a-wuk*]
      hey! you.masc I-LK+DAT:IND.SP.REP IMPV.2pers-listen:DIR.SP.REP
      [ata wa-na]   [mən   maː   waːk]
      then say-ACT.FOC+3fem.sgBAS.NP   you.masc NEG   listen+NEG
      'Hey! You listen to me_i!' she_i thus said, you are not listening!

As in the examples (18), (20) and (22) above, the semi-direct speech
report in (24) has features of both direct and indirect speech: second
person imperative is a token of direct speech report, and the form of
the addressee, 'me', is a token of indirect speech (the mother had said
'her', in (23)). The interjection *sa!* 'Hey!' is another token of direct
speech in (24). However, (24) differs from the other examples of semi-
direct speech discussed so far in that the token of indirect speech
reflects the perspective of the real Current Speaker (the care-taker),
and not that of the Original Speaker (the mother). (24) is an example of a semi-direct speech report of Type II: the person shift is done
here in agreement with the person of the Current Speaker: the Current Speaker—coreferential with the addressee in (24)—is expressed
as 'me'.

The Current Speaker (that is, the narrator of the story) was of no
relevance for person marking in (18), (20) and (22). So, the person of a
participant within a speech report was shifted, to mark coreferentiality
with the secondary Original Speaker, a 'surrogate' Current Speaker.

The imperative intonation of (17) and of (23) was preserved in the
semi-direct speech reports in (18) and (24). This 'mimicking' effect is a
feature of direct, and not of indirect, speech reports both in Manambu
(see Table 9.3), and cross-linguistically (see Wierzbicka 1974; Clark
and Gerrig 1990).

Within a semi-direct speech report, free pronouns shift to fit in with
the perspective of the Original Speaker (tokens of semi-direct speech
of Type I, exemplified in (18), (20), and (22)) or with that of the Current Speaker (tokens of semi-direct speech of Type II, exemplified in
(24)). Tokens of direct speech can be free pronouns, or bound forms
of pronominal cross-referencing.

All the instances of semi-direct speech always imply an actual speech
event. This is in contrast to direct speech reports which have a plethora
of other meanings, to do with intention, reason and counting—see
(10)–(13) above. The speech report introducer *ata* is optional (see
(22)) These features bring semi-direct speech reports closer to indirect than to direct speech. Semi-direct speech reports of Type I and

Type II do not show any differences between themselves with respect to any of these features.

Table 9.4 features a comparison between semi-direct, direct, and indirect speech reports, in terms of the defining properties outlined in Table 9.3 above.

The person shift in semi-direct speech is partly shared with direct speech, and partly with indirect speech. Of the further ten properties differentiating direct and indirect speech reports, semi-direct speech reports share four with direct speech, and four with indirect speech. Semi-direct speech reports occur only in statements and commands (but not in questions), while indirect speech is limited to commands, and direct speech may contain commands, questions, or statements (property 8). Discontinuous semi-direct speech reports have not been attested (property 6). That is, semi-direct speech reports indeed occupy a 'middle ground' between direct and indirect speech.

Semi-direct speech is recognizable through the shifts in personal deixis, rather than in spatial or temporal deixis. The conditions under which semi-direct speech occurs in Manambu provide a partial explanation.

2.3.2. *How to use a semi-direct speech report in Manambu: a summary*

All the instances of semi-direct speech in Manambu fall into two types, in agreement with §1.2 above:

Type I. The secondary Original Speaker—or the surrogate Current Speaker—is involved in the speech report, as the subject of an intransitive verb (18), as the possessor (20), or as the object (22). The 'real' Current Speaker (that is, the narrator of the story) is of no relevance in the person shift.

Type II. The Current Speaker is involved in the speech report, as the object (24).

In all the examples, the tokens of indirect speech are free pronouns, while the tokens of direct speech can be free or bound.

The use of semi-direct speech as an alternative to either direct or indirect report is not obligatory. Rather, it has a pragmatic effect: it occurs in situations when the speaker is under stress and particularly focussed on their own well-being. In (18), the girl is about to be kid-napped by a stranger. In (20), the two orphaned children are being

Table 9.4. Semi-direct, direct and indirect speech reports in Manambu:
a comparison

PROPERTIES OF SPEECH REPORT	DIRECT SPEECH	SEMI-DIRECT	INDIRECT SPEECH
1. Shift in personal, temporal or spatial deixis	no	partial: shift in free pronouns	yes
2. Co-extensive with a clause	not necessarily		yes
3. Speech report introducer *ata* 'then, thus'	yes (as in (22))		no
4. A pause between reporting verb and the speech report	optional		no
5. Vocatives and exclamations	yes		no
6. Discontinuous speech report	possible	not attested	no
7. Speech report can precede or follow the reporting clause	yes	always precedes	
8. Types of speech acts reported	statements, questions and commands	statements and commands	only commands
9. Can be conventionalized	yes	no	
10. Implies a speech event	not necessarily	always	
11. Different forms of verb in speech reports mark involvement of the Original Speaker in performing activity	no	possible	

robbed of their things by their nasty cousins, which makes them concerned about their things and where they are. In (22), the girl is afraid of being devoured by a man. And in (24), the care-taker is desperate because the naughty child would not listen. Examples (18)–(22) come from the climactic parts of narratives each of which is crucial for the rest of the story. Semi-direct speech is a stylistic device; it does not have the function of disambiguating who did what to whom.

That is, semi-direct speech can thus be considered a strategy for marking the involvement of the Original Speaker or of the Current Speaker in a situation which affects them (note that either one or the other is marked as a first person). The function of semi-direct speech reports is to allow the Current Speaker or the narrator to simultaneously 'index' two speech events: the current one and the former one. This tends to happen when the former speech event is relevant to the current situation, or is the climactic part of the story, or when it is appropriate to highlight the relevance of the participants in the speech event. This may be why semi-direct speech is focussed on person shift, rather than on shifts in time and space.[6]

3. BEYOND MANAMBU: SEMI-DIRECT SPEECH WORLD-WIDE

Semi-direct speech can be a stylistic, or a discourse-organizing option, as in Manambu and in a number of languages from Africa and from the New Guinea area (§3.1). Or it can be obligatory, under certain conditions (§3.2).

3.1. *Optional semi-direct speech*

The phenomenon of semi-direct speech as an alternative to direct and indirect speech was first described for African languages. While in indirect speech reports the person reference must 'shift' to the perspective of the narrator, there is no such shift in direct speech reports and in quotations. And in semi-direct speech, the reference for some participants is shifted, while for others it is not (see Hedinger 1984; Jackson 1987; Noss 1988; and Wiesemann 1990).

---

[6] I am grateful to Carol Genetti for suggesting this idea.

We first discuss semi-direct speech of Type I, whereby person marking within a semi-direct speech report can be shifted to the perspective of the Original Speaker. We then consider semi-direct speech of Type II, whereby the person reference is shifted to the perspective of the Current Speaker.

3.1.1. *Semi-direct speech of Type I: Person shift to the perspective of the Original Speaker*

An oft-quoted example of semi-direct speech comes from Akɔɔse (a Bantu language from Cameroon: Hedinger 1984: 91–2). (25) illustrates direct speech, and (26) contains a straightforward indirect speech report. Note that in Akɔɔse any speech report is preceded by a reporting particle (*bán* in (25) and (26)) which distinguishes person and number of the Original Speaker. The direct speech report contains a vocative phrase: this is a typical feature of direct speech, but not of indirect speech reports:

Akɔɔse

(25) [Bé-lángé   bá   nέn   bán]   [à-mwέ'έ   bán
      they-told   them   this   RP:pl   VOC-friends   RP:pl
      sê-dɔɔ́   nyí   à-wóŋ]
      we-like   you   to-marry
     They said to them, 'Friends, we would like to marry you'

(26) [éĉê   ŋgɔ̀ndédè   é-kwéntené   bán]   [bé'wón   bɔ̀]
      those   girls   they-agreed   RP:pl   they.will.marry   them
     Those girls agreed to marry them (Lit. Those girls agreed (saying that)
        they will marry them)

Another option is a semi-direct speech report (called 'combined speech' by Hedinger 1984: 92), shown in (27). The Original Speaker is referred to with a third person pronoun. Had it been direct speech, first person would be expected. This is thus a token of indirect speech. The addressee is referred to with a second pronoun, just as in the original speech. This is a token of a direct speech report. In the first clause of the speech report, the complex pronoun ('you and she') combines a token of direct speech report ('you') and that of an indirect speech report ('she'). The second person plural agreement on the verb is a token of direct speech, and so is the vocative form of 'husband'.

(27) [mwàád   à-lângì   ǹjóm   ǎ]   [à-ǹjóm
      wife   she-tells   husband   RP:3sg   VOC-husband(DIR.SP.REP)
      ngánè   *nyî-dyĕ*   *nén…*
      you(DIR.SP.REP)+she(IND.SP.REP)   2pl:DIR.SP.REP-stay 'like.this'….
      ǎ   m̀bwé'ɛ   *mɔ́-'wéɛ́*   ǎ
      RP:3sg   day.when   she'll-die:IND.SP.REP   RP:3sg
      é-kɛ̀   *é-lɔ́géd*   *mé*
      you-go:DIR.SP.REP   you-leave:DIR.SP.REP   her:IND.SP.REP
      á   *son*   *tê]*
      locative   grave   in
      The wife said to her husband, 'Husband, since we have stayed like
      this…the day when I die, go and put me in a grave' (lit. Husband,
      since you and she you-plural-have stayed like this, the day when
      she dies, you go and you put her in a grave)

Vocative phrases can occur in semi-direct speech reports in Akɔɔse,
just as they do in direct speech. This is hardly surprising, since vocatives 'refer' to the addressee, whose marking is the same in direct and
in semi-direct reports.[7] Whether semi-direct speech shares any further features—such as temporal, spatial and deictic reference—with
direct and/or with indirect speech reports remains an open question
(as noted by Hedinger 1984: 94).

Using a semi-direct speech report in lieu of indirect or direct speech
in Akɔɔse, Gbaya (Noss 1988: 105, 111) and other African languages
(Wiesemann 1990: 77–8) is the speaker's choice. As Noss (1988:
110–11) observed for Gbaya narratives, the interplay of direct, indirect
and semi-direct ('combined') discourse is a literary device used by the
performer 'to develop his plot'. In Wiesemann's (1990: 78) words, this
reflects 'a manner of speaking current in conversation'—as a stylistic
option.

---

[7] Additional complications to do with logophoricity in Akɔɔse—largely independent
of semi-direct speech—are discussed in Hedinger (1981, 1984). Some languages,
such as Goemai (Chadic: Hellwig 2006, 2011), have a special kind of speech report
construction with a special set of logophoric pronouns in the speech report; their
choice depends on coreferentiality between the subject of the reporting clause and
that of speech complement. Such constructions combine properties of indirect speech
(the use of logophoric, rather than independent pronouns) and of direct speech (lack
of shift of any deictic categories other than person). A speech report can contain
vocatives and interjections, and can even mimic the original author—this makes it
similar to what we expect 'direct speech' to be. Such speech reports are different from
semi-direct speech reports discussed here in that they involve logophoric markers. In
addition, Goemai also has indirect speech reports (a subtype of complement clauses),
and emerging direct speech reports, as an innovation widespread in the speech of
young speakers of this language.

The use of tokens of direct and of indirect speech in Akɔɔse is similar to Manambu in that free pronouns appear as tokens of indirect speech, while bound pronouns are tokens of direct speech. The complex free pronoun ('you and she' in (27)) combines both.

A significant difference between choice of tokens of direct and indirect speech reports in Akɔɔse and Manambu lies in the treatment of the Original Speaker in Type I of semi-direct speech. In Manambu, the Original Speaker is cast as first person, while in Akɔɔse this is cast as third person.[8]

---

[8] This goes hand-in-hand with the statement by Donald Webster, about Abidji (Kwa, Ivory Coast): 'Any reference to the speaker of a quotation inside the quotation is made by indirect reference, and any reference to the person spoken to is made by direct reference' (Grimes 1975: 321). Similar examples have been reported by Hyman (1978), for Aghem, by Perrin (1974), for Mambila, by Hill (1995) for Adioukrou, and by Jackson (1987) for Tikar.

Instances of optional semi-direct speech occur in other languages. An example is found in Old Russian (Fennell and Obolensky 1969: 33), in the *Tale about Boris and Gleb* (c. early 1200):

(i) Se   slyshavshi,   Novgorodcy   re:ša
     this+neuter.ACC having.heard   Novgorodians.NOM.PL   said
        Yaroslav-u,   [jako   zautra
        Yaroslav-DAT.SG   that   next.day
        perevezemsja   na   nj]
        go.across+1pl.FUT:DIR.SP.REP   onto   him:IND.SP.REP
     Having heard this, Novgorodians said to Yaroslav, (that) the next day we
        would go across onto you (lit. That we will go across onto him)

To what extent such semi-direct speech structures were common in Old Russian is an open question. They are not mentioned in the existing grammars where speech reports are discussed only very briefly (see Vlasto 1986: 203–5, Borkovskij and Kuznetsov 1965: 525; and Matthews 1960: 222–3). I am grateful to Jonathan Clarke for drawing my attention to this example, and to Noel Brackney and Ian Press for commenting on it.

Galo (Tibeto-Burman: Post 2008) displays a similar structure: the object pronoun, '3-ACC', is a token of indirect speech, while the 'self-directed' imperative form (which can be roughly translated as 'cut-me-off') is a token of direct speech:

(ii) [bɨɨ-əm   ilɨɨ =əm
      3-ACC:IND.SP.REP   stone=ACC
        pá-pàk-láa-ku-ka]
        chop-OFF-IPTV.SELF/SPEAKER.DIRECTED:DIR.SP.REP-COMPL-ADVZ
        ə́m-dùu-ku   na=na
        tell-IMPERF-COMPL   DECL=DECL
     She₁ told them [to cut her₁ free from the rock, see]

MacDonald (1990a: 35) mentions semi-direct speech in Tauya (Brahman family, Papua New Guinea); however, the examples are difficult to interpret. Semi-direct speech is not mentioned in her reference grammar of the language (MacDonald 1990b). Logophoric pronouns in some Daghestanian languages occur in structures similar to semi-direct speech (cf. Kibrik 1977: 238; 316–17 on Archi; Kalinina 2001: 550–1; Ljutikova 2001: 652–8, on Bagvalal).

3.1.2. *Semi-direct speech of Type II: Person shift to the perspective of the Current Speaker*

Semi-direct speech as an optional choice has been documented for a number of languages from the Papuan area (many of them from the Highland regions of New Guinea). Unlike Manambu and the African languages, all these Papuan languages typically have just direct speech reports, and no indirect speech report as an alternative option.

In all semi-direct speech report constructions the Current Speaker is involved in the speech report. The reference to the Current Speaker is shifted to their perspective (and not to that of the Original Speaker).

Consider (28), from Usan (Numugenan family, Madang-Adalbert range: Reesink 1993: 220). The Current Speaker ('I') is the addressee within the speech report; it is expressed with a token of indirect speech report ('to me') fused with the imperative form. The free pronoun within the speech report is a token of direct speech—it reflects what 'he' (the Original Speaker, different from the Current Speaker, 'me') had actually said:

Usan
(28)   [Wo$_i$ eng ba di]   [ye$_j$ yeis-ib$_i$]
       he   this   take come:up I:DIR.SP.REP give:me:IND.SP.REP-sg:FUT:SS
       qamb$_i$ [ba di-arei]
       say:SS   take come:up-3sgFAR.PAST
       He$_i$ brought this up in order to give to me$_j$ (lit. He brought this up saying: I=Original Speaker$_i$ will give it to me=Current Speaker$_j$)

In (29), also from Usan (Reesink 1987: 258–9), the first person 'refers to a group of children of which the Current Speaker is a part, and the third person plural refers to the children's parents':

(29)   wuri   [wau   qei   ini-nob   ir-i
       they   child   some   us-with:IND.SP.REP   ascend-CAUS
       in-wâgâr]
       us:IND.SP.REP-leave.pl.IMPV:DIR.SP.REP
       [qâmb] [maribig-umir   eng Boui ne   Memind]
       say.SS   appoint-3persFAR.PAST the Boui and Memind
       They (parents) appointed Boui and Memind saying 'May the children (that is, Boui and Memind) leave us (=a group which includes the Current Speaker)

The token of indirect speech, 'us', is coreferential with the group which includes the Current Speaker (not the Original Speaker) and is expressed as an argument of a postposition, and also a bound pronoun on the verb. The token of direct speech is expressed in the imperative form of the verb itself.

Similar examples come from Lower Grand Valley Dani (Dani family, Papuan area: Bromley 1981: 244). The Current Speaker, 'I', is the object of the speech report.

Lower Grand Valley Dani
(30) [*n-asuwok*]-olvk-at
      me:IND.SP.REP-let's.kill.later:DIR.SP.REP-having.said-PREDICATE
      ykhy-lakoukwha]
      saying-they:were:FAR.PAST
      They used to make plans to kill me (lit. They_i (=Original Speaker) were saying having said 'Let's kill me_j (=Current Speaker) later'

The token of indirect speech is coreferential with the Current Speaker, 'I', and is expressed as a bound pronoun on the verb. The token of direct speech is expressed in the imperative form of the verb 'kill' within the speech report.

In (31), from the same language, the Current Speaker, 'I', is the addressee within the direct speech report, and is cast as 'me' (rather than as 'him/her' or 'you' as was said in the original speech). The subject of the speech report is also 'I'. Both tokens of direct speech ('I') and of indirect speech reports ('me') are expressed as bound pronouns on the verb (Bromley 1981: 245):

(31) [*wo'nesik-ylvk*]
          move-let.me.transfer.it.to.me:DIR.SP.IND.SP
          [eken?]
          having.said.did.you(sg).say
      Did you_i say that you_i were planning to give it to me_j? (Lit. did you_i (=Original speaker) say 'I_i am planning to give (i.e. move.let.transfer) it to me_j (=Current Speaker)?')

In the descriptions of Usan and Lower Grand Valley Dani, semi-direct speech reports are presented as occasional alternatives to the usual direct speech reports.[9] There is no information as to how semi-direct speech compares to direct speech, in terms of the use of vocatives, 'mimicking effect', pauses, or any other potentially criterial features (as was described for Manambu, in Table 9.4 above). The exact conditions under which semi-direct reports are preferred are equally unknown, and require further investigation for these languages. The feature they share is overt marking of the Current Speaker's role in a speech report quoted by them.

We can recall, from the discussion following Table 9.2, that speech report constructions with incomplete person shift such as *$John$ $said$ '$I_{CurrentSpeaker}$ saw $Fred$' or *$I_{CurrentSpeaker}$ $said$ '$She_{CurrentSpeaker}$ saw $Fred$' are unacceptable in English. (They would be fine if understood as indirect speech reports with the linker *that* omitted.) However, these constructions—analogous to the semi-direct speech attested in Papuan languages—do occur in imperative constructions.

Consider the following example, from colloquial British English. The Current Speaker is talking about an adminstrator who has told the Current Speaker to come and see him.

(32) I_{CS} rang up Paul$_i$, and Paul$_i$ said '$Come_{CS}$ *and see him$_i$*'

What Paul had said was *Come and see me* (see (33a)). In the speech report construction in (32) the second person imperative form *come* is kept just as Paul might have uttered it. The Current Speaker ('I') is the addressee. This lack of shift of person is a token of direct speech. But the free pronominal form of the addressee, *me*, has been changed to *him* to fit in with the perspective of the Current Speaker. This is a token of indirect speech.

Straightforward direct and indirect speech report constructions corresponding to (32) are given in (33a) and (33b–d) respectively, for comparison. These are considered grammatical English, while the con-

---

[9] In Bromley's words, 'the person reference of any personal object-marking prefixes is interpreted from the standpoint of the speaker in all cases, so that in this construction, and only here, there occur verb forms which have first person object markers, referring to the speaker or the speaker with others, and also first person subject markers, where these refer to the addressee or any other non-speaker, since the marked subject person category is not interpreted from the standpoint of the speaker but of the subject of the superordinate verb' (1981: 244).

struction in (32)—albeit used—is rejected by many as an 'ungram-matical slip of the tongue'.[10]

(33a)   I rang up Paul, and Paul said: *'Come and see me'*

(33b)   I rang Paul, and Paul said that I should come and see him

(33c)   I rang Paul, and Paul told me to come and see him

(33d)   I rang Paul, and Paul said to come and see him

The speech report in (32) shares another feature with direct speech reports—its 'theatrical effect'. As Clark and Gerrig (1990: 772) put it, quotations are 'demonstrations', and they often convey not just the words, but the intonation, the look, the gestures and so on; 'the internal structure of quotation is really the structure of what is being depicted, and that can range from the raging of a person to the racket of a machine'. In (33a) the Original Speaker mimicked the administrator's high-pitched voice and his broad Australian accent. This mimicking is perfectly possible with direct speech reports—as in (33a)—but not with indirect speech—as in (33b) and (33c). Along similar lines, the administrator's high-pitched voice was mimicked in (32). This is a major reason why (32) cannot be considered an instance of indirect speech report with *to* omitted.

A similar example of a command directed at the Current Speaker and cast as a semi-direct speech report is (34). The speaker had broken her contact lenses, the doctor was alarmed and told her to make an appointment as soon as possible. What the doctor actually had said was *Make an appointment with me.* The speaker reports this as:

(34)   And she_i said, [*make*_{CS=ADDRESSEE} *an appointment with her_i as soon as possible*]

The speech report in (34) is similar to that in (32) in that the imperative form of the verb, *make*, is identical to what had actually been said and can be seen as a token of direct speech report. The free pronoun, *her*, has been changed to fit in with the perspective of the Current Speaker, and is a token of indirect speech.

---

[10] I have recorded half-a-dozen instances of such uses, from native or near-native speakers of British and Australian English. No such examples have been located in the existing web-based corpora.

Another speaker told me how he came to the Australian North and got married, and then his new father-in-law suggested he should bring his family closer to where the in-laws lived and build a house there. The speaker phrased it as follows: 'My father-in-law said 'Bring my family in and build a house''. Here, 'my' reflects the perspective of the Current speaker, while the command form belongs to what the father-in-law is quoted as saying.

A somewhat different example was recorded in the speech of a toddler. Sam was at the time 2 years 9 months old, and quite fluent for his age. His mother was trying to show us what he could say, and kept asking him: 'And what does Daddy say to you?' 'G'day, mate'. 'And what does Granny say to you?' 'Hello, dear'. 'And what does Mummy say to you? Sam, wash your hands?' To this last question Sam replied:

(35)   Mummy says: 'Sam_{CS}, $wash_{CS=ADDRESSEE}$ my_{CS} hands'

Just like in (32) and (34), the imperative, *wash*, appears within the speech report in exactly the same form as Mummy had used it. It is a token of direct speech. But the possessive *my* is changed according to the perspective of Sam, the Current Speaker (rather than the Original Speaker's, Mummy), and is a token of indirect speech.[11]

All the instances in English which contain shift to the Current Speaker's perspective involve commands. Just like direct speech reports, these semi-direct speech constructions can contain vocatives, and mimics what has been said. The functions of these constructions and the pragmatic implications require further investigation. Examples (32), (34) and (35) illustrate that the inclusion of Current Speaker in speech report—resulting in the emergence of marginal semi-direct speech constructions—is a reality in everyday varieties of English.

We now turn to the few instances whereby semi-direct speech is obligatory.

---

[11] Note that Sam has never been a pronoun-reversing child (in the sense of Chiat 1982, 1986; cf. Hanson 2000): he did not used to employ 'I' instead of 'you' or 'you' instead of 'I'. The relevance of 'semi-direct' speech for child language acquisition deserves further study.

3.2. *Obligatory semi-direct speech*

Two languages, both from the New Guinea Highlands area, have been described as having semi-direct speech as an obligatory construction: Gahuku, from the Gorokan family (Deibler 1971, 1976), and Dom, from the Chimbu family (Tida 2006).[12] Semi-direct speech is obligatory if the Current Speaker is first person and is also the addressee or the object within the speech report. In all other cases, direct speech is the only option.

Gahuku (Deibler 1971: 115; 1976: 110–18) is said to have just straightforward direct speech reports, in all but one context. If the speech report is made by first person subject who is also the addressee in the reported speech, the second or third person is shifted to first, to fit in with the perspective of 'I', the Current Speaker.

If (36) were a bona fide direct speech construction, we would have expected 'you' in lieu of 'me'. In (36), the Original Speaker had said 'We will seize your hands'. This appears in the speech report in (36) (Deibler 1976: 115) as 'We will seize my hands'. The person reference of 'we' is determined by the perspective of the Original Speaker of 'we will seize your hands'. The person reference of 'my' is determined by the perspective of the Current Speaker.

The first person plural marker on the verb 'seize' within the speech report is a token of direct speech: this is exactly what the Original Speaker, 'you', had said. The first person singular in 'my hands' is coreferential with the Current Speaker and can be considered a token of indirect speech, since the person has 'shifted':

Gahuku
(36) [*NIgizatoq*   *al-it-UNE*]
      my.hands.at:IND.SP.RP   take-FUT-1pl:DIR.SP.REP
      [L-iki   niahe]
      say-SUCCESSIVE.ACTION   are.you?
      Are you saying: 'We will seize your hands?' (lit. Are you$_i$ saying: 'We$_i$ will seize my$_{CS}$ hands?')

---

[12] This construction was also described for Golin, a dialect of Dom (Loughnane 2003, 2005). Tida, who produced a comprehensive grammar of the language based on several years of fieldwork in the Chimbu province (2006), provides a fuller account than Loughnane who was only able to work with one speaker in Melbourne during a limited period of time.

In (37) (Deibler 1971: 109), the third argument of the verb 'give' is coreferential with the Current Speaker, and its person reference is 'shifted' to the Current Speaker's perspective. What was said in the original speech report was 'I'll give it to you now'. The speech report within (37) is cast as 'I'll give it to us (=Current Speaker) now'. 'I' remains as in the original speech report, and thus can be considered a token of a direct speech report. 'Us' includes the Current Speaker ('he') and retains his perspective. The Current Speaker is the addressee.

(37) [Lelliq   nemoqza],   [*mota*   *limitove*]
      ours   is.but   now   I'll.give.to.us:DIR.SP.REP.IND.SP.REP
      [lokake]
       after.he.said
      It is ours, but after he said 'I'll give it to you(plural) now'...(lit. After
      he_i said 'I_i'll give it to us_CS now...')

In (38), the addressee of 'open' (Deibler 1971: 110) is co-referential with the Current Speaker. A few further, similar examples are in Deibler (1976: 115).

(38) [*gapo hamagokoq gahe segelatove*]   [loko]
      road only.one   door I'll.open.for.us DIR.SP.REP.IND.SP.REP saying
      [amuza   nomolako]
       strength   as.you.are.putting
      ...As you are striving to open the door of a single way for us...(Lit.
      As you_i are putting strength saying 'I_i will open the door of a single
      way for us_CS')

Along similar lines, in Dom (Tida 2006: 219) semi-direct speech is obligatorily used when the Current Speaker is the object or the addressee of the speech report. In (39), the free pronoun is a token of direct speech report, and the bound pronoun ('me') is a token of indirect speech, from the perspective of the Current Speaker. The 'reporter' is expressed as a token of indirect speech—this is similar to Manambu.

(39) [˩ta   ˩na   *kar-Val*]   ˥d
      a   I(excl):DIR.SP.REP   see-FUT.1sg:IND.SP.REP   QUOT
      ˀu-na-ga
      come-FUT-2sgSUB
      (One) of you$_i$ who would come (here) saying 'I$_i$ will see him$_{CS}$(=Current
      Speaker)' (lit. I$_i$ (=Original Speaker:IND.SP.REP) will see me$_{CS}$ (=Cur-
      rent Speaker:DIR.SP.REP))[13]

In all other circumstances, straighforward direct speech reports are used.
Note that, unlike other New Guinea languages mentioned here, Dom
employs a special quotative marker to introduce any speech report.

3.3. *Parameters of variation in semi-direct speech reports*

Semi-direct speech reports can be an option; or they can be obligatory.
They appear to coexist with direct and with indirect speech reports in
just two languages where a semi-direct speech report is an optional
choice: Manambu and Akɔɔse. 'Original-Speaker-oriented' semi-direct
speech of Type I has been attested in Manambu and Akɔɔse. 'Current-
Speaker-oriented' semi-direct speech of Type II has been attested
in Usan, Lower Grand Valley Dani, Manambu, Gahuku,[14] and Dom.
Manambu differs from other languages discussed here in that it combines the two types of semi-direct speech. English has semi-direct
speech constructions of Type II, limited to commands. Tokens of
direct and indirect speech can be encoded by free pronouns, bound
pronouns, or both. In Colloquial English, the imperative verb is a token
of direct speech, and the free pronoun is a token of indirect speech.

The parameters of variation in semi-direct speech constructions of
two types are summarized in Table 9.5.

The existence of Current-Speaker-oriented semi-direct speech constructions confirms the importance of the Current Speaker for a comprehensive typology of speech reports—despite the fact that for some
languages, such as English (exemplified in §1.2), marking coreferentiality with the Current Speaker appears superfluous.

---

[13] ˩, ˩, ˥, ˀ are tone marks (Tida 2006).
[14] In Deibler's (1971: 109) words, 'A verb-affix pronominal form in the quoted
speech whose referent is the person or persons who are doing the quoting [that is,
the speaker—A. A.] is a first-person pronoun instead of a second person as would
have been used by the original speaker'.

Table 9.5. Parameters of variation in semi-direct speech constructions

PARAMETERS FOR SEMI-DIRECT SPEECH		EXAMPLE LANGUAGES
Original-speaker-oriented: Type I		Manambu, Akɔɔse
Current-speaker-oriented: Type II		Usan, Lower Grand Valley Dani, Colloquial English, Gahuku, Dom
Obligatory or optional	stylistic option	Manambu, Akɔɔse, Usan, Lower Grand Valley Dani, Colloquial English
	obligatory	Gahuku, Dom
Existence of indirect speech as a special speech report	yes	Manambu, Akɔɔse, Colloquial English
	no	Usan, Lower Grand Valley Dani, Gahuku, Dom
Form of the token of indirect speech	free pronoun	Manambu, Akɔɔse, Dom, English
	bound pronoun	Lower Grand Valley Dani, Usan, Gahuku

We will now compare the two types of semi-direct speech reports with instances which look superficially similar: 'mixed' speech reports, and the phenomenon of 'logophoricity'.

3.4. *Semi-direct speech and 'mixed' speech reports*

Semi-direct speech reports containing tokens of direct and indirect speech are reminiscent of 'mixed' direct and indirect speech (see Mittwoch 1985: 140–2; called 'mixed direct and indirect quotations' by Partee 1973). Consider the following examples, all from written sources. R. M. W. Dixon describes how the Jamamadí people of Southern Amazonia came to be converted to Christianity by the Campbells, a missionary team (Dixon 2011: 288). The mixed direct and indirect speech is in italics.

(40)   An intruding Branco had been shot by the Jamamadí at the end of the airstrip. But he was such an evil fellow that they really did fear his spirit. *The Campbells said [that Jesus is all powerful]* INDIRECT SPEECH REPORT *and [only he can protect you—better convert double quick!]* DIRECT SPEECH REPORT'

The direct speech report here is unlikely to be a verbatim quotation, but it has all the trappings of direct speech: lack of person shift and imperative form. Some authors put direct speech report inserts within quotes, as in (41) (Mittwoch 1985: 140) and (42) (*Weekend Australian Magazine*, March 17–18 2007: 14):

(41)   He$_i$ assures the reader that during the journey he$_i$ wrote down 'in the evening what during the day I$_i$ had seen…'

(42)   Noxon started doing his research 'in order to understand myself'

Such 'mixed' constructions are used to achieve a stylistic effect— making the narrative more vivid. These occur predominantly in written style. Unlike semi-direct speech of Type I described above, the identity between the Original Speaker and a participant within the speech report is optional. Unlike semi-direct speech reports of Type II, the Current Speaker's perspective is irrelevant.

3.5. *Semi-direct speech and logophoricity*

The phenomenon of logophoricity (identified in numerous African languages, and first introduced by Hagège 1974) involves a special set of forms reserved for indirect speech clauses. They indicate that one of the referents of the embedded speech clause (often, but not always, the subject) is coreferential with one of the participants in the reporting ('matrix') clause. That is, examples such as (2a) and (2b) from English would be explicitly differentiated by different forms of 'he'—one coreferential with the Original Speaker, as in (2a), and one not, as in (2b).

Consider logophoric pronouns in Donno Sɔ, a Dogon language from Burkina Faso (Culy 1994a) (in bold type). In (43), the referent of 'he' is neither Anta nor Oumar. In (44) 'he' is Oumar.[15]

Donno Sɔ
(43)   Oumar   [Anta   wo-ñ   waa   be]   gi
       Oumar   Anta   3sg-OBJ   seen   AUX   said
       Oumar$_i$ said that Anta$_j$ had seen him$_k$

---

[15] Alternatively, logophoricity can be expressed with verbal cross-referencing, or with a clitic (see Hyman and Comrie 1981: 24; and an overview by Curnow 2002b, c). This phenomenon is not confined to Africa: a so-called conjunct-disjunct person marking in Tibeto-Burman and Barbacoan languages has essentially the same function (see a summary in Aikhenvald 2004: 133–4).

(44) Oumar   [Anta   **inyem'**-ñ waa   be]   gi
       Oumar   Anta   LOG-OBJ seen AUX said
       Oumar_i said that Anta_j had seen him_i

As pointed out by Wiesemann (1990: 78–9), logophoric reference is primarily employed in a situation where 'third person identification refers to any participant other than the speaker of the original speech act'. The instances of semi-direct speech of Type I and Type II discussed above do not—and cannot—serve the function of differentiating referents. They mark coreferentiality of a participant within the speech report with the Original Speaker, or with the Current Speaker. Note that current-speaker-oriented semi-direct speech differs from 'classical' logophoricity—which concerns a third-person speaker and a participant within the speech report—in that it includes marking of the Current Speaker.

An additional difference between semi-direct speech of Type II and logophoricity lies in the syntactic functions of the speech report participant coreferential (or not) with the Original Speaker. Logophoric pronouns are typically tied to the function of subject, or object. In contrast, reference to 'Current Speaker' in optional semi-direct speech of Type II spans a variety of participants (O in (24) from Manambu, in (30) from Lower Grand Valley Dani and in (39) from Dom; addressee in (28) from Usan, (31) from Lower Grand Valley Dani and (32) from English; possessor in (35) from English).

Obligatory semi-direct speech of Type II is closer to logophoricity in that the Current Speaker has to be in the addressee or direct object function within the speech report (see (36)–(38) from Gahuku; and (39) from Dom). That is, semi-direct speech can be seen a marker of co-refentiality between the Current Speaker and a particular participant within the speech report.

3.6. *Semi-direct speech and 'first-person logophoricity'*

An analogy can be drawn between semi-direct speech of Type II and so-called 'first person logophoricity'. In some African languages with logophoric pronouns, if the Orginal Speaker is the subject of the speech report, first person marking may appear in the speech report. This is illustrated with (45), also from Donno Sɔ (Culy 1994b: 123). The person of the possessor is cast as if it were an indirect speech report (with a logophoric pronoun indicating the identity of Oumar and 'he', the possessor). First person marking on the verb is coreferential with the Original Speaker, Oumar, and reflects what one would expect in a direct speech report.

(45) Oumar   [{*minnɛ*   *inyemɛ* }   *mɔ*
      Oumar   field   LOG:IND.SP.REP   POSS
      gɨndɨzɨm]   gi
      regard:PROG:1sg:DIR.SP.REP   said
      Oumar said that heᵢ will look at hisᵢ field (lit. Oumar said 'I-will-look at his field')

This 'first person logophoricity' (Curnow 2002b: 3–5) serves the same function as a logophoric pronoun—it indicates that an argument (often subject, but sometimes also an object) within a speech report is coreferential with the Original Speaker. It is indeed reminiscent of Type I of semi-direct speech.[16]

A similar instance of first person-only logophoricity has been documented for Central and East Hokkaido dialects of Ainu (Bugaeva 2008: 41). If the Original Speaker is identical to the subject of the direct speech report, the inclusive pronoun 'I and you' is used, rather than the singular pronoun. The verb appears in the plural form:

(46) wa ne   eper   ene   Ø=itak   i,   [*anokay… kamuy mosir ine*
      and this bear   like.this 3S=say   NMZR   INCL   god   land to
      paye=an]   sekor   Ø=ne
      go.PL=INCL.S   QUOT   3A=COP
      The bear said: 'I shall go to the land of gods (=die)' (lit. The bear said: 'We (I+you+s/he/they) shall go to the land of gods')

This is comparable to what Wiesemann (1990: 78) refers to as 'direct reporting of the use of third person to refer to first or second person as a manner of speaking, such as […] *Somebody is hungry around here* meaning "I am hungry" *Somebody has not finished his work* meaning "you didn't finish"'. The difference lies in the fact that in examples like (46) from Ainu the inclusive pronoun is an obligatory choice and not a stylistic option.

---

[16] This is also reminiscent of conjunct-disjunct person marking (see Curnow 2002a, d; Hale 1980; and the summary in Aikhenvald 2004: 123–8).

There is thus a superficial similarity between first-person logophoricity in (45)–(46) and the semi-direct speech of Type I. But there are also two major differences.

Firstly, semi-direct speech of Type I is optional—in all the instances surveyed it is a stylistic option used to mark the Original Speaker's involvement in the event (see §2.3.2, for Manambu).

Secondly, the choice of a logophoric pronoun correlates with a syntactic function of the participant within the speech report coreferential with the Original Speaker (that is, the choice of a logophoric pronoun is determined by whether it is the subject or the object). In contrast, in languages with semi-direct speech of Type I the Original Speaker can have a plethora of syntactic functions within a speech report, including:

- (i) S (intransitive subject), as in (18), from Manambu;
- (ii) O, as in (27), from Akɔɔse, and (22), from Manambu; and
- (iii) possessor, as in (20), from Manambu.

In addition, as can be seen from the analysis of Manambu (§2.3.1), semi-direct speech can be considered a separate speech report which shares some features with direct, and some with indirect speech. Semi-direct speech of Type I is a means of marking the Original Speaker's involvement. For languages with logophoricity this has been described as an obligatory mechanism, which has no such discourse functions. Whether or not once semi-direct speech becomes obligatory, it acquires additional, logophoric, functions remains an open question.[17]

4. To Conclude

A major difference between direct and indirect speech lies in the way the person of the author of the original speech is cast. In direct speech, the person is expressed exactly as it was in the original speech report. In indirect speech, the person reference is shifted to the perspective of

---

[17] Semi-direct speech reports may be obligatory under additional circumstances, independently of person value of the reporter. Slave (Athabaskan: Rice 1986, 1989: 1273–89) has a class of 'direct discourse determining verbs' reminiscent of semi-direct speech: with these, 'Simon says that you hit him' translates as 'Simon says you hit me'. See Chapter 8.

the Current Speaker. There is a third option—a 'middle ground' situation known as 'semi-direct' speech—with incomplete person shift.

Speech report constructions with incomplete person shift can be of two types. Type I, which tends to be optional, indicates the involvement of the Original Speaker in the speech report. There appear to be hardly any restrictions on the syntactic functions of the participant—coreferential with the Original Speaker—within the speech report: this is what distinguishes semi-direct speech from classical logophoric constructions.

Type II, which may be optional or obligatory, indicates coreferentiality of the Current Speaker—rather than the Original Speaker—with a participant within the speech report. This brings an additional dimension to the typology of speech report constructions: the necessity of including the perspective of Current Speaker as a parameter for classification and analysis of speech reports. Such constructions occur in English—albeit marginally (in English they are restricted to commands).

Semi-direct speech of Type II may be compared to first-person logophoricity, in that the two do a similar job, but with respect to different participants. While logophoricity indicates that an argument within a speech report is coreferential with the Original Speaker, semi-direct speech of Type II indicates that an argument within a speech report is coreferential with the Current Speaker.

The Manambu data are particularly instructive: they indicate that optional semi-direct speech reports of Type I and Type II may be significantly different from both direct and indirect speech. Semi-direct speech in this language can be considered a strategy for marking Original Speaker's, or Current Speaker's, involvement in a situation which affects them.

To what extent this also applies to other languages with optional semi-direct speech constructions remains an open question. Most languages with optional semi-direct speech have just direct speech reports. The existing grammars provide no information on how semi-direct speech compares to direct speech in terms of the potential 'mimicking' effect, semantic extensions not directly presupposing a speech event, and further properties.

A further question relates to the development and spread of semi-direct speech constructions. Like many other categories, speech report constructions are easily diffused. Logophoricity is an areal, rather than a genetic, property spread across unrelated African languages (as demonstrated by Güldemann 2001, 2002, 2003; see Frajzyngier 1985 on Chadic languages). Further examples of areally diffused speech reports abound. The emergence of indirect speech reports in Maale is the result of influence from Amharic; traditional Maale has only direct speech report constructions (Amha 2001: 199–200). In Evenki, clauses with indirect speech reports had to be nominalized; under Russian influence, Evenki allows the use of verbal indicative forms in indirect speech (Nedjalkov 1997: 1–3). And Modern Goemai has developed direct speech reports under influence from Hausa (Hellwig 2011).

Both Gahuku and languages of the Chimbu family (which include Dom and Golin), where semi-direct speech of Type II is obligatory, are spoken in the New Guinea Highlands. Does this shared feature reflect a diffusional pattern? And can shared semi-direct speech patterns in Manambu (from the Sepik area), Lower Grand Valley Dani (spoken further west in West Papua), and Usan (spoken in Madang Province, bordering on the Sepik area) be attributed to a contact-induced change? These questions remain open until further studies become available.

PART B

EXPLAINING LANGUAGE

CHAPTER TEN

NAIVE LINGUISTIC EXPLANATION

R. M. W. Dixon

Languages show similar basic vocabularies but differ in the wealth of words they have for specialized domains. All peoples surely have similar perception of colour and taste, yet languages show considerable variation in the numbers of colour terms and taste terms they contain. Members of different cultures probably have similar perception of colour matching and similar appreciation of taste distinctions, but some are able to talk about these things better than others—they have a more developed vocabulary in that area.

The same applies to language. All human beings have an appreciation of their native language—they will comment on whether something is grammatical or felicitous or appropriate to say in a certain situation. All cultures have some sort of metalanguage for talking about the lexicon—a word for 'word' or 'name', which enables them to talk about the meanings of words and say that a certain word is not appropriately used in a particular context or is a borrowing from another language.

People's appreciation of language extends to phonetic, phonological, and grammatical as well as to lexical matters. But most speakers have no meta-language for discussing phonetics, phonology, or grammar. In his classic article, 'The Psychological Reality of Phonemes,' Sapir (1933) described how native speakers can reveal their perception of the phonological system of their language not by discussing this in a scientific way but simply by the sorts of orthographic conventions they adopt. Tony, his Southern Paiute interpreter, wrote [páβa'] as pa·pa', indicating that this medial [β] corresponds to the same phoneme as the initial [p]. John Whitney, Sapir's Sarcee interpreter, suggested that [dìní] ended in a t, which in fact the underlying form does. The final t is realized when followed by a suffix beginning with a vowel, for example, [dìnít'i], but is not pronounced in the 'absolute' (i.e., unsuffixed) form of the word.

Similar things happen in the case of grammar, as many field workers can attest. A speaker of a language may want to communicate some point to a linguist but lacks the metalanguage for doing this. He cannot say: 'Look, the reason you can't understand that sentence is that you're thinking the second word is a noun. It isn't, it's a verb. Think in those terms and you will understand it.' Speakers of out-of-the way languages generally do not have words for 'noun', 'verb' and the like.

However, intelligent native speakers usually find some 'lateral means' of getting their message through to the linguist. This chapter describes four examples of such 'naive linguistic explanation' from my fieldwork in Australia.

First Example

In July 1989, I recorded from Bessie Jerry, a native speaker of the Girramay dialect of Dyirbal (in northeast Australia), a dreamtime legend that explains the origin of death. As I have been working on the language on and off since 1963, I was able to transcribe the story on my own and then check with Bessie that I had done it correctly and ask about a couple of points that bothered me. One concerned the sentence, as I had transcribed it:

balay-jilu	bayi	guyi-bi-n	bana-ŋga
THERE-EMPHATIC	HE	dead-BECOME-NON.FUTURE	water-LOCATIVE
mulu-ŋga		buniŋga	
end-LOCATIVE		firewood-LOCATIVE	

I understood what was being described. A young man has been killed by his brother but then gets up and comes home to his mother, bringing a piece of wood that he puts on the fire. As it burns shorter and shorter, he becomes sicker and sicker. He dies just as the end of the piece of wood is consumed by the fire.

The first three words are 'right there he died'. The last two make up a noun phrase—*buni* 'fire, firewood' and *mulu* 'end', both in locative case, 'at the end of the firewood'. That was quite clear. But what on earth was *bana-ŋga* 'at/in the water' doing in the sentence? I asked Bessie and she immediately saw my difficulty.

In fact, *bana-ŋga* here is not 'water-LOCATIVE' but a homonym consisting of *ban* (a short form of the feminine determiner *balan*) plus accusative -*ña* (which by a morphophonological rule reduces to just -*a* after a nasal) plus locative -*ŋga*. The message Bessie wanted to get across to me was:

buni 'firewood' is feminine and it is here accompanied by a feminine determiner, which agrees with it in case; you know that a determiner, such as masculine *bayi* or the feminine—which has long form *balan* and short form *ban* in free variation—must take the suffix *-ña* before locative inflection. With a masculine determiner you'd get *bayi-ña-ŋga* and here it is feminine *ban-a-ŋga*. (Dixon 1972: 260)

But, although Bessie Jerry was a highly intelligent person, she did not have this technical vocabulary. How, then, was she to get the message through? What Bessie said was: *'banaŋga, balanaŋga'*. She used the longer form of the feminine determiner, *balan* plus *-a-* plus *-ŋga*. The light suddenly dawned—I realized that *balanaŋga* could only be *balan-a-ŋga* and that *banaŋga* here was *ban-a-ŋga*. Bessie smiled that, once again, she had been able to 'put me on the right track.'

Second Example

In 1984, Bessie Jerry had been helping me transcribe and translate the words of Dyirbal songs. This was not an easy task because songs often include archaic words as well as some words that are only used in songs (and only have meaning in the context of a song). Also, the grammar of song poetry can be slightly different from that of everyday speech. I had recorded many of the songs 17 or more years earlier (and the singers were now dead). Bessie often had to have a song replayed several times before she could pick out all the words (I would generally send her a cassette in advance of my field trip, so that she would have time to listen to it at leisure). And if this task was hard for Bessie, you can imagine that it was highly demanding for me.

One Gama-style song included the words: *wambiɲu ŋaŋgarr gurrundulu*. We'd worked out that *gurrundulu*, a common noun meaning 'cricket', is in this song the proper name of a dog; *ŋaŋgarr* is an adjective 'waiting, watching.' The form *wambi* I knew as a noun 'wooden pillow'; *-ɲu* is the genitive suffix used for alienable possession. (Inalienable possession—marking whole-part relationships—is shown just by apposition, with no suffix.)

The word *wambiɲu* had me completely puzzled. How could a pillow inalienably possess anything? And, if it did, how did this fit in with the meaning of the song?

Now in Dyirbal, word classes are basically quite distinct; only very seldom does one get a situation as in English where a form can function as both noun and verb (e.g., *stone, laugh*). There is also very little homonymy in the dictionary of about 5,000 entries which I have compiled. Also, nouns and verbs each have a rich set of inflections, which are by and large distinct (Dixon 1972: 42, 247).

But there are *a few* homonyms and *wambi* is one—it is both a noun 'wooden pillow' and an intransitive verb 'to lean'. One of the few endings that exists both on a noun and on a verb is - *ŋu*, genitive suffix with nouns and marking a relative clause when used on a verb. In this song, *wambi-ŋu* is a verb: '(the dog) who was leaning (as he waited and watched)...'

What Bessie wanted to tell me was: 'you've got the wrong *wambi* here; this is the verb *wambi-* 'to lean', not the noun *wambi* 'pillow'. But she does not have words like 'noun' and 'verb' either in Girramay or in her English. What she said was: '*wambiŋu, wambiñu.*' Although -*ŋu* is a suffix on both nouns and verbs, -*ñu* is only used with verbs, indicating 'non-future tense' for the conjugation to which *wambi-* belongs. By giving another paradigmatic form of the verb *wambi-*, Bessie very efficiently 'told' me that *wambi-* is here a verb rather than a noun. Everything now made sense.

THIRD EXAMPLE

I finished a grammar of Dyirbal in 1971 (published as Dixon 1972) and then began to work intensively on its northerly neighbour, Yidiñ. Both languages have a 'comitative' nominal suffix— -*ji* in Yidiñ, and -*ba* (in some dialects) or -*bila* (in other dialects) for Dyirbal. I knew that in Dyirbal the comitative can translate English *with*, as in 'He's standing with a stick' (i.e., 'he stand-NON.FUTURE stick-COMITATIVE'), or *have*, as in 'He has a beard (i.e., 'he beard-COMITATIVE') (Dixon 1972: 222–23).

I then discovered that the suffix -*ji* in Yidiñ covers the same meanings as -*ba* ~ -*bila* in Dyirbal and more besides (Dixon 1977: 294–300). For instance, 'moon-COMITATIVE' can mean 'by moonlight'. In October 1972, on the way to my second major fieldwork on Yidiñ, I stopped in to see George Watson, consultant for the Mamu dialect of Dyirbal, partly to say hello and partly to ask about comitative. I wondered if I might have missed something in writing the grammar of Dyirbal, whether in fact comitative in that language has as wide a range of meaning as it does in Yidiñ.

Now Dyirbal has a number of nominal suffixes, including LOCATIVE (same in all dialects): *-ŋga* onto a disyllabic stem ending in a vowel; *-ga* onto a trisyllabic or longer stem ending in a vowel; *-ba* after *m*, *-da* after *n*, *-ja* after *y* or *ñ*; *-ra* onto a stem ending in *l*, *r*, or *rr* (with loss of this *l*, *r*, or *rr*), and COMITATIVE (no phonological conditioning): *-bila* in southern dialects (Jirrbal and Girramay) and *-ba* in northern dialects (Mamu and Ngajan).

The word for 'moon' in Mamu is *gagalum*. I asked George if one could say *ŋaja* ('I') *waymbañu* ('am going walkabout') *gagalum-ba*, trying to discover whether comitative *-ba* could be used with the same sense as comitative *-ji* in Yidiñ.

The difficulty—which George saw before I did—is that in Mamu comitative and locative fall together on a stem ending in *m*. Thus, *gagalum-ba* is ambiguous between locative and comitative senses. George is familiar with southern dialects of Dyirbal (he had a Girramay wife and, later, a Jirrbal wife) and he proceeded to clarify my questions by reference to Jirrbal. Here, the word for 'moon' is *gagara*, with comitative *gagara-bila* and locative *gagara-ga*. I was informed that you can say *ŋaja waymbañu gagaraga* (with locative) 'I'm going walkabout by moonlight' but that *ŋaja waymbañu gagarabila* (with comitative) is nonsensical. It could only be used, said George, if 'you had the moon in your pocket'. It turned out that I had not missed anything—the comitative in Dyirbal does have a more restricted meaning than that in Yidiñ.

But the interesting thing was how George resolved the difficulty caused by comitative and locative having identical allomorphs after a stem ending in *m* in Mamu. He would have liked to have said: '*gagalum-ba* is acceptable here in the locative sense but not in the comitative' only he did not have these technical terms available. So he transferred my questions into another dialect, in which this neutralization does not occur.

FOURTH EXAMPLE

All the native speakers of Australian languages that I have worked with have also known some English, but they were not familiar with such terms as grammar and grammatical. What they did was metaphorically extend the meaning of some other word in order to make a linguistic statement. John Tooth, speaker of Warrgamay, used to tell

me 'it doesn't rhyme', as his way of saying that a sentence I had created
was not grammatical.

Willie Seaton, the last speaker of Nyawaygi (see Dixon 1983), was
an exceptional teacher, who took pains to explain his language to me
in the clearest possible way. When I took down *gurrijala* 'eaglehawk',
he told me not to confuse it with *wurrijala* 'barramundi (a fish)', and
then mentioned that *gawiga* was another name for 'barramundi'. Willie Seaton did not have in his vocabulary the term 'synonym', but he
explained the idea to me through an example from English: '*wurrijala* and *gawiga*, that's just the same thing, just like you say *man* or
bloke'.

He drew attention to other minimal pairs: *wurruwurru* 'ibis (a wad-
ing bird)', with a trilled rhotic, written as 'rr', and *wuruwuru* 'frog',
which has a continuant rhotic, written as 'r'. In October 1977, I was
checking the transitive verb *buymbi-* 'to lick', which belongs to Conjugation I and has unmarked inflection *buymbi-ña*. Seaton confirmed
this and then volunteered that there was a similar verb for 'to paint',
whose unmarked inflection was also *buymbi-ña*, only it was a slightly
different word. He was obviously thinking of some way to communicate to me what this difference was.

To appreciate the difficulty of Seaton's task, one must understand
a little of the complexity of the verbal system in Nyawaygi. There are
seven conjugations, with at least nine inflections in each. Disyllabic
verbs are confined to three conjugations, which are illustrated in Table
10.1. It can be seen that the unmarked inflection is identical across all
three of these classes.

Now in Nyawaygi, the sequence *-iy-* must be followed by a vowel.
There is a morphophonological rule that states that a *y* is simply
dropped between *i* and a following consonant. Thus, for stems ending

Table 10.1. Conjugational classes for disyllabic verbs in Nyawaygi

| | conjugation | | |
	1	2	3
example verb	'cut'	'return'	'die'
UNMARKED	gunba-ña	bana-ña	wula-ña
IRREALIS	gunba-lma	bana-yma	wula-ma
PAST	gunba-laña	bana-yaña	wula-waña

in *i*, from Conjugation 2, irrealis is simply -*ma* (as it always is for Conjugation 3).

My corpus contains 57 verbs of Conjugation I and all are transitive. I have 25 forms in Conjugation 3 and all are intransitive. Conjugation 2 is smaller. Before this session with Willie Seaton, I had 11 verbs in the second class and all were intransitive.

Seaton used *buymbi-* 'to paint' in transitive constructions and I would have guessed that it was in Conjugation I, as is *buymbi-* 'to lick'. But he insisted that there was a difference and was plainly searching for a way to tell me about it. In order to get the irrealis form I asked how one would say 'I'll paint him by-and-by'. Seaton said *buymbima* and then—trying to get his point across—added *buymbiyama, buymbima, buymbiyama, buymbima.*

In fact, *buymbi-* 'to paint' is a transitive verb belonging to Conjugation 2 (the only such in my small corpus). If the root had ended in *a*, then a *y* would have appeared in the irrealis, but it ends in *i*, and the underlying sequence -*iym*- must be reduced to -*im*-. What Seaton did was to say the *y*, adding a vowel between it and the following *m*, to try to convey to me that there was an underlying *y* (even though the phonotactics did not allow it to surface in this instance), before going back to the correct irrealis form *buymbima*. At this stage, I did not understand what he was doing. But then, when I elicited the past tense and got *buymbiyaña*, the whole thing became clear. If Willie Seaton had had the appropriate metalanguage available he might have said: 'note that *buymbi-* "to paint" is unusual in that it is a transitive verb in Conjugation 2, and also in having a final *i*, so that the conjugational marker *y* only appears when there is a following vowel, as in past inflection.' (This is notable. Of the 57 Conjugation 1 roots I gathered, 7 end in *i* and 50 in *a*; of the 25 Conjugation 3 roots, 17 end in *i* and 8 in *a*; all the Conjugation 2 roots in my corpus end in *a* except for *buymbi-* 'to paint'.) Seaton had offered *buymbi-* (class 2) 'to paint' as a syntactic minimal pair with *buymbi-* (class I) 'to lick', and he took it upon himself to explain this difference. Not having available suitable vocabulary to talk about it, he demonstrated the difference by putting in an underlying *y*, *buymbiyama* (with a vowel to produce a sequence -*yam*- and avoid the disallowed -*ym*-) and then dropped it, finishing with the actual irrealis form of 'to paint', *buymbima*.

Conclusion

All field linguists need a certain degree of expertise and wit. But they also require the assistance of a native speaker who is dedicated to teaching the structure of the language and helping to uncover generalizations. In my experience, most such consultant-teachers are as intelligent and as intellectually creative as the linguist and could be doing the linguist's work if they had had the same educational opportunities. Their job is in some ways harder than the linguist's, because they have to communicate structural information without having available an appropriate metalanguage. The ways in which they achieve this—as illustrated by the four examples given here—can be ingenious and revealing.

CHAPTER ELEVEN

MULTIPLE MARKING OF SYNTACTIC FUNCTION AND POLYSYNTHETIC NOUNS IN TARIANA

Alexandra Y. Aikhenvald

Multiple dependent marking in a noun phrase implies that 'every case-marked constituent passes its case to all of its dependents or co-constituents which bear cases marking their own functions as well as the cases of their heads' (Nichols 1992: 62). This 'multiple-layered' case marking is found in some Australian languages, and has been dealt with in a classic paper by Dench and Evans (1988); see also Evans (1995a) and Dixon (2002). This involves simultaneous marking of two distinct clausal functions on one noun phrase, known as 'double case', providing an exception to Nichols' (1986: 104–5) statement that while 'many languages have polysynthetic verbs, there are no polysynthetic nouns'.

Polysynthetic inflectionally-complex nouns are found in other languages which combine head- and dependent-marking properties. For instance, in Tariana, a previously undescribed Arawak language from Northwest Amazonia, both nouns and verbs are inflectionally complex. Tariana allows sixteen affixed positions in a verbal word, and fifteen in a noun. The structure of the noun is recursive: that is, the same category may be marked more than once, while verb structure is not recursive.

This double marking of distinct syntactic functions has to be distinguished from marking one syntactic function twice within a noun phrase.

I will show that Tariana allows both phenomena—that is, in some instances, two distinct clausal functions can be marked on one noun phrase; while in others a noun phrase takes two case markers which combine to indicate one syntactic function.

Double marking of syntactic function can be also found within a noun phrase. In Tariana, if a noun phrase contains another noun phrase as a modifier the noun class agreement with two distinct 'heads'—the head of the embedded noun phrase, and the head of the embedding noun phrase—gets marked on the modifier.

Thus, Tariana consistently follows the principle of multiple-layered marking of syntactic function, both within a clause, and within a noun phrase. Note that the double marking of syntactic function is distinct from marking the same function twice.

§1.1 of this chapter deals with the nominal and verbal categories, and the structure of nouns and verbs in Tariana. The dependent marking case system in Tariana is considered in §1.2. Syntactic function of one noun phrase marked twice is discussed in §2.1. In §2.2 I look at double marking of syntactic function within a clause. Multiple-layered agreement within a NP is considered in §2.3. Conclusions are given in §3.

1. GRAMMATICAL BACKGROUND

1.1. *Structure of nouns and verbs in Tariana*

Tariana[1] is a polysynthetic language which combines head-marking morphology with elements of dependent marking. The open classes are nouns, verbs and adjectives; the latter share most categories with nouns (see note 7).

Nouns and verbs have partly different and partly similar sets of grammatical categories. Nominal categories include possession, diminutive, augmentative, pejorative, number and tense, while verbal categories cover cross-referencing, valency-changing and tense-aspect-evidentiality. Note that nouns have only three values for tense (past, future and Ø-marked present) and one for extralocality ('elsewhere'), while verbs have eleven values of tense-evidentiality (with an obligatory specification of the source of information: whether the event or a state was seen, perceived with means other than seeing, inferred from some non-firsthand evidence, or reported).

[1] Tariana, from the North Arawak subgroup of the Arawak language family, is spoken by about 100 people in the Vaupés river basin, north west Amazonia, Brazil. This chapter is based on data obtained during fieldwork on North Arawak and East Tucanoan languages of the Upper Rio Negro, Brazil, in 1991–1997. My text corpus of Tariana consists of appr. 700 pp. (135 stories of different genres). I am grateful to all my teachers of Tariana—Cândido, José, Jovino, Graciliano and Olívia Brito. Special thanks go to R.M.W. Dixon, Alan Dench and Tim Curnow for comments and discussion, and to Suzanne Kite for technical assistance.

Diagram 11.1. Noun structure in Tariana
(– suffixal boundary, = clitic boundary)

---

1. Possessive prefix, or negative *ma-*, or relative *ka-*
2. ROOT
3. Gender-sensitive derivational suffix
4. Classifier as a derivational suffix (may be more than one for nouns with an inanimate referent)
5. Plural marker
6. Pejorative =*yana* (± plural -*pe*)
7. Approximative =*iha* 'more or less'
8. Diminutive =*tuki* (or diminutive plural =*tupe*)
9. Tense (past =*miki*, future =*pena*) and locality (=*wya* 'extralocal: participant in a place distinct from where the speech act is')
10. Classifier as an agreement marker (more than one is possible)—see §2.3
11. Oblique cases (=*ne* 'comitative-instrumental'; -*se* 'locative')
12. Contrastive =*se*
13. Coordinative =*misini*, =*sini* 'also'
14. Focussed A/S =*ne*
15. Topical non-Subject =*nuku*

Noun structure in Tariana is shown in Diagram 11.1. Nouns are divided into subclasses depending on which structural 'positions' they have. Some nouns can contain more than one root. Position 1 is restricted to inalienably possessed (prefixed) nouns; position 3 is restricted to nouns with human referents. Suffixes or enclitics which occupy one structural position do not cooccur in one word (e.g. two oblique cases: position 11; or diminutive: position 8). Classifiers (positions 4 and 10) can be used recursively (see §2.3). Positions 11 and 14 are never filled at the same time (see §1.2); however, 14 and 15 are sometimes filled simultaneously (§2.2).

Categories realised in positions 1–4 can be considered as characteristic of the head noun, while positions 5–15 are filled once per noun phrase; they can be considered as belonging to a 'phrasal' level. That is, in a sense, not just nouns but noun phrases in Tariana can be considered inflectionally complex, as we will demonstrate in §2.

In (1) below 13 structural positions are filled (note that the recursive plural marking -*pe* after pejorative -*yana* counts as one position). Square brackets indicate the syntactic structure.

(1)   1   2   3   4   5   6   8   9   10 11 12   13   15
          [[[nu-phe-ru-ma-pe=yana-pe=tupe=miki]-ite]=ne=se=misini=nuku]
          1sg-older.sibling-fem-CL:FEM-PL=PEJ-PL=DIM:PL=PAST:PL=
          CL:PERSON=COMIT=CONTRAST=ALSO=TOP.NON.A/S
          with this very person belonging to my bad little older sisters, too

There are three main types of predicates in Tariana—simple predicates, serial verb constructions, and complex predicates. Every verbal
root is either ambitransitive of A=S$_a$ type (prefixed) or intransitive
of type S$_o$ or of type S$_{io}$ (both prefixless). Simple predicates have one
prefix position and up to eight suffix positions. In the scheme below,
positions marked with * do not appear with prefixless verbs. Diagram
11.2 shows the verb structure.

Diagram 11.2. Verb structure in Tariana
(1–10 are suffixes; 11–16 are enclitics which allow variable ordering
and are optional.)

---

 *1. Cross-referencing prefixes or negative *ma-* or relative *ka-*
  2. ROOT
 *3. Thematic syllable
  4. Causative *-i*
 4a. Complete involvement of O *-ta* (only appears after *-i*)
  5. Negative *-(ka)de*
 *6. Topic-advancing *-ni*, or Passive *-kana*, or Purposive *-hyu* or Resultative
     -karu
  7. Verbal classifiers
  8. Benefactive *-pena*
 *9. Reciprocal *-kaka*
 10. Relativizers or nominalizers
 11. Mood (imperative, frustrative, conditional)
 12. Tense and evidentiality
 13. Aktionsart (manner or extent of action, e.g. 'split open', associated
     action)
 14. Aspect (completive, durative, repetitive, etc)
 15. Degree—augmentative (also meaning 'indeed'), diminutive, approxima-
     tive ('more or less')
 16. Switch-reference and clause-chaining

---

(2) illustrates a simple predicate with 12 positions filled.

(2)   1   2   4 4a 5   9   11   12   13   14   15 16
ma-thuka-i-ta-kade-kaka=tha=pidana=bosa=niki=pu=ka
NEG-break-CAUS-CAUS-NEG-REC=FRUSTRATIVE=REM.P.REP=
    SPLIT.OPEN=COMPL=AUG=SUBORDINATE
While (they) apparently did not break each other by splitting open
totally indeed in vain...

The difference between the structure of a noun and the structure of
the verb is that only noun structures are recursive, while verb structures are not. That is, the same nominal category may be marked more
than once on a noun or within a NP, while all verbal categories are
expressed just once on a predicate. This multiple marking of syntactic
function is of several distinct types. This is the topic of the remainder
of this chapter.

1.2. Dependent marking case system in Tariana

Unlike most other Arawak languages, Tariana has a case system for
both core and oblique arguments of verbs. All the case markers appear
once per NP; they go onto the last constituent of an NP.

The case morphemes combine reference to the grammatical function of an argument and to the discourse status of a referent. There
are two core cases. One of these, a clitic -ne (slot 14 in Diagram 11.1),
marks the subject (A/S) if this is a foregrounded participant in contrastive focus to another participant, or if the subject is reintroduced
as a main participant in the discourse and contrastive. The subject
marked with -ne has to be definite or referential; that is, it cannot have
a generic referent.

A zero-marked non-focussed subject is exemplified in (3).

(3)   pa-ita   tʃãri   di-kapi-pidana   di-pisa
      one-CL:ANIM   man   3sgnf-hand-REM.P.REP   3sgnf-cut
      One man cut his hand

In (4) the A argument, *nawiki* 'person' (in bold type), is marked with
-*ne* since this key participant of the story is contrasted to another key
participant—an evil spirit who kept coming and eating the fruit the
man was collecting.

(4) kiya-ku   hiniri   di-hwa-ka   di-ka
    strong-PERSISTENT ukukí.fruit   3sgnf-fall-SUB   3sgnf-see
      di-niwa   di-waketa
      3sgnf-collect   3sgnf-join+CAUS1−CAUS2
      di-yã-nhi-pidana   dihya   **nawiki-ne**
      3sgnf-stay-ANTERIOR-REM.P.REP   he   man-FOC.A/S
    The man (not anybody else) saw that the ukukí fruit was falling down
    a lot (and) was collecting them) (while the evil spirit was trying to
    steal the fruit)

The -*ne* marker on the subject often serves to disambiguate who said
what to whom, as a marker of turn-taking in longish series of dia-
logues (of the type: he$_i$ said, he$_j$ said, he$_i$ said). This is illustrated with
(5a–c). The subjects are in bold type.

(5a) di-wasa-hu   di-a   di-sape-pidana   **diha   ne:ri**
     3sgnf-jump-AWAY 3sgnf-go 3sgnf-speak-REM.P.REP **he   deer**
     He, the deer, jumped away and spoke

(5b) nuhua   wi:nu-ka   kwe-botha-ka   di-a
     I   hit.target-SUB what-COND-REC.P.VIS 3sgnf-go
      pi-na   di-a-pidana   **diha   nawiki-ne**
      2sg-OBJ   3sgnf-say-REM.P.REP **he   man-FOC.A/S**
     If I hit the target, what would happen, said **he, the man**

(5c) ikasu-botha-ka   pi-ñare   phia   di-a-pidana
     now-COND-REC.P.VIS   2sg-disappear you   3sgnf-say-REM.P.REP
      di-ha   ne:ri-ne
      he   deer-FOC.A/S
     Now you would have disappeared, said **he**, **the deer**

Any non-subject constituent which is a nominated discourse topic—
that is, what the sentence is about—or presents given rather than new
information, has to be marked with a clitic -*nuku* 'topical non-subject'
(see examples further on in this section). Non-subject constituents
can be in the function of O (direct object), recipient, addressee, or in
any oblique function (see below, and Aikhenvald 1994b). In addition,
-*nuku* is obligatory with definite referents (as in (8)).

There are different sets of case morphemes for nouns and for personal pronouns (which include first person, second person and impersonal pronouns and third person pronouns with animate referents).
These pronouns take the -*na* case marker for non-subject function. If
a personal pronoun with an animate referent is topical, it takes -*nuku*.
Table 11.1 shows the system of core case marking. The morphemes

Table 11.1. Grammatical relations and core cases in Tariana

Grammatical function	Discourse status	Nouns	Pronouns
subject (A/S)	non-focussed	-Ø	
	focussed	-ne	
non-subject (Non-A/S)	non-topical	-Ø	-na
	topical	-nuku	

used with nouns can also mark complement and subordinate clauses (which are nominalizations: see Aikhenvald 2003).

(6) illustrates a non-topical pronominal constituent in a non-subject function marked with the suffix -na.

(6) di-na   du-na   du-hĕ-ta-pidana
     3sgnf-OBJ   3sgf-OBJ   3sgf-see+CAUS1–CAUS2–REM.P.REP
     She showed her to him *or* She showed him to her

Non-topical non-pronominal constituents in a non-subject function are unmarked. The O ('canoe') in (7), from a story about a bride-price for women, refers to canoes in general; canoes are not what this story is about.

(7) ita-whya   naha   nheta   naka
     canoe-CL:CANOE   they   3pl+bring   3pl+arrive
     They bring canoes (as bride-price, among other things)

A pronominal, or a non-pronominal constituent in a non-subject function which is the topic of a narrative gets marked with a clitic -nuku. In (8) the addressee, 'women', is topical and definite; this example comes from a story about women who lost their hair.

(8) hĩ   tʃari   kadawa   di-mayè-na
     DEM:ANIM   man   Kadawa   3sgnf-lie+CAUS-REM.P.VIS
     hanupe   **ina-nuku**
     much   woman:PL-TOP.NON.A/S
     This man Kadawa lied a lot to these women

In (9), the pronominal addressee 'he', marked with -nuku, is highly topical: the story is about him.

(9) phia   hĩ   fiʒau   aros   di-a-pidana
     you   DEM:ANIM   beans   rice   3sgnf-say-REM.P.REP
     diha-nuku   pi-besita   pi-sue   puaya-mia
     he-TOP.NON.A/S   2sg-choose   2sg-stay+CAUS   separately-ONLY
     You, he (the chief) said to **him** (the protagonist of the story), separate
     and put these beans and rice apart

Table 11.1 shows that Tariana is basically nominative-accusative, with overt case-marking indicating the syntactic function of an argument the use of which is dependent on discourse properties of arguments.

A dependency between the occurrence of a case morpheme and the discourse status of its noun is well attested in the languages of the world—it is found, for instance, in Turkish (see Nilsson 1985), in Hebrew (see Kirtchuk 1993) and in the East Tucanoan languages spoken in the same area as Tariana (see Aikhenvald 1994b for an overview). It can be argued that the morpheme *-nuku* 'topical non-subject' in Tariana should be considered a topic marker used on non-subjects, and not a case marker (unlike, for instance, Turkish). The following arguments can be put forward against this. Firstly, *-nuku* is obligatory with definite referents. Second, if a pronominal constituent is topical—as in (9)— *-nuku* is the only overt marker of its syntactic function (Addressee), and, again, cannot be omitted.

There are also two oblique cases, locative and instrumental-comitative.[2] Table 11.2 shows oblique cases. While nouns distinguish two oblique cases, pronouns have only one.[3]

Table 11.2. Oblique cases in Tariana

Case	Nouns	Pronouns
Locative	*-se*	<doesn't exist>
Instrumental-comitative	*-ne*	*-ine*

---

[2] As I have shown elsewhere (Aikhenvald 1996), the case marking system in Tariana is most probably the result of an areal diffusion from the neighbouring East Tucano languages.

[3] For a detailed analysis of the semantics of locative and of instrumental-comitative see Aikhenvald (1994b, 2003).

The locative case marked on nouns with -*se* is illustrated in (10).

(10) na-pidana   uni-se
      3pl+go-REM.P.REP   water-LOC
      They went into water

The instrumental-comitative case, marked with -*ne* on nouns, is shown
in (11).

(11) ne   ita-whya-ne   di-uka   di-rahta
      then   canoe-CL:CANOE-INSTR   3sgnf-arrive   3sgnf-sail
      Then he arrived on a canoe

The instrumental-comitative case marker differs from the focussed
subject marker -*ne* in two ways. First, the focussed subject marker is
an enclitic (it receives a secondary stress), e.g. *nuhuá-nè* 'I-focussed',
while the instrumental-comitative is a suffix, and has no stress. Second,
the instrumental-comitative has two distinct forms—-*ne* with nouns
and -*ine* with pronouns, while the focussed subject marker has just
one form with both nouns and pronouns (see Tables 11.1 and 11.2).

The oblique case markers are not totally obligatory; they can be
omitted if understood from the context. In (12) the locative -*se* is
omitted since the locative meaning is clear from the context.

(12) ha-niri   **inipuku**   ka:-kali
      parent-MASC   garden   REL+go-PAST.PARTICIPLE
        di-dia-ka   di-nu-pidana
        3sgnf-return-SUB   3sgnf-come-REM.P.REP
      When the father who had gone to the garden came back…

In (13) the locative case marker is omitted from *Papuri* 'the Papuri
river' as from all place names which are inherently locational.[4] The
clitic -*nuku* marks this constituent since it is topical.

(13) papuri-nuku   na-wa   na:-pidana
      Papuri-TOP.NON.A/S   3pl-enter   3pl+go-REM.P.REP
      They (the Tariana forefathers) came onto the Papuri river

---

[4] Locative case can be used for clarification, even on an inherently locational
noun.

2. MULTIPLE MARKING

2.1. *Marking one syntactic function twice: oblique cases and* -nuku *'topical non-subject'*

A noun phrase can be marked with the instrumental case, or with the locative case, and receive an additional suffix -*nuku*, if it is topical; that is, if it satisfies the conditions for the use of -*nuku*. Thus, the same 'non-subject' syntactic function is marked with two morphemes: a 'specific' one showing a locative, or instrumental/comitative meaning, and a 'generic' one referring to the 'non-subjecthood' of the argument to be marked together with its discourse status.

(14) comes from a story about a shaman whose body was severely injured by another shaman (disguised as a jaguar) who takes his spirit away (so that the first shaman 'dies' with his spirit, before his body actually dies as well). The first shaman comes home and tells his grandchildren his body is also going to die (literally, he is going to die with his body). After that he does 'die with his body'. The word for 'body' takes instrumental case -*ne* and topical non-subject marker -*nuku* (in bold type), since it is the topic of a long stretch of the narrative.

(14) di-yāmi-kha   **ha-idaki-ne-nuku**
      3sgnf-die-AWAY   **DEM:INAN-CL:BODY-INSTR-TOP.NON.A/S**
      He died with his body

In (15) a hunter is talking about going back to his own house (marked with locative -*se*) the 'improvement' of which is what the story is about; since this locative constituent is topical, it receives -*nuku* following the locative case.

(15) nu-hña nu-dia   nhua **nu-ya-dapana-se-nuku**
      1sg-eat 1sg-return I   **1sg-POSS-CL:HABITAT-LOC-TOP.NON.A/S**
      I'll go back to eat (my catch) in my very house

In the instances described here, -*nuku* is used as a 'generic' marker of non-subject syntactic function for a topical argument, while the locative or the instrumental case indicates the 'specific' syntactic role of the oblique argument within the 'non-subject' domain. The two markers combine to indicate one syntactic function of a noun phrase within one clause. In contrast, in examples (8) and (9) above -*nuku* is the only means of indicating the non-subject syntactic function of a core argument.

2.2. *Double marking of syntactic function within clauses*

Double marking of syntactic function occurs when a core argument of a complement clause takes a case marker, and the complement clause also takes a case-marker for its syntactic function in a higher clause.

All complement and subordinate clauses in Tariana are nominalizations, and they can take case-markers.[5] Complement clauses occupy the O (direct object) slot, while subordinate clauses—marked with the subordinator -*ka* or with switch-reference sensitive sequencing enclitics, with meanings such as 'after', 'because', 'since'—occupy the oblique slot. Like any nominal or nominalization, a complement or a subordinate clause can be topical, and thus be marked with -*nuku* 'topical non-subject'.[6]

(16) illustrates a topical subordinate clause which takes -*nuku* clitic; it is topical because the action of putting a magic shirt on is what changes the whole course of the story. The subject (A) of this subordinate clause is marked with the focussed subject marker, clitic -*ne*, because the participants who are supposed to be watching are contrasted with other participants of the story. Square brackets indicate the scope of -*nuku* which is the whole clause.

(16) dihya   dhita   di-ña-pidana
      he   3sgnf+take   3sgnf-put.on-REM.P.REP
      [nha-ne   na-ka-ka]-nuku
      they-FOC.A/S   3pl-see-SUB-TOP.NON.A/S
      He (the man) took (the magic shirt) and put it on, while they (the girls,
      NOT anyone else) were looking

If the predicate of the topical subordinate or a complement clause is omitted (being retrievable from the context) and its A/S is contrastive, the A/S constituent can take focussed subject marker -*ne* followed by -*nuku*, thus creating the situation of double marking of syntactic function on one noun phrase. This is illustrated with (18). Square brackets indicate the scope of case marking. (18) is a continuation of (17); the

---

[5] This property is shared with the East Tucanoan languages (cf. the description of case-marked nominalised complement clauses in Tucano by Ramirez 1997).
[6] They cannot take oblique cases.

388   ALEXANDRA Y. AIKHENVALD

verb 'see' is omitted in (18) because it is easily retrievable from the
context.

(17)   [[diha-ne]   di-ka-ka-nuku]
       [[he-FOC.A/S]   3sgnf-see-SUB-TOP.NON.A/S]
          sidua-na-pidana
          arrow-CL:VERT-REM.P.REP
       For him (i.e. the evil spirit) (looking) it was an arrow

(18)   [[diha-ne]-nuku]   mawali-pidana
       [[he-FOC.A/S]-top.non.a/s]   snake-REM.P.REP
       For him (i.e. the man) (looking) it was a snake

Similarly, in (19), which describes 'eating', the omitted predicate of the
subordinate temporal clause is understood as the verb of eating. The
constituent marked for double syntactic function is in bold type, and
the square brackets indicate the scope of case marking.

(19)   di-a-pidana   yawi-nuku   iri-peri,
       3sgnf-give-REM.P.REP   jaguar-TOP.NON.A/S   red-COLL
          [[diha-ne]-nuku],   **[[ne:ri-ne]-nuku]**,
          he-FOC.A/S-TOP.NON.A/S   deer-FOC.A/S-TOP.NON.A/S
          hipole-peri-ne   di-dia-pidana
          green-COLL-INSTR   3sgnf-stay-REM.P.REP
       He (the deer) gave the red (ripe) ones (i.e. bananas) to the jaguar,
          when he (was eating), when the deer (was eating), he only got (lit.
          remained with) green ones

In (20), the predicate of the complement clause was omitted when
the clause was repeated. (20a) is the first occurrence, and (20b) is the
second one.

(20a) nha-ne   neka-ka-nuku   nu-ka-ka
       they-FOC.A/S   3pl+laugh-SUB-TOP.NON.A/S   1sg-see-REC.P.VIS
       I have seen them laugh

(20b) **nha-ne-nuku**   nu-ka-ka
       they-FOC.A/S-TOP.NON.A/S   1sg-see-REC.P.VIS
       I have seen them (do something, that is, laugh)

One noun phrase in (18), (19) and (20b) takes the marking for two
distinct syntactic functions in two clauses, one embedded within the
other. This multiple-layered marking of syntactic function is quite
different from having two morphemes indicating the same function
illustrated in §2.1.

2.3. *Multiple agreement within a noun phrase*

Double marking of syntactic function within a noun phrase in Tariana consists in marking agreement more than once, with different 'heads', one embedded within the other.

Tariana has an extensive system of noun classes and classifiers (Aikhenvald 1994b, and 2000b, 2003). Noun class markers can be used on any word in a modifier function to mark agreement with the head noun. In (21) a noun class marker is used on the adjective 'good'.

(21) pani-si   mača-dapana
      house-NPOSS   good-CL:HABITAT
      a good house

In (22), the noun class marker *-puna* 'stretch' is used on a connective *kayi* 'like, thus' and on the demonstrative (in bold type),

(22) di-a-pidana   di-musu-kha   di-a
      3sgnf-go-REM.P.REP   3sgnf-go.out-AWAY   3sgnf-go
      ha-puna   i-thirikuna   **kayi-puna**
      DEM:INAN-CL:STRETCH   INDEF-near   like-CL:STRETCH
      i-thirikuna-nuku
      INDEF-near-TOP.NON.A/S
      He came out near this (stretch of road), near something (which looked) like a road

If a noun phrase is used as a modifier to a noun, a noun class marker is attached to the last word of the noun phrase to mark agreement with the head noun. In (23), the possessive noun phrase 'medicine for diarrhoea' (in square brackets) is used to modify the head noun, 'chestnut tree'. The classifier *-na* 'VERTICAL', which marks the agreement with the head noun, 'tree', is attached to the end of the modifying noun phrase.

(23) pui-na   [tsuli   i-tape]-na
      chestnut.tree-CL:VERT [diarroea   INDEF-MEDICINE]-CL:VERT
      chestnut tree, (which is) a medicine against diarrhoea

If the last noun of a modifying noun phrase already contains a noun class marker to agree with its own head, the noun class marker which marks agreement with the head of the embedding noun phrase will simply follow it. In (24) the modifier within the modifying noun phrase, 'flowering' in 'flowering like a curved vine', contains the noun class agreement marker -*kha* 'CL:CURVED'. This modifier also takes the noun class agreement marker -*na* 'CL:VERTICAL', to agree with the head of the embedding noun phrase, *heku-na* (tree-CL:VERTICAL) 'tree'.[7] The modifying noun phrase is in square brackets.

(24) heku-na   [bebi-kha   kayu kewi-kha]-na
      tree-CL:VERT [vine-CL:CURVED like   REL+flower-CL:CURVED]-CL:VERT
      a tree flowering like a curved vine

This stacking of classifier agreement usually involves only two 'levels', as in (24). More complicated structures, such as (25), are rare. In (25), the noun phrase of (24) is a modifier to the head, 'leaf', and it takes the appropriate noun class agreement marker -*phe* 'CL:LEAF.LIKE'.

(25) pana-phe   [heku-na   [bebi-kha   kayu
      leaf-CL:LEAF.LIKE [tree-CL:VERT [vine-CL:CURVED   like
        kewi-kha]-na]-phe
        REL+flower-CL:CURVED]-CL:VERT]-CL:LEAF.LIKE
      a leaf of a tree flowering like a curved vine

Thus, agreement in noun class is marked twice in (24), and three times in (25). It reflects agreement 'on different levels': that with the head of embedded noun phrase(s), and that with the head of the 'embedding' noun phrase of a higher level.

3. DISCUSSION

I have shown that Tariana has two distinct phenomena whereby morphemes of the same class cooccur. One is marking more than one syntactic function of one noun phrase. This covers

---

[7] Noun class markers also appear on the head nouns, as derivational suffixes: see Aikhenvald (1994a). As mentioned in §1, adjectives share most categories with nouns; one of the differences between the two lies in the function of noun class markers. When used on nouns, they are similar to derivational suffixes, and when used on adjectives, they mark agreement with the head noun (cf. discussion of similar 'double' derivational and inflectional functions of classifiers in Yagua by Payne 1990c).

(a) marking two clausal functions of a constituent: the function it has within a lower (embedded) clause and the function of the lower clause within a higher (embedding) clause;

(b) marking two (or more) functions within a noun phrase: if a noun phrase contains another noun phrase (consisting of a head and a modifier) as a modifier, the agreement in noun class with both heads gets marked on a modifier in the end of the modifying noun phrase: there is agreement with the head of the embedded noun phrase, and also with the head of the 'embedding' noun phrase.

The other phenomenon involves combining two morphemes to refer to the same syntactic function of a noun phrase: one, a locative or an instrumental-comitative case marker, provides a specific meaning, while the other, -*nuku* 'topical non-subject', indicates the generic 'non-subjecthood' combined with the indication of the discourse status of the noun phrase.

The principle of 'double' marking of syntactic function—that within a lower clause, and that within a higher clause,—is similar to the 'multiple-layered' case marking in Australian languages described by Dench and Evans (1988). However, in Australian languages such as Kayardild, Martuthunira and Panyjima noun phrases regularly receive multiple inflection. That is, the case suffixes 'code recursive dependencies: case values can be percolated down from main clause to subordinate clause' (Dench and Evans 1988: 44). In contrast, multiple inflection of a noun phrase in Tariana —whereby structural positions 14 and 15 in Diagram 11.1 are filled simultaneously—is the result of ellipsis of the predicate of a nominalised clause.

The double marking of syntactic function within a noun phrase has surface similarities to the stacking of adnominal cases in Australian languages. Cf. (26), from Martuthunira (Dench and Evans 1988: 6):

(26) kapunmarni-marta   jirli-wirriwa-marta
      shirt-PROPRIETIVE   arm-PRIVATIVE-PROPRIETIVE
      having a shirt without sleeves

Adnominal cases in Australian languages—such as genitive, privative, proprietive ('having')—relate two nominals within a NP. However, this case stacking is totally different from the 'double agreement' in Tariana discussed in §2.3.

Double marking of agreement with heads of different levels is highly unusual from a cross-linguistic perspective. It may be useful to compare double marking of noun class in Tariana with other instances of 'double' marking of noun class across the world (see further details in Aikhenvald 2000b).

The so-called 'preprefixation' found in marking overt noun class and noun agreement in some Bantu languages creates a 'double marking' of noun class. For instance, in Nyanja, a Bantu language of Malawi, some nouns have an archaic noun class prefix as a part of their form, and take a different noun class prefix as a productive mechanism. A few adjectives copy both prefixes (Stump 1993: 176).[8]

(27) ka-n-khuku   ka-ka-kulu
      CL12-CL9-chicken   QUAL12-CONC12-large
      a large chicken

However, this is different from Tariana which displays a 'multiple layer' agreement with multiple head: in Nyanja agreement is with one head, but it gets marked twice.

Some Australian languages have a different kind of double-marking of a noun class. It is restricted to the noun class marking of inalienably possessed nouns in possessive constructions. For instance, in Nungali possessed body parts take two prefixes: one noun class prefix—which comes closer to the root—reflects the noun class of the possessor, while the other prefix—which precedes the first one—corresponds to the noun class of the possessed noun itself. In (28) (Evans 1994: 3; Bolt, Hoddinott and Kofod 1971: 70) the possessed noun 'ear' has two noun class prefixes: the Class IV prefix marks its inherent class and the Class I prefix marks agreement with the possessor, 'man'.

(28) ni-ya-manga   d-uŋunin
      CLIV:NEUT-CL1:MASC-ear   CL1:MASC:ABS-man
      the man's ear

Unlike Tariana, semantic restrictions on cooccurrence of noun class prefixes with possessed body parts which take double noun class mark-

---

[8] One is labelled qualifying (restricted to head-modifier agreement), and the other concordial (also used in verb-argument agreement).

ing in Nungali are linked to the semantics of possessive constructions. Unlike Tariana, there is no simultaneous agreement with two heads.

We conclude that the multiple-layered agreement in Tariana noun phrases is unique—at least, in terms of our knowledge of the languages of the world at this point in time.

The principle of 'double' marking of syntactic function—that within a lower clause, or an embedded noun phrase, and that within a higher clause, or an embedding noun phrase—appears to apply consistently in Tariana. The 'multiple-layered' marking of syntactic function and of agreement demonstrates the inflectional complexity of noun phrases in Tariana, which mirrors syntactic structure in morphological structure and allows inflections (both case markers and noun class agreement markers) to specify their syntactic environments simultaneously at different levels. A number of recent studies have argued against a strict separation of the syntactic and morphological components of the grammar (cf. Baker 1985, 1995, Corbett 1987, Anderson 1992, and many others). The phenomena described for Tariana provide further justification for this line of argument.

CHAPTER TWELVE

PALIKUR AND THE TYPOLOGY OF CLASSIFIERS

Alexandra Y. Aikhenvald and Diana Green

This chapter describes an unusual and complicated system of genders and classifiers in Palikur (North Arawak, Brazil and French Guiana). It has three genders (masculine, feminine and neuter); gender assignment is based on a combination of semantic features (humanness, animacy, size and shape). There are two or three gender choices depending on construction type. There are also five distinct types of classifiers: numeral classifiers; verbal classifiers (with two subsets—those occurring on stative verbs, which are frequently used as modifiers in NPs, and those occurring on transitive verbs); locative classifiers (used as adpositions), and possessive classifiers (i.e. generic nouns used in possessive constructions with some alienably possessed nouns). Different noun classification devices have different functions and scopes; all except possessive classifiers overlap in their semantics. Classifiers provide cross-categorization of nouns and help the language to structure concepts. Throughout the chapter, the types of genders and classifiers in Palikur are placed in typological perspective.

1. Introduction

Amazonian languages are known for their complicated and unusual systems of noun classification devices. Often, there is more than one type of classifier combined with genders (for examples of some of these systems see Derbyshire and Payne 1990; Aikhenvald 1994a, and Aikhenvald 2000b). The same morphemes may be used in several classifier functions, and sometimes there are up to five or six different sets of noun classification devices.

These languages are important from the point of view of a broad typological perspective on classifiers. Many questions need to be addressed. How many different kinds of classifiers can cooccur in one language? What are their functions, and semantics? How do they interact? Are they obligatory? Are the same, or different morphemes used in different functions? These, and other questions can only be answered after a close look at the complex classifier systems of individual Amazonian languages which is what this chapter aims to do.

Here we propose to describe one of the world's richest systems of noun classification devices—that found in the Palikur language of Brazil.[1] This highly unusual system has five kinds of classifiers, which coexist with two sets of genders. Genders and classifiers can cooccur within one grammatical word—though agreement in gender, and in classifiers, follow different principles. We will then look at how different noun classification devices interact in one language with respect to their functional properties, semantics and origin.

The chapter is organized as follows. A brief sketch of the typological framework used for our analysis of noun classification devices is given in §2. The next five sections describe Palikur. Gender assignment and the principles of gender agreement are considered in §3. Numeral classifiers are analyzed in §4. Verbal classifiers and their use with transitive and with stative verbs are considered in §5. An unusual type of classifier found on locative adpositions is described in §6. Finally, classifiers used to characterize the possessed noun in a possessive noun phrase are described in §7. We evaluate the properties of classifiers and genders in Palikur, in a typological perspective, in the last section of the chapter.

2. NOUN CLASSIFICATION DEVICES

2.1. *Outline of a typology*

Almost all languages have some grammatical means for the linguistic categorization of nouns and nominals. The term 'classifiers' will be used here as an 'umbrella' label for the continuum of noun categorization devices.

---

[1] Palikur is a North Arawak language spoken by over a thousand people in northern Brazil (state of Amapá) and in French Guiana. We would like to express gratitude to our many Palikur friends who provided texts on which this study is based and who patiently answered our many questions, especially Raimunda Ioio. We owe thanks to R.M.W. Dixon, Des Derbyshire and David Payne for comments and discussion, and to Suzanne Kite for technical assistance. This chapter was based upon thirty years of linguistic and translation programs for Palikur people by Diana and Harold Green. The analysis and write-up is the joint work of the two authors.

The term 'classifier systems' is used to denote a continuum of methods of noun categorization. Well-known systems, such as the lexical numeral classifiers of South-East Asia, on the one hand, and the highly grammaticalized gender agreement classes of Indo-European languages, on the other, are the extremes of this continuum. They can have a similar semantic basis; and one can develop from the other.

During the last two decades, there have been a number of proposals for a semantic and grammatical typology of noun classifying systems (e.g. Denny 1976; Allan 1977; Dixon 1982, 1986; Craig 1986a, b, 1992). Recently the typological parameters of classifiers and other agreement categories have had to be revised in the light of new data, especially those from previously undescribed South American Indian languages (e.g. Derbyshire and Payne 1990; Craig 1992; Corbett 1991).

Classifiers and noun classification systems have, for a long time, been a particular focus of interest in functional typology. They provide a unique insight into how people categorize the world through their language. The study of classifiers and noun classification systems is intrinsically connected with a great many issues which are crucial in modern linguistics, such as agreement; processes in language development and obsolescence; the distinction between inflection and derivation; and types of possessive constructions.

The typology of noun classification devices given below is based on different morpho-syntactic contexts specific for each type.[2]

- Some languages have grammatical agreement classes, based on such core semantic characteristics as animacy, sex, or humanness. They are called *noun classes, or genders*. The number of noun classes varies—from two, as in Portuguese or French, or three, as in Palikur (see §3), to ten, as in Bantu, or even to several dozen, as in some North Arawak languages of South America (Aikhenvald 1994a, 1996). Noun classes, or genders, can be more or less semantically transparent, and their assignment can be based on semantic, morphological and/or phonological criteria.
- Some languages have special morphemes which occur affixed to a numeral, or a quantifier. They categorize the noun in terms of its

---

[2] These types also correlate with the morphological status of each morpheme, their semantics, origin, grammaticalization pattern, and whatever other grammatical and discourse categories they interact with. Issues concerning further rationale for this typology of classifiers are approached in Aikhenvald (2000b).

animacy, shape, dimensionality, arrangement and other properties. These are *numeral classifiers* (see Craig 1992). Numeral classifiers are relatively frequent in isolating languages of Southeast Asia, and in North Amazonian languages of South America.

- *Noun classifiers* categorize the referent noun with which they cooccur. The semantic relationship between the classifier and the noun is generic-specific, e.g. Yidiñ, an Australian language (Dixon 1982: 192ff) *bama waguja* (person man) 'a man'. These can be independent lexemes as above, or they can appear as affixes on a noun. They are typically found in Australian, Austronesian, Mayan and a few South American languages (see Aikhenvald 2000b; Sands 1995).
- A special morpheme in a possessive construction can characterize the way the possessed noun relates to the possessor. This is illustrated below, with examples from Fijian, an Austronesian language (Lichtenberk 1983: 157–8). Such morphemes, in bold type in (1) and (2), are called *relational classifiers*. Relational classifiers are found in Oceanic languages, and in a few South American languages—see Aikhenvald (1994a).

(1) na   me-**qu**   yaqona
    ARTICLE   CL:DRINKABLE-my   kava
    my kava (which I intend to drink)

(2) na   no-**qu**   yaqona
    ARTICLE   CL:GENERAL-my   kava
    my kava (that I grew, or that I will sell)

There may be a special morpheme which characterizes a possessed noun in a possessive construction, as in (3), from Tariana, a South American language from the Arawak family. This is a *possessive classifier*.

(3) tsinu   nu-ite
    dog   1sg-CL:ANIMATE
    my dog

Possessive classifiers may also be generic nouns (with possessive affixes attached to them).[3] They are obligatory with certain nouns which can not take possessive affixes; these often include fruit, plants, or animals.

---

[3] Classifier constructions of this type are reminiscent of the generic-specific relationship between a noun classifier and a noun, as exemplified by Yidiñ above.

This is illustrated with (4), from Apalai, a Carib language from Northern South America (Koehn and Koehn 1986: 85–6; see also Carlson and Payne 1989).

(4) a-napy-ry   paruru
     2sg-POSS CL:FRUIT-POSS   banana
     your banana (lit. your fruit: banana)

Classifiers in possessive constructions are often employed only with alienably possessed nouns, but this is not necessarily so.[4] In very few languages, special morphemes characterize the possessor; these are *possessor classifiers*.

- *Verbal classifiers* are affixed to the verb, or incorporated into the verb; they categorize a noun, which is typically in S/O function, in terms of its shape, consistency, and animacy. Example (5) from Waris, a Papuan language (Brown 1981: 96) shows how the classifier *-put-* 'round objects' is used with the verb 'get' to characterize its O argument, 'coconut'. Verbal classifiers may occur before the verb root, as in (5). In other languages they follow a verb root (see Aikhenvald 1994a: 426, and §5).

(5) sa   ka-m   put-ra-ho-o
     coconut   1sg-to   V.CL:ROUND-get-BENEFACTIVE-IMPERATIVE
     Give me a coconut (lit. coconut to-me round one-give)

These are found in a number of North American Indian languages (such as Athapascan), northern Australian languages of Arnhem Land (Sands 1995), some Papuan languages and a number of South American Indian languages. The use of verbal classifiers may correlate with classificatory noun incorporation as a marker of verb-argument agreement (cf. Mithun 1984: type IV).

There are two further, rarer kinds of classifiers.

- *Locative classifiers* occur on locative adpositions, or adverbs, and characterize the head noun in terms of its animacy or shape.[5] So far

---

[4] Contrary to Carlson and Payne (1989). For an example, see Aikhenvald (1994a).
[5] The existence of this type was suggested by Allan (1977); and later questioned by Croft (1994) who did not have access to the South American languages discussed here.

these have only been found in a limited number of South American languages. The data of Palikur are crucial in arguing for this type as a separate classifier type—see §6 below.

- Another rare type of classifiers are *deictic classifiers* which occur with deictic markers such as demonstratives and articles. They are found in a few South American and North American Indian languages (e.g. Siouan: Barron and Serzisko 1982), and possibly in Teop (an Austronesian language from Bougainville: Mosel and Spriggs (1992)); more argumentation in favour of these as a separate type is given in Aikhenvald (2000b).

A number of the general statements which have been made in the past about different types of classifiers have since been shown to be incorrect. Some of the previously accepted universals and general tendencies do not hold any more. For example, Dixon (1982: 220) said that languages can not have classifiers and gender as separate categories, and that 'no example is known of a language with two distinct systems of noun classes' (also see Craig 1986a, b). Recent work on South American and Papuan languages shows that classifiers and genders do in fact cooccur, and that languages can have more than one distinct system of classifiers which coexist with more than one complicated and semantically non-transparent gender system. Palikur, a North Arawak language of Brazil, is an extreme example of such a language.

2.2. *Coexistence of different classifier types in one language*

There are two ways in which different types of noun classification devices can coexist in one language.

- (A) One set of morphemes is used in different classifier functions. Systems of this kind are attested in South American, Papuan and Austronesian languages. See Aikhenvald (1994a), Senft (1996), and Onishi (1994).
- (B) There are several different sets of morphemes used in different classifier functions (as outlined in §2.1).These may partly overlap in form and/or semantics. They may differ in the conditions of their use; that is, whether they are obligatory or not. Sometimes, their semantics is the same, but the form is different; sometimes it is the other way around.

In this chapter we will investigate Palikur[6] which has an ample array of distinct types of classifiers. It is one of the richest noun classification systems yet described in terms of how many distinct types of classifiers it possesses.

Palikur has a system of genders (two, or three, depending on the type of construction). There are also five more types of classifiers:

- numeral classifiers;
- verbal classifiers with two subsets:
  —those occurring on stative verbs frequently used as modifiers in NPs;
  —those occurring on transitive verbs;
- locative classifiers;
- possessive classifiers, i.e. generic nouns used in possessive constructions with some alienably possessed nouns.

Different grammatical systems of agreement based on different semantic parameters coexist in quite a few languages of the world. Most frequently, there are two (or, in rarer cases, more) concordial systems either for different classes of grammatical units, or for different classes of units and different types of agreement—such as verb-argument and head-modifier agreement (for a useful discussion of differences between these two agreement types see Anderson 1992: 106). In a number of South American and Australian languages, there is a small set of sex-based and animacy-based genders realized in verb-argument constructions. A larger set of animacy and shape-based noun classes is used in head-modifier agreement (Aikhenvald 1994a: 415–6).[7] Systems of these two kinds were called 'split agreement' systems in Aikhenvald (1994a: 415–9).

---

[6] Some important typological characteristics of Palikur are summarized in Appendix 1. An early and tentative statement of the basic grammar of Palikur can be found in Green and Green (1972).

[7] Another possibility is for two agreement systems to be used at the same time with the same class of grammatical units. There are usually different agreement types or at least different rules of agreement (as in Paumarí, an Arawá language from Brazil; see brief discussion in Aikhenvald 1994a: 417, and Aikhenvald 1999 and 2009e). Few languages allow 'double' marking of genders (or noun classes) and classifiers in the same morpho-syntactic environment. A few examples of this are discussed in Aikhenvald (1994a: 417–8).

Palikur is another example of a language of this kind. Palikur uses different set of gender distinctions (two or three) depending on types of agreement and the element on which the agreement is marked (known as the 'target' of agreement: see Corbett 1991: 189ff). There is a general tendency to have more gender-like distinctions with personal pronouns, cross-referencing elements, or sometimes demonstratives, and fewer in other contexts. This is also the case in Palikur—see §3 and §8.

3. GENDER IN PALIKUR

Gender forms in Palikur are briefly characterized in §3.1. Gender assignment is described in §3.2, and gender agreement in §3.3. Unusual typological properties of Palikur genders are outlined in §3.4.

3.1. *Gender forms*

Gender in Palikur is realized through agreement of the head-modifier kind, and of the predicate-argument kind. Typically for an Amazonian language, gender is usually not marked on the head noun itself.[8] Gender agreement is obligatory and every noun has fixed gender.[9]

Three gender agreement forms (masculine, feminine and neuter) are found in head-modifier constructions on demonstratives (see Table 12.1); they are also found in predicate-argument constructions on third person cross-referencing affixes and independent pronouns (see Appendix 2). See §3.3.1.

Two gender agreement forms (feminine, and masculine-neuter or non-feminine) are found with a number of verbal 'gender-sensitive' suffixes in predicate-argument agreement with the subject (A/S) and head-modifier agreement if a modifier is a stative verb. Palikur has

---

[8] There are just a few agent nominalizations which distinguish masculine and feminine gender, e.g. *amepi-yo* 'thief (woman)', *amepi-ye* 'thief (man)'. There are also elements of men's and women's speech, e.g. *ahadje* 'men's response: I am going', *ye* 'women's response' (also characterized by higher pitch). These phenomena are excluded from our discussion here.

[9] There is one word which has double gender (in the sense of Corbett 1991: 67). *Bakimni* 'child' is usually assigned to feminine gender when the sex is not known. If the referent is specific and the sex is known, then it triggers feminine, or masculine agreement, e.g. *ig bakimni gi-mana* (this:m child 3sg m-food) 'this (male) child's food'.

no special morphological class of adjectives; stative verbs are used as modifiers. See §3.3.2.

3.2. *Gender assignment*

Gender assignment principles are mixed semantic and phonological (cf. Corbett 1991). *Semantic* principles of assignment are not totally transparent (see Figure 12.1). The main semantic division which governs gender assignment is ANIMACY.

ANIMATE nouns divide into HUMAN and NON-HUMAN. Gender assignment of human nouns is governed by sex: males are masculine, and females are feminine. Heavenly bodies (sun, moon, stars, planets), thunder and lightning belong to masculine gender, because according to traditional legends they were once men.

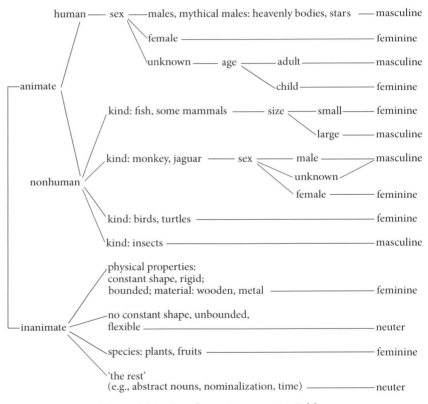

Figure 12.1. Gender assignment in Palikur

Gender assignment of non-human nouns is determined by their nature:

- Certain kinds of animate beings—e.g. birds, turtles and butterflies—are feminine.
- Sex of species determines gender choice for some large animals, e.g. monkeys, dogs and jaguars: males are masculine and females are feminine. If sex is unknown, masculine gender is used.
- Size of species determines gender choice for fish and some animals:[10] small ones tend to be feminine, and large ones tend to be masculine, e.g. *tamanwa* 'anteater' (from Portuguese *tamandoa*) is masculine, and a smaller animal, *tat* 'armadillo' (from Portuguese *tatú*) is feminine.

Gender assignment to non-human animates can also depend on their value and on speakers' attitude. Feminine gender assignment is associated with positive value, while masculine gender goes together with negative feelings. The rat is a small animal; however, it is assigned masculine gender because it is looked upon as dirty and bad. But a cute little baby rat would be referred to as feminine. Along similar lines, turtles are usually feminine; but a turtle which is a nuisance and has to be got rid of would be referred to as masculine. One of our consultants explained that all insects are masculine in spite of their small size 'because none of them are any good for food' and all they do is bother people, eat crops and cause sickness.

If the sex of a person is unknown, masculine gender is used for an adult, and feminine for a child. The term for 'person', *hiyeg*, is always masculine. A mixed group is masculine unless it is specified that a woman is among them in which case the group is referred to as feminine. For instance, a married couple is always referred to as *eg-kis* 'she-pl'. Consequently, neither masculine nor feminine gender can be considered functionally unmarked (for markedness in gender see Alpher 1987; Aikhenvald 2000b).

A large proportion of nouns with inanimate referents—including natural phenomena, abstract nouns and nominalizations—are assigned to neuter gender, e.g. *ahin* 'path', *arikna* 'thing', *abektey* 'example',

---

[10] For instance, large carrion-eating birds are masculine.

barewka 'beauty'. Words which refer to time are also neuter, e.g. *hawkri* 'day', *paka* 'week'. All plants and fruits are feminine.

Gender assignment of other inanimate nouns is partially based on SHAPE, CONSISTENCY and MATERIAL.

- Nouns which refer to objects with CONSTANT SHAPE, and which are RIGID and BOUNDED, are feminine. Consequently, all round, square, concave objects with a fixed shape are feminine, e.g. *umuh* 'canoe', *tumawi* 'cuya: an indigenous cup'. So are objects made of wood and metal, e.g. *nosuwyeg* 'a metal pan', *tip* 'rock', and *kasivag* 'machete'. Natural phenomena which are considered to have a definite height and depth and boundaries are feminine—river, waterfall, fire, waves and tornados.
- Nouns which refer to FLEXIBLE, UNBOUNDED objects without CONSTANT SHAPE are neuter, e.g. *kwak* 'manioc meal', *ah* 'wood', *un* 'water, liquid', *payt* 'leaf roof; house', *panye* 'basket'.

The following 'minimal pairs' illustrate this principle. *Parakwam* is neuter if it means 'clay' and feminine if it means 'ceramic piece, pot'; *ah* is neuter if it means 'wood' and feminine if it means 'tree'. A natural star is masculine, while a metal star is feminine, and a paper star or a star drawn on paper is neuter.

The following phonological principles of gender assignment are also at work. These principles are important for gender assignment of loans from French-based creole and Portuguese. The gender of the source language is usually overridden by these phonological principles. Masculine human nouns usually end in *-e* or *-i*. Neuter nouns can end in any vowel or consonant. Loan nouns which end in *-o* or *-u* are usually feminine in gender, e.g. *marto* 'hammer' (from French Creole *marto*), *sitru* 'lemon' (from French Creole *citrō*), *tattu* 'armadillo' (variant of *tat*; from Portuguese masculine *tatu*).[11] Nouns which end in *-a* or *-i* are usually given neuter gender, e.g. *karta* 'paper' (from

---

[11] There may be an historical explanation for this phonological principle of gender assignment. Proto-Arawak had a feminine (non-masculine) affix *-u/o* which is still preserved in the form of Palikur gender-sensitive suffixes (Table 12.3), and in some lexical items, e.g. *tino* 'woman', cf. Proto-Arawak *čina-ru* 'woman' (Payne 1991: 426).

Portuguese feminine *carta*); *kamisa* 'cloth; shirt' (from Portuguese feminine *camisa*); *simis* 'shirt' (from French *chemise*).[12]

Neuter agreement forms are often used with inanimate nouns independently of their gender. This has been observed in texts (e.g. (10) below) and among younger speakers.[13] This reflects a synchronic tendency to make gender assignment more semantically motivated.

3.3. *Gender agreement*

3.3.1. *Three agreement forms*
Three gender agreement forms are found in head-modifiers NPs with demonstratives as modifiers; see Table 12.1. Other modifiers (quantifiers, indefinites and interrogatives) have no gender agreement (Green and Green 1972: 64). Gender agreement with demonstratives is illustrated in (6)–(8).

(6)	ner	awayg	this man[14]
	this:M	man	
(7)	no	tino	this woman
	this:F	woman	
(8)	ini	ahin	this path
	this:N	path	

Table 12.1. Demonstratives in Palikur (singular)

	in speaker's hand	near to speaker and to hearer	far from speaker and near hearer or vice versa	far from both, visible	very far from both, not visible
masc	*ner*	*ner*	*nop*	*netra*	*nere*
fem	*no*	*no*	*nop*	*notra*	*nore*
neut	*inin*	*ini*	*nop*	*inetra*	*inere*

---

[12] However, semantics overrides phonology. *Nawiy* 'boat' (from Portuguese masculine *navio*) could be expected to be neuter, but is in fact feminine—as a metal object with constant shape.

[13] A fifteen-year old girl monolingual in Palikur spontaneously assigned neuter gender to feminine *suyeg* '(black) metal pan', and to masculine *warapyu* 'little star'; she then corrected herself.

[14] Examples are given in an underlying form, to avoid the complications of phonological changes.

In predicate-argument constructions, third person cross-referencing affixes and independent pronouns have three gender agreement forms as given in Table 12.2. See discussion of different cross-referencing markers in Appendixes 1 and 2.

Gender agreement with the subject, with possessor—as in (9)—, or the argument of an adposition is also obligatory.

(9) ig   Karumaya   ig   Uhokri   gi-wat-ni
     3m   Karumaya   3m   God   3sgm-sent.one-POSS
     This (man) Karumaya was the God's messenger

Neuter cross-referencing is commonly used in texts to mark agreement with an inanimate head noun. In (10), the agreement with the demonstrative modifier is feminine; the agreement with the cross-referencing possessor is neuter.

(10) eg   gi-waw-ni   nawene-wa   a-humwa-ni
     this:f   3sgm-rattle-POSS   different:nf-EMPH   3sgn-form-POSS
     This (feminine) rattle of his had a different form

3.3.2. *Two gender agreement forms*

On verbs, gender agreement appears on a number of suffixes (given in Table 12.3). These suffixes distinguish two agreement forms—one for masculine and neuter (non-feminine), and one for feminine. For a few individual lexical items gender agreement is realized via internal vowel change (*o* 'feminine'; *e, a* 'masculine/neuter').

Table 12.2. Cross-referencing affixes and independent pronouns

	prefixes	suffixes	independent pronouns
1sg	*nu-*	*-un*	*nah*
2sg	*pi-*	*-pi/ep*	*pis*
1pl	*u-*	*-u/wi*	*wis*
2pl	*yi-*	*-yi/ey*	*yis*
3 m	*gi-*	*-gi/ig*	*ig*
3 f	*gu-*	*-gu/ig*	*eg*
3 n (see Appendix 2)	*a-, ga-, ni-*	*-ni/in*	*in*

Table 12.3. Gender marking on verbs in Palikur

	masculine/neuter (nf)	feminine (f)
Continuative	-ne	-no
Continuative prolonged	-nene	-nano
Non-completed frustrated action	-pa-ri	pa-ru
Inchoative	-pi-ye	-pi-yo
Durative	-ye	-yo
Individual lexical items	miyap 'he/it dies'[15]	miyop 'she dies'
	nemnik 'approach'	nomnik 'approach'
	nawene-wa 'different'	naweno-wa 'different'

This type of gender agreement is obligatory in predicate-argument constructions and is always with A/S (subject). (11) illustrates gender agreement with the subject marked on the continuative suffix.[16]

---

[15] Feminine and non-feminine genders are distinguished in a nominalization of the verb 'die': gi-mire-mni 'his/its death'; gu-miro-mni 'her death'. This nominalization contains a gender-sensitive nominalizer of a Proto-Arawak origin: -re (non-feminine), -ro (feminine).

[16] The gender-sensitive suffixes are not used in negative clauses in Palikur. This means that there are fewer aspect choices in negative clauses than in positive ones. Consider the following examples. Gender agreement is marked on the durative suffix which is typically used with stative verbs (i). In (ii), it is suppressed.

(i) tino   barew-yo
     woman   be pretty/clean-DURf
     The woman is pretty
(ii) tino   ka-barew
     woman   NEG-be pretty/clean
     The woman is not pretty

However, gender agreement is obligatory in negative clauses with emphatic contrastive negation (marked by both negative prefix ka- and a negative suffix -ma), as illustrated in (iii).

(iii) tino   ka-barew-yo-ma
      woman   NEG-be pretty/clean-DURf-NEG
      The woman is not pretty at all

There are a few more limitations on gender agreement. These are linked to the choice of the aspectual form of a verb. There are a few stative verbs which are idiosyncratic in that they do not combine with either durative or continuative. Such are pohe 'black' and kisepehe 'cold, tasteless'. Other stative verbs which refer to colours or physical properties do not have this idiosyncrasy. Sometimes the non-occurrence of a stative verb with a gender-sensitive suffix may be due to phonological restrictions. For instance, hiwiye 'shiny' does not take durative -ye/-yo, probably because ye is a part of its stem (masc. huwi-ye, fem. huwi-yo).

(11) gi-waw-ni   eg-yer-wa   waw
      3sgm-rattle-POSS   3sgf-true-EMPH   rattle
          waymaviya-no   eg
          underworld+PERT-CONTf   3f
      His rattle (feminine) was a true underworld one

Gender agreement of animate nouns with a stative verb as a modifier
in a noun phrase is illustrated in (12) and (13). Agreeing forms are in
bold type.

(12) **barew-yo**   tino
      be pretty/clean-DURf   woman
      a pretty woman

(13) eg   ipeg-pita   hiyeg   **barew-ye**
      3f   look-V.CL:IRREG   person   **beautiful-DURnf**
      She looked a beautiful person all over

Gender agreement with an animate noun (*hiyeg* 'person) on the verb
(*miyap* 'he dies') and with an inanimate noun (*yuwit* 'word') on *barew-
ye* 'beautiful-durative non-feminine', a stative verb in a modifier function, is shown in (14).

(14) kuri   a-pit   hiyeg   **miyap**   ig-kis   awna
      now   3sgn-before   person   **die:3sgnf**   3m-PL   speak
          barew-ye-nen   yuwit   ku   pariye   pes
          beautiful-DURnf-ONLY   word   SUB   that   come out
      Now before a person dies they speak beautiful words that come out

3.4. *Typological properties of Palikur genders*

Palikur has a gender system with two or three agreement forms
depending on the type of construction, and the type of agreement.
More agreement forms are distinguished in demonstratives and personal pronouns than in gender-sensitive verbal affixes, thus creating
a peculiar and typologically quite unusual 'split' system of gender
marking (i.e. different forms and categories for different construction
types). However, if viewed in a broad typological perspective, this system is not so peculiar. There is an almost universal tendency to distinguish more gender agreement forms with third person pronouns and/
or with deictics than with modifiers from open classes.

In many languages of the world a gender opposition is found only in
personal pronouns (e.g. English; Kaingang, a Jê language from South

Brazil; Rikbaktsa, a Macro-Jê language from Central Brazil; Kakua, a Makú language from Colombia—see Aikhenvald 2000b; numerous languages from south-east and east-central Australia, e.g. Diyari, Pitta-Pitta, Yandruwanhtha, Wangkumara, Galali, Awabakal, and Gadjang—Dixon 2002). In other languages, such as Dyirbal, an Australian language from North Queensland, noun classes are restricted to deictic markers. Waurá and Yawalapiti, two Xinguan Arawak languages from Brazil, from the same family as Palikur, distinguish masculine and feminine genders only in deictics which are also used in the function of third person pronouns (Aikhenvald 1996: 165–7).[17]

As seen in §3.2, gender assignment in Palikur is semantically complex. It is sex-based for humans; for other animates it is based on species, size and sex. For inanimates, it is based on a combination of physical properties—consistency, boundedness and shape, or form (see Figure 12.1). Neuter has some properties of a residue class (abstract nouns and nominalizations, non-classifiable otherwise, are neuter).

The use of physical properties in gender assignment for inanimate nouns is fairly well attested in the languages of the world. Typical properties associated with feminine gender are small size and round shape (as in some Afroasiatic languages, e.g. Dasenech, Oromo, Amharic, or East-Nilotic languages Turkana, and Camus (Heine 1982); and languages from the East Sepik region of Papua New Guinea, e.g. Alamblak (Bruce 1984) and Manambu (Aikhenvald's field data)). In harmony with this, masculine gender tends to be associated with long, big and rigid objects. (cf. also Croft 1994). Palikur is unusual in that feminine gender is assigned to inanimate nouns if they have constant shape and are rigid or bounded. But unlike the masculine gender in the above mentioned cases, neuter gender in Palikur can be viewed as a semantically residual category which is used if a referent does not satisfy the criteria for other genders.

---

[17] The use of one form for masculine and neuter gender agreement with gender-sensitive verbal suffixes reminds us of a phenomenon known as 'concordial super-classing' in Australian linguistics (Sands 1995: 264–5) where fewer agreement forms are used with some modifiers, such as demonstratives. Unlike Palikur, however, superclassing in Australian languages often has a discourse function: fewer agreement forms are used when the head noun has a general reference, or is backgrounded.

4. NUMERAL CLASSIFIERS

Palikur has twelve numeral classifiers of sortal type, and six classifiers of mensural type.[18] The assignment of numeral classifiers is semantically based, and fairly straightforward. Every noun in Palikur has to take a numeral classifier. Unlike verbal classifiers (see §5), numeral classifiers are obligatory (with a cardinal number). The semantics of numeral classifiers is analyzed in §4.1. Their morphological form and usage are described in §4.2. Some typological properties of numeral classifiers in Palikur are given in §4.3.

4.1. *Semantics of numeral classifiers*

Numeral classifiers in Palikur are of sortal type (§4.1.1), and of mensural type (§4.1.2). Classifiers derived from body parts share properties with both (§4.1.3).

4.1.1. *Semantics of sortal numeral classifiers*

The basic semantic opposition in numeral classifiers is animate vs inanimate (see Croft 1994, on the universal character of animacy in numeral classifiers; for some exceptions see Aikhenvald 2000b). Animate classifiers fall into masculine and feminine types, and these are sex-based.

Palikur has an obligatory 'double marking' of animacy and of gender on the cardinal numbers 'one' and 'two' which accompany an animate head-noun. The assignment of gender which governs the agreement on cardinal numerals is much more semantically transparent than the assignment of gender discussed in §3.1. It is sex-based. Heavenly bodies (sun, moon) are masculine, as shown in Figure 12.1. There is no marking for gender on classifiers used with inanimate nouns. That is, there is a generic 'animate' classifier, *-p*; but there is no generic inanimate form. The way gender agreement operates on numeral classifiers

---

[18] The choice of a sortal classifier depends on inherent or temporary properties of the referent of the noun. Mensural classifiers correspond to measure terms in non-classifier languages, and describe the ways referents can be quantified. Distinguishing sortal and mensural classifiers and establishing a distinction between quantifiers and mensural classifiers is a recurrent problem in analyzing classifier languages (see Adams 1989). Mensural classifiers in Palikur are morphologically distinct from quantifiers, which are a separate closed class; they do not show any agreement with the head noun (e.g. *yuma* 'none', *aynesa* 'few', *ka aynsima* 'many', *madikte* 'all': Green and Green 1972: 64).

used with animate masculine and feminine nouns is illustrated in (15) and (16).

(15) paha-p-ru   tino   one woman
      one-NUM.CL:ANIM-f   woman

(16) paha-p-ri   awayg   one man
      one-NUM.CL:ANIM-m   man

An inanimate head noun cannot take gender agreement on numeral classifiers, even though it may trigger gender agreement on demonstratives or verbs. The noun 'path' has neuter gender (see (8)). There is no gender agreement in (17).

(17) paha-tra   ahin   one path
      one-NUM.CL:EXTENDED   path

The noun *warik* 'river' is feminine (see §3.2). (18) shows how this noun does not take a gender agreement marker with a numeral because it is inanimate.

(18) paha-tra   warik   one river
      one-NUM.CL:EXTENDED   river

These examples demonstrate that gender distinctions on numeral classifiers show only a partial overlap with the gender system marked on predicates and modifiers discussed in §3. We will return to this in §8.

The assignment of inanimate numeral classifiers is based on physical properties of the referent: shape, which goes with consistency (flexible); dimensionality, which goes together with consistency (rigid, flexible), shape and material; and boundedness. There are also three specific classifiers based on the nature of the referent.

The semantic organization of classifiers in Palikur is shown in Figure 12.2. Palikur is rich in geometrical terms (Green 1996). There is a term for each numeral classifier based on dimensionality, form or boundedness. These are given in square brackets in Figure 12.2. Dimensionality in numeral classifiers in Palikur has three values. Classification of one-dimensional objects combines reference to their consistency (rigid); classification of three-dimensional objects combines reference to material. Thus, consistency is a secondary parameter in Palikur numeral classification.

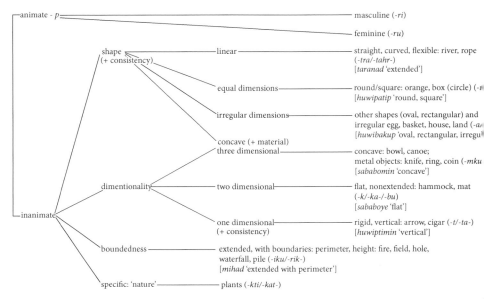

Figure 12.2. Semantics of Palikur sortal numeral classifiers. (The first form given for each classifier is the form that occurs with the number 'one', the second with 'two', and the third with other numbers.)

The classifier *-t/-ta* is used for vertical objects, as in (19). It can also be used as a kind of residue classifier, with otherwise 'unclassifiable' abstract nouns,[19] as in (20). Numbers are in bold type.

(19) ig   ka-daha-ni   **paha-t**   ah
       3m   ATT-for-POSS   **one-NUM.CL:VERT**   stick
       He had a stick

(20) **paha-t**   yuwit
       one-NUM.CL:VERT   word
       one word

Shape has four values: linear, equal dimensions, irregular or unequal dimensions, and concave. Classifier 'concave' is the only example of semantic extension from a prototype: it is applied to concave objects traditionally made of wood, and to a few newly introduced ones made

---

[19] Possibly the two are just homonyms (see Green 1996); *-t* is also a suffix which appears on numerous abstract nouns, so one can not exclude that the classifier *-t* is a repeater.

of metal (e.g. bowls, and ships). Following the extension by material, it also applies to other metal objects, all introduced by Europeans, such as knives and coins. Extension of this sort is fairly typical in noun classification systems (see Downing 1996; and Lakoff 1986).

One classifier is used for objects extended in any dimension and with boundaries; it applies to flat fields, or three-dimensional holes and waterfalls, or one-dimensional things, such as piles. There is just one specific classifier, for plants.

4.1.2. *Semantics of mensural classifiers*

Mensural classifiers in Palikur occur in the same position on cardinal numbers as do sortal classifiers; they display a similar morphological behaviour (infixed to 'two', suffixed to other numbers). They refer to the way the objects are arranged; one classifier refers to 'parts', and one to 'sides'. Their choice only indirectly correlates with intrinsic animacy- or dimensionality-related properties of objects. Only the classifier for 'group' can be used with human and with animate referents; the classifier for 'tied bundles or strings' is typically used with inanimates or dead animates, e.g. fish. See Figure 12.3.

Classifier *-bru* 'group' can be used with human referents (21), non-human animates (22) and inanimates (23).

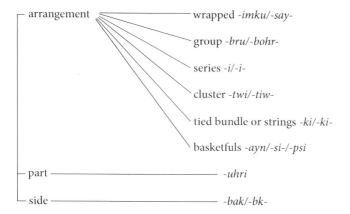

Figure 12.3. Semantics of Palikur mensural numeral classifiers. (The first form given for a classifier is the form that occurs with the number 'one', the second with 'two', and the third with other numerals.)

(21) **paha-bru-me**   tipik   iwasa-e-gi-kis
    one-NUM.CL:GROUP-CONTRAST   leave   observe-COMPL-3m-PL
    One group (of people) will leave and observe them (Arara Indians)

(22) **paha-bru**   upayan
    one-NUM.CL:GROUP   duck
    one flock of ducks

(23) **pi-bohr-a**   bot
    two-NUM.CL:GROUP-two   boot
    two pairs of boots

Other mensural classifiers are not used with animate referents. Classifier *-i* 'series' is used with spans of time, e.g. *paha-i mtipka* (one-NUM. CL:SERIES night) 'one night', with *paka* 'week' as in (31), or with other referents which come in a series, e.g. *paha-i kahikanau* (one-NUM. CL:SERIES breath) 'one breath'.

4.1.3. *Semantics of numeral classifiers derived from body parts*
The two classifiers derived from body parts can be used both as sortal, and as mensural classifiers. They are 'mouth, mouthful' (*-biyu/-biy*) and 'hand, handful' (*-uku/wok*). As sortal classifiers they are 'unique', i.e. they refer to just one object, as in (24).

(24) pi-wok-na   i-wak-ti
    two-NUM.CL:HAND-two   INDEF-hand-NPOSS
    two hands

They can also be used as mensural classifiers, as in (25).

(25) paha-uku-wa   kumat
    one-NUM.CL:HAND-EMPH   beans
    one handful of beans

4.2. *Morphological form and usage of numeral classifiers*

Palikur has numbers from one to ten.[20] Classifiers are suffixed to all numerals, with the exception of 'two': there they are infixed between

---

[20] Unlike the majority of other Arawak languages, Palikur has a decimal number system. Numbers eight and nine are derivations of seven (seven plus one, and seven plus two); all the rest can be considered separate stems. For a more detailed analysis of numeral classifiers, and of the counting system in Palikur, see Green (1996).

the first and the second syllable. This morphological difference in the behaviour of 'two' as opposed to other numbers is not uncommon in North Amazonian languages. A similar phenomenon is found in Warekena of Xié (North Arawak: Aikhenvald 1998).

Some numeral classifiers combine only with numbers one and two, some only with 'one', and some with numbers up to ten. Their morphological forms are often suppletive. For a language with numeral classifiers, there are typically more classifier distinctions for numbers one and two than there are for higher numbers (see §8). Morphological divisions of numeral classifiers are shown in Table 12.4. The first form occurs with 'one', the second one with 'two', and the third one with other numbers.

Table 12.4. Morphological divisions of numeral classifiers

Classifiers used with 'one'	part -*uhri* wrapped -*imku*
Classifiers used with 'one' and 'two' Classifiers with suppletive forms:	animate: -*p* (m -*ri*; f -*ru*)/-*ya* irregular shape -*a*/-*sa*- round/square -*u*/-*so*-: stone, box
Classifiers with same form for both numbers	vertical: -*t*/-*ta*- body part 'hand' -*uku*/-*wok*- side -*bak*/-*bk*- group -*bru*/-*bohr*- series -*i*/-*i*- basketfuls -*ayh*/-*si*/-*psi*
Classifiers used with numbers up to ten One form for one/two, different form for rest:	flat -*k* ~ -*ka*[21]-/-*bu*
One form for all	linear flexible -*tra* ~ -*tahr*- concave -*mku* ~ -*muk*- bounded -*iku* ~ -*rik*- plant -*kti* ~ -*kat*- body part 'mouth' -*biyu* ~ -*biy*- cluster -*twi* ~ -*tiw*- tied bundle -*ki* ~ -*ki*-

---

[21] Forms separated by ~ are allomorphs.

Inanimate nouns can be used with several different classifiers, depending on the semantic aspect of a polysemous noun. The use of different numeral classifiers results in meaning change. See (26)–(27). Classifiers are in bold type.

(26) nah   ka-daha-ni   **paha-kti**   pilatno
     1sg   ATT-for-POSS   **one-NUM.CL:PLANT/TRUNK**   banana
     I have one banana (plant)

(27) ba   pis   muwaka   ax   **paha-t**
     INTER   2sg   want   eat   **one-NUM.CL:VERT**
     Do you want to eat one (banana fruit)?

Classifiers can be used headlessly as anaphoric devices.

(28) kuri   a-pim   inin   **paha-p-ri**
     now   3n-during   **this:n**   **one-NUM.CL:ANIM-m**
       miyap   takuwa-nek   **paha-p-ri-me**
       die:nf   tomorrow-PROB   **one-NUM.CL:ANIM-m-CONTRAST**
     Today one dies, tomorrow the other one

(29) ig-kis   keh   **pi-ta-na**   ay-ta
     3m-PL   make   **two-NUM.CL:VERT-two**   there-DIR
     They made two (litres of honey) there

Both mensural and sortal classifiers, when used headlessly, can have an adverbial function. 'One' with a sortal classifier and -*rumpi* 'sequence' used headlessly means 'one by one' in (30).

(30) uwas   tuguh-e   **pahou-rumpi**
     orange   fall-COMPLETIVE   **one+NUM.CL:ROUND-SEQUENCE**
     Oranges fell one by one

Mensural classifiers when used headlessly can have a fairly idiosyncratic meaning. *Paha-i* 'one-QUANTIFIER:SERIES' is normally used with periods of time as is shown in (31).

(31) ig   ker-ye   **paha-i**   paka   ka-te
     3m   fight-DUR:nf   **one-NUM.CL:SER**   week   NEG-UNR
       miyap
       die:nf
     He fought for one week without dying yet

When used headlessly, it means '(at) once, all of a sudden' (32).

(32) **paha-i-e**   ig   miyap
    one-NUM.CL:SER-COMPL   3m   die:nf
    Suddenly he died

This lexicalization appears to be a unique property of numeral classifiers not found with other classifier types (see §8).

Number 'one' can be used almost like an indefinite article, e.g. *paha-p-ru tino* (one-NUM.CL:ANIM-f woman) 'a woman'

As yet, little is known as to the origin of numeral classifiers in Palikur. One classifier for linear flexible objects, -*tra*, is related to the verbal root *tara-* 'extended' (Green 1996: 12). Three specific classifiers come from full nouns (i.e. 'repeaters'): -*kat* from *akat* 'trunk, stem'; -*wok* 'NUM.CL: hand' from -*wak* 'hand', and -*biyu* 'NUM.CL:mouth' from -*biy* 'mouth'. The classifier for flat objects, -*bo* (used with numbers bigger than two) is similar to a verbal classifier with the same semantics (see Figure 12.4).

4.3. *Typological properties of numeral classifiers in Palikur*

Numeral classifiers fall into several subclasses according to (a) whether they are used only with numbers one and two, or with other numbers (up to ten) as well; and (b) whether the classifier has the same form for one, two, and other numbers, or these forms differ. More classifier distinctions are found with lower numbers (one and two) than with higher numbers. This follows the universal principle whereby lower numerals take more classifiers than higher numerals. In some languages (e.g. Minangkabau, a Malayo-Polynesian language: Marnita 1996) classifiers are obligatory only with one and two. In the majority of classifying South American languages classifiers are always used with numbers one and two, more rarely with three and four (see Aikhenvald 1996; 2000b).

Numeral classifiers are obligatory in NPs which contain numbers. Different classifiers can be used with inanimate nouns depending on what aspect of their semantics is to be highlighted. Numeral classifiers have no other functions.

5. Verbal Classifiers

Verbal classifiers are suffixes which appear on the verb[22] to characterize the S/O constituent in terms of its shape and other physical properties (see §2.1). General properties of verbal classifiers in Palikur are discussed in §5.1. The following two sections, §5.2 and §5.3, discuss verbal classifiers with stative and transitive verbs.

Another closed class of morphemes—incorporated body parts—can occur in the same slot as classifiers in the structure of stative and of transitive verbs. Their properties are analyzed and contrasted with verbal classifiers in §5.4. In §5.5 we will show that incorporated body parts do show certain tendencies of developing into classifiers. A typological perspective on verbal classifiers in Palikur is given in §5.6.

5.1. General properties of verbal classifiers in Palikur

Verbal classifiers in Palikur are typologically unusual in two ways.

- First, there are effectively two sets of verbal classifiers which display some formal and semantic differences. One set is used on stative verbs to refer to the S, or to the head noun if a stative verb is used as a modifier. The other is used on transitive verbs, to refer to the O of transitive verbs; the same set refers to the derived S of detransitivized passive verbs.[23]
- Second, the use of verbal classifiers is restricted to certain semantic types of transitive verbs, and of stative verbs.

The assignment of verbal classifiers is semantic, and shape-based. There are no distinctions based on animacy; all animate nouns are treated as 'irregular-shaped'.[24] Verbal classifiers can be used without the overt NP. Similarly to numeral classifiers, an inanimate noun can

---

[22] Palikur has a complicated verb structure, with one prefix position and eight suffix positions: O prefix or negation + root+ (i) VERBAL CLASSIFIERS or INCORPORATED BODY PARTS; (ii) REFLEXIVE, RECIPROCAL; (iii) DESIDERATIVE; (iv) 'RANGE OF ACTION' (wide range, limited action, etc.); (v) DIRECTIONALS, NUMBER OF A/S (action while subject is moving, action by individual subjects, or by dual subjects etc); (vi) ASPECT (completive, inceptive, etc.) (vii) OBJECT; (viii) INTENTIONAL, IRREALIS, SUPERLATIVE, EMPHATIC.

[23] Palikur is one of the few Amazonian languages with a passive derivation where an underlying agent can be stated—see examples in the text.

[24] This is not uncommon in verbal classifier systems—contrary to Croft (1994).

be used with different classifiers depending on the aspect of the S/O constituent that is involved in the action.

All verbal classifiers are optional. They are used (a) if the corresponding constituent (S or O) is fully involved in the activity, or displays a full degree of a 'property'; or (b) if the action/state involves the whole surface of the object.

The forms and semantics of verbal classifiers are given in Figure 12.4. If a classifier is used with transitive verbs as well as with stative ones, the first form is the one used with a stative verb, and the second one is used with a transitive verb (surface differences are due to morphophonological processes). Classifiers used with stative verbs only are marked with an asterisk.[25]

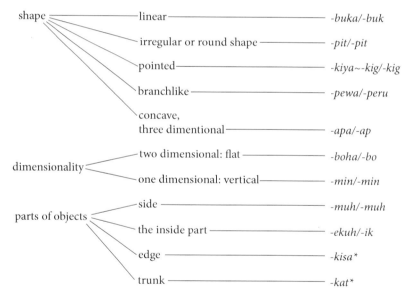

Figure 12.4. Palikur verbal classifiers. (The first form given is used with stative verbs; if a second form is given, it is used with transitive verbs.)

---

[25] There are possibly a few more classifiers which are restricted to just one stative verb, *pugum-/pugub/pugu-* 'large, thick, big'. These are: *-w-* 'vertical objects' (e.g. manioc squeezer, arrow, pencil: (v)), *-r-* 'extended broad objects' (e.g. field, plate, road: (vi)), *-rawk-* 'fire, wave' (vii) and *-tw-* 'cluster of small things, e.g. beads, banana or açai fruit (viii)':

(v) yuwivra   pugum-w-ad
     bamboo   large/thick-CL:VERTICAL-AUGMENTATIVE
     The bamboo is thick

Semantically, verbal classifiers are based on the form and dimensionality of objects.²⁶ Classifiers used with stative verbs distinguish more parts of objects. They have a few more, subtler distinctions. Classifier *-kig* 'pointed objects' is used with transitive verbs for *-kisa* 'sharp edge' (on stative verbs). Classifier *-min* used with transitive verbs covers one dimensional thin and rigid objects, e.g. tree trunks (classified with *-kat* on stative verbs).²⁷

The origin of most verbal classifiers is unknown. At least three come from parts of the body, or parts of a plant: *-kig*—'edge' is related to *-kig* 'nose'; *-pewa/peru* 'branch-like' is related to *-peru* 'branch' (cf. *a-peru* 'on a branch'), and *-kat* is related to *akat* 'trunk (of a tree)'. See §5.4.

5.2. *Verbal classifiers on stative verbs*

Verbal classifiers are used on stative verbs of the following semantic types (following Dixon 1991: 78–79):

(i)   dimension, e.g. *pugum* 'thick', *imuw* 'tall';²⁸
(ii) physical property, e.g. *mtibdi* 'soft', *ivat* 'stiff', *kiki* 'smooth', *kiyaw* 'sharp, abrasive (of cloth)', *miyaw* 'blunt', *barew* 'clean; pretty', *patauh* 'dirty, not pretty', *dax* 'stained';

(vi)   was   pugub-r-ad
       field   large/thick-CL: EXTENDED.BROAD-AUGMENTATIVE
       The field is broad

(vii) tiket   pugub-rawk-ad
       fire   large/thick-CL: FIRE, WAVE-AUGMENTATIVE
       The fire is big/broad

(viii) pilatno   pugu-tw-ad
       banana   large/thick-CL: CLUSTER-AUGMENTATIVE
       The stalk of banana is big
    ²⁶ The classifier 'irregular shape' is by far the most frequently used. It is also used to refer to objects of different shapes and may be considered functionally unmarked.
    ²⁷ Compare *-min* on a transitive verb 'split' with *-kat* on a stative verb:
(ix)   wis-uh   bak-mina-e-gu
       1pl-EXCL   split-V.CL:VERTICAL-COMPL-3f OBJ
       We split it (a tree, or a stick)
(x)   pilatno   pugum-akat-yo
       banana   large/thick-V.CL:TRUNK-DURf
       Banana tree is thick
    ²⁸ Not all nominal modifiers belonging to the semantic group of dimension are stative verbs; some of them are nouns. Such is the case of *nops-ad* 'big' (size-AUG); *nops-esa* 'small' (size-DIMINUTIVE) and *mih-ad* 'deep' (deepness-AUG). Being nouns, these modifiers do not take classifiers.

(iii) colour, e.g. *puhi* 'black', *sey* 'white', *duruweh* 'red', *ayeweye* 'blue, green', *kuwikwiye* 'yellow'.

Stative verbs of other semantic groups such as speed, age, difficulty, qualification, human propensity and value do not cooccur with classifiers.[29]

Verbal classifiers have a limited use as derivational affixes; when added to some nouns they transform them into colour terms, e.g. *aha-mna-bo-ye* (leaf-V.CL:FLAT-DURnf) 'leaf-coloured', or 'green'.

Verbal classifiers are only used if the stative verb describes the complete involvement of the S, or the head of a head-modifier construction. In (33), a classifier is used to indicate the complete blackness of the bird's feathers. (In the examples below, classifiers are in bold type).

(33) gu-sipri   puhi-**pti**[30]-ye
     3sgf-feather   black-**V.CL:IRREG**-DURnf
     Her (bird's) feathers are black all over; are completely black

The use of classifier may imply higher degree of quality. In (34) the classifier is used because the man is **very** handsome.

(34) ay-ne-wa   ig   awayg   pes
     here-SAME-EMPH   3m   man   come.out
       ig   ipeg   barew-**pit**-ye   awayg
       3m   look   beautiful-**V.CL:IRREG**-DURnf   man
     Immediately the man came out (into the garden). He (woman's brother)
     looked and saw: it was an absolutely handsome man (without defects,
     handsome in every way)

The same term *barew* in the sense of 'clean' is illustrated with (35) (from a text about Arara Indians). Verbal classifiers are often accompanied by the suffix *-apa-* 'total involvement of S/O', to emphasize the

---

[29] The only exception may appear to be *barew* 'good, pretty' which may be considered as belonging to value type; however, its other meaning is 'clean', and the meaning 'good, pretty' can be considered as a semantic extension of 'clean'. These meanings of *barew* are illustrated in (12, 13, 14, 34); the same item is used in the meaning 'clean' in (35). The stative verb *kabay* 'good' which is only used for value judgements does not take classifiers.

[30] Both *-pti-* and *-pita-* are allomorphs of *-pit.*

completeness of an action, or quality. (35) describes the 'savage' Arara Indians who wore no clothes, and:

(35) gi-ay-tak -kis-me   barew-**pit**-apa-e
      3m-some-EL-PL-CONTRAST   clean-**V.CL:IRREG**-TOTAL-COMPL
        gi-tew-kis
        3m-head-PL
      Some however [had] shaven heads (lit. some, their heads were com-
      pletely clean)

In (36) the classifier is used while the noun to which it refers is omitted. The complete involvement of the S is marked twice—with a 'repetitive' marker on the verb (as an intensive marker: Green and Green
1972), and with the classifier.

(36) eg   wanak-e-ka   a-kak   ini   mawru
      3f   tie-COMPL-PASS   3n-with   this:n   cotton
      barew   tamak-ka   eg   tamak-ka   barew
      beautiful   paint-PASS   3f   paint-PASS beautiful
      ka-si-si-**pita**-e
      ATT-REP-feather-**V.CL:IRREG**-COMPL
      It (the shaman's rattle: feminine) was tied with a cotton string. It was
      painted beautifully. It had feathers on it (all over)

5.3. *Verbal classifiers on transitive verbs*

Verbal classifiers are used with transitive verbs which imply direct
physical contact with the object. These are:

- physical actions such as: 'grab', 'wash', 'dry', 'hit', 'rub', 'peel', 'touch',
  'sweep', 'eat', 'bite', 'sting', 'tie', 'untie', 'blow on', 'shoot', 'split', 'burn',
  'carry'.
- positional verbs such as 'hang', 'stand', or 'lie'.

They are also used with telic verbs such as 'look' (as opposed to 'see').
Accordingly, classifiers are not used with verbs denoting mental processes, such as think or remember, or verbs which do not involve
direct physical contact with the object, such as 'see', 'hear', or 'say'.

Verbal classifiers are only used if the object does not have to be
completely involved in the action. They are not used with the verb
'kill', since it always involves the whole object—'non-complete' killing is not killing at all. Verbal classifiers are used to refer to O, as

in (37) and (40); to derived S of passives, as in (41); and reflexives, as in (38).

Verbal classifiers are not obligatory. As mentioned in §5.1, they have to be used if the O, or the derived S (of reflexive or passive) is completely involved in the action, cf. (37) and (38).

(37) yak-**pit**-apa-e-gu-kis   nikwe
    sting-**V.CL:IRREG**-TOTAL-COMPL-3f-PL   therefore
    So (the killer bees) stung them all over (their bodies)

(38) ig   pituk-**mina**-wa   a-r-iw
    3m   break.out-**V.CL:VERT**-REFL   3n-EP-away.from
    He broke (himself) out of the cord (lit. He broke his own vertical parts,
      i.e. arms and legs, which were tied by a cord)

The following pairs of examples illustrate the opposition between doing the action 'a little', as in (39), and doing it with the object completely involved, as in (40). The narrator unties the cotton string which was wound around the head of a shaman's rattle a little bit in (39), and then he unties it completely to see if it is a fake, in (40). Only in the latter case is the classifier *-pit* 'irregular shape' used.

(39) nikwe   nah   watak-e   ini   mawru
    therefore   1sg   untie-COMPL   this:n   cotton
    So I untied the cotton string (a little)

(40) nah   watak-**pita**-e   nah   watak-pita-e
    1sg   untie-**V.CL:IRREG**-COMPL   1sg   untie-V.CL:IRREG-COMPL
     ka-yes-te
    ATT-size-COMPAR
    I untied the string, I untied it more

Classifiers tend to be used if the noun in O or derived S function is the topic. (41) comes from the same text as the previous two examples. The classifier is used on 'tie' in (41) because the noun, the 'head' of the rattle is the topic of this stretch of the text.

(41) gu-apitiw   wanak-**pita**-ka   a-kak   mawru
    3f-head   tie-**V.CL:IRREG**-PASS   3n-with   cotton
    The head [of the rattle] is tied with cotton (all over)

Classifiers can also be used if the O or the derived S is unusual, as a kind of focus marker. The verb 'cook' is rarely used with verbal classifiers (because it presumably always implies complete involvement of the object; cooking a little is not cooking). However, the classifier is used in (42) in which the serpent is cooking a person which is an unusual object to cook.

(42) eg   iw-e-gi   ay-ta-re   nikwe-ni   eg
     3f   take-COMPL-3m   there-DIR-ANA   therefore-PAUSAL   3f
           bat-ha-kis   un   awah-wa-ye   un   a-daha-ni
           seated-VBZR-CAUS   water   hot-?-DURm   water   3n-for-POSS
           sakah-**pita**-e-gi
           cook-**V.CL:IRREG**-COMPL-3m
     She (snake) took him (man) there [and] put hot water on to cook him

5.4. *Incorporated body parts and classifiers*

Incorporated body parts occur in the same slot as verbal classifiers, and with the same types of stative and transitive verbs. The same morphemes appear on stative, and on transitive verbs—see Table 12.5. However, they display a number of significant differences from verbal classifiers.

Body part incorporation in Palikur is not productive—incorporated body parts are a closed set. Incorporated body parts either formally coincide with the full nouns, or are reduced forms of these.

The position incorporated body parts occupy in Palikur verbs is rather unusual for an Amazonian language. In quite a few languages in the Amazon incorporated body parts are placed preverbally (e.g. Mundurukú (Tupí), Yanomami, Tupí-Guaraní, Panoan, Nadëb (Makú))—see Aikhenvald (1996). In Palikur they occur post-verbally.

Incorporated body parts can not cooccur with verbal classifiers since they go in the same slot (see Green and Green 1972, on verb structure

Table 12.5. Incorporated body parts

With stative verbs	With transitive verbs	full noun	gloss
-duk	-duka	-duk	chest
-kug	-kuga	-kugku	foot
-ok	-oka	-wak	hand
-tiw	-tew	-tew	head
-ot	-(h)ot(a)	-utyak	eye
-bi	-biya	-biy	mouth
-tip	-tipa	-tip	top (lid)

in Palikur). Incorporated body parts and verbal classifiers differ in the following aspects of their morphosyntactic behaviour.

(i) While verbal classifiers only characterize the S or O constituent, but do not replace it, incorporated body parts have the function of the O of a transitive verb, or the S of a stative verb. There is no overt NP in the O function then (unless it is a possessor, see (ii)).

(43) kuri   ig   hakis-**ota**-ne   han   akiw
     now   3m   rub-**EYE**-CONTnf   thus   again
     He continued rubbing his eyes again

(ii) If a verb contains an incorporated body part in the O slot (note that body parts in Palikur are obligatorily possessed), the possessor is raised to direct object. This is a well-known strategy in incorporating languages (type II in Mithun 1984; cf. also Evans 1996). The possessor may be cross-referenced on the verb with an object suffix, as in (44), or it may be expressed with a full NP as in (45).

(44) ig-kis   hapis   patuk-**ot**-bet-h-e-gi
     3m-pl   shoot   burst-**EYE**-MULTIPLE-INT-COMPL-3m
     They shot his eyes out (lit: they eye-shot-him)

(45) nikwe   ig   ariya-e   ta   a-r-ot-r-iku-t
     therefore 3m   heat.up-COMPL   DIR   3n-EP-eye-EP-inside-DIR
       tiket   a-daha-ni   hakis-**ota**   bakimni-ayh
       fire   3n-for-POSS   rub-**EYE**   child-PL
     Therefore he heated it (brushwood) up in the fire in order to rub the
       eyes of the children (lit. eye-rub the children)

(iii) If a stative verb contains an incorporated body part, there is always a possessed-possessor relationship between the body part and the subject. This is different from the function of verbal classifiers used in the S slot of a stative verb. This difference is illustrated with (46) and (47); (46) contains a verbal classifier, and (47) an incorporated body part. (48) is another example of body-part incorporation on a stative verb. While verbal classifiers refer to a particular shape-related property of the S, incorporated body parts show a part-whole relationship with the S.

(46) in   barew-**buk**
     this:n   clean-**V.CL:LINEAR**
     This (the cord) is clean

(47) eg   barew-**kug**
     3f   clean-**FOOT**
     She is clean-footed (i.e. her feet are clean)

(48) ig   barew-**tiw**
     3m   clean-**HEAD**
     He is bald (lit. clean-headed)

Body part incorporation is not obligatory, unlike some other South American Indian languages.[31] The conditions under which body part incorporation is used are different from the conditions of use of verbal classifiers. A body part in O function does not get incorporated if it refers to one, individual body part. In (49), the narrator's spirit tells him to put just one hand in the water, and so there is no body part incorporation.

(49) subuk   pi-wak   a-hakwa-t   un
     submerge 2sg-hand   3n-in.WATER-DIR   water
     Put your hand in the water

The following two examples illustrate the difference between a non-incorporated individual incorporated body part ('one eye' in (51)) and a non-incorporated one ('both eyes' in (50)):

(50) nah   sukuh-**hot**-aw
     1sg   wash-**EYE**-REFL
     I washed (all) my eyes (lit. I eye-washed myself)

(51) nah   sukuh   nu-uty-ak
     1sg   wash   1sg-eye-REC
     I washed one eye (lit. I washed one eye)

An incorporated body part and a non-incorporated one (with the same reference) in O function can cooccur, if the complete involvement of a body part has to be focussed on. This is shown in (52).

(52) nah   sukuh-**hot**-aw   nu-uty-ak
     1sg   wash-**EYE**-REFL   1sg-eye-REC
     I washed **both of my eyes** (and not ears)

---

[31] For instance, in Yanomami (Ramirez 1994) obligatorily possessed body parts are always incorporated into the verb.

A body part is not incorporated if it is in contrastive focus, as in (53). This example comes from a story considered very humorous by the Palikur. Here one bird takes the man by his feet, and the other one takes him by his head. The point of focussing on body parts is that it is funny: the humming bird cannot normally grab or carry anyone.

(53) eg   tukus   kamax   gi-kugku   eg-me   karuw
     3f   humming.bird   catch   3m-foot   3f-CONTRAST   hawk
       kamax   gi-tew-ha   eg-kis   amara-e   gi-kak
       catch   3m-head-POSS   3f-pl   fly-COMPL   3m-with
     The humming bird caught hold of his feet. The hawk grabbed his head.
       They flew away with him

Incorporated body parts and verbal classifiers are thus used under different semantic conditions. While the use of a classifier is linked, basically, to the completeness of involvement of the O/S in the action, the use of an incorporated body part implies the lack of individuation of a noun in the O/S function, and its non-focussed status.

Another important difference in behaviour between incorporated body parts and verbal classifiers concerns possibilities of lexicalization of the former. Only incorporated body parts can get lexicalized with certain verbs. That is, they may result in the creation of unique idiomatic expressions in which the meaning of the whole can not be determined on the basis of the meaning of the parts. This happens both with transitive verbs (54), and with stative verbs (55). Nothing of this sort ever happens with verbal classifiers.[32]

(54) kamax-**duk**-aw
     grab-**CHEST**-REFL
     He had a quick snack (lit. he grabbed his own chest)

(55) nah   barew-**wok**
     1sg   clean-**HAND**
     I am poor, destitute (lit. I am clean-handed)

---

[32] Example (48), with an incorporated body part, and (xi) below, with a verbal classifier, are another 'minimal pair':
(xi)   gi-tew   barew-pit
       3m-head   clean-V.CL:IRREG
       His head is clean (well-washed, or clean-shaven)

5.5. *Similarities between verbal classifiers and incorporated body parts*

In §5.4 we focussed on how incorporated body parts and verbal classifiers differ in their morphosyntactic behaviour, conditions of use and semantic effects, and lexicalization processes.

Verbal classifiers and incorporated body parts have the following properties in common:

- morphosyntactic conditions (S/O; same verb types);
- same slot in verb structure

Besides these, there are a few more similarities between verbal classifiers, and incorporated body parts.

Verbal classifiers allow reclassification of the noun depending on the part of the object which is in focus. Consider (56), from a story about canoe-making. The overt reference to *umuh* 'canoe' is omitted; but it is cross-referenced with the third person feminine object pronoun on the verb. This sentence contains two occurrences of the verb *bak* 'split'. The first one refers to splitting the whole of the canoe, and the classifier *-min* is used to refer to its vertical shape. The second one, *-muh* 'edge', is used to refer to the sides of a log out of which a canoe is being made.

(56) wis-uh   bak-**mina**-e-gu
    1pl-EXCL   split-**V.CL:VERT**-COMPL-3f
      bak-**muh**-kis-e-gu
      split-**V.CL:SIDE**-CAUS-COMPL-3f
    We split it (a log) apart, chip its sides smooth

(57) and (58) illustrate a similar phenomenon with stative verbs.

(57) barew-**muh**   umuh
    clean-**V.CL:SIDE**   canoe
    clean-sided canoe[33]

---

[33] The distinction between a clause and an NP is marked with constituent order. (xii) is a clause as compared to the NP in (57):
(xii) umuh   barew-muh
    canoe   clean-V.CL:SIDE
    The canoe is clean-sided

(58) barew-**kig**   umuh
      clean-**V.CL:EDGE**   canoe
      clean-edged canoe

A part-whole relationship between the noun and the classifier in these examples is reminiscent of the role incorporated body parts play in (45), (47) or (48). Incorporated body parts can sometimes be used to characterize the shape of the noun in O function. This is what verbal classifiers usually do. One such example is (59). The incorporated body part, *hot* 'EYE', can be interpreted in two ways: either as possessor raising, similar to (45), or as referring to a round-shaped inside part ('eye') of a wound.

(59) ig   sukuh-**hot**-e   busukne
      3f   wash-**EYE**-COMPL   wound
      She washed the centre (lit. 'eye') of the wound

Thus, there is a certain tendency for incorporated body parts to be used similarly to verbal classifiers; conversely, verbal classifiers also show functional similarities with incorporated body parts. We mentioned at the beginning of §5 that at least two verbal classifiers derive from parts of the body, or from parts of plants. There is, then, a certain tendency for body parts to get grammaticalized as verbal classifiers. This is a typologically well-attested phenomenon. (See Mithun 1984, on 'classificatory' noun incorporation. See also Evans (1996: 76–78) on the two distinct functions body parts have in Mayali, an Australian language: that of verbal classifiers, and that of incorporated body parts.)

5.6. *Verbal classifiers in Palikur in a typological perspective*

In Palikur, verbal classifiers divide into two groups—those which are used with stative verbs, and those which are used with transitive verbs. Among stative verbs, only those which refer to dimension, physical propensity and colour, take classifiers. Among transitive verbs, classifiers are used only with those which imply a possibility of a direct physical contact with the object (or derived S of a passivized verb).

Note that, despite a superficial similarity, 'side' in the English translation ('clean-sided', 'clean-edged') can not be considered incorporation or an instance of a classifier; see Mithun (1984).

Thus, verbal classifiers are used to focus on the shape of an object completely involved in an activity; apparently properties related to form and dimensionality are only important when direct physical contact is implied. There is an analogy to suppletive classificatory verbs in some North American Indian languages, notably Athabascan and Iroquoian, and also in some languages of Central and South America, e.g. Ika, from Colombia (Frank 1990). Suppletive classificatory verbs in Athabascan languages refer to *concrete objects*, and they describe 'objects at rest, in motion, being handled, being dropped, or falling' (Carter 1976: 24). In Ika, they refer to location or 'handling' of an item (i.e. putting or carrying).

Unlike Athabascan languages or Ika, every noun in Palikur can be classified. However, classifiers are not obligatory, and their use depends on completeness of involvement of the O, or S, or on its status in the discourse. Having two sets of verbal classifiers which have some formal and semantic differences, one for stative verbs and the other one for transitive verbs, is another typologically rare property of Palikur. In a way, this can be compared to the way two sets of verbal classifiers operate in some North Athabascan languages. Languages like Koyokon (Axelrod forthcoming; Thompson 1993) have classificatory verb stems and verbal classifiers prefixed to verbs. Classificatory verbs are suppletive stems which are used depending on the shape of the S of some stative verbs (mostly positional verbs), and of the O of some transitive verbs (mostly verbs of eating and manipulation). Two prefixed verbal classifiers (labeled 'genders' in the Athabascan linguistic tradition) refer to an S/O argument, characterizing it in terms of its shape (round and elongated). Verbal classifiers in Palikur differ from classifiers in Athabascan languages in that in Palikur the two sets overlap, and their use is not obligatory.

6. LOCATIVE CLASSIFIERS

Palikur has a set of morphemes which function as locative adpositions,[34] meaning 'on' or 'in'. Their choice depends on the shape and boundedness

---

[34] See Appendix 2, on how the choice of a postposition or a preposition depends on the discourse function of the head noun.

of the head noun.[35] These morphemes, called locative classifiers, display certain formal and semantic similarities with other classifier morphemes used in different contexts. The semantics and other properties of locative classifiers are discussed in §6.1. A cross-linguistic perspective on locative classifiers is given in §6.2.

6.1. *Properties of locative classifiers in Palikur*

Similarly to verbal classifiers but unlike numeral classifiers, locative classifiers do not make any formal distinctions for animate and inanimate nouns (see §6.2, on locative classifiers in other languages which also have no animacy distinctions). Locative classifiers are based on shape, dimensionality and boundedness. The classifier *-bet* used for unbounded substances (e.g. mud, clay, faeces) also plays the role of a residue classifier: it is used for otherwise unclassifiable items.[36] These include abstract nouns, such as thoughts, dirt, darkness, coolness, suffering. There are two specific classifiers: 'water' and 'road, river'.

Locative classifiers in Palikur and their semantics are shown in Figure 12.5. These morphemes when used as locative adpositions mean 'on' or 'in'. They are illustrated in (60) and (61). The person, number and gender of the head noun can be cross-referenced on them (see Appendix 2). They can also cooccur with the following locative suffixes to form directionals, elatives, and perlatives: *-t* 'directional: into, to' (62), *-tak* 'elative: from', *-iu* 'perlative: along'. In the examples below locative classifiers are in bold type.

(60) pis   keh   paha-t   arab   pi-wan-**min**
      2sg   make   one-NUM.CL:VERT   shield   2sg-arm-**on.VERT**
      You make a shield on your arm

(61) ig-kis   ute-e-gi   ig   motye
      3m-pl   find-COMPL-3m   3m   wasp
          ay-h-te   **a-peru**   ah
          there-INT-DISTAL   **3n-on.BRANCH LIKE**   tree
      They found the wasps on the tree

---

[35] Since they combine the functions of classifiers and those of adpositions they could be called classificatory adpositions, following the analogy of 'classificatory' verbs in North American Indian languages, such as Athapascan and Cherokee.

[36] The classifier *-bet* is also used to refer objects which consist of multiple parts, e.g. caviar (which consists of many eggs), cotton (with its many fibers), or clothing (many pieces).

432   ALEXANDRA Y. AIKHENVALD AND DIANA GREEN

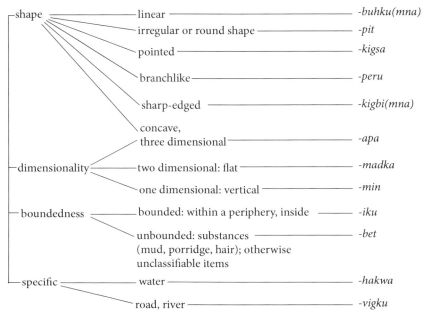

Figure 12.5. Palikur locative classifiers

(62) wis-uh   tarak-e-gu   **a-hakwa-t**   un
      1pl-EXCL   push-COMPL-3f   **3n-in.WATER-DIR**   water
      We push it (the canoe) into the water

In an adpositional phrase, the head can be omitted. Then a locative classifier is used headlessly, e.g.

(63) ka-daha-ni   warukma   **gu-madka**
      ATT-for-POSS   big.star   **3f-on.FLAT**
      It (rattle: feminine, flat) had a big star on it

Further examples of *-madka* 'on: FLAT' are in Appendix 2.
    Similarly to numeral and verbal classifiers, locative classifiers allow variable classification of a noun. That is, different locative classifiers can be used depending on which characteristics of a noun are focussed on.[37]

---

[37] (63) is also such an example. Rattle is usually classified as 'irregular shaped'. In this case, the star was glued to its flat side, and this is why locative classifier *-madka* 'on.flat' is used.

Consider the following examples. In (64), a locative classifier 'linear' is used with *akati* 'cord' to indicate that crows are sitting along it; vertical *-min* is used in (65) since no 'horizontal extension' of a cord is implied. Number marking with non-humans is optional in Palikur. Note that 'along' in (64) presupposes a plural reading for the subject 'crow', and 'on' in (65) presupposes that 'crow' is singular. Thus, one can infer a singular or plural reading from a classifier choice.

(64) yu   bat   a-buhkumna   paha-tra   akati
     crow   sit   **3n-on.LINEAR**   one-NUM.CL:LINEAR   cord
     Crows sat on/along a (horizontal) cord

(65) yu   bat   a-**min**   paha-tra   akati
     crow   sit   3n-**on.VERT**   one-NUM.CL:LINEAR   cord
     A crow sat on a (vertical) cord

Unlike numeral classifiers, locative classifiers can be sometimes used as derivational affixes, e.g. *ma-hakwa* (?-in.WATER) 'lake'; *paraw-hakwa* (waves-in.WATER) 'ocean'. More commonly, they cooccur with a derivational suffix *-ya* 'pertaining to', e.g. *pi-duk-madka-ya* (2sg-chest-on. FLAT-PERTAINING) 'the flat part of your chest, your breast plate', *a-kig-bimna-ya* (3n-on.EDGE-PERTAINING) 'its frame'.

There is another set of locative adpositions which contain body parts. Their use is similar to locative classifiers, however, unlike locative classifiers they are always accompanied by another locative morpheme, e.g. *-nume-ku* (lips-LOC) 'in a doorway, along the banks of a river, or along the road'; *-ot-gik* (eye-LOC) 'in the 'eye', i.e. round middle part of (a wound, a fire, etc)'; *-tew-ha* (head-LOC) 'on top of the head; a protruding part'. It appears that body parts are developing into locative classifiers, in the same way as some of them are developing into verbal classifiers. See §5.4. Little is known about the origin of locative classifiers. Two of them probably originated from body parts. *-kigsa* 'on.POINTED' is related to *-kig* 'nose'; *-vigku* 'on.ROAD, RIVER' derives from *-vigik* 'bone, marrow'.

6.2. *Cross-linguistic perspective on locative classifiers*

Locative classifiers are an exteremely rare phenomenon in the languages of the world—see §2.1. In Palikur, they coccur with oblique case-markers. Similarly to numeral classifiers, but unlike verbal ones, they are obligatory. Unlike numeral classifiers, they can be used as derivational suffixes.

Regular correlations between the shape of the head noun and the choice of an adposition have been noticed in a number of other North Amazonian languages.[38] Sometimes locative classifiers are analyzable, and sometimes they are not.

One such example is from Lokono (Arawak) (Aikhenvald 1996; Pet 1987: 37ff). Here there is a smallish set of postpositions the choice of which correlates with the physical properties of the noun: *loko* 'inside' (a solid or empty object); *koborokon* 'inside' (animate being); *kolokon* 'inside' (fire or light).

The correlation between the choice of a postposition, and the shape, or consistency of the head noun is typical for a number of Carib languages (e.g. Apalai, Hixkaryana, Macushi and Wai Wai—see Derbyshire 1999). Table 12.6 is from Apalai (Koehn and Koehn 1986: 100).

Dâw (Makú, Northwest Amazonia: Martins 1994: 53ff) has four locative postpositions, the choice of which is determined by the shape and consistency of the head noun. Two of them are exemplified below. Locative classifiers are fused with locational markers, just like in Palikur. In (66), *ked* 'in:HOLLOW' is used with a noun *canoe*. In (67), *miʔ* 'in:LIQUID' is used with a noun 'river'. (68) is ungrammatical.

(66) xoo-ked
      canoe-IN:HOLLOW
      in a canoe

Table 12.6. Locative classifiers in Apalai

	in/on	into/onto	via/from
liquid	kua-o	kua-ka	kua-e
fire	hta-o	hta-ka	hta-e
small container	a-o	a-ka	a-e
large place	ta-o	ta-ka	ta-e
flat place	po	po-na	po-e
pole shape	poko	pokoi-na	pokoi-no
river	na-o	na-ka	na-e
hammock	tapo	tapo-na	tapo-e

---

[38] All typological statements are based on the analysis of systems of classifiers and genders in over 300 languages of the world undertaken in Aikhenvald (2000b). Data on Arawak systems were summarized in Aikhenvald (1996).

(67) nââx-pis-mî?
    water-small-IN:LIQUID
    in a small river

(68) *xoo-mî?
    canoe-IN:LIQUID

The classificatory postposition *mî?* 'in:LIQUID' is cognate with the noun *mi* 'water' in Nadëb, a language from the same family (Silvana Martins, p.c.).

Palikur seems to be the only language in which some of the locative classifiers are used in other functions (such as numeral and verbal classifiers)—see Table 12.8. In other languages, different adpositions are used depending on the shape and other physical properties of the head noun.

7. CLASSIFIERS IN POSSESSIVE CONSTRUCTIONS

7.1. *Properties of possessive classifiers in Palikur*

Another set of classifiers in Palikur which is completely independent of the classifier types outlined above are classifiers used in a possessive NP to characterize the possessed noun.[39] Unlike other classifiers and genders, not all nouns in the language require a possessive classifier. Their use is restricted to alienably possessed referents of nouns which can not take possessive affixes—similarly to (4) in §2.1, from Apalai. The semantic relationship between the classifier and the possessed noun is generic-specific. Referents are classified depending on their functions, or the ways they can be handled: fruit can be eaten, or planted; animals can be domesticated, or caught for food. See Table 12.7.

7.2. *Palikur possessive classifiers in a typological perspective*

Palikur has five generic terms used as possessive classifiers with alienably possessed nouns. This system of possessive classifiers is similar to the ones found in other languages (e.g. Yuman, or Uto-Aztecan,

---

[39] Palikur also has possessive markers on alienably possessed nouns which go back to proto-Arawak relational classifiers; however, it is not clear whether they have any classificatory function in Palikur (as they do have in other Arawak languages, e.g. Baniwa of Içana: Aikhenvald 1994a: 410).

Table 12.7. Possessive classifiers in Palikur

CLASSIFIERS	SEMANTICS	EXAMPLES
-pig	'pet'; used with domesticated animals	*gi-pig pewru* (3m-pet dog) 'his dog'; *gi-pig mutom* 'his sheep';
-mana	'food'; used with fruit and vegetables	*pi-mana uwas* (2sg-food orange) 'your orange';
-mutra	'plant'	*n-amutra pilatno* (1sg-plant banana) 'my plant-banana' (the one I planted);
-win	'catch; animal caught to eat'	*nu-win arudiki* (1sg-catch tapir) 'my catch-tapir' (the tapir I caught);
-kamkayh	'child'	*nu-kamkayh awayg* (1sg-child boy) 'my son', *nu-kamkayh tino* (1sg-child woman) 'my daughter'.

or Carib: see Carlson and Payne 1989, for more examples). Unlike all other classifier systems in Palikur, not all nouns have a possessive classifier.

This system is strikingly similar to possession in Carib languages (Macuxi, Apalai; cf. Derbyshire 1999), and in Island Carib (Aikhenvald 1999), a North Arawak language which suffered a strong Carib influence. It is in some ways atypical of Arawak languages. Bearing in mind long term (and not too peaceful!) contacts of Palikurs with Galibi and, possibly, other Carib peoples, one may hypothesize that Palikur perhaps acquired possessive generics under the Carib influence. It is, however, not impossible that possessive classifiers developed in Palikur as an independent phenomenon, as they probably did in Nadëb, a Makú language from the Middle Rio Negro (Weir 1984), or Kipeá-Kiriri, an extinct Macro-Jê language formerly spoken in north-eastern Brazil (Rodrigues 1999).

8. Palikur Genders and Classifiers: An Evaluation

Palikur has a system of genders, and several types of classifiers. An overview of the properties shared by these noun classification devices, and the ways in which they differ is given in §8.1. The semantics of classifiers of different types is contrasted in §8.2. Some ideas as to their origins are offered in §8.3. A summary is presented in §8.4.

8.1. *Overall comparison of the systems*

Numeral classifiers, verbal classifiers with two subtypes, and locative classifiers in Palikur show a degree of congruence—i.e. the same forms are used in some instances, and there is a significant overlap in semantics. There is a significant overlap between the inventories of verbal and locative classifiers, and some overlap with numeral classifiers. Genders and possessive classifiers are independent. See Table 12.8.

Noun classification systems differ on a number of points, but they also have some properties in common. These are discussed below. The two sets of verbal classifiers show the same properties. These properties are summarized and contrasted in Table 12.9.

(a) *Morphological form*
Noun classification devices in Palikur differ in morphological complexity. Genders have two or three agreement forms depending on the type of construction they are used in. There are also a few morphologically irregular gender forms (see Table 12.3). Numeral classifiers fall into several subgroups depending on what numbers they are used with; some are used just with number 'one', some with numbers 'one' and 'two', and some with other numbers as well. Unlike gender systems, restrictions on the number of forms every numeral classifier has are idiosyncratic for each particular classifier (see Table 12.4). Several numeral classifiers have suppletive forms. Classifiers of other types do not have restrictions on how many forms they have; they do not have any morphological irregularities.

Classifiers differ in their morphological status. Verbal and numeral classifiers are bound morphemes. Numeral classifiers may be suffixes, or infixes (to number 'two'). Verbal classifiers are suffixes. Gender markers can be suffixes, or prefixes, or infixes (see Tables 12.1 and 12.2). Possessive and locative classifiers have a different status. Locative classifiers are either attached to the noun or are used independently with a person-marking prefix. Possessive classifiers always have a person-marking prefix.

Locative classifiers are used as derivational suffixes. Genders and verbal classifiers have a limited use as derivational markers (cf. Note 8). Other classifiers are not used this way.[40]

---

[40] Unlike other multiple classifier systems, e.g. Yagua (Payne 1990c), or Tariana (Aikhenvald 1994a) in which every classifier can be used as a derivational affix.

Table 12.8. Numeral, verbal and locative classifiers

Semantics	Numeral classifiers		Verbal classifiers		Locative classifiers
			with stative verbs	with transitive verbs	
animate	-p				
round, square		-u/-so	-pit	-pit	
irregular shape		-a/-sa			-pit
side			-muh	-muh	
vertical objects	-t/-ta-		-min	-min	-min
rigid, thin			-ah		
flat	-k/-ka-/-bu		-boha	-bo	-madka
concave; numeral classifier: metal	-mku/-muk		-apa	-ap	-madka
edge			-kiya		-kigbi
pointed			-kisa	-kig	-kigsa
linear; numeral classifier: long and extended	-tra/-tahr-/-bu		-buka	-buk	-buhku(-mna)
road, river					-vigku
the inside part of; NUM.CL: extended with boundaries	-iku/-rik		-eku	-ik	-iku
tree, plant, trunk	-kti/-kat		-kat	-min	-pew
tree, branch-like			-pewa	-peru	-peru
water			-it	-it	-kakwa

Table 12.9. Properties of classifiers and genders

	genders	numeral cl	verbal cl (2 sets)	locative cl	possessive cl
formal overlap with other noun classification devices	no	partly yes	yes	yes	no
different number of morphological forms depending on construction type	yes	no	no	no	no
different number of morphological forms depending on classifier	no	yes	no	no	no
irregular forms	yes (limited)	yes	no	no	no
derivational functions	yes	no	no	yes	no
bound morphemes	yes	yes	yes	no	no
prefixes, suffixes, infixes	prefixes, suffixes, infixes	suffixes, infixes	suffixes	n/a	n/a
every noun 'classified'	yes	yes	yes	yes	no
obligatory use	yes	yes	no	yes	yes
cooccurrence with other noun classification devices in one morphological word	yes	no	yes	yes	no

(b) *Function*

All noun classification devices in Palikur, including gender and possessive classifiers, do not have to cooccur with an overt NP, i.e. they can all be used anaphorically. All of them allow variable classification of nouns depending on which shape characteristic is in focus. This shows that classifiers are not semantically redundant; they add information to the noun (cf. Denny 1986; Downing 1996: 93).

All classifiers can be used anaphorically. Together with gender they play a major role in tracking participants in Palikur discourse. This is typical for noun classification devices (see Aikhenvald 1994a: 428–29).

(c) *Usage*

Every noun in Palikur is assigned a gender, or a numeral, verbal or locative classifier. Only some nouns are assigned a possessive classifier.

The marking of gender, numeral classifiers and locative classifiers are obligatory, while the use of verbal classifiers depends on whether the S, or the O constituent is completely involved in the action (see §5).

(d) *Cooccurrence with other noun classification devices*

Gender marking can cooccur with verbal classifiers and with locative classifiers, in one morphological word (cf. (34)). Gender marking does not cooccur with numeral classifiers (since there is a gender distinction in numeral classifiers; however, it applies only to animate nouns and is more semantically transparent). There is no special gender marking on possessive classifiers; gender is cross-referenced on the third person prefix to a possessive classifier.

The use of several systems of noun classification devices contributes to the complexity of Palikur discourse (cf. gender and a locative classifier in one clause in (61), a locative and a numeral classifier in (60), and gender and a numeral classifier in (28)).

8.2. *Semantics of noun classification devices*

The semantics of numeral, verbal and locative classifiers shows a significant overlap, while the choice of genders and possessive classifiers is determined by rather different properties. These properties are summarized in Table 12.10. 'Yes' or 'no' given in brackets indicates the secondary importance of a given parameter.

Table 12.10. Semantics of classifiers and genders

semantic parameter	genders	numeral classifiers	verbal classifiers	locative classifiers	possessive classifiers
animacy	yes	yes	no	no	no
humanness	yes	yes	no	no	no
dimensionality	(no)	3 values	4 values	3 values	no
shape	yes	4 values	6 values	6 values	no
material	yes	(yes)	no	no	no
boundedness	yes	yes	no	yes	no
material	yes	(yes)	no	no	no
function	no	no	no	no	yes
semantic extensions	yes	yes	no	no	no
default class	yes	yes	yes	yes	no

The choice of a classifier is usually semantically based and transparent. Semantic principles are rather more complicated with regard to gender assignment since many more semantic features are encoded in a smaller number of morphemes (see Figure 12.1). Numeral classifiers of the sortal type show a semantic extension from form or dimensionality to material: the classifier *-mku / -muk* is used for concave objects, and also for objects made of metal. Semantic extensions of this sort are not found in verbal, locative, or possessive classifiers. They are found in gender assignment; we have seen in §3 how a metal star was assigned feminine gender because of the material it is made of; 'natural' stars are masculine. Of the other classifiers, only numeral classifiers have an overt animacy distinction. They also mark the sex of animate nouns.

Sortal classifiers categorize nouns in terms of their shape, dimensionality, and boundedness. There are three specific classifiers ('plants', 'hand' and 'mouth'). Mensural classifiers categorize nouns in terms of ARRANGEMENT (cf. Allan 1977).

DIMENSIONALITY has three values for numeral and locative classifiers, and four values for verbal classifiers: there are two classifiers for one-dimensional objects. Locative and verbal classifiers have very similar distinctions in FORM (note that the verbal classifier for objects with sharp edges is used only with stative verbs). Numeral classifiers distinguish fewer forms, and on different principles: objects with equal dimensions (round or square) are distinguished from irregular-shaped ones. BOUNDEDNESS is used in numeral and locative classifiers, but in different ways; only locative classifiers have a special term for unbounded substances.

The semantic closeness of verbal and locative classifiers goes together with their formal similarity—see Table 12.8. However, it is hard to decide which function is the original one.[41] The ways dimensionality, form and boundedness are encoded in numeral classifiers are reflected in the 'ethnogeometry' of Palikur. There are geometrical terms in the language which correspond to each dimensionality, form and bound-edness-based classifier. There are no such terms which could corre-spond to verbal or locative classifiers.

The semantic parameters used in most classifier systems include CONSISTENCY. This parameter appears as a secondary feature in numeral classifiers in Palikur. It is the most important one in assign-ing gender to inanimates based on their physical properties. The clas-sification of nouns into genders is based on a combination of different semantic features which only partly overlap with features used in numeral, verbal and locative classifiers. Nouns are divided into gen-ders according to their animacy; animates are divided into humans and non-humans. Animate non-human nouns are assigned genders by their species, kind, sex and size, and inanimate ones by consistency, shape, boundedness, and material.

FUNCTION is encoded exclusively in possessive classifiers. Only possessive classifiers encode a generic-specific (or superordinate-sub-ordinate) relationship between the two nouns.

Genders and numeral, verbal and locative classifiers have a class which includes otherwise unclassifiable nouns and can be considered a default, or residue class. Possessive classifiers do not have such a category.

8.3. *Origin of classifiers and genders*

Classifiers differ in their etymologies. A few numeral and verbal clas-sifiers originated from full nouns used in classifier functions (called 'repeaters': Aikhenvald 2000b). Possessive classifiers are generic nouns ('pet', 'catch', 'child', 'plant' and 'food'). Feminine and masculine gen-der markers -*o* and -*e* originated in Proto-Arawak gender marked demonstratives, also used as third person pronouns (see Payne 1991, on Proto Arawak feminine *-u*, masculine *-i*). Palikur innovated a

---

[41] Since there are reasons to believe that locative classifiers in Palikur are the result of areal diffusion from Carib languages, one might assume that verbal classifiers are older (see §8.3).

third gender, neuter. Neuter gender marker -*a*- could have developed as the result of reanalysis of a non-specific 'impersonal' prefix *a*- found in some other North Arawak languages (e.g. Bare, Guajiro: Aikhenvald 1999).[42]

Another aspect of the Palikur classifier system concerns grammaticalization of body parts. Different body parts grammaticalize as different classifiers. 'Mouth' and 'hand' become numeral classifiers both of sortal, and of mensural types, presumably due to the functional use of mouth and hand in measuring operations. 'Head' and 'nose' are grammaticalized as verbal and locative classifiers, possibly, due to their perceptually salient position; this is a case of polygrammaticalization (a term used in Craig 1991). 'Bone, marrow' became a specific locative classifier (for roads and rivers).

Since numerous North Arawak languages have systems of numeral and verbal classifiers, these classifiers in Palikur could have been inherited from the proto-language as categories—see Aikhenvald (1996). However, since other North Amazonian languages also have rich systems of numeral, and of verbal classifiers, in this case it is not easy to distinguish areal diffusion from genetic inheritance.

The emergence of a small set of possessive generic classifiers, and of locative classifiers can be explained as the result of areal diffusion. In both cases, the most likely source of areal influence would be the Carib languages with which Palikur had a long history of contact.

8.4. *Summary*

Palikur has six systems of noun classification devices: genders, numeral classifiers, two sets of verbal classifiers, locative classifiers, and possessive classifiers. Genders and possessive classifiers are independent and do not interrelate to the other systems in the way that the other systems do among themselves.

---

[42] A similar scenario for the genesis of noun classes in Iroquoian languages was suggested by Chafe (1977). In Pre-Proto-Northern Iroquoian cross-referencing prefixes developed a human-nonhuman opposition: for agents, the erstwhile nonspecific prefixes were reinterpreted as 'human' (Chafe 1977: 505). A later addition of a masculine singular form triggered the split of a 'human' category into masculine and feminine (Chafe 1977: 506).

Different noun classification devices have different functions[43] and different scope. A three-gender system is used with pronouns and in head-modifier agreement with a demonstrative as a modifier. A two-gender system is used to mark agreement with A/S (subject) on verbs and in head-modifier agreement with stative verbs in modifier function.

Numeral classifiers are used in NPs containing numerals. Their function is enumeration and quantification. Possessive classifiers are used in possessive NPs; locative classifiers are used in locative NPs. Verbal classifiers have the predicate (or the clause) as their scope, and appear on verbs referring to O/S.

Noun classification devices differ in their semantics. Only verbal classifiers have a pragmatic effect—they correlate with topicality and contrastiveness and completeness of involvement of S, or O (for verbal classifiers used with transitive verbs) or S (for verbal classifiers used with stative verbs). Classifiers also differ in their origin and morphological status. These correlations, summarized in Table 12.11, show semantic and functional differences between noun classification devices in Palikur.

How unusual is Palikur in having so many different sets of morphemes in different functions? Having more than one noun classification device is not uncommon among the languages of the world (see Aikhenvald 2000b). Quite a few have two. For instance, languages often have noun classes (genders) and numeral classifiers (e.g. Dravidian, Indic). Noun classes and noun classifiers coexist in some Australian languages, e.g. Wardaman and Ngan'gityemerri (Sands 1995). Noun classes and verbal classifiers coexist in the Australian languages Gunbarlang and Mayali (Evans 1996); numeral and relational classifiers cooccur in a number of Oceanic languages (Mokilese, Ponapean, Truquese).

Few languages have three or more systems of noun classification. Dâw (Makú: Martins 1994) has noun classifiers, locative classifiers, and classifiers in possessive constructions.[44] Baniwa (North Arawak)

---

[43] These functions include those worked out by Croft (1994): determination; enumeration; possession, relevant for possessive classifiers; spatial predication. Since at least some of them are too vague we did not use them.

[44] Among Guaicuruan languages from Argentina, Toba (Klein 1978, 1979) has deictic classifiers and noun classifiers, and classifiers in possessive constructions. Possibly, Pilagá (Vidal 1997) has a similar system.

Table 12.11. Semantic and functional properties and origin of classifiers

Classifier	Function	Scope	Semantics	Pragmatic effect	Origin
genders	head-modifier agreement in NP; A/S agreement in clause	NP : three genders with pronouns and demonstratives; two genders with stative verbs as modifiers clause (two genders)	animacy, physical properties	—	deictic/third person enclitic: Proto-Arawak
numeral classifiers	quantification, enumeration	NP	animacy, physical properties, nature	—	
verbal classifiers with non-stative verbs	O/S agreement	clause	physical properties, parts of objects	complete involvement or topicality/ contrast of O/S	some come from nouns, e.g. body parts
verbal classifiers with stative verbs	S agreement				
locative classifiers	location	NP	physical properties, 'typical' locations	—	
possessive classifiers	possession	NP	function, way of handling	—	generic nouns

has two genders, relational classifiers, a large set of noun classes, and another set of morphemes used as numeral and verbal classifiers which largely overlaps with noun class markers. This is quite common in Arawak languages (see Aikhenvald 1996, Shephard 1997).

In all these cases, classifiers provide cross-categorization of nouns. Classifiers serve to provide additional information about a noun's referent, and also to organize entities into classes or groups. The taxonomies expressed by classifier systems differ not only from those encoded by nouns; they also differ from one another. As Benton (1968: 142–3) put it, in his analysis of the system of two classifier types in Truquese, an Austronesian language, 'the classifiers…thus at the same time provide a means for ordering the universe, and a method for structuring concepts'.

This can be illustrated with the following example. Along with a rich system of shape-based classifiers, Palikur has comparatively few stative verbs of such semantic groups as dimension. The same lexical item, *pugum-/pugub-/pugu-* can be translated as 'thick', 'broad', 'large', and 'big', and further semantic distinctions are made with classifiers.

We have seen that Palikur is an instance of a multiple classifier system which displays extreme precision in combining different sorts of reference to physical and other inherent properties of entities encoded in distinct classifiers.

APPENDIX 1

TYPOLOGICAL CHARACTERISTICS OF PALIKUR

Typically for a North Arawak language, Palikur is polysynthetic, predominantly suffixing with a few prefixes. It is agglutinating with a strong fusional tendency and complicated morphophonological rules. It is basically nominative-accusative. Grammatical relations are expressed through pronominal cross-referencing. Cross-referencing suffixes usually mark the pronominal O of a transitive verb. With some verbal aspects (inchoative and abilitative) the O is marked with a prefix instead of a suffix. There is also a set of cross-referencing prefixes which are used to mark the possessor, and the argument of a postposition.

Constituent order tends to be AVO, SV; Possessor-Possessed; Adjective-Head noun. However, there is considerable freedom in order. The same item can be used as a preposition and as a postposition depending on its discourse status—see Appendix 2.

Unlike the vast majority of North Arawak languages, Palikur does not have the split ergative pattern of split-S type in marking grammatical relations with cross-referencing affixes (see Dixon 1994). In other Arawak languages, split ergative marking is based on division of intransitive verbs into active (S_a) and stative (S_o) types. It goes along the following lines:

  A = S_a: marked with cross-referencing prefixes
  O = S_o: marked with cross-referencing suffixes or enclitics (see Aikhenvald 1996)

In Palikur, cross-referencing suffixes are used to mark the pronominal O of a transitive verb (69).

(69) Ig   umeh-p-ig
      3m   kill-COMPL-3m
      He killed him

A full NP can not cooccur with a pronominal suffix unless it is focussed. In (70), O is expressed with a full NP, and there are no cross-referencing suffixes on the verb.

(70) Ig   umeh-e   kaybune
      3m   kill-COMPL   snake
      He killed a snake

In (71), the NP ('you') in O function is focussed, and so it cooccurs with a cross-referencing suffix. Similar techniques are found in other Arawak languages, e.g. Warekena of Xié (Aikhenvald 1998).

(71) Nah   kabeywot-ep-yi   yis
      1sg   conciliate-COMPL-2plO   2pl
      I will conciliate **you** (and nobody else)

There is only one instance where the O suffixes are used to mark S in Palikur. When interrogatives are used in the predicate slot, the pronominal S is cross-referenced with the suffixes. This is shown in (72).

(72) pariye-ki-ap
      who/what-EMPH-2sg S=O
      Just who are you?

This is probably the only trace of the Proto-Arawak split-ergativity retained in Palikur. Curiously, young people tend to employ independent personal pronouns (normally used for marking all subjects) in these constructions, as shown in (73).

(73) pariye-ki   pis
      who/what-EMPH   2pl
      Just who are you?

APPENDIX 2

CROSS-REFERENCING AND ADPOSITIONS IN PALIKUR

Cross-referencing affixes and independent pronouns are given in Table 12.2 (§3.3.1). Number distinctions in third person are marked on independent pronouns only when they have an animate referent: *ig-kis* 'they masculine', *eg-kis* 'they feminine'. Exclusive and inclusive suffixes are used with first person plural.

There are three neuter cross-referencing markers: *a-* 'non-integral', *ga-* 'integral' and *ni-* 'definite'. Third person neuter 'non-integral' *a-* is by far the most widely used, and it can be considered the unmarked one. See (10) above (note that the glosses are simplified). The 'definite' neuter cross-referencing prefix *ni-* is used when the head noun of the adposition or the subject is omitted but has been mentioned in the previous sentence. The difference between *a-* and *ni-* is illustrated with (74) and (75). The occurrences of these two prefixes with the adposition *-pit* 'on.IRREGULAR' are in bold type.

(74) puwikne   manuk   akiw   **a-pit-it**   kewgihri
      animal   cross   again **3n.NON.INT-on.IRREG-DIR**   island
      The animals cross over again to the islands (from the mainland)

(75) inakni   gi-w-n   ka-waditnevyenen-ma
      that:n   3m-word-POSS   NEG-worthless-NEG
        nah   kamax-wa   **ni-pit-it**
        1sg   lean-REFL   **3n.DEF-on.IRREG-DIR**
      That word of his is not worthless. I trust it (lit. I lean myself on it)

Neuter *a-* can also be used when the head noun is omitted. Then, the adposition has a more generic reference, e.g. *ni-hakwe-t-e* '3nDEF-in.

WATER-DIR-COMPL' 'into the water' (previously mentioned), *a-hakwe-t-e* '3nNON.INT-in.WATER-DIR-COMPL' 'into water, into liquid'.

The following pairs of examples illustrate the difference in meaning between neuter 'integral' *ga-* (76), (78), (80) and 'non-integral' *a-* (77), (79), (81). It correlates with alienable vs inalienable possession, and with part-whole relationship.

(76) payt   ga-lapota
      house   3n.INTEG-door
      the door of a house (as part of a house)

(77) payt   a-lapota
      house   3n.NON.INT-door
      the door of a house (lying on the ground, and not necessarily attached
         to the house)

In (78) the cover of the book is considered its integral part. In (79), in contrast, it is just a dustjacket.

(78) kagta   ga-mar-bo
      book   3n.INTEG-skin-FLAT
      a book's cover (part of the book)

(79) kagta   a-mar-bo
      book   3n.NON.INT-skin-FLAT
      an empty book's cover, a dustjacket

In (80), 'a branch of a tree' is considered a part of a tree, and in (81) it is just firewood.

(80) ah   ga-tawni
      tree   3n.INTEG-branch
      tree branch (part of a tree)

(81) ah   a-tawni
      tree   3n.NON.INT-branch
      tree branch (used for firewood)

Etymologically, prefix *a-* in Palikur may be connected with *a-* used for A/S and possessors in a number of other North Arawak languages, e.g. Guajiro, Añun *a-* 'non-referential A/S'; Bare *a-* (Aikhenvald 1995, 1999) 'focussed A/S$_a$', and *a-* as a prefix on a main verb in an auxiliary construction in Lokono and Island Carib (Peter van Baarle p.c.).

The use of adpositions as prepositions or as postpositions in Palikur depends on the discourse status of the head noun. Cross-referencing is obligatory with prepositions whether the head noun is present or absent; but when the same item is used as a postposition, cross-referencing is omitted. This is reminiscent of the situation in other North Arawak languages, such as Baniwa of Içana, Bare and Warekena (see Aikhenvald 1998, 1999).

The following 'minimal' pair shows that postpositions are used when the head noun is not individualized, and the adpositional phrase refers to an habitual activity. In (82), 'in the field' implies that the 'field' is not individualized. The sentence describes the habitual activity of a woman. Note that *was-madka* is pronounced as a single phonological word.

(82) eg   ka-annipwi-yo   was-**madka**
      3f   ATT-work-DURf   field-**in**.FLAT
      She worked in the field

Prepositions are used if the head noun is individualized. Person, number and gender of the head noun are obligatorily cross-referenced on a preposition. This is illustrated with (83). In (83), *was* 'field' has nothing to do with any habitual activities associated with a field; the example comes from a story of a Palikur man who was part of a pacification team carefully crossing the Arara Indians' field while trying to make contact with them.

(83) wis-uh   pes   amew-e   ay-ta-re
      1PL-EXCL   come.out   sneak.up-COMPL   there-DIR-ANAPHORIC
      a-madka   in   gi-was-ra-kis
      3n.NON.INT-in.FLAT   this.N   3m-field-POSS-PL
      We went out stealthily there across their (Araras') field

CHAPTER THIRTEEN

ZERO AND NOTHING IN JARAWARA

R. M. W. Dixon

1. INTRODUCTION—ZERO AND NOTHING IN PĀṆINI

The analytic device called 'zero' in modern linguistics has its origin in Pāṇini's analysis of Sanskrit. He uses the term *lopa* to describe a blank in a grammatical pattern. 'This blank or lopa is in several places treated as having a real existence and rules are made applicable to it, in the same way as any ordinary substitute that has an apparent form' (Vasu 1891, 1: 56). Bloomfield (1933: 209) applies this idea to English and suggests that, in *sheep*, 'the plural-suffix is replaced by *zero*—that is, by nothing at all.'

The idea of 'zero' (written as ø) is nowadays used in a variety of different—and sometimes confusing—manners. I suggest (pace Bloomfield) that a distinction should be made between:

(a) zero, referring to an empty (and blank) slot in grammar (this to be shown by 'ø'); and
(b) nothing, the absence of anything (this to be shown by a space, or by '{nothing}').

Note that an empty slot is something.

It is relevant to quote in full the relevant sūtras from Pāṇini's *Aṣṭādhyāyī* (the translation is Vasu 1891, 1: 55–56):

1.1.60   The substitution of a blank (*lopa*) signifies disappearance.
1.1.61   The disappearance of an affix when it is caused by the words *luk, ślu* or *lup* are designated by those terms respectively.
1.1.62   When elision of an affix has taken place (*lopa*), the affix still exerts its influence, and the operations dependent upon it take place as if it were present.
1.1.63   Of the base (*anga*) whose affix has been elided by use of any of the three words containing lu [that is, *luk, ślu, lup*], the operations dependent on it do not take place, regarding such base.

I understand this to mean that *lopa* indicates a zero allomorph of a suffix, an empty slot (or blank) where the suffix would be expected to be. Sūtra 62 states that this blank functions in many ways as a non-zero suffix in its position would, and sūtra 63 states that elisions called *luk, ślu* or *lup* do not have this property. In confirmation, Monier-Williams' (1899: 904) dictionary of Sanskrit includes within its entry for *lopa*: 'when *lopa* of an affix takes place, a blank is substituted, which exerts the same influence on the base as the affix itself, but when either *luk* or *ślu* or *lup* of an affix is enjoined, then the affix is not only dropped, but it is also inoperative on the base.'[1]

   In terms of the distinction suggested here, Pāṇini's *lopa* represents what I would call (a) zero, whereas *luk, ślu* and *lup* correspond to (b) nothing. In §6, a morphological distinction between zero and nothing will be illustrated for Jarawara, from the small Arawá family of southern Amazonia. But first it will be useful to survey some of the varying uses of zero and of nothing.

2. Phonological Change

English *knee* was originally pronounced with initial /kn/, later simplified to just /n/. This kind of change is sometimes written as $k > \emptyset$; that is, k being replaced by zero. In terms of the parameters adopted here, this is not an appropriate use of the term zero. There is no justification for saying that the modern form /ni:/ involves an underlying consonant cluster, with its initial slot being left empty. The change should be described as $k >$, or $k >$ {nothing}.

---

[1] Note that Pāṇini did not employ the word for 'zero' in Sanskrit (see Allen 1955: 113). According to the *Oxford English Dictionary* the earliest use of 'zero' as a grammatical term in English is in Vasu's 1891 translation of the *Aṣṭādhyāyī*. It occurs in the sentence immediately preceding that quoted in the first paragraph above: 'In Sanskrit Grammar, this 'lopa' is considered as a substitute or ădesa and as such this grammatical *zero* has all the rights and liabilities of the thing which it replaces.' Vasu's introduction of the term 'zero' was unfortunate; 'gap' or 'blank' might have been preferable. However, the usage is now too deeply ingrained to be overturned.

   For further useful discussion of Pāṇini's *lopa*, etc., see Subrahmanyam (1999: 45–6, 148, 176–7).

3. Syntactic Constructions

Zero may legitimately be used to represent an empty slot in a syntactic construction (which is a syntagmatic chain). A clear example is *John came in and ø sat down*, where the subject slot of the second clause is left empty. In terms of the syntactic conventions of English, the subject of the second clause—realized by zero—is taken to be identical with the subject of the first.

Other circumstances in which zero may be employed as a syntactic tool in English include sentences such as *John ate an apple and Mary ø an orange, I like sour milk better than fresh ø*, and *You were running faster than I was ø* (Bloomfield 1933: 252). The zeros here should be reconstituted as *eat*, *milk* and *running* respectively. One way of describing these examples is to say that an underlying element is replaced by zero through a rule of ellipsis (there is a multitudinous literature on this).

4. Morphological Structures

Generally, every word should include a root, which typically may be flanked by a number of prefixes and/or suffixes. There can be special circumstances under which a root slot is left empty; one could say that here the root has a zero alternant. It is highly unusual for a root to have zero form in every circumstance. Roberts (1997) does report such a situation in Amele (Gum family, Papua New Guinea). In this language a verb takes pronominal suffixes referring to (in this order): direct object, indirect object, oblique object and subject. 'Give' is realized simply by a complex of bound pronouns in regular form, but with indirect object preceding direct object (the indirect object pronoun could be regarded as a surrogate root to which the other bound forms are attached).

My Jarawara corpus includes about 700 verb roots. One of these makes up no less than 17 per cent of the textual occurrences of verbs. This is *-ka-* 'be in motion'; it shows a number of irregularities. There is a verbal suffix *-ke ~ -ki* 'coming'. As might be expected, it occurs most frequently with the verb *-ka-* 'be in motion', the combination being equivalent to the English verb *come*. When there is no prefix (which is when the subject is third person singular), we get the straightforward root-suffix combination *ka-ke*, as in:

(1)   bati   ka-ke
      father   be.in.motion-COMING
      Father is coming

However, if there is a pronominal prefix (for instance, *o-* for first person singular subject), the root slot is left blank (Dixon 2004b: 148):

(2)   o-ø-ke
      1sg:SUBJECT-be.in.motion-COMING
      I am coming

Since *-ka-* is the only root which may have zero realization, one infers that the empty root slot in (2) is realization of 'be in motion'.

There are two ways of describing this:

(a) Saying that 'be in motion' has zero realization when preceded by a prefix and followed by the 'coming' suffix.
(b) Saying that the underlying structure of (2) is *o-ka-ke*, and the *-ka-* drops from this sequence (the root slot then becoming a blank).

We can note that the 'coming' suffix has form *-ke* when preceded in its phonological word by one or three syllables and *-ki* when preceded by two or four syllables; it can conveniently be represented as *-kI*, where *I* is a morphophoneme realized as *i* or *e*. Under analysis (b), the underlying form of (2) would be *o-ka-kI*; if the *-ka-* did not drop, it would be realized as *o-ka-ki*. We would have to specify that the rule omitting *-ka-* applies before the rule specifying realization of the morphophoneme. However, under analysis (a) there are no concerns of this sort, suggesting that (a) is to be preferred.

§§3–4 have discussed zero elements in syntagmatic strings—in a syntactic construction in §3 and in a morphological structure in §4. We can now look at the most pervasive use of zero, which is as realization of a term (or as one of the alternative realizations of a term) in a paradigmatic system.

5. GRAMMATICAL SYSTEMS

A grammar includes a number of closed systems, each consisting of a limited number of terms. The function and meaning of each term is defined with respect to the functions and meanings of the other terms in its system. For example, in a typical three-term number system, something which is neither 'singular' nor 'plural' is recognized to be 'dual'.

One term in a system may have zero realization in all environments; this produces an empty slot (a 'blank') in the place where the system is realized. The blank has contrastive value, just as do the other terms in the system, which have non-zero realization. Consider the regular inflection for number of an English noun, such as *dog*:

(3) SINGULAR   *dog-ø*   referring to just one dog
     PLURAL   *dog-s*   referring to two or more dogs

Singular, marked by zero (a blank in the slot available for number suffix in the template of noun structure in English), has the specific meaning of referring to a single individual, in contrast to plural, which has the specific meaning of referring to more than one individual. Consider:

(4) The dog-ø stands in the yard

(5) The dog-s stand in the yard

The noun *dog-ø*, as subject, selects the third person singular present/generic ending, orthographic -*s*, on the verb, whereas noun *dog-s* selects the non-third-singular ending -*ø*.

There are two ways in which zero plays a role within grammatical systems. Zero may be the sole realization of a term, as for singular on nouns in English. Or zero may be one of a number of alternative realizations (an allomorph) of a term. Plural is shown by orthographic -*s* on most count nouns in English, but by zero on a few, including *sheep* (also *deer, fish* and a few others). Corresponding to (4–5), we get:

(6) The sheep-ø stands in the yard

(7) The sheep-ø stand in the yard

Number agreement with the third singular ending -*s* on the verb in (6) shows that the ø on *sheep* in (6) is the invariant realization of singular number, while agreement with the non-third-singular ending -*ø* on the verb in (7) shows that the ø on *sheep* in this sentence is the zero allomorph of plural.

For another example, consider inflections on an English verb. We have:

(8)
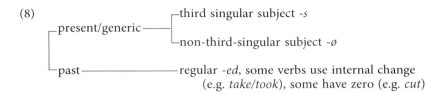

With a regularly inflecting verb, such as *slice*, we get:

ENDING ON VERB
(9) generic, third sg subject, *-s*   John slice-s the bread each morning

(10) generic, non-third-sg subject, *-ø*   I slice-ø the bread each morning

(11) past, *-ed*   John slice-d the bread yesterday

(12) past, *-ed*   I slice-d the bread yesterday

The sentences corresponding to (9–12) for a verb, such as *cut*, which has zero allomorph for past tense are:

ENDING ON VERB
(13) generic, third sg subject, *-s*   John cut-s the bread each morning

(14) generic, non-third-sg subject, *-ø*   I cut-ø the bread each morning

(15) past, *-ø*   John cut-ø the bread yesterday

(16) past, *-ø*   I cut-ø the bread yesterday

In (14), the *ø* on *cut* is the invariant realization of the present/generic term in the tense system. In (15–16), the *ø* on *cut* is the allomorph, for this verb, of the past term in this system. Quoted outside of an instance of use, *cut-ø* is ambiguous between present/generic and past values. But, within a sentence, the identity of the zero is likely to be clarified by the other items present. In (16), time adverb *yesterday* indicates that the *ø* here is an allomorph of past, while in (14) the time adverb *each morning* shows that the *ø* on *cut* is the present/generic term.

We have seen that there are two uses of zero within a grammatical system:

(a) The sole realization of a term—for example, singular in the number system for nouns in English, and present/generic with a non-third-singular subject in the tense system for verbs.

(b) One of the alternative realizations of one (or more) terms in a system—for example, plural in the number system and past in the tense system.

It would not be possible for there to be two terms in a system both having entirely zero realization, type (a). However, there could be two terms of type (b), each having a zero allomorph (in different, or in overlapping, circumstances). And, as illustrated for *sheep* and *cut*, a system can have one term of type (a) and one (or more) of type (b). This leads to potential ambiguity, which is likely to be resolved from the discourse context.

5.1. *Markedness*

It is often said that zero is linked to markedness. For example: 'within a grammatical correlation a zero affix cannot be steadily assigned to the marked category and a "nonzero" (real) affix to the unmarked category' (Jakobson 1990: 157).

In point of fact, one needs to distinguish two kinds of markedness within grammar:

(i) Formal markedness. A term with invariant zero form is the formally unmarked member of its system.
(ii) Functional markedness. This relates to context of use. The marked term(s) are only used with specific meanings, in restricted contexts, whereas the unmarked term may be used with a general meaning in general contexts.

Formal and functional markedness do not necessarily coincide. Consider the inflectional system on verbs in Dyirbal, illustrated for *bani-* 'come':

(17) positive imperative   bani-ø
      negative imperative   bani-m
      present/past   bani-ñu
      future   bani-ñ
      purposive   bani-gu

Positive imperative is realized by zero and is the formally unmarked term in the system. But the present/past, *baniñu*, is the functionally unmarked form. Whenever a speaker wishes to refer to a verb (without

R. M. W. DIXON

recourse to whether it is imperative, purposive, past, present or future) they will use *baniñu* as citation form.[2]

5.2. *Obligatory system, including zero, versus optional system*

There can be, say, three possible forms for a word—with suffix X, or with suffix Y, or with no suffix. There are then two possible analyses:

(a) An obligatory three-term system, with two of the terms having suffixal realization and the third term being realized by zero.
(b) An optional two term system, with the terms realized by suffixes X and Y. When a word is used with no suffix at all, this indicates that the system has not been applied.

In contrast to the 'zero' analysis, (a), we could call (b) a kind of 'nothing' analysis.

Which analysis should be preferred depends on whether or not the root with no suffix has a specific meaning, a value contrastive to (and complementary with) those of the words with suffix X and with suffix Y, or whether it simply bears a general meaning, independent of those relating to X and Y.

Many languages have a grammatical system which must or can specify the type of evidence on which a statement is based. As with other systems, one term can have zero realization. There is a three-term evidentiality system in Bora (Bora-Witoto family, Colombia; data from Aikhenvald 2004: 44).

(18) TYPE OF EVIDENCE   REALIZATION
      visual   zero
      inferential   clitic *ʔha*
      reported   clitic *βa*

---

[2] The account given here applies to the southern dialects of Dyirbal. Northern dialects have the same forms of inflections, but differ in how they assign time reference to them:

INFLECTION	SOUTHERN DIALECTS	NORTHERN DIALECTS
-ñu	present/past	past
-ñ	future	present/future

Interestingly, the citation form is present/past, *baniñu*, for southern dialects but present/future, *baniñ*, for northern dialects. That is, the inflection whose reference includes present time is always the functionally unmarked term in the system.

Here zero has a specific meaning, visual evidence, complementary to the inferential and reported meanings of the other two terms in the system, each realized by a non-zero clitic. Analysis (a) is plainly appropriate for the obligatory system of evidentiality in Bora (one term of the system having zero realization).

This can be contrasted with evidentiality specification in Retuarã (Tucanoan family, Colombia; data from Aikhenvald 2004: 49). There are three non-zero markers onto verbs:

(19) TYPE OF EVIDENCE   REALIZATION
      auditory   suffix *-ko*
      reported   suffix *-re*
      assumed   suffix *-rihi*

But, in addition, a verb may bear none of these three suffixes. Is this a zero, a fourth term in the system? It is not, the reason being that a verb with none of these suffixes does not carry a specific meaning. It simply indicates that no specification of evidentiality is being made (a 'nothing'). A verb with no suffix can be used if in fact the evidence was auditory or reported or assumed, but the speaker does not choose to specify this; and it must be employed when the evidence was of some other type (for instance, visual). It will be seen that analysis (b) is appropriate for Retuarã; there is an optional evidentiality system, all of whose terms have non-zero realization. The system need not be applied; then we get nothing in the way of information about type of evidence.

The number system on nouns in English is of type (a), the term with zero realization having a specific value (singular) in contrast to that of the formally marked term (plural). This is an inflectional system, obligatory on each count noun. We can repeat (3):

(3) SINGULAR   *dog-ø*   referring to just one dog
     PLURAL   *dog-s*   referring to two or more dogs

Now compare this with ways of marking number on nouns in Dyirbal, for example, on *guda* 'dog':

(20) (a) *guda*   any number of dogs (one, two or more)

     (b) *guda-jarran*   two dogs, a pair of dogs

     (c) *guda-guda*   many dogs (generally, three or more)

This is not a grammatical system of number marking, similar to that in English. In (20c), reduplication indicates plurality; since there is a specific marker for dual, illustrated in (20b), reduplication is generally (but not exclusively) used for a group of more than two individuals. Dyirbal has a set of stem-forming affixes to a noun; they include *-jarran* 'two, a pair of'—in (20b)—and also *-gabun* 'another', *-mumbay* 'all (and only)' and *-bajun* 'really, very' (Dixon 1972: 221–32, 243–243).

The point to note is that the plain noun with neither suffix nor reduplication, in (20a), indicates nothing about number. It could not be considered a term in a number system in the way that zero (indicating singular) can be for English. (To specify singular reference in Dyirbal, one must simply modify the noun with number adjective *yuŋgul* 'one'; that is, *guda yuŋgul* 'one dog'.)

Mithun (1986) provides a fascinating account of differing systems of bound pronouns. In some languages, an argument is obligatorily realized by a bound pronoun, optionally augmented by a noun phrase; if one term in the paradigm of bound pronouns—say third person singular—has zero realization, then the absence of an overt realization in the bound pronominal slot implies third person singular. In other languages, an argument may be realized either by a bound pronoun or by a noun phrase. There may be no bound pronoun for third person singular, so that a noun phrase has to be included to indicate this argument. Here the absence of an overt realization in the bound pronominal slot carries no implication of third person singular reference (that is, there is no term in the system with zero realization).

6. ZERO AND NOTHING IN JARAWARA

Pāṇini's discussion, summarized in §1, is also appropriate for Jarawara. The masculine form of the 'continuous' suffix can be assigned zero form (Pāṇini's *lopa*); in contrast, the masculine form of polar interrogative corresponds to one of Pāṇini's *lu* elisions, being nothing.

First we need to supply a little grammatical background.

6.1. *Some Basic Grammatical Information*

Jarawara has two genders: f(eminine), the functionally unmarked choice, and m(asculine). These are not shown on a noun itself but by agreement of modifiers within a noun phrase, and on the verb. Verbal agreement is with the pivot (grammatical topic) of the clause. This is in A function in one kind of transitive clause (an A-construction) and in O function in another kind (an O-construction). All the examples below involve intransitive clauses, where the pivot is in S function, or copula clauses where the pivot is in CS (copula subject) function.

Most verbal suffixes have distinct feminine/masculine forms, e.g. declarative -*ke*/-*ka*. For example, with nouns *mati* 'mother' and *bati* 'father' and intransitive verb *tafa* 'eat':

(21) mati$_S$ tafa-k**e**   Mother eats

(22) bati$_S$ tafa-k**a**   Father eats

A verb whose root ends in *a* (and a number of suffixes, including negator -*ra*) maintain a constant form when non-final, as in (21–22). However, when word-final, they do agree with the pivot in gender—*a* is maintained for feminine and raised to *e* for masculine agreement. Thus:

(23) mati$_S$ taf**a**   Mother eats

(24) bati$_S$ taf**e**   Father eats

6.2. *Zero realization of masculine form of 'continuous' suffix*

The 'continuous' suffix appears to have form -^{i}*ne* (where the *i* replaces a preceding *a*) for feminine and zero (ø) for masculine (Dixon 2004b: 187). Thus, when followed by declarative:

(25) mati$_S$ tafi-ne-ke   Mother is eating

(26) bati$_S$ tafa-ka   Father is eating

When there is no following declarative suffix, we get:

(27) mati$_S$ tafi-ne   Mother is eating

(28) bati$_S$ tafa   Father is eating

These forms can be explained by the following analysis:

(27') tafa-^{i}ne
       eat-CONTINUOUS:f

(28') tafa-ø
       eat-CONTINUOUS:m

In 'eat-CONTINUOUS:m', the root-final vowel *a* is not word-final; it is followed by the zero allomorph of the continuous suffix for masculine gender. It is because of this zero element that the root-final *a* of *tafa* is not word-final and is thus not raised to *e* in order to show masculine agreement, as it is in (24).

6.3. *Masculine polar interrogative is not zero, but nothing*

The situation is rather different for the polar interrogative mood suffix (Dixon 2004b: 410–11). This has feminine form *-ᶦni*, as in the copula clause (including negative suffix *-ra*):

(29) ratena$_{CS}$ ama-ri-ni?
      flashlight(f)   be-NEGATIVE-POLAR.INTERROGATIVE:f
      Isn't it a flashlight?

Here negative suffix *-ra-* plus feminine polar interrogative *-ᶦni-* gives *-ri-ni-*. The corresponding question with masculine agreement is:

(30) afiao$_{CS}$ ama-re?
      plane(m)   be-NEGATIVE:m
      Isn't it a plane?

We could suggest that the masculine form of the polar interrogative is zero. But if this were the case we would get:

(31) ama-ra-ø
      be-NEGATIVE-POLAR.INTERROGATIVE:m

And the zero would stop the raising of the *a* of negator *-ra* to *e* to mark masculine gender agreement.

But we do get this raising. The only thing to conclude is that the masculine form of the polar interrogative is not zero, but nothing. The *a* of negative suffix *-ra* does count as word-final, since nothing follows it, and is raised to *e* to mark masculine agreement. In the morphology of Jarawara—as in Sanskrit (and probably many other languages)—there appears to be a distinction between zero and nothing.[3]

---

[3] Contini-Morava (2006) presents a very similar analysis of noun class prefixes in Swahili, in terms of zero and nothing.

PART C

ENGLISH GRAMMAR AND LEXICOLOGY

CHAPTER FOURTEEN

PRONOUNS WITH TRANSFERRED REFERENCE

R. M. W. Dixon*

For almost 30 years, there has been occasional mention in the literature[1] of the first person pronoun having varying reference at different places within a single sentence, but no real attempt has been made to explain such cognitive dissonance. My aim here is to further articulate the problem, exploring which syntactic functions a pronoun can be in for this 'transfer of reference', and whether the transfer may also apply to plural first person and also to second person pronouns.

If a bit of discourse describes someone, A, taking on the identity of someone else, B (in a dream, or as a hypothetical state-of-affairs) the reference of a pronoun within this discourse may be transferred from A to B.

In the late 1960s, Jim McCawley (JM) came up with a sentence along the following lines:[2]

(1)   I dreamt I was Brigitte Bardot ‖ and I kissed me, ‖ and then I woke up
       JM   JM   →   BB   BB   JM   JM

In the portion of the sentence between the ‖'s, the reference of *I* is changed from the speaker, Jim McCawley, to Brigitte Bardot. Note that, although the clause *I kissed me* has the first person pronoun as both subject and object, the *me* cannot be replaced by *myself*. The reason is that *I* and *me* are not coreferential, *I* referring to Brigitte Bardot

* Thanks are due to Haj Ross for a bibliographic reference, to Nicholas Evans for a suggestion at an oral presentation of this material, and to Alexandra Aikhenvald for detailed and perceptive comments.

[1] Among a number of other discussions, Fauconnier (1997: 14–6, 161–4) mentions sentences along the lines of *If I were you, I would hire me*. However, neither he nor others pursue the grammatical possibilities associated with such constructions.

[2] Lakoff (1970: 27) quotes 'McCawley's celebrated example' as *I dreamed that I was Brigitte Bardot and that I kissed me*. Lakoff then says that he finds the problems thrown up by this example 'very mysterious, and I have no idea of how to account for them. But one thing is clear. Referential indices will not do the job.'

R. M. W. DIXON

and *me* to the speaker. The transfer of reference ceases at the second ‖, so that in the final clause *I* refers once again to the speaker.

Taubman (2003: 15) quotes Nikita Khrushchev as saying, to the meeting of the Central Committee which dismissed him:

(2)   I understand that my role doesn't exist anymore, but if
     NK   NK
       I were you, ‖ I wouldn't dismiss me entirely ‖
       NK → CC CC   NK

In a recent newspaper article, Sally Satel (2008: 30) wrote of how, needing a kidney transplant, she looked at the profiles of deserving people with the same need and mused on what her attitude might be were she (SS) a kidney donor (KD):

(3)   Were I were a prospective kidney donor, ‖ even I wouldn't
       SS   →   KD   KD
       have picked me ‖
          SS

In the 1942 film *Casablanca*, the Chief of Police (CP) says something like the following to the character played by Humphrey Bogart (HB):

(4)   If I were a woman and I were not around, ‖ I'd be in love with you ‖
     CP →   W   CP   W   HB

Missing out the negative from the second clause of (4), we might get:

(5)   If I were a woman and I were around, ‖ I'd be in love with me ‖
     CP →   W   CP   W   CP

Along similar lines, I once heard a husband (H) say to his wife (W), who had told him she would call on her mobile phone to let the husband know which train he should meet:

(6)   If I were you, ‖ I wouldn't call me until I got to the station,‖ and you
      H → W W   H   W   W
       found out what train you are going to catch
              W

The transfer of reference—with 'I' (the husband) assuming the identity of 'you' (the wife)—extends between the two ‖'s. Pronominal reference

in the final clause is the same as in the first clause, with *you* referring
to the wife.

Thus far, all instances of transfer have involved the first person singular pronoun in subject function. But it does extend further. Consider
a scenario in which John (J) served a spell in prison before meeting
and marrying Mary (M). Before getting married, he wonders whether
he should confess his nefarious past, but decides not to. Later, Mary
does find out, from some other source, and is upset. Mary then says
to her husband:

(7)   If I had been you, ‖ I'd have told my story to me before I married
      M   →   J J   J   M   J
      me,‖ but you didn't
      M   J

Here the transfer applies also to the possessor *my* within the object NP.

It thus appears that the transfer can apply to a first person subject,
or to a possessor which is coreferential with such a subject.

All the sentences thus far have involved the singular first person
pronoun. But transfer of reference is also possible with first person
plural, as in:

(8)   If we were the NSF, ‖ we'd give us/our project a big grant, ‖
      A →   NSF   NSF   A
      but we're not
      A

Transfer can apply to the subject of a passive clause. Suppose that John
is easily deceived and Mary is more canny. John has just been swindled
and ruefully tells Mary:

(9)   If I had been you, ‖ I wouldn't have been taken in by the con-man, ‖
      J   →   M M
      since I am pretty gullible and you are less so
        J   M

However, transfer would be less felicitous if the second clause of (9)
were in active rather than passive form:

(10) ?If I had been you, ‖ the con-man wouldn't have taken me in,‖ since
       J   →   M   M
      I am pretty gullible and you are less so
      J   M

That is, transfer appears to be possible into subject function, as in (1–9) but not—for most native speakers of English—into object function, as in (10).

So the principle appears to be:

> A pronoun whose normal reference is A may have its reference transferred to B if the discourse includes a 'transfer statement' along the lines of 'if A were B' or 'if A had been B' or 'I dreamt A was B'. This transfer applies to a (singular or plural) first person pronoun in (underlying or derived) subject function, and to a possessor within the same clause which relates to such a transferred-reference pronoun.

In certain circumstances, the transfer may be optional. Suppose that Tom is about to pull up some prickly bushes. His friend John suggests that Tom should take care so that the prickles do not injure his hands. John could say either of the following two sentences (with the same meaning and pragmatic effect):

(11) (a)   If I were you, ‖ I'd wear my gardening gloves ‖
            J →   T   T   T

(11) (b)   If I were you, ‖ I'd wear ‖ your gardening gloves
            J →   T   T   T

In (11a) the possessor within the object NP in the second clause also has transferred reference, along with the subject of this clause. In (11b) transfer is confined to the subject, the possessor having 'normal' (non-transferred) meaning. For (11a) the scope of the transfer extends to the end of the second clause whereas for (11b) it finishes after *wear*.

Suppose that Tom's gardening gloves are old and torn, whereas John has a new pair which he offers to Tom. John could say:

(12) If I were you, ‖ I'd wear‖ '*my* gardening gloves
          J →   T   T   J

That is, John is saying: 'If I (John) were you (Tom), then I (Tom) would wear my (John's) gardening gloves'. John achieves this message through stressing *my* in (12)—shown by '—indicating reversion of reference. In contrast, *my* in (11a) is unstressed, indicating continuation of reference transfer.

Another difference is that *own* could be inserted after *my* in (11a), indicating that the possessive pronoun is co-referential with the subject of its clause: *If I were you, ‖I'd wear my own gardening gloves ‖*. In contrast, it is not permissible to insert *own* after *my* in (12) since here *my* is not co-referential with the subject of its clause.

Note that the possessive pronoun in (7) could *not* have normal reference, as it does in (12). This is, one could not say:

(7) (b)   *If I had been you, ‖¹ I'd have told ‖² your story ‖³ to me before I
     M   →   J   J   J   M   J
        married me, ‖⁴ but you didn't
           M   J

Sentence (7b) would involve discontinuous transfer of reference, between ‖¹ and ‖² and between ‖³ an d ‖⁴, but not between ‖² and ‖³. This appears not to be acceptable.

So far we have discussed transfer of reference for first person pronouns, to second person in (2), (6)–(7), (9) and (11)–(12), and to some other participant in (1), (3)–(5) and (8). But there are two pronouns referring to speech act participants.[3] We should enquire whether transfer of reference can also apply to a second person pronoun? It appears that this may be possible, although it is less common—and more difficult to process—than transfer involving a first person pronoun. Whereas several of the examples already given were observed—(2)–(4), (6), and (11a/b)—all of those below, involving transfer applying to a second person pronoun, have been thought up.

One could use second person in place of first person in (1). Suppose that Jim McCawley said to George Lakoff (GL):

(13)   I dreamt you were Brigitte Bardot ‖ and you kissed you ‖
    JM   GL   →   BB   BB   GL
    and then I woke up
        JM

---

[3] 'Third person' pronouns are of a quite different nature from first and second person forms. I follow Benveniste (1971a: 198, 217) in considering that '"the third person" is not a "person", it is really the...form whose function is to express the *non-person*'. (That is, it is not a speech act participant.) However, when there is a term referring to 'non-person' in the same paradigm as first and second person pronouns, then the custom is to refer to it as 'third person'. It is first and second persons which form a natural class, so that it is relevant to enquire to what extent anything which is a property of first person may also apply for second person pronouns.

A second person pronoun could also be used in place of first person in (8):

(14) If you were the NSF, ‖ you'd give you/your project a big grant, ‖
      A   →   NSF   NSF   A
    but you're not
      A

For another example, suppose that John is someone who typically tells everyone everything. He finds out that his friend Tom has been keeping an important secret from him and berates Tom for it. Tom's response is:

(15) If you were me, ‖ would you have trusted you with the/your secret, ‖
     J   → T   T   J   T
    knowing how indiscrete you are?
                   J

Suppose that John is someone who never signs anything without a great deal of thought whereas Mary is impulsive and tends to sign everything placed before her. John says to Mary, with transferred reference for first person pronoun:

(16) If I were you,‖ I wouldn't sign the contract, ‖ but you will
    J → M M   M

Or, with the same scenario, Mary could employ transferred reference for second person pronoun:

(17) If you were me,‖ you wouldn't sign the contract, ‖ but I will
    J   → M M   M

All of the examples above have been statements. Transfer of reference would not be possible in a command. It may, however, be possible—in limited circumstances—in a question. For example:

(18) If you were Brigitte Bardot, ‖would you kiss you?‖
     A →   BB   BB   A

and:

(19) If you were the NSF, ‖would you give you/your project a big grant? ‖
          A   →   NSF   NSF   A

This provides a brief overview of how transferred reference can be used for first person pronouns in subject function (and, to a more limited extent, for second person pronouns in subject function) in English statements and questions. The transfer is motivated by the creation of an 'alternative world', introduced by a conditional copula construction of the form 'if I/you were X' or else 'I dreamt that I/you were X'.

It would be interesting to explore to what extent transferred reference can be utilised in other European languages, with structures similar to that of English, and also in languages of quite different profile, including those with an inclusive/exclusive distinction for first person non-singular pronouns, and also for languages with obligatory bound pronouns.

CHAPTER FIFTEEN

COMPARATIVE CONSTRUCTIONS IN ENGLISH

R. M. W. Dixon*

1. Introduction

The prototypical comparative scheme—which is found in most (but not all) human languages—involves comparing two participants in terms of the degree of some gradable property relating to them. There are three basic elements: the two participants being compared, and the property in terms of which they are compared.[1] Consider the sentence:

(1)   John   is   more   famous   than   Bill
      COMPAREE   INDEX   PARAMETER   MARK   STANDARD

The participants are:

COMPAREE—that which is being compared, here *John*

STANDARD of comparison—what the comparee is being compared against, here *Bill*

The property is:

PARAMETER of comparison—here *famous*

A prototypical comparative scheme will generally also include:

INDEX of comparison—here *more* (with a different choice of adjective it could be *-er*)

---

* I have benefited from the most helpful comments on a draft of this chapter from Alexandra Y. Aikhenvald, Kate Burridge, Andrew Butcher, Stig Johansson and Jerry Sadock. And from the participants in the Workshop on Comparative Constructions at the Research Centre for Linguistic Typology in 2004.
[1] See Dixon (2008a) for a general discussion and cross-linguistic typology of comparative constructions.

Within any clause, there must be some marking of the function of each argument. In English the Comparee is subject (shown by its position before the verb), with the Standard of comparison receiving special marking. We get:

MARK of the grammatical function of the Standard—*than*

This chapter deals with comparative constructions in my dialect of educated British English. It begins, in §2, with consideration of the form of the index of comparison, and the conditions for using *more* or *-er* or either. There is then discussion of comparison of adverbs, and of the superlative index with both adjectives and adverbs. The syntax of comparatives is the topic of §3. Two brief sections then mention inherently comparative expressions, and the verb *compare*. (Note that I basically follow the transcriptional system of Jones (1956), who documents a dialect of educated British English very similar to my own.)

2. FORM OF THE INDEX OF COMPARISON

We can exemplify positive and negative instance of the prototypical comparative scheme in English by:

(2a) John is fatter than Tom

(2b) John is less fat than Tom

(2c) John is more intelligent than Tom

(2d) John is less intelligent than Tom

These are copula clauses with the Parameter of comparison being an adjective, in copula complement function. The positive Index of comparison is either a suffix *-er*, /-ə(r)/, or a modifier *more*, /mɔ:/ or /mɔə/. There are corresponding superlative Indexes *-est*, /-əst/ or /-ist/, and *most*, /moust/. The negative index of comparison has a single form, comparative *less*, /les/, and superlative *least*, /li:st/.

The origin of the periphrastic Indexes *more, most, less* and *least* is interesting. In Old English, the adjectives *micel* 'big' and *lȳtel* 'little' had the following paradigm:

	PLAIN	COMPARATIVE	SUPERLATIVE
'big'	micel	māra	mǣst
'little'	lȳtel	lǣssa	lǣst

The form *micel* dropped out of use (being replaced by *big*), but its comparative and superlative were retained as general periphrastic Indexes for adjectives which do not take *-er* or *-est* (and for some that do). The comparative and superlative of *little* took the same path, becoming dissociated from the adjective *little*. For the comparative of *little* one just had to use *smaller* and *smallest*. Only recently have new comparative and superlative forms, *littler* and *littlest*, started to come into use.

Besides being used for qualitative comparison, *more* and *less* also have a quantitative sense, as in *Three times three is more than six plus two*, *There are more people in Sydney than in Melbourne*, and *He drinks less (beer) than he used to*.

English still retains irregular paradigms for three adjectives:

PLAIN	COMPARATIVE	SUPERLATIVE
good	better	best
bad	worse	worst
far	farther/further	farthest/furthest

Regular comparative and superlative forms *older* and *oldest* have now replaced the original irregular forms *elder* and *eldest*. The latter are retained in frozen lexical items such as *the elders of the church / the tribe* and *elder brother / sister*. In a prototypical comparative construction, only *older* (and *oldest*) may be used.

The Indexes can be modified. For example:

(3) a bit
     a little bit   *plus* fatter / more intelligent / less fat / less intelligent
     much
     very much

An Index of comparison may also be preceded by an adverb such as *even, simply, really,* or *kind-of*.

When used in a prototypical comparative construction such as (1–2)—with two participants and one property—some adjectives only take *-er* (for example, *big, kind*), some only take *more* (*intelligent, beautiful*), while others may take either (*friendly, stupid*) as the Index of comparison. When two properties are compared with respect to one participant, in a non-prototypical comparative construction, we get:

(4) Mary is more kind than intelligent

One cannot say **Mary is kinder than intelligent*. That is, when the first adjective in a construction like (4) is one which would normally take *-er* (or an irregular comparative), it must in this context take *more*. This is discussed further in §3. (Note that whereas the prototypical comparative construction is found in many language, a non-prototypical construction such as (4) occurs in far fewer languages.)

Whether a given adjective may take *-er* or *more* in a prototypical comparative construction is almost predictable.[2] It depends on a combination of factors:

- the phonological form of the adjective;
- its frequency of usage in the language;
- whether or not it refers to a property which is, in a logical sense, gradable.

The most basic parameter is phonological form, as set out in Table 15.1. During and after commentary on the Table, I will refer to the other two factors. Note that parentheses around /ə/ or ✓ in Table 15.1 indicate that this is a less preferred possibility.

The orthographic form *-er* has the following phonological forms:

—(i) /-gə/ after a monosyllable ending in /ŋ/; for example, *long*, /lɔŋ/, *longer*, /lɔŋgə/.
—(ii) /-ə/ elsewhere. That is, after a consonant other than /ŋ/, as in *wide*, /waid/, *wider*, /waidə/. And after a vowel other than /ə/, as in *grey*, /grei/, *greyer*, /greiə/; *true*, /tru:/, *truer*, /tru(:)ə/; *pretty*, /priti/, *prettier*, /pritiə/.

A set of adjectives have orthographic form ending in *r* or *re* with the last vowel being /ə/. In some dialects—particularly in Scotland and the USA—a final /r/ is generally pronounced. However, in standard English and Australian varieties, the /r/ is only pronounced before a suffix, clitic or following word (within the same intonation group) which begins with a vowel. We thus get /-rə/, as realisation of comparative *-er* after /ə/; for example, *dear* /diə/, *dearer*, /diərə/; *tender*, /tendə/, *tenderer*, /tendərə/; *obscure*, /əbskjuə/, *obscurer*, /əbskjuərə/.

All allomorphs of *-er* take a linking /r/ before a word commencing with a vowel within the same grammatical constituent, so long as a pause does not intervene; for example, *smaller elf*, /smɔːlər elf/.

---

[2] Bauer (1994: 51–61) presents a study of how the use of *more* and *-er* may have changed over the past century (without arriving at any firm conclusions).

Table 15.1. Choice of -er or more

SET	FORM OF ADJECTIVE	EXAMPLES	-er HAS FORM:	CAN more BE USED
A	Monosyllabic			
	end in /ŋ/	long, strong, young	/-gə/	—
	end in another consonant	big, wide, hard, kind, quiet, rude, brave, calm, cheap, coarse, loose	/-ə/	—
	end in /ə/	fair, clear, dear, square, sure, pure	/-rə/	((✓))
	end in another vowel	dry, free, new, raw, slow, grey	/-ə/	—
B	Disyllabic, monomorphemic, ending in vowel or syllabic /l/			
	end in /i/	heavy, pretty, happy, busy, easy	/-ə/	—
	end in /ou/	yellow, hollow, narrow	/-ə/	(✓)
	end in syllabic /l/	simple, humble, gentle, noble, subtle	/-ə/	(✓)
	end in plain /ə/	clever, bitter, tender	/-rə/	✓
	end in /uə/	demure, secure, obscure, mature	/-rə/	✓
C	Disyllabic, bimorphemic, ending in vowel			
	end in suffix -y, /-i/	cloudy, hungry, lazy, lucky, dreamy	/-ə/	✓
	end in suffix -ly, /-li/	friendly, lonely, lively, lovely, manly	/-ə/	✓
D	All others			
	Disyllabic and longer, end in consonant	famous, superb, public, foreign, golden, careful, difficult, splendid	—	✓
	Exceptions	stupid, solid, wicked, pleasant, polite, common, handsome	/-ə/	✓ ✓
	Trisyllabic and longer, end in vowel	ordinary, familiar, peculiar, extraordinary, necessary	—	✓
E	Adjectives with prefix un- or im-			
	from set A	unkind, unfair	(/-ə/)	✓
	from set B	unhappy	(/-ə/)	✓
	from set C	unfriendly	(/-ə/)	✓
	from set D	uncommon	(/-ə/)	✓
		unpleasant, impolite	—	✓

We can now comment on the sets in Table 15.1 (leaving aside for the time being some adjectives—such as *right* and *real*—which would be expected to take *-er* but don't, on semantic grounds).

SET A. Monosyllabic forms, ending in a consonant or a vowel. These take *-er* and, as a rule, use this form exclusively (rather than *more*) in the prototypical comparative construction. (Some speakers do nowadays use *more*, as an alternative to *-er*, with monosyllabics ending in /ə/, such as *fair* and *clear*.)

Two exceptions are *well* (no speaker accepts **weller*) and *ill* (some speakers accept *iller*, many do not). These are the only common monosyllabic adjectives ending in a high or mid vowel plus /l/ (*cruel*, which takes *-er*, is generally /kruəl/); this may constitute a phonological factor which accounts, in part, for these exceptions. Another factor may be that *well* was originally an adverb, being later extended to adjective function.

SET B. Disyllabic monomorphemic forms, ending in a vowel or syllabic /l/. All take *-er*. A disyllabic form is preserved for all save those ending in /ə/, which—with the 'linking *r*'—add /-rə/; for example, *clever*, /klevə/, *cleverer*, /klevərə/.

Some adjectives in set B may use *more* as an alternative to *-er*. This applies most to those ending in /uə/ or in plain /ə/ where, for example, either of *securer* and *more secure* and either of *cleverer* and *more clever* is acceptable. *More* may be used with forms which end in /ou/, or in syllabic /l/, but the *-er* form is generally preferred; for example, *hollower* rather than *more hollow*, *gentler* rather than *more gentle*. For a less frequent item, such as *mellow* or *subtle*, the *more* alternative may be preferred. Forms ending in /i/ are pretty well restricted to *-er*; one seldom hears *more heavy*.

Although most disyllabic adjectives ending in plain /ə/ take *-er* (*clever*, *bitter*, *tender*), *silver* and *eager* do not. *Silver* is relatively uncommon as an adjective and scarcely used in a comparative construction (one says *more silvery* rather than *more silver*); in addition, the *-il* may be a factor (recall that *well* does not take *-er* and *ill* scarcely does). *Eager* is a common word, often used in comparatives, but only with *more*. **Eagerer* is quite unacceptable, and it is hard to explain why this should be (the long vowel may be a factor, but this is very much speculation).

Disyllabic forms ending in syllabic /l/ generally take -*er*; for example, *simple*, /simpl/, *simpler*, /simplə/. Those which end in /əl/ (*loyal, royal, formal*) count as disyllabic consonant-final and are confined to *more*. *Evil* may have the form /i:vl/ or /i:vil/; it does not take -*er*, suggesting that /i:vil/ calls the tune. *Idle*, /aidl/ satisfies the criterion for -*er*, with a final syllabic /l/; the fact that it is confined to *more* may be due to interference from the noun *idler* (derived from verb *idle*).

There are a few disyllabic adjectives ending in syllabic /n/, such as *rotten* and *sudden*. Unlike those ending in syllabic /l/, most of these are pretty well confined to *more*; *rottener* is rather marginal and **suddener* quite unacceptable. (There is time adverb *often*—with no corresponding adjective—which allows both *oftener* and *more often*.)

SET C. Disyllabic forms ending in a vowel, which include suffix -y or -ly (the only vowel-final suffixes that derive disyllabic adjectives); for example, *friendly, cloudy*. These are like monomorphemic disyllabic forms ending in /i/ (such as *happy*) in taking -*er*. They differ from them in that they may also occur with *more*. Thus, *more friendly* and *more cloudy* as alternatives to *friendlier* and *cloudier*.

SET D. Adjectives not included in sets A-C. Generally, these do not take -*er*. For example, disyllabic forms ending in a consonant, such as *famous, superb, public, foreign, direct*, and *golden*; trisyllabic or longer terms ending in a consonant, such as *elastic, careful, difficult, splendid* and *experimental*; and trisyllabic or longer forms ending in a vowel, such as *ordinary, familiar, peculiar, extraordinary* and *necessary*.

There are a number of exceptions here, disyllabic or longer forms ending in a consonant (none ending in a vowel) which would be expected from their phonological form not to take -*er* but in fact do so, as an alternative to *more*. The main exceptions are:

    stupid, solid, wicked
    pleasant, polite
    common, handsome

There are a number of factors which may go some way towards explaining these exceptions. Firstly, there appears to be a preference for antonyms to behave in the same way. One can say *cleverer, ruder* and *hollower* (sets A and B) and so also *stupider, politer* and *solider*. Another factor is that these are very common, everyday adjectives. A full explanation (in the sense of something which could have been predicted) is not possible. These are exceptions, although not totally surprising exceptions.

It will be seen that five of the exceptions end in /d/ or /t/. When one tries out -er on other adjectives from set D, which are normally confined to *more*, different results are obtained depending on the final segment. Forms ending in a labial or velar stop or /s/ cannot possibly take -er—*superber, *elasticer and *famouser sound totally unacceptable. However, frequently-used adjectives ending in an alveolar stop are not quite as bad. One could imagine the scope of -er being extended so that *rapider, honester, completer* and *profounder* (which are currently quite unacceptable) should come into circulation. That is, the final alveolar stop in *stupid, solid, wicked, pleasant* and *polite* may be one of several factors enabling these adjectives to take -er.

SET E. Adjectives with prefix un-. Generally, if an adjective takes -er then it is likely still to do so after the addition of negative prefix *un-*. However, *more* is always an alternative, and often the preferred alternative.

For sets A and B, *more* is seldom used with *kind, fair* and *happy*, but it is with *unkind, unfair* and *unhappy*. A form such as *more unfair* will often be preferred over *unfairer*. The negated form of *friendly*, from list C, has comparatives *more unfriendly* and *unfriendlier*, and here *more unfriendly* will often be preferred. Some of the exceptions in set D do have *un-* antonyms. One can say *uncommoner*, although *more uncommon* is generally preferred. And *more unpleasant, more impolite* are generally used rather than the odd-sounding *unpleasanter* and *impoliter*.

Frequency has a role here. *Noble* (from set B) is not a very common lexeme; one can say *nobler or more noble*. The negative adjective *ignoble* is a rather obscure item; if this were to be used in a comparative construction, *more ignoble* would have to be used (rather than **ignobler*). Another factor is length; adding *un-* lengthens the stem and—as a rule—the longer a form, the less likely it is to accept -er.

We can now look at semantic reasons for the exclusion of certain adjectives from those that take -er. This relates to their gradability. The adjectives mentioned in Table 15.1, and in the discussion above, are fully gradable. But others are not. We can recognise three classes.

Class (a). Cannot be graded; do not occur with *more* or *-er*. These include:

> first, last, second, opposite

Class (b). Adjectives which, by their meaning, should not really be gradable; however, speakers do use them in comparative constructions. Even though for some of them the phonological form relates to set A or set B, they only occur with *more*, never *-er*.

This class includes (phonological set in parentheses):

right (A)	wrong (A)
real (A)	fake (A)
dead (A)	alive (D)
male (A)	female (D)
ready (B)	
single (B)	

And also the following from set D: *correct, equal, extreme, perfect, proper* and *unique*.

Basically, something should either be right or not, real or not, dead or not, male or not, single or not, and so on. On logical grounds, one should not compare two items in terms of such a property. But people do. The interesting fact is that while most of these adjectives have a phonological form which should accept *-er*, only *more* may be employed. If neither Mary nor Jane are married, then both are single. However, one can say *Mary (who lives alone) is more single than Jane (who shares an apartment with her boyfriend).* Or *John was more right than Peter*, if John got every detail correct but Peter only the outline. Or *He was more dead than I had realised* (the body was starting to decompose).

Class (c) involves *true* and *false*, adjectives which also refer to properties that should not be gradable. They are monosyllables which should take *-er*, not *more*. *True*, at least, can be used with *-er*, but also with *more*, which is not normally available for monosyllables. *False* is only used with *more*.

For those adjectives which may take either *-er* or *more*, there are doubtless various factors which assist in determining which should be used. I have uncovered one of these. In (3) some of the modifiers to a comparative were listed. Those adjectives which may use *more* or *-er* can have *a bit* or *a little bit* or *much* with either of the possibilities. But not *very much*; this always selects the *more* comparative, if a choice is available. For example:

$$\text{very much more} \begin{Bmatrix} \text{handsome} \\ \text{stupid} \\ \text{friendly} \end{Bmatrix} \textit{in preference to} \quad \text{very much} \begin{Bmatrix} \text{handsomer} \\ \text{stupider} \\ \text{friendlier} \end{Bmatrix}$$

Those adjectives which are generally confined to *-er*, do retain this with *very much*; for example, *very much bigger / fatter / dearer / drier*.

2.1. *Comparative adverbs*

The Parameter of comparison may be a manner adverb rather than an adjective, as in:

(4) John spoke more quietly than Mary (spoke)

Here the Comparee is *John spoke* and the Standard of comparison *Mary spoke*, with the Parameter being *quietly*, the Index of comparison *more*, and the Mark of the standard *than*.

Most adjectives form an adverb by the addition of suffix *-ly*.[3] The language does not allow adverbial suffix *-ly* and comparative suffix *-er* to co-occur. There are thus a number of relations between comparative adjective and comparative adverb. Table 15.2 sets out the main possibilities, with (a–d) exemplifying large classes of forms and (e–h) providing a fullish list of exceptions. The rows in the table will be commented on in turn.

There are some adverbs which are not derived from an adjective but which do form a comparative. These include time adverbs *late* and *soon* (both take *-er*) and *often* (which takes *-er* or *more*).

---

[3] I am here describing Standard English. Various dialectal variants can use a plain adjective in adverbial function, as in *He talked rude/bad* rather than *He talked rudely/ badly*. I have not systematically investigated such dialects.

Table 15.2. Comparative forms of adjectives and adverbs

	ADJECTIVES		ADVERBS	
	PLAIN	COMPARATIVE	PLAIN	COMPARATIVE
(a)	rude	ruder	rudely	more rudely
	happy	happier	happily	more happily
(b)	stupid	stupider *or* more stupid	stupidly	more stupidly
(c)	direct	more direct	directly	more directly
(d)	friendly	friendlier *or* more friendly	—	—
(e)	quick	quicker	quick *or* quickly	quicker *or* more quickly
	slow	slower	slow *or* slowly	slower *or* more slowly
(f)	good	better	well	better
	bad	worse	badly	worse
(g)	fast	faster	fast	faster
	hard	harder	hard	harder
	early	earlier	early	earlier
	late	later	late	later
(h)	long	longer	long *or* lengthily	longer *or* more lengthily

—(a) An adjective which forms its comparative with -*er*, and derives an adverb with -*ly*, adds *more* to the adverb for comparison.

—(b) An adjective which may use -*er* or *more* for the comparative, and derives an adverb with -*ly*, again adds *more* to the adverb for comparison.

—(c) Those adjectives which use *more* for comparative, and form an adverb with -*ly*, also use *more* for comparison of the adverb.

—(d) Adjectives derived with suffix -*ly* (from set C of Table 15.1) constitute a class of exceptions. They cannot take adverb-forming suffix -*ly*; it appears that two suffixes -*ly*, even though with different meanings, are not permitted. There is no adverb **friendlily* corresponding to adjective *friendly*, for instance. One simply has to use a phrasal adverb—*in a friendly way* with, for the comparative, either *in a friendlier way* or *in a more friendly way*.

—(e) The two basic SPEED adjectives, *quick* and *slow*, have comparatives *quicker* and *slower*. They form adverbs in regular fashion by adding -*ly*; just occasionally, the plain adjective can be used in adverbal function—*walk quick/slow* as an alternative to *walk quickly/slowly*. In keeping with this, the comparative adverb may be either *quicker/slower* or *more quickly/slowly*.[4]

—(f) The two main VALUE adjectives, *good* and *bad*, have irregular comparatives, *better* and *worse*. *Good* also has an irregular adverb, *well*, while *bad* shows the regular form *badly*. The comparative adjectives are also used as comparative adverbs, *better* (rather than **more well*) and *worse* (rather than **more badly*). For example, *Mary sings better/worse than John.*

---

[4] This variation is beginning to extend to other forms; for example, some people may say *John spoke ruder than Mary*, as an alternative to *John spoke more rudely than Mary*.

—(g) A number of adjectives maintain the same form in adverbial function—*fast, hard, early* and *late*. (There are forms *hardly* and *lately*, with quite different meanings, but no forms **fastly* or **earlily*.) In accord with this, the comparative adjectives are also used as comparative adverbs.

—(h) *Long* behaves in an unusual manner. There is no adverb **longly*; instead, either the adjective *long* or else *lengthily* (derived from the nominalisation *length*) are employed. For example, *He talked long/lengthily on that topic*. The comparative adverb can be based on either of these, as in *He talked longer/more lengthily than Mary*. (One could, alternatively, employ phrasal adverb *at length* and its comparative *at greater length*.)

2.2. *Form of the superlative index*

Basically, every adjective which forms a comparative with *-er* has a corresponding superlative with *-est*. Those employing *more* for comparative use *most* for superlative.

Jespersen (1933: 227) states: 'the superlative does not indicate a higher degree than the comparative, but really states the same degree, only looked at from a different point of view.' Whereas a comparative adjective typically makes up the whole of a copula complement argument and relates together two participants of equal status, as in (1–2), a superlative effectively identifies a unique individual. The superlative form of an adjective typically modifies a noun in an NP which is marked by the definite article *the*. Compare:

(5) John is better / more intelligent than each of the other boys in the class

(6) John is the best / most intelligent boy in the class

Most has two quite different grammatical functions. It can be, as in (6), a general superlative like *-est*, and it can also be an intensifying modifier, with a meaning similar to *very* or *really*. Compare the intensifying use of *most* in (7) with the superlative use in (8):

(7) He is most famous

(8) He is the most famous person (in town)

Famous is an adjective which forms its superlative with *most*. The difference between the two senses of *most* becomes morphologically apparent with an adjective which only takes *-est*, as in (10), or one which may take either *-est* or *most*, as in (12).

(9)   Your mother was most brave (throughout the ordeal)

(10) Your mother was the bravest person (in town) (throughout the ordeal)

(11) She was most friendly

(12) She was the friendliest / most friendly person (in town)

Sentence (10) involves a superlative, expressed by *-est* with *brave*. However, *bravest* could not be used in (9) since here *most* has an intensifying meaning. Similarly for (12) and (11).

   A comparative can be used in a similar syntactic frame to a superlative, as in:

(13) John is the cleverer of the twins

(14) John is the cleverest of the triplets

In many cases, a comparative is employed when two participants are involved and a superlative for more than two. However, people do use a superlative for reference to a set of two; one hears *John is the cleverest of the twins*. And the idiom *put your best foot forward* can not be rephrased as **put your better foot forward*.

2.3. *Superlative adverbs*

Superlative adverbs follow the same formal pattern as comparatives, set out in Table 15.2. One simply uses *-est* in place of *-er* (/ist/ or /əst/ replacing the /ə(r)/ of *-er*) and *most* in place of *more*. However, superlative adverbs are used much less than comparative adverbs. A typical syntactic position is following the core constituents of a clause, as in:

(15)

He speaks French
$\left\{ \begin{array}{l} \text{(the) best} \\ \text{(the) slowest} \\ \text{(the) most fluently} \\ \text{(the) most carefully} \end{array} \right\}$
of all the boys in the class

It was remarked that a superlative adjective typically occurs in an NP with *the*. As can be seen in (15), a superlative adverb is typically preceded by *the*, although this can be omitted.

3. THE SYNTAX OF COMPARATIVE CONSTRUCTIONS

There are basically three Indexes of comparison in English—*more* (*than*), *less* (*than*), and *as…*(*as*). Consider:

(16) John is more intelligent than Fred

(17) Fred is less intelligent than John

(18) John is as intelligent as Fred

Sentences (16) and (17) have the same meaning—that John's level of intelligence is greater than Fred's. Sentence (18) states that the levels of intelligence are the same.[5]
    Under negation we get:

(19) John is not more intelligent than Fred

(20) Fred is not less intelligent than John

(21) John is not so/as intelligent as Fred

Both (19) and (20) state that Fred's level of intelligence is the same as or greater than John's. And (21) states that John's level of intelligence is below that of Fred. That is, negation of '(the same) as' implies less, never more. Jespersen (1933: 224) points out that: 'comparisons with *less* are not very frequent; instead of *less dangerous than*, we often say *not so dangerous as*, and whenever there are two adjectives of opposite meaning we say, for instance, *weaker than*, rather than *less strong than*.'
    More (*than*), *less* (*than*) and *as* (*as*) have a quantitative as well as a qualitative sense, the equality Index then becoming *as many/much as*. The Indexes can link NPs within an NP. For example:

(22) *More* men *than* women
      Less (or *fewer*) men *than* women ⎫   voted for the president
      As many men *as* women ⎭

(23)
                                  ⎧ *more* whiskey *than* gin
      Last year, Japan imported   ⎨ *less* whiskey *than* gin
                                  ⎩ *as much* whiskey *as* gin

An alternative to *as many as* is *as few as*. Then, *As few men as women voted for the president* states that a small number of men, and about the same small number of women, cast their vote for him. Similarly, an alternative to *as much as* is *as little as*. This provides a paradigm for quantity terms:

---

[5] Huddleston and Pullum (2002: 1101) state that (18) 'is consistent with' John having a higher level of intelligence than Fred. This is erroneous. It would require something like *John is at least as intelligent as Fred*.

(24)

	PLAIN	COMPARATIVE	SUPERLATIVE
COUNTABLE MASS	many much	more	most
COUNTABLE MASS	few little	less	least

The comparative and superlative of *few* can be *fewer* and *fewest* (forms preferred by prescriptivists), as alternatives to *less* and *least*.

Quantitative comparison relates items in terms of their size. In contrast, qualitative comparison relates items in terms of some shared property or state or activity. The prototypical comparative construction is exemplified in (1–2) but the full possibilities are considerably wider. In essence, any two clauses can be compared—by *more* (*than*), *less* (*than*) or *as* ... (*as*)—provided that

—(i)   each clause is of the same construction type;
—(ii) the clauses describe comparable properties, states or actions.

The possibilities are illustrated in:

(25)

a Mary dances	*i* more than	*a* John sings
b Mary speaks French	*ii* more often than	*b* John speaks German
c Mary designs gardens	*iii* better than	*c* John constructs gardens
d Mary writes stories	*iv* more slowly than/ slower than	*d* John paints pictures
e Mary likes jazz		*e* John dislikes rock
f Insincerity annoys Mary	*v* more vigorously than	*f* Jealousy irks John

The Parameters and Indexes of comparison illustrated in (25) are:

—(i)   quantity—*more than, less than, as much as*;
—(ii) time—*more often than, less often than, as often as*;
—(iii) VALUE—*better than, worse than, as well/badly as*:[6]

---

[6] Note that there is also the phrasal preposition *as well as*. The comparative *as well as* is unambiguous in *Mary speaks French as well as John speaks German*. However, the reduced version *Mary speaks French as well as John* is ambiguous between a comparative reading (the excellence of Mary's speaking French is on a par with

—(iv) SPEED—*more slowly than* or *slower than, less slowly than* or *less slow than, as slowly as* (and similarly for *quick, fast*);

—(v) adverbs derived from other adjectives; for example, *more vigorously than, less vigorously than, as vigorously as.*

Note that not every comparative adverb can be appropriately marked with every pair of clauses. For example, (ii) and (v) are only marginally possible with e-e and f-f, while (iv) is not possible at all.

In (25), clause pairs (a) are intransitive with different subjects and verbs; (b) are transitive with the same verb but different subjects and objects; (c) have the same object but different subjects and verbs; and clauses (d–f) differ in all constituents.

The paired clauses have the same structure and similar meanings; the actions or states which the clauses describe are comparable. A little mixing could be possible between the left-hand and right-hand columns in (25); for instance, it may be possible to contextualise *Mary dances better than John speaks German.* But other clause types are scarcely comparable. One could not expect to hear **Mary writes stories more than John dislikes rock,* or **Mary likes jazz more than jealousy irks John.* It will be seen that a comparative construction cannot include a verb from the semantic type LIKING in one clause and a verb from the type ANNOYING in the other clause (for semantic types, see Dixon 1991, 2005).

If the two clauses share everything but the subject NP, then everything but the subject can be omitted from the second clause, as in:

(26) Mary speaks French more fluently than John (speaks French)

Similarly, if the two clauses share everything but the object NP, then everything but the object can be omitted from the second clause, as in:

(27) Mary speaks French more fluently than (Mary speaks) German

It is possible to choose subject and object NPs such that ambiguity might result. For example:

(28) John loves you more than Mary (loves you)

---

the excellence of John's speaking French) and a prepositional reading (Mary speaks French and John does so too).

(29) John loves you more than (John loves) Mary

The syntactic function of a core NP in English is shown by its position relative to the verb. Once the verb is omitted, this criterion is lost so that in *John loves you more than Mary* it is hard to tell whether Mary is subject or object of the second clause. The ambiguity could be resolved by saying either *John loves you more than Mary does* or *John loves you more than he does Mary*.

The compared clauses in examples just discussed had just core—subject and object—arguments. There may, of course, also be peripheral arguments. And the two clauses in a comparative construction could be identical save for a peripheral argument. For example:

(30) John tells stories to children more than (John tells stories) to adults

The Index of comparison, *more*, can remain between the two clauses, as in (30), or it can be moved to precede the peripheral argument in the first clause, giving *John tells stories more to children than to adults*. Similarly with time adverbs (*in the morning more than in the afternoon*, or *more in the morning than in the afternoon*) and space adverbs (*in the garden more than in the house*, or *more in the garden than in the house*).

The constructions just discussed have included intransitive and transitive clauses. We can now examine the comparison of copula clauses, which shows a rather different grammar. Consider the following underlying structures:

(31) [John is sincere] more than [Fred is loyal]

(32) [John is a fighter] more than [Fred is a tactician]

(33) [John is the brains behind the enterprise] more than [Fred is the driving force]

In (31), involving two clauses each with an adjective as copula complement, the Index *more* cannot remain between the clauses, but must be moved to immediately precede the copula complement of the first clause. That is, in place of (31), which is unacceptable, we have:

(31') John is more sincere than Fred is loyal

When the copula complement is an NP—either indefinite as in (32) or definite as in (33)—*more* may remain between the clauses, as in (32–3) or it may be moved to position before the copula complement of the first clause, as in:

(32') John is more (of) a fighter than Fred is a tactician

(33') John is more the brains behind the enterprise than Fred is the driving force

In (32') *of* may optionally intrude between *more* and the indefinite NP *a fighter*.

Less and *as much* behave exactly like *more*; for example, *John is less sincere than Fred is loyal*; and either *John is a fighter as much as Fred is a tactician* or *John is as much (of) a fighter as Fred is a tactician*. Note that *more (than), less (than)* and *as much (as)* are the only Indexes which may be involved in the comparison of copula clauses.

As with the comparison of transitive and intransitive clauses, repeated constituents may be omitted. For example:

(34) John is more sincere than Fred (is sincere)

(35) John is more sincere than (John is) loyal

And similarly for clauses like (32–3) involving NPs as copula complement.

Sentence (34) is a prototypical comparative construction, where two participants are compared in terms of a property. In contrast, (35) is a non-prototypical comparative, where two properties are compared in relation to one participant. From the discussion just provided, it might be inferred that prototypical and non-prototypical constructions are of similar status, being reduced in similar ways from a biclausal construction such as (31).

The adjectives used for illustration thus far in this section form their comparative with *more*. When we examine the behaviour of adjectives which employ the suffix -*er*, a clear difference between prototypical and non-prototypical comparatives emerges. Let us employ *rude* as copula complement in the first clause of a comparative construction. Underlying

(36) [John is rude] more than [Mary is insensitive]

is realised as

(36') John is ruder than Mary is insensitive

That is, the Index of comparison, *more*, is moved into juxtaposition with the adjective *rude*, producing *ruder*, in (36'). If the two clauses have the identical copula complement, we get:

(37) John is ruder than Mary

This is the prototypical comparative construction.

The non-prototypical comparative construction comes about when the two clauses in (36) have the same subject, which can be omitted. We get (a sentence similar to (4) above):

(38) John is more rude than insensitive

In this non-prototypical comparative construction, *more* plus *rude* may NOT be replaced by *ruder*; that is, *John is ruder than insensitive* is not an acceptable sentence.

There is thus an important grammatical difference in English between the kind of comparative construction which is termed prototypical, since it is found in the majority of languages, and the type termed non-prototypical, since it occurs in a minority of languages. In English, an adjective which takes comparative *-er* must assume this form within a prototypical comparative construction, where two participants are related in terms of one property, as in (37). But in a non-prototypical construction, such as (38), where two properties are related to one participant, an adjective which may otherwise take *-er* has here to occur with *more*.

There are many variants on the construction types presented here. Alongside

(39) Fred's wife is more beautiful than Peter's

we can get

(40) Fred has a more beautiful wife than Peter

Using an adjective which may take *-er, prettier* could be substituted for *more beautiful* in both (39) and (40). These are variants of the proto-typical comparative, involving two participants and one property, and so require *-er* on an adjective of the appropriate kind.

4. INHERENTLY COMPARATIVE EXPRESSIONS

English has a number of terms which are inherently comparative, effectively fusing Parameter and Index into one form. These include:

(a) Adjectives *superior (to)* and *inferior (to)* are etymologically related to morphological comparatives in Latin. They have a similar meaning to *more than* and *less than*, but both Comparee and Standard must be nominalisations. For example, *John's intelligence is superior to Mary's (intelligence)*, alongside *John is more intelligent than Mary*.

(b) Transitive verbs such as *exceed* and *surpass* basically indicate a comparison of quantity, as in *The number of men exceeds the number of women*. Subject and object can be nominalisations of adjectives; we can have either of:

(41) Mary's industriousness surpasses John's

(42) Mary surpasses John in industriousness

Constructions of this kind are more idiomatic in the passive, with the addition of *only*, as in *John's ignorance is exceeded only by his stupidity*.
   Verbs such as *outdo* and *outperform* may occur in a construction like (42), but not in one like (41).

(c) While verb *like* corresponds to adjective *good* (for example, *I like jazz* relates to *(I think) jazz is good*), verb *prefer* corresponds to comparative adjective *better* (*I prefer jazz to rock* relates to *(I think) jazz is better than rock*). *Prefer* is thus an inherently comparative verb. As grammatical support for this, compare:

COMPARATIVE ADJECTIVE	PLAIN VERB	INHERENTLY COMPARATIVE VERB
better	like	prefer
much better	*much like	much prefer
very much better	very much like	very much prefer

The inherently comparative verb *prefer* can be modified by *much*, like a comparative adjective, unlike the corresponding plain verb *like*.[7]

(d) The grammatical combination *would rather* (which behaves quite differently from adverb *rather*) is also an inherent comparative, and marks the Standard of comparison with *than*. Parallel to *I prefer walking to running*, one can say *I would rather walk than run*.

(e) The grammatical combination *even better* serves to link sentences and has a comparative sense. One person could suggest *Why don't we go to the cinema*. Another might respond: *Even better, why don't we go to the theatre*. A further degree of gradation is shown by use of *better still*. A third person could then say: *Better still, let's go to the opera*. The most extreme grade involves *best of all*, as in *Best of all, we could stay at home and watch a video*.

5. The Verb *Compare*

The verb *compare* has the person who makes the comparison as subject, with the Comparee and Standard expressed through the object argument. This can be a plural NP or it may involve coordination using *and*. For example:

(43) The lecturer compared
$$\begin{cases} \text{the various Roman generals} \\ \text{Caesar and Augustus} \end{cases}$$

The Parameter may be implicit (generals are presumably compared in terms of generalship) or explicitly stated through a peripheral constituent, as in:

(44) The travel agent compared Bali and Tahiti
$$\begin{cases} \text{as holiday destinations} \\ \text{in terms of life-style} \end{cases}$$

An alternative construction is to have just the Comparee as O of *compare*, and state the Standard through a following NP marked by *with*:

---

[7] These remarks apply to positive sentences. Interestingly, negatives are somewhat different, since one can say *I don't much like it*, corresponding to *I very much like it* (but scarcely **I don't very much like it*, save in a particular contrastive context).

(45) The travel agent compared Bali with Tahiti $\begin{cases} \text{as holiday destinations} \\ \text{in terms of life-style} \end{cases}$

Sentence (45) can involve promotion of object to subject slot in the presence of an appropriate adverb or negation (similar to a sentence such as *These cars sell well*), giving:

(46) Bali $\begin{cases} \text{doesn't compare} \\ \text{compares favourably} \end{cases}$ with Tahiti $\begin{cases} \text{as a holiday destination} \\ \text{in terms of life-style} \end{cases}$

This shows that in (45) the O NP of compare is just *Bali* (rather than *Bali with Tahiti*), since only *Bali* is promoted into subject position in (46). Note also that it is appropriate to include *as holiday destinations* (plural) in (44) but *as a holiday destination* (singular) in (45).

Promotion to subject is also possible from (44), giving *Bali and Tahiti compare favourably as holiday destinations*. (The topic of 'promotion to subject' is discussed in Dixon 1991: 322–35, 2005: 446–58.)

BIBLIOGRAPHIC NOTE

There is a perceptive discussion of comparatives in Jespersen's (1933: 219–29) chapter on 'Degree'. A wide array of example sentences are in Huddleston and Pullum (2002: 1099–170) and Declerck (1991: 342–5).

CHAPTER SIXTEEN

FEATURES OF THE NOUN PHRASE IN ENGLISH

R. M. W. Dixon

1. INTRODUCTION

The following is a summary of the elements which may precede the head of an NP in Modern English (this is taken from Dixon 2005: 26):

(*a*) an adverb which modifies a complete NP, e.g. *even, simply, really*; or *what a* or *such a*;

(*b*) a predeterminer, e.g. *all (of), some (of), both (of), one (of), another (of), any (of), one-quarter (of)*;

(*c*) a determiner, which can be
   (i) an article (*the, a*),
   (ii) a demonstrative (e.g. *this, those*), or
   (iv) a possessor word or NP (*my, John's, the old man's*);

(*d*) a superlative (*tallest, most beautiful*), a comparative (*taller, more beautiful*); or an ordering word (*next, last*) and/or a cardinal number (*three*) or a quantifier (*many, few*) or qualifier (*some, any*);

(*e*) an ordinal number, e.g. *fourth*;

(*f*) one or more adjectival modifiers; an adjective here may be modified by an adverb (such as *simply, really* or *very*);

(*g*) one or more modifiers describing composition (e.g. *wooden*), origin or style (e.g. *British*), purpose/beneficiary (e.g. *rabbit* in *rabbit food, medical* in *medical building*).

Although only one element may be chosen from slots (a), (b), (c) and (e), there may be more than one in the other slots. Examples with two or three selections from slot (d) are: *many taller entrants* and *two next fastest horses*.

Note that (iii) within slot (c) is left blank here and will be shown in §3 to be filled by *the same*. But before turning to this, in §2 we discuss articles.

2. The Articles in English

The label 'article' was used for a word class in Classical Greek which had two members—what we would call 'definite article' (the 'preposed article') and what we would call 'relative pronoun' (the 'postposed article'). These two grammatical words showed similar morphology, having gender, number and case inflections. The definite article had evolved from a demonstrative. There was nothing corresponding to 'indefinite article'. No class of articles was recognised for Latin, nor for Old English.

Modern English has *the*, which developed from a demonstrative in Old English, and *a(n)*, which developed from a reduction of the cardinal number *one*. Almost every grammarian of Modern English groups *the* and *a(n)* together, either as part of a major word class (generally adjective, but pronoun and preposition have also been suggested—see Michael 1970: 350–61) or as a separate class.

2.1. *Articles as a grammatical system in Modern English*

It is the custom to group together English *the* and *a(n)* as articles, and to say that they occur as determiners, in slot (c) of NP structure. For *the*, this is the same slot as demonstratives, from which the definite article evolved. And (c) must be the slot for *the* since it can precede a full array of choices from slot (d); for example, *the* (c) *next* (d) *two* (d) *fastest* (d) *horses.*

Many examples of complex NPs including *a(n)* could be explained equally well whether *a(n)* were in slot (c) or in slot (d). Compare *a taller man* and *a last prayer* with *three* (d) *taller* (d) *men* and *one* (d) *last* (d) *prayer*. The justification for placing *a(n)* in slot (c) lies in NPs such as *a* (c) *shorter* (d) *last* (d) *prayer*; sentences such as **one shorter last prayer* or **three shorter last prayers* are scarcely acceptable (they could only be produced in the most contrived circumstances).

Note that any of the items in slot (b) can be followed by *the* from slot (c) plus a head noun in plural inflection; for example *all/some/both/one/any/one-quarter of the dogs. A(n)* can only be used with a singular noun and so is not possible (save in highly unusual contexts) after most slot (b) items; one would not normally say, for instance, **all/some/any of a dog*. However, fractions may be followed by *a(n)* plus a singular noun, as in *one-quarter of a cake.*

The quantifiers *many* and *few*, in slot (d), pattern with numbers and may be preceded by *the*—see (34–5). However, *some* and *any*, from the same slot, behave quite differently (note that these items are semantically and functionally different from *some (of)* and *any (of)* in slot (b)).

The quantifiers *some* and *any*—as in *I saw some boy(s) in the park, I didn't see any boy(s) in the park*—cannot be preceded by either article. *Some* and *any* are similar to *a(n)* in referring to unspecified member(s) of a set (they differ from *a(n)* in not being restricted to singular reference); we do not get **a some* or **an any*, since this would involve double marking of 'unspecified'. And since *some* and *any* represent something which is not identified, they cannot co-occur with *the*.

2.2. *Their meaning and function*

Although they are mutually exclusive, which justifies their being placed in one grammatical system, the two articles have quite different roles in the grammar. Their central meanings are:

- *the* indicates that the referent of the NP it occurs in should be identifiable to the addressee;
- *a(n)* refers to one unspecified member of a set of countables (for example, it can occur with *coin* or *ripple*, but not with *money* or *mud*).

Note that quite different factors are involved in the two specifications. That for *the* does not relate to number or countability; an NP with *the* can involve a countable or uncountable noun, and if a countable it may be marked with singular or plural inflection.

Now compare:

(1)   He's the winner

(2)   He's a winner

(1) is incomplete; if it is not clear from the context or preceding discourse, one should specify what he is the winner of; for example *of the two o'clock race*. In contrast (2) is an acceptable sentence without any context being supplied. It would mean, at the least, that he won one thing once; in fact (2) will often be taken to mean that he wins habitually.

There are certain written styles which often omit *the* but in contrast retain *a(n)*. A significant number (but a minority on my shelf) of cookery books find little need for the definite article in their recipes. For example (underlining the omissions and retentions):

(3)   Clean ___ cauliflower…Transfer ___ mixture to **a** soufflé dish…Bring ___ water to **the** boil again

Headline writers in newspapers typically omit *the* and all forms of *be*—whether copula or auxiliary—to save space (they will retain them if space is available). Examples include:

(4)   ___ drug squad __ hit by ___ leader's departure
(5)   ___ night Africa came alive to ___ magic of Ali

However, as in recipes, *a(n)* is seldom omitted from headlines, as shown by:

(6)   ___ dip in ___ iodine level ___ **a** worry
(7)   Parole ___ **a** distinct hope for prisoner

One sometimes comes across a paradigm of the articles, something like:

	INDEFINITE	DEFINITE
SINGULAR	*a(n)*	*the*
PLURAL	ø or *some*	*the*

This is misconceived. Firstly, number is not relevant for *the* and it is misleading to refer to it. Secondly, there is no clear non-singular equivalent of *a(n); many* or *(a) few* could be suggested just as well as zero or *some*, but none of these is really appropriate.

2.3. The *and demonstratives*

Demonstratives *this/these* and *that/those* can function as a complete NP or as a determiner, in slot (c). Some occurrences of a demonstrative as determiner may be substituted by *the* with no substantial difference in meaning.

Demonstratives have two kinds of anaphoric function—substitution anaphora and textual anaphora (see Dixon 2003).

(a) SUBSTITUTION ANAPHORA. Here the anaphoric NP (which includes the demonstrative) substitutes for a full NP, which could have been repeated in place of the anaphoric constituent. For example (using bold type for both the anaphoric NP and the NP it is anaphoric on):

(8)   He gets **a large salary**, but **that/this salary** doesn't meet all his needs

(9)   She died on **Thursday** and (on) **that afternoon** they had a party

In (8), *the* could be used in place of *that* or *this*. Similarly in (9), but note that with the demonstrative one can say either *that afternoon* or *on that afternoon* whereas with the definite article one must say *in the afternoon*. In versions of (8) and (9) with the definite article, *the salary* and *the afternoon* are uniquely specified—the large salary that he gets, and the afternoon of the day she died, Thursday. In summary, a demonstrative in slot (c), with substitution anaphoric function, can generally be replaced by *the*.

(b) TEXTUAL ANAPHORA. This involves an NP with a demonstrative which refers back not to an NP but to a proposition which is typically a clause but could be a lengthy stretch of discourse. For example:

(10)   **He drinks excessively** and for **that reason** Mary left him

(11)   **He doesn't study** and **this behaviour** worries Mary

The definite article *the* may not substitute for a demonstrative in textual anaphoric function. It appears that only a deictic determiner may be used, referring back to something larger in extent than an NP.

There is plainly considerable variation across different genres of spoken and written English, but examination of a selection of samples suggests that something like half the occurrences of demonstratives as determiners could be replaced by *the*.[1] For example, many utterances

---

[1] For example, *this* cannot be substituted by *the* in *Our city store is having a sale later this month*.

employ a deictic for a uniquely recognisable referent, which could equally well be specified by *the*, as in:

(12) This (/the) suit fits well

(13) Where did you buy that (/the) hat?

(14) Did you get that (/the) cheque which I sent?

(15) I chose that (/the) solution which I considered most appropriate

(16) With regard to human observation this (/the) world has neither a beginning nor an end

The demonstrative *that* has a further sense as intensifier with an adjective or adverb, a function which is not open to *the*; for example, *He was that angry, I've never seen anyone behave that stupidly*. And, in an appropriate context, *that* or *this* may modify a proper noun with derogatory overtones, as in *Who's this Mrs Smith who wants to see me?* and *Igor hates that Josef Stalin*.

The can be used with a proper name in completely different circumstances, when identifying one of a number of people (or rivers, etc.) that share the same name. For example, *I mean the Murray River just south of Tully, not the big Murray River in the south*.

Whereas about half of the instances of demonstratives as determiners (in the textual samples I examined) may be replaced by *the*, only a very small number—less than five per cent—of the instances of *the* could be replaced with a demonstrative. These include:

(17) He noticed fossilised fish remains embedded in the rock; the (/these) remains suggested that volcanic activity had raised the rock

Here *the remains*, an instance of substitution anaphora, could be replaced by a deictic anaphora, *these remains*. Another example is:

(18) He arrived on a Thursday and by the (/that) Saturday had settled the estate

Other instances of possible substitution of a demonstrative for *the* involve a slight addition of meaning. Consider:

(19) She sat outside in the hot sun

One could say *in that hot sun*, with *that* adding a deprecatory sense of the hot sun not being a good thing. And in

(20)   The Smiths always vote Republican

the refers to a particular group of people called Smith. One could, alternatively, say, *Those Smiths always vote Republican*, with *those* implying a negative attitude towards them.

Slot (c) of NP structure involves a choice between an article, a demonstrative and a possessor. In quite a few instances, *the* can be replaced by an appropriate possessor, as in:

(21)   She took him by the (/his) hand

(22)   How's the (/your) family

(23)   How's the (/your) wife

(24)   The (/my) wife'll be along later

It is interesting (and surely socially significant) that *husband* could not be substituted for *wife* in (23–24). One can only say *your/my husband*, rather than **the husband*.

Generally, *the* is used to identify the unique referent of the NP in which it occurs, as in *The best (one) of all, The first in line*, and:

(25)   After the election, the winning candidate will be the president for the next four years

Certain abstract nouns (and some adjectives when functioning as NP head) take *the*; for example:

(26)   I think a lot about the future

(27)   Don't dream of the impossible!

And *the* can also have generic reference, as in (see also §2.5):

(28)   The telephone is a mixed blessing

(29)   Do you play the piano?

There are some grammatical constructions which require one or more definite articles. These include the correlative comparative, as in *The longer the better*, *The more the merrier* and *The more hours you work the more we'll pay you* as well as set expressions like *(He's) the worse for drink*.

The can be used with a noun at its introductory mention, if a unique referent is understood. For example, *The vicar knocked on the door*, *The boss always reads the paper on the train in the morning*, and *Beware of the dog!*

Generally, if the head of an NP is a common noun then it will take *the* for referential specification. If the head is a proper noun, this should have unique reference, so no article is required. However, a number of common nouns referring to geographical features or buildings are often omitted when modified by a proper name, so that the NP now consists just of the proper noun. An interesting feature is that a definite article which was required by the common noun head is retained when the common noun is omitted. For instance:

(30)   the Atlantic (ocean)   the Amazon (river)   the Hilton (hotel)
       the Louvre (gallery)   the Andes (mountains)   the Hebrides (islands)

Another point of interest is that when the common noun is omitted, its plural ending may be transferred to the proper noun, as in *the Shetland islands*, yielding *the Shetlands*.

In Sir William Jones's famous speech of 1786, he mentions *the Sanscrit language* and then just *the Greek* and *the Latin*,[2] following the same principle as in (30). During the last two centuries this habit of including *the* before the name of a language has dropped out of use.

The has a further role, indicating that something is the best of its kind. In Classical Greek, the definite article was used in exactly this way, so that 'The Poet' was used to refer to Homer and 'The Stagirite' for Aristotle (considered the most esteemed person to come from Stagira) (Harris 1765: 223.) Similar use of the definite article in Modern English is seen in *This is the life!* and *It'll be the event of the year!*

---

[2] 'The *Sanscrit* language, whatever be its antiquity, is of a wonderful structure; more perfect than the *Greek*, more copious than the *Latin*, and more exquisitely refined than either, yet bearing to both of them a stronger affinity, both in the roots of verbs and in the forms of grammar, than could possibly have been produced by accident…' (Italics in original.)

Americans speak of *the president* and everyone on earth refers to *the sun* and *the moon*. The first Sherlock Holmes short story, 'A scandal in Bohemia', commences: 'To Sherlock Holmes she is always *the* woman' (italics in original).

There is an interesting contrast between the inclusion and omission of *the* before the name of a limited set of institutions. Compare:

(31)   The choirboy is going to church/school

(32)   The plumber is going to the church/school

In (31) the boy is going to church to take part in a service or to school to take part in lessons, while in (32) the plumber is going to mend a burst pipe. For the plumber, the church/school is simply a building which, like almost all buildings, has pipes that can burst, and so it is appropriate to include *the* in (32). However, *the* is omitted—as in (31)—when someone is going to an institution to take part in the normal, defining business of that institution.

In British English, the definite article can be omitted after an appropriate preposition with a small number of names of institutions. The main ones are:

(33)   after *to, from, in, at* before   *school, church, college, university*
        after *to, from, in*   before   *town, prison, hospital, theatre* (only for
                                           operating theatre in a hospital)

Other dialects of English show variation. For example, in American English, *the* cannot be omitted from before *hospital* (Trudgill and Hannah 1982: 61).

Note that *the* can also be omitted from *He's lying in (the) bed* and *He's getting out of (the) bed* since these are prototypical activities with respect to a bed. But it is not possible to omit *the* from *He's sitting on the bed* or *He loves jumping on the bed*.

In summary, we have seen that:

- the definite article *the* developed from demonstratives;
- many instances of demonstratives in texts can be replaced by *the* with no appreciable difference in meaning (for example, *the* may be used in place of a demonstrative in substitution anaphora, but not in textual anaphora);

- rather few textual instances of *the* may be replaced by a demonstrative; where this is possible, it often involves a certain difference of meaning or emphasis;
- *the* serves to uniquely identify the referent of the NP it occurs in (irrespective of countability or number); it also occurs in set constructions such as *The more he eats the less he speaks*;
- *the* may be dropped from between one of a set of locational prepositions and one of a small set of nouns describing institutions, as in *The elderly patient is still in theatre.*

2.4. A(n) *and the number modifier one*

The indefinite article *a(n)* developed out of *one*, used as a number modifier in slot (d) of NP structure. Indeed, one function of *a(n)* is to be the unstressed equivalent of *one*. Consider an NP *X rabbit(s)*, where *X* is a number or quantifier. We can focus on the identity of *X*, as in column (a)—where the number or quantifier is stressed (shown by ')—or on *rabbit(s)*, as in (b)—where the noun is stressed.

(34) (a)   (b)
      'one rabbit   a 'rabbit
      'two rabbits
      'five rabbits
      'twenty rabbits   }   ø 'rabbits
      'many rabbits
      'few rabbits

Regular count nouns in English take an obligatory number inflection, with zero suffix for singular and -*s* for plural. If the actual non-singular number is not to be specified, nothing precedes 'rabbits. With singular number, and stress on 'rabbit, *one* must be replaced by *a*.

Note that any of the expressions in (34) may be identified by preposing *the*, giving:

(35) (a)   (b)
      the 'one rabbit   the 'rabbit
      the 'two rabbits
      the 'five rabbits
      the 'twenty rabbits   }   the 'rabbits
      the 'many rabbits
      the 'few rabbits

Since *the* simply precedes everything else in (35), we might expect *the a 'rabbit*. However, *the* and *a* make up a single grammatical system and are mutually exclusive, so that we just get *the 'rabbit* (see §2.6).

One can also place *this/these* or *that/those* or a possessor before each of the NPs in (34), and again *a* is dropped after *this* or *that* or a possessor. Only one choice may be made from slot (c) in NP structure, covering demonstratives, possessors and the two articles.

Note that it is possible to have *the* and *a* in the same complex NP:

(36)   The more than 'two million/'one million/a 'million people who voted for John were disappointed when he did not get elected

But here *more than a 'million* functions as a complex modifier within the NP; *the* and *more than a 'million* are modifiers to *people*. The essential point is that *the* and *a* are not direct members of the same constituent, and they are not contiguous.

Consider the question:

(37)   Could a 'boy lift that plank

and two possible answers:

(38)   No, (a 'boy couldn't) but a 'man could
(39)   No, ('one boy couldn't) but 'two boys could

The words in parentheses could be omitted but if included serve to make explicit the contrast—in (38) between *'man* and *'boy* (each with the unstressed form *a*) and in (39) between *'one boy* and *'two boys* (with the number stressed). These examples clearly show that *a* functions here as the unstressed variant of *one*.

Examining text samples across different genres, there are just a few instances of *one* in slot (d). For example:

(40)   You get maybe 'one authentic talent in every 'hundred students

The point of employing (stressed) *'one* here is the contrast with *'hundred* (also stressed); the contrast requires *one*, rather than *a*. Consider also:

(41)   She said 'one short word: "Good".

The emphasis here is on the fact that a single word was given, and stress falls on 'one. If the focus was on the length of the word, stress would go on 'short and one would be replaced by a: She said a 'short word: "Good".

When a single item is to be focussed on, a common means is to use one of (slot b) followed by the (slot c) in preference to one (slot d), as in:

(42)   This is one of the assumptions behind the American revolution

(43)   It is one of the great achievements of my sporting career

One could substitute a(n) for one of the—-s, with more felicity in the case of (42) than for (43). Such a replacement simply removes the focus from being on a single item from the full set of items.

There are circumstances in which a can replace one with little difference in meaning or emphasis. For example:

(44)   They have four dogs and one (/a) cat

However, there are set expressions where only one is possible, such as one day soon.

Only about five per cent of the instances of a(n) in the textual samples were replaceable by one. These include:

(45)   About a (/one) third of the way into the debate...

(46)   He didn't pay him a (/one) cent

(47)   It was only an (/one) hour

In each instance, when one is used in place of a, it attracts stress away from the following lexeme.

The great majority of instances of a(n) could not, in the textual context in which they occur, be replaced by one. Consider first:

(48)   He lives in a palace

(49)   An ink that will dry easily

One could only be substituted for a(n) here if a contrast were introduced, as with one... another or one... two:

(50)   He lives in 'one palace and works in 'another

(51)   'One ink that will dry easily and 'two that won't

However, the great majority of instances of *a(n)* do not implicitly relate to *one*. The indefinite article simply indicates an unspecified member of a set, as in *He is a cheat, Is this a red wine?, A frown darkened his face*. Note, though, that only nouns which are countable may be preceded by *a(n)*. One can say

(52)   I have a right to know

since *right* is countable (one can say, *I know my rights*). But one cannot say **He made the offer with a sincerity*, since *sincerity* is not countable. (There are, however, set expressions with *a* plus a non-countable noun, as in *(do it) with a vengeance*.)

  A(n) also has a somewhat unusual use, preceding a human propensity adjective which modifies a proper name or title, as in:

(53)   An emotional Marilyn Monroe came forward to accept the award

(54)   A delighted chairman of the board told shareholders there had been a record profit

In such instances, the article relates to the adjective rather than to the head of the NP; in essence, the chairman was in a delighted mood.

  And there are a number of set phrases which include *a(n)*, including:

what a (shame)	a few (of)
such a (disaster)	a lot (of)
many a (slip)	a little (of)
much of a (size)	a bit of a

The indefinite article is used to mean 'for each', as in *a dollar a day, sixpence a dozen*, and the set phrase *two at a time*.

  As pointed out by Jespersen (1933: 177) 'while *little* and *few* are negative terms, *a little* and *a few* are positive.' Two of his examples are:

(55)   There are few mistakes in his papers (less than one might expect, i.e. praise)

(56)   There are a few mistakes in his papers (there should have been none, i.e. criticism)

In appropriate circumstances, a noun following a number in slot (d) may be omitted, leaving the number as, effectively, head of the NP. For example:

(57)   one man taller than me

(57')   one taller than me

(58)   two men taller than me

(58')   two taller than me

Following the paradigm in (34), we could replace *one man* by *a man* and *two men* by *men*, giving:

(59)   a man taller than me

(60)   men taller than me

However, *man/men* could not be omitted from (59–60), as they can be from (57–58); that is, we cannot have an NP **a taller than me* or **taller than me*. That is, *one* can be a modifier as in (57) or a head noun as in (58) but *a(n)* may only be a determiner.

There are two forms *one* which can function as a complete NP: the generic pronoun—as in *One shouldn't do that*—and the number—as in (57') and in *I'll have one but give Mary two* (for these NPs it could be suggested that a following head noun, understood by speaker and addressee, has been omitted).

Such a *one*, which is effectively NP head, can be preceded by *a(n)* if a modifier intervenes:

(61)   (a)   Have one last drink before you go

        (b)   Okay, I'll have **a** last **one**, if you make it **a** small **one**

Sentence (61b) is acceptable in all varieties of English. One can also get *a* plus *one* with nothing intervening in some colloquial varieties. For example:

(62)   You're a one (for the ice-cream)!

(63)   He's a one (for making eyes at girls)!

The meaning is 'indulge in it a lot', with jocular overtones. (Note that one would not be likely to say, *I'm a one*.) The adjective *real* may be included: *You're/He's a real one for*...

Since the indefinite article *a(n)* developed from the number *one*, it would be expected to take some time before *a(n)* became sufficiently grammatically detached for it to be able to occur with *one*. The first stage would be as in (61b), with *a(n)* and *one* separated by another word. The final stage, as in (62–3) with the sequence *a one*, appears to be just being introduced in colloquial speech and will no doubt in due course work its way up into formal (and written) styles.

In summary, we have seen that:

- the indefinite article *a(n)* developed from *one* used as a number modifier in an NP;
- in some occurrences, *a(n)* still functions as an unstressed variant of *one*;
- *a(n)* has a non-contrastive sense; it must be substituted by *one* if there is a contrast such as *one... two* or *one... another*;
- in most instances of use, *a(n)* has moved away from association with *one* and simply indicates an unspecified member of a set;
- *a(n)* can still only be used—like *one*—with countable nouns;
- the indefinite article has a special grammatical function in constructions like *A happy Franklin D. Roosevelt accepted the nomination*; and in phrases like *a bit of a muddle*.

2.5. *Generic use of articles*

As mentioned in §2.3, *the* is often used in a generic sense, as in (28), (29), *The aeroplane has revolutionised travel* and *I dislike the bagpipes*. In addition, *a(n)*, or just the plural form of a countable (or the unmarked form of a countable), can be used with a generic sense. Compare:

(64)   The fox is a cunning animal   [comparing the prototypical fox to other animals]

(65)   A fox is a cunning animal   [any unspecified member of the set of foxes]

(66)   Foxes are cunning animals   [the whole class]

The bracketed comments provide an explanation of the meaning of each sentence. But (64), (65) and (66) can have equivalent pragmatic import.

In different contexts, only some of the generic possibilities may be felicitous. For example:

(67) A cat is more vigilant than a dog

(68) Cats are more vigilant than dogs

(69) *?The cat is more vigilant than the dog

It seems that, with respect to vigilance, one can compare unspecified members of the classes of cats and dogs, or the entire classes, but scarcely the prototypical animals.

And compare (with explanations similar to those for (64–6))

(70) You can't trust a Hun

(71) You can't trust Huns

(72) You can't trust the Hun

with

(73) You can't trust a cat

(74) You can't trust cats

(75) *You can't trust the cat

The fact that one can say (72) but not (75) is due to the fact that *the Hun* refers to the entire nation of Huns, meaning that one cannot trust the leaders of this nation. There is no equivalent interpretation of *the cat*. (Note that in each of these sentences *you* has a generic sense, in keeping with the generic nature of the statements. The sentences would not be felicitous if *I* or *she* or *John* were substituted for *you*.)

This would be a fertile field for further research.

2.6. *Underlying sequence of articles*

Since *the* and *a(n)* are mutually exclusive, in instances where one might expect a sequence of articles, only one may appear. (This discussion is based on Jespersen 1949: 468–9.)

(i)   Underlying *the* plus *a*. As shown in (34–5) of §2.4, where *the* plus *a* would be expected, we get just *the*.

(ii) Underlying *a* plus *the*. If there are several paintings by Raphael called *The Madonna and Child*, one could say:

(76)   I looked at a [The] Madonna and Child by Raphael

In each of (i) and (ii), the first of an underlying sequence of articles is retained: *the a* becomes *the* and *a the* comes out as *a*.

We can also get a sequence of underlying *the the*, as in (78) or *a a*, as in (80), in each instance reducing to just one occurrence.

(77)   He lives at the end of Bedford Street nearest to The Strand

(78)   He lives at the [The] Strand end of Bedford Street

(79)   I have a suitcase which is a little heavier than yours

(80)   I wish I had a [a] little heavier suitcase

In summary, although *the* and *a(n)* relate to the same slot in NP structure, their grammatical properties show considerable differences.

3. The Grammatical Status of *the same*

Why is it that *same* must be accompanied by the definite article *the* when used as a copula complement, whereas *different* never is. Compare:

(81)   Today's message is [the same] as yesterday's message

(82)   Today's message is [different] from yesterday's message

When used as modifier within an NP, *same* must again be preceded by *the*:

(83)   The same message came today

Different is most frequently preceded, within an NP, by indefinite article *a*:

(84)   A different message came today

However, it is possible to use *the* with *different*. Suppose that every day for three months the same message had appeared on your computer screen. Then one day a different message is found there. The following day, yesterday's message appears again, You can say:

(85)   The different message came again today

Or you can even include both *the same* and *different*, in this order:

(86)   The same different message came again today

One can get two adjectives together in an NP—for example, *the little white house*, and *a nasty wet day*—but not, as a rule, two from the same semantic type. Does the fact that *the same* and *different* may co-occur, as in (86), suggest that *the same* is not really an adjective at all, but instead some other kind of modifier within an NP?

To respond to this question, we shall first survey the set of adjectives which require two arguments, then examine the difference of meaning between *the same* and *identical*, before studying how *the same* slots into the structure of an NP and examining its grammatical properties.[3]

3.1. *Adjectives which require two arguments*

Most adjectives—in English and in every other language—simply modify a noun. But there is a small set which indicate a relation between two arguments. Using X and Y for the arguments, one can say either:

(87)   X be ADJECTIVE PREPOSITION Y

or

(88)   X and Y be ADJECTIVE

For example, *different (from)* may occur in either of:

(89)   Today's message is different from yesterday's message
(90)   Today's message and yesterday's message are different

---

[3] Huddleston (2002: 1137–40) provides an excellent discussion of *same* within 'comparative constructions', a quite different matter from that investigated here.

The constructions for *equal (to)* are illustrated by:

(91)   In a right-angled triangle, the square on the hypotenuse is equal to the
       sum of the squares on the other two sides

(92)   In a right-angled triangle, the square on the hypotenuse and the sum
       of the squares on the other two sides are equal

Adjectives relating to two arguments differ concerning which pre-
position(s) they require for occurrence in framework (87). The set
includes:

(93)   identical (to/with)   different (from/than/to)
       similar (to)   dissimilar (to/from)
       equal (to/with)   separate (from)
       related (to)   independent (of)
       comparable (to/with)   consistent (with)
       simultaneous (with)   concurrent (with)

At first glance, *the same (as)* appears to belong in this set of adjectives.
For instance, one can say either of:

(94)   Today's message is the same as yesterday's message

(95)   Today's message and yesterday's message are the same

In this respect, *the same (as)* does pattern like adjectives *different* and
identical. Once we look further, however, differences emerge. But
before delving further into grammar, we can compare the meanings
of *the same (as)* and *identical (to/with)*.

3.2. *Meaning contrast between* the same *and* identical

The difference between the canonical meanings of *the same (as)* and
identical (to) is perfectly straightforward:

- If 'X and Y are the same', then X = Y. That is, there is only one entity
  involved.
- If 'X and Y are identical', then there are two entities (that is, it is
  not the case that X = Y). The two entities are very similar in certain
  respects so that it can be difficult to tell them apart.

A grammarian of English will say that determiners and possessors go
into the same slot in NP structure. That is, determiners go into slot

(c) and possessors also go into slot (c)—see §1. One cannot say that determiners and possessors go into identical slots since only one slot is involved, not two.

'Identical twins' are not one person but two people who it is difficult to tell apart. This is why we use *identical* here rather than *the same*. In contrast, the 'morning star' and the 'evening star' are not two identical stars but one and the same star (the planet Venus) which is accorded different names depending on the time of day at which it is observed.

The canonical meanings of *the same* and *identical* are thus quite clear. There is, as is always the case, extension of meaning in everyday usage, such that in some circumstances *the same* and *identical* may be used interchangeably.[4] For example. if someone is comparing his stamp collection with that of a friend, he may exclaim (with pointing):

(96)   This stamp of mine is the same as that stamp of yours

Strictly speaking, the collector should have used *is identical to* rather than *is the same as*. But since two stamps are being considered (rather than just one), the meaning is clear. Quite often *the same* is used as an abbreviation for *the same in* [some] *respect*. For instance, if one hears *The houses in that street are all the same*, it would probably be inferred that they are of the same design. The Germanic term *same* is far more frequent[5] than the Romance borrowing *identical* and, related to this, it has wide extensions of meaning.

However, there are many situations in which only one of *the same* and *identical* may be employed, as illustrated by the examples given a little earlier.

Identical is like *different* in that it may be preceded by definite article *the* or indefinite article *a*, whereas *same* may not occur with *a*.

Just as *the same* may be used with *different*, so it may be used before *identical*. For example:

(97)   The same (set of) identical twins came to Tom's party as to Laura's party

---

[4] Dictionaries are typically lax in distinguishing meanings of semantically similar words. The second edition of the *OED* (Simpson and Weiner 1989), for instance, gives as definition of *identical* 'the same, the very same: said of one thing (or set of things) viewed at different times or in different relations' and for *same* it says 'the ordinary adjectival and pronominal designation of identity'. The *Cobuild Dictionary* aims to define less frequent words in terms of more frequent ones. For *identical* it states 'things that are identical are exactly the same' (Sinclair 2001: 774).

[5] The *Cobuild Dictionary* (Sinclair 2001: xiii–xv, 774, 1373) lists *same* in frequency Band 5, while *identical* is in Band 2.

It is clear that *identical* belongs to the set of double-argument adjectives illustrated in (93). We will see that *the same* has a different grammatical status; that is, it is not an adjective. *The same* can usefully be referred to as an 'identifier'.

3.3. *Which structural slot is appropriate for* the same?

Looking back at the structure of an NP presented in §1, the appropriate slot for identifier *the same* is (c)—alongside articles, demonstratives and possessors—whereas *different, identical* and other items from (93) are in slot (f). One says *the same* (c) *two* (d) *messages* but *the* (c) *two* (d) *different* (f) *messages.*[6] Other exemplars of ordering are:

(98) [The same three different messages] appeared on the screen today as
            c   d   f
      yesterday

(99) She brought along with her [the same most idiotic third husband as last
                                         c   d   e
      year]

Note that *different* (slot f) can be preceded by a possessor (slot c):

(100) Your different approach to the problem is most refreshing

In contrast. *the same* may not co-occur with a possessor; one cannot say *your the same or *the your same or *the same your. This is consistent with *the same* and possessors both belonging to slot (c), from which only one item may be selected. (All that is possible is to combine *the same* and a possessor in some other way, for instance, *The same old approach of yours is not at all helpful.*)

   Although *same* is normally preceded by *the*, it can take a demonstrative instead—*this, that, these* or *those*. For example:

(101) These same miners are on strike again

(102) He was wearing that same tie as at the previous interview

---

   [6] It is sometimes possible to permute the order of elements in an NP, for semantic and/or pragmatic reasons, but this always receives special stress marking. Thus, if one were talking about sets each consisting of two messages, one could conceivably say *the different 'two messages*. This non-standard ordering would be marked by placing special stress on *two*.

We can now interpolate set (iii), into slot (c) of NP structure, as set out in §1:

(iii) an identifier (*the same* or *this/that/these/those same*)

In the interests of concision, for the remainder of this chapter *the same* will be used as an abbreviation covering all of *the/this/that/these/those same*.

3.4. *Special properties of the identifier* the same

Grammars are never absolutely tidy. We have analysed *the same* as an identifier in slot (c-iii) of NP structure. Nevertheless, *the same* does share properties with the set of two-argument adjectives from slot (f). For example, each of them can be followed by post-head PREPOSITION-plus-NP within the NP for which they are a pre-head modifier:

(103)   [The same message [as yesterday's]] appeared on the screen today

(104)   [A similar message [to yesterday's]] appeared on the screen today

(105)   [A different message [from yesterday's]] appeared on the screen today

An NP head may be followed by *the same* or *different* which are, in fact, the first elements of a reduced relative clause. For example:

(106)   [Two messages [(which are) the same as yesterday's]$_{RC}$] appeared on the screen

(107)   [Two messages [(which are) different from yesterday's]$_{RC}$] appeared on the screen

This is a property which *the same* and *different* share with most adjectives. For instance:

(108)   [A new message [(which is) impossible to understand]$_{RC}$] just arrived

Many adjectives form an adverb by adding *-ly* (for details see Dixon 2005: 381–5). This applies to the double-argument adjectives in (93). One can say *John made his decision independently (of Mary)* and *Tom behaved similarly (to Kate)*. It is interesting that *the same* may function as an adverb (without any derivational suffix being added). Compare (examples from Huddleston 2002a: 1138):

(109)   She treats them all differently

(110)   She treats them all identically

(111)   She treats them all the same

Some speakers would prefer to say *He treats them all in the same way*, rather than (111). However, constructions such as (111) are fairly well attested although they may be of recent origin,[7] created by analogy with sentences like (109–10).

   Having pointed out several respects in which *the same* behaves like adjectives, we can mention one way in which it shares a grammatical property with demonstratives. Substitution anaphora (Dixon 2003: 83–5, 111–2) may involve a demonstrative:

(112)   John has ordered coffee and I'll have that too

The same may also be used as a substitution anaphor:

(113)   John has ordered coffee and I'll have the same

Different and *identical* (and other double-argument adjectives) lack this property.

   We can now turn to consideration of *the same* as copula complement, as illustrated at the beginning of this section by sentence (81).

3.5. The same *as copula complement*

A copula complement may consist of an NP or of an adjective. A further way in which *the same* patterns with adjectives is that it may make up a copula complement on its own, as in (repeating (81)):

(114)   Today's message is [the same] as yesterday's message

(115)   Today's message and yesterday's message are [the same]

The interesting point is that, even when functioning as copula complement, *same* must still be accompanied by *the* (a demonstrative would not be appropriate in this context).

---

   [7] This is based on examination of the considerable corpus in the *OED* entry for *same*.

Instead of (114) and (115), one could say:

(114')   Today's message is [the same message] as yesterday's (message)

(115')   Today's message and yesterday's message are [the same message]

It could be suggested that (114') and (115') are the underlying structures for (114) and (115). In order not to state the word *message* three times it is omitted from the end of (115). And in (114) it is stated after *yesterday's* instead of after *the same* (although it is understood to be in underlying structure after *the same*).

But, whether or not this analysis is accepted, it is a fact that this is another way in which *the same* behaves like an adjective, although in terms of position it is a determiner (slot c) within NP structure.

Once again, *same* requires a preceding *the*. This applies to *same* in all contexts in which it occurs. Examples from the *OED* show that *same* has required a preceding *the* from the earliest stages of the language. However, we could not regard *the-same* as a single syntagmatic unit since *very* can intrude between definite article and *same*—*the very same message*. Maybe the association between *the* and *same* has some similarities to that between the two elements of a verb such as *bring in*. The phrasal verb *bring in* is a single lexical item but its components need not occur contiguously—alongside *The farmer brought in the cows* we get *The farmer brought the cows in*.

3.6. *Summary*

We have been discussing the 'identifier' *the same* and *this/that/these/those same* which involve *same* preceded by the article *the*—from slot (c-i) in NP structure—or a demonstrative—from slot (c-ii). (We use *the same* as abbreviation for these five forms.)

- As regards position within an NP, *the same* belongs in slot (c). It is mutually exclusive with possessors—also in slot (c)—and may be preceded by items from slots (a–b) and followed by items from slots (d) on.
- *The same* may function as substitution anaphor, like demonstratives which also belong to slot (c).
- *The same* shares an important property with double-argument adjectives (from slot f)—it may be followed by preposition plus NP.

- Like adjectives (in slot f) *the same* may be the first element of a reduced relative clause.
- Like many adjectives, *the same* has limited function as an adverb (and retains its form for this function, not taking derivational suffix *-ly* as adjectives do).
- Like adjectives, *the same* can make up a complete copula complement.

We see that the identifier item *the same* has unique form, including definite article *the* (or, in some contexts, a demonstrative). It functions in some ways like a determiner and in other like an double-argument adjective.

ACKNOWLEDGEMENTS AND SOURCES

I have benefited from the most helpful comments on a draft of this chapter from Alexandra Y. Aikhenvald and Kate Burridge.

For §2, on articles. information in many grammars and dictionaries was consulted. Christophersen (1939), Jespersen (1949) and Declerck (1991) were of especial value.

Breban (2010) has an instructive account of the history of *same*; see also the further references listed therein.

CHAPTER SEVENTEEN

TWICE AND CONSTITUENCY

R. M. W. Dixon*

1. Introduction

Dictionaries, be they twice as awful as many are, could scarcely improve (worsen) on the *OED*'s ingenuous comment in its entry for *twice*: 'in all senses now the regular substitute for the phrase *two times*'.

Consider the following:

(1)   The best two times to see kangaroos are dusk and dawn

(2)   We saw kangaroos twice yesterday

In (2) the *OED*'s precept does apply—one *could* say *two times* but it would sound awkward, *twice* being greatly preferred.[1] However, in (1) *two times* must remain and cannot be replaced by *twice*.

It is basically a matter of lexicon. The noun *time* in English has three distinct senses in which it can be modified by numbers.[2]

* *time₁* refers to a temporal location, as in (1) and:

(3)   Even those four/two times I saw him up close I didn't realise he was blind

---

* I have benefited from the most helpful comments on a draft of this chapter from Alexandra Y. Aikhenvald, Laurie Bauer and Kate Burridge. Useful information comes from Quirk, Greenbaum, Leech and Svartvik (1985: 1139).

[1] Judgments in this chapter are based on my and my senior colleagues' usage of British and Australian English. Younger speakers of Australian English, and speakers of varieties of American English, nowadays show a marked tendency to use *two times* rather than *twice*.

[2] Other senses of time include: (a) duration, as in *for a long time*; (b) a bounded period, as in *My time is limited*; and (c) specification, as in *It is now eight o'clock New York time*.

We cannot here replace *two times* by *twice*.

- *time₂* refers to frequency as in (2) and:

(4) Even when I saw him up close four times/twice I didn't realise he was blind

Here *twice* is preferred to *two times*.

- *time₃* refers to quantity, as in:

(5) Tom saw four times/twice the number of kangaroos that we saw

(6) Mary earns four times/twice my salary

The rule is straightforward:

— For a number X which is greater than three, X *times* is used whether the noun *time* refers to temporal location, as in (3), frequency, as in (4) or quantity, as in (5)–(6).
— The underlying collocation *two times* is generally replaced by *twice* when *time* refers to frequency or quantity, but seldom for *time₁*, temporal location.[3]
— Relating to *three*, the archaic-sounding *thrice* can be used in the same circumstances as *twice* (for frequency and quantity, never for temporal location) although nowadays *three times* is generally preferred.

Thrice will not be mentioned again; it may be used wherever *twice* can be, in all examples below.

And, corresponding to the smallest number of all, *one*, there is *once*. This is used, like *twice* (and *thrice*), with *time₂*, the frequency sense, as in:

(7) We saw kangaroos once yesterday

---

[3] Note that the *OED* gives an example from 1907 of *twice* replacing *two times₁*: 'T. Cobb in Story-Teller 93/1 *Judging by Lady Kitty's demeanour the last twice they had met.*' This would not be judged appropriate by many speakers of Standard English today, *two times* being required rather than *twice*. However, a search of the *Google* does turn up a few instances similar to this; for example *The twice I was wrong.* This would not be considered acceptable by the majority of speakers.

One cannot be used with the quantity sense, *time₃*, so there is no *once* referring to quantity.

Corresponding to (5) one could only say something like *Tom saw the same number of kangaroos as we did*, and corresponding to (6), something like *Mary earns the same salary as me*.

Number *one* is seldom used with *time₁*, referring to temporal location. One simply says *the time*, as in *The time to see kangaroos is at dusk*. It *is* possible to say *one time₁*, by way of emphasising a unique occurrence; this is likely to be accompanied by emphatic *do*. For example: *The one time I did see him up close I didn't realise he was blind.*

Once has a range of other meanings—not paralleled by *twice*—which fall outside the purview of the present study.[4] For example, it can indicate 'at one time' or 'on one occasion' as in *I once saw Winston Churchill*. *Once* can be added to temporal linker *when* or conditional linker *if*, and the *when* or *if* may then be omitted from the combination, leaving *once* as a clause linker. For instance: *The judge will soon deliver his verdict (when) once he examines the evidence.* And so on.

We will now survey the three senses of *time* identified above. §2.1 describes the temporal location sense, for which it is seldom possible to substitute *twice* for *two times*. §§2.2–3 discuss the replacement of *two times* by *twice* in the frequency and quantity senses. §3 examines comparative constructions featuring these two senses of time—*twice* may be used in some but not in others. This relates to constituency within a construction type.

2. THREE SENSES OF *TIME*

2.1. *The temporal location sense*, time₁

In the temporal location sense, the noun *time₁* typically occurs as head of an NP (in a core argument slot), accompanied by an article or demonstrative. For example:

(8)   The (first/last/next) time(s) that I saw John, I noticed that he was sick

(9)   Those (other) times that we met, you seemed to ignore me

---

[4] See the survey in Payne. Huddleston and Pullum (2007).

A number could be inserted when *time₁* occurs with the definite article or a demonstrative—*The first/last/next two times that I saw John*...and either *Those two other times that we met*...or *Those other two times that we met*...(this could be used if we met in batches of two times, say at Christmas and New Year annually).

A limited set of modifiers may occur with *time₁*. Besides *first, last, next* and *other*, illustrated in (8)–(9), there is *only*, as in:

(10)   The only two times I saw Mary she was laughing

There may also be a superlative, as *The best two times*...in (1).

We may also get *only* or *just* or *even* preceding the definite article or demonstrative as in (3) and:

(11)   Only the first two times are you allowed to enter without paying

(12)   Just those two times when the boss was out did we get to play with the computer

The temporal location sense may also occur with the indefinite article, but there cannot then be a number modifier, for example, *A time I will never forget is when we climbed the mountain.* And *time₁* may be modified by a number with no preceding article or demonstrative, as in:

(13)   Two times I particularly remember are when you broke your leg and fractured your arm

In none of these sentences can *two times* be replaced by *twice*. However, if *two times* is preceded just by *the* (with no *first, last, next, other, only, just* or *even*) then some speakers can use *twice* as an alternative to *two times*. For example:

(13a)   The two times/twice I particularly remember are when you broke your leg and fractured your arm

2.2. *The frequency sense*, time₂

The phrase *X times*, where *X* is a number and *times* the frequency sense of the noun, can function as head of an NP which is in a core argument slot. *Two times₂* is then replaced by *twice*, as in:

(14)   Four times/twice in a lifetime suffices for most people

However, *X times₂* most often functions as a sentential adverb. It can occur at any of the three positions in clause structure available to sentential adverbs (Dixon 2005: 386):

- I, as initial element in the clause;
- F, as final element in the clause;
- A, after the first word of the auxiliary.

These may be illustrated in:

(15)   I John has A criticised me F

The single word adverb *twice* may with equal felicity be placed in any of the three slots. A two-word phrase, such as *four times*, is preferred in slots I and F. It could be used at A, but sounds a little awkward there.

There are instances of *X times* (referring to frequency) in more complex constructions, where *twice* may be used instead of *two times*. For example, *X times₂* may be modified by a relative clause, or a prepositional phrase, or something like *altogether*. Consider:

(16)   He kicked the dog   { four times }   { that I noticed }
                           { two times }   { in the morning }
                           { twice   }   { in succession }
                                            { in all   }
                                            { altogether   }

Or *X times₂* can be preceded by *just* or *only*:

(17)   He kicked the dog   { just }   { four times }
                           { only }   { two times }
                                      { twice   }

We may also get:

(18)   He did it   { four times }   too often
                   { two times }
                   { twice   }

Twice can be used in all of (16)–(18) since here *time* refers to frequency. But it is also possible to retain *two times*. Note that in each of these sentences the following or preceding elements modify the whole of the *X times* element. It may be the complexity of the whole adverbial phrase which allows for the retention of *two times* here, as an alternative to *twice*.

There are frequency expressions involving *X times* with respect to a unit of time. For example:

(19)   He waters the lawn $\left\{\begin{matrix} \text{four times} \\ \text{twice} \end{matrix}\right\}$ $\left\{\begin{matrix} \text{a} \\ \text{every} \\ \text{each} \end{matrix}\right\}$ $\left\{\begin{matrix} \text{day} \\ \text{week} \\ \text{month} \end{matrix}\right\}$

Two times would not be likely to be used in such a context, *twice* being preferred.

There is an alternative way of saying (19), with *twice* modifying an adverb derived from a period-of-time noun:

(20)   He waters the lawn twice daily/weekly/monthly

One would not be likely to say *two times daily*. And in fact *four times daily* does not sound terribly felicitous. With a two-word frequency designation such as *four times*, one of the alternatives set out in (19) may well be preferred.

Frequency specifications may also be included as the first element of a compound, such as *four-times-married* or *twice-married* (not **two-times-married*).[5]

However, when *two* is not adjacent to the noun *times*, although it does modify it, there is no possibility of using *twice*. This is illustrated in:

(21)   He kicked the dog two separate times

Both *two* and *separate* modify *times*, but rules of surface ordering require *two* to precede *separate*. Since *separate* intervenes between *two* and *times$_2$*, these words may not be replaced by *twice*.

---

[5] Payne, Huddleston and Pullum (2007: 594–6) recognise three senses of *twice*: 'numerical' (my 'frequency'); 'multiplier' (my 'quantity') and what they call 'term of office', illustrated by *the twice President of the United States* and *the thrice Lord Mayor of London*.

We can now consider the following, where *X times₂* is linked either to *or more* or to *more*:

	(a)	(b)
(22)	four or more times	four times or more
	two or more times	twice or more (scarcely *two times or more)
(23)	four more times	four times more
	two more times	twice more (scarcely *two times more)

In column (a), *or more* and *more* modify the number, *X*, whereas in (b) they modify *X times*. The interesting point is that, in (b), the final placement of *or more* and *more* allows *times* to immediately follow *two*, and *two times* is here replaced by *twice*.

It can be seen that, for the examples discussed thus far, every instance of the frequency sense of *time* modified by number *two* is replaceable by *twice*—optionally in (16)–(18) but pretty obligatorily elsewhere. That is, replacement occurs whenever no other word intervenes between *two* and *times*. We will see in §3 that things are a little different in comparative constructions.

2.3. *The quantity sense*, time₃

Whereas the frequency sense of *time* most often occurs within an adverbial expression, the quantity sense generally occurs at the beginning of an NP which is in core argument function (or else makes up a whole NP). Examples include (5)–(6) and:

(24)   [Four times two] is eight

(25)   [Twice two] is four

(26)   [Five times/twice the number of troops which we presently have available] would not suffice for us to beat the enemy

(27)   John is [four times/twice the size he ought to be]

In each of these, *twice* is used in place of *two times*. One would not expect to employ *two times* in (26) or (27). However, *two times* is equally good in (25)—*Two times two is four*. This is by analogy with other components in the arithmetic tables taught in schools (which are, after all, called 'times tables').

There is an alternative to *twice* in the quantity sense—*double* may be used rather than *two times* in each of (5)–(6) and (25)–(27), with essentially the same meaning. Similarly, *treble* can be used in place of *thrice* or *three times*, and *quadruple* in place of *four times*. Similar forms exist for higher numbers but, as the quantity increases, so the frequency of usage decreases—*quintuple, sextuple*, and so on. And note that *double* may not be used in place of *two times* or *twice* in any of the comparative constructions discussed at examples (b) and (c) in the next section.

3. COMPARATIVE CONSTRUCTIONS

Both frequency and quantity senses of *time* may feature in comparative constructions. Beginning with quantity, we can contrast (repeating (5) as (28a)):

(28a)   Tom saw four times/twice the number of kangaroos that we saw

(28b)   Tom saw four times/twice as many kangaroos as we saw

(28c)   Tom saw four/two times more kangaroos than we saw

(29a)   Mary earns four times/twice what I earn

(29b)   Mary earns four times/twice as much as I earn

(29c)   Mary earns four/two times more than I earn

What we find here is that *twice* must be used in place of *two times* in the (a) sentences and also in the (b) sentences, involving *as many as* (for a countable noun such as *kangaroos*) or *as much as* (for a mass noun such as *money*). However, *twice* may not replace *two times* in the (c) sentences, involving *more than*.

Adjectives can also feature in comparative constructions involving the quantity sense of *time*. For example:

(30b)   That car sells four times/twice as fast as this model

(30c)   That car sells four/two times faster than this model

(31b)   John is four times/twice as handsome as Tom

(31c)   John is four/two times more handsome than Tom

Once more, *twice* must be used in the (b) constructions, involving *as...as*, but cannot occur in the (c) sentences which feature the comparative form of an adjective, *faster* or *more handsome*. The (c) clauses cannot include *twice*, only *two times*. But they sound awkward with *two times*. Whereas for *three times* or *four times* (or some high number) either the (b) or the (c) construction may be used, in the case of *two times* there is a marked preference to employ construction (b), with *twice*.

The factors relating to whether or not *two times* must be replaced by *twice* relate to constituency within the copula complement. The syntactic structures of (31b) and (31c) are:

(31b')   John is [four times/twice] as handsome as Tom

(31c')   John is four/two [times more handsome] than Tom

In the (b) constructions *four/two* forms one constituent with *times*, and this permits *two times* to be replaced by *twice*. However, in (c) *more handsome* forms a constituent with *times* and the number modifies *times more handsome*. We see that *two* and *times*, although contiguous in surface structure, belong in different constituents. This blocks the replacement of *two times* by *twice*. The same argumentation applies for each of (28)–(30).

It also applies for comparisons involving the frequency sense of *time*. We can contrast:

(32b)   John visits his mother [four times/twice] as often as Fred does

(32c)   John visits his mother four/two [times more often] than Fred does

Once more, the fact that *times more often* forms one constituent in the (c) construction, with the number modifying this constituent, means that *two* and *times* belong to different constituents, and this blocks the replacement of *two times* by *twice* in (32c). Sentence (32c) with *two times* is acceptable but sounds very awkward. We get a similar situation to that described above for the quantity sense—whereas (32b) and (32c) are equally acceptable for *four times*, when the number of frequencies involved is two, the preferred alternative is (32b).

4. CONCLUSION

Some instances of *two times* may be replaced by *twice*, but for others
this is scarcely possible. There are two factors determining this. First,
the noun *time* should refer to frequency or quantity, not to temporal
location. And secondly, *two* and *times* must belong to the same syntactic constituent for the sequence to be replaceable by *twice*.

CHAPTER EIGHTEEN

AUSTRALIAN ABORIGINAL WORDS IN DICTIONARIES— A HISTORY

R. M. W. Dixon

1. Introduction

Over 400 words have been borrowed from the Aboriginal languages of Australia into Australian English, some into other varieties of English and thence into other languages. A chronological account is provided of how English dictionaries have dealt with the commonest loans— *kangaroo, boomerang, koala, dingo, wombat* and a few more. There is comparison with the way in which loans from American and African languages were treated. Although there were c 250 distinct indigenous languages in Australia, words taken from them were marked just as 'Aboriginal' or 'native Australian' until the publication of the second edition of the unabridged *Random House Dictionary* in 1987, of *The Australian National Dictionary* in 1988 and of *Australian Words in English, their Origin and Meaning* in 1990.[1] The final question is: after full etymologies were provided, in 1987–1990, how did dictionaries handle this new information.

In summary, until the late 1980s dictionaries across the world paid scant attention to providing etymologies for words borrowed from the Aboriginal languages of Australia. There was a good deal of reliable primary source material available, but little use was made of it. This lack of attention was due in part to racist denigration of Aboriginal people, their cultures and languages. My own long-term research has involved gathering together extensive primary source materials (both published and unpublished) on each of the c 250 distinct languages

---

[1] Abbreviations used in this chapter are: AAWE, Australian Aboriginal Words in English; ACD, American College dictionary; AND, Australian National Dictionary; COD, Concise Oxford dictionary; DAE, Dictionary of American English; EWD, Encyclopedic World Dictionary; OED, Oxford English Dictionary; OUP, Oxford University Press; SOED, Shorter Oxford English Dictionary.

which were spoken at the time of European invasion (which com-
menced in 1788). These materials provided the basis for establishing
which language each loan word came from, and its original form and
meaning in the source language. For some now-extinct languages all
we have is a handful of word lists from the nineteenth century. By
comparing variant spellings of a single word (and knowing something
of the linguistic profiles of the transcribers) it is possible to reconsti-
tute—with a fair degree of confidence—the original phonetic form of
the word.

Reliable etymological information was published in the late 1980s
and has been copied correctly in a number of modern dictionaries.
But other dictionaries have exhibited a careless and unscholarly attitude, making errors or omissions in the information they now purvey.
The author has been the main person responsible for the production
of reliable etymological information. He expresses the hope that this
information will in the future be treated with respect and reproduced
fully and accurately.

About 430 words in common usage in varieties of English are loans
from the Aboriginal languages of Australia. They include *jarrah* (from
Nyungar, spoken around Perth, Western Australia) for the tree *Eucalyptus marginata*, whose hard reddish-brown timber is much prized
for furniture-making, *yabby* (from Wemba-wemba, in western Victoria) for freshwater crayfish of the genus *Cherax*, and *brolga* (from
Kamilaroi, in eastern New South Wales) for the tall, graceful crane
Grus rubicundus. About sixty of the loans come from Dharuk, the
language spoken around Sydney, and another sixty from Nyungar, at
Perth. In all around seventy-five languages have supplied loans into
English (of the 250 or so distinct languages spoken in Australia at the
time of the invasion by Europeans in 1788).

For almost 200 years after the first colonisation of Australia, no dictionary of English gave the language from which any of these loans
were taken, let alone its original form and meaning in that language.
Entries for words from Australian languages were just noted as 'Australian Aboriginal' or 'native Australian'. This is rather like lumping
together all loans into English from French, German, Spanish, Turkish, Hungarian, Russian, Greek etc., as 'European'. Then, in 1987, the
second edition of the unabridged *Random House Dictionary* published
etymologies for about a hundred items.

In 1990, full information on about 400 loans from Australian languages was published in *Australian Aboriginal Words in English, their Origin and Meaning, AAWE* (Dixon et al. 1990). Recently, in the second edition of this book (Dixon et al. 2006), the number of attested loans was increased to 430. The purpose of the present essay is to document how etymologies of words from Australian languages have been dealt with—in dictionaries emanating from the USA, the UK and Australia—both before and after their first publication in 1987 in the *Random House Dictionary*. Interestingly, not only did an American dictionary take the lead in providing etymologies, we also find that, since etymologies became generally available, American dictionaries have been best at reproducing them accurately.

§2 provides information on the five most common loans, which can be used as a yardstick against which to measure how dictionaries deal with native Australian words. §3 then provides a brief chronological overview of how dictionaries have dealt not only with loans from Australian languages but also with those from the native languages of the Americas and of Africa. The second edition of the unabridged *Random House Dictionary*, in 1987, the *Australian National Dictionary* (*AND*), in 1988, and the first edition of *Australian Aboriginal Words in English* in 1990, are discussed in §4. Then, in §5, we look at how dictionaries in the USA, in the UK, and in Australia have—during the past two decades—handled the information that is now in free circulation. §6 describes the second edition, in 2006, of *AAWE* and then §7 provides a brief conclusion.

2. THE FIVE MOST COMMON LOANS FROM AUSTRALIAN LANGUAGES

Most of the 400 loans from Australian Aboriginal languages are used only in Australian English, some of them only in a particular part of the continent where some fairly rare tree or animal is found. A fair few have been taken into the English varieties spoken in Britain and North America. And a handful have found their way into other languages. Five words feature in dictionaries of Dutch, French, German, Portuguese and Russian, cast into a phonological form appropriate for that language. It will be useful to begin by providing information about these words—*kangaroo, boomerang, koala, dingo*, and *wombat*. (This is adapted from Dixon et al. 2006: 57–64, 175–7, 64–5, 54–5, 78–9.)

(1) Kangaroo /kæŋgəˈru/

In 1770, when Captain James Cook's vessel the 'Endeavour' was damaged on the Great Barrier Reef, he had to spend some time on shore in order to make repairs. The town now located at this place on the North Queensland coast is called Cooktown, the river which there flows into the sea is the Endeavour River.

Cook and his party (which included scientist Joseph Banks) observed a number of large marsupials. He described one in particular, a peculiar animal 'of a light mouse Colour and the full size of a Grey Hound, and shaped in every respect like one, with a long tail, which it carried like a Grey Hound; in short I should have taken it for a wild dog but for its walking or running, in which it jump'd like a Hare or Deer.' Cook elicited *kangaroo* or *kanguru* as the name for the animal. The actual form in the local language, Guugu Yimidhirr, is *kaŋurru* (or *gaŋurru*, since *k* and *g* are in free alternation in this language) and it appears that it is the name for the male of the large black or grey kangaroo species, *Macropus robustus*. However, this was wrongly supposed by Cook and his party to be the name for any species of kangaroo or wallaby (any member of the Macropodid family), and became widely used in that fashion. In Guugu Yimidhirr the word has a single consonant, velar nasal *ŋ*, between first and second vowels. This was transcribed as 'ng' and then naturally pronounced in English as *ŋg*, with a *g* inserted after the *ŋ*. (See Cook 1955: 398–9; also see Dixon 1980: 8–10, 378 and further references listed there.)

In 1820 Captain Phillip P. King visited the Endeavour River. He plainly established good relations with the Guugu Yimidhirr people and took down a vocabulary that agreed with Cook's in every word except one. Instead of *kangooroo* he was given a word transcribed as 'min-ār', 'mee-nuah', or 'mēn-ū-āh' (King 1827, vol. 2: 632–5). Some people thought that Cook and Banks had made a mistake and it was even suggested that when asked the name of the animal a Guugu Yimidhirr person had said 'I don't understand' or 'I don't know', this being the true meaning of *kangaroo*. (As if any member of the tribe would not know the name for the animal! This is rather like suggesting that a speaker of British English would not be able to supply the name *dog*.)

The pioneer ethnologist Walter E. Roth wrote a letter to the *Australasian* newspaper, published 2 July 1898, pointing out that *gang-oo-roo* was the name in Guugu Yimidhirr for a species of kangaroo, but this newspaper correspondence apparently went unnoticed by lexicographers. Finally, the observations of Cook and Roth were confirmed when linguist John Haviland (1974) undertook an intensive study of Guugu Yimidhirr and again recorded *kaŋurru* (or *gaŋurru*). Haviland also pointed out that the word recorded in 1820 must have been *minha* 'edible animal'. King probably pointed at several species of kangaroo other than the large black variety, and the Guugu Yimidhirr might not have connected his pronunciation /kæŋgəˈru/ with the word /ˈkaŋurru/ or /ˈgaŋurru/.

When Governor Phillip brought the First Fleet of white settlers (convicts and their marine guards) to Sydney in 1788, Joseph Banks provided his manuscript vocabulary of the 'New Holland language', without specifying in what part of the continent it had been taken down. Phillip mistakenly thought that it must have been taken down near Sydney (or perhaps that a single language was spoken over the whole continent). Members of the First Fleet employed the word *kangaroo* in talking to the local Aborigines, and must have used it in connection with a variety of marsupials. The Sydney people thought they were being taught the English word for 'edible animal'; when cattle were unloaded the Aborigines enquired whether they were *kangaroo*.

The story doesn't end there. Several decades later, when Europeans settled along the Darling River in northern New South Wales, the English word *kangaroo* (an original loan from Guugu Yimidhirr) was taken over into the Baagandji language (with the form *gaaŋgurru*) as the name for the introduced animal 'horse'.

The word *kangaroo* is used in dozens of combinations, including *kangaroo closure*, a method adopted in Parliamentary committees by which the chairman is permitted to select what amendments they consider to be relevant to the question and 'jump over' those they think are not worth considering, and *kangaroo bar*, a strong metal bar or frame mounted at the front of a vehicle to reduce damage to the vehicle in the event of a collision with an animal, particularly a kangaroo. The Australian Rugby League football team is known as the *Kangaroos*, and a part of Earl's Court in London, where many Australian immigrants live, is known as *Kangaroo Valley*. The term *kangaroo court*, for an improperly constituted court having no legal standing (which may disregard or parody established principles of law or moral rights), originated in the USA about 1850.

(2) Boomerang /ˈbuməræŋ/
The first settlers at Sydney, in 1788, noted that members of the local
Dharuk[2] tribe used a crescent-shaped implement which they at first
thought must be a type of sword or 'scimitar'. Closer observation
showed that the boomerang was thrown as a missile in hunting or in
war, or just for play.

There are, basically, two varieties of boomerang: (a) The hunting/
fighting boomerang, which is used for hunting animals and fighting
people. It may be held in the hand or thrown. This type of boomerang does not, when thrown, return to the sender. (b) The returning
boomerang, which is not a weapon, but is used primarily for sport
and amusement. Australian Aboriginal languages often have different
terms for the two varieties. However, the English word *boomerang* is
typically used for both varieties.

It appears that the Sydney tribe only used type (a), the hunting and
fighting weapon.[3] A number of spellings are given for the original
form(s) of this word.—*bumarit* on the coast at Sydney; *bumarañ* and
bumarin further inland.[4] It has been inferred that the original name in
Dharuk is most likely to have been *bumariñ*, which became adopted
into English as *boomerang*.[5] (However, this etymology is far less certain in its details than those for *kangaroo, koala, dingo* and *wombat*.)

This unusual implement is found over most of Australia (being missing from just a few small regions, see the map in Dixon 2002: 13–4)
and has come to be recognised as a characteristic of the Aboriginal
people of the continent. This word is used in many combinations
(though nothing like so many as *kangaroo*). For example, *boomerang*

---

[2] A single Aboriginal language was spoken on the coast around Sydney/Port Jackson
and for some way inland. Matthews (1901) gathered information on an inland dialect
which he called 'Dharruk'. (There is about 80% vocabulary in common between the
inland and Sydney dialects.) The convention has arisen of using 'Dharuk' as a convenient designation for the entire tribal group and its language. Note that the local group
around Sydney appears to have been called 'Eora' (in various spellings).

[3] Troy (1994: 43) glosses *bumarit* as 'boomerang for fighting' and adds 'sword or
scimitar shaped large piece of heavy wood used as a weapon for hand-to-hand fighting or thrown.' And Attenbrow (2002: 88) further states: 'items called "swords" and
"scimitars" were non-returning boomerangs.'

[4] Sources are: 'boo-mer-rit' in Anon (n.d.); 'būmarin' in Ridley (1875: 105),
'bumarañ' in Matthews (1901: 159).

[5] Nash (2009) discusses the etymology of *boomerang*. But note that he appears to
conflate 'the language of the Turawal tribe of the Georges River' (speaking a dialect of
what we refer to as the Dharuk language) and 'Tharawal', a quite different language.

cheque, a cheque that 'bounces', and *boomerang leg*, a disease characterised by flattening and forward bowing of the shinbone.

(3) Koala /koʊˈalə/
In Dharuk, at Sydney, this mainly nocturnal marsupial was called
kulawañ or just *kula*. As the word was taken into English it was at
first spelled *coola* or *koola* or *koolah*. Then a new spelling *koala* came
into use, probably due to scribal error from *koola*. Towards the end of
the nineteenth century both names—*koola* and *koala*—were in use but
koola gradually dropped out, being replaced by (the basically erroneous) *koala*.

The koala has also been called *monkey bear, native bear, tree-bear*,
and *koala bear*. It is sometimes said that *koala* is a word which means
'doesn't drink' in 'the Aboriginal language'; this is without foundation.
(Many people in Australia wrongly believe that there was one 'Aboriginal language' spoken in Australia, when there were in fact around 250
distinct languages, each as different from its neighbours as are French
and German.)

(4) Dingo /ˈdɪŋgoʊ/
Speakers of Dharuk, the Sydney language, used the name *warrigal* for
wild dogs that roam across Australia, and *din-gu* for domesticated
warrigal. In English, *dingo* is used for all indigenous Australian dogs,
whether wild or domesticated. (*Warrigal* is a lesser-used loan into
English, an alternative to *dingo*; it was also used to refer to 'wild' or
unacculturated Aborigines.)

There are a number of colloquial combinations which include the
word *dingo*. For example, a *dingo's breakfast* is 'a pee and a good look
round'.

(5) Wombat /ˈwɒmbæt/
Like *boomerang, koala* and *dingo*, this is a loan from Dharuk. The original form in that language was *wambad, wambaj*, or *wambag* (these
may possibly have been variant pronunciations in different dialects
of Dharuk). It is used to describe any of three thickset, burrowing,
plant-eating marsupials of southern and eastern Australia, including
Tasmania—the *common wombat* (*Vombatus ursinus*), the *northern
hairy-nosed wombat* (*Lasiorhinus krefftii*), and the *southern hairy-
nosed wombat* (*Lasiorhinus latifrons*).

The word *wombat* is also used to describe either 'a slow or stupid person' or 'one who burrows'. As a verb, *to wombat* means 'to dig or tunnel, like a wombat'.

3. DICTIONARIES UNTIL 1987

We can examine how early dictionaries dealt with some of the most important loans into English from American and African languages, and then consider the treatment accorded to words taken from the indigenous languages of Australia.

3.1. *Samuel Johnson and his predecessors*

Dictionaries have always copied from each other in rather shameless fashion (see the instances quoted in Burchfield 1989: 155–65). Samuel Johnson's magnum opus of 1755 is sometimes cited as a model of originality, yet it relies heavily on precursors.

During the sixteenth century there were produced a number of bi- and multi-lingual dictionaries linking English with French or Latin (or both). The first monolingual English dictionary was *A Table Alphabeticall...of Hard...Wordes...*, by Robert Cawdrey, published in 1604 (new edition 2007). More than a dozen further dictionaries (each building on the work of its predecessors) appeared between Cawdrey and Johnson.[6] For a fair number of less common words Johnson simply repeated (in most cases—but not always—with due acknowledgement) entries from his predecessors, notably Nathan Bailey's excellent compilation *Dictionarium Britannicum, or a More Compleat Universal Etymological English Dictionary than any Extant*, of 1730.

It is instructive to see how Johnson dealt with loans from indigenous words of the Americas and of Africa which had become established in English by his time. There is no entry for *opossum* or *squaw*, each of which had appeared in print at least half a dozen times between 1610 and 1720. Johnson does have entries for *moose, cannibal, canoe, maize* (which come from languages of the Americas) and *banana* (from Africa) but without any attempt at etymology.

---

[6] Discussions and full bibliographic details are in Starnes and Noyes (1946); Mathews (1933); Hulbert (1955); and Murray (1900). Alston (1966) provide a complete bibliography of all English dictionaries from 1604 to 1797.

There are just two loan words—that are from indigenous languages of the West Indies—for which he mentions a source. *Hammock* 'a swinging bed' was said to come from the Saxon word *þamaca*. In this Johnson simply copied Bailey who provided the definition 'a hanging Bed for Sailors on Ship-Board' and etymology 'of hammaca, *Sax.*' This is in error; the word comes from an Arawak language of the West Indies, being first borrowed into Spanish as *hamaca* and thence into English as *hammock* (Aikhenvald 1999: 71–2; Oliver 1989). For *tobacco*, Bailey gave: 'of Tobago, an island in America, whence Sir Francis Drake brought it into England'. Johnson follows Bailey in briefly stating 'from Tobaco or Tobago in America'. (Modern knowledge suggests that the English term *tobacco* was taken over from Spanish *tabaco*, which was a loan from the Carib language spoken in Haiti. The similarity with island name *Tobago* appears to be coincidental.)

Bailey included 500 diagrams, mostly for mathematical terms such as 'acute angle'. Johnson had none, thus commencing the English tradition that illustrations should have no place in a dictionary.

3.2. *Noah Webster*

Many virtues are rightly attributed to Noah Webster's magnum opus of 1828 *An American Dictionary of the English Language*...However, being 'American', in the fullest sense of the word, cannot be one of them. Webster paid great attention to etymologies of words taken from languages such as Russian, Welsh, Latin, Italian, Spanish, Portuguese, French and Arabic but scarcely any to loans from the indigenous languages of the Americas. There is no entry at all for *squaw* and entries without any etymology for *opossum* and *cannibal*. *Moose* is simply stated to be 'a native Indian name' (in fact, it comes from an Algonquian language). *Canoe*—actually from Arawak and Carib languages of the West Indies, a loan into Spanish and then into English—is reported to be from French and Spanish and eventually from Latin *canna* 'a tube or cane', which is wrong. The origin of *hammoc* is given as 'Spanish, Portuguese' (which is half right), and that of *tobacco* is said to be '*Tabaco*, a province of Yucatan in Spanish America'—which at least relates to roughly the right part of the world. For *maiz*—also in fact from an Arawak language—the full entry reads: 'A plant of the genus Zea, the native corn of America, called Indian corn. [In the Lettish and Livonic languages, in the north of Europe, *mayse* is bread. *Tooke*. In Ir[ish] *maise* is food; perhaps a different orthography of *meat*.]' Webster's was the first dictionary to include words borrowed from Australian languages; he includes *kangaroo* and *wombat*, but with no etymology.

3.3. *James Murray and* The Oxford English Dictionary

Inspired by Webster's achievement, the Philological Society in London commissioned an absolutely comprehensive dictionary of every word in the English language, with dated citations indicating its range of meanings and use, together with full etymological information. *A New English Dictionary on Historical Principles*—with James Murray as the main editor—was published in ten volumes, beginning in 1888 and finishing in 1928, with a supplement in 1933. (Oxford University later changed the title to *The Oxford English Dictionary—OED*.) The scholarly principles followed were impeccable. Readers around the world sent in around five million slips with quotations. Selecting from these, 1,827,306 illustrative quotations were included in the dictionary (Winchester 2005: xxiii) and for each one of these Murray insisted that it be re-checked against the original source to ensure accuracy.

Words from American languages were well served by Murray.[7] *Squaw* is from Narragansett, an Algonquian language of Massachusetts; *opossum* from an Algonquian language of Virginia; *cannibal* comes from Spanish *canibal*, involving suffix *-al* added to *Canib*, an alternative name for the Carib ethnic group of the West Indies, who were believed to be people-eaters. Respectable etymologies were provided for *moose, canoe, maize, hammock*, and *tobacco* plus many more words taken from the languages of the Americas.

Banana was borrowed in the sixteenth century from a West African language; it is mentioned by both Johnson (1755) and Webster (1828), with no etymology given (in fact, later scholars have found it difficult to pinpoint exactly which language was the source). Other words from African languages were taken into English in the eighteenth century—including *chimpanzee*, from a Bantu language, and *gnu*, from a Bushman language—and in the nineteenth—including

---

[7] There have been a number of recent studies concerning the methodology employed in the *OED* (including Mugglestone 2000, 2005). Interestingly, attention has not been directed at the treatment of words from outside the familiar languages of Europe. The fully revised 3rd edition of the *OED* (now in progress and expected to take several decades to complete) is attempting to provide full and accurate etymologies for words taken from less familiar languages.

raffia, from Malagasy, and *tsetse* (fly), from Tswana (or Setswana), the national language of Botswana. All of these receive sound etymological treatment from Murray and his collaborators.

Words from Australian languages were introduced into English soon after the initial colonisation of 1788. As mentioned above, Webster (1828) has entries for just *kangaroo* and *wombat*, but with no etymology. James Murray included several dozen Australian loans in his large work, but the information about their origin was sometimes poor and inconsistent. Consider the following six words, all of which came from Dharuk, the language spoken at Port Jackson (now called Sydney):

- *wallaby, waratah*, 'a plant with a striking red flower', and *wombat* were given just as 'native Australian (name)'
- *boomerang* as 'adoption or modification of the native name in a lang. of the aborigines of N. S. Wales'
- *dingo* as 'native Australian name in an obs. dialect of N. S. Wales'
- *corroboree*, 'a dance ceremony', was given as 'native name in the now extinct language of Port Jackson, New South Wales'. (In fact, Dharuk was not extinct at that time.)

Only *corroboree* is identified as from the Port Jackson language. The *OED* quotes Collins as one source for *boomerang*. The vocabulary in Collins (1793) is labelled 'New South Wales' but there is a strong implicaton that it relates to Port Jackson. His word list also includes *wallaby, waratah, wombat* and *dingo*. Other sources also identify these as from Port Jackson. Rather than just *corroboree*, all six words should have been identified as coming from the Port Jackson language.

Several loans are now known to be from Wiradhuri, a language spoken in west central New South Wales: *quandong*, 'a small tree with bright red fruit' is given as 'Aboriginal Australian'; *kookaburra*, 'a kingfisher' as 'native Australian'; *gang-gang* (or *gangan*), 'a grey cockatoo', as 'native word'.

For *kangaroo*, the *OED* says 'stated to have been the name in a native Australian lang.', the caution perhaps reflecting the ideas, mentioned in §2, that Cook and Banks might have erred. At the least, one would think, it should be indicated which part of Australia the word was 'stated' to have come from.

It is interesting to speculate on the *OED*'s poor treatment of the origins of loans from Australian languages, at a time when detailed information was being provided for those from American and African languages. Two factors may be responsible. First, the condescending attitude which the English adopted towards Australia, looking upon it as a culture-less colony. Secondly, the disdain which white Australians evinced for the Aboriginal inhabitants, regarding them as 'scarcely human'.

The Shorter Oxford English Dictionary or *SOED* (Little et al. 1933) was essentially an abridgement of Murray's great work. It correctly repeated his etymologies for loans from American and African languages. But those from Australian languages fared even worse than they had in the larger dictionary. *Kangaroo* retained its 'said to be', while *wallaby, waratah, wombat* and *corroboree* were cited just as 'native Australian' (*corroboree* losing its link to the Port Jackson language), and *boomerang* and *dingo* were each 'native name in N. S. Wales'. (*Quandong, kookaburra* and *gang-gang* were omitted, presumably as part of the condensation process involved in creating a shorter dictionary.)

Oxford University Press provided a wealth of smaller dictionaries, including the best-selling *Concise Oxford Dictionary*. The fourth edition of the *COD* (Fowler 1951) compares rather unfavourably with its contemporary competitors from across the Atlantic in relation to loans from American and African languages. For example, *squaw, moose, tobacco* and *tsetse* were each accorded the etymology 'native' while *opossum* was 'Amer.-Ind.'. It would be hard to imagine shorter shrift being accorded loans from Australian languages than that by the *SOED*, but the *COD* did succeed in doing so. The etymology 'native' sufficed for *wombat* and *corroboree* and also for *boomerang* and *dingo* (these latter two being now deprived of their location 'N. S. Wales'), while *wallaby* received 'Austral.' The recurrent qualifier for *kangaroo* was varied to 'perh. native Austral.'. (*Waratah* was omitted.)

3.4. *H. L. Mencken, and* The Dictionary of American English

Across the Atlantic, words from the indigenous languages of the Americas received further attention in *A Dictionary of American English on Historical Principles* or *DAE* (Craigie and Hulbert 1938–44) and in H. L. Mencken's masterpiece *The American Language, an Enquiry into the Development of Language in the United States*. This was first published in 1919, being gradually revised and expanded. The fourth edition, in 1936, has a fine section on 'the first loan-words'; this was greatly expanded in Mencken's *Supplement 1* (1945) providing a commentary on information contained in the *DAE*. By mid-century, dictionaries of English published in America—including *Webster's Third* (Gove 1961)—routinely included reliable information concerning loans from the indigenous languages of America. As in England, words from Australian languages were simply described as 'native Australian', with no information on language or geographical provenance.

3.5. *Early work in Australia*

There had been some relevant publications in Australia, but of rather poor quality. In 1898, Edward E. Morris (who was Professor of English, French and German languages and literatures in the University of Melbourne) published *Austral English, a Dictionary of Australasian Words, Phrases and Usages*, with a number of dated citations for each word. He includes around 150 loans from Australian languages. Often, the illustrative quotations indicate the area in which the donor language was spoken. Just occasionally, nineteenth-century sources do mention a language name. For instance *coolamon* comes from *kūlūman* 'seed vessel or basket' in the Kamilaroi language (Ridley 1875: 25). Morris includes Ridley's mention but says that this word comes from the 'Kamilaroi Dialect of New South Wales', despite Ridley having used the designation 'language'. There was (and still is) a common belief among many white Australians that Aborigines speak 'dialects' whereas Europeans speak 'languages'. Morris himself refers to 'the Aboriginal language' (for example, p. 497) implying that he considers there to have been a single language spoken across the continent, with many dialects. (As mentioned before, there were in fact about 250 distinct languages, each mutually unintelligible with the others.) Compilers of the *OED* refer quite often to Morris but information on the language from which *coolamon* came was not taken up; the *OED Supplement* gives just 'native name' for *cooliman/coolamon*.

When Morris ventured beyond listing quotations, quite often fantasy took over. *Budgerigar*, the name of the small yellow parrot *Melopsittacus undulatus*, also comes from Kamilaroi, spoken some hundreds of miles north of Sydney. Morris does not say which location the bird comes from, but puts forward a gratuitous suggestion that the first part of the name is related to '*bŭdgeri* or *boodgeri* in the Port Jackson [Sydney] dialect'. The 1933 *OED* supplement incorrectly interprets this as 'Native Australian ("Port Jackson dialect", Morris *Austral English*)'

f. *budgeri, boodgeri* good + *gar* cockatoo'. This bird name is *not* decomposable and it does *not* come from Dharuk, the Port Jackson language. (Note also that the *OED* omits the haček over the first *u* in Morris' *bŭdgeri*.)

The loan word *waddy* 'an Aboriginal war club' comes from *wadi* in Dharuk, the Sydney language. This is well attested in Morris' illustrative quotations. Yet he states that 'many now hold that it is the English word *wood*, mispronounced by Aboriginal lips.' Morris illicitly suggests that the loan *woomera* 'an implement used to propel a spear' is etymologically connected with *boomerang*. There are many further pieces of misinformation, of these types, in the Morris volume.

Sidney J. Baker's *The Australian Language: an Examination of the English Language and English Speech as used in Australia, from Convict Days to the Present, with Special Reference to the Growth of Indigenous Idiom and its Use by Australian Writers* (1945) was no doubt modelled on Mencken. The two paragraphs (p. 311) devoted to 'native contributions' are pitiful. He simply lists (with no elaboration) two dozen words from 'native dialects', including *boomerang, corroboree, kookaburra, waddy* and *woomera* (but not *budgerigar, coolamon, dingo, gang-gang, kangaroo, koala, quandong, wallaby, waratah*, or *wombat*, among many others). This despite the fact that fuller information was available in primary source materials.

In 1966 there appeared *Australian English, an Historical Study of the Vocabulary, 1788–1898*, a revision of W. S. Ramson's 1961 PhD dissertation. This is a little better than its predecessors. A number of loans are, correctly, attributed to Port Jackson, and *kangaroo* to the Endeavour River. But only a hundred loans from Australian languages are mentioned (some just in a list). He does not try to establish which tribe or language each loan came from—in fact, Ramson continues the tradition of referring to Aboriginal languages as 'dialects'—although a comprehensive catalogue and map of Australian Aboriginal tribes had by then been published (Tindale 1940) with detailed references to the source materials available for each.

3.6. The Macquarie Dictionary

Dictionaries of English published in the USA (and also the *OED*, in England) had taken on responsibility for dealing with loans from the indigenous languages of the Americas. Surely there should be an Australian dictionary which would assume this role for loans from the indigenous languages of Australia? Oxford University Press did, it is true, put out Australian editions of some of their most popular dictionaries, but no improvements were made on the empty etymology 'native'. Then, in 1981, the first edition of *The Macquarie Dictionary* (edited by Arthur Delbridge) was advertised, billed as 'the first comprehensive dictionary of Australian English'. To tell the story fully, we must go back 34 years, and note that while every dictionary is to some extent based on its predecessors, some are more so than others.

In 1947, Random House in New York published *The American College Dictionary* (*ACD*), edited by Clarence L. Barnhart 'with the assistance of 355 Authorities and Specialists'. This was a highly professional work, a concise but comprehensive dictionary of 1432 pages, with narrow margins and frequent illustrative drawings. Adequate etymologies were given for words from languages of the Americas and of Africa. There were a small number of loans from Australian languages, all described simply as 'native Australian'—*boomerang, corroboree, dingo, koala, kookaburra, quandong, wallaby, wombat,* and just a few more. (For *kangaroo* the entry gave '? native Australian'.) The *ACD* was reprinted many times, and formed the basis for the larger dictionaries which Random House was to embark on in future decades (Stein 1966; Flexner 1987).

Then, in 1971, Paul Hamlyn in London published the *Encyclopedic World Dictionary* (*EWD*), edited by Patrick Hanks. The introduction to *EWD* states 'we were fortunate in being able to secure the right to use the definitions and principles' of the *ACD*. A careful examination shows that the *EWD* actually *is* the *ACD*, anglicised in slight degree. Just about all the good features of the *ACD* were retained; for example, two of the six introductory essays—those on 'Treatment of Etymologies' by Kemp Malone, and on 'Synonyms and antonyms' by Miles L. Hanley—were retained, and a further two added. The illustrations were kept, an unusual feature for a dictionary published in the UK. The 'anglicisation' undertaken for the *EWD* did involve the addition of several dozen further loans from Australian languages, including *budgerigar, brolga, waratah, bilby* 'a burrowing marsupial' and *bettong* 'a rat-kangaroo'. All these additions were words that had been included in the *OED* and were again described just as 'native Australian'.

Ten years later Australia comes into the picture. *The Macquarie Dictionary*, published in 1981 and styling itself 'The National Dictionary of Australia', was in essence the English *EWD* (which was in essence the American *ACD*), slightly Australianified. This genesis is vaguely acknowledged on page 13 of the first edition of the *Macquarie* by its editor Arthur Delbridge: 'Naturally, we could not prepare a book of this size without having access to another good dictionary for use as its base. We were fortunate in having access to the *Encyclopedic World Dictionary*, published by Hamlyn in England in 1971. This dictionary was itself based on the well-known *American College Dictionary*, first published in 1969.' (This date is erroneous; the *ACD* was first published in 1947.) However, from its second edition (1991) on, the *Macquarie* includes no mention of its antecedents.

It is instructive to compare the three dictionaries. The vast majority of entries are identical or very nearly so. However, the *Macquarie* differs from its predecessors in three important respects.

(a) The *ACD* includes many small illustrations with informative captions. For example, the first illustration bears the caption: 'Aardvark, *Orycteropos afer* (Overall length 5 to 6 ft., tail 2 to 2½ ft.)'; and the caption to the second illustration is 'Chinese abacus (Each vertical column = one integer; each bead in group A = 5 when lowered; each bead in group B = 1 when raised; value of this setting is 203,691,500.)' The *EWD* repeats the drawings and captions exactly. The *Macquarie* retains the illustrations but their captions are simplified to a single word: 'aardvark' and 'abacus' respectively. (And similarly throughout the volume.) Perhaps they decided that their Australian readers would not be interested in the zoological name of the aardvark, or would not be able to understand the principles of use for an abacus.

(b) The *ACD* includes entries for countries and major cities across the world, with information on their population and many small but useful maps. These are repeated (with population figures updated) in the *EWD*. All such information is omitted from the *Macquarie*.

(c) After a number of common words, the *ACD* and the *EWD* provide several lines of synonyms, and sometimes also antonyms, with discussion of their meaning and use. All these are omitted from the *Macquarie*.

The first edition of the *Macquarie* was reviewed by Robert Burchfield (1982), editor-in-chief of the *Oxford English Dictionary*, in Melbourne's leading newspaper *The Age*.[8] He comments on its 'occasional charm-

---

[8] Burchfield's review is mentioned on p. 55 of Ramson (2002), which is essentially the story of how the *AND* came to be produced.

ing unawareness of the standard professional requirements of reputable lexicography outside Australia.' And he points out that around 93 per cent of the entries were from the *ACD* and the *EWD*, with about seven per cent being original, the addition of distinctively Australian words or meanings.

In a later publication, Burchfield (1989: 153) closely examines and compares the three dictionaries, observing 'what emerges with the utmost clarity is that the exact wording and ordering of senses has been carried over, and deemed appropriate, from an American dictionary of 1947 to a British one of 1971 and then to an Australian one of 1981 [the *Macquarie*].' He concludes that 'the primary derivativeness of the dictionary was fudged, not by the blurb-writers, but by the editor-in-chief, Professor A. Delbridge himself.'

The seven per cent of words added for the *Macquarie* did include quite a few more loans from Australian languages. But were specific etymologies offered? No, not a one. Those which are in the *OED*—and a number more besides—were again accorded the empty designation 'Aboriginal', no attempt being made to discover which language each word came from. Other words that come from Australian languages were not even identified as 'Aboriginal'; for example, *boodie* 'a burrowing rat-kangaroo', *mardo* 'an Aborigine (name used in Western Australia)', and *mulloway* 'a large edible fish' (see Dixon et al. 2006: 52,169,94).

A 'Specialist Consultant on Aboriginal Languages' was listed, a well-known linguist who had himself published a good grammar of the Alyawarra language from Central Australia (Yallop 1977), and who was well aware that there had been around 250 distinct languages spoken across the continent. Despite having an expert consultant, no attempt had been made to identify the language (or even the region) from which each loan came.

4. FROM 1987 TO 1990

In 1978, W. S. Ramson of the Australian National University announced a project to compile an *Australian National Dictionary* (*AND*), a 'dictionary of australianisms on historical principles' to be published in 1988, which would be the two hundredth anniversary of European settlement in Australia. I agreed to assist in providing etymologies for loan words from indigenous languages. Since it was known that many of the most important loans came from Dharuk, the Sydney language, in 1980 Ramson employed linguistics student David Wilkins to work on these etymologies, utilising the comprehensive materials which I had assembled on the language.

Meanwhile, over in America, Random House was preparing the second edition of their large 'unabridged' dictionary—with Stuart Berg Flexner as Editor in Chief—and in June 1984 James Rader, Senior Editor (Etymology), requested my assistance in obtaining specific etymologies for a list of words claimed to be 'Native Australian'. Rader sent photocopies of the entries in the *OED* for about eighty words; there were no etymologies but the *OED* quotations might be a help in working out which geographical region, and then which language, each word related to. (Dictionaries invariably make use of all the information provided by their competitors, and try to improve on it.)

About 35 of the loans were from Dharuk, for which etymologies had been furnished by Wilkins. Utilising the files I had been building up since 1973 (with the assistance of grants from the Australian Research Grants Committee)—which gathered together all published and unpublished materials on each of the 250 Australian languages— Research Assistant Claire Allridge was able to trace the origin of a further 70 loans. I checked, expanded and corrected these etymologies, sending off a packet of 105 etymology slips to Random House in November 1984 (with a copy to Ramson for the *AND*).

In acknowledging these, Rader wrote: 'Since commercial dictionaries seem to plagiarize each other shamelessly, I suspect that these etymologies, once they appear, will also turn up in other dictionaries, without any acknowledgement of their authorship. Perhaps you or Ms. Allridge should consider publishing these in a more scholarly format, so that your work will at least get a certain amount of recognition in terms of priority.' (Dr. Johnson had generally made acknowledgement when taking over information from other dictionaries, but unfortunately that practice has now fallen out of fashion.) I replied that we were simply happy to make these etymologies available, and that anyone would be welcome to use them. In hindsight—if I had known what the future was to bring (see §5 below)—it would have been sensible to add 'so long as they are quoted correctly'.

In 1985, Ramson prepared a list of about 300 further putative loans from Aboriginal languages, and employed Linda McFarlane and Lysbeth Ford to search through my files for etymologies. Thus the *AND*, in 1988, became the second dictionary—after the unabridged *Random House Dictionary* (Flexner 1987)—to specify which language each loan word came from, and its original phonetic form and meaning.

Unfortunately, Ramson had just used the materials provided by research assistants, without getting me to check them, or checking them himself. As a result, a number of howlers had crept in. Two can be mentioned:

• (a) Edward John Eyre, on pp. 252–4 of the second volume of his *Journal of Expeditions of Discovery*...(1845), discusses types of fish caught around Moorunde, on the Murray River (where the Ngayawung language was spoken). His narrative then continues:

> Another very favourite article of food, and equally abundant at a particular season of the year, in the eastern part of the continent, is a species of moth which the natives procure from the cavities and hollows of the mountains in certain localities. This, when roasted, has something of the appearance and flavour of an almond badly peeled. It is called in the dialect of the district, where I met with it, Bōōguōn.

Eyre had here switched his attention from Moorunde on the Murray River to the Snowy Mountains, about 800 miles distant to the southeast, where the Ngarigo language was spoken. However, the switch of area was not noticed by the research assistant, and the *AND* wrongly assigns *bogong* to the Ngayawung language.

• (b) *Murlonga* 'white man who sexually exploits Aboriginal women' first appeared in print in the *Bulletin* magazine in 1912. A research assistant noticed that in Yolngu, spoken in the far north of the continent, *munaŋa* is 'white person'. The *AND* gives this as the possible etymology. But *murloŋa* could not have come from Yolngu since this tribe did not have contact with Europeans until the 1930s. (It is unclear what the origin of *murlonga* is; if it does come from an Australian language, we have not been able to pinpoint the source.)

In 1988, Oxford University Press and the Australian National University established 'The Australian National Dictionary Centre' at the ANU. This would produce Australianified versions of standard dictionaries such as the *COD*, and also specialised monographs on aspects of Australian lexicography. Ramson, appointed first director of the Centre, and I thought up a volume which would expand the information on loans from Australian languages contained in the *AND*. This was to be *Australian Aboriginal Words in English, their Origin and Meaning* (*AAWE*). Together with Ramson, I mapped out a detailed plan of the volume, and again made available my archive of materials on the 250 autochthonous languages of Australia, plus my expertise on these matters. Ramson's Centre hired Mandy Thomas, then an undergraduate studying anthropology and linguistics, to do the ground work. There were two preliminary chapters—an introduction to what Australian languages are like, and thumb-nail sketches of the two dozen languages from which the greatest number of loans had come. Then Chapter 3 (157 pages) providing full information on about 400 loans—alternative spellings in English, the language of origin with form and meaning there, meaning in English and date of first attestation, plus an illustrative quotation (most of these were from the *AND*, a few being from other sources). This was followed by a chapter by Ramson on how loans were used once they had been accepted into English, and a final brief peek in the opposite direction—how Australian languages have taken in loan words from English.

Some of the etymologies were deucedly tricky. For instance, in 1938 the Australian poet Rex Ingamells formed a literary group which he called the jindyworobaks, explaining that ' "Jindyworobak" ' is an aboriginal word meaning 'to annex, to join', and I propose to coin it for a particular use. The jindyworobaks, I say, are those individuals who are endeavoring to free Australian Art from whatever alien influences trammel it, that is, to bring it into proper contact with its material.' (Ingamells and Tilbrook 1938: 4). Several research assistants had been unable to discover which of the 250 indigenous languages of Australia the word *jindyworobak* had been taken from. I approached this problem by speculating on which book with lists of Aboriginal words might have been readily available to Ingamells in 1938. Perhaps, *The Vanished Tribes*, by James Devaney, which had been published in 1929. Sure enough, Devaney's 'glossary' (pp. 237–46) includes 'Jindy-worabak—To annex; to join'. Devaney does not give a source, but perusal of his complete word list reveals that he had copied it from Daniel Bunce's vocabulary of the Melbourne language in his *Language of the Aborigines of the Colony of Victoria and other Australian Districts* (1859: 2) where the spelling *Jindi woraback* was used.

Drafts of the book were circulated to experts on Australian Aboriginal languages, and on the mammals, reptiles, birds, fishes, insects and plants of the continent. We wanted the volume to be accessible to high school students and so elicited feed-back from one such.

I undertook a thorough reassessment of all the etymologies, and revised and rewrote the book, so that it should have a homogeneous style. *AAWE* was published in hardback in October 1990, being issued as a paperback eighteen months later (and reprinted in 1995).

5. AFTER 1990

With the 2nd edition of the unabridged *Random House Dictionary* in 1987, the *AND* in 1998 and *AAWE* in 1990, there were now three sources from which other dictionaries could draw for etymologies of loan words into English from the indigenous languages of Australia.

How they did so will be briefly considered—firstly dictionaries published in the USA, then those in the UK, and finally lexicographic works in Australia.

5.1. *In the USA*

Two major competitors of Random House took note of etymologies provided for words from Australian languages, and copied them absolutely correctly. The tenth edition of *The Merriam-Webster Collegiate Dictionary* (Mish 1995) only includes a few nouns of Australian origin but for these the information is given exactly as in Random House—name of the language the word was taken from, its location, and the form of the word in that language. Similar comments apply for the third edition of *The American Heritage Dictionary of the English Language* (Soukhanov 1992).

But high standards are not necessarily maintained. The paperback version of the fourth edition of the *American Heritage Dictionary*, 2001 (published by Bell, a division of Random House) gives 'Guugu Yimidhirr (Australian) *gaŋgurru*' for *kangaroo*. The third edition had correctly cited *gaŋuru* (with no g following the ŋ) and had specified a location 'Aboriginal language of north-east Australia'. For *boomerang* the paperback version of the fourth edition gives the original form correctly ('Australian *bumariñ*') but does not mention language name or location; the third edition had been more helpful, with 'Dharuk (Aboriginal language of southeast Australia) *bumariñ*'.

5.2. *In the UK*

Oxford University Press, at Oxford, is the major world producer of dictionaries. Both *AAWE* and the *AND* were published by OUP's Australian branch. Indeed, during the preparation of the *AND*, Ramson was in close contact with dictionary headquarters in Oxford. The Oxford dictionaries thus had a head start—an internal link to the new work on etymologies of loans from Australian languages. (They didn't have to buy the *AND* or *AAWE* or the second edition of the unabridged *Random House Dictionary*, and peruse them in detail, as other dictionary makers would have had to.) One would expect the stable of Oxford dictionaries to seamlessly incorporate the new information. Such expectations were not fulfilled.

In the mid-1990s I noticed that a new dictionary, just out from OUP, still gave 'probably a native Australian name' for *kangaroo*. Thinking that the retention of this outmoded entry must be an oversight, I wrote to the dictionary people at Oxford, pointing out the recent work which had been done (under OUP's auspices), and suggested that mentioning the language from which *kangaroo* was taken should be a *sine qua non*. The letter sent in return stated that the omission of a full etymology for *kangaroo* had been deliberate, concluding: 'this sort of detail would not be welcomed by our readers'.

The second edition of *The Oxford English Reference Dictionary* (Pearsall and Trumble 1996) is an impressive 1765-page volume (plus sixteen pages of coloured maps). But consider the entries for the two most common loans from Australian languages:

- boomerang... [Dharuk *umariny*].
- kangaroo... [*ganurru* name of a specific kind of kangaroo in an extinct language of N. Queensland].

For *boomerang* the first letter of the original name in Dharuk has been omitted; it should, of course, be *bumariny*. For *kangaroo* the form given is also wrong: it should be *gaŋurru* (or *gang-urru*) rather than *ganurru*. And why not say that this was originally the name for 'a large black or grey kangaroo, probably specifically the male *Macropus robustus*' (see §2 above)?

One wonders why the language of origin was stated for some loans but not for others. Was this done at random, or was there a principle involved? Detailed study of this dictionary suggests that a guiding principle was in operation. We can note that the language of origin, Dharuk, was stated for *boomerang* but not that for *kangaroo* (it is Guugu Yimidhirr). This dictionary does in fact have an entry for Dharuk: 'an Aboriginal language of the area around Sydney, Australia, now extinct'. A hypothesis now occurs as to the principle that may have been followed. Quite a few of the loans included in this dictionary are from Dharuk, so it was perhaps thought worthwhile to specify this language in the etymologies and to include an entry for the language name. But *kangaroo* is the only word (in this dictionary) coming from Guugu Yimidhirr. It appears that the principle involved was that a language name would not merit an entry unless it had supplied more than one loan. And if there was no entry for Guugu Yimidhirr, then this language could not be specified as the source of *kangaroo*, even though this is the best-known loan of all from an Australian language. (And, in fact, the Guugu Yimidhirr language is *not* extinct.)

This principle does apply in the majority of instances. For instance, *coolabah* 'species of Eucalyptus', which is a loan from the Gabi-Gabi language, is just given as 'Aboriginal'. It appears that *coolabah* is the only loan from Gabi-Gabi included in the dictionary, and there is no entry for the language name Gabi-Gabi. There is an entry for language name Wiradhuri, and the two Wiradhuri loans included in this dictionary—*corella* 'a type of white cockatoo', and *kookaburra* 'a kingfisher'—are correctly identified as 'Wiradhuri'. (The original Wiradhuri word from which *kookaburra* was taken is given by the *Random House Dictionary*, *AND* and *AAWE* as *gugubarra*. The *Oxford Reference Dictionary* gives the form as *guguburra*, which is erroneous.)

However, there do appear to be a small number of exceptions to application of the principle. There is an entry for the language name Kamilaroi. And the dictionary does include four words borrowed from Kamilaroi—*budgerigar, brolga, bora* 'initiation ceremony, initiation site', and *mulga* 'type of Acacia plant'. But each of these words is given as 'Aboriginal' (rather than as 'Kamilaroi').

Other dictionaries published in England fare even less well. A volume marketed in 2005 as *The Collins Australian Dictionary* has for *boomerang* 'from a native Australian language' and for *kangaroo* 'probably from a native Australian language'—the same as thirty years earlier.

5.3. *In Australia*

For the second edition of *The Macquarie Dictionary*, in 1991, editor Arthur Delbridge requested permission to include etymologies from Australian languages provided in *AAWE*, and he did acknowledge this in his Introduction. However, the etymologies weren't always copied accurately. To mention just one error, *AAWE* states that *pademelon*, the name of a species of wallaby, comes from *badimaliyan* in Dharuk; *Macquarie* gives the original form as *gadimalion*, writing *g* instead of *b* and *o* in place of *ya* (the mis-spelling is maintained in the 2001 edition).

The Australian National Dictionary Centre (which was responsible for the *AND* and *AAWE*) produces Australian editions of standard Oxford works. Sadly, the second edition of *The Australian Concise Oxford Dictionary* (Hughes et al. 1992) doesn't accurately reproduce all etymologies for words from Australian languages. In pronunciations provided for English words, this dictionary uses the phonetic symbol 'ŋ'. In English orthography, 'ng' sometimes represents /ŋg/—as in *finger* /fɪŋgə/—and sometimes /ŋ/—as in *singer* /sɪŋə/. Use of a phonetic alphabet with 'ŋ' resolves this potential ambiguity.

However, the symbol 'ŋ' is (unaccountably) avoided in specifying the original forms in languages from which loans were taken. The sequence 'ng' is employed, but sometimes this is used instead of /ŋ/ and other times instead of /ŋg/. For example, the source in Dharuk for *wonga-wonga* 'a ground-feeding grey and white pigeon', which should be /waɲa-waɲa/, is given as 'wanga-wanga'—this could be interpreted as either /waɲa-waɲa/ or /waŋga-waŋga/. The source in the Dharawal language for *bangalow* 'a tall species of palm tree', which should be /baŋgala/, is given as 'bangala'—this could be interpreted as either /baɲala/ or /baŋgala/. The original Guugu Yimidhirr form from which *kangaroo* was taken is /kaɲurru/ or /gaɲurru/; here a really wrong form is given: 'ganurru'. And there are some loans for which the original language is mentioned, but not what the original form was in that language.

The same principles appear to have been followed in the second edition of *The Australian Oxford Dictionary* (Moore 2004). This again avoids using 'ŋ' for representing words in Australian Aboriginal languages, with the same results as reported in the last paragraph. Except that the origin for *kangaroo* is now given as 'gangurru' which could be representing either /gaɲurru/ or /gaŋgurru/. There are also quite a number of omissions of the original form in the donor language.

Consider the following etymologies given for the name of the twining plant, *alunqua*:

- *AAWE* (Dixon et al. 1990: 112): 'Aranda, Alice Springs region, *alaŋgwe*, the name for the fruit (the vine itself is called *aljeye*).'
- *The Australian Concise Oxford Dictionary* (Hughes et al. 1992: 31): 'Aranda, the name for the fruit (the vine itself is called *aljeye*).'
- *The Australian Oxford Dictionary* (Moore 2004: 36): 'Arrernte'.

The 1992 dictionary states that the English name for the vine comes from the Aranda name for the fruit the vine bears, but fails to quote

AUSTRALIAN ABORIGINAL WORDS IN DICTIONARIES

the source word in Aranda, *alaŋgwe*. The 2004 dictionary just gives the language name ('Arrernte' is a variant spelling of 'Aranda' preferred by speakers nowadays), nothing else.

So goes progress, not always forwards.

6. New edition of *Australian Aboriginal Words in English*

It is appropriate to prepare a new edition of a standard reference work about every fifteen years. So, in collaboration with Bruce Moore—who took over as Director of the Australian National Dictionary Centre on Ramson's retirement in the mid-1990s—a new edition of *AAWE* was published in 2006 (Dixon et al. 2006). About 30 further loans from Australian languages were added and some etymologies improved in the light of new knowledge (but not those for any of the better-known words). The whole work was revised and updated, with many new illustrative quotations being added, plus with a short new chapter on how already-existing English words had their meanings extended to describe aspects of Australian Aboriginal life and culture.

7. Conclusion

The first European settlers in Australia, commencing at Port Jackson (now called Sydney) in 1788, published good accounts of Aboriginal society and artefacts, and reliable vocabularies. These materials were little used by dictionary-makers and, until 1987, every loan from an indigenous Australian language was noted just as 'native Australian'. Full etymological information was made available, for the first time, in the second edition of the unabridged *Random House Dictionary* in 1987, in the *Australian National Dictionary*, in 1988, and in *Australian Aboriginal Words in English, their Origin and Meaning*, in 1990. As always happens, other dictionaries have copied the new materials. Those in the USA have, for the most part, done so systematically and accurately, while dictionaries in the UK and in Australia have been less reliable.

When thinking of buying a new dictionary, a number of factors must be weighed. One which I always pay attention to is: are accurate etymologies given for *kangaroo* and other words from Australian languages?

BIBLIOGRAPHY

Aaron, Uche. 1996/1997. 'Grammaticalization of the verb "say" to future tense in Obolo', *Journal of West African Languages* 26: 87–93.

Abbott, Miriam. 1991. 'Macushi', pp. 23–160 of Derbyshire and Pullum 1991.

Abdul-Fetouh, H. M. 1969. *A morphological study of Egyptian Colloquial Arabic.* The Hague: Mouton.

Ackerman, Farrell and John Moore. 1999. 'Syntagmatic and paradigmatic dimensions of causee encoding', *Linguistics and Philosophy* 22: 1–44.

—— and—2001. *Proto-properties and grammatical encoding.* Stanford: CSLI.

Adams de Liclan, Patsy and Stephen Marlett. 1991. 'Antipasivo en Madija (Culina)', *Revista Latinoamericana de Estudios Etnolingüísticos* 6: 36–48.

Adams, Karen L. 1989. *Systems of numeral classification in the Mon-Khmer, Nicobarese and Aslian subfamilies of Austroasiatic.* Canberra: Pacific Linguistics.

Adams, Karen and Alexis Manaster-Ramer. 1988. 'Some questions of topic/focus choice in Tagalog', *Oceanic Linguistics* 27: 79–101.

Adelaar, Willem F. H. 2004. *The languages of the Andes.* Cambridge: Cambridge University Press.

Aikhenvald, Alexandra Y. 1987. *Strukturno-tipologicheskaja klassifikacija berberskih jazykov. Sintaksis. Kratkaja istoria klassifikacij berberskih jazykov. Resuljtaty strukturno-tipologicheskoj klassifikacii berberskih jazykov. (A Structural and Typological Classification of Berber Languages. Syntax. A short history of classifications of Berber languages. The results of a structural and typological classification of Berber languages.)* Publication 9 of the Department of Languages of the Institute of Oriental Studies of the Academy of Sciences of the USSR. Moscow: Nauka.

—— 1994a. 'Classifiers in Tariana', *Anthropological Linguistics* 34: 407–65.

—— 1994b. 'Grammatical relations in Tariana', *Nordic Journal of Linguistics* 7: 201–18.

—— 1995. *Bare.* Munich: Lincom Europa.

—— 1996. 'Areal diffusion in North-West Amazonia: the case of Tariana', *Anthropological Linguistics* 38: 73–116.

—— 1998. 'Warekena', pp. 215–439 of Derbyshire and Pullum 1998.

—— 1999. 'The Arawak language family', pp. 65–106 of Dixon and Aikhenvald 1999.

—— 2000a. 'Transitivity in Tariana', pp. 145–72 of Dixon and Aikhenvald 2000.

—— 2000b. *Classifiers: A typology of noun categorization devices.* Oxford: Oxford University Press.

—— 2001. 'Areal diffusion, genetic inheritance and problems of subgrouping: a North Arawak case study', pp. 167–94 of Aikhenvald and Dixon 2001.

—— 2002a. *Language contact in Amazonia.* Oxford: Oxford University Press.

—— 2002b. 'A typology of clitics, with special reference to Tariana', in R. M. W. Dixon and Alexandra Y. Aikhenvald (eds.), *Word: a cross-linguistic typology*, 42–78. Cambridge: Cambridge University Press.

—— 2003. *A grammar of Tariana, from north-west Amazonia.* Cambridge: Cambridge University Press.

—— 2004. *Evidentiality.* Oxford: Oxford University Press.

—— 2006a. 'Serial verb constructions in typological perspective', pp. 1–87 of Aikhenvald and Dixon 2006.

—— 2006b. 'Serial verb constructions in Tariana', pp. 178–201 of Aikhenvald and Dixon 2006.

—— 2006c. 'Complement clause types and complementation strategies in Tariana', pp. 178–203 of Dixon and Aikhenvald 2006.

—— 2007a. 'Typological dimensions in word formation', in Timothy Shopen (ed.), *Language typology and syntactic description*, 2nd ed., vol. 3, 1–65. Cambridge: Cambridge University Press.

—— 2007b. 'Linguistic fieldwork: setting the scene', in Alexandra Y. Aikhenvald (ed.), *Linguistic Fieldwork*. A Special issue of *Sprachtypologie und Universalienforschung* 60: 1–11.

—— 2008a. *The Manambu language from East Sepik, Papua New Guinea*. Oxford: Oxford University Press.

—— 2008b. 'Information source and evidentiality: what can we conclude?', in Mario Squartini (ed.), Special issue on *Evidentiality between lexicon and grammar*, *Rivista di Linguistica* 19: 207–27.

—— 2009a. 'Eating, drinking and smoking: a generic verb and its semantics in Manambu', pp. 92–108 of Newman 2009.

—— 2009b. 'Language contact along the Sepik River', *Anthropological Linguistics* 50: 1–66.

—— 2009c. 'Semantics and grammar in clause linking', pp. 380–402 of Dixon and Aikhenvald 2009.

—— 2009d. 'Syntactic ergativity in Paumarí', in Samuel Dyasi Obeng (ed.), *Topics in descriptive and African linguistics. Essays in honor of Distinguished Professor Paul Newman*, 111–27. Munich: Lincom Europa.

—— 2009e. 'Gender and noun class in Paumari' in a typological perspective', pp. 111–270 Eithne B. Carlin and Simon van de Kerke (eds.) *Linguistics and archaeology in the Americas*, 239–52. Leiden: Brill.

—— 2010. *Imperatives and commands*. Oxford: Oxford University Press.

—— 2011. 'Grammaticalization of evidentiality', 2 pp. 602–10 Heiko Narrog and Bernd Heine (eds.), *Handbook of evidentiality*. Oxford: Oxford University Press.

—— 2015. *The art of grammar*. Oxford: Oxford University Press.

Aikhenvald, Alexandra Y. and R. M. W. Dixon (eds.). 2001. *Areal diffusion and genetic relationship: Problems in comparative linguistics*. Oxford: Oxford University Press.

—— and —— (eds.). 2003. *Studies in evidentiality*. Amsterdam: John Benjamins.

—— and —— (eds.). 2006. *Serial verb constructions: a cross-linguistic typology*. Oxford: Oxford University Press.

Aissen, Judith and David Perlmutter. 1983. 'Clause reduction in Spanish', in David Perlmutter (ed.), *Studies in Relational Grammar*, vol. 1, 360–403. Chicago: The University of Chicago Press.

Akiba, Katsue. 1977. 'Switch reference in Old Japanese', *Berkeley Linguistics Society Proceedings* 3: 610–19.

Alexander, Ruth M. 1988. 'A syntactic sketch of Ocotepec Mixtec', pp. 151–304 of Bradley and Hollenbach 1988.

Algeo, John. 1977. 'Blends, a structural and systemic view', *American Speech* 82: 47–64.

Allan, Keith. 1977. 'Classifiers', *Language* 53: 284–310.

Allen, W. S. 1955. 'Zero and Pāṇini', *Indian Linguistics* 16: 106–113.

Alpher, Barry. 1987. 'Feminine as the unmarked grammatical gender: Buffalo girls are no fools', *Australian Journal of Linguistics* 7: 169–187.

Alsina, Alex. 1992. 'On the argument structure of causatives', *Linguistic Inquiry* 23: 517–55.

—— 1996. *The role of argument structure in grammar: Evidence from Romance*. Stanford: CSLI.

Alsina, Alex and Smita Joshi. 1991. 'Parameters in causative constructions', *Chicago Linguistic Society* 27: 1–16.

Alston, R. C. 1966. *The English dictionary (A bibliography of the English language from the invention of printing to the year 1988*, vol. 5). Leeds: E. J. Arnold.

Amberber, Mengistu. 1996. 'A grammatical summary of Amharic', RCLT internal document, ANU.
—— 2009. 'Quirky alternations of transitivity: The case of ingestive predicates', pp. 45–64 of Newman 2009.
Ameka, Felix. 1991. 'Ewe: its grammatical constructions and illocutionary devices', PhD thesis, ANU.
—— 2009. 'Likpe', in Coding participant marking, edited by Gerrit Dimmendaal, 239–79. Amsterdam: John Benjamins.
Amha, Azeb. 2001. The Maale language. Leiden: CNWS.
Andersen, Torben. 1988. 'Ergativity in Päri, a Nilotic OVS language', Lingua 75: 289–324.
Anderson, Gregory. 2004. 'The languages of Central Siberia: Introduction and overview', in Edward J. Vajda (ed.), Languages and prehistory of Central Siberia, 1–120. Amsterdam: John Benjamins.
Anderson, Stephen R. 1971. 'On the role of deep structure in semantic interpretation', Foundations of Language 7: 387–96.
—— 1992. A-morphous Morphology. Cambridge: Cambridge University Press.
Anonymous, n. d. 'Vocabulary of the language of N. S. Wales in the neighbourhood of Sydney (Native and English, but not alphabetical)'. Notebook filed together with the notebooks of William Dawes (and doubtless associated with them). Marsden collection 41645(c)/(d), School of Oriental and African Studies library, University of London.
Anonymous. 1969. Chichewa: Intensive course. Liongwe, Malawi: Likuni Press.
Aronoff, Mark. 1992. 'Noun classes in Arapesh', in Geert Booij and Jaap van Marle (eds.), Yearbook of morphology 1991, 21–32. Dordrecht: Kluwer.
Asher, R. E. 1985. Tamil. London: Croom Helm.
Asher, R. E. and T. C. Kumari 1997. Malayalam. London and New York: Routledge.
Attenbrow, Val. 2002. Sydney's Aboriginal past: investigating the archaeological and historical records. Sydney: UNSW Press.
Austin, Peter. 1981a. A Grammar of Diyari, South Australia. Cambridge: Cambridge University Press.
—— 1981b. 'Case marking in southern Pilbara languages', Australian Journal of Linguistics 1: 211–26.
—— 1981c. 'Switch-reference in Australia', Language 57: 309–34.
—— 1997. 'Causatives and applicatives in Australian Aboriginal languages', in Kazulo Matsumura and Tooru Hayasi (eds.), The dative and related phenomena, 165–225. Tokyo: Hiutzi Syobo.
Axelrod, Melissa. Forthcoming. 'Gender and aspect in Koyokon'.
Bailey, N. 1730. Dictionarium Britannicum, or a more compleat universal etymological English dictionary than any extant…London: T. Cox.
Bakaev, Ch. H. 1966. 'Kurdskij jazyk [Kurdish language]', in V. V. Vinogradov (ed.), Jazyki narodov SSSR: Indoevropejskie Jazyki [Languages of the peoples of the USSR: Indo-European languages], 257–80. Moscow: Nauka.
Baker, Mark. 1985. 'The mirror principle and morphosyntactic explanation', Linguistic Inquiry 16: 373–416.
—— 1995. The polysynthesis parameter. New York: Oxford University Press.
Baker, Sidney J. 1945. The Australian language: an examination of the English Language and English speech as used in Australia, from convict days to the present, with special reference to the growth of indigenous idiom and its use by Australian writers. Sydney: Angus and Robertson.
Bamgboṣe, Ayo. 1986. 'Reported speech in Yoruba', pp. 77–97 of Coulmas 1986a.
Barentsen, Adrian. 1996. 'Shifting points of orientation in Modern Russian: Tense selection in "reported perception"', pp. 15–55 of Janssen and van der Wurff 1986a.

Barnes, Janet. 1984. 'Evidentials in the Tuyuca verb', *International Journal of American Linguistics* 50: 255–71.

Barnhart, Clarence L. (ed.). 1947. *The American College dictionary*. New York: Random House.

Barron, Roger and Fritz Serzisko. 1982. 'Noun classifiers in the Siouan Languages', in Hansjakob Seiler and F. J. Stachowiak (eds.), *Apprehension: Das sprachliche Erfassen von Gegenständen*. Teil II. *Die Techniken und ihr Zusammenhang in Einzelsprachen*, 85–105. Tübingen: Gunter Narr.

Barz, Richard K. and Diller, Anthony V. N. 1989. 'Classifiers and standardisation: Some South and South-east Asian comparisons', in David Bradley (ed.), *Papers in South-East Asian Linguistics* No. 9: *Language policy, language planning and sociolinguistics in south-east Asia*, 155–84. Canberra: Pacific Linguistics.

Basu, Dwijendranath. 1955. 'On the negative auxiliary in Bengali', *Indian Linguistics* 15: 9–13.

Bauer, Laurie. 1983. *English word-formation*. Cambridge: Cambridge University Press.

—— 1994. *Watching English change, an introduction to the study of linguistic change in Standard Englishes in the twentieth century*. London: Longman.

—— 1996. 'No phonetic iconicity in evaluative morphology', *Studia Linguistica* 50: 189–206.

Bauer, Laurie, and Rodney Huddleston. 2002. 'Lexical word-formation', pp. 1621–777 of Huddleston and Pullum 2002.

Bauer, Winifred. 1993. *Maori*. London: Routledge.

Beachy, Marvin D. 2005. *An overview of Central Dizin phonology and morphology*. Masters thesis, University of Texas at Arlington.

Beck, David. 2002. *The typology of parts of speech systems: the markedness of adjectives*. New York: Routledge.

Benton, Richard A. 1968. 'Numeral and attributive classifiers in Truquese', *Oceanic Linguistics* 7: 104–146.

Benveniste, Emile. 1971a. *Problems of general linguistics*, translated by Mary E. Mack. Coral Gables: University of Miami Press. [Original: *Problèmes de linguistique générale*. 1966. Paris: Editions Gallimard.]

—— 1971b. 'Delocutive verbs', pp. 239–46 of Benveniste 1971a.

Berg, van den, Helma. 1995. *A grammar of Hunzib*. Munich: Lincom Europa.

Berlin, Brent. 1968. *Tzeltal numeral classifiers: a study in ethnographic semantics*. The Hague: Mouton.

Berry, Keith. and Christine Berry. 1999. *A description of Abun: A West Papuan language of Irian Jaya*. Canberra: Pacific Linguistics.

Besnier, Niko. 1992. 'Reported speech and affect on Nukulaelae atoll', in Jane H. Hill and Judith T. Irvine (eds.), *Responsibility and evidence in oral discourse*, 161–81. Cambridge: Cambridge University Press.

—— 2000. *Tuvaluan*. London: Routledge.

Bhat, D. N. S. n. d. 'Functional constraints on word-formation rules'. Ms.

Blake, Barry J. 1979. 'Pitta-Pitta', pp. 182–242 of Dixon and Blake 1979.

—— 1987a. *Australian Aboriginal grammar*. London: Croom Helm.

—— 1987b. 'Subordinate verb morphology in western Queensland', in Donald C. Laycock and Werner Winter (eds.), *A world of language: papers presented to Professor S. A. Wurm on his 65th birthday*, 61–8. Canberra: Pacific Linguistics.

—— 1993. 'Verb affixes from case markers', *La Trobe University Working Papers in Linguistics* 6: 33–58.

—— 1999. 'Nominal marking on verbs: some Australian cases', *Word* 50: 299–317.

—— 2001. *Case*. 2nd ed. Cambridge: Cambridge University Press.

Bloomfield, Leonard. 1917. *Tagalog texts with grammatical analysis*. Urbana, IL: University of Illinois.

—— 1933. *Language*. New York: Holt.

—— 1962. *The Menomini language*. New Haven and London: Yale University Press.

Blust, Robert. 2003. 'Three notes on early Austronesian morphology', *Oceanic Linguistics* 42: 438–78.

Boeder, Winfried. 2002. 'Speech and thought representation in the Kartvelian (South Caucasian) languages', pp. 4–48 of Güldemann and von Roncador 2002.

Bolt, Janet E., William G. Hoddinott and Frances M. Kofod. 1971. *An elementary grammar of the Nungali language of the Northern Territory.* Mimeo.

Borg, Albert and Maria Azzopardi-Alexander. 1997. *Maltese.* London: Routledge.

Borgman, Donald M. 1990. 'Sanuma', pp. 17–248 of Derbyshire and Pullum 1990.

Borkovskij, V. I. and P. S. Kuznetsov. 1965. *Istoricheskaya grammatika russkogo jazyka. [Historical grammar of the Russian language].* Moscow: Nauka.

Boroditsky, Lera. 2000. 'Metaphoric structuring: understanding time through spatial metaphors', *Cognition* 75: 1–28.

Bowden, John. 2001. *Taba: Description of a South Halmahera language.* Canberra: Pacific Linguistics.

Bradley, C. Henry. and Barbara E. Hollenbach (eds.). 1988. *Studies in the syntax of Mixtecan languages,* vol. 1. Dallas: Summer Institute of Linguistics and the University of Texas at Arlington.

—— and —— (eds.). 1990. *Studies in the syntax of Mixtecan languages,* vol. 2. Dallas: Summer Institute of Linguistics and the University of Texas at Arlington.

Brambila, David S. J. 1953. *Gramática Rarámuri.* Mexico: Editorial Buena Prensa.

Breban, Tine. 2010. 'Reconstructing paths of secondary grammaticalisation of *same* from emphasising to phoricity and single-referent-marking postdeterminer uses', *Transactions of the Philological Society* 108: 68–87.

Breen, J. G. 1981. 'Margany and Gunya', pp. 274–393 of Dixon and Blake 1981.

Breeze, Mary J. 1990. 'A sketch of the phonology and grammar of Gimira (Benchnon)', in Richard J. Hayward (ed.), *Omotic language studies,* 1–67. London: School of Oriental and African Studies.

Broadwell, George Aaron. 1990. 'Extending binding theory: a Muskogean case study', PhD dissertation, University of California at Los Angeles.

Bromley, H. Myron. 1981. *A grammar of Lower Grand Valley Dani.* Canberra: Pacific Linguistics.

Brown, D. Richard. 1994. 'Kresh', in Peter Kahrel and René van den Berg (eds.), *Typological studies in negation,* 163–89. Amsterdam: John Benjamins.

Brown, Penelope and Stephen Levinson. 1987. *Politeness.* Cambridge: Cambridge University Press.

Brown, Robert. 1981. 'Semantic aspects of some Waris predications', in Karl J. Franklin (ed.), *Syntax and semantics in Papua New Guinea languages,* 93–124. Ukarumpa: Summer Institute of Linguistics.

Bruce, Les. 1984. *The Alamblak language of Papua New Guinea (East Sepik).* Canberra: Pacific Linguistics.

—— 1988. 'Serialisation: from syntax to lexicon', *Studies in Language* 12: 19–49.

Buchstaller, Isabelle. 2005. 'Putting perception to the reality test: The case of *go* and *like*', *University of Pennsylvania Working Papers in Linguistics* 10(2): 61–76.

—— 2006. 'Social stereotypes, personality traits and regional perception displaced: Attitudes towards the "new" quotatives in the U.K.', *Journal of Sociolinguistics* 10: 362–81.

Bugaeva, Anna. 2008. 'Reported discourse and logophoricity in Southern Hokkaido dialects of Ainu', *Gengo kenkyu [Journal of the Linguistic Society of Japan]* 133: 31–75.

Bugenhagen, Robert D. 1995. *A grammar of Mangap-Mbula: an Austronesian language of Papua New Guinea.* Canberra: Pacific Linguistics.

Bunce, Daniel. 1859. *Languages of the Aborigines of the Colony of Victoria and other Australian districts, with parallel translations and familiar specimens in dialogue,* 2nd ed. Geelong: Thomas Brown.

Burchfield, Robert. 1982. 'Opening Words: Review of *The Macquarie Dictionary*'. *The Age,* 1st March 1982, 'Monthly Review Section', pp. 10–11.

—— 1989. *Unlocking the English language*. London: Faber and Faber.

Burgess, Donald. 1984. 'Western Tarahumara', in Ronald W. Langacker (ed.), *Southern Uto-Aztecan grammatical sketches*, 1–150. Dallas: Summer Institute of Linguistics and University of Texas at Austin.

Burling, Robbins. 1965. 'How to use a Burmese numeral classifier; Context and meaning', in Melford E. Spiro (ed.), *Cultural anthropology*, 243–65. Glencoe, Ill.: Free Press.

—— 2004. *The language of the Modhupur Mandi (Garo)*. New Delhi: Bibliophile South Asia.

Burridge, K. 2001. *Blooming English*. Sydney: ABC books.

Bybee, Joan, Revere Perkins and William Pagliuca. 1994. *The evolution of grammar: Tense, aspect and modality in the languages of the world*. Chicago: University of Chicago Press.

Bybee, Joan, John Haiman and Sandra A. Thompson (eds.). 1997. *Essays on language function and language type, dedicated to T. Givón*. Amsterdam: John Benjamins.

Campbell, Barbara. 1985. 'Jamamadi noun phrases', in David Lee Fortune (ed.), *Porto Velho workpapers*, 130–65. Brasília: Summer Institute of Linguistics.

Campbell, Lyle and Marianne Mithun (eds.). 1979. *The languages of Native America: Historical and comparative assessment*. Austin: University of Texas Press.

Carlin, Eithne B. 2004. *A grammar of Trio, a Cariban language of Suriname*. Frankfurt am Main: Peter Lang.

Carlson, Robert. 1994. *A grammar of Supyire*. Berlin: Mouton de Gruyter.

Carlson, Robert and Doris L. Payne. 1989. 'Genitive classifiers', in *Proceedings of the fourth annual Pacific Linguistics Conference*, 89–119. Eugene, OR: University of Oregon.

Carroll, Peter J. 1976. 'Kunwinjku: a language of western Arnhem Land', MA thesis, ANU.

Carter, Robin M. 1976. 'Chipewyan classificatory verbs', *International Journal of American Linguistics* 42: 24–30.

Casad, Eugene. 1984. 'Cora', in Ronald W. Langacker (ed.), *Southern Uto-Aztecan grammatical sketches*, 151–459. Dallas: Summer Institute of Linguistics and University of Texas at Arlington.

Cawdrey, Robert. 1604. *A table alphabeticall, conteyning and teaching the true writing, and vnderstanding of hard vsuall English wordes, borrowed from the Hebrew, Greeke, Latine, or French, &c. with the interpretation thereof by Plaine English words, etc.* London: Edmund Weauer. [New edition 2007, with Introduction by John Simpson. Oxford. Bodleian Library.]

Chafe, Wallace L. 1967. *Seneca morphology and dictionary*. Washington: Smithsonian Press.

—— 1977. 'The evolution of third person verb agreement in the Iroquoian languages', in Charles N. Li (ed.), *Mechanisms of syntactic change*, 493–524. Austin: University of Texas Press.

Chafe, Wallace and Johanna Nichols (eds.). 1986. *Evidentiality: The linguistic coding of epistemology*. Norwood, NJ: Ablex.

Chapman, Shirley and Desmond C. Derbyshire. 1991. 'Paumarí', pp. 161–354 of Derbyshire and Pullum 1991.

Charney, J. O. 1993. *A grammar of Comanche*. Lincoln: The University of Nebraska Press.

Chelliah, Shobhana. 1997. *A grammar of Meithei*. Berlin: Mouton de Gruyter.

Chiat, S. 1982. 'If I were you and you were me: The analysis of pronouns in a pronoun-reversing child', *Journal of Child Language* 9: 359–79.

—— 1986. 'Personal pronouns', in P. Fletcher and M. Garman (eds.), *Language acquisition*, 339–55. Cambridge: Cambridge University Press.

Christaller, J. G. 1875. *A grammar of the Asante and Fante language called Tshi (Chwee, Twi) based on the Akuapem dialect with reference to the other (Akan/Fante) dialects.* Basel: The Basel Evangelical Missionary Society.

Christophersen, Paul. 1939. *The articles, a study of their theory and use in English.* Copenhagen: Einar Munksgaard, and London: Oxford University Press.

Chung, Sandra, and Alan Timberlake. 1985. 'Tense, aspect and mood', pp. 202–58 of Shopen 1985c.

Churchill, Winston S. 1951. *The Second World War*, vol. IV. *The hinge of fate*. London: Cassell.

Churchward, C. Maxwell. 1953. *Tongan grammar.* London: Oxford University Press.

Clark, Eve V. and Herbert H. Clark. 1979. 'When nouns surface as verbs', *Language* 55: 767–811.

Clark, Herbert H. and Richard J. Gerrig. 1990. 'Quotations as demonstrations', *Language* 66: 764–805.

Clarke, Jonathan E. M. 2005. 'Speech report constructions in Russian', *Acta Linguistica Hungarica* 52: 367–81.

Cole, Peter. 1982. *Imbabura Quechua.* Amsterdam: North-Holland.

Collinder, Björn. 1965. *An introduction to the Uralic languages.* Berkeley and Los Angeles: University of California Press.

Collins, David. 1793. *An account of the English Colony in New South Wales...*, 2 vols. London: T. Cadell Jun. and W. Davies.

Comrie, Bernard. 1976a. 'The syntax of causative constructions', pp. 261–312 of Shibatani 1976a.

—— 1976b. *Aspect.* Cambridge: University Press.

—— 1976c. 'In defense of spontaneous demotion: the impersonal passive', in Peter Cole and Jerrold M. Sadock (eds.), *Syntax and semantics*, vol. 8, *Grammatical relations*, 47–58. New York: Academic Press.

—— 1981a. *Language universals and linguistic typology.* Oxford: Blackwell.

—— 1981b. 'Ergativity and grammatical relations in Kalaw Lagaw Ya (Saibai dialect)', *Australian Journal of Linguistics* 1: 1–42.

—— 1985. 'Causative verb formation and other verb-deriving morphology', pp. 309–48 of Shopen 1985c.

—— 1989. *Language universals and linguistic typology.* 2nd ed. Oxford: Blackwell.

—— 2000. 'Valency-changing derivations in Tsez', pp. 360–74 of Dixon and Aikhenvald 2000a.

—— 2003. 'Causatives', in William J. Frawley (ed.), *International Encyclopedia of Linguistics*, 2nd ed., vol. 1, 281–3. New York: Oxford University Press.

Comrie, Bernard and Maria S. Polinsky (eds.). 1993. *Causatives and transitivity.* Amsterdam: John Benjamins.

Comrie, Bernard and Sandra A. Thompson. 1985. 'Lexical nominalization', pp. 349–98 of Shopen 1985c.

Contini-Morava, Ellen. 2006. 'The difference between zero and nothing', in Joseph Davis, Radmila J. Gorup, and Nancy Stern (eds.), *Advances in functional linguistics, Columbia school beyond its origins*, 211–22. Amsterdam: John Benjamins.

Cook, James. 1955. *The voyage of the Endeavour, 1768–1771*, edited by J. C. Beaglehole. Cambridge: Cambridge University Press.

Cooreman, Ann. 1982. 'Topicality, ergativity, and transitivity in narrative discourse: Evidence from Chamorro', *Studies in Language* 6: 341–74.

—— 1987. *Transitivity and discourse continuity in Chamorro Narratives.* Berlin: Mouton de Gruyter.

Corbett, Greville G. 1987. 'The morphology/syntax interface', *Language* 63: 299–345.

—— 1991. *Gender.* Cambridge: Cambridge University Press.

—— 2000. *Number.* Cambridge: Cambridge University Press.

Coulmas, Florian (ed.). 1986a. *Direct and indirect speech*. Berlin: Mouton de Gruyter.
—— 1986b. 'Direct and indirect speech in Japanese', pp. 161–78 of Coulmas 1986a.
—— 1986c. 'Reported speech: some general issues', pp. 1–28 of Coulmas 1986a.
Craig, Colette G. (ed.). 1986a. *Noun classes and categorization*. Amsterdam: John Benjamins.
—— 1986b. 'Jacaltec noun classifiers', *Lingua* 70: 241–84.
—— 1991. 'Ways to go in Rama', pp. 455–92 of Traugott and Heine 1991, vol. 2.
—— 1992. 'Classifiers in a functional perspective', in Michael Fortescue, Peter Harder and Lars Kristofferesen (eds.), *Layered structure and reference in a functional perspective*, 277–301. Amsterdam: John Benjamins.
Craigie, William A. and James A. Hulbert (eds.). 1938–1944. *A dictionary of American English on historical principles*. 4 vols. Chicago: University of Chicago Press.
Creamer, Mary Helen. 1974. 'Ranking in Navajo nouns.' *Diné Bizaad Naníl'ı̨́i̧h, Navajo Language Review* 1(1): 29–38.
Croft, William. 1990. *Typology and universals*. Cambridge: Cambridge University Press.
—— 1994. 'Semantic universals in classifier systems', *Word* 45: 154–71.
Crowley, Terry. 1998. *An Erromangan (Sye) grammar*. Honolulu: University of Hawaii Press.
Cuervo, Maria Cristina. 2003. 'Structural asymmetries but same word order: The dative alternation in Spanish', in Anna Maria Di Sciullo (ed.), *Asymmetry in grammar*, 117–44. Amsterdam: John Benjamins.
Culy, Christopher. 1994a. 'Aspects of logophoric marking', *Linguistics* 32: 1055–94.
—— 1994b. 'A note on logophoricity in Dogon', *Journal of African Languages and Linguistics* 15: 113–25.
—— 2002. 'The logophoric hierarchy and variation in Dogon', pp. 201–10 of Güldemann and von Roncador 2002.
Curnow, Timothy. J. 1997. 'A grammatical summary of Awa Pit', RCLT internal document. ANU.
—— 2002a. 'Conjunct/disjunct systems in Barbacoan languages,' *Santa Barbara Papers in Linguistics* 11: 3–12.
—— 2002b. 'Three types of verbal logophoricity in African languages', *Studies in African Linguistics* 31: 1–25.
—— 2002c. 'Verbal logophoricity in African languages', in Peter Collins and Mengistu Amberber (eds.), *Proceedings of the 2002 Conference of the Australian Linguistic Society*. http://www.als.asn.au.
—— 2002d. 'Conjunct/disjunct marking in Awa Pit', *Linguistics* 40: 611–27.
Daguman, Josephine S. 2004. 'A grammar of Northern Subanen', PhD thesis, La Trobe University.
Dahl, Östen. 1985. *Tense and aspect systems*. Oxford: Blackwell.
Davies, John. 1981. *Kobon*. London: Routledge.
Davies, William. 1981. 'Choctaw clause structure', PhD dissertation, University of California at San Diego.
—— 1986. *Chocktaw verb agreement and universal grammar*. Dordrecht: Reidel.
Day, Christopher. 1973. *The Jacaltec language*. Bloomington: Indiana University and The Hague: Mouton.
De Roeck, Marijke. 1994. 'A functional typology of speech reports', in Elisabeth Engberg-Pedersen, Lisbeth F. Jakobsen and Lone S. Rasmussen (eds.), *Function and expression in functional grammar*, 331–51. Berlin: Mouton de Gruyter.
De Wolf, Charles M. 1988. 'Voice in Austronesian languages of Philippine type: passive, ergative or neither?', pp. 143–93 of Shibatani 1988.
Declerck, Renaat. 1991. *A comprehensive descriptive grammar of English*. Tokyo: Kaitakuska.
Deibler, Ellis W. Jr. 1971. 'Uses of the verb "to say" in Gahuku', *Kivung* 4: 101–10.

—— 1976. *Semantic relationships of Gahuku verbs*. Norman, OK: Summer Institute of Linguistics and University of Oklahoma.

DeLancey, Scott. 2003. 'Classical Tibetan', pp. 25–69 of Thurgood and LaPolla 2003.

Delbridge, Arthur (ed.) 1981. *The Macquarie Dictionary*. Sydney: Macquarie Library.

—— (ed.). 1991. *The Macquarie Dictionary*, 2nd ed. Sydney: Macquarie Library.

Dench, Alan C. 1991. 'Panyjima', pp. 125–244 of Dixon and Blake 1991.

—— 1995. *Martuthunira: a language of the Pilbara region of northern Australia*. Canberra: Pacific Linguistics.

—— 2009. 'The semantics of clause linking in Martuthunira', pp. 261–84 of Dixon and Aikhenvald 2009.

Dench, Alan C. and Nicholas Evans. 1988. 'Multiple case-marking in Australian languages', *Australian Journal of Linguistics* 8: 1–47.

Denny, J. Peter. 1976. 'What are noun classifiers good for?', *Chicago Linguistic Society* 12: 122–32.

—— 1986. 'The semantic role of classifiers', pp. 297–308 of Craig 1986.

Derbyshire, Desmond C. 1979. *Hixkaryana*. Amsterdam: North-Holland.

—— 1985. *Hixkaryana and linguistic typology*. Dallas: Summer Institute of Linguistics and the University of Texas at Arlington.

—— 1999. 'Carib', pp. 23–64 of Dixon and Aikhenvald 1999.

Derbyshire, Desmond C. and Doris L. Payne. 1990 'Noun classification systems of Amazonian languages', pp. 243–72 of Payne 1990.

Derbyshire, Desmond C. and Geoffrey K. Pullum (eds.). 1986. *Handbook of Amazonian languages*, vol. 1. Berlin: Mouton de Gruyter.

—— and —— (eds.). 1990. *Handbook of Amazonian languages*, vol. 2. Berlin: Mouton de Gruyter.

—— and —— (eds.). 1991. *Handbook of Amazonian languages*, vol. 3. Berlin: Mouton de Gruyter.

—— and —— (eds.). 1998. *Handbook of Amazonian languages*, vol. 4. Berlin: Mouton de Gruyter.

Deutscher, Guy. 2000. *Syntactic change in Akkadian: the evolution of sentential complementation*. Oxford: Oxford University Press.

—— 2006. 'Complement clause types and complementation strategies in Akkadian', pp. 159–77 of Dixon and Aikhenvald 2006.

Devaney, James. 1929. *The vanished tribes*. Sydney: Cornstalk.

Diakonoff, Igor M. 1988. *Afrasian languages*. Moscow: Nauka.

Dill, Lisa B. 1986. 'English prepositions: the history of a word class', PhD dissertation, University of Georgia.

Dimmendaal, Gerrit J. 1983. *The Turkana language*. Dordrecht: Foris.

—— 2001. 'Logophoric marking and represented speech in African languages as evidential hedging strategies', *Australian Journal of Linguistics* 21: 131–57.

Dirr, A. 1912. 'Rutulskij jazyk [The Rutul language].' *Sbornik Materialov dliya Opisaniya Plemen Kavkaza* (Tbilisi) 42(3): 1–204.

Dixon, R. M. W. 1968. 'The Dyirbal language of North Queensland', PhD thesis, University of London.

—— 1972. *The Dyirbal language of North Queensland*. Cambridge: Cambridge University Press.

—— 1977. *A grammar of Yidiɲ*. Cambridge: Cambridge University Press.

—— 1979. 'Delocutive verbs in Dyirbal', in Paul. J. Hopper (ed.), *Studies in descriptive and general linguistics: Festschrift for Winfried P. Lehmann*, 21–38. Amsterdam: John Benjamins.

—— 1980. *The languages of Australia*. Cambridge: Cambridge University Press.

—— 1981. 'Warrgamay', pp. 1–145 of Dixon and Blake 1981.

—— 1982. *Where have all the adjectives gone? and other essays in semantics and syntax*. Berlin: Mouton.

—— 1983. 'Nyawaygi', pp. 430–525 of Dixon and Blake 1983.

—— 1986. 'Noun classes and noun classification in typological perspective', pp. 105–112 of Craig 1986.

—— 1988. *A grammar of Boumaa Fijian*. Chicago: University of Chicago Press.

—— 1991. *A new approach to English grammar, on semantic principles*. Oxford: Clarendon Press.

—— 1994. *Ergativity*. Cambridge: Cambridge University Press.

—— 1995. 'Fusional development of gender marking in Jarawara possessed nouns', *International Journal of American Linguistics* 61: 263–94.

—— 1997. *The rise and fall of languages*. Cambridge: Cambridge University Press.

—— 1999. 'Semantic roles and syntactic functions: the semantic basis for a typology', *Chicago Linguistic Society* 25(2): 321–41.

—— 2000. 'A typology of causatives: form, syntax and meaning', pp. 30–83 of Dixon and Aikhenvald 2000.

—— 2002. *Australian languages: their nature and development*. Cambridge: Cambridge University Press.

—— 2003. 'Demonstratives, a cross-linguistic typology', *Studies in Language* 27: 61–112.

—— 2004a. 'Adjective classes in typological perspective', pp. 1–49 of Dixon and Aikhenvald 2004.

—— 2004b. *The Jarawara language of southern Amazonia*. Oxford: Oxford University Press.

—— 2005. *A semantic approach to English grammar*. 2nd ed. Oxford: Oxford University Press.

—— 2006a. 'Serial verb constructions: conspectus and coda', pp. 338–350 of Aikhenvald and Dixon 2006.

—— 2006b. 'Complement clause types and complementation strategies in typological perspective', pp. 1–48 of Dixon and Aikhenvald 2006.

—— 2006c. 'Complement clause types and complementation strategy in Jarawara', pp. 93–114 of Dixon and Aikhenvald 2006.

—— 2007. 'Field linguistics, a minor manual'. *Linguistic Fieldwork* (edited by Alexandra Y. Aikhenvald). Special issue of *Sprachtypologie und Universalienforschung* 60(1): 12–31.

—— 2008a. 'Comparative constructions: a cross-linguistic typology', *Studies in Language* 32: 787–817.

—— 2008b. 'Deriving verbs in English', *Language Sciences* 30: 31–52.

—— 2009. 'The semantics of clause linking in typological perspective', pp. 1–55 of Dixon and Aikhenvald 2009.

—— 2010a. *Basic linguistic theory*, vol. 1, *Methodology*. Oxford: Oxford University Press.

—— 2010b. *Basic linguistic theory*, vol. 2, *Grammatical topics*. Oxford: Oxford University Press.

—— 2011. *I am a linguist*. Leiden: Brill.

—— 2012. *Basic linguistic theory*, vol. 3, *Further grammatical topics*. Oxford: Oxford University Press.

—— 2014. *Making New Words. Morphological Derivation in English*. Oxford: Oxford University Press.

—— Ms. 'Transitive verbs derived from verbs by prefix *va'a-* in Boumaa Fijian'.

Dixon, R. M. W. and Alexandra Y. Aikhenvald. 1997. 'A typology of argument-determined constructions', pp. 71–113 of Bybee, Haiman and Thompson 1997.

—— and —— (eds.). 1999. *The Amazonian languages*. Cambridge: Cambridge University Press.

—— and —— (eds.). 2000a. *Changing valency: Case studies in transitivity*. Cambridge: Cambridge University Press.

—— and —— 2000b, 'Introduction', pp. 1–29 of Dixon and Aikhenvald 2000a.

—— and —— (eds.). 2004. *Adjective classes: a cross-linguistic typology*. Oxford: Oxford University Press.

—— and —— (eds.). 2006. *Complementation: a cross-linguistic typology*. Oxford: Oxford University Press.

—— and —— (eds.). 2009. *The semantics of clause linking: a cross-linguistic typology*. Oxford: Oxford University Press.

Dixon, R. M. W. and Barry J. Blake (eds.). 1979. *Handbook of Australian languages*, vol. 1. Canberra: ANU Press and Amsterdam: John Benjamins.

—— and —— (eds.). 1981. *Handbook of Australian languages*, vol. 2. Canberra: ANU Press and Amsterdam: John Benjamins.

—— and —— (eds.). 1983. *Handbook of Australian languages*, vol. 3. Canberra: ANU Press and Amsterdam: John Benjamins.

—— and —— (eds.). 1991. *The Handbook of Australian languages*, vol. 4. Melbourne: Oxford University Press.

—— and —— (eds.). 2000. *The Handbook of Australian languages*, vol. 5. Melbourne: Oxford University Press.

Dixon, R. M. W., W. S. Ramson, and Mandy Thomas. 1990. *Australian Aboriginal words in English, their origin and meaning*. Melbourne: Oxford University Press.

Dixon, R. M. W., Bruce Moore, W. S. Ramson, and Mandy Thomas. 2006. *Australian Aboriginal words in English, their origin and meaning*, 2nd ed. Melbourne: Oxford University Press.

Dol, Philomena. 1999. *A grammar of Maybrat, a language of the Bird's Head, Irian Jaya, Indonesia*. Leiden: University of Leiden.

Dolgopolsky, A. B. 1991. 'Kushitskie jazyki [Cushitic languages]', in *Languages of Asia and Africa*, vol. 4, 3–147. Moscow: Nauka.

Donohue, Mark. 1999. *A grammar of Tukang Besi*. Berlin: Mouton de Gruyter.

Douglas, Wilfrid H. 1981. 'Watjarri', pp. 197–272 of Dixon and Blake 1981.

Downing, Pamela. 1996. *Numeral classifier systems: The case of Japanese*. Amsterdam: John Benjamins.

Dowty, David R. 1972. 'Studies in the logic of verb aspect and time reference in English', PhD dissertation. University of Texas at Austin.

—— 1979. *Word meaning and Montague Grammar: The semantics of verbs and times in generative semantics and in Montague's PTQ*. Dortrecht: Reidel.

Drabbe, Peter. 1955. *Spraakkunst van het Marind, Zuidkust Nederlands Nieuw-Guinea*. Wien-Moedling: Drukkerij Missiehuis St. Gabriël.

—— 1957. *Spraakkunst van het Aghu-dialect van de Awjutaal*. The Hague: Nijhoff.

—— 1959. *Kaeti en Wambon, Twee Awju-dialecten*. The Hague: Nijhoff.

Dressler, Wolfgang. 1968. *Studien zur verbalen Pluralität*. Vienna: Hermann Böhlaus.

Driem, George van. 1987. *A grammar of Limbu*. Berlin: Mouton de Gruyter.

—— 1993. *A grammar of Dumi*. Berlin: Mouton de Gruyter.

Du Bois, John. 1987. 'The discourse basis of ergativity', *Language* 63: 805–55.

Du Feu, Veronica. 1996. *Rapanui*. London: Routledge.

Duff-Tripp, Martha. 1997. *Gramatica del Idioma Yanesha' (Amuesha)*. Lima: Instituto Lingüístico de Verano.

Dunn, M. 1999. 'A Grammar of Chukchi', PhD thesis, ANU.

Durie, Mark. 1986. 'The grammaticization of number as a verbal category', *Berkeley Linguistics Society Proceedings* 12: 355–70.

—— 1997. 'Grammatical structures in verb serialisation', in Alex Alsina, Joan Bresnan and Peter Sells (eds.), *Complex Predicates*, 289–354. Stanford: CSLI.

Dutton, Tom. 1996. *Koiari*. Munich: Lincom Europa.

Eades, Domenyk. 2005. *A grammar of Gayo: a language of Aceh, Sumatra*. Canberra: Pacific Linguistics.

Ebert, Karen. 1986. 'Speech reporting in some languages of Nepal', pp. 145–59 of Coulmas 1986a.

Edmonson, Barbara W. 1988. 'A descriptive grammar of Huastec (Potosino dialect).' PhD dissertation, Tulane University.

Engelenhoven, Aone van. 2004. *Leti: a language of Southwest Maluku*. Leiden: KITLV Press.

England, Nora C. 1983. *A grammar of Mam, a Mayan language*. Austin: University of Texas Press.

Enk, Gerrit J. van and Vries, Lourens de. 1997. *The Korowai of Irian Jaya: Their language in its cultural context*. New York: Oxford University Press.

Erelt, Mati. 2002. 'Does Estonian have the jussive?', *Linguistica Uralica* 2: 110–17.

―― 2007. 'Structure of the Estonian language: Syntax', in Mati Erelt (ed.), *Estonian language*, 93–129. Tallinn: Estonian Academy.

Evans, Bethwyn. 2003. *A study of valency changing devices in Proto Oceanic*. Canberra: Pacific Linguistics.

Evans, Nicholas. 1994. 'The problem of body parts and noun class membership in Australian languages', *University of Melbourne Working Papers in Linguistics* 14: 1–8.

―― 1995a. 'Multiple case in Kayardild: Anti-iconic suffix ordering and the diachronic filter', in Frans Plank (ed.), *Double case. Agreement by suffixaufnahme*, 396–428. New York: Oxford University Press.

―― 1995b. *A grammar of Kayardild, with historical-comparative notes on Tangkic*. Berlin: Mouton de Gruyter.

―― 1996. 'The syntax and semantics of body part incorporation in Mayali', in Hilary Chappell and William McGregor (eds.), *The grammar of inalienability. A typological perspective on body part terms and the part-whole relation*, 65–109. Berlin: Mouton de Gruyter.

―― 2003. *Bininj Gun-Wok. A pan-dialectal grammar of Mayali, Kunwinjku and Kune*. 2 vols. Canberra: Pacific Linguistics.

Eyre, Edward John. 1845. *Journals of expeditions of discovery into Central Australia and overland from Adelaide to King George's Sound in the years 1840–1*...London: T. and W. Boone.

Faraclas, Nicholas G. 1996. *Nigerian Pidgin*. London: Routledge.

Fauconnier, Gilles. 1997. *Mappings in thought and language*. Cambridge: Cambridge University Press.

Feldman, Harry. 1986. *A grammar of Awtuw*. Canberra: Pacific Linguistics.

Fennell, John and Dimitri Obolensky. 1969. *A historical Russian reader. A selection of texts from the XIth to the XVIth centuries*. Oxford: Clarendon Press.

Feoktistov, A. P. 1966. 'Mordovskije jazyki [Mordvin languages]', in *Yazyki narodov SSSR, Tom. III: Finno-Ugorskije i Samodijskije jazyki [Languages of the peoples of the USSR, vol. III: Finno-Urgric and Samoyed languages]*, 172–220. Moscow: Nauka.

―― 1975. Mordovskije jazyki [Mordvin languages]', in *Osnovy Finno-ugorskogo jazykoznanija: Pribaltijsko-finskije, Saamskij and Mordovskije jazyki [Foundations of Finno-Ugric linguistics: Balto-Finnic, Saami and Mordvin languages]*, 248–345. Moscow: Nauka.

Feuillet, Jack 1996. 'Réflexions sur les valeurs du médiatif', in Z. Guentchéva (ed.), *L'Énonciation médiatisée*, 71–86. Louvain-Paris: Éditions Peeters.

Fischer, John L. 1969. 'Honorific speech and social structure. A comparison of Japanese and Ponapean', *The Journal of the Polynesian Society* 78: 417–22.

Fleck, David W. 2002. 'Causation in Matses (Panoan, Amazonian Peru)', pp. 375–415 of Shibatani 2002a.

―― 2006. 'Antipassive in Matses', *Studies in Language* 30: 541–73.

―― Forthcoming. *A grammar of Matses*. Berlin: Mouton de Gruyter.

Flexner, Stuart Berg (editor in chief). 1987. *The Random House dictionary of the English language*, 2nd ed., unabridged. New York: Random House.

Floyd, Rick. 1999. *The structure of evidential categories in Wanka Quechua*. Dallas: Summer Institute of Linguistics and University of Texas at Arlington.

Foley, William A. 1986. *The Papuan languages of New Guinea*. Cambridge: Cambridge University Press.

—— 1991. *The Yimas language of New Guinea*. Stanford: Stanford University Press.

Foley, William A. and Mike Olson. 1985. 'Clausehood and verb serialisation', pp. 17–60 of Nichols and Woodbury 1985.

Foley, William A. and Robert D., Van Valin, Jr. 1984. *Functional syntax and universal grammar*. Cambridge: Cambridge University Press.

Ford, Kevin and Dana Ober. 1991. 'A sketch of Kalaw Kawaw Ya', in Suzanne Romaine (ed.), *Language in Australia*, 118–42. Cambridge: Cambridge University Press.

Ford, Lysbeth Julie. 1998. 'A description of the Emmi language of the Northern Territory of Australia', PhD thesis, ANU.

Fortescue, Michael. 1984. *West Greenlandic*. London: Croom Helm.

—— 1992. 'Morphophonemic complexity and typological stability in a polysynthetic language family', *International Journal of American Linguistics* 58: 242–8.

Fowler, H. W. (ed.). 1951. *The concise Oxford Dictionary of Current English*. 4th ed., revised by E. McIntosh. Oxford: Clarendon Press.

Fox, Barbara and Paul J. Hopper (eds.). 1994. *Voice: form and function*. Amsterdam: John Benjamins.

Frajzyngier, Zygmunt. 1982. 'Indefinite agent, passive and impersonal passive: a functional study', *Lingua* 58: 267–90.

—— 1985. 'Logophoric systems in Chadic', *Journal of African languages and linguistics* 7: 23–37.

—— 1989. *A grammar of Pero*. Berlin: Dietrich Reimer.

—— 2001. *A grammar of Lele*. Stanford: CSLI.

—— 2002. *A grammar of Hdi*. Berlin: Mouton de Gruyter.

Frank, Paul. 1990. *Ika syntax*. Dallas: Summer Institute of Linguistics and the University of Texas at Arlington.

Frawley, William. 1992. *Linguistic semantics*. Hillsdale, NJ: Lawrence Erlbaum.

Freudenburg, Allen. 1970. *Grammar essentials: Boiken language*. Ms. Ukarumpa.

—— 1979. *Grammar sketch: Boiken language, Yangoru dialect*. Ms. Ukarumpa.

Friedman, Victor A. 1986. 'Evidentiality in the Balkans: Bulgarian, Macedonian and Albanian', pp. 168–87 of Chafe and Nichols 1986.

Gabas, Nilson, Jr. 1999. 'A grammar of Karo, Tupí (Brazil)', PhD dissertation, University of California at Santa Barbara.

Gary, Judith O. and Saad Gamal-Eldin. 1982. *Cairene Egyptian Colloquial Arabic*. Amsterdam: North-Holland.

Genetti, Carol. 1986. 'The development of subordinators from postpositions in Bodic languages', *Berkeley Linguistics Society Proceedings* 12: 387–400.

—— 1991. 'From postposition to subordinator in Newari', pp. 227–56 of Traugott and Heine 1991, vol. 2.

—— 2005. 'The participial construction of Dolakhā Newar: Syntactic implications of an Asian converb', *Studies in Language* 29: 35–87.

—— 2006. 'Complement clause types and complementation strategy in Dolakha Newar', pp. 137–58 of Dixon and Aikhenvald 2006.

—— 2007. *A reference grammar of Dolakha Newar*. Berlin: Mouton de Gruyter.

Genetti, Carol and Laura D. Crain. 2003. 'Beyond preferred argument structure: sentences, pronouns and given referents in Nepali', in John W. Du Bois, Lorraine E. Kumpf and William J. Ashby (eds.), *Preferred argument structure: Grammar as architecture for function*, 197–224. Amsterdam: John Benjamins.

Gentner, Dedre, Mutsumi Imai and Lera Boroditsky. 2002. 'As time goes by: Evidence for two systems in processing space and time metaphors', *Language and Cognitive Processes* 17: 537–65.

Gerdts, Donna B., and Kaoru Kiyosawa. 2005a. 'The function of Salish applicatives'. *Proceedings of the 10th Workshop on the Structure and Constituency of Languages*

of the Americas, University of British Columbia Working Papers in Linguistics
17: 84–94.
—— and —— 2005b. 'Halkomelem psych applicatives', *Studies in Language* 29: 329–62.
—— and —— 2007. 'Combinatorial properties of Salish applicatives', *Papers for the 42nd International Conference on Salish and Neighbouring languages, University of British Columbia Working Papers in Linguistics* 20: 176–219.
Gildea, Spike. 1998. *On reconstructing grammar. Comparative Cariban morphosyntax.* New York: Oxford University Press.
Gippert, J. 1978. *Zur Syntax infinitivischen Bildungen in den indogermanischen Sprachen.* Frankfurt am Main: Peter Lang.
Givón, Talmy. 1979. *On understanding grammar.* New York: Academic Press.
—— 1982. 'Preface', in Paul J. Hopper (ed.), *Tense-aspect: between semantics and pragmatics.* Amsterdam: John Benjamins.
—— 1990. *Syntax: a functional-typological introduction,* vol. 2. Amsterdam: John Benjamins.
—— (ed.). 1994. *Voice and inversion.* Amsterdam: John Benjamins.
Goddard, Cliff. 1983. 'A semantically-oriented grammar of the Yankunytjatjara dialect of the Western Desert language', PhD thesis, ANU.
Goddard, Ives. 1967. 'The Algonquian independent indicative', in *Contributions to Anthropology: Linguistics* 1: 66–106. Ottawa: National Museum of Canada.
—— 1979a. *Delaware verbal morphology: A descriptive and comparative study.* New York: Garland.
—— 1979b. 'Comparative Algonquian', pp. 70–132 of Campbell and Mithun 1979.
Göksel, Asli and Celia Kerslake. 2005. *Turkish. A comprehensive grammar.* London: Routledge.
Golato, Andrea. 2000. 'Und ich so/und er so [and I'm like/and he's like]: An innovative German quotative for reporting on embodied actions', *Journal of Pragmatics* 32: 29–54.
Golovko, Evgenij V. 1993. 'On non-causative effects of causativity in Aleut', pp. 385–90 of Comrie and Polinsky 1993.
Golúscio, Lucía A. 2007. 'Morphological causatives and split intransitivity in Mapudungun', *International Journal American Linguistics* 73: 209–38.
Gonçalves, Cristina H. R. C. 1987. *Concordância em Mundurukú.* Campinas: Editora da Unicamp.
González Ñáñez, Omar. 1997. 'Gramática de la lengua Warekena', PhD dissertation, Universidad Central de Venezuela.
Gorbet, Larry. 1973. 'Case markers and complementizers in Diegueño', *Working Papers on Language Universals* 11: 219–22.
—— 1976. *A grammar of Diegueño nominals.* New York: Garland.
—— 1979. 'The case marking of Diegueño complement clauses', *International Journal of American Linguistics* 45: 251–66.
Gordon, Lynn. 1980. '-*k* and -*m* in Maricopa', in Pamela Munro (ed.), *Studies in switch-reference, UCLA Papers in Syntax* 8, 110–43.
—— 1986. 'The development of evidentials in Maricopa', pp. 73–88 of Chafe and Nichols 1986.
Gove, Phillip B. (editor in chief). 1961. *Webster's third new international dictionary of the English language, unabridged.* Springfield, MA: G. and C. Merriam.
Grande, B. M. 1972. *Vvedenie v sravniteljnoe izuchenie semitskikh jazykov [Introduction to the comparative study of Semitic languages].* Moscow: Nauka.
Green, Diana. 1996/1994. 'O sistema numérico na língua Palikur', *Boletim do museu Goeldi* 10: 261–303.
Green, Diana and Harold Green. 1972. *Surface grammar of Palikur.* Brasília: Summer Institute of Linguistics.

Greenberg, Joseph H. 1963. 'Some universals of grammar with particular reference to the order of meaningful elements', in Joseph H. Greenberg (ed.), *Universals of language*, 73–113. Cambridge, MA: MIT Press.

—— 1966. *Language universals*. The Hague: Mouton.

—— 1991. 'The Semitic "intensive" as verbal plurality: a study of grammaticalization', in Alan S. Kaye (ed.), *Semitic studies in honor of Wolf Leslau*, 577–87. Wiesbaden: Harrassowitz.

Grimes, Joseph E. 1975. *The thread of discourse*. The Hague: Mouton.

Guillaume, Antoine. 2008. *A grammar of Cavineña*. Berlin: Mouton de Gruyter.

Güldemann, Tom. 2001. *Quotative constructions in African languages: a synchronic and diachronic survey*. Habilitationsschrift, Leipzig University.

—— 2002. 'When "say" is not *say*: the functional versatility of the Bantu quotative marker *ti* with special reference to Shona', pp. 253–88 of Güldemann and von Roncador 2002.

—— 2003. 'Logophoricity in Africa: an attempt to explain and evaluate the significance of its modern distribution', *Sprachtypologie und Universalienforschung* 56: 366–87.

—— 2008. 'The 'Macro-Sudan belt': towards identifying a linguistic area in northern Sub-Saharan Africa', in Bernd Heine and Derek Nurse (eds.), *A linguistic geography of Africa*, 151–85. Cambridge: Cambridge University Press.

Güldemann, Tom and Manfred von Roncador (eds.). 2002. *Reported discourse. A meeting ground for different linguistic domains*. Amsterdam: John Benjamins.

Güldemann, Tom, Manfred von Roncador and Wim van der Wurff. 2002. 'A comprehensive bibliography of reported discourse', pp. 363–415 of Güldemann and von Roncador 2002.

Gurubasave Gowda, K. S. 1975. *Ao grammar*. Mysore: Central Institute of Indian Languages.

Haberland, Hartmut. 1986. 'Reported speech in Danish', pp. 219–53 of Coulmas 1986a.

Hagège, Claude. 1974. 'Les pronoms logophoriques', *Bulletin de la Société de Linguistique de Paris* 69: 287–310.

—— 1982. *La structure des langues*. Paris: Presses Universitaires de France.

Haig, Geoffrey. 2001. 'Linguistic diffusion in present-day Anatolia: from top to bottom', pp. 195–224 of Aikhenvald and Dixon 2001.

Haiman, John. 1980. *Hua: a Papuan language of the Eastern Highlands of New Guinea*. Amsterdam: John Benjamins.

—— 1983. 'Iconic and economic motivation', *Language* 59: 781–819.

—— 1985. *Natural syntax*. Cambridge: Cambridge University Press.

Haiman, John and Sandra A. Thompson (eds.). 1988. *Clause combining in grammar and discourse*. Amsterdam: John Benjamins.

Hajek, John. 2004. 'Adjective classes: what can we conclude?', pp. 348–61 of Dixon and Aikhenvald 2004.

Hakulinen, Auli and Fred Karlsson. 1979. *Nykysuomen lauseoppia*. Helsinki: Suomalaisen Kirjallisuuden Seura.

Hakulinen, Lauri. 1961. *The structure and development of the Finnish language*, translated by John Atkinson. Bloomington: Indiana University.

Hale, Austin. 1980. 'Person markers: Finite conjunct and disjunct verb forms in Newari', in *Papers in South-East Asian linguistics* vol. 7, 95–106. Canberra: Pacific Linguistics.

Hale, Kenneth. 1973. 'A note on subject-object inversion on Navajo', in Braj B. Kachru. Robert B. Lees, Yakov Malkiel and Angelina Petrangeli (eds.), *Issues in linguistics: Papers in Honor of Henry and Renée Kahane*, 300–9. Urbana, IL: University of Illinois Press.

—— 1982. 'Some essential features of Warlpiri verbal clauses', in S. Swartz (ed.), *Papers in Warlpiri grammar, in memory of Lothar Jagst*, 217–315. Darwin: Summer Institute of Linguistics.

Hanks, Patrick (ed.). 1971. *Encylopedic world dictionary*. London: Paul Hamlyn.

Hanson, Rebecca. 2000. 'Pronoun acquisition and the morphological feature geometry', *Calgary Working Papers in Linguistics* 22: 1–14.

Harris, James. 1765. *Hermes: or, a philosophical inquiry concerning language and universal grammar*. 2nd ed. London: J. Nourse and P. Valliant.

Harrison, Sheldon. 1982. 'Proto-Oceanic *aki(ni)* and the Proto-Oceanic periphrastic causatives', in Amran Halim, Lois Carrington and S. A. Wurm (eds.), *Papers from the Third International Conference on Austronesian Linguistics*, vol. 1, *Currents in Oceanic*, 179–230. Canberra: Pacific Linguistics.

Harrison, Simon J. 1993. *The mask of war*. Manchester: Manchester University Press.

Härtl, Holden. 2001. *CAUSE und CHANGE: Thematische Relationen und Ereignisstrukturen in Konzeptualisierung und Grammatikalisierung*. Berlin: Akademie.

Haspelmath, Martin. 1989. 'From purposive to infinitive—a universal path of grammaticization', *Folia Linguistica Historica* 10: 287–310.

—— 1990. 'The grammaticization of passive morphology', *Studies in Language* 14: 25–72.

—— 1993a. 'More on the typology of inchoative/causative verb alternations', pp. 87–120 of Comrie and Polinsky 1993.

—— 1993b. *A grammar of Lezgian*. Berlin: Mouton de Gruyter.

—— 1994. 'Passive participles across languages', pp. 151–77 of Fox and Hopper 1994.

—— 1995. 'The converb as a cross-linguistically valid category', in Martin Haspelmath and Ekkehard König (eds.), *Converbs in cross-linguistic perspective*, 1–55. Berlin: Mouton de Gruyter.

—— 1997. *From space to time: temporal adverbials in the world's languages*. Munich: Lincom Europa.

Haude, Katharina. 2006. 'A grammar of Movima', PhD thesis, Radboud University, Nijmegen.

Haviland, John. 1974. 'A Last Look at Cook's Guugu Yimidhirr Word List', *Oceania* 44: 216–32.

—— 1979. 'Guugu Yimidhirr', pp. 27–180 of Dixon and Blake 1979.

Hawkins, Robert E. 1998. 'Wai Wai', pp. 25–224 of Derbyshire and Pullum 1998.

Hayward, Richard J. 1990. 'Notes on the Aari language', in Richard J. Hayward (ed.), *Omotic language studies*, 425–93. London: School of Oriental and African Studies.

Healey, Phyllis M. 1964. 'Teleéfoól quotative clauses', in *Papers in New Guinea Linguistics* vol. 1, 27–34. Canberra: Pacific Linguistics.

Heath, Jeffrey. 1976. 'Antipassivization: a functional typology', *Berkeley Linguistics Society Proceedings* 2: 202–11.

—— 1978. *Ngandi grammar, texts and dictionary*. Canberra: Australian Institute of Aboriginal Studies.

—— 1984. *Functional Grammar of Nunggubuyu*. Canberra: Australian Institute of Aboriginal Studies.

Hedinger, R. 1981. 'The pronouns of Akɔɔse', *Studies in African linguistics* 12: 277–90.

—— 1984. 'Reported speech in Akɔɔse', *The Journal of West African languages* 14: 81–102.

Heinämäki, Orvokki. 1984. 'Aspect in Finnish', in Casper de Groot and Hannu Tommola (eds.), *Aspect bound. A voyage in the realm of Germanic, Slavonic and Finno-Ugric aspectology*, 153–176. Dordrecht: Foris.

Heine, Bernd. 1982. 'African noun class systems', in Hansjakob Seiler and Christian Lehmann (eds.), *Apprehension*, Teil I. *Das sprachliche Erfassen von Gegenständen*, 189–216. Tübingen: Gunter Narr.

Heine, Bernd and Tania Kuteva. 2002. *World lexicon of grammaticalization*. Cambridge: Cambridge University Press.

Hellwig, Birgit. 2006. 'Complementation in Goemai', pp. 204–23 of Dixon and Aikhenvald 2006.
—— 2011. *A grammar of Goemai (a West Chadic language of Nigeria)*. Berlin: Mouton de Gruyter.
Hercus, L. A. 1982. *The Bāgandji language*. Canberra: Pacific Linguistics.
Hetzron, Robert. 1969. *The verbal system of Southern Agaw*. Berkeley and Los Angeles: University of California Press.
Hewitt, B. G. 1979. *Abkhaz*. Amsterdam: North-Holland.
Hewitt, B. G. and S. R. Crisp. 1986. 'Speech reporting in the Caucasus', pp. 121–43 of Coulmas 1986a.
Hill, H. 1995. 'Pronouns and reported speech in Adioukrou', *The Journal of West African languages* 25: 87–106.
Hill, Jane H. 2005. *A grammar of Cupeño*. Berkeley and Los Angeles: University of California Press.
Hills, Robert A. 1990. 'A syntactic sketch of Ayutla Mixtec', pp. 1–260 of Bradley and Hollenbach 1990.
Hinds, John. 1986. *Japanese*. London: Croom Helm.
Holes, Clive. 1990. *Gulf Arabic*. London: Routledge.
Hollenbach, Barbara. E. 1992. 'A syntactic sketch of Copala Trique', in C. Henry Bradley and Barbara. E. Hollenbach (eds.), *Studies in the Syntax of Mixtecan Languages*, vol. 4, 173–341. Dallas: Summer Institute of Linguistics and the University of Texas at Arlington.
Holm, David. 2006. 'The semantics of clause linking in Manchu'. Paper presented at RCLT.
Hopper, Paul J. and Sandra A. Thompson. 1980. 'Transitivity in grammar and discourse', *Language* 56: 251–99.
Huang, Yan. 2002. 'Logophoric marking in East Asian languages', pp. 211–26 of Güldemann and von Roncador 2002.
Hübschmannová, Milena and Vít Bubeník. 1997. 'Causatives in Slovak and Hungarian Romani', in Yaron Matras, Peter Bakker and Hristo Kyuchkov (eds.), *The typology and dialectology of Romani*, 133–45. Amsterdam: John Benjamins.
Huddleston, Rodney. 2002a. '13. Comparative constructions', pp. 1097–1170 of Huddleston and Pullum 2002.
—— 2002b. 'Content clauses and reported speech', pp. 947–1030 of Huddleston and Pullum 2002.
Huddleston Rodney and Geoffrey K. Pullum (chief authors). 2002. *The Cambridge grammar of the English language*. Cambridge: Cambridge University Press.
Hudson, Richard. 1976. 'Beja', in M. Lionel Bender (ed.), *The Non-Semitic languages of Ethiopia*, 97–132. East Lansing, MI: African Studies Center, Michigan State University.
Hughes, J. M., P. A. Mitchell and W. S. Ramson (eds.), 1992. *The Australian concise Oxford dictionary*, 2nd ed. Melbourne: Oxford University Press.
Hulbert, James R. 1955. *Dictionaries, British and American*. London: Andre Deutsch.
Huttar, George and Mary L. Huttar. 1994. *Ndyuka*. London: Routledge.
Huumo, Tuomas. 2010. 'Nominal aspect, quantity and time: the case of the Finnish object', *Journal of Linguistics* 46: 83–125.
Hyman, Larry M. 1978. 'Phonology and noun structure', in Larry M. Hyman (ed.), *Aghem grammatical structure*, 1–72. Los Angeles: University of Southern California.
Hyman, Larry M. and Bernard Comrie. 1981. 'Logophoric reference in Gokana', *Journal of African languages and linguistics* 3: 19–37.
Hyslop, Catriona. 2001. *The Lolovoli dialect of the North-east Ambae language, Vanuatu*. Canberra: Pacific Linguistics.

Iggesen, Oliver. 2005. *Case-asymmetry: A world-wide typological study on lexeme-class-dependent deviations in morphological case inventories*. Munich: Lincom Europa.

Ikola, Osmo. 1961. *Lauseopin kysymyksiä. Tietolipas* 26.

Ikoro, Suanu. 1996. 'A grammatical summary of Swahili', RCLT internal document, ANU.

—— 1997. 'A grammatical summary of Igbo', RCLT internal document, ANU.

Ingamells, Rex and Ian Tilbrook, 1938. *Conditioned culture*. Adelaide: E. W. Preece.

Itkonen, Erkki. 1976. 'Über das Objekt in den finnisch-wolgäischen Sprachen', *Finnisch-Ugrische Forschungen* 39: 53–213.

Ivanov, V. V. and Gamkrelidze T. V. 1984. *The Indo-european language and Indo-europeans*. Tbilisi: Tbilisi University Press.

Jackson, E. 1987. 'Direct and indirect speech in Tikar', *Journal of West African Languages* 17: 98–109.

Jacobsen, William H., Jr. 1983. 'Typological and genetic notes on switch-reference systems in North American Indian languages', in John Haiman and Pamela Munro (eds.), *Switch- reference and universal grammar*, 151–83. Amsterdam: John Benjamins.

—— 1985. 'The analog of the passive transformation in ergative-type languages', pp. 176–91 of Nichols and Woodbury 1985.

—— 1986. 'The heterogeneity of evidentials in Makah', pp. 3–28 of Chafe and Nichols 1986.

Jakobson, Roman. 1971. 'Shifters, verbal categories and the Russian verb' in his *Selected writings*, vol. 2, *Word and language*, 130–43. The Hague: Mouton. [Reprinted in Jakobson 1984, 41–58.]

—— 1984. *Russian and Slavic grammar studies 1931–1981*, Linda R. Waugh and Morris Halle (eds.). Berlin: Mouton.

—— 1990. *On language*. Linda R. Waugh and Monique Monville-Burston (eds.). Cambridge, MA: Harvard University Press.

Janssen, Theo A. J. M. and Wim van der Wurff (eds.). 1996a. *Reported speech: forms and functions of the verb*. Amsterdam: John Benjamins.

—— and—1996b. 'Introductory remarks on reported speech and thought', pp. 1–11 of Janssen and van der Wurff 1986a.

Jarkey, Nerida. 1991. 'Serial verbs in White Hmong: a functional approach', PhD thesis, University of Sydney.

Jauncey, Dorothy. 1997. 'A grammar of Tamambo', PhD thesis, ANU.

Jeffers, Robert J. 1975. 'Remarks on the Indo-European infinitives', *Language* 51: 133–48.

Jelinek, Eloise. 1989. 'The case split and pronominal arguments in Choctaw', in László Marácz and Pieter Muysken (eds.), *Configurationality: The typology of asymmetries*, 117–41. Dordrecht: Foris.

Jendraschek, Gerd. 2006. 'Clause fusion in Iatmul: from cleft sentences to highlighting constructions'. Seminar presented at RCLT.

Jespersen, Otto. 1933. *Essentials of English grammar*. London: George Allen and Unwin.

—— 1949. *A modern English grammar on historical principles*, Part VII, *Syntax*. London: George Allen and Unwin, and Copenhagen: Ejnar Munksgaard.

Johnson, Audrey F. 1988. 'A syntactic sketch of Jamiltepec Mixtec', pp. 11–150 of Bradley and Hollenbach 1988.

Johnson, Samuel. 1755. *A dictionary of the English Language*...London: J. and P. Knapton, T. and T. Longman, C. Hitch and L. Hawes, A. Millar, and R. and J. Dodsley.

Jones, Daniel. 1956. *English pronouncing dictionary*, 11th ed. London: Dent, and New York: Dutton.

Joseph, Brian D. and Irene Philippaki-Warburton. 1987. *Modern Greek*. London: Routledge.

Kachru, Yamuna. 1976. 'On the semantics of the causative construction in Hindi-Urdu', pp. 353–69 of Shibatani 1976a.

Kakumasu, James. 1986. 'Urubu-Kaapor', pp. 326–403 of Derbyshire and Pullum 1986.

Kalinina, E. Yu. 2001. 'Aktantnye predlozhenija', in A. E. Kibrik, K. I. Kazenin, E. A. Ljutikova and S. G. Tatevosov (eds.), *Bagvalinskij jazyk: Grammatika. Teksty. Slovari*, 512–53. Moscow: Nasledie.

Kammerzell, Frank and Cursten Peust. 2002. 'Reported speech in Egyptian: Forms, types and history', pp. 289–322 of Güldemann and von Roncador 2002.

Kany, Charles. 1944. 'Impersonal *dizque* and its variants in American Spanish', *Hispanic Review* 12: 168–77.

Karlsson, Fred. 1983. *Finnish: an essential grammar*. London: Routledge.

Keating, Elizabeth. 1998. *Power sharing. language, rank, gender, and social space in Pohnpei, Micronesia*. Oxford: Oxford University Press.

Keen, Sandra. 1983. 'Yukulta', pp. 190–304 of Dixon and Blake 1982.

Keenan, Edward L. 1984. 'Semantic correlates of the ergative/absolutive distinction', *Linguistics* 22: 197–223. [Reprinted as pp. 166–94 of Keenan 1987.]

—— 1985. 'Passive in the world's languages', pp. 243–81 of Shopen 1985a.

—— 1987. *Universal grammar: 15 essays*. London: Croom Helm.

Keesing, Roger. 1985. *Kwaio grammar*. Canberra: Pacific Linguistics.

Kendall, Martha B. 1975. 'The /-k/, /-m/ problem in Yavapai syntax', *International Journal of American Linguistics* 41: 1–9.

Kenesei, Istvab, Robert M. Vago and Anna Fenyvesi. 1998. *Hungarian*. London: Routledge.

Kennedy, Rod. 1984. 'Semantic roles: the language speaker's categories (in Kala Lagaw Ya)', *Papers in Australian linguistics* vol. 16, 153–70. Canberra: Pacific Linguistics.

Kettunen, Lauri. 1943. *Vepsän murteiden lauseopillinen tutkimus*. Helsinki: Suomalais-Ugrilainen Seura.

Keyser, Samuel Jay and Thomas Roeper. 1984. 'On the middle and ergative constructions in English', *Linguistic Inquiry* 15: 381–416.

Kibrik, A. E. 1977. *Opyt strukturnogo opisanija archinskogo jazyka*. Tom II. *Taksonomicheskaja grammatika*. Moscow: Izdateljstvo Moskovskogo Universiteta.

Kibrik, Andrej A. 1996a. *Godoberi*. Munich: Lincom Europa.

—— 1996b. 'Transitivity in lexicon and grammar', pp. 107–46 of Kibrik 1996a.

Kiefer, Ferenc. 1986. 'Some semantic aspects of indirect speech in Hungarian', pp. 201–17 of Coulmas 1986a.

Kimball, Geoffrey D. 1991. *Koasati grammar*. Lincoln: University of Nebraska Press.

King, Gareth. 1993. *Modern Welsh*. London: Routledge.

King, Phillip P. 1827. *Narrative of a survey of the intertropical and western coasts of Australia performed between the years 1818 and 1822*. London: John Murray.

Kiparsky, Paul. 1998. 'Partitive case and aspect', in Miriam Butt and Wilhelm Geuder (eds.), *The projection of arguments: lexical and compositional factors*, 265–307. Stanford: CSLI.

—— 2001. 'Structural case in Finnish', *Lingua* 11, 315–76.

Kirsner, Robert S. 1976. 'On the subjectless "pseudo-passive" in Standard Dutch and the semantics of background agents', in Charles N. Li (ed.), *Subject and Topic*, 385–415. New York: Academic Press.

Kirtchuk, Pablo. 1993. '/?et / ou ne pas /?et/: l'actant Y en hébreu et au-dela', *Actances* 7: 91–136.

Kisseberth, Charles W. and Mohammad Imam Abasheikh. 1977. 'The object relationship in Chi-Mwi:ni, a Bantu language', in Peter Cole and Jerrold M. Sadock (eds.), *Syntax and Semantics*, vol. 8, *Grammatical Relations*, 179–218. New York: Academic Press.

Kittilä, Seppo. 2009. 'Causative morphemes as non-valency increasing devices', *Folia Linguistica* 43: 67–94.

Klaas, B. 2002. 'Reported commands in Lithuanian compared to Estonian', *Linguistica Uralica* 2: 118–25.

Klaiman, Miriam H. 1991. *Grammatical voice*. Cambridge: Cambridge University Press.

Klamer, Marian A. F. 2000. 'How report verbs become quote markers and complementisers', *Lingua* 110: 69–98.

—— 2002. '"Report" constructions in Kambera (Austronesian)', pp. 323–40 of Güldemann and von Roncador 2002.

Klein Harriet E. M. 1978. *Una grammatical de la lengua Toba: morphologia verbal y nominal*. Montevideo: Universidad de la Republica, Division Publicaciones y Ediciones.

—— 1979. 'Noun classifiers in Toba', in Madeleine Matthias (ed.), *Ethnology: Boas, Sapir and Whorf revisited*, 85–95. The Hague: Mouton.

Klein, Jared S. 1984. 'Review of *Stative and middle in Indo-European* by Jay H. Jasanoff', *Language* 60: 131–8.

Klumpp, Deloria. 1990. *Piapoco grammar*. Colombia: Summer Institute of Linguistics.

Koehn, Edward and Sally. 1986. 'Apalai,' pp. 33–127 of Derbyshire and Pullum 1986.

Konow, Sten. 1909. 'The Tibeto-Burman family', in George A. Grierson (ed.), *Linguistic survey of India*, vol. III, *Tibeto-Burman family*. Part 1, 1–13. Calcutta: Government of India. [Reissued by Motilal Banarsidass, Delhi.]

Kooyers, O. 1974. 'Washkuk grammar sketch', *Working Papers in New Guinea Linguistics* 6, 5–74.

Kornfilt, Jaklyn. 1997. *Turkish*. London: Routledge.

Krishnamurti, Bh. and Brett A. Behnam. 1998. 'Konḍa', pp. 241–69 of *The Dravidian languages*, edited by Sanford B. Steever. London: Routledge.

Kroskrity, P. V. 1993. *Language, history, and identity: Ethnolinguistic studies of the Arizona Tewa*. Tucson: The University of Arizona Press.

Kruspe, Nicole. 2004. *A grammar of Semelai*. Cambridge: Cambridge University Press.

Kulikov, Leonid I. 1999. 'Split causativity: Remarks on correlations between transitivity, aspect, and tense', in Werner Abraham and Leonid Kulikov (eds.), *Tense-aspect, transitivity and causativity*, 21–42. Amsterdam: John Benjamins.

Kumakhov, Mukhadin and Karina Vamling. 1995. 'On root and subordinate clause structure in Kabardian', *Lund University Department of Linguistics, Working Papers* 44: 91–110.

Kuryłowicz, Jerzy. 1964. *The inflectional categories of Indo-European*. Heidelberg: Winter.

Kvavik, Karen H. 1986. 'Characteristics of direct and reported speech prosody: Evidence from Spanish', pp. 333–60 of Coulmas 1986a.

Laanest, Arvo. 1975. *Sissejuhatus Läänemeresoome keeltesse* [*Introduction to Balto-Finnic languages*]. Tallinn: Eesti NSV Teaduste Akadeemia (Estonian Academy of Sciences). An abridged version published as: pp. 5–121 of *Pribaltijsko-finskije jazyki. Osnovy Finno-Ugorskogo jazykoznanija; Pribaltijsko-finskije, Saamskij and Mordovskije jazyki (Foundations of Finno-Ugric Linguistics; Balto-Finnic, Saami and Mordvin languages)*. 1975. Moscow: Nauka.

Laki, Pauline Yuaneng Agnes Luma and Alexandra Y. Aikhenvald. Forthcoming. *Manamb kundi: a dictionary of the Manambu language*.

Lakoff, George. 1970. 'Counterparts, or the problem of reference in transformational grammar', in Susumu Kuno (ed.), *Mathematical linguistics and machine translation*. Report NSF-24, pp. 23–37. Cambridge, MA: The Computation Laboratory of Harvard University.

—— 1986. 'Classifiers as a reflection of mind', pp. 13–52 of Craig 1986.

Landeweerd, Rik and Co Vet. 1996. 'Tense in (free) indirect discourse in French', pp. 141–62 of Janssen and van der Wurff 1986a.

Langacker, Ronald W. 1976. *Non-distinct arguments in Uto-Aztecan*. Berkeley and Los Angeles: University of California Press.

Langdon, Margaret. 1977. 'Semantics and syntax of expressive "say" constructions in Yuman', *Chicago Linguistic Society* 13: 1–11.

—— 1979. 'Some thoughts on Hokan with particular reference to Pomoan and Yuman', pp. 592–619 of Campbell and Mithun 1979.

Langdon, Margaret and Pamela Munro. 1979. 'Subject and (switch-) reference in Yuman', *Folia Linguistica* 13: 321–44.

LaPolla, Randy J. 1995. 'On the utility of concepts of markedness and prototypes in understanding the development of morphological systems', *The Bulletin of the Institute of History and Philology, Academia Sinica* 66: 1149–86.

—— 2004. *A grammar of Qiang with annotated texts and glossary*. Berlin: Mouton de Gruyter.

—— 2006. 'Clause linking in Dulong-Rawang'. Paper presented at RCLT, 24 May 2006.

Larjavaara, Matti. 1991. 'Aspektuaalisen objektin synty', *Virittäjä* 95: 372–407.

Larson, Mildred L. 1984. *Meaning-based translation. A guide to cross-language equivalence*. Lanham: University Press of America.

Larsson, Lars-Gunnar. 1983. *Studien zum Partitivgebrauch in den ostsee-finnischen Sprachen*. Uppsala: Acta Universitatis Upsaliensis.

Leech, Geoffrey and Jan Svartvik 1975. *A communicative grammar of English*. London: Longman.

Lees, Aet. 2004. 'Partitive-accusative alternations in Balto-Finnic languages', *Proceedings of the 2003 Conference of the Australian Linguistic Society* (www.newcastle.edu.au/aschool/lang-media/news/als2003/proceedings.html).

Lehmann, Christian. 1988. 'Towards a typology of clause linkage', pp. 181–225 of Haiman and Thompson 1988.

Lehmann, Thomas. 1993. *A grammar of Modern Tamil*. Pondicherry: Pondicherry Institute of Linguistics and Culture.

Leslau, Wolf. 1995. *Reference grammar of Amharic*. Wiesbaden: Harrassowitz.

LeSourd, Phillip S. 1995. 'Diminutive verb forms in Passamaquoddy', *International Journal of American Linguistics* 61: 103–34.

Levin, Beth and Malka Rappaport Hovav. 1995. *Unaccusativity: at the syntax-lexical semantics interface*. Cambridge, MA: MIT Press.

Lewis, Geoffrey. 1967. *Turkish grammar*. Oxford: Clarendon Press.

Li, Charles N. 1986. 'Direct and indirect speech: A functional study', pp. 29–45 of Coulmas 1986a.

Lichtenberk, Frantisek. 1983. 'Relational classifiers', *Lingua* 60: 147–176.

—— 1991a. 'Semantic change and heterosemy in grammaticalization', *Language* 67: 479–509.

—— 1991b. 'On the gradualness of grammaticalization', pp. 37–80 of Traugott and Heine 1991, vol. 2.

—— 1993. 'Causatives and applicatives in Oceanic'. Paper at the First International Conference on Oceanic Linguistics. Port Vila, Vanuatu.

—— 2009. 'The semantics of clause linking in Toqabaqita', pp. 239–60 of Dixon and Aikhenvald 2009.

Little, William, H. W. Fowler and J. Coulson (eds.). 1933. *The Shorter Oxford English Dictionary, on historical principles*. Revised and edited by C. T. Onions. Oxford: Clarendon Press.

Ljutikova, E. A. 2001. 'Anaforicheskie sredstva', in A. E. Kibrik, K. I. Kazenin, E. A. Ljutikova and S. G. Tatevosov (eds.), *Bagvalinskij jazyk. Grammatika. Teksty. Slovari*. 615–81. Moscow: Nasledie.

Long, R. 1965. 'The English "conjunctions"', *American Speech* 42: 163–177.

Longacre, R. E. 1985. 'Sentences as combinations of clauses', pp. 235–86 of Shopen 1985c.
Loughnane, Robyn. 2003. 'Reported speech in Golin (a Papuan language of New Guinea)', BA Honours thesis, University of Melbourne.
—— 2005. 'Reported speech constructions in Golin', in Nicholas Evans, Jutta Besold, Hywel Stoakes and Alan Lee (eds.), *Materials on Golin: Grammar, texts and dictionary*, 132–51. Department of Linguistics and Applied Linguistics, University of Melbourne.
Lowe, Ivan and Ruth Hurlimann. 2002. 'Direct and indirect speech in Cerma narrative', pp. 91–108 of Güldemann and von Roncador 2002.
Lynch, John, Malcolm D. Ross and Terry Crowley (eds.). 2002. *The Oceanic languages*. London: Curzon.
Lyons, John. 1966. 'Towards a 'notional' theory of the "parts of speech"', *Journal of Linguistics* 2: 209–36.
—— 1977. *Semantics*. vol. 2. Cambridge: Cambridge University Press.
McCawley, James. 1978. 'Conversational implicature and the lexicon', in Peter Cole (ed.), *Syntax and semantics*, vol. 9, *Pragmatics*, 245–60. New York: Academic Press.
MacDonald, Lorna. 1988. 'Subordination in Tauya', pp. 227–46 of Haiman and Thompson 1988.
—— 1990a. 'Evidentiality in Tauya', *Language and Linguistics in Melanesia* 21: 31–46.
—— 1990b. *A grammar of Tauya*. Berlin: Mouton de Gruyter.
McGinnis, Martha. 2001. 'Variation in the phrase structure of applicatives', *Linguistic Variation Yearbook* I, 105–46.
McGinnis, Martha and Donna B. Gerdts. 2004. 'A phrase-theoretic analysis of Kinyarwanda multiple applicatives', in Sophie Burelle and Stanca Somesfalean (eds.), *Proceedings of the 2003 LA Annual Conference*, 154–65. Université de Quebec: Département de linguistique et de didactique des langues.
McGregor, William. 1994. 'The grammar of reported speech and thought in Gooniyandi', *Australian Journal of Linguistics* 14: 63–92.
McKay, Graham R. 1975. 'Rembarrnga, a language of central Arnhem Land', PhD thesis, ANU.
Mahapatra, B. P. 1979. *Malto: an ethnosemantic study*. Mysore: Central Institute of Indian Languages.
Maldonado, Ricardo and E. Fernando Nava L. 2002. 'Tarascan causatives and event complexity', pp. 157–95 of Shibatani 2002a.
Mallinson, Graham. 1986. *Rumanian*. London: Routledge.
Mallinson, Graham, and Barry J. Blake, 1981. *Language typology: Cross-cultural studies in syntax*. Amsterdam: North-Holland.
Marchand, Hans. 1969. *The categories and types of present-day English word-formation*. Munich: C. H. Beck.
Marnita, Rina A. 1996. 'Classifiers in Minangkabau', MA thesis, ANU.
Martin, Jack. 1991. 'Lexical and syntactic aspects of Creek causatives', *International Journal of American Linguistics* 57: 194–229.
—— 2000. 'Creek voice: Beyond valency', pp. 375–403 of Dixon and Aikhenvald 2000.
Martin, Jack and Pamela Munro. 2005. 'Proto-Muskogean morphology', in Heather K. Hardy and Janine Scancarelli (eds.), *Native languages of the southeastern United States*, 299–320. Lincoln: University of Nebraska Press.
Martin, Samuel E. 1975. *A reference grammar of Japanese*. New Haven: Yale University Press.
Martins, Silvana A. 1994. 'Análise da morfosintaxe da língua Dâw (Maku-Kamã) e sua classificação tipológica', MA thesis, Universidade Federal de Santa Catarina.

Masica, Colin. 1976. *Defining a linguistic area: South Asia.* Chicago: University of Chicago Press.

Maslova, Elena. 2003. *A grammar of Kolyma Yukaghir.* Berlin: Mouton de Gruyter.

Massamba, David P. B. 1986. 'Reported speech in Swahili', pp. 99–119 of Coulmas 1986a.

Mathews, M. M. 1933. *A survey of English dictionaries.* London: Oxford University Press.

Matisoff, James A. 1973. *The grammar of Lahu.* Berkeley and Los Angeles: University of California Press.

Matras, Yaron. 2002. *Romani. A linguistic introduction.* Cambridge: Cambridge University Press.

Matteson, Esther. 1965. *The Piro (Arawakan) language.* Berkeley and Los Angeles: University of California Press.

Matthews, P. H. 1997. *The concise Oxford dictionary of linguistics.* Oxford: Oxford University Press.

Matthews, R. H. 1901. 'The Dharuk language'. *Journal and Proceedings of the Royal Society of New South Wales* 35: 155–60.

—— Ms. 'Field notebooks'. Mitchell Library, Sydney.

Matthews, Stephen and Virginia Yip. 1994. *Cantonese: a comprehensive grammar.* London: Routledge.

Matthews, W. K. 1960. *Russian historical grammar.* London: Athlone.

Matzel, Klaus. 1987. *Einführung in die singalesische Sprache.* Wiesbaden: Harrassowitz.

Meillet, Antoine. 1912. 'L'évolution des formes grammaticales', *Scientia 12/26* (Milan). [Reprinted in his *Linguistique historique et linguistique générale*, 130–148. Paris: C. Klincksieck. 1951.]

—— 1964. *Introduction à l'étude comparative des langues indo-européennes.* Alabama: University of Alabama Press.

Mencken, H. L. 1919. *The American language, a preliminary inquiry into the development of English in the United States.* New York: Alfred A. Knopf.

—— 1936. *The American language, an inquiry into the development of English in the United States.* 4th ed. New York: Alfred A. Knopf.

—— 1945. *The American language, an inquiry into the development of English in the United States. Supplement 1.* New York: Alfred A. Knopf.

Merlan, Francesca. 1982. *Mangarayi.* Amsterdam: North-Holland.

—— 1983. *Ngalakan grammar, texts and vocabulary.* Canberra: Pacific Linguistics.

—— 1994. *A grammar of Wardaman, a language of the Northern Territory of Australia.* Berlin: Mouton de Gruyter.

Merlan, Francesca and Alan Rumsey. 1991. *Ku Waru. Language and segmentary politics in the western Nebilyer Valley, Papua New Guinea.* Cambridge: Cambridge University Press.

—— and —— 2001. 'Aspects of ergativity and reported speech in Ku Waru', in Andrew Pawley, Malcolm Ross and Darrell Tryon (eds.), *The boy from Bundaberg: studies in Melanesian linguistics in honour of Tom Dutton*, 215–31. Canberra: Pacific Linguistics.

Michael, Ian. 1970. *English grammatical categories, and the tradition to 1800.* Cambridge: Cambridge University Press.

Miller, Amy. 2001. *A grammar of Jamul Tiipay.* Berlin: Mouton de Gruyter.

Miller, Marion. 1999. *Desano grammar.* Dallas: Summer Institute of Linguistics and University of Texas at Arlington.

Mish, Frederick G. (editor in chief). 1995. *Merriam-Webster's collegiate dictionary*, 10th ed. Springfield, MA: Merriam-Webster.

Mithun, Marianne. 1984. 'The evolution of noun incorporation', *Language* 60: 847–94.

—— 1986. 'When zero isn't there', *Berkeley Linguistics Society Proceedings* 12: 195–211.

—— 1999a. *The languages of Native North America*. Cambridge: Cambridge University Press.

—— 1999b. 'Noun and verb in Iroquoian languages', in Bernard Comrie and Petra Vogel (eds.), *An anthology of word classes*, 379–420. Berlin: Mouton de Gruyter.

—— 2000. 'Valency-changing derivation in Central Alaskan Yup'ik', pp. 84–114 of Dixon and Aikhenvald 2000.

—— 2001. 'Understanding and explaining applicatives', *Chicago Linguistic Society* 37(2): 73–97.

Mittwoch, Anita. 1985. 'Sentences, utterance boundaries, personal deixis and the E-hypothesis', *Theoretical Linguistics* 12: 137–52.

Monier-Williams, Sir Monier. 1899. *A Sanskrit-English dictionary, etymologically and philologically arranged, with special reference to cognate Indo-European languages*. Oxford: Clarendon Press.

Moore, Bruce (ed.). 2004. *The Australian Oxford dictionary*, 2nd ed. Melbourne: Oxford University Press.

Moravcsik, Edith. 1972. 'On case markers and complementizers', *Working Papers on Language Universals* 8: 151–152.

Morphy, Frances. 1983. 'Djapu, a Yolngu dialect', pp. 1–188 of Dixon and Blake 1983.

Morris, Edward E. 1898. *Austral English, a dictionary of Australasian words, phrases and usages*. London: Macmillan.

Moscati, Sabatino (ed.). 1969. *An introduction to the comparative grammar of the Semitic languages: Phonology and morphology*. Wiesbaden: Otto Harrasowitz.

Mosel, Ulrike. 1984. *Tolai syntax and its historical development*. Canberra: Pacific Linguistics.

Mosel, Ulrike and Ruth Spriggs. 1992. 'A grammar of Teop'. Ms.

Motsch, W. 1994. 'Word-formation: compounding', in R. E. Asher and J. M. Y. Simpson (eds.), *The encyclopedia of language and linguistics*, vol. 9, 5021–4. Oxford: Pergamon Press.

Mous, Maarten. 1993. *A grammar of Irakw*. Hamburg: Helmut Buske.

Mufwene, Salikoko S. 1980. 'Bantu class prefixes: inflectional or derivational?', *Chicago Linguistic Society* 16(1): 246–258.

Mugglestone, Lynda 2005. *Lost for words: The hidden history of the Oxford English dictionary*. New Haven: Yale University Press.

—— (ed.). 2000. *Lexicology and the OED: Pioneers in the untrodden forest*. Oxford: Oxford University Press.

Munro, Pamela. 1978. 'Chemehuevi "say" and the Uto-Aztecan quotative pattern', in Donald R. Tuohy (ed.), *Selected papers from the 14th Great Basin anthropological conference*, 149–71. Socorro, NM: Ballena Press.

—— 1982. 'On the transitivity of "say" verbs', in Paul J. Hopper and Sandra A. Thompson (eds.), *Syntax and semantics*, vol. 15. *Studies in transitivity*, 301–19. New York: Academic Press.

Murray, James A. H. (ed.). 1888–1933. *A new English Dictionary on historical principles, founded mainly on the materials collected by the Philological Society*. 10 vols., plus supplement. Oxford: Clarendon Press. [Later retitled by the publishers *Oxford English Dictionary*.]

—— 1900. *The evolution of English lexicography*. Oxford: Clarendon Press.

Naess, Åshild. 2009. 'How transitive are EAT and DRINK verbs?', pp. 27–44 of Newman 2009.

Nagano, Yasahiko. 2003. 'Cogtse Gyarong', pp. 469–89 of Thurgood and LaPolla 2003.

Nash, David, 2009. 'Australian Aboriginal words in dictionaries: a reaction', *International Journal of Lexicography* 22: 179–88.

Nedjalkov, Igor. 1997. *Evenki*. London: Routledge.

Nedyalkov, V. P. and G. G. Silnitsky. 1973. 'The typology of morphological and lexical causatives', in Ferenc Kiefer (ed.), *Trends in Soviet theoretical linguistics.* 1–32. Dordrecht: Reidel.

Newman, John (ed.). 2009. *The linguistics of eating and drinking.* Amsterdam: John Benjamins.

Newman, Paul. 1990. *Nominal and verbal plurality in Chadic.* Dordrecht: Foris.

—— 2000. *The Hausa language: An encyclopedic reference grammar.* New Haven: Yale University Press.

Nichols, Johanna. 1986. 'Head-marking and dependent-marking grammar', *Language* 62: 56–119.

—— 1992. *Linguistic diversity in space and time.* Chicago: University of Chicago Press.

Nichols, Johanna and Anthony C. Woodbury (eds.). 1985. *Grammar inside and outside the clause.* Cambridge: Cambridge University Press.

Nicklas, T. D. 1974. 'The elements of Choctaw', PhD dissertation, University of Michigan at Ann Arbor.

Nikolaeva, Irina and Maria Tolskaya. 2001. *A grammar of Udihe.* Berlin: Mouton de Gruyter.

Nilsson, Brita. 1985. *Case marking in Turkish.* University of Stockholm.

Noonan, Michael. 1992. *A grammar of Lango.* Berlin: Mouton de Gruyter.

—— 1997. 'Versatile nominalizations', pp. 373–94 of Bybee, Haiman and Thompson 1997.

—— 2001. 'Direct speech as a rhetorical style in Chantyal'. Paper presented at the Workshop on Tibeto-Burman languages, University of California at Santa Barbara.

Nordlinger, Rachel and Louise Sadler. 2004. 'Nominal tense in cross-linguistic perspective', *Language* 80: 776–806.

Noss, Philip A. 1988. 'Speech, structure and aesthetics in a Gbaya tale', *Journal of West African Languages* 18: 97–115.

O'Grady, Geoffrey N., C. F. and F. M. Voegelin. 1966. 'Languages of the world: Indo-Pacific Fascicle 6', *Anthropological Linguistics*, vol. 8, no 2.

Ohori, Toshio. 1996. 'Case markers and clause linkage: towards a semantic typology', in Eugene Casad (ed.), *Cognitive linguistics in the redwoods: The expansion of a new paradigm in linguistics*, 693–712. Berlin: Mouton de Gruyter.

Olawsky. Knut J. 2001. 'A grammar summary of Dagbani', RCLT internal document.

—— 2006. *A grammar of Urarina.* Berlin: Mouton de Gruyter.

Oliver, José R. 1989. 'The archaeological, linguistic and ethnolinguistic evidence for the expansion of Arawakan into northwestern Venezuela and northeastern Colombia', PhD dissertation, University of Illinois.

Onishi, Masayuki. 1994. 'A grammar of Motuna. Bougainville, Papua New Guinea', PhD thesis, ANU.

—— 1996a. 'A grammatical summary of Ainu', RCLT internal document, ANU.

—— 1996b. 'A grammatical summary of Japanese', RCLT internal document, ANU.

—— 1997. 'A grammatical summary of Bengali', RCLT internal document, ANU.

—— 2000. 'Transitivity and valency-changing derivations in Motuna', pp. 115–44 of Aikhenvald and Dixon 2000.

Overall, Simon. 2008. 'A grammar of Aguaruna'. PhD thesis, La Trobe University.

Palmer, F. R. 1957. 'The verb in Bilin', *Bulletin of the School of Oriental and African Studies* 19: 131–159.

—— 1984. *Grammar.* 2nd ed. Harmondsworth: Penguin.

—— 1986. *Mood and modality.* Cambridge: Cambridge University Press.

Palmer, L. R. 1954. *The Latin language.* London: Faber and Faber.

Pandharipande, Rajeshwari V. 1997. *Marathi.* London: Routledge.

Partee, Barbara H. 1973. 'The syntax and semantics of quotation', in Stephen Anderson and Paul Kiparsky (eds.), *A Festschrift for Morris Halle*, 410–18. New York: Holt, Rinehart and Winston.

Patz, Elisabeth. 1991. 'Djabugay', pp. 245–347 of Dixon and Blake 1991.

—— 2002. *A grammar of the Kuku Yalanji language of North Queensland*. Canberra: Pacific Linguistics.

Pawley, Andrew K. 1993. 'A language which defies description by ordinary means', in William A. Foley (ed.), *The role of theory in language description*, 87–129. Berlin: Mouton de Gruyter.

—— 1987. 'Encoding events in Kalam and English: different logics for reporting experience', in Ross Tomlin (ed.), *Coherence and grounding in discourse*, 329–60. Amsterdam: John Benjamins.

—— 2006. 'Where have all the verbs gone? Remarks on the organisation of languages with small, closed verb classes'. Paper at 11th Binnenial Rice University Linguistics Symposium, 16–18 March 2006.

Payne, David L. 1991. 'A classification of Maipuran (Arawakan) languages based on shared lexical retentions', pp. 355–500 of Derbyshire and Pullum 1991.

Payne, Doris L. (ed.). 1990a. *Amazonian linguistics: Studies in lowland South American languages*. Austin: University of Texas Press.

—— 1990b. 'Morphological characteristics of lowland South American languages', pp. 213–41 of Payne 1990a.

—— 1990c. *The pragmatics of word order: typological dimensions of verb initial languages*. Berlin: Mouton de Gruyter.

—— 1994. 'The Tupí-Guaraní inverse,' pp. 313–40 of Fox and Hopper 1994.

—— 2004. 'A construction grammar view of clause combining in Maa'. Paper presented at 35th Annual Conference on African Linguistics, Boston.

Payne, Doris L. and Thomas E. Payne. 1990. 'Yagua', pp. 249–474 of Derbyshire and Pullum 1990.

Payne, John, Rodney Huddleston and Geoffrey K. Pullum. 2007. 'Fusion of functions: The syntax of *once, twice* and *thrice*', *Journal of Linguistics* 43: 565–603.

Payne, Thomas E. 1994. 'The pragmatics of voice in a Philippine language: Actor-focus and goal-focus in Cebuano narrative', pp. 317–64 of Givón 1994.

Pearsall, Judy and Bill Trumble (eds.). 1996. *The Oxford English reference dictionary*, 2nd ed. Oxford: Oxford University Press.

Perlmutter, David M. 1978. 'Impersonal passives and the unaccusative hypothesis', *Berkeley Linguistics Society Proceedings* 4: 157–89.

Perlmutter, David M. and Paul M. Postal. 1984. 'The 1-advancement exclusiveness law', in David M. Perlmutter and Carol G. Rosen (eds.), *Studies in relational grammar*, vol. 2, 81–125. Chicago: University of Chicago Press.

Perrin, M. 1974. 'Direct and indirect speech in Mambila', *Journal of Linguistics* 10: 27–37.

Persson, Gunnar. 1988. 'Homonymy, polysemy and heterosemy: the types of lexical ambiguity in English', in Karl Hyldgaard-Jensen and Anne Zettersten (eds.), *Symposium on Lexicography III*, 269–80. Tübingen: Niemeyer.

Pet, William J. A. 1987. 'Lokono (Dian), the Arawak language of Suriname: a sketch of its grammatical structure and lexicon', PhD dissertation, Cornell University.

Peterson, David A. 2007. *Applicative constructions*. Oxford: Oxford University Press.

Peterson, Glenn. 1993. 'Kanengamah and Pohnpei's politics of concealment', *American Anthropologist* 95: 334–52.

Piper, Nick. 1989. 'A sketch grammar of Meryam Mir', MA thesis, ANU.

Pittman, Richard S. 1948. 'Nahuatl honorifics', *International Journal of American Linguistics* 91: 236–9.

Plaisier, Heleen. 2006. 'A grammar of Lepcha', PhD thesis, University of Leiden.

Plank, Franz (ed.) 1991. *Paradigms: the economy of inflection*. Berlin: Mouton de Gruyter.

Plank, Franz and Wolfgang Schellinger. 1997. 'The uneven distribution of genders over numbers: Greenberg Nos. 37 and 45', *Linguistic Typology* 1: 53–101.

Plungian, Vladimir. 1995. *Dogon*. Munich: Lincom Europa.
Poppe, Nikolaus. 1951. *Khalkha Mongolische Grammatik mit Bibliographie, Sprachproben und Glosssar.* Wiesbaden: Franz Steinet.
Post, Mark. 2007. 'A grammar of Galo', PhD thesis, La Trobe University.
—— 2009. 'The semantics of clause linking in Galo', pp. 74–95 of Dixon and Aikhenvald 2009.
Postal, Paul M. 1977. 'Antipassive in French', *Lingvisticae Investigationes* 1: 333–74.
Premper, Waldfried. 1987. *Kausativierung im Arabischen (Arbeiten des Kölner Universalien-Projekts* 46). Cologne.
Pustet, Regina. 1995. 'Obviation and subjectivization: The same basic phenomenon? A study of participant marking in Blackfoot', *Studies in Language* 19: 37–72.
Pylkkänen, Liina. 2008. *Introducing arguments.* Cambridge, MA: MIT Press.
Quirk, Randolph, and C. L. Wrenn. 1957. *An Old English grammar*, 2nd ed. London: Methuen.
Quirk, Randolph, Sidney Greenbaum, Geoffrey Leech and Jan Svartvik. 1985. *A comprehensive grammar of the English language.* London: Longman.
Ramirez, Henri. 1994. *Le parler Yanomamí des Xamatauteri.* Paris.
—— 1997. *A fala Tukano dos Yepâ-masa.* Tomo I. *Gramática.* Tomo II. *Dicionário.* Tomo III. *Método de aprendizagem.* Manaus: Inspetoria Salesiana Missionária da Amazônia.
Ramson, W. S. 1961. 'An historical study of the Australian vocabulary', PhD thesis, University of Sydney.
—— 1966. *Australian English, an Historical Study of the Vocabulary, 1788–1898.* Canberra: Australian National University Press.
—— (ed.). 1988. *The Australian National Dictionary, a dictionary of Australianisms on historical principles.* Melbourne: Oxford University Press.
—— 2002. *Lexical images, the story of the Australian National Dictionary.* Melbourne: Oxford University Press.
Reesink, Ger P. 1987. *Structures and their functions in Usan, a Papuan language of Papua New Guinea.* Amsterdam: John Benjamins.
—— 1993. '"Inner speech" in Papuan languages', *Language and Linguistics in Melanesia* 24: 217–25.
—— 1999. *A grammar of Hatam, Bird's Head Peninsula, Irian Jaya.* Canberra: Pacific Linguistics.
Refsing, Kirsten. 1986. *The Ainu language: The morphology and syntax of the Shizunai dialect.* Aarhus: Aarhus University Press.
Rehg, Kenneth L. 1981. *Ponapean reference grammar.* Honolulu: University of Hawaii Press.
Rennison, John R. 1997. *Koromfe.* London: Routledge.
de Reuse, Willem J. 1994. 'Noun incorporation', in R. E. Asher (ed.), *The encyclopedia of language and linguistics*, vol. 9, 2842–7. Oxford: Pergamon Press.
Rice, Keren. 1986. 'Some remarks on direct and indirect speech in Slave (Northern Athapaskan)', pp. 47–76 of Coulmas 1986a.
—— 1989. *A grammar of Slave.* Berlin: Mouton de Gruyter.
Ridley, William. 1875. *Kámilarói and other Australian languages.* Sydney: Government Printer.
Roberts, John R. 1987. *Amele.* London: Croom Helm.
—— 1997. 'GIVE in Amele', in John Newman (ed.), *The linguistics of giving*, 1–33. Amsterdam: John Benjamins.
Robins, R. H. 1959. 'Nominal and verbal derivation in Sundanese', *Lingua* 8: 337–69.
Rodrigues, Aryon D. 1999. 'Macro-Jê languages', pp. 165–206 of Dixon and Aikhenvald 1999.
Romaine, Suzanne and Deborah Lange. 1998. 'The use of *like* as a marker of reported speech and thought: A case of grammaticalization in progress', in Jenny Cheshire

and Peter Trudgill (eds.), *The sociolinguistics reader*, vol. 2, *Gender and discourse*, 240–77. London: Arnold.

Rose, Françoise 2003. 'Morphosyntaxe de l'émérillon, une langue tupi-guarani de Guyana française', Thèse de Doctorat en Sciences du Langage, Université Lumière Lyon II.

—— 2005. 'Le syncrétisme adpositions/subordonnants: Proposition de typologie syntaxique', *Faits de Langues* 28: 205–16.

Rose, Françoise and Antoine Guillaume. 2010. 'Sociative causative markers in South-American languages: a possible areal feature' pp. 383–402 of *Essais de typologie et de linguistique générale. Mélanges offerts á Denis Creissels*, edited by F. Floricic. Lyon: École normale supérieure de Lyon.

Rosen, S. 1989. 'Argument structure and complex predicates', PhD dissertation, Brandeis University.

Rosenbaum, P. 1967. *The grammar of English predicate complement constructions.* Cambridge, MA: MIT Press.

Roth, Walter E. 1897. *Ethnological studies among the north-west-central Queensland Aborigines.* Brisbane: Government Printer.

—— 1898. 'The word "kangaroo"', Letter to the editor of *The Australasian*, 2 July 1898, p. 33.

Rubino, Carl. 1998a. 'A grammatical summary of Ilocano', RCLT internal document, ANU.

—— 1998b. 'A grammatical summary of Tagalog', RCLT internal document, ANU.

Rumsey, Alan. 1982. *An intra-sentence grammar of Ungarinjin, north-western Australia.* Canberra: Pacific Linguistics.

—— 1990. 'Wording, meaning and linguistic ideology', *American Anthropologist* 92: 346–61.

—— 1994. 'On the transitivity of "say" constructions in Bunuba', *Australian Journal of Linguistics* 14: 137–53.

—— 2000. 'Bunuba', pp. 35–152 of Dixon and Blake 2000.

Rutgers, Roland. 1998. *Yamphu: Grammar, texts and lexicon.* Leiden: CNWS.

Saeed, John. 2003. *Semantics*, 2nd ed. London: Blackwell.

Sakita, Tomoko I. 2002. 'Discourse perspectives on tense choice in spoken-English reporting discourse', pp. 173–98 of Güldemann and von Roncador 2002.

Saksena, Anuradha. 1980. 'The affected agent', *Language* 56: 812–26.

—— 1982a. 'Case marking semantics', *Lingua* 56: 335–43.

—— 1982b. *Topics in the analysis of causatives with an account of Hindi paradigms.* Berkeley and Los Angeles: University of California Press.

—— 1982c. 'Contact in causation', *Language* 58: 820–31.

Saltarelli, Mario. 1988. *Basque.* London: Routledge.

Sands, Kristina. 1995. 'Nominal classification in Australia', *Anthropological Linguistics* 37: 247–346.

—— 2000. 'Complement clauses and grammatical relations in Finnish', PhD thesis, ANU.

Sands, Kristina and Lyle Campbell. 2001. 'Non-canonical subjects and objects in Finnish', in Alexandra Y. Aikhenvald, R. M. W. Dixon and Masayuki Onishi (eds.), *Non-canonical marking of subjects and objects*, 251–306. Amsterdam: John Benjamins.

Sapir, Edward. 1922. 'The Takelma language of southwestern Oregon', in Franz Boas (ed.), *Handbook of American Indian Languages*, Part 2, 1–296. Washington: Smithsonian Institution.

—— 1933. 'La realité psychologique des phonèmes', *Journal de Psychologie Normale et Pathologiques* 30: 247–65. [English version in David G. Mandelbaum (ed.), *Selected writings of Edward Sapir in language, culture and personality*, 46–60. Berkeley and Los Angeles: University of California Press.]

Satel, Sally. 2008. 'Desperately seeking a kidney', *The Weekend Australian Magazine*, February 16–17, pp. 27–31.

Saxena, Anju. 1988. 'On syntactic convergence: the case of the verb "say" in Tibeto-Burman', *Berkeley Linguistics Society Proceedings* 14: 375–88.

Saxton, Lesley. 1998. 'Complement clauses in Dogrib', in Leanne Hinton and Pamela Munro (eds.), *Studies in American Indian languages: Description and theory*, 204–11. Berkeley and Los Angeles: University of California Press.

Say, Sergei. n.d. 'Between causation and intention: Semantic bleaching of causatives in Kalmyck dependent clauses'. Ms.

Scatton, Ernest A. 1984. *A reference grammar of Modern Bulgarian*. Columbus, OH: Slavica.

Schachter, Paul. 1985. 'Parts-of-speech systems', pp. 1–61 of Shopen 1985a.

Schachter, Paul and Fe T. Otanes. 1972. *Tagalog reference grammar*. Berkeley and Los Angeles: University of California Press.

Schaub, Willi. 1985. *Babungo*. London: Croom Helm.

Schauber, Ellen. 1979. *The syntax and semantics of questions in Navajo*. New York: Garland.

Schauer, Stanley and Junia Schauer. 2000. 'El yucuna', in María Stella González de Pérez and María Luisa Rodríguez de Montes (eds.), *Lenguas indígenas de Colombia: Una visión descriptiva*, 515–32. Santafé de Bogotá: Instituto Caro y Cuervo.

—— 2005. *Meke kemakánaka puráka'aloji. Wapura'akó chu, eyá karíwana chu. Diccionario bilingüe yukuna-español español yukuna*. Bogotá: Editorial Fundación para el Desarrollo de los Pueblos Marginados.

Schneider-Blum, Gertrud. 2009. 'Alaaba', in Gerrit J. Dimmendaal (ed.). *Coding participant marking: Constuction types in twelve African languages*, 55–96. Amsterdam: John Benjamins.

Schöttelndreyer, Burkhard. 1980. 'Person markers in Sherpa', in *Papers in South-East Asian linguistics*, No. 7, 125–30. Canberra: Pacific Linguistics.

Seki, Lucy. 2000. *Gramática da língua Kamaiurá*. Campinas: Editora da Unicamp.

Senft, Gunter. 1996. *Classificatory particles in Kilivila*. New York: Oxford University Press.

Sharma, Suhnu Ram. 2001. 'A sketch of Rongpo grammar', in Yasuhino Nagano and Randy J. LaPolla (eds.), *New research on Zhangzhung and related Himalayish languages*. Bon Studies 3, 195–270. Osaka: National Museum of Ethnology.

Sharp, Janet. 2002. *A grammar of Nyangumarta*. Canberra: Pacific Linguistics.

Shephard, Glenn. Jr. 1997. 'Noun classification and ethnozoological classification in Machiguenga, an Arawakan language of the Peruvian Amazon', *Journal of Amazonian Languages* 1: 29–57.

Shibatani, Masayoshi (ed.). 1976a. *Syntax and semantics*, vol. 6, *The grammar of causative constructions*. New York: Academic Press.

—— 1976b. 'The grammar of causative constructions: a conspectus', pp. 1–40 of Shibatani 1976a.

—— 1985. 'Passives and related constructions', *Language* 61: 821–48.

—— (ed.). 1988a. *Passive and voice*. Amsterdam: John Benjamins.

—— 1988b. 'Voice in Philippine languages', pp. 85–142 of Shibatani 1988a.

—— 1990. *The languages of Japan*. Cambridge: Cambridge University Press.

—— 1991. 'Grammaticization of topic into subject', pp. 93–133 of Traugott and Heine 1991, vol. 2.

—— (ed.). 2002a. *The grammar of causation and interpersonal manipulation*. Amsterdam: John Benjamins.

—— 2002b. 'Introduction: Some basic issues in the grammar of causation', pp. 1–22 of Shibatani 2002a.

Shibatani, Masayoshi and Prashant Pardeshi. 2002. 'The causative continuum', pp. 85–126 of Shibatani 2002a.

Shields, Jana K. 1988. 'A syntactic sketch of Silacayoapan Mixtec', pp. 305–449 of Bradley and Hollenbach 1988.

Shopen, Timothy (ed.). 1985a. *Language typology and syntactic description*, vol. I, *Clause structure*. Cambridge: Cambridge University Press.

—— (ed.). 1985b. *Language typology and syntactic description*, vol. II, *Complex constructions*. Cambridge: Cambridge University Press.

—— (ed.). 1985c. *Language typology and syntactic description*, vol. III, *Grammatical categories and the lexicon*. Cambridge: Cambridge University Press.

Siewierska, Anna. 1984. *Passive: a comparative linguistic analysis*. London: Croom Helm.

Simpson, J. A., and Weiner, E. S. C. (eds.). 1989. *The Oxford English dictionary*, 2nd ed. Oxford: Oxford University Press.

Simpson, Jane. 1988. 'Case and complementizer suffixes in Warlpiri', in Peter K. Austin (ed.), *Complex sentence constructions in Australian languages*, 205–218. Amsterdam: John Benjamins.

Skorik, P. Ja. 1961. *Grammatika čukotskogo jazyka*. Tom. 1 [*Grammar of the Chukchi language*, vol. 1]. Moscow and Leningrad: Izdatel'stvo akademii nauk SSSR.

Small, Priscilla C. 1990. 'A syntactic sketch of Coatzospan Mixtec', pp. 261–479 of Bradley and Hollenbach 1990.

Smith, Ian and Steve Johnson. 2000. 'Kugu Nganhcara', pp. 355–489 of Dixon and Blake 2000.

Sneddon, James N. 1996. *Indonesian reference grammar*. Sydney: Allen and Unwin.

Sohn, Ho-min. 1994. *Korean*. London: Routledge.

Solnit, David. 1997. *Eastern Kayah Li: Grammar, texts, glossary*. Honolulu: University of Hawai'i Press.

Soukhanov, Anne H. (executive editor). 1992. *The American Heritage dictionary of the English language*, 3rd ed. Boston: Houghton Mifflin.

Staalsen, Phil. 1965. *Iatmul grammar sketch*. Ms. Ukarumpa.

Starke, Gunter. 1985. 'Zum Modusgebrauch bei der Redewiederaufgabe in der Presse', *Sprachpflege* 34: 163–5.

Starnes, De Witt T. and Gertrude E. Noyes, 1946. *The English dictionary from Cawdrey to Johnson, 1604–1755*. Chapel Hill: The University of North Carolina Press.

Stebbins, Tonya N. 2001. 'A grammatical summary of Sm'algyax', RCLT internal document.

Steever, Sanford B. 2002. 'Direct and indirect discourse in Tamil', pp. 91–108 of Güldemann and von Roncador 2002.

Stein, Jess (editor in chief). 1966. *The Random House dictionary of the English language*. New York: Random House.

Steinhauer, Hein. 1986. 'Number in Biak: Counterevidence to two alleged language universals (a summary)', in Paul Geraghty, Lois Carrington and S. A. Wurm (eds.), *FOCAL I: papers from the Fourth International Conference on Austronesian Linguistics*, vol. 1, 171–3. Canberra: Pacific Linguistics.

Stirling, Lesley. 1998. 'Isolated *if*-clauses in Australian English', in Peter Collins and David Lee (eds.), *The clause in English: In honour of Rodney Huddleston*, 273–294. Amsterdam: John Benjamins.

Stump, Gregory T. 1993. 'Reconstituting morphology: The case of Bantu prefixation', *Linguistic Analysis* 23: 169–204.

Subrahmanyam, P. S. 1999. *Pa:ninian linguistics*. Tokyo: Institute for the Study of languages and Cultures of Asia and Africa, Tokyo University of Foreign Studies.

Sulkala, Helana and Merja Karjalainen. 1992. *Finnish*. London: Routledge.

Suzuki, Yasushi. 2002. 'The acceptance of "free indirect discourse": A change in the representation of thought in Japanese', pp. 109–20 of Güldemann and von Roncador 2002.

Svantesson, Jan-Olof. 1983. *Kammu morphology and phonology*. Lund: University of Lund.

Szemerényi, Oswald. 1970. *Einführung in die vergleichende Sprachwissenschaft.* Darmstadt: Wissenschaftliche Buchgesellschaft.
—— 1996. *Introduction to Indo-European linguistics.* Oxford: Clarendon Press.
Tamura, Suzuko. 2000. *The Ainu language.* Tokyo: Sanseido.
Tarmo, Tiiu. 1981. 'The direct object in Estonian', BA Honours thesis, ANU.
Taubman, William. 2003. *Khrushchev: The man and his era.* New York: W. W. Norton.
Tauli, Valter. 1980. *Eesti grammatika.* Uppsala: Finsk-ugriska Institutionen.
Taylor, Charles. 1985. *Nkore-Kiga.* London: Croom Helm.
Taylor, Gerald. 1990. *Introdução à língua baniwa do Içana.* Campinas: Editora da UniCamp.
Ten Cate, Abraham P. 1996. 'Modality of verb forms in German reported speech', pp. 189–211 of Janssen and van der Wurff 1986a.
Tepljashina, T. I., and V. I. Lytkin, 1976. 'Permskije jazyki [Permic languages]' in *Osnovy Finno-Ugorskogo jazykoznanija; Marijskij, Permskije i Ugorskije jazyki [Foundations of Finno-Ugric Linguistics; Mari, Permic and Ugric languages]*, 97–228. Moscow: Nauka.
Terrill, Angela. 2003. *A grammar of Lavukaleve.* Berlin: Mouton de Gruyter.
Thomas, David D. 1971. *Chrau grammar.* Honolulu: University of Hawaii Press.
Thomas, Dorothy M. 1969. 'Chrau affixes', *Mon-Khmer Studies* 3: 90–107.
Thompson, Chad. 1993 'The areal prefix hu- in Koyukon Athabaskan', *International Journal of American Linguistics* 59: 315–333.
Thompson, Laurence C. and M. Terry Thompson. 1992. *The Thompson language.* University of Montana Occasional Papers in Linguistics, No. 8.
Thompson, Sandra A. 1987. 'The passive in English: a discourse perspective', in Robert Channon and Linda Shockley (eds.), *In honor of Ilse Lehiste*, 497–511. Dordrecht: Foris.
Thompson, Sandra A. and Robert E. Longacre. 1985. 'Adverbial clauses', pp. 171–234 of Shopen 1985b.
Thomsen, Marie-Louise. 1984. *The Sumerian language: An introduction to its history and grammatical structure.* Copenhagen: Academic Press.
Thornes, Timothy J. 2003. 'A Northern Paiute grammar with texts', PhD dissertation, University of Oregon.
Thurgood, Graham and Randy J. LaPolla (eds.). 2003. *The Sino-Tibetan languages.* London: Routledge.
Tida, Syuntarô. 2003. 'Quotative construction in Dom: Parameters of direct-indirect speech'. Presentation at RCLT.
—— 2006. 'A grammar of the Dom language, a Papuan language of Papua New Guinea', PhD thesis, University of Kyoto.
Tiersma, Peter M. 1982. 'Local and general markedness', *Language* 58: 832–49.
Timberlake, Alan. 1986. 'Hierarchies in the genitive of negation', in Richard D. Brecht and James S. Levine (eds.), *Case in Slavic*, 338–60. Columbus, OH: Slavica.
Tindale, Norman B. 1940. 'Distribution of Australian Aboriginal tribes', *Transactions of the Royal Society of South Australia* 64: 140–231.
Toman, J. 1992. 'Compounding', in William Bright (ed.), *International encyclopedia of linguistics*, vol. 1, 286–8. New York: Oxford University Press.
Tonhauser, Judith. 2006. 'The temporal semantics of noun phrases: Evidence from Guaraní', PhD dissertation, Stanford University.
Topping, Donald M. 1973. *Chamorro reference grammar.* Honolulu: University of Hawaii Press.
Tosco, Mauro. 1999. 'A grammatical summary of Dhaasanac', RCLT internal document, ANU.
Trask, R. L. 1993. *A dictionary of grammatical terms in linguistics.* London: Routledge.

Traugott, Elizabeth C. 1982. 'From propositional to textual and expressive meanings:
    some semantico-pragmatic aspects of grammaticalization', in Winfried P.
    Lehmann and Yakov Malkiel (eds.), *Perspectives on historical linguistics*, 245–71. Amsterdam:
    John Benjamins.
Traugott. Elizabeth C. and Bernd Heine (eds.). 1991. *Approaches to grammaticalization*,
    2 vols. Amsterdam: John Benjamins.
Travis, Catherine. 2006. '*Dizque*: A Colombian evidentiality strategy', *Linguistics* 44:
    1269–98.
Troy, Jakelin. 199 4. *The Sydney Language*. Flynn, A. C. T.: The author.
Trubetzkoy, N. S. 1962. *Principles of phonology*, translated by Christiane A. M. Baltaxe.
    Berkeley and Los Angeles: University of California Press. [Translation of *Grundzüge
    der Phonologie*, 3rd ed. Göttingen: Vanderheck and Ruprecht. 1962.]
Trudgill, Peter, and Jean Hannah, 1982. *International English, a guide to varieties of
    Standard English.* London: Arnold.
Tsarfaty, Reut. 2007. 'Participants in action: Aspectual meanings and thematic
    relations interplay in the semantics of Semitic morphology', in Henk Zeevat and
    Balder Ten Cate (eds.), *Proceedings of the Sixth International Tbilisi Symposium on
    Language, Logic and Computation*. Batumi, Georgia.
—— Forthcoming. 'Connecting causative constructions and aspectual meanings: A case
    study from Semitic derivational morphology', in Paul Dekker and Michael Franke
    (eds.), *Proceedings of the Fifteenth Amsterdam Colloquium, ILLC/Department of
    Philosophy*, University of Amsterdam.
Tsonope, Joseph. 1997. A grammatical summary of Setswana', RCLT internal
    document, ANU.
Tuldava, Juhan. 1994. *Estonian textbook*. Bloomington: Research Institute for Inner
    Asian Studies.
Tveite, Tor. 2004. *The case of the object in Livonian: A corpus based study*. Helsinki:
    The Finno-Ugrian Department of Helsinki University.
Underhill, Robert. 1976. *Turkish grammar.* Cambridge, MA: MIT Press.
Vajda, Edward J. 2004. *Ket*. Munich: Lincom Europa.
Valenzuela, Pilar M. 2003. 'Transitivity in Shipibo-Konibo grammar', PhD dissertation,
    University of Oregon.
Vallauri, E. L. 2004. 'Grammaticalization of syntactic incompleteness: Free conditionals
    in Italian and other languages', *SKY Journal of Linguistics* 17: 189–215.
Van Breugel, Seino. 2006. 'Similarities in verbal and nominal morphology in Atong'.
    Paper presented at a meeting of Sino-Tibetan Special Interest Group, La Trobe
    University.
—— 2014. *A grammar of Atong*. Leiden: Brill.
Van Der Mark, Sheena. 2007. 'A grammar of Vinitiri', PhD thesis, La Trobe
    University.
Van Valin, Robert D., Jr. 1993. 'A synopsis of role and reference grammar', in Robert
    D. Van Valin, Jr. (ed.), *Advances in role and reference grammar*, 1–164. Amsterdam:
    John Benjamins.
Vasu, Śrīśa Chandra. 1891. *The Aṣṭādhyāyī of Pāṇini* Allahabad: Indian Press.
Veselinova, Ljuba N. 2003. 'Suppletion in verb paradigms: bits and pieces of a puzzle',
    PhD dissertation, Stockholm University.
—— 2005. 'Verbal number and suppletion', in Martin Haspelmath, Matthew S. Dryer,
    David Gil and Bernard Comrie (eds.), *The world atlas of language structures*, 326–9.
    Oxford: Oxford University Press.
Vidal, Alejandra. 1997. 'Noun classification in Pilagá', *The Journal of Amazonian Lan-
    guages* 1: 58–111.
Vlasto, A. P. 1986. *A linguistic history of Russia to the end of the eighteenth century*.
    Oxford: Clarendon Press.
Voort, van der, Hein. 2000. 'A grammar of Kwaza', PhD thesis, University of Leiden.

Vries, Lourens J. de. 1990. 'Some remarks of direct quotation in Kombai', in Harm Pinkster and Inge Genee (eds.), *Unity in diversity: papers presented to Simon C. Dik on his 50th birthday*, 291–309. Dordrecht: Foris.

Wälchli, Bernhard. 2000. 'Infinite predication as marker of evidentiality and modality in the languages of the Baltic region', *Sprachtypologie und Universalienforschung* 53: 186–210.

Wali, Kashi and Omkar N. Koul. 1997. *Kashmiri. A cognitive-descriptive grammar.* London: Routledge.

Walker, Alan T. 1982. *Grammar of Sawu.* Jakarta: Badan Penyelenggara Seri NUSA, Universitas Atma Jaya.

Walsh, Michael. 1976. 'The Murinypata language of north-west Australia', PhD thesis, ANU.

Watkins, Calvert. 1998. 'Proto-Indo-European: Comparison and reconstruction', in Anna Giacolone-Ramat and Paolo Ramat (eds.), *The Indo-European languages*, 25–73. London: Routledge.

Watkins, Laurel. 1984. *A grammar of Kiowa.* Lincoln: University of Nebraska Press.

Watters, David E. 2002. *A grammar of Kham.* Cambridge: Cambridge University Press.

—— 2005a. *Kusunda grammar (a language isolate of Nepal).* Kathmandu: National Foundation for the Development of Indigenous Nationalities.

—— 2005b. 'Kusunda: a typological isolate in South Asia', in Yogendra Yadava, Govinda Bhattarai, Ram Raj Lohani, Balaram Prasain and Krishna Parajuli (eds.), *Contemporary issues in Nepalese linguistics*, pp. 375–396. Kathmandu: Linguistic Society of Nepal.

—— 2009. 'The semantics of clause linking in Kham', pp. 96–117 of Dixon and Aikhenvald 2009.

Weber, David J. 1986. 'Information perspective, profile, and pattern in Quechua', pp. 137–55 of Chafe and Nichols 1986.

—— 1989. *A grammar of Huallaga (Huánuco) Quechua.* Berkeley and Los Angeles: University of California Press.

Webster, Noah. (ed.). 1828. *An American dictionary of the English Language...* New York: S. Converse.

Weir, E. M. Helen. 1984. 'A negação e outros tópicos da gramática Nadëb', MA thesis, Universidade Estadual de Campinas.

Wendel, Thomas D. 1993. 'A preliminary grammar of Hanga Hundi', MA thesis, University of Texas at Arlington.

Werner, H. 1997a. *Die ketische Sprache.* Wiesbaden: Harrassowitz.

—— 1997b. *Das Jugische (Sym-Ketische).* Wiesbaden: Harrassowitz.

Whitney, William Dwight. 1891. *Sanskrit grammar.* Leipzig: Breitkopf and Härtel.

Wierzbicka, A. 1974. 'The semantics of direct and indirect discourse', *Papers in Linguistics* 7: 267–307.

Wiesemann, U. 1990. 'A model for the study of reported speech in African languages', *Journal of West African Languages* 20(2): 75–80.

Wilkinson, Melanie. 1991. 'Djambarrpuyngu, a Yolngu variety of northern Australia', PhD thesis. Sydney University.

Williamson, Kay. 1963. *A grammar of the Kolokuma dialect of Ịjọ.* Cambridge: Cambridge University Press.

Williamson, Kay and Roger Blench. 2000. 'Niger-Congo', in Bernd Heine and David Nurse (eds.), *African languages. An introduction*, 11–42. Cambridge: Cambridge University Press.

Wilson, Patricia R. 1980. *Ambulas grammar.* Ukarumpa: Summer Institute of Linguistics.

Wilson, Peter J. 1992. *Una descripción preliminar de la gramática del Achagua (Arawak).* Bogotá: Instituto Lingüístico de Verano.

Winchester, Simon. 2005. *The meaning of everything, the story of the Oxford English Dictionary*. Oxford: Oxford University Press.

Winter, Werner. 1976. 'Switch-reference in Yuman languages', in Margaret Langdon and Shirley Silver (eds.), *Hokan studies: Papers from the First Conference on Hokan languages*, 165–174. The Hague: Mouton.

Witherspoon, Gary. 1977. *Language and art in the Navajo universe*. Ann Arbor: University of Michigan Press.

—— 1980. 'Language in culture and culture in language', *International Journal of American Linguistics* 46: 1–13.

Wolff, John U. 1973. 'Verbal inflection in Proto-Austronesian', in Andrew B. Gonzalez (ed.), *Parangal Kay Cecilio Lopez*, 71–91. Quezon City: Linguistic Society of the Philippines.

Wunderlich, D. 1997. 'Cause and the structure of verbs', *Linguistic Inquiry* 28: 27–68.

Yallop, Colin. 1977. *Alyawarra, an Aboriginal language of Central Australia*. Canberra: Australian Institute of Aboriginal Studies.

Zaugg-Corelli, Silvia. 2008. 'Converbs in Yemsa', in *From Siberia to Ethiopia: Converbs from a cross-linguistic perspective*, 221–55. Zürich: ASAS.

Zimmer, Karl R. 1976. 'Some constraints on Turkish causativization', pp. 399–412 of Shibatani 1976a.

Zuckermann, Ghil'ad. 2006. 'Direct and indirect speech in straight-talking Israeli', *Acta Linguistica Hungarica* 53: 467–81.

Zwicky, Arnold M. 2002. 'I wonder what kind of construction that this example illustrates', in D. Beaver, Luiz Castillas Martinez, Brady Clark and Stefan Kaufman (eds.), *The construction of meaning*, 219–48. Stanford: CSLI.

AUTHOR INDEX

LANGUAGE INDEX

SUBJECT INDEX

absolutive   146–50, *see also* ergative-absolutive

accusative   146–50, *see also* nominative-accusative

adjectives   102, 224–8, 402, 473–81, 491–518

derivation of   230, 271–6, 280–9, *see also* word-class-changing derivations

semantic types of   102, 227, 243, 272, 276, 282, 323, 407, 420–1, 429, 482, 506, *see also* age, colour, dimension, human propensity, physical property, value

adjectivization, *see* adjectives, derivation of

adjuncts, *see* peripheral arguments

adpositions   395, 398–9, 430–51, 481–3, 494, 521–6, *see also* postpositions, prepositions

adverbs   276–80, 294, *see also* word-class-changing derivations

age as a semantic type of adjectives   421, *see also* adjectives, semantic types of

agglutinating language   29, 102, 110, 171, 200, 446

agglutinative language, *see* agglutinating language

allative-instrumental   35–8, 102

ambitransitive, *see* transitivity

anaphor(a)   498–503, 516

animacy   74, 157, 178, 405–6, 409–13, 416–46, *see also* gender, reference classification

antipassive   46–51, 76–85, 146–7

applicative   44–58, 76–80, 86–90, 93–7, 112–15, 138–40, 207–8, 244–5, *see also* argument-transferring derivations, valency-changing derivations

apprehensive   14–16, 21–8

areal diffusion   95, 109, 318, 324, 365–6, 384, 442–3, *see also* borrowing, language contact

areal feature   315, 318, 324, 365

argument-determined constructions   44–80

argument-focussing constructions   58–65, 76–80

argument-manipulating constructions   66–72, 76–80

argument-transferring derivations   44–58, 76–80, *see also* applicative, causative

article   494–510, 521–2

aspect   10, 24–8, 223, 225

and adjectivizations   273

and case   26–8, 30–2

and nominalizations   257–8

and other grammatical systems   170–3, 179–83, 189–200

augmentative   6, 137, 223, 378–98, 420, 428

Australian Aboriginal words in dictionaries   529–54

basic linguistic theory   80

body parts   227, 233, 242, 392, 410, 414–15, 418–19, 424–30, 433, 443–5

boomerang, the etymology of   529, 531, 534–5, 538–53

borrowing   246, 269, 279, 369, 513, 529–54, *see also* loan

boundedness as a parameter in classifiers   409–12, 430–2, 441–2, *see also* classifiers

boundedness of event   26, 172

case   1–43, 102, 110, 170, 175–6, 181–2, 187–202, 222, 256–7, 298, 381–5, *see also* grammatical relations

causal meaning   21–2

causative   46–58, 76–80, 86–142, 227, *see also* argument-transferring derivations, valency-changing derivations

as meaning of a word-class-changing derivation   233–4, 238–41

origin of   96–7

child language   356

classifiers   6–7, 173–4, 178–9, 223, 256, 269, 378–90, 394–450

clause linking   1–4, 8–23, 33–40, 167–8, *see also* coordination, pivot

cognitive states, verbs of, *see* verbs of perception and cognition

colour as a semantic type of adjectives   102, 243, 323, 407, 421, 429, *see also* adjectives, semantic types of

oblique case 1–40
onomatopoeia 221, 239–41, 244, 318, 325
order (in the Algonquian linguistic tradition) 75–6

parameter of comparison 472–93
participial clause 279, 314–15
participle 22, 42, 182, 193, 227, 270–3, 279, 282, 288, 385
partitive case 26–31, 181
passive 46–51, 58, 66–71, 76–85, 258, 429, 491
    impersonal passive 50–1
peripheral arguments 45, 52–5, 62, 65, 93–4, 144, 149, 217–18, 223–71, 488
periphrastic constructions 47, 58, 97–9, 109, 138, 190, 270, 273, 473–4
person 170–3, 176–81, 184–200, 308, 328–32, 446–50
person shift in speech reports 290–2, 306–8, 324–5, 328–66
phonological change 452–3
phonological difference between nouns and verbs 226
physical property as a semantic type of adjectives 243, 272, 276, 282, 420, see also adjectives, semantic types of
pivot 58–66, 80, 148–50
pluractional 155–6
plural 150–59, see also number
polarity 170–2, 178–84, 189, 193–202, 259, 265, see also negation
polyfunctional roots 228–30
polysynthesis 377–394, 446
possession 176, 223, 260–3, 300–1, 392–3
    classifiers in possessive constructions 397–8, 435–6, see also relational classifiers
postpositions 430–5, 446–51, see also adpositions, prepositions
    as markers of clause linking 16, 23, 41–2
precategorial roots 228–9
prepositions 430–5, 446–51, see also adpositions, postpositions
    as markers of clause linking 16, 23, 41–2
preprefixation 392
privative case 7, 245, 251, 259, 272, 274, 391
privative derivation 274
progressive 232, 243, 263

promotion to subject 70–3
pronoun-reversing children, see child language
pronouns 357–60, 382–3, 460, 465–71
proprietive 7, 25, 233, 236–8, 274, 342–6, 358, 391
proximate-obviative 75–6, 80
purposive 3, 12–19, 25, 30–40

quantifier 155, 172, 263, 396, 405, 410–15, 494–6
quotation 290–2, 299–308, 313–23, 328–34, 348, 351, 355, 359–61
quotative evidential 291, 298–9, 304–8, 318–20

realis 15, 19, 21, 190, see also irrealis
reality status, see irrealis, realis
reanalysis 23–8, 34, 110, 141, 246–7, 269–70, 279–82, 287, 291, 443, see also reinterpretation
reciprocal 51, 176, 235–8, 380, 418
reconstruction 119–20, 138–42
reduplication 7, 29, 99, 118, 141, 156–7, 223, 228–9, 232, 283, 286, 460
reference classification 170, 173, 181–200, 203, see also animacy, gender, classifiers
referential status of arguments 73–6, see also inverse systems
referring expressions 229–30
reflexive 51, 151, 166, 175–6, 293, 300–1, 418, 423
reinterpretation 24–8, 38–9, 246, 273, 278–80, 323, see also reanalysis
relational classifiers 397–8, 435–6, see also possession
reported evidential 304–8, see also quotative evidential
reporting verb 290, 296–9, 300–14, 325–8, 335–40, 347

same subject marking, see switch reference
secondhand evidential, see reported evidential
semantic roles 205–20
semi-direct speech 327–66
serial verb construction 97, 100, 109, 111, 114–15, 151, 317, 380
similarity as a meaning of derived verbs 235–9, 274–6, 282, 314, 319–20
songs, language of 371–2

Printed in the United States
By Bookmasters